Hitler

Satan's Socialist Messiah

The False Pride of a Nation
The Allied Crusade To Peace

The Apostasy of the German Church
A Warning to America Today

Book 2

Clive Dennis Louden

Calvary Presbyterian Church Trinity Sunday

Indiana, PA— Jimmy Stewart's home church June 3, 2012
Rev. David J. Hanna

THE ORDER OF SERVICE FOR THE WORSHIP OF GOD
Welcome to worship at Calvary Church. We ask that you take the time to prepare your hearts and minds for worship.

Chapel of the Fallen Angels Mighty Eighth Air Force Museum

Carillon Dedication Honoring Dr. & Mrs. William Clark, Jr. May 16, 2003
WELCOME   LT. GEN. C. G. SHULER, JR.
REMARKS   JUDGE BEN SMITH
PLAQUE DEDICATION

REMARKS & DEDICATION   Dr. S. William Clark, III, Dr. James D. Clark, sons
Dr. and Mrs. S. William Clark, Jr. were tireless supporters of the Chapel of the Fallen Eagles. The project was dear to their hearts. Funding for the Chapel's carillon was made possible by their generous gift. Today, we proudly honor Mrs. Clark and remember Dr. Clark with this dedication. Pooler, Georgia a Savannah suburb.

What Are the 95 Theses of Martin Luther?

GOT QUESTIONS Internet

Answer: "The "95 Theses" were written in 1517 by a German priest and professor of theology named MARTIN LUTHER. His revolutionary ideas served as the catalyst for the eventual breaking away from the Catholic Church and were later instrumental in forming the movement known as the Protestant Reformation. Luther wrote his radical "95 Theses" to express his growing concern with the corruption within the Church. In essence, his Theses called for a full reform of the Catholic Church and challenged other scholars to debate with him on matters of church policy. "One of the major issues that concerned Luther pertained to the matter of church officials selling "indulgences" to the people as a means of releasing them from having to exact PENITENCE for their misdeeds. Indulgences were also claimed by the Church to limit the amount of time the purchaser's loved one would have to spend in "PURGATORY". [This is based on a passage in Macabees in the inter-testament Apocrypha accepted by the Roman Catholic and Eastern Orthodox churches not the mainstream Protestant churches because it is not an accepted canonical writing. Jesus Gospel is a FREE gift to faithful believers. YOU CAN'T BUY YOUR SALVATION through wealth or your self righteous works. However, through your faith in JESUS' GOSPEL one is asked to do good works in Jesus' spirit.]
CHURCH DOGMA: "As soon as the penny [pnenning] jingles into the money box, the soul flies out (of purgatory)." Luther felt that these church officials were teaching people that they could literally buy their way into the kingdom of God or buy God's favor. His belief was that the papacy had deteriorated to the point that people were being led to believe in man-made doctrines. The Pope had the power to limit or do away with penances imposed by the clergy, but he did not have

the power to bring about the interior contrition that leads to salvation. Only God could do that. Indulgences are positively harmful, according to the Theses, since they induce a false assurance of peace, and cause the recipients to neglect true repentance."

AN IRONIC OXYMORON OR PROVIDENCE? The Pope promoted indulgences to obtain money from the poor German peasants to build the magnificent ST. PETER'S Cathedral in Rome which they could never visit. When I was 15, in July 1958, my German Lutheran mother Elisabeth Frank took me and my brother Paul Thomas into St. Peter's Cathedral. A beautiful humanistic symbol of Michelangelo's vision of the creation of Adam in God's image.]

"Luther published his "95 Theses" fully realizing that he faced excommunication and even death for protesting the traditions and beliefs of the Catholic Church. To do so was considered heresy against God. Luther's "95 Theses" became highly sought after by the populace and were soon translated into German [from Latin] for the common people to read. The [new] printing press then enabled the wide distribution of the Theses, provoking in people more disenchantment with the ways of the Catholic Church."

[A monk, across the Elbe River in another district, named Tetzel drew people to his dramatic Hell fires show. Luther's Theses brought HOPE to the peasants and Tetzel returned to Rome and was rebuked by the Pope for his failure to allow the Germans to become a "heretical" insubordinate free-willed people.]

"In 1521, Pope Leo X excommunicated Luther from the Catholic Church and declared him a heretic. Luther was so despised by the church that a death warrant was issued, giving anyone permission to kill him. However, Luther was given protection by PRINCE FREDERICK OF SAXONY, a staunch defender of Luther. [He was very wealthy and possessed one of the largest collections of "Christian" relics which he renounced after receiving the first native tongue German language BIBLE not in Latin. Luther hidden in the Wartburg Castle translated the New Testament from Greek into German in a providential 10 months.] "Hidden in one of Frederick's castles, Luther began producing a translation of the Bible into the German language. Ten years later it was finally completed." [This included the longer Old Testament Hebrew Torah and Tenach prophetic HIStories.]

"It was in 1529, some 12 years after Luther had nailed his Theses to the church door, that the word "Protestant" became a popular term describing those who supported Luther's protests against the Church. These opponents of the Church declared their allegiance to God and protested any loyalty or commitments to the emperor. Thereafter, the name "Protestant" was applied to all who argued that the Church be reformed. Luther died in 1546 with his revolutionary Theses forming the foundation for what is known today as the Protestant Reformation." [Luther was a Biblical reformer and didn't want to create a Lutheran denomination. This would have been anathema to him. Luther would have been distressed to learn that today there are more than 15,000 "denominations". This is in America where religious tax free status can be obtained easily including cults like Scientology which became wealthy tax free entities. A PARADOX of FREEDOM OF RELIGION? Some churches have become mega-churches and some have become fraudulent to their faithful believers. Jesus spoke of Apostasy in the END-TIMES when there will be false Christs and Messiahs who would deceive even the ELECT. Many denominations have mostly members of the same nationalistic, ethnic or racial similarities. This is not the biblical fellowship which Jesus preached about having his disciples go throughout the world and bring the Good News Gospel to all people throughout the world ——————THE GREAT COMMISSION.

PERSONAL BELIEFS: I was confirmed on my 15th birthday at Emanuel Lutheran church in Hudson, NY in May 1958. My mother convinced our Lutheran pastor Grissliss, who was Lithuanian and had been in a Communist jail, to have an "unorthodox" joint communion with my brother who was 12 1/2, because we were going to Germany in June. My mother may have also known that I had difficulty memorizing and we had to recite some of Luther's creed. My brother Paul Thomas had a good memory and even acted in plays. In college in southern Maine a French Catholic area my roommate talked me into singing in the Baptist choir with his French/Canadian "Catholic" girl fiend Esther. In Air Force I went to Heidelberg Army chapel with a Baptist girl from Lake Oswego, Oregon who lived with civilian cousins who worked for BUNKER REMO at the Army HQ. She had lived in Philippines jungle with IGORET headhunters! Later, they were in the movie APOCALYPSE NOW who MARLON BRANDO lived with. Sheri also served in a missionary in India and Israel. After being discharged from the Air Force in April 1969, I didn't attend my local Lutheran church because at my grandmother's funeral and burial in Old Chatham the pastor asked me why I didn't attend church services? He had previously called my mother and asked her if I could take his daughter to her senior prom because her "boyfriend" couldn't attend? As they say in the military services NEVER VOLUNTEER! The worst date I ever had a pastor's daughter. OY WEH. He was not the pastor who confirmed me. I liked Pastor Grissliss, I believe my mother said he went to Trinity College in Hartford, CT and then Duke University? I dated several Catholic girls because of my Italian-American roommate at Andrews AFB in 1965-66 who was from Bayonne, NJ. I went to some Italian weddings where they married Jewish doctors and lawyers. I was invited to be part of a wedding party of his high school friend Jerry Tackas and his red haired "Irish" wife. I had dated her Irish-American Barnard college maid of honor Joanne Lynch from Middletown, NJ. The wedding was at Infant Jesus Catholic Church in Port Jefferson on Long Island. Recently, I asked a fellow employee where he was from and he said Port Jefferson. He said he and his wife were married in that Church! We both live near Fredericksburg, VA. I asked James if he knew where Setuaket, Long Island was and told him that TV/film actor KEVIN JAMES lived there. He said we both went to St. James high school not at the same time. Small World. Jerry the groom and his wife Valerie told me they met at Geordie's Disco in the upper East Side of Manhattan. I had been to other discos in Westchester and Connecticut. Geordie's is where I met my future Jewish wife Sandy. I later found postcards from Germany to my mother 1935-1939 and one in 1935 showed she lived in the exact same area for awhile before going to a refugee home in Amityville, Long Island. The upper East Side 80s was the Yorkville German section of New York City.]

I have attended weddings and services in almost all denomination churches except Mormon. Then after my son's Sabbath Bar Mitzvah on Nov. 10, 1990, on Luther's birthday we left Temple Beth Shalom in Fredericksburg, VA. I had attended a Missouri Synod Lutheran Church in Triangle, VA, not far from where I worked. My first day at the Concordia Lutheran Church was on the day of Pentecost May 1989. PROVIDENCE. The day before Saturday my wife, son and daughter had visited the Children's Holocaust Museum in Washington, DC. Today, I drive the 39 miles only on big Lutheran holy days. I attend a multi-denominational Bible church 3 miles away in my community now for about five years. The Lake of the Woods Church its pastors, Bible study, congregation, 25 member choir, pipe organ and smaller praise chapel are AWESOME!]

I believe this synopsis of Luther's Reformation by GOT QUESTIONS would be considered KOSHER by my Missouri Synod Lutheran Church which strictly maintains Luther's original 95 Theses and Augsburg Confession. In the early 1800s some German Lutherans came to America after the Reformed-Lutheran state evangelical church was formed. This became today's Lutheran Church Missouri Synod begun in Missouri.

I am now a Judeo-Christian as my testimony and witness reveal.

A CONFESSING CHURCH

"Today is an important date on the Lutheran calendar, even though it isn't well celebrated. It is the 488th anniversary of the presentation of the Augsburg Confession of Faith, one of the most influential documents of the Reformation. On this day in 1530, this confession was read before Holy Roman Emperor Charles V in Augsburg, Germany

Called a "founding manifesto" of the church, it was written by Philip Melanchthon with Martin Luther's approval (Luther could not attend because he was under a ban of the empire and subject to arrest.) Its 28 articles consist of 21 statements of doctrine and 7 declarations of abuses in the church and demands for reforms.

As the beating Gospel heart of Christ's mission. It states,"People cannot be justified before God by their own strength, merits, or works. People are freely justified for Christ's sake, through faith, when they believe that they are received into favor and that their sins are forgiven for Christ's sake. By His death, Christ made satisfaction for our sins. God counts this faith for righteousness in His sight." (Article IV)   PorTals Prayer

THE LUTHER ROSE

Letter to Lazarus Spengler, Coburg, July 8, 1530
Grace and peace in Christ!
Honorable, kind, dear Sir and Friend! Since you ask whether my seal has come out correctly, I shall answer most amiably and tell you of those thoughts when (now) come to my mind about my seal as a symbol of my theology.

There is first to be a cross, black (and placed) in a heart, which should be of its natural color, so that I myself would be reminded that Faith in the Crucified saves us. For if one believes from the Heart he will be justified. Even though it is a black cross, (which) also should hurt us, yet it leaves the Heart in its (natural) color (and) does not ruin nature; that is, (the Cross) does not kill but keeps (man) alive. For the just man lives by Faith, but by Faith in the Crucified One. Such a Heart is to be in the midst of a WHITE ROSE, to symbolize that FAITH GIVES JOY, COMFORT, AND PEACE; in a word it places the believer into a White joyful Rose; for (this Faith) does not give Peace and Joy as the world gives and, therefore, the Rose is to be in a Sky-Blue field, (symbolizing) that such Joy in the Spirit and in Faith is a beginning of the future Heavenly Joy; it is already a part (of Faith), and is grasped through Hope, even though not yet manifested. And around this field is a Golden Ring, (symbolizing) that in Heaven such blessedness lasts forever and has no end, and in addition is precious beyond all Joy and goods, just as gold is the most valuable and precious metal.

May Christ, Our Dear Lord, be with your Spirit until the life to come. AMEN
[Spengler, Nuremberg Reformation leader wrote hymn "All Mankind Fell in Adam's Fall"]

"The LUTHER SEAL or LUTHER ROSE is a widely recognized symbol for Lutheranism. It was the seal that was designed for [pastor] MARTIN LUTHER at the behest of Prince JOHN FREDERICK, in 1530, while Luther was staying at COBERG FORTRESS during the DIET OF AUGSBURG. LAZARUS SPENGLER, to whom Luther wrote an interpretation below, sent Luther a drawing of the seal. Luther saw it as a compendium or expression of his theology and faith, which he used to authorize his correspondence. Luther informed PHILIP MELANCHTHON on September 15, 1530 that the Prince had personally visited him in the Coburg fortress and presented him with a signet ring, presumably displaying the seal."   Wikipedia

Luther's interpretation of the Seal—"In a July 8, 1530 letter to Lazarus Spengler, Luther interprets his seal: Grace and peace from the Lord. As you desire to know whether my painted seal, which you sent to me, has hit the mark, I shall answer most amiably and tell you my original thoughts and reason about why my seal is a symbol of my theology. The first should be a black cross in a [RED] heart, which retains its natural color, so that I myself would be reminded that faith in the Crucified saves us. "For one who believes from the heart will be justified" (Romans 10:10). Although it is indeed a black cross, which mortifies and which should cause pain, it leaves the heart its natural color. It does not corrupt nature, that is, it does not kill but keeps alive. "The just shall live by faith" (Romans 1:17) but by faith in the crucified. Such a heart should stand in the middle of a white rose, to show that faith gives joy, comfort, and peace. In other words, it places the believer into a white, joyous rose, for this faith does not give peace and joy like the world gives. (John 14:27). That is why the rose should be white and not red, for white is the color of the spirits and the angels (cf. Matthew 28:3; John 20:12). Such a rose should stand in a sky-blue field, symbolizing that such joy in the spirit and faith is the beginning of the heavenly future joy, which begins already, but is grasped in hope, not yet revealed. And around this field is a gold ring, symbolizing that such blessedness in Heaven lasts forever and has no end. Such blessedness is exquisite, beyond all joy and goods, just as gold is the most valuable, most precious and best metal. This is my compendium theologiae [summary of theology]. I have wanted to show you in good friendship, hoping for your appreciation. May Christ, our beloved Lord, be your spirit until the life hereafter. Amen"   Wikipedia

Components of the seal connected to Luther earlier than 1530—"A single rose had been known as Luther's emblem since 1520 when WOLFGANG STOECKEL in Leipzig published one of Luther's sermons with a woodcut of the reformer. This was the first contemporary depiction of Martin Luther. Luther's doctor's ring displayed a heart like shield, the symbol of the HOLY TRINITY."   Wikipedia

Use in Byzantine Rite Lutheranism—"Churches of Byzantine Rite Lutheranism, the Ukrainian Lutheran Church, use the Luther Rose with an Orthodox Cross in the center."

Use in Coats of Arms—there are 8 German/Austrian coats of arms with Luther Rose.

In June 2017, after the READING, PA, WORLD WAR II Air/Army reenactment I drove to Indiana, Pennsylvania actor JAMES STEWART'S birthplace. I left Reading after the Swing Fever Big Band finished playing the songs the bands played during the war. At the end of the music many of the men and women dressed in military uniforms including American, British, Canadian, Russian, Serbian and even German, and civilians in period clothing joined hands in a large circle in the General SPAATZ hanger. General TOOEY SPAATZ was commander of the 8th Air Force his home is in BOYERTOWN, PA, 10 miles from Reading. When the war in Europe ended he was sent to the Pacific and his 20th AAF ended World War II, with General CURTIS LEMAY'S firebombing of Japan's cities and the use of two atomic bombs. In 1947, SPAATZ became the first chief of staff of the newly created Air Force.

The final song the Swing Fever band plays is WE WILL MEET AGAIN which is sung by all in memory of the departed veterans of World War II. At gas station I met a man related to JAMES STEWART who gave me directions to Indiana, PA, his hometown.

PERSONAL SMALL WORLD STORY: I arrived at Indiana, PA about 3 AM and stopped at a 24 hr. store. I meet two students there and told them I was going to visit the JAMES STEWART museum and go to his Presbyterian church in the morning. I told them I had been at the Reading World WAR II airshow and was finishing a book about ADOLF HITLER trying to destroy Christianity.

One of the young men told me a remarkable story how his mother's very distant German relative named KRUG was related to the man who painted the LUTHER ROSE for MARTIN LUTHER! He told me he was considered a heretic by the Roman Catholic church and like Luther had to go into hiding to protect his life. I didn't know the HIStory of the Luther Rose then and checked the Internet and found the letter from Martin Luther to LAZARUS SPENGLER.

After I said I had many World War II stories the other boy asked me if I was going to have anything about KURT VONNEGUT who was in the DRESDEN FIRE BOMBING RAID, as an American soldier prisoner there, which he tells about in his best selling book "SLAUGHTERHOUSE FIVE— The Children's Crusade"? I said yes, I tell his amazing providential story. He then asked. "Will you put his extraterrestrials in your book?" I said, I have included the extraterrestrial's question to Billy Pilgrim, "According to the Gospel of Matthew the man named Jesus said he was for the brotherhood of Humankind and said don't hate your neighbor or enemies. Why do Christians kill each other?" This is a paraphrase not actual text from Vonnegut's book. In the movie FOOTLOOSE actor KEVIN BACON questions why Christians were banning the book SLAUGHTERHOUSE FIVE, a "'classic." The town preacher, JOHN LITHGOW is against dancing, rock music, the main theme of the film, because of an earlier fatal accident.

I attended a service at Stewart's beautiful Presbyterian church with a Tiffany stained glass window with the Roman Centurion JONATHAN and a disciple?

SMALL WORLD STORY: A young man Matthew, now an Elder, in my Concordia Missouri Synod Lutheran church in Triangle, VA. I meet his father who graduated from Indiana University, PA. He said he was stationed in Germany in the US Army. He was attached to a liaison unit with the small Luxembourg Army. He and his family and his son, as a child, lived at Bitburg AB housing in 1991, 22 years after I left. Matthew graduated from Kent State University.

Lutheran-Missouri Synod Communion Registration Card

Concordia Lutheran Church Triangle, Virginia

"Take eat, this is my Body...Drink it all of you, this is my Blood"
"Given and shed for you for the remission of sins."

These words from Luther's Small Catechism express our belief and teaching about: Holy Communion:
HOLY COMMUNION IS the body and blood of our Lord Jesus Christ, given with bread and wine, instituted by Christ; Himself, for us to eat and drink.

THE BENEFITS OF THIS SACRAMENT are pointed out by the words, given and shed for you for the remission of sins.These words ensure us that in the sacrament: we receive forgiveness of sins, life and salvation. For when there is forgiveness of sins there is also life and salvation. Fasting and other outward preparations serve a good purpose, however, a person is well prepared and worthy who believes these words:

"Given and shed for you for the remission of sins."

"All who believe these words are invited to participate. But, anyone who does not believe these words, or doubt them is neither prepared nor worthy, for the words FOR YOU require simply a believing heart." - Martin Luther

If you believe the above statements, please sign below and come forward at the direction of the usher (children are welcome to come forward with a parent)

"When Jesus says, This IS MY body," He is using a special form of grammar. Normally in Koine Greek, one would assume the verb TO BE and simply say, "Thus He is drawing special attention to a reality. He is saying for emphasis:

"THIS REALLY AND TRULY IS MY BODY!"

PERSONAL ANALYSIS: It's so simple. Why do people question this? In the sixteenth century Zwingli and Calvin said that the LORD'S SUPPER is ONLY SYMBOLIC. Even Melanchthon, Luther's best friend, caved in to pressure and published an altered version of the Augsburg Confession that was acceptable to the Reformed. By the 19th century, Lutheran congregations were being pressured—even forced—to accept compromise on the LORD'S SUPPER "for the sake of HARMONY." [After Napoleon's defeat the German Lutheran church merged with the Calvinist/Reformed church becoming the State German Evangelical Lutheran church. Some Lutherans left the mother church in Germany moving to Missouri forming the Missouri Synod keeping Luther's and original Augsburg Confession beliefs also rejecting the Reformed concept of COMMUNION.]
Many Lutheran churches chiseled "U.A.C." on their cornerstone. It stands for "UNALTERED AUGSBURG CONFESSION." It is a way of saying, "We teach that CHRIST IS TRULY PRESENT in the LORD'S SUPPER. HIS BODY AND BLOOD TAKE AWAY SINS. COME AND EAT!"

COMMUNION CARD GOSPEL CONCLUSION

'We are really sinners. We need the REAL FORGIVENESS that comes with the REAL BODY AND BLOOD of the REAL CHRIST that are given to US in the LORD'S SUPPER.
And that is what we have THANK GOD!
LORD JESUS, thank you for coming to us in bread and wine of HOLY COMMUNION. AMEN"
[As written in Lutheran-Missouri Synod "PorTals of Prayer" Nov. 13, 2017. Read Matthew 26:26-29 & Psalm 51:1-10 Jesus said, "Take, eat THIS IS MY BODY!"]
[The very precise Greek language was used in JUDEA during the Roman occupation because it was the language of trade brought there under ALEXANDER THE GREAT of Macedonia's rule. Latin was used only by the Romans. The local Jewish language was Aramaic. Hebrew was used by the Temple pharisees, priests and rabbis because it was the written language of the TORAH and TENACH and the prophets in their HOLY SCRIPTURES OLD TESTAMENT.]
PERSONAL STORY: When I took several nighttime lessons to become a member of my Lutheran-Missouri Synod church Concordia I was with two ladies Joyce was born Catholic, then Baptist. I don't know "Charlie" Charline's religious background. One lesson by Pastor James Knill was about Communion. He explained that in the Missouri Synod church we believe literally what JESUS revealed to his 11 Disciples at the LAST SUPPER was that his BODY AND BLOOD taken in HOLY COMMUNION was not symbolic but was Jesus actual presence! My pastor explained the Greek definition of IS which really meant IS! I remarked, "President Clinton had just made the word IS a national and world wide word of providence. In his Congressional impeachment testimony Clinton testified, "It depends what the definition of IS IS!" HIStory?   [ISIS?]
My pastor said the Missouri Synod is the ONLY CHURCH denomination professing this Biblical truth! I questioned him on this unbelievable truth. He said the Roman Catholic also believes this

but they only give the BODY not the BLOOD. Their dogma considers the round thin wafer as JESUS' BODY which also "contains" HIS BLOOD? I have been to Catholic masses and do recall only the priest drinks the BLOOD from the cup of wine. Does anyone read the Bible? Hollywood has often portrayed the LAST SUPPER based on the true Biblical GOSPEL. My church uses kosher Manechevitz wine. Grape juice is also provided and today gluten free wafers are provided. I believe most Christians believe that their Communion service is real not a "symbolic" ritual. I HOPE. Jesus knows what is in a believer's heart and doesn't care about church denomination dogma. Jesus biggest enemy was not Romans or Pontius Pilate, whose wife had a dream about Jesus, and told Pilate to free Jesus. Pilate, a brutal governor, did not find the pharisees case against Jesus a reason for a death sentence. Then the mob probably Jewish Zealots, who realized Jesus wasn't the conquering Messiah, maybe some were motivated or paid by the pharisees, maybe some were the angry pagan money lenders and pagan Moabites and Amorites who may have believed that Jesus may have been just a devout Old Testament Jew who was speaking against their idolatry and miraculous healings and raising people from the dead which their idols couldn't possibly imitate. So they shouted, CRUCIFY HIM! Then Pilate, to avoid rioting, invoked a Hebrew Passover law which allowed freeing a prisoner. The mob yelled free BARABBAS, a zealot who had possibly killed Roman soldiers! Not a Hollywood ending? The Old Testament has some 140 scriptures related to Jesus life's SUFFERING MESSIAHSHIP! Isaiah 53. The epitaph "CHRIST KILLER!' is an OXYMORON. Jesus "death" was DEICIDE. It was pre-ordained PREDESTINED by GOD THE FATHER. Read Jesus THE HUMAN SON's FINAL PRAYER in the Getsemeny Garden praying to HIS FATHER to relieve him from his painful human future death. Then the Temple guard came and arrested Jesus after JUDAS kisses JESUS to identify Him for his 30 silver coins as prophesied in the Old Testament which began JESUS PASSION OF THE CROSS. The New Testament GOOD NEWS GOSPEL tells the "rest of the story."
Even Hollywood films know or knew this.

HOLY COMMUNION SERVICE

Lake of the Woods multi-denomination Bible Church

INVITATION   Pastor
PRAYER OF CONFESSION (UNISON)
Almighty God, Father of our Lord Jesus Christ, we confess that we have sinned against You in thought, word, and deed by what we have done and what we have left undone.
We have not loved You with our whole hearts; we have not loved our neighbors as ourselves. We are truly sorry, and we humbly repent. Forgive us all that is past; and grant us Your Son our Lord Jesus Christ's sake. Amen.
MOMENT OF SILENT PRAYER All
PRAYER FOR PARDON   Pastor
COMFORTING WORDS   Pastor
PRAYER OF CONSECRATION   Pastor
PRAYER OF HUMBLE ACCESS (UNISON)
O Merciful Lord, we do not come to this table trusting in our righteousness, but in Your great mercy.
We are not worthy to gather up the crumbs under Your table, but let us partake of this Sacrament of Jesus Christ, so that we may grow into His likeness, and dwell in Him, and He in us. Amen.
DISTRIBUTION OF ELEMENTS

(Please hold the elements [wafer and cup] until all of the congregation can partake of the Communion together. Note that grape juice is in the center ring and wine in the outer ring of each tray.)

PRAYER OF THANKSGIVING (UNISON):

Eternal Father, we give You thanks for Your gift of salvation through Jesus Christ.
Grant that we may go into the world in the strength of Your Holy Spirit to give ourselves to others and to serve You with gladness of heart, through Christ our Lord.   Amen.

Boy Who Brought GOD to Hollywood HIS Day in Church
THE ONE AND ONLY

"I believe with all my Heart that if YOU were the ONLY PERSON on EARTH, the LORD JESUS CHRIST would still have descended to this planet, been born of a VIRGIN, and DIED on the Cross for YOU. That's how very special and unique you are in His Heart."

Pastor David Jeremiah Turning Point

When the famous Hollywood producer CECIL B. DEMILLE, was a boy of 10, his father sent him off to attend a special Christian service at their church, It was a small church, and in an effort to stimulate interest in the community, the church leaders had announced holiday services every morning for a week during the Christmas season. Since the church didn't have a full-time pastor, guest ministers were recruited. Young Cecil braved the wintery weather and walked into the small wooden chapel to discover he was the ONLY parishioner who had shown up. He was the congregation. He took his seat with some anxiety, and at the appointed hour the minister walked to the pulpit.

The man had a strong, kindly face and a prominent red beard. He looked down at the boy, smiled, and commenced the service as if the church were packed. He read the lessons, and Cecil read the responses to the liturgy. The minister preached a short Sermon and talked earnestly to the boy. When the time came for the offering, Cecil stepped into the isle and dropped his nickel into the collection plate. That's when something happened that Cecil B. DeMille never forgot. As he offered his coin, the preacher stepped off the platform and placed his hand on the boy's head. "I can still feel the thrill and sensation of his gentle touch." DeMille later wrote. "IT WON MY BELIEF AND STRENGTHENED MY FAITH. THE SPIRIT OF TRUTH WAS IN THE CHURCH WITH US THAT MORNING."   "A Boy's Finest Memory," by Cecil B. DeMille in THE GUIDEPOSTS CHRISTIAN TREASURY (Carmel, NY; Guidepost, 1973}

"Sometimes we feel like we're the only one feeling as we do, sitting in our pew, going through our particular season of life. But on the first Christmas, the Lord Jesus stepped off Heaven's platform, came down to where you were, and placed His hand of Grace on your head. Had you been the only one on the planet, He would have still made the trip. And as we love and worship him this season, we can feel the thrill and sensation of His gentle touch, as gentle as the softly falling snow." TURNING POINT DAVID JEREMIAH

SMALL WORLD STORY: I met a lady from Washington, North Carolina whose father was a pastor there and knew this story about Cecil B. DeMille.

"LUTHER": A MOVIE FOR OUR TIME

The "Lutheran Witness" Missouri Synod magazine September 2003
"Luther" To Open Nationwide Sept. 26

"Luther," the new motion picture about the life and times of Martin Luther, is scheduled for release Sept. 26 and will open in more than 300 movie theaters nationwide."
HOLLYWOOD PROVIDENCE: British actor JOSEPH FIENNES was chosen to portray the monk/pastor/reformer MARTIN LUTHER. Fiennes confesses, "At that time MY GOD was soccer/football!" I believe Jesus and Martin Luther will bless him for his remarkable "acting" portrayal of Luther. Sadly, few people even Lutherans saw the movie. Fiennes later is "chosen" for RISEN (2011) portraying the centurion Roman soldier Pontius Pilate orders to find Jesus' missing body. His character allegedly had seen Jesus on the cross and ordered a soldier to pierce Jesus Heart proving JESUS was deceased. Gaius Cassius Longinus, a German Centurion, historically actually did this fulfilling two Old Testament prophecies of the Jewish suffering messiah. Fiennes is later stunned when he sees Jesus alive with His disciples. As a faithful Roman soldier he had hoped to leave hot, dusty Israel to retire to a beautiful villa near Rome. Fiennes goes AWOL from the Roman army. Is this acting or a strong belief, conviction about his role's message? Providently, Fiennes made a film THE LAST RACE about Scottish Presbyterian pastor ERIC LIDDELL, who in the film CHARIOTS OF FIRE (1980) about the 1912 Paris OLYMPIC GAMES, refuses to run his 100 meter race because it is scheduled on the Sabbath/Sunday. His story gets front page headlines and national support. Would it today? The British Olympic committee and even King of England tell pastor Liddell he must honor king and country. He refuses, choosing his GOD JESUS. Another track teammate offers Liddell his more difficult 300 meter race which Liddell hadn't trained for. Liddell wins the Gold medal, for Jesus. Joseph Fiennes in THE LAST RACE (2017) portrays pastor Liddell returning to his birthplace China as a missionary. The film ends with a starved and sick Liddell in a Japanese army prison camp being offered freedom. He refuses his pardon telling the commander to release a pregnant mother instead. Liddell passes soon afterward on February 22, 1945. My German mother's birthday was February 22,1915, 30 years old. George Washington's birthday. The Episcopal church has made February 22, a feast "saints" day in pastor ERIC LIDDELL's memory.

IS THE HANDMAIDEN'S TALE SACRILEGIOUS?

JOSEPH FIENNES largest role is in the three season TV series as a commander in a futuristic dystopian United States. The HANDMAIDEN'S TALE was written as a book by a Canadian woman check Wikipedia. After all of Fiennes great Christian roles as MARTIN LUTHER, the Centurion who finds Jesus alive, and missionary Olympic winner ERIC LIDELL who in the LAST RACE dies in a Japanese prison in China. Providentially, the film was only shown in Communist China as a propaganda film for China's still great hatred towards Japan for killing some 20,000,000 Chinese people mostly civilian. Fiennes is an actor and I doubt from his previous roles he identifies with his character.
PERSONAL CONNECTION: Actress ANN DOWD portrays the stern but caring head mistress of her "hand maidens". She tased one for insubordination. In the film AMAZING ANIMALS she is the head librarian at TRANSYLVANIA UNIVERSITY where a rare AUDUBON bird paintings is on secure display. In the movie she resists college thieves who tase her and she pees in her pants. What goes around comes around? ACTING. Dad graduated there in June 1942, I visited the library in 2017, and was given a card by the librarian who was tased! This was before the film and

I didn't know about the rare book. HOLLYWOOD STORY: Dowd's husband was LADY GAGA'S movie acting coach.

PROVIDENTIAL REST OF THE STORY: I checked Wikipedia to read about the film THE LAST RACE and was surprised to see it wasn't shown to the Western world? Apparently, the Chinese Communist government took control of it! Providentially, not to eliminate a story about a true example of what Jesus wants Christians to become, NOT JUST PASTORS. The Chinese Communist government is using Pastor/missionary ERIC LIDDELL's MARTYRDOM story as propaganda to show how evil the Japanese were in World War II. It is believed 20,000,000 to 25,000,000 Chinese were killed by the Japanese army in the war. Most of those who died were from military forces, biological weapons, starvation and diseases. They were civilian women, children and the elderly. I read a historical email that revealed today "half" of China's TV shows are still showing Japanese atrocities revealing a continued hatred for the Japanese, 75 years. History
Fiennes, you must know this? His wife is Spanish and he is now Catholic. His earlier films were ENEMY AT THE GATES (2001) portraying a Communist commissar during the cataclysmic battle of STALINGRAD. His love interest was fellow Communist RACHEL WEISZ who loved Russian sniper JUDE LAW, in ELIZABETH as JOHN ROLFE. Today, JOSEPH FIENNES has as an actor gone to the other extreme as a sinister commissar leader in a dystopian America in the HANDMAIDEN's TALE.
Also as a young SHAKESPEARE IN LOVE with new, young actress GWYNTH PALTROW, "chosen" by "ME-TOO" predator producer HARVEY WEINSTEIN. She was dating young actor BRAD PITT at that time. Brad you should have punched Weinstein out like you wanted to do. Many in Hollywood knew this and one actress even said it during the ACADEMY AWARDS. Is anyone listening? Brad you were THELMA AND LOUISE's young male hero. Your former wife ANGELINA JOLIE would have kicked Weinstein where it really hurts that would have ended it. Angelina's dad JON VOGT would have killed Weinstein. Loved Angelina as LARA CROFT in two TOMB RAIDER films with her dad JON VOGT. I heard on ET, Entertainment Tonight, you did aerial acrobatic scenes even stunt men couldn't do. Talented Swedish actress ALICIA VIKANDER was also amazing as LARA CROFT. I spent a night in her hometown GOTEBERG in late June 1973, when I shipped my new SAAB 99 EMS to America. Read my BITBURGER PILS story about your IRISH husband FASSBENDER, MAGNETO, born in Heidelberg, drinking a BITBURG PILS and then he kills three Nazis. Evil "Nazi" experimental doctor actor KEVIN BACON who is happily married to KIRA SEDGWICK, a Jewish American actress. Sedgwick was TOM CRUISE's high school girl friend in the movie BORN ON THE FOURTH OF JULY based on my Long Island Massapequa/Amityville neighbor RON KOVIC's sad Vietnam experience. Read my personal story about Kovic. Cruise, born on July 3, should have won the best actor Academy Award Oscar. Don't feel bad Tom legendary actors KIRK DOUGLAS and PETER O'TOOLE also didn't "win" an OSCAR with many nominations. The voting system may not always be fair but sometimes I do agree.
Read my providential "connection" to the SIX DEGREES OF SEPARATION of KEVIN BACON through his many Hollywood films. I can connect to where it started in Pennsylvania. Love WIKIPEDIA and its HYPER LINKS connections amaze me. FOOTLOOSE dancing started BACON's career. It is interesting to see the TNT channel commercial for Hollywood great moments film clips with its great dancing scenes including Bacon in FOOTLOOSE. Ironically, the infectious raucous background dancing music is unknown except for being used as a raucous London street dancing opener for zany comedian MIKE MYERS spy spoof THE SPY WHO SHAGGED ME. A big band record fan, I bought this song SOUL BOSSA NOVA in college in 1963, when the gentle Bossa Nova was very popular. BIG BAND BOSSA NOVA was recorded by the

great QUINCY JONES big band. I just found this album in my 2,000+ LP collection and enjoyed playing it. I was disappointed by many clicks and pops from dust. My large CD collection is pure music. Jones was an early friend of RAY CHARLES, who inspired him to form his own tremendous big band. JAIME FOX you deserved the Academy Award for your portrayal of RAY CHARLES. Charles passed just before the film's premier, but must have HEARD your outtakes. Of course, he couldn't have SEEN the movie. I saw and heard Ray Charles in the Portland, Maine concert hall in August 1962. The audience was 95% white. He had THREE top 10 chart hits I CAN'T STOP LOVING YOU, BORN TO LOSE, and YOU DON'T KNOW ME toping even the BEATLES! Charles tells the ABC/Paramount record company executives he wanted to record a COUNTRY AND WESTERN album with his big band and chorus. They retorted: "'Ray that is not your type of music." Ray Charles, Jaime Fox, retorts, "It doesn't say that in my contract!" I heard Charles again at a WOLF TRAP concert just before he passed. Have many of his albums,a music legend. Charles was popular during a time when both the North and South were still very racist and prejudicial. Ray Charles cancels his sold out appearance in Atlanta, Georgia, because the audience was segregated not allowing any Negroes to attend. Charles rendition of GOD BLESS AMERICA is a classic. CHARLES being blind could not racially profile his avid music fans. Born again, wealthy slave ship captain JOHN NEWTON wrote one of the greatest Christian hymns AMAZING GRACE testifying "ONCE I WAS BLIND NOW I CAN SEE."

I became a devoted LES & LARRY ELGART, both Jewish, big band fan in March 1960, when my dad bought me my first LP THE BAND OF THE YEAR 1954, Elgart album featuring the BANDSTAND BOOGIE which was ABC TV's DICK CLARK AMERICAN BANDSTAND theme song broadcast across America to America's young ROCK AND ROLL dance enthusiasts waiting to hear all the new singers at 4:00 PM. My dad knew well the American Bandstand theme song because as ABC's New York City's senior Master Control room engineer (1949) he connected the show from ABC's Philadelphia Dick Clark's dancing studio affiliate. I visited the Dick Clark music museum in Pigeon Forge, Tennessee, and took photos of all the pictures of Dick Clark with all of America's popular singers who owe him their breakouts. The barn museum has been torn down because of the "NOISE" of visiting band performances. I saw an unmarked big bus turn into the Clark museum road on July 4, 2007, the night CHARLIE DANIELS band played there. It was next to Dollywood Theme park. My wife and I watched the fireworks at nearby Gatlinburg and heard county bands and "Rocky Top" recorded nearby.

Read my story of how I almost knocked DICK CLARK down in the ABC basement hallway where I got his autograph in August 1960. I didn't tell my dad that I almost accidentally knocked down ABC's and America's most beloved personality.

RACHEL WEISZ married DANIEL CRAIG "JAMES BOND" in 2011.

Brad Pitt was Paltrow's boyfriend in SEVEN with detective MORGAN FREEMAN. They both pursue the elusive SEVEN DEADLY SINS revenge murder KEVIN SPACEY. My dad went to Nantucket Island in the 1970s, to hear his friend Roger Johnson play the Hammond organ at CAPTAIN TOBY's restaurant. They capture Spacey and then Pitt receives a Special Delivery package with Paltrow's decapitated head inside it. In REVENGE Pitt shots and kills Spacey completing the 7th DEADLY SIN REVENGE! Receiving an ACADEMY AWARD MERLE STREEP holds up her OSCAR and shouts "Harvey Weinstein you are my god!" Hollywood this is not a parable. Jesus loves everyone but Jesus wants you to be careful who you choose as gods (God's 1st Commandment), choose your friends wisely, beware of drugs, including "prescription", MICHAEL JACKSON and ELVIS, and alcohol and marijuana/cigarettes can diminish your rationality. JOHNNY DEPP, a good child actor and an enigmatic adult actor. Were you using drugs or alcohol when you slurred your words saying "When is the last time an actor killed a president? But, I'm not an actor, I LIE for a living." Today, is this your script?" You and LEONARDO DICAPRIO were good kids in WHAT'S EATING GILBERT GRAPE? You should portray

GOETHE'S DR. FAUSTUS who sold his soul to the devil for PRIDEFUL FAME for 23 years. He was able to "reverse" his deal in the last minute. Jesus will allow TRULY repentant sinners forgiveness. However, don't take his Grace in vain because HE will know your TRUE HEART on JUDGMENT DAY.

LUTHER MOVIE TELLS WHY HE BEGAN REFORMATION

"The motion picture is bound to cause higher visibility for MARTIN LUTHER and for Lutherans, and that's wonderful," says Rev. Tom Lapacka, executive director of the Synod's Board of Communications Services.

Shot on at least 10 sets in 20 locations around Germany, italy and the Czech Republic, "Luther" was co-produced by Thrivent Financial for Lutherans and Neue Film production of Berlin, Germany.

The films stars JOSEPH FIENNES (SHAKESPEARE IN LOVE, ELIZABETH, ENEMY AT THE GATE) as MARTIN LUTHER, ALFRED MOLINA (FRIDA, CHOCOLAT), as indulgence seller TETZEL, and two-time Academy Award winner Sir PETER USTINOV (SPARTACUS, TOPKAPI). The movie's director is ERIC TILL.

SPECIAL EDITION BOOK: As complements to the film, Concordia Publishing House is producing a number of resources including a special edition of LUTHER: BIOGRAPHY OF A REFORMER., by Frederick Nohl. A 224-page hardcover book at $14.99.

CPH interim President and CEO Paul T. McCain describes the book as "a very clear, direct and simple biography, with many full-color pictures from the movie, that will fill in many gaps and articulate much more clearly the essential truths the movie covers."

McCain said that he is "convinced that this movie is "convinced that this work really will open doors for people interested in Lutheranism, wanting to learn more about Martin Luther. his life and work. It will provide a valuable tool for years to come to help portray the essential truths of the Lutheran Reformation. —Joe Isenhower Jr.

A MAN FOR THIS SEASON

by Uwe Siemon-Netto—UPI religion editor

LUTHER—MARTIN LUTHER's discovery of a merciful God comes through in a new film that's also riveting entertainment. Photo: Martin Luther (Joseph Fiennes) translates the Bible into German [from original Greek not Latin] while hiding out in the Wartburg castle. "Luther" portrays events with attention to detail and considerable historical accuracy.

"It's a pity that the title A MAN FOR ALL SEASONS is taken (a brilliant movie about Sir THOMAS MORE, a Roman Catholic martyred at the hand of King HENRY VIII). It would be a perfect title for the first full-length feature film in half a century about Martin Luther, which opens in 300 theaters nationwide on Sept. 26.

Ah well, let's call Luther a "Man for This Season" then—the right man for our manic era, a time of "cafeteria religion," an era whose statement of faith seems to be "HERE I STAND—and here, and there, and here."

So, to whom shall we turn to guide us out of post-modernity's labyrinth of creeds? This marvelously fast paced film suggests the person who ranked third on A & E's and LIFE magazine's lists of the most influential people of the last millennial [1,000 years]—even though 78 per cent of Americans don't know who he was: Dr. Martin Luther. Hence the actual, very simple title of this new film, "Luther."

"HERE I STAND"

"It so happens that the same quality that cost Sir Thomas More his life is what makes Luther so important for us. Both men's faith did not permit them to waffle. The relationship between God and man does not allow for choice, there is but one option. As Luther, played superbly by English actor JOSEPH FIENNES (Shakespeare in Love), said in 1521 before the Imperial DIET OF WORMS, risking death at the stake: "Unless I am convicted by Scripture and plain reason...my conscience is captive to the Word of God: I cannot and will not recant anything, for to go against conscience is neither right nor safe. God help me. Amen."

MARTIN LUTHER DEFENDER OF WESTERN DEMOCRACY

"Maybe Luther added, "Here I stand"; maybe that's just something pamphleteers edited into their reports immediately after WORMS. It doesn't really matter. These words sum up who LUTHER was; that's why the filmmakers, thankfully, inserted them into their amazingly accurate and detailed account of the Worms standoff without which WESTERN DEMOCRACY AS WE KNOW IT WOULD NEVER HAVE DEVELOPED.

"HERE I STAND"—by GOD, these words churn up one's guts and send shivers down one's spine! Even if this was a dreary documentary, this brief scene would still win over hundreds of thousands. But "LUTHER" is anything but dull. It is so fast-moving that some who previewed it wondered if it might confuse the audience, which I doubt. It is breathtakingly filmed. It has humor and charm and wonderfully authentic aphorisms (Luther: "In ROME you can buy sex and salvation) [shows unmarried "celibate" priests with prostitutes]. It keeps you on the edge of you seat, wondering at first— to be reassured later-about Luther's sanity.

"It also makes you wish dolefully that we were governed by men like those German princes, who toward the movie's end bowed their heads to Emperor CHARLES V at the AUGSBURG DIET of 1530—no, not in deference, but showing their readiness to be decapitated for the sake of the Gospel. O that in these decadent days, when the dirtiest fingers fumble with the words of God presuming to conform it to their own foul desires, we would hear dialogue like this:

"Emperor Charles: "YOUR MINISTERS WILL NOT PREACH AND YOU WILL OUTLAW THESE BIBLES IN THE COMMON LANGUAGE AND DECLARE ANYONE WHO POSSESSES ONE AN ENEMY OF THE STATE."

PHILIP OF HESSE: "We will not stop our ministers from PREACHING THE WORD."

JOHN OF SAXONY:"We will not outlaw the new Bible"translated by Luther into German.

CHARLES: "As a sign of your loyalty to ME, tomorrow you shall march in the CORPUS CHRISTI procession to the Cathedral and worship. All of you—in the Roman manner."

GEORGE OF BRANDENBURG: "We will not, my Lord."

CHARLES: "You... shall know my sword!"

GEORGE OF BRANDENBURG: "Before I let anyone take away the Word of God and ask me to deny my belief, I will kneel and let him strike off my head..."

"At this point, a filmmaker mindful of his audience's stereotypical pangs, might have gone out in Augsburg's streets break in LUTHER'S ANTHEM, "A MIGHTY FORTRESS IS OUR GOD." Director ERIC TILL doesn't do that. In fact, he only hints at Luther's musical accomplishments, which later influenced BACH and all the classical German composers. Yes, somewhere in the movie a group of worshippers sings '"OUT OF THE DEPTH I CRY TO YOU." But that's it. Clearly, "Luther" is not about Luther the musician."

14

"Nor is it about Luther the family man, although a hint at the immense influence of the Lutheran parsonage on Western civilization might be particularly welcome at a time when there are suggestions in some quarters that it might be OK for the parsonage to be inhabited by a him and a him or a here and a hereafter."

"But Luther the musician, or Luther the family man, would make great topics for separate films or installments of a television series, as would, alas, the old and sick Luther's against the Jews. Let's rejoice that this movie ends at a point when, with PHILP MELANCHTON's presentation of the AUGSBURG CONFESSION, the Reformer was at the pinnacle of his ministry and in the loving arms of a still youthful KATHARINA von BORA, played superbly by CLAIRE FOX, also English."

"Thankfully, Luther's chief message was that of the Gospel (which for some inexplicable reason played only fifth fiddle in an uninspiring Luther documentary on PBS this summer). Doubtless there are also other reasons to revisit the FATHER OF THE REFORMATION—the magnificent realism of his two-kingdoms theology, for example which would bring some sanity to postmodern times. But that HIS DISCOVERY OF A MERCIFUL GOD should come across what is also excellent entertainment—therein lies the filmmaker's genius."

"I have often wondered what effect great men of faith might have on artists who played them or performed their works. Thomas Quasthoff, the crippled German base-baritone, once said when he sang Christ's part in BACH'S SAINT MATTHEW PASSION he stopped being an agnostic. JOSEPH FIENNES, WHOSE CHURCH IS BY HIS OWN acknowledgment SOCCER, was made to ponder his own faith while acting Luther."

"You can't get away from it if you embrace this man," Fiennes told an interviewer. "I have found faith to play a big part in my life." This comes across forcefully in the way he masters the massive, threefold task of showing Luther's discovery of his personal relationship to God, the application of this discovery as priest and professor, and his concern with how much his accomplishments would last after his death. FOR LUTHER FULLY EXPECTED TO BE MARTYRED."

A POWERFUL JOURNEY

"If you think this kind of heavy-duty stuff can never be turned into a riveting film, stand corrected. In the opening scene YOU WILL LITERALLY BE SUCKED INTO THE TERRIFYING THUNDERSTORM THAT MADE A SCARED MARTIN LUTHER VOW TO BECOME A MONK, IF SPARED. Later you are tempted to identify with his fellow Augustinian monks, sniggering at Luther, shaking with fear over his sinfulness, spills the altar wine during his first consecration of the EUCHARIST. Then you see him in Rome, that "circus sewer and brothel clerics," stumbling disgustedly across whoring monks."

"You—yes, you! will experience with Luther the wise guidance of his Superior, JOHN von STAUPITZ (BRUNO GANZ), who makes him discover the liberating message of salvation by God's Grace through faith in Christ."

PROVIDENTIAL HISTORY: Staupitz was Luther's "JOHN THE BAPtTIST" anointing him on his unknown mission. Bruno Ganz born in beautiful ZURICH, Switzerland March 22, 1941, was "Germany's" greatest actor. In the film DOWNFALL (2004) his bunker portrayal of ADOLF HITLER, the year after portraying STAUPITZ, is the most realistic sorry Sir ANTHONY HOPKINS THE BUNKER, you are Welsh not Germanic. DOWNFALL was nominated for BEST FOREIGN LANGUAGE film at the 77th ACADEMY AWARDS. His portrayal of Hitler's rage after his generals failure to obey his orders spawned a series of INTERNET MEMES. I have the DVD its plot is based on Hitler's longtime secretary TRAUDL JUNGE's personal diary of Hitler's last days before Hitler's and his mistress EVA BRAUN's suicide on WALPURGIS "Devil's" NIGHT April 30, 1945, 10 days after Hitler's 56th birthday.

Ganz was a HOLOCAUST survivor law professor in the movie THE READER (2008) where KATE WINSLET is imprisoned for a Holocaust war crime she didn't commit, because she couldn't read and wouldn't admit this fact because of her pride. One of Ganz's students RALPH FIENNES, had been her teenage lover who read to her an older woman. He knows her truth but as a law student cannot help her. RALPH FIENNES, is Joseph's brother. His most notorious role was as the inhumane SS DEATH CAMP commandant in SCHINDLER's LIST. Schindler was portrayed by Irish actor LIAM NEESON. Fiennes also was evil and demented in the movie RED DRAGON.

Ganz portrayed a Nazi "cloning" doctor in the movie THE BOYS FROM BRAZIL (1978). GREGORY PECK portrays evil Dr. JOSEF MENGELE trying to clone another Hitler also using home environment euthenics. The only evil role beloved actor Gregory Peck played. Sir LAURENCE OLIVIER portrayed a Nazis hunter based on SIMON WIESENTHAL, who located and captured ADOLF EICHMANN in Argentina.

Ganz in UNKNOWN (2011) is a former STASI German communist agent who helps LIAM NEESON, a doctor whose wife disappears in Berlin. Nesson befriends a German taxi driver DIANE KRUGER. She was born in a little German town near Hannover/Hameln about 10 miles north of where my German grandfather is buried in the World War I section of the cemetery in Gronau. I visited his grave in June 1968, coming from Hannover and passed near Kruger's birthplace. Wikipedia her many films. HELEN OF TROY was great but not in $. Sorry BRAD PITT, ORLANDO BLOOM, ERIC BANA.

Ganz in FAUST. His last role before his death was in A HIDDEN LIFE, as a Nazi judge.

"You will, like Luther recoil, recoil during the magnificent scenes of JOHN TETZEL's sale of indulgences. You will sit among the superbly costumed congregants in Luther's church, having eye contact with him as he thunders from the nave—which is historically incorrect (he would have not used the pulpit) but cinematographically very effective—against this perversion of the Gospel. You will laugh with his Wittenberg students as he ridicules the folly of collecting relics: "18 of the 12 apostles are buried in Spain alone!"

"Sometimes dramatic films have to take some liberties with history, and "Luther" has some of those. As Luther hides in the WARTBURG [Castle] translating the NEW TESTAMENT into German, for example, two appalling events—the 1521 iconoclast riots and the 1525 PEASANTS' WARS—seem to flow into one. But the message comes across clearly. Luther's struggles and deep remorse over this film he horrors his REFORMATION have triggered, including the slaughter of 50,000 to 100,000 rebels.

"But that's precisely the point of this film: What history courses and even the most wonderful books cannot accomplish, succeeds here. In two gripping hours, you literally become part of one of the most dramatic biographies in Human History, a tale with enormous heights but also great lows most of us would shy away from. Within minutes you switch from breathlessness as you partake in the wild boar hunt of the extravagant Pope LEO X, who excommunicated Luther, to the calm and wily warmth of Saxony's prince elector FREDERICK THE WISE, who saved his "little monk," as he called him, and thus changed History."

"The inexorable Sir PETER USTINOV plays this ruler with so much allure and humor that he seems a prime candidate for an OSCAR AS BEST SUPPORTING ACTOR. In one of the movie's loveliest scenes, Luther enters Frederick's study to hand him the first print of the New Testament in German. As he engages the prince in dialogue, the aged Frederick impatiently snaps his fingers, asking with a childlike smile, "Do you think I can have my present now?"

PERSONAL USTINOV STORY: My dad said one night leaving the ABC TV Master Control room he had to take a cab because it was cold. He said Peter Ustinov got out of the cab. Dad said the seat was still warm. Ustinov, a Russian Baptist, in SPARTACUS took KIRK DOUGLAS baby and wife to safety and pass by Spartacus crucified on a Roman Cross. I AM SPARTACUS! When a child I saw QUO VADIS where Roman Emperor NERO portrayed by Ustinov burns Rome, to rebuild it, and blames it on the Christians who then puts Christians in the Coliseum where the Romans watch them killed by hungry lions. The Romans gave the people bread and circuses in the Coliseum Circus Maximus. Is America becoming like Rome? Rome was a Republic.

"This film's all about this gift's magnitude—it is a drama about the Gospel of Christ made available not just sages but to all, which is why Luther's deed enthralled all of Germany and the rest of Europe in the 16th Century. Such are the vagaries of History, though, that in much of Germany, Luther is recognized merely as a historical giant, while his true significance as a Christian prophet seems widely forgotten."

"But here comes yet another twist: So catastrophic is Germany's spiritual decline of the last decades that its Roman Catholic Church has joined its Protestant sister in promoting this film about the Father of the Reformation. As Cardinal KARL LEHMANN, chairman of the German Conference of Catholic Bishops, once told me, "We, too, recognize Luther as a great teacher of the faith."

"Ironically, in the much more religious United States, a leading film distributor told Dennis Clauss, executive producer of the film and corporate projects leader with Thrivent Financial for Lutherans, the movie's sponsor: "Great! I'll handle this,——-

"IF YOU LEAVE OUT THE CHRIST STUFF."

"It is amazing how confused movie moguls can be! "CHRIST STUFF"— THAT'S WHY WE WANT TO SEE THIS FILM; that's why you want to fret, smile and rejoice with Luther, and do battle on his side; that's why he is the MAN FOR THIS SEASON. HIS RENAISSANCE [Reformation] does not come to soon."

Magazine article photos: Diet of Worms—"I cannot and will not recant." Luther's defense of his writings before the Diet of Worms in April 1521 is faithfully and dramatically portrayed in the movie. Luther's declaration of faith could well have meant his death by fire at the stake. Photo: Luther (Joseph Fiennes) throws onto a fire the papal bull excommunicating him from the Roman Catholic Church. Photo: English actress Claire FOX superbly plays former nun Katharina von Bora, who became Martin Luther's wife. [She is face to face with Fiennes holding hands. Claire began her acting career at the National Theater alongside renowned actress Dame JUDI DENCH.] Photo: The movie has received a PG-13 rating. The scenes of the peasant war are graphically presented, along with several images of executions. Photo: Although quite young when he presided over the Diet of Worms in 1521, Charles V (Torben Liebrecht) was one of the most powerful men in Europe, and not someone a lowly monk should defy. He imposed an imperial ban, declared Luther an outlaw. [He had recently completed his Roman Catholic Confirmation which was strict because he would become the DEFENDER OF THE FAITH for Pope LEO X. It was possible Frederick, Charles older uncle was to be elected as Emperor.] Photo: Sir Peter Ustinov plays Elector Frederick the Wise. In this scene, Luther (Joseph Fiennes) presents him with a first print of the New Testament in German. Although such an event probably never happened, the scene underscores how Luther made the Gospel available to everyone. Photo: Luther praying—It is clear in the movie that it is Christ to whom Luther points for hope and salvation and who is the focus of his work. Photo: The movie concludes with Luther at the pinnacle of his ministry and in a blessed marriage to Katharina.

Wikipedia Review of movie Luther Budget: $30,000,000 Box office $29,413,900

Wikipedia Film INACCURACIES: "The film portrays congregants seated in PEWS. In reality, pews were not a common church fixture until after the Reformation." "In the film, Luther refers to Bible passages by the book, chapter, and verse. However, the Bible was not divided into verses until

1551, an even then the divisions were not ubiquitous until the GENEVA BIBLE. It is assumed that this was done in order that discerning viewers might easily locate the text to which Luther refers." [The archbishop of Mainz during the Diet of Worms, palace was in MILTENBERG am MAIN, my grandmother picturesque hometown. The oldest inn in Germany is there, In August 1958, my German grandfather showed me the cave where legendarily SIEGFRIED KILLED the DRAGON in Miltenberg. My mother showed me in the woods stone columns the Romans were going to use to build a bridge across the Main River

Dr. Uwe Siemon-Netto is religion editor for United Press International UPI, a member of Mount Olivet Lutheran Church, Washington, D.C.   September 2003

"LUTHER" A Film Review of Its Historicity

Rev. Dr. Eric W. Gritsch September 2003 a letter from my mentor Gettysburg Seminary

"Though well directed, acted and dramatically impressive, some caution needs to be exercised when the film might be used for education based on historical evidence. There is always room for "dramatic license", but when dealing with such influential historical figures as MARTIN LUTHER a fundamental loyalty to historical facts must be preserved.

I only focus on some basic facts which have been ignored, indeed abused, in the sequence of portraying Luther as a man who changed world History, as the film correctly assumes."

1. Luther's first first celebration of the Mass revealed his great anxiety about the priestly power to bring Christ from heaven to the altar. He wanted to leave the altar, but was signaled by his prior to continue. There is no evidence that he spilled the wine. Moreover, his father attended with many members of the family, gave 20 guilders as a gift to the monastery and, despite some criticism of Luther for becoming a monk rather than a lawyer, the father stayed and enjoyed the celebration. He did not leave after a public outburst of anger, as the film alleges.

2. "The Uprising of the Peasants made Luther so angry that he called for their killing as a divine mandate since the peasants identified the freedom in the gospel with violent liberation from their feudal landlords. About 5,000 peasants were finally massacred in the so-called battle of Frankenhausen, Saxony; their "noble: opponents lost six men. The spiritual leader of the rebellious peasants in Saxony was not Calstadt, but THOMAS MUENTZER who was executed. All rebellious peasants in German territories numbered about 60,000. About 6,000 were killed, not 100,000, as the film alleges.

3. "The Augsburg Confession was developed and drafted by Melanchthon who met with and was supported by the princes and other officials. Luther met with princes a year after the Diet of Augsburg, in 1531 at Smalcald when supporters founded the military Smalcald League to defend themselves against Catholic attacks. Luther never met with princes in connection with the Augsburg Confession and had no leading role in its production, as the film alleges."

4. Luther and FREDERICK THE WISE had only a relationship through Spalatin in order to protect the prince from any accusation of personal contact with the heretical professor. Consequently, Luther never saw him (except from a distance at the DIET OF WORMS in 1521). The moving scene of Luther handing the prince the German Bible never took place, as the film alleges."

5. "Luther at the Wartburg is the one part of his life when he agreed to hide, indeed change his appearance by being disguised as a German knight known as "Squire George" ("Junker Joerg"). While it is not necessary to show Luther with beard and knightly dress (though it would have

enhanced the film), it is important that he returned to WITTENBERG on his own, against the orders of Frederick the Wise. The prince did not issue a call for his return, as the film alleges."

"Other minor historical flaws could be pointed out, such as the use of a legend that his spouse "Katie" had been smuggled in herring barrels with other nuns into Wittenberg. It is uncertain where the nuns were hidden during their secret journey, Some sources talk about empty barrels, other add "herring". But no Luther scholar has confirmed the "smelly" part of the story."

"Instead of highlighting a legend, the film could have portrayed in some fashion one of the most dramatic events in Luther's career, the LEIPZIG DEBATE on July 4, 1519 with JOHN ECK—the only occasion when he was granted his wish for a FREE, SCHOLARLY DISPUTATION. The AMERICAN AUDIENCE would have enjoyed this "Fourth of July" event in Luther's life."

"It should have been easy to receive some expect technical advice for the prediction of such a significant film which after all, was sponsored by Lutherans in the United States and in Germany. History itself is a powerful medium. In the case of Luther, the historical facts themselves are just as dramatic as any film maker could make them through "dramatic license" without much concern for historicity."

Austrian Rev. Eric W. Gritsch, Ph.D. Emeritus Professor of Church History Gettysburg Lutheran Seminary FIRST director of the Institute for Luther Studies (1961-1994), Member of the Forum for German Culture Zion Church of the City of Baltimore.

Professor Gritsch was my mentor and sent me this review from the Internet and his last book on Luther's anti-semitism. I told him about my Lutheran mother and asked him many questions about Hitler which were historical, religious and theological.

LUTHER'S LIFE IN OUTLINE

Nov. 10, 1483—A son born to Hans and Margarethe Luther in Eisleben, Saxony, Germany
Nov. 11, 1483—The child baptized Martin, in honor of St. MARTIN OF TOURS.
April, 1501—Martin entered the University of ERFURT.
1502—Received the bachelor of arts degree.
Feb. 1505—Received the master of arts degree and began studying law.

July 3, (ca.) 1505—Luther, almost struck by lightening, vowed to become a monk.
July 17, 1505—Entered Augustinian cloister in Erfurt, Ordered by his superiors to continue his studies in theology, Luther re-entered the University of Erfurt.
April 4, 1507—Ordained a priest; thereafter became a teacher of theology.
1508—Transferred to the University of Wittenberg.
1510—Visited Rome as traveling companion of another monk.
Oct, 19, 1512—July 1513—Most probable time when Luther discovered the true meaning of the Gospel through study of Romans 1:17 justification by FAITH ALONE.

1516 (ca.)—Became priest of the City Church in Wittenberg, plus his academic duties.
Oct. 31, 1517—Tacked the 95 Thesis "On the Power of Indulgences" to Castle Church door, in Wittenberg.

April 26, 1518—Held discussions at the Augustinian chapter house in HEIDELBERG.
Aug. 7, 1518—Ordered to Rome for examination on the charge of heresy.
Oct. 12-14, 1518—Examination held at Imperial Diet in Augsburg through intervention by Luther's prince, FREDERICK THE WISE. Luther refused to recant.

July 4-8, 1519—Debate with JOHANN ECK at the University of LEIPZIG.

June 15, 1520—Threatened with excommunication by papal bull.

Jan. 2, 1521—Luther banned by papal bull.

April 17-18, 1521—Appeared before Emperor CHARLES V at the DIET OF WORMS.

May 25, 1521—Luther and his cause banned as HERETICAL, by the EDICT OF WORMS issued by the IMPERIAL DIET.

1521-1522—Spent nearly a year at the WARTBURG CASTLE of his protector, Frederick the Wise. During this time know as JUNKER JORG, Luther began translating the Bible into German.

March, 1522—Returned to Wittenberg to stop an outbreak of radicalism initiated by fellow-monks and academic colleagues.

1524-1525—Luther, considering social and political revolution as rebellion against God, refused to support the PEASANT'S WAR.

June 13, 1525—Martin Luther married Katherina von Bora, a former nun he had sheltered at Wittenberg. Their marriage was blessed with six children. In addition, they gave a home to 11 orphans.

Oct. 1-3, 1529—Debate at MARBURG, Germany with ULRICH ZWINGLI concerning the LORD'S SUPPER.

1529—Published SMALL CATECHISM and LARGE CATECHISM. Luther published almost 400 works in his lifetime.

1530—AUGSBURG CONFESSION, authored chiefly by PHILIP MELANCHTHON. (The ban of the Edict of Worms prevented Luther from sharing directly in the deliberations that produced the Confession.)

1537—Publish SMALCAL Articles, Luther's most characteristic summary of his faith.

1546—Return to Eisleben to arbitrate a dispute between the counts of Mansfeld.

Feb. 18, 1546 —Luther died in Eisleben following a heart attack.

[My Lutheran German mother Elisabeth Frank's birthday Feb. 22, 1915 in Frankfurt.]

(Based on "MARTIN LUTHER," Wilhelm Pauck, Encyclopedia Americana, 1964; and ABOUT MARTIN LUTHER, Channing L. Bete Co., Inc. Greenfield, MA)

MARTIN LUTHER WAS UNINTENTIONAL REBEL

George W. Cornell AP Religious Writer THE FREE LANCE-STAR Dec. 21, 1983

"A big, hearty, earthy man with a razor wit and a flair for plain words, MARTIN LUTHER sat at the head of a long dining table laden with home-grown victuals and rimmed by admiring students, usually some fellow professors and neighbors, his children and his wife, "my Lord Kate." "He savored those occasions, the good conversation, the good food, song and beer and assorted good companionship."   [Gemetlichkeit]

"Looking back on the whirlwind he had loosed in 16th-century Christianity, he says, "I did not intentionally undertake this arduous affair," but it happened as if by "DIVINE PLAN" through unforeseen "successive occasions." His purpose was not to attack the pope, but to counter the blasphemous voice of the hucksters," he says."   [Indulgences]

"But "the papists wrote remarkable things against me and I had to defend myself...When I was provoked I went ahead like a horse with blinders on...Well, God led us wondrously out of all that

and, for 20 years now, has held my head above the water without my understanding how."
"Thus a reflective Luther reminisced about his work that had fired the PROTESTANT REFORMATION, that unleashed principles of RELIGIOUS LIBERTY, that curbed Rome's political power over Western Europe, that spurred initial Roman Catholic reforms that eventually culminated in the SECOND VATICAN COUNCIL of 1962-65, which strongly influenced the course of History."

"Christians, whether Protestant or Catholic, cannot disregard the person and the message of this man," says a 1983 evaluation by a joint Catholic-Lutheran international team of scholars. "He is beginning to be honored in common as a witness to the Gospel, a teacher of the faith and a herald of spiritual renewal."

"Both tough and tender, he would write playful, sentimental note to his children and wife, but he could also be crude, stubborn and cantankerous, and in old age, venomous about Jews whom he once had praised as the "chosen people God" through whom divine revelation came." [Luther was angry when the Jewish people didn't accept his reformed biblical Christianity which would end their centuries of persecution as "CHRIST KILLERS" which was an Oxymoron to Jesus sacrifice for Humankind's sins.]

"His later vilification of them is acknowledged by modern admirers as a sad lapse."

"While he did not want to divide the Church, his initially respectful but rebuffed attempts to stop some blatantly slanted practices gradually swelled into a bitter, fulminating battle of mutual denunciations that fanned an isolated spark into a fire. It swirled in diverse forms through Northern Europe and England and at root precipitated the PILGRIM migration to America."

"The various branches of Protestantism "all stem in some measure" from Luther, writes Protestant biographer Roland Bainton. Lutheran JAROSLAV PELIKAN says Luther "more than any other man, changed the map of Christendom.""

"When it all started, the sportsman pope of the MEDICI family, LEO X, dismissed it indifferently as "some quarrel of monks.""

"But the isolated dispute, exacerbated by ignored appeals, published blasts, cutting debates, threats, imperial court hearings, overblown accusations and recriminations that hardened both sides, whipped into a tidal wave of reforms that overflowed the banks of Roman Catholicism and proliferated in Protestant churches."

"A candid, learned and fervently devout Roman Catholic priest, Luther was a magnetic teacher whose dauntless convictions hurled him into a world of drama. He was a tireless writer with masterful literary gifts, his translation of the BIBLE into German compared to SHAKESPEARE; a warm, loving family man, a prolific HYMN COMPOSER, [A MIGHTY FORTRESS IS OUR GOD] a compassionate pastor and counselor to people in trouble."

"The year 1983 marked the widely celebrated 500th anniversary of Luther's birth on Nov. 10, 1483, in Eisleben [ice love] Germany.

[Luther was baptized in Eisleben's St. Peter and Paul Church (the original font survives) on November 11, 1483, SAINT MARTIN'S birthdate, who was his namesake. Read my St. Martin dream about Jesus which inspired him to create Roman Catholic CHAPLAINS for soldiers. Luther preached his last sermon at St. Andreas Church in Eisleben where he passed on Feb. 18, 1546. My German mother born Feb. 22, 1915.]

PROVIDENTIAL HISTORY: LUDWIG GEYER was born in the little hamlet of Eisleben, Luther's birthplace. He was the stepfather of composer RICHARD WAGNER, whose biological father had died six months after his birth. Geyer was author of a stage play THE SLAUGHTER OF THE INNOCENTS in Leipzig which inspired Wagner's interest in the theater. On his death bed Geyer asked Wagner's mother "has he perchance a talent for music?" However, until Wagner heard a BEETHOVEN symphony was Wagner profoundly inspired to learn music, as a young teenager. Wagner arguably created the most spectacular theatrical Operas in history. Geyer was born Jan.

21, 1779, my father's birthday Jan. 28,1919 — Geyer passed on   Sept. 30, 1821— my German mother Elisabeth Frank passed, when I was at Bitburg Sept. 30, 1967. My brother Paul Thomas was born Sept. 30, 1945, in Lexington, KY in St. JOSEPH hospital where I was born on May 4, 1943. GEORGE CLOONEY was born in St. Joseph's on May 7, 1961. My granddaughter, and cousin Benjamin were born on Sept. 30, 2005 in Fredericksburg, VA, and Orlando, Florida. Read my other September 30 dates.

"The son of a miner and foundry owner. Luther finished the University of ERFURT and his father wanted him to become a lawyer, a tribe he later deplored as always mouthing justice but knowing nothing   of   it."

"Man's   only   comprehensive   justice,"   he   says,   "is   humility."

"As a self-critical youth, keenly conscientious and introspective, he was walking home one evening when an overhanging cloud unleashed a shuddering bolt of lightning near him. He cried out in terror, "Help, St. ANNE, I promise to become a monk!"

[St. Anne, was the mother of Mary mother of Jesus. Anne's name appears in the apocryphal GOSPEL OF JAMES circa 150 A.D. According to tradition, Saint Anne was born in Bethlehem, and married JOACHIM of NAZARETH. In the proto-evangelium of JAMES, Joachim is described as a rich and pious man, who regularly gave to the poor. At [Jerusalem] Temple, Joachim's sacrifice was rejected, as the couple's childlessness was interpreted as a sign of divine displeasure. Joachim consequently withdrew to the desert, where he fasted and did penance for 40 days. Angels then appeared to both Joachim and Anne to promise a child."]   Wikipedia

"Joachim later returned to Jerusalem and embraced Anne at the CITY GATE, located in the walls of Jerusalem. An ancient belief held that a child born of an elderly mother who had given up hope of having offspring was destined for great things. Parallels occur in the OLD TESTAMENT in the case of HANNAH, mother of SAMUEL." Wikipedia [Also, SARAH and ABRAHAM, ISSAC. In the NEW TESTAMENT ELISABETH mother of JOHN THE BAPTIST with Temple priest ZECHARIA.]

"HEBREW HANNAH means "favor, grace"; etymologically the same as ANNE who had also been childless." In LUTHERAN PROTESTANTISM, it is held that Martin Luther chose to enter religious life as an AUGUSTINIAN FRIAR after crying out to St, ANNE while endangered by lightning."

"Martin Luther: His Road to Reformation, 1482-1521" Martin Brecht (1985). "Anne receives little attention in the Latin Church prior to the late 12th century, dedications to Anne in Eastern Christianity occur as early as the 6th century." Wikipedia

KORAN Connection: "Anne (Arabic Hannah) is also revered in Islam, recognized as a highly spiritual woman and as the mother of Mary. She is noted named in the QUR'AN, where she is referred to as "The wife of 'IMRAN'. [Joachim] The QUR'AN describes her remaining childless until her old age. She prayed for a child and eventually conceived…Expecting the child to be a male, Hannah [Anne] vowed to dedicate him to isolation and service in the Second Temple. However, Hannah bore a daughter, and named her Mary. Her words upon delivering Mary reflect her status as a great mystic, realizing that while she had wanted a son, this daughter was God's gift to her."

> Then, when she brought forth she said: My Lord! Truly I
> Brought her forth, a female. And God is greater in knowledge
> Of what she brought forth. And the male is not like the female…
> So her Lord received her with the very best acceptance. And
> Her bringing forth caused the very best to develop in her.
>   [Koran Sura 3:36-37 trans Laleh Bakhtiar]   Wikipedia

The Koran states that Anne's daughter MARY CONCEIVED ISSA-JESUS THROUGH A VIRGIN BIRTH. However, Islam and Koran claim Jesus only as a great Prophet and teacher. ISLAM and JUDAISM cannot conceive or accept the Christian TRINITARIAN GOD-HEAD. Their belief is in a

MONOTHEISTIC single CREATOR god ALLAH not a sacrificial forgiving GOD through his SON JESUS CHRIST.

THE THREE MARY'S AT THE CROSS RELATED TO ST. ANNE

"In the late Middle Ages, legend held that Anne was married three times: first to Joachim, than to CLOPAS and finally to a man named SOLOMAS and that each marriage produced one daughter: MARY, MOTHER OF JESUS, MARY OF CLOPAS, and MARY SALOME, respectively. The sister of Saint Anne was SOBE, mother of ELIZABETH [elderly mother of JOHN THE BAPTIST].
PROVIDENTIAL FACT: The church of ST. ANNE of DUPRE in QUEBEC city is a church of miraculous healings like LOURDES in France.
[It is providential that these three women would be at the Crucifixion but this historical story makes them all related to Anne who was the mother of Mary. They are all named by the youngest disciple JOHN, who Jesus from the Cross, tells John to care for his mother. One question: Anne was unable to have children and gave birth to Mary divinely through God's intervention. Anne's two other daughters through two other husbands would make it appear that Joachim was infertile because of his age.]
"In an Augustinian monastery, as a diligent, acute student, Luther spent so long confessing his every minor, possible sin that his superior [Father Staupitz] told him to wait until he had something needing forgiveness. Ordained in 1507, he was persuaded to take a doctorate in theology and Biblical literature. Afterward at an extraordinarily young age, he became a professor at the University of Wittenberg."
"But gnawing doubts assailed him about his strenuous effort to bolster it by fasting and penitential exercises. In his spiritual crisis, he dealt with the Bible, which he had habitually read through twice yearly, now the Epistles of Paul resonated with new force."
"Their point was that faulty human beings are redeemed only "by faith" in the "sheer mercy" of God offered through Christ. Luther proclaimed; "I felt myself to be reborn and to have gone through open doors into paradise."
"The bracing, central message, "Sola fides," became the watch-word of the subsequently burgeoning PROTESTANT REFORMATION—that "only faith" justifies errant human beings through God's freely given Grace, that they can't merit or earn it, but that while unacceptable themselves, they need only to accept their acceptance. It is totally "A GIFT," PAUL puts it, "received by faith apart from works."
"A Catholic-Lutheran theological team, after five years' study of the issue, in 1983 reached "fundamental consensus" on that position — that "our entire hope" of salvation "depends wholly on the great mercy of God in Christ, the one mediator between God and fallen humanity," and not on human works or merit."
"But "justifying faith…necessarily issues in good works," the agreement says. As Luther himself put it, "good works do not make a man good, but a good man does good works."
"Other main themes of the Reformation, summed up in phrases, "SOLA CHRISTUS"—
"only Christ" as the basis of REDEMPTION—and "SOLA SCRIPTURA"—"ONLY SCRIPTURE" as the basic rule of faith—also have gained new standing in contemporary Catholicism through concepts stressed by the Second Vatican Council.
"It also, in a shift from the past, affirmed the need of continual church reform, recognized the universal priesthood of believers, along with the ordained priesthood of believers, along with the ordained priesthood, upheld religious liberty and ordered worship in the language of the people instead of Latin—all advocated by Luther."
"His "magnificent religious values need to be appreciated by all," says Catholic Archbishop John

Whealon of Hartford, Conn. "He was a Catholic, a Christian, loyal to the church, to her creeds and her sacraments." Of the Church rupture, Whealon notes that in Luther's time, "there was much decadence in the church," with the pope then more concerned with politics, money and power than   religion."

"The situation that ignited the conflict occurred in 1517 when Albert, a youth of 23 and member of a German dynamic line, paid to the papacy a fee of 43,000 gulden, borrowed from the Fugger banking house, to obtain control of a third church region as archbishop of MAINZ, with both ecclesiastical   and   civil   powers."

"So that he could repay the bank, the pope authorized Albert to sell indulgences in his territory for a period of eight years. Half the revenues would go to Rome to help the pope rebuild ST. Peter's Basilica, in addition to the 43,000 gulden already paid."

"Among the vendors dispatched by Albert was Dominican monk JOHANN TETZEL, offering indulgences to cancel out purgatorial punishment sins both for those living and their dead relatives and friends. He even added an advertising jingle, "As soon as the coin in the coffer rings, the soul from Purgatory springs." [PURGATORY was "a limbo" between Heaven and Hades is in the Apocrypha text in Maccabees.]

"Luther heard of it in disgust. He drafted a paper in ecclesiastical Latin of 95 THESES protesting the practice, and circulated it for consideration by German bishops. Legend says he also, on ALL SAINTS EVE, Oct. 31, 1517, affixed his theses to the WITTENBERG castle door, in accord with custom   for   presenting   issues   for   debate."

[Today, this date is celebrated as HALLOWEEN, Hallowed Eve, when people wore scary masks which scared off devils or demons part of Germany's medieval folklore.]

"In any case, while he sought only theological discussion, the new medium of the printing press spread his protest and it swiftly became a sensation throughout Germany. The pope eventually ordered him tried for heresy, and a papal legate and others accused Luther of denying the pope's full authority. This Luther then proceeded to do, although agreeing to a moratorium in public discussion."

"The truce was broken by other goading accusations and, amid escalating argument, the pope issued a bull giving Luther 60 days to recant or suffer "our excommunication and anathema" under "the wrath of Almighty God.""

"Before Luther had even seen the bull, he was put on trial April 16, 1520, before the HOLY ROMAN EMPEROR CHARLES V and princes of the German states at the DIET OF WORMS, demanding   that   he   "repudiate   your   books   and   the   errors   they   contain.""

"Under two days of intimidating examination, Luther finally took his unbudging, forthright position: "Since then your majesty and your lordships desire a simple reply, I will answer without horns or teeth. Unless I am convicted by Scripture and plain reason — I do not accept the authority of popes and councils, for they have contradicted each other — MY CONSCIENCE IS CAPTIVE TO THE WORD OF GOD. I cannot and will not recant anything, for to go against conscience is neither right or safe. God help me, Amen. Here I stand. I cannot do otherwise."

"Shortly afterward, the EDICT OF WORMS condemned Luther as a "convicted heretic" to be seized, not to be harbored by anyone, and ordered his books be destroyed."

'However, a band of armed supporters of Luther, realizing his life was in danger, whisked him forcibly into hiding at WARTBURG CASTLE where he remained for two years, studying, writing, translating the Bible into German, while most people assumed him dead."

"Eventually, under protection of the prince of SAXONY, FREDERICK THE WISE, Luther returned to Wittenberg, resuming work as teacher and pastor, still wearing a cassock. But he called it non-essential."

"He was in his 40s, three years after his return to Wittenberg, when a practical situation induced him to marry. One of several nuns he had helped get resettled and find husbands, KATHARINA

von BORA, held out for Luther himself, and he finally gave in."
"She supervised their big household, with him alternatively calling her "master," "lord," "grand wizard" or "my chain." She called him "doctor," They had a close, warm family for 20 years before he died with six children. 'I would not swap my Kate for France with Venice thrown in,' he said."
"He was involved in negotiating various agreements that consolidated the "Protestant estates in the empire. Basically a conservative man, he opposed the peasant uprisings of that period and also the fragmentation of various new sects, such as ANABAPTISTS and others that denied Christ's real presence in the LORD'S SUPPER.""
"He objected to his own followers calling themselves LUTHERANS, as they did,"
"Once, in retrospect about the movement he started, he mused, "It was the opposition that caused it all. If they had been moderate, what might they have accomplished. Nor can I claim to have been a good teacher or preacher. You have to find a better nail for your horseshoe than that.""

PREACHER JOHNATHAN EDWARDS INSPIRED THE GREAT AWAKENING IN AMERICA

C.S. [Clive] LEWIS INSTITUTE REPORT Spring 2001
PROFILES IN FAITH JOHNATHAN EDWARDS (1703-1758)
Dr. Art Lindsley Scholar-in-Residence
"The power of his preaching lay in the vivid imagery in his sermons."

"Edwards has been variously evaluated as the greatest philosopher/theologian America has ever produced or else caricatured as a monster who delighted in tormenting his congregation with hell fire and damnation preaching, that even his opponents recognized his genius. Who was this man who caused such extreme reactions?"
"Edwards was born into a pastor's family October 5, 1703. He was the only son, and had 10 sisters, each of the sisters was about six feet tall, and he was referred to as Timothy Edwards' "Sixty 60 feet of daughters." Johnathan also grew tall and thin."
"He was admitted to Yale at 13 years of age, graduated at 17 and continued there to study for the ministry at Yale Seminary. In 1726, he became assistant minister in his grandfather's church at Northampton, Massachusetts, where he remained for most of his adult life."
"Although he is know as a powerful preacher and one who was instrumental in the GREAT AWAKENING in AMERICA, he was not the fiery preacher conveyed by his most famous sermon, "SINNERS IN THE HANDS OF AN ANGRY GOD." His voice was not very powerful, since he never used loud volume or dramatic gestures to make his points. The power of his preaching lay in the vivid imagery in his sermons. He believed that people would remember that which was made most vivid to their senses. It was this "rhetoric of sensation" that made his sermons effective."
"In SAMUEL HOPKINS' "LIFE OF EDWARDS he says, "He commonly spent 13 hours, every day, in his study…As part of his daily devotion he rode his horse into the woods and would walk alone meditating.""
"Johnathan drew up 70 RESOLUTIONS that he regularly reviewed in order to maintain his spiritual edge. They include:
"Resolved, Never to do anything out of revenge."
"Resolved, to study the Scriptures so steadily, constantly and frequently, as that I may find, and plainly perceive myself to grow in the knowledge of the same."

"Resolved, Never to give over, nor in the least to slacken my fight with my corruptions, however unsuccessful I may be."
Resolved, that I will do whatsoever I think to be most to God's Glory."

"Never to do anything which I should be afraid to do, if it were the last hour of my life."

"Where Edwards was socially stiff, his wife SARAH was socially adept. Where he was intellectual and sometimes abstract, she was practical and concrete. They complemented each other well. They had 11 children. In 1900, a reporter tracked down 1,400 descendants and found they included 13 college presidents, 65 professors, two graduate school deans, 80 holders of public office, including three senators and three governors of states. They had written 135 books, included many bankers, heads of business, and many missionaries."

"Edwards became the president of Princeton [college of New Jersey] when a smallpox epidemic began. He volunteered to try the then new experimental smallpox vaccination. He soon passed from smallpox. He is buried there. Two daughters reveal his last words.

"Give my kindest love to my dear wife, and tell her that the uncommon union which was so long subsisted between us has been of such a nature as I trust is spiritual and therefore will continue forever."

"Martyn Lloyd-Jones comments:

"No man is more relevant to the present condition of Christianity than Jonathan Edwards…He was a mighty theologian and a great evangelist at the same time…He was preeminently the theologian of revival. If you want to know anything about true revival. Edwards is the man to consult."

IRONIC HISTORY FACT: AARON BURR, SR., was Johnathan Edward's son-in-law, he had married Esther Edwards which made Edwards the grandfather of their son AARON BURR, later Vice President of the United States. Burr was almost indicted for treason and is infamous for his duel with ALEXANDER HAMILTON who Burr killed at Weehauken, New Jersey opposite Manhattan. Dueling was legal but not promoted. Burr's father had been president of Princeton and persuaded Edwards to succeed him.

SINNERS IN THE HANDS OF AN ANGRY GOD

"This was a sermon written by British Colonial Christian theologian Jonathan Edwards, preached to his own congregation in Northampton, Massachusetts, to unknown effect, and again on July 8, 1741 in ENFIELD, Connecticut. It combines vivid imagery of Hell with observations of the world and citations of the Scripture. It provided a glimpse into the theology of the FIRST GREAT AWAKENING of 1730-1755. This is a typical sermon of the Great Awakening, emphasizing the teaching that Hell is real—a place that actually exists. Edwards hoped that the imagery and language of his sermon would awaken audiences to the horrific reality of Hell that awaits them should they continue living without calling on Christ to be saved. The underlying point is that God has given humans a chance to confess their sins. Edwards said that it is the mere will of God that keeps wicked men from the depths of Hell. This act of restraint has given humans a chance to believe and trust in Christ." Wikipedia

DOCTRINE—"There is nothing that keeps wicked men at any one moment out of Hell, but the mere pleasure of God."

"Most of the sermon's text consists of ten "commandments":
1. God may cast wicked men into Hell at any given moment.

2. The wicked deserve to be cast into Hell. Divine justice does not prevent God from destroying the wicked at any moment.
3. The wicked, at the moment, suffer under God's condemnation to Hell.
4. The wicked on earth—at this very moment—suffer a sample of the torments of Hell. The wicked must not think, simply because they are not physically in Hell, that God (in Whose hand the wicked now reside) is not—at this moment—as angry with them as He is with those miserable creatures He is now tormenting in Hell, and who—at the very moment—do feel and bear the fierceness of His wrath.

5. At any moment God shall permit him, Satan stands ready to fall upon the wicked and seize them as his own.
6. If it were not for God's restraints, there are, in the souls of wicked men, hellish principles reigning which, presently, would kindle and flame out into hellfire.
7. Simply because there are not visible means of death before them at any given moment, the wicked should not feel secure.
8. Simply because it is natural to care for oneself or to think that others may care for them, men should not think themselves safe from God's wrath.
9. All that wicked men may do to save themselves from Hell's pains shall afford them nothing if they continue to reject Christ.
10. God has never promised to save us from Hell, except for those contained in Christ through the covenant of Grace,

"Edwards ends the sermon with one final appeal: "Therefore let everyone that is out of Christ, now awake and fly from the wrath to come." According to Edwards, only by returning to Christ can one escape the stark fate he outlines."

"Edwards was interrupted may times during the sermon by people moaning and crying out, "What shall I do to be saved?"   Wikipedia

[This was not his home church and was due south probably a couple of days by horse. Edwards was informed that this church and its members were becoming weak in their faith like Asia Minor's church at LAODECIA. This church encouraged Edwards to begin an evangelical REVIVAL known as THE GREAT AWAKENING in British colonial America. Ironically, many of these church congregations comprised members who had come to America for religious freedom from Britain's State Anglican church.]

PERSONAL SMALL WORLD PROVIDENTIAL STORY: On May 3, 2019, I had just gotten gas in East Hartford, Connecticut. I asked a man how to get back onto the Interstate. He said, "I am not from here, I am from Enfield." I said that is where the famous Johnathan Edwards church is located. He retorted, "It is today liberal." I told him I was writing a book about my Lutheran mother leaving Hitler's Germany and how Hitler was trying to destroy Christianity. He said. "Read the book HITLER'S CROSS by Pastor Lutzer." I said, "I read it in 2002, it is the best book on the subject." PROVIDENCE?

INVENTING THE GREAT AWAKENING

Frank Lambert book reviewed by Helena M. Wall History Book Club Midsummer 1999
"If he GREAT AWAKENING were a movie, it would be RASHOMON. [1950, Japanese Samurai film by Kurosawa considered one of the greatest films "Roshomon effect". Hero actor Toshiro Mifune, 150 films, was born in Qingdao, Shandong, China, occupied by the Japanese army after it was seized from German control in World War I. His parents were Methodist missionaries. He was born April 1, 1920, he passed Dec. 24, 1997. My Jewish daughter was born Dec. 24, 1975.]
"Few events — if we can even call it an event—in Colonial American history have elicited so many clashing perceptions and irreconcilable interpretations as this series of religious revivals, occurring primarily in New England and New Jersey, in the late 1730s and early 1740s. To revivalists, the Awakening was "an extraordinary and mighty work of God's special Grace," a "shower of Divine blessing." Its fruits were "wonderful," in every sense of that term, transforming society and saving souls. "When once the Spirit of God began to be so wonderfully poured out in the general way through that town," Jonathan Edwards wrote of the Northampton Revival. "People had soon done with their old quarrels, backbitings, and intermeddling with other men's matters." To judge the power of the Awakening, Edwards thought, one need only observe that "it was no longer the tavern" that drew local crowds, "but the Minister's House, that was thronged far more than ever the Tavern had been meant to be."

"A DANGEROUS SHAM?"

"But to its opponents, the so-called Awakening was a dangerous sham, a DELUSION that generated "enthusiastic Heat" and "Commotion in the Passions," while failing to reform hearts and minds. "Tis not evident to me," wrote Charles Chauncey, one of the most influential anti-revivalists, "that Persons…have a better Understanding of Religion, a better government of their Passions, a more Christian Life to their Neighbor, or that they are more decent and regular in their Devotions toward God." Indeed, evangelical ministers seemed to their opponents to be no more than snake-oil salesman. A "Sett of Rhapsodists—Enthusiasts—Bigots—Pedantic, illiterate, impudent Hypocrites,"
"Historians have generally been kinder to the revival movement, beginning with the minister-scholar, Joseph Tracy, who first used the term "Great Awakening" in the 1840s; in fact, several modern historians have seen the Awakening as an engine of social change and an important INFLUENCE on the AMERICAN REVOLUTION."
PROMOTING THE WORK OF GOD— "First, the revivalist "discovered a thing hidden,"
in this case a genuine "work of God"; Second, they were active instruments in promoting that work, designing a program intended to spur a spiritual awakening, and significantly, spreading the news of that awakening. Revivalists used pamphlets, broadsides, conversion narratives, and newspapers to transform accounts of local revivals into a larger, unified story of a single intercolonial "general Awakening."
"As Lambert shows, the invention of the Great Awakening was a heavily contested process, with revivalists and anti-revivalists struggling to control its interpretation." It was also a continuing process, as later evangelicals reinterpreted the Awakening for their own purposes."
Frank Lambert is Associate Professor of History at Perdue University author of "Pedlar in Divinity: George Whitefield and the Transatlantic Revivals, 1731-1770."
Helena Wall is Professor of History at Pomona College author of "Fierce Communion Family & Community in Early America."

SUBTLE SEDUCTION

WHY SOME CHRISTIANS ARE TURNING TO THE NEW AGE

George Hague THE PLAIN TRUTH magazine September 1993

"The scene: a bookstore in an upscale shopping district. During the day the store does a brisk business, Customers scurry to find titles and store clerks ring up the sales. But tonight is different."

"Several people entering the store are not here to buy books, but to exchange ideas. They assemble downstairs in the clean, well-lighted basement room."

"There's a construction worker, a homemaker, a college student, a retired fisherman. In all, 15 people from five ethnic backgrounds."

"Welcome to the New Age and its hottest movement—study groups that use the book A COURSE IN MIRACLES as a guide."

"With more than 1,200 pages, a royal blue cover and gold stamped lettering, the book looks like a BIBLE, even laid out in a chapter and verse. This resemblance is intentional after all, the Course claims as its author the central person of the Bible, none other than Jesus Christ himself."

"According to the preface of the book. A COURSE IN MIRACLES was "CHANNELED" to a psychiatrist who took a sort of cosmic dictation from "THE VOICE." The dictation began in 1965 and took seven 7 years."

"People heard about the book from friends of friends. It quietly swept the country, selling more than 750,000 copies since its first mass printing in 1976."

"Gradually, readers began to form study groups, posting public invitations in bookstores, cafes and laundromats. More than 1,000 study groups have sprung up around the world but since there is no formal structure to the movement, no one knows the number.

Each group is like a school-yard game, with one difference: Even the least athletic person is invited to play."

INSIDE THE COURSE—The title, A Course in Miracles, does not refer to wonders like the parting of the Red Sea or the turning of water into wine. Instead, it refers to something more dramatic— a change of heart and way of thought. On the surface this miracle seems like that of Christian conversion. But there are major differences!"

"In the basement: The study group gathers in a circle, sitting on folding metal chairs. They forsake comfort of the body to find comfort of the mind. And make no mistake, that is what they find, Though this comfort is ephemeral, to these people, it's something."

"The teacher begins the lecture: What you need to say to yourself is. 'From this moment on, I'm going to GIVE UP MY OPINION and INTERPRETATION of EVERYTHING.' "

"Thus begins an introspective pep talk filled with religious jargon and pop psychology. Tonight the emphasis is on forgiving—FORGIVING FRIENDS, PARENTS, MATES, CO-WORKERS and, most of all, YOURSELF."

"But this forgiveness with a twist. According to A Course of Miracles, SIN DOES NOT EXIST, SO WHAT IS THERE TO REPENT OR FORGIVE? As the teacher said, "Sin is like an obnoxious child. If you ignore it, it will go away."

"According to the Course, the whole physical world, including our bodies, IS AN ILLUSION. This sweeping foundational principle has far reaching consequences."

"Though the Course TALKS ABOUT CHRIST, THE HOLY SPIRIT, THE ATONEMENT and PRAYER, it comes to dramatically different conclusions than the Bible. In several places in the book it even offers commentary on biblical scriptures, or as the Course states, "the UPSIDE-DOWN thinking in the New Testament."

"Some of this "upside-down thinking" regards the Crucifixion, and how, according to the Course, "the Apostles often misunderstood it.""

"As one teacher of the Course put it: "Jesus DID NOT SUFFER and DIE for our sins.""

"This idea flagrantly contradicts the Bible "For Christ died for sins once for all, the righteous for the unrighteous, to BRING YOU TO GOD." (1 Peter 3:18)."

"Thus A Course in Miracles is a perversion and HERESY of the central message of the Gospel. For the unchurched to believe the philosophy of this book is one thing. They do not know the Gospel of Salvation. For Christians to believe is another matter."

"Christians have read the Bible, heard sermons, attended Bible studies. Of all people, they should understand the Gospel. Why do some FALL FOR THE FANTASIES of A Course in Miracles?"

"Back to the basement: Each person, in turn, reads out loud from the Course. The teacher occasionally interrupts to comment on the passage and asks for responses from the group. As the meeting goes on, the participants disclose their inner thoughts and feelings."

"Despite having different ethnic, social and economic backgrounds, the members of the group do have things in common—pain, hurt, emptiness, guilt. Most of all guilt. The teacher interrupts: 'We haven't been bad, we haven't sinned, we're just doing the best we can. The promise of this way of thinking is peace." In other words, forget about your guilt, because it does not exist since SIN DOES NOT EXIST. Voila! Peace of mind."

"Every week the members of the group return to this basement to be convinced of this illusion. They long to believe anything that will some-how undo their past mistakes and pain. For these people, the PEACE OF MIND can only come through Jesus Christ is elusive (as it is for some Christians)."

CHRIST AND PEACE—The evening before the crucifixion, Jesus Christ was comforting his disciples, promising them he would send them the HOLY SPIRIT. He equated the Holy Spirit with peace: "Peace I leave with you; my peace I give you. I do not give to you as the world gives. Do not let your hearts be troubled and do not be afraid." John 14:27.

"A person living in peace is not burdened by guilt. The removal of this guilt and the fear it brings is a great gift from Jesus Christ."

"The apostle PAUL, in his epistle to the Colossians, explained how we can have our guilt removed so we can live in peace. Christ and his sacrifice, Paul wrote: "For God was pleased to have all his fullness dwell in Him, and through Him to reconcile to himself all things on earth or things in Heaven, by making peace through His blood, shed on the cross." Colossians 1:19-20."

"Paul continued in verse 22, God "has reconciled you by Christ's physical body through death to present you Holy in His sight, without blemish and free from accusation." And in verse 23, "This is the Gospel that you heard and that has been proclaimed.""

"The fact that Jesus Christ, God in the flesh, died for our sins and that we can receive forgiveness for our sins by accepting his sacrifice through faith, is the central message of the Gospel. The acceptance of the Gospel brings the Christian to a new life through the Holy Spirit—a life not burdened by guilt, "Free from accusation," Paul called it."

"Though several of the people are Christians, and some attend worship services, for some reason they feel the Gospel message is not enough to assuage their guilt."

"At one point in the meeting, the teacher turned the discussion to judgment and criticism. she made a negative comment about a church she once attended. Many agreed with a knowing smile."

"Their smiles and nods were a sad commentary. These people had attended Christian churches, but did they hear the Gospel?"

"Apparently not. From their comments, they heard judgments on hair lengths, clothing styles, musical tastes, political platforms and personal interests. Instead of the good news, they heard condemnation, criticism, you'd better-shape-up, toe-the-line."

"They heard catch phrases like "turn or burn" to scare them into repentance to escape hellfire. They heard slogans like "get right or get left," so they would change their lives before a soon-coming RAPTURE or GREAT TRIBULATION.'

"Such preaching and teaching overshadow the Gospel of forgiveness—that after we walk in newness of life by accepting the blood of Jesus Christ and His atoning work on the cross for our past   sinful   mistakes."

"Before going to this meeting, I was a bit apprehensive. What would I find? People sitting on Persian   carpets   mumbling   mantras?"

"No, instead I found normal people who for some reason couldn't stomach Christianity as it's served up to them in their neighborhood churches."

"Can we blame them for not being interested in someone's personal agenda—a laundry list of personal tastes and dislikes—that some attach to the Gospel of Christ?"

"The Gospel is not like some Congressional legislation burdened with dozens of special interests clauses. If we present it as such, we drive the flock from the church to basements where they study books like A Course in Miracles."

"This book is not the only New Age writing that has made its way into the lives of some Christians. Several NEW AGE ideas have found fertile ground."

"How can we help our friends, perhaps even our own children, from falling for the deceptive lure of the NEW AGE MOVEMENT?"

STUMBLING BLOCKS—An allure of the New Age for some is the movement's lack of condemnation and value judgments. In the New Age, you don't make mistakes. Life is more like a   series   of   value-free   experiments."

"Jesus Christ, however, does offer a life of subjective, ad hoc values. God has standards. A partial list of them is recorded in the Ten Commandments."

"As a teacher of the ways of God, the Church has the responsibility to take stands on moral issues—fornication, adultery, lying, stealing, murder."

"The Church must not compromise on these issues. But, at the same time, the Church must apply mercy   when   dealing   with   people   who   sin."

"Jesus Christ, himself, gave a wonderful example of this balance when dealing with the woman caught in adultery. His words."If any one of you is without sin, let him be the first to throw a stone at her." John 8:7, should ring in our ears when we deal with individuals who have spiritual problems."

"After the teachers of the law and the Pharisees left in shame, Christ told the woman: "Neither do I condemn you…Go now and leave your life of sin" (verse 11). In our dealings with people who sin and repent, we must be careful not to exact a punishment God himself does not require."

"We must be all the more careful when making decisions about matters not covered in the Bible. Paul called such marginal topics "disputable matters,"

"In the first verses of Romans 14, Paul addresses the subject of personal convictions and individual beliefs of Christians. Among other beliefs, some Church members in Rome believed it a sin to eat meat."

"Paul's judgment on the issue was not to take a dogmatic stand on the matter. "Who are you to judge someone else's servant?" (verse 4), he asked."

"It seems that as long as the issues did not become divisive. Paul was content to leave these matters alone. He urged the Roman Christians not to dwell on these points."

"Later, in verse 12-13, he wrote: "Each of us will give an account of himself to God. Therefore let us stop passing judgment on one another. Instead, make up your mind not to put any stumbling block   or   obstacle   in   your   brother's   way.

"All people responsible to teaching the Word of God—ministers, parents, laypersons—should regularly question themselves to see if they are laying unnecessary obstacle before those who teach."

"For example, some Christians have judged their brothers or sisters in Christ for such offenses as their choice of music, their methods of child rearing, their clothing styles, the   height of their shoes, for growing a beard. Need I go on?"

'Everyone will not dress in the same styles, will not rear their children according to the same theories, will not eat the same types of food, will not listen to the same types of music and will not support the same social programs."

"When he summed up his discussion on "disputable matters," the apostle Paul wrote, "Accept one another, just as Christ accepted you, in order to bring praise to God." Romans 15:7

NEW AGE CELEBRATION—MARIANNE WILLIAMSON

"Los Angeles: The NEW AGE is heady wine, even for a Hollywood crowd. It was December 21, the night of the NEW AGE Christmas gala presided over by the guru, counselor-to-the stars [Hollywood not Heavenly] MARIANNE WILLIAMSON."

"MS Williamson is author of the best-selling book A RETURN TO LOVE. She calls her publications a   book   report   on   the   New   Age   classic   A   COURSE   ON   MIRACLES."

"When Williamson walked out onto the stage, the capacity crowd at the Wilshire Ebell Theatre exploded with thunderous applause. Ms. Williamson is a hybrid mix of charismatic preacher, street-smart executive and stand-up comedian."

"That night, her spiritual message, based on the principles of the book A COURSE IN MIRACLES, was an allegory of Christ's conception and birth."

"According to her interpretation, we can fulfill the role of Mary by allowing the Holy Spirit to enter us, and we can give birth in Christ, who is not another person, but, much to our surprise, IS US. In short, her message—the Course's message—is that we are all Christs if we would only recognize the fact."

"If, to you, this sermon sounds radically different from the message of the New Testament, you're right. As Ms. Williamson said in the theater in Los Angeles. "The ego turned Jesus' teachings into a   religion."

"Translated her statement means that the Apostles of Christ got his message wrong in their New Testament writings, so Jesus tried again, this time by channeling his teachings through a New York   psychiatrist."

"One teacher of the Course wrote, in the pamphlet titled AN INTRODUCTION TO THE COURSE OF MIRACLES, that the Course is "clearly intended not as a restatement, but as a purification, of traditional Christianity." That's a bold statement indeed."

"As Dean Halverson, a critic of the New Age philosophy wrote, "Anyone who believes the Course is compatible with Christianity either does not understand the Course or Christianity or both," (Spiritual Counterfeits Project 7, No. 1, page 23)

WHAT IS THE NEW AGE?

"The New Age movement can be expensive or lucrative, depending on which side of the cash register you're on. But behind the glitzy advertising that offers METAPHYSICS in exchange for hard cash, there can be some serious philosophy. Pinning this philosophy down, however, is difficult."

"Even the title "New Age movement" is misleading. The name gives the impression of a unified, cohesive group. That is not the case. There is no hierarchical or congregational system to which

"Thus, many "NEW AGERS" don't like that title at all. They feel it groups too many divergent belief systems—shamanism, Wicca [witches], pop psychology and Eastern religions, to name just a few—under the same umbrella. They have a point."

"As a general rule, however, most New Age groups hold the following beliefs in common:

* "All is one" or universal oneness. This tenant implies that everything, living and inanimate, seen and unseen, is of one essence. And, that this essence is the ultimate reality and divinity."
* Humans are divine. This unbiblical idea stems from the above premise. In other words, humans, as part of the Universal Oneness, are themselves divine."
* The belief that humans suffer from a type of spiritual amnesia, having forgotten that they are part of the Oneness and divinity."
* This ignorance (of being god) is the enemy, not any supposed evil. In an attempt they are god, humans must seek enlightenment via any number of methods—meditating, [channeling], chanting, listening to esoteric music, seeking mystical knowledge, using mind-altering drugs— whatever works."

Suggested reading: UNDERSTANDING THE NEW AGE by Russell Chandler, Word Publishing 1988. In his book Mr. Chandler accurately and responsibly discusses the New Age movement for a Christian audience."

[Adam and Eve were divine creations of God who ate the "forbidden fruit" actually wisdom from the tree of life/knowledge which Satan proclaimed: "Will make you gods."

"GLOSSARY:—ALLEGORY: A story that symbolically represents another meaning than what is apparently stated.

CHANNELING: To receive spiritual messages from a "higher plane," often in an altered state of mind, such as a trance.

GURU: A religious leader or a spiritual guide.

HERESY: A belief contrary to Christian doctrine.

MANTRA: A mystical phrase repeated over and over in meditation to bring about an altered sate of mind.

SHAMANISM: Most often used as a general term for native religions that do not spring from the Judeo-Christian heritage, where a holy person uses magic in an attempt to influence gods, demons and ancestral spirits.

WICCA: An ancient religion from Northwestern Europe that uses magic to communicate with the deity and influence events. Called witchcraft, it is strongly oriented to nature."

A COURSE FOR MIRACLES—combined volume—Preface-Text—Workbook for Students— Manual for Teachers—Classification of Terms-Supplements published by the Foundation for Inner Peace editors Helen Schucman, Bill Thetford, Kenneth Wapnick 1976 Viking pub. 1,333 pages [original 1,200 pages no workbook written in 7 years.]

"Helen Schucman was born Helen Dora Cohn July 14, 1909 in New York City her parents were both half-Jewish they were non-observant. Her mother Rose Black dabbled in THEOSOPHY [psychic Madame Blavatsky, who also inspired Hitler's occultism]. She also studied various expressions of Christianity such as CHRISTIAN SCIENCE and the UNITY SCHOOL OF CHRISTIANITY. However, it was the family housekeeper, Isabel who had the the deepest religious influence on Schucman while she was growing up. In 1921, when she was 12, she visited LOURDES, France, where she had a spiritual experience, and in 1922 she was baptized as a BAPTIST. Later in life, she considered herself an ATHEIST. [Vanity Fair] In May 1933, she married, in a 10-minute ceremony in a local rabbi's office. Her husband Louis owned bookstores on "BOOK ROW" in Manhattan, used books on Park Avenue between UNION SQUARE and

ASTOR PLACE. [From 1970-1974, I bought 2,000? books at THE STRAND BOOKSTORE at 9TH and Broadway. It was the best bookstore in New York City. In a TV movie MARILYN MONROE, when married to Jewish author/playwriter ARTHUR MILLER (THE CRUCIBLE), tells Miller that she buys her books at THE STRAND bookstore.] "The only Book Row store surviving today is the STRAND." Wikipedia

"Schucman was a clinical psychologist and research psychologist and professor of medical psychology at Columbia University 1958-1976. She is best known for having "SCRIBED" with help of colleague William Thetford the book A COURSE IN MIRACLES (1st edition, 1975), the contents of which she claimed had been given her by an inner voice she identified as Jesus. However, at her request, her role as its "writer" was not revealed to the general public until after her death." Wikipedia

"A Course in Miracles was written as a collaborative venture between Schucman and William Thetford. In 1958 Schucman began her professional career at Columbia-Presbyterian Medical Center in New York City as Thetford's research associate. In the spring of 1965, at a time when their weekly office meetings had become so ostentatious that they both dreaded them, Thetford suggested to Schucman that "THERE MUST BE ANOTHER WAY". Schucman believed that this interaction acted as a stimulus, triggering a series of inner experiences that were understood by her visions, dreams, and heightened imagery, along with an "inner voice" which she identified as JESUS. She said that on Oct. 21, 1965, an "inner voice" told her: "This is A COURSE IN MIRACLES, please take notes." Schucman said that the writing made her very uncomfortable, though it never seriously occurred to stop." The next day, she explained the events of her "note taking" to Thetford. To her surprise, Thetford encouraged her to continue the process, He offered to assist her in typing out her notes as she read them to him. The transcription the next day repeated itself regularly for many years to come. In In 1972, the dictation of the three main sections of the Course were completed." Wiki

PROPHETIC CONNECTIONS: ADOLF HITLER dictated MEIN KAMPF—MY STRUGGLE in LECHFELD PRISON TO RUDOLPH HESS during Hitler's 9 months in jail. Hess typed Hitler's evil manuscript on a Remington typewriter which he allegedly obtained from the wealthy Jewish ROTHCHILD banking family? Hitler became wealthy with the book's royalties.

KARL MARX wrote his MARXIST/SOCIALIST/COMMUNIST book in England alone in a basement. He was incensed by the exploitation of preteen children in coal mines and women in textile factory sweatshops. Reforms took many years. I was given a copy of a self published book about JESUS, BARABBAS and KARL MARX a prophetic book, it said Marx was a satanist. I met the man at the Fairfax Station Baptist Church where, I was reading the historical sign about CLARA BARTON having her hospital there during the SECOND MANASSAS battle, it was Easter evening. It was Easter Providence?

CONVERSATIONS WITH GOD best selling book a movie about the author interviewing god who looked like a businessman. The author also appeared on Oprah's TV show.

JOHNATHAN LIVINGSTON SEAGULL RICHARD BACH 1973 number 1 book. The film showed beautiful California shore and mountains. but was a box office flop. Allegedly a "smart" seagull was seen and snagged at Fisherman"s Wharf restaurant according to NY DAILY NEWS reporter REX REED. They had no CGI computer tech or a robotic bird available. The mechanical metallic OWL in BATTLE OF THE TITANS with PERSEUS HARRY HAMLIN was comical. NEIL DIAMOND wrote the songs and SOUNDTRACK the best selling recording in 1974. I was at a record store in NYC on 42nd Street. The record salesmen said that few records being recorded because of the ARAB OIL EMBARGO, except for Diamond's Seagull record. I bought it and have the CD. It is a NEW AGE opera or "CANTATA". I have been to a Diamond concert in D.C. he is an amazing performer. At the historic ERASMUS HIGH school in Brooklyn Diamond sang in the chorus with BARBRA STREISAND. In Diamond's autobiography he devotes two chapters to how he visited INDIA to get a spiritual HINDU-BUDDHIST musical theme which is the basis for the NEW AGE. At his concert a lady told me he had just become a Christian. I have an audio book recording LP narrated by the great Irish actor RICHARD HARRIS. He reveals when Johnathan breaks the seagull speed record he enters the NEW AGE. The story is anti-Christian revealing how he left the communal flock after being ostracized because he self-actualized himself.

RICHARD BACH had the background to write about how a seagull could fold his wings back and be like a hawk and fly faster. He was a Republic F-84 jet pilot in the New Jersey Air Guard. I have a paper back book he wrote STRANGER TO THE GROUND 1964, about his flying and tells about being sent to Chaumont AB in France. There is a map in the book which shows Ramstein and Spangdahlem Air Bases in Germany. He doesn't show Bitburg AB, where I was stationed 1966-1969. Bach told TIME an ENTITY in the FORM OF A BIRD inspired him to write JONATHAN LIVINGSTON SEAGULL.

THE BEATLES made a visit to INDIA and their music was transformed. Their song IMAGINE has been called anti-Christian or atheist because it proclaims: "Imagine there is no god." The multi millionaire BEATLES sang "no possessions" which Jesus warned "Our hearts are where our treasures are." You can't take it with you. Give to the poor.

STEVE JOBS: Visited India during his first stage of deadly cancer. His mindset brain may have been enlightened by a sage guru and the fact that his allotted time was eminent. He motivated his brilliant innovative engineers to create the iPod, iPad and then the iPhone, iCloud, and the high tech world went viral and APPLE became the first TRILLION dollar corporation. I remember in 1983, I was told the PC and Microsoft were winners and Apple Macintosh were losers. The computers were like baby toys then.

When STEVE JOBS passed I and my church congregation were stunned to hear Jobs as part of Pastor Knill's sermon. He said his father gave him up for adoption as a baby, but wanted him to have a Christian family. His adoptive family were Missouri Synod Lutheran which is a very strict Biblical Christian denomination. In the two JOBS films he was a very authoritarian CEO whose demeanor was threatening to innovate and complete projects some which failed. Many of his employees became millionaires and some could afford to retire or pursue their own interests.

OPRAH WINFREY has had many NEW AGE authors and gurus on her very popular TV show. They speak in very positive "save the world" ecological ways, but are often radical environmentalists who believe Capitalism especially Big Oil and inefficient cars are destroying the Earth with pollution and Global Warming. America's is Energy independent with the most Natural Gas LP and oil/gasoline of any nation. Therefore, America's energy costs are the lowest of any industrial nation encouraging Americans to buy family Vans, SUVs, Jeeps, Crossovers, muscle cars, and America's favorite, the workhorse multi-purpose truck. Economy cars don't sell because gasoline is cheap.

Oprah attended the same church in Chicago as Barack Obama and his family. His United Church and Rev. WRIGHT created a stir when SEAN HANNITY showed his anti-America sermon where he falsely preached: "G-D DAMN AMERICA." The liberal, secular media apparently agreed and decided not to run the video clip of Rev. Wright because it would reflect poorly on presidential candidate Obama's 20 yrs. in his church.

"Throughout the 1980s annual sales of the book steadily increased each year; however the largest growth in sales occurred in 1982 after MARIANNE WILLIAMSON discussed the book on THE OPRAH WINFREY SHOW, with more than 2,000,000 copies sold. The book has been called everything from "New Age psychobabble" to a "Satanic seduction" to "the New Age bible." Wikipedia

THE AQUARIAN CONSPIRACY—PERSONAL AND SOCIAL TRANSFORMATION IN THE 1980S

"The 1980 book's title THE AQUARIAN CONSPIRACY led to some confusion, having to do with astrology only to the extent of drawing from the popular conception of the "AGE OF AQUARIUS" succeeding a dark "Piscean" age. The word conspiracy she used in its liberal sense of "breathing together" as one of her great influences, the philosopher PIERRE TEILHARD de CHARDIN, had done before her."   Wikipedia

"Unabashedly positive in its outlook, the book was praised by such diverse figures as philosophical writer ARTHUR KOESTLER who called it "stunning and provocative," commentator MAX LERNER, who found it "drenched in sunlight," and United Nations Secretary-General ROBERT MULLER, who described it as "remarkable" and "epoch-making." Psychologist CARL RODGERS credited her [MARILYN FERGUSON] with having "etched, in unforgettable vividness, the intricate web of changes shaping the inevitable revolution in our culture," and said the book "gives the pioneering spirit the courage to go forward. Philosopher and [Eastern] religious scholar JACOB NEEDLEMAN predicted that the book would help to make "NEW AGE" thinking "more understandable and less threatening" to the general public in America. This was born out by its success, as THE AQUARIAN CONSPIRACY steadily climbed to the best-seller list and its viewpoint began seeping into the popular culture. Before long the book was being credited as "the HANDBOOK OF THE NEW AGE" (USA Today) and a guidepost to a philosophy "working its way increasingly into the nation's cultural, religious, social, economic and political life." (New York Times)

"The book was translated into some 16 languages. In 1985 she was featured as a keynote speaker at the UN-sponsored "SPIRIT OF PEACE" conference, where she appeared along with MOTHER TERESA and the DALAI LAMA of Tibet."

RELIGIOUS CRITICISM—"Such validation did not come without a price. Ferguson was attacked in some quarters for excessive optimism. Others alleged that her "NEW" ideas were merely a repackaging of old notions of positive thinking, and some saw the "NEW AGE" (a term Ferguson herself seldom used) as merely extending the self-absorption that had marked much of the 1970s, most persistently, some religious groups contended that the "conspiracy" was an attempt to subvert Christian views. This view, most notably expressed by author CONSTANCE CUMBEY in her 1983 book THE HIDDEN DANGERS OF THE RAINBOW, was restated as recently as 2007, when one online essayist wrote that the Christian church "rightly discerned the New Age movement, as outlined in Ferguson's book, to be demonically inspired in anticipation of the ultimate unveiling of…the ANTICHRIST. It was inaccurately alleged that Ferguson was raised and confirmed a Lutheran, had written the book at the behest of the Stanford Research Institute with the goal of overtaking western culture with Eastern mysticism."

IMPACT—"Indirectly supporting both Ferguson and her critic, the New Age movement, as popularly understood, did thrive in the 1980s and into the 1990s, though this was partially through such pop-cultural manifestations as the autobiographical works of actress SHIRLEY MACLAINE and the "HARMONIC CONVERGENCE" festival in 1987."

PERSONAL STORY: When I began research Hitler's plan to replace Christianity with Nazis Socialism in September 1982, I went to a local bookstore in 1983. I asked a young girl cashier, if they had any books about Hitler and Christianity. She said they had just received Cumbey's Hidden Dangers of the Rainbow. This book was shocking, there was a chapter comparing the unknown to me New Age philosophy to Nazi beliefs and dogma. I have bought many Christian books, some self published, soon afterward. All were well researched historical and current factual books. Cumbey was a lawyer.

"Marilyn Ferguson was born in Grand Junction, Colorado April 5, 1930. She was a "founding" member of the Association of Humanistic Psychology and edited the well-regarded science newsletter BRAIN/MIND BULLETIN from 1975-1996. She became friends with inventor BUCKMINSTER FULLER, spiritual author RAM DASS and billionaire TED TURNER. Ferguson's work also influenced Vice President AL GORE, who participated in her informal network while a senator and latter met with her in the White House during BILL CLINTON'S presidency." Wikipedia

AL GORE'S book A BALANCED NATURE highlighted abuses of the environment which the FBI found annotated by the UNI-BOMBER which inspired or instigated him to send letter bombs to people working at polluting chemical companies. His Manifesto letter sent and printed by the New York Times was read by his brother who connected the thoughts and he informed the FBI. The NEWS MUSEUM has TED KACZYNSKI's large empty bookcase on display. I took a photo. The museum closed in December 2019.

OUT ON A LIMB and other SHIRLEY MACLAINE best selling books made her the most famous NEW AGE guru. The two part ABC TV OUT ON A LIMB show had her on Monday night sitting on MALIBU BEACH behind her home. Her New age artist friend DAVID, probably David S was a New Age author, where he hesitatingly gets her to call herself god.They may have met at the New Age village at FINDHORN (New Age Vatican City} near the northern tip of Scotland. It is near INVERNESS which is actress KAREN GILLIAN's hometown. I went through it in 1973. Gillian is the red haired girl in the two JUMANJI films with the ROCK JOHNSON, KEVIN HART and JACK BLACK. The first JUMANJI was filmed in Berwick, Maine near my college, DUNST, WILLIAMS.

AVOIDING ANGELIC ERRORS

"Let no one cheat you of your reward, taking delight in false humility and worship of angels, intruding into those things which he has not seen, only puffed up in his fleshly mind." Colossians 2:18

"Gnosticism was a heresy in the early years of Christianity which, among its many errors, created a list of spirit beings (angels) who came from God and through whom man might approach God. When Paul wrote his letter to the Colossians, a church particularly infected with the Gnostic heresy, he made a point of warning against being tempted to worship angels."

"Two major world religions—Mormonism and Islam—cite the role of angels in relating so-called divine revelation to the religions' respective founders, JOSEPH SMITH and MUHAMMAD. While angels are present throughout the Bible, there is one difference between biblical angels and these others: Biblical angels never dictated divine revelation to the authors of the Scriptures. The Bible states clearly that "holy men of God [Prophets] spoke as they were moved by the Holy Spirit" (2 Peter 1:21)—not as they were dictated to by angels."

"It is a false teaching to ascribe to angels roles that Scripture does not give them. Interpreting their place in God's economy is dishonoring to the God who created them."
TURNING POINT   Pastor David Jeremiah

HISTORIC FACT: ISLAM and the MORMON CHURCH OF LATTER DAY SAINTS are the fastest growing religions. Abortion of any baby is illegal and in Islam a death penalty.

Dr. Schweitzer Laments Nazis Church as Antichrist

Dr. ALBERT SCHWEITZER, also a Lutheran pastor as was his father, in Alsace, France, saw early the failure of the German churches to resist HITLER and the Nazis. He spoke sadly to a group gathered at his French Equatorial African (Gabon) hospital proclaiming: "With the rise of Hitler, and the silence of the churchmen, with only a few notable exceptions, I came to realize that the church could not be counted upon to withstand the State or the culture in which it held a privileged position. I had always wondered that after 2,000 years, a church dedicated to following the PRINCE OF PEACE had not found a means of resisting and overcoming the war spirit and the military machines. When, after the rise of Hitler, good, conscientious churchmen began writing me to stop communicating with them, and pleading 'If you come to Europe, please do not visit me.' I understood that the church which is supported by the State cannot withstand the State, but becomes a tool of it! The great churches could not be relied upon, something within me died, and I thought, what is left? As I looked about me, I realized only a few small sects, the historically grounded heretical, or dissenting sects, the Unitarians and the Quakers were the only real hope—they and the new modern spirit of humanism which might rekindle the true Spirit of Jesus."

[Contributed by ERICA ANDERSON, Albert Schweitzer Friendship House, Great Barrington, MA, circa 1970. Erica, a Jewish refugee from Vienna, Austria, received the documentary Academy award in 1958, for her film on Dr. Schweitzer's African hospital and his Reverence for Life for all animals ethic.]

Schweitzer Inspired by the book/play THE DEPUTY

"The German play write ROLF HOCHHUT in his highly critical play "THE DEPUTY" dramatizes the failure of the powerful Catholic Church in being more forceful in its attitude toward the known unchristian deeds of the NAZI REGIME. In June 1963, Dr. Schweitzer received a copy of "The Deputy" from the German publisher Rowohlt Verlag. Schweitzer recalling the tragic events leading to World War II wrote to Rowohlt: "I was an active witness of the FAILURE which took place in those days, and I believe we must concern ourselves with this great problem of the events of History. We owe this to ourselves, for our failure made us all participants in the guilt of those days. After all, the failure was not that of the Catholic Church alone, but that of the Protestant Church as well.The Catholic Church has greater guilt for it was an organized supranational power."

The FAILURE OF THE GERMAN CHURCHES

"On-third of Germany's population was Roman Catholic and 85 per cent of Austria's population was Catholic. WYTHE WILLIAMS in 'RIDDLE OF THE REICH" (1938) in the chapter "GOD AND HITLER" proclaims: "The record of relations between the Catholic Church and the Nazi state machine has born one of friction. For the Vatican may arrive at compromise but will not take orders from lay dictators when they profess themselves active pagans or atheists, engage in vigorous anti-religious campaigns, and even proclaim their own credos as the state religion and their persons as supernatural."

UNHOLY CONCORDANT WITH HITLER'S NAZI THIRD REICH

"On July 20, 1933, the Nazi government signed a Concordant with the Vatican which "guaranteed" the freedom of the CATHOLIC FAITH and the Church's right "to regulate her own affairs." signed by the papal secretary of state. Monsignor PACELLI, later POPE PIUS XII. The Concordant was broken whenever it suited the Nazis. It also gave Hitler's regime prestige it badly needed. On June 2, 1945, POPE PIUS XII speaking to the Sacred College defended the Concordant and denounced the evolution of NATIONAL SOCIALISM into an "ARROGANT APOSTASY FROM JESUS CHRIST, THE DENIAL OF HIS DOCTRINE and HIS WORK OF REDEMPTION, THE CULT OF VIOLENCE, THE IDOLATRY OF RACE AND BLOOD, THE OVERTHROW OF HUMAN LIBERTY AND DIGNITY."   Catholic encyclopedia

CATHOLIC ENCYCLOPEDIA HITLER BIOGRAPHY

Read in September 1982 which initiated my research for this book

HITLER, ADOLF
"Chancellor of *Germany: b. Braunau am Inn, Upper Austria, April 20, 1889; d. Berlin, April 30, 1945. His father, Alois Hitler (1837-1903), a minor customs official, was industrious and frugal, but lukewarm in his religion. His mother, Klara (Poelzl) Hitler (1860-1907), a devout Catholic, was Alois third wife.

"CAREER TO 1933. Adolf received the Sacrament of Confirmation in 1904, but rarely attended church. During his early education at the Benedictine monastery in Laubach and at the public schools in LINZ. He was unwilling to apply himself to studies. He opposed adamantly his family's wish that he prepare for a career as a civil servant. In 1907 he left Linz for Vienna, where he sought unsuccessfully to enter the academy of Fine Arts. He earned a meager livelihood as a painter of postcards and grew embittered toward life and society. During these years in Vienna (1907-13), which he called the unhappiest of his existence, he developed his outlook on the world. It was characterized by ANTI-SEMITISM, DISDAIN FOR DEMOCRACY, and for individual liberty, idealization of brute force, and passionate pan-German nationalism. After 6 years of army service, during which he was gassed in World War I, he returned to Munich, where he had resided (1913-14). Germany's defeat dismayed and disillusioned him; it was the result, he claimed, of a "STAB IN THE BACK.""

"Hitler laid the foundation for overthrowing the Versailles Treaty by converting the German Workers' Party into the National Socialist German Workers' party (NSDAP) in 1920. From then until 1933 Hitler's history coincided with his party's history. After the abortive Beer Hall Putsch (Nov. 8 and 9, 1923), Hitler was imprisoned for 8 months in the LANDSBERG fortress. He utilized his time to compile notes for MEIN KAMPF [My Struggle] (2 v. Munich 1925-27); Eng. tr. New York 1941). This book, which went through numerous editions and which was translated into many languages, publicized the basic ideas and ambitions and goals that Hitler sought later to realize by political action.[Book royalties made Hitler wealthy.] References to the Catholic Church in Mein Kampf describe it only as a model for the authoritarian, inflexible state that Hitler proposed to create." [Senator CRANSTON published critical passages court blocked.]

NAZI SOCIALISM TO REPLACE CHRISTIANITY

"HITLER'S AIM WAS TO SUPPLANT FAITH IN CHRISTIANITY BY FAITH IN *NATIONAL SOCIALISM. ONCE THIS GOAL WAS ATTAINED HE EXPECTED to ANNIHILATE THE CHURCH AS AN INSTITUTION."   Catholic Encyclopedia

"Few Catholics were attracted to the NSDAP during the 1930s, but the Nazi gains in 1930, caused the German bishops to warn Catholics against the movement. In the elections of 1932 and 1933 they urged Catholics to support Catholic candidates and forbade them to vote for the Nazis."

HITLER AS DICTATOR—When Hitler became chancellor of the Third Reich (January 30, 1933), he reaffirmed Germany's traditional foundations. He [Hitler] asserted that his government regarded Catholicism and Protestantism as the most important factors for the support of the German ethos and that it would devote itself to sincere cooperation between Church and State (March 24, 1933). He seemed to be fulfilling these promises when he concluded a CONCORDANT with the HOLY SEE (July 20, 1933) that permitted free, public exercise of the Catholic religion. So numerous were the violations of its provisions, however, that *PIUS XI ISSUED THE ENCYCLICAL Mit brennender Sorge [with burning sorrow] 1937, which made clear the fundamental irreconcilability of Catholicism and Nazism. It protested the closing of Church-related schools, the seizures of property belonging to religious orders, the discrediting of religion by means of trials (1936) concerning foreign exchange and immorality, and the identifying of loyalty to Christianity with disloyalty to the Fatherland."

"German bishops in sermons and pastoral letters frequently and forcefully opposed racism, totalitarianism, euthanasia laws, compulsory membership in Hitler youth organizations, and interference with Catholic schools. In 1933, however, the bishops lifted the ban against Catholic membership in the NSDAP. Desirous to avoid charges of "political Catholicism," they abstained from direct attacks on Hitler and concentrated on assailing the neopagan ideology currently in favor and those persons who were striving to lead the Fuehrer astray."

"During his triumphant years (1938-41) Hitler gave the impression of personal restraint in his relation with the churches. He persuaded most Germans that he was a genius raised up to advance their national ambitions. His diplomatic and military victories increased their confidence in his [Hitler's] ultimate success. Distasteful aspects of Nazism were commonly blamed on others. One of Hitler's greatest accomplishments was his achievement of the ANSCHLUSS with Austria (1938); it resulted in a hero's welcome to Vienna, the city that had repudiated the youthful Hitler."

"World War II brought increasing pressures on the home front and inevitably affected Hitler's relations with the churches. Thousands of Catholic priests and Protestant pastors were imprisoned. Yet Cardinal FAULHABER, Bishop CLEMENS von GALEN, and Bishop KONRAD von PREYSING, the three most outspoken critics of the regime, were never arrested."

"According to the best reports available, Hitler shot himself to death as Russian troops approached Berlin and left orders for his body to be cremated." [April, 30, 1945]

   CATHOLIC ENCYCLOPEDIA   published by Catholic University Washington, D.C.

This Catholic Encyclopedia historical biography of ADOLF HITLER revealed to me the unspoken truth that Hitler planned to destroy Christianity not just Judaism. I read this in September 1982. In my WITNESS/TESTIMONY, I explain my providential events which directly preceded this revelation. I had "converted" to Judaism in October 1974, for my Nov. 9, 1974 Temple wedding in Brooklyn, booked in April. I didn't know this date was Chrystal Night, Nov. 9, 1938, when the Nazis openly persecuted Germany's/Austria's Jewish people. My son was born on Nov. 8, 1977, and had his BAR MITZVAH, "confirmation", on the Sabbath Nov. 10, 1990. Martin Luther was born on Nov.10,1489. My wife is a secular Jewess and we then left the Reform Temple Beth Shalom,

House of Peace, in Fredericksburg. I had been attending some Concordia Missouri Synod Lutheran services in Triangle, Virginia, since PENTECOST Sunday May 1989.

[I have dozens of detailed World War II books historically and personally describing what happened to Christians and the Jewish people during the war. Reviewing this short biography of Adolf Hitler, I give great credit to the researcher/writer in explaining it all concisely in only one page. History is said to be written by the VICTORS. This shows the reason for churches' limited opposition, but also their "powerlessness" even though it proclaims Hitler planned to replace Christianity with Nazism, an Apocalyptic Threat.
I believe the author wrote this as a "guilt" failure of the Roman Catholic as a penance.

Neo-orthodox Barth "Reforms" European Church Liberalism

"Neo-orthodox theology was born of a protest and reaction against the dominant liberalism of the 19th and 20th Century, KARL BARTH's commentary on "The Epistle to the Romans", published in 1919, and in revised edition in 1922, was the trumpet call of dialectical theology which subsequently became the new or new-orthodoxy."
"It is significant that Barth's famous commentary on Romans was a product of the crisis of THE GREAT WAR, World War I. The liberal theological vision of the SOCIAL GOSPEL, the building of the kingdom of God on Earth, the progress of culture united with Christianity—this great vision collapsed as the Christian nations of Europe, the flower of the world culture, plunged the world into the most destructive war thus far in HIStory. The synthesis of Christianity and culture and the optimistic belief in human progress and the continued perfectibility of human society was, as a result of the Great War, World War I, partially or totally discredited in the eyes of Christendom and the Western world. It was denounced as unrealistic, blind to the reality of sin and evil, and lax about the Truth of the Christian Faith." Ibid p 96
"Neo-orthodoxy sought to rescue Christianity from the general dissolution of Western culture by going behind the era of nineteenth century liberalism to the Reformation of the sixteenth century and the period of Protestant orthodoxy in the seventeenth and eighteenth centuries. Hence the name 'new-orthodoxy'. The period of Protestant orthodoxy had been the subject of liberal theological criticism. Therefore, new-orthodox theologians found it to be a helpful weapon in their struggle against liberalism. And by claiming to be the true heirs of MARTIN LUTHER, JOHN CALVIN, and the Reformation, new-orthodox thinkers sought to brand liberalism as a dangerous innovation and a disastrous deviation from biblical faith of the Reformation." Ibid p 98
My friend CHRISTOPHER NIEBUHR, son of the renounced new-orthodox theologian REINHOLD NIEBUHR, told me as a child he lived in an apartment down the hall from PAUL TILLICH on New York City's Riverside Drive near President Grant's tomb. I sat with Gen. ULYSSES GRANT's great grandson Grifiths at Mary Washington university's GREAT LIVES book lecture on a General MacArthur biography. His grandfather graduated from West Point class of 1903 with MacArthur. He said, "My grandfather had a photographic memory but MacArthur received top honor in the class."
Reinhold Niebuhr was dean of the ecumenical UNION THEOLOGICAL SEMINARY in Manhattan. The professors at Union gave a tithe offering to bring professor Tillich to America from Hitler's anti Christian Germany where his new-orthodox biblical beliefs could not be preached or taught. Christopher still remembers smelling his cigar smoke.

Moral Man and Immoral Society

"MORAL MAN AND IMMORAL SOCIETY: A STUDY IN ETHICS AND POLITICS is a 1932 book by REINHOLD NIEBUHR, a Protestant theologian at UNION THEOLOGICAL SEMINARY (UTS) in New York City, NY. The thesis of the book is that people are more likely to sin as members of groups than as individuals."

Niebuhr wrote the book in a single summer. He drew his book's contents from his experience as a pastor in Detroit, Michigan, prior to his professorship at Union. The book attacks liberalism, both secular and religious, and is particularly critical of JOHN DEWEY and also the SOCIAL GOSPEL. Moral Man and Immoral Society generated much controversy and raised Niebuhr's public profile significantly. Initial reception of the book by liberal Christian critics was negative, but its reputation soon improved as the RISE OF FASCISM throughout the 1930s was seen as having been predicted in the book. Soon after the book's publication, PAUL LEHMANN gave a copy to DIETRICH BONHOEFFER, who read it and was impressed by the book's thesis but disliked the book's critique of pacifism.

The book eventually gained significant readership among American Jews because, after a period of considerable anti-theological sentiment among Jews in the United States, many Jews began to return to the study of theology and, having no Jewish works of theology to read, turned to Protestant theological works." Wikipedia

HISTORY FACT: "Rev. PAUL LEHMANN obituary in the NEW YORK TIMES Mar. 2, 1994, by Wolfgang Saxon cites: "His character was shaped by the experience of being the closest American friend and soul mate of the German theologian DIETRICH BONHOEFFER. The men met as students at Union Theological and he saw off Mr. Bonhoeffer in 1939 as he embarked for Germany after a second visit here.

By then Mr. Bonhoeffer had become a leader in MARTIN NIEMOLLER's CONFESSING CHURCH of Protestants opposed to the Nazi regime. The breakaway group was suppressed and Mr. Bonhoeffer took his ministry underground and joined the resistance. He was hanged the month before the war ended in 1945 for his part in plotting against HITLER."

"A Presbyterian minister Professor Lehmann was associated with Princeton Theological Seminary, Harvard University Divinity School, Union Theological Seminary and Wellesley women's college. He was the son of a German Protestant pastor who immigrated from the UKRAINE and became president of Elmhurst College, Illinois. Paul graduated from OHIO STATE University and Union Theological, where he received a doctorate in 1936."

"Having studied with both REINHOLD NIEBUHR and in Germany with KARL BARTH, Professor Lehmann was particularly interested in the ethical issues surrounding the Christian-Marxist dialogue, war and peace." Wikipedia

"Paul Lehmann's work has nurtured in generations of students the discernment of God's humanizing action in the social controversies of current events," said Christopher Morse, Bonhoeffer professor at Union Theological. "For Lehmann, the GOD who is now at hand calls all humanity to be on hand in the struggles for freedom in their time."

"Active in politics throughout his career, his opposition to MCCARTHYISM led him to become founding chairman of the Emergency Civil Liberties Committee in 1951. It was formed by 150 clergymen, educators, professionals to safeguard Constitutional rights. He firmly rejected insinuations that some of its leaders acted as fronts for Communists."

DEALS WITH THE DEVIL

"If you are the SON OF GOD..."   Matthew 4:3,6
Also read Matthew 4:1-11 + Psalm 91

"A famous fable tells of [GOETHE'S] FAUST, who wanted to be the smartest man. A devil makes a deal with him. Faust can have great knowledge in exchange for his soul. When death approaches, Faust refuses Christ's mercy. He feels honor bound to the deal he made.

Every one of us has made a deal with the devil. We agree to a life separated from God for fleeting rewards. In sin, we believe that we are missing out unless we make devilish deals. Faith knows the larger picture. Every deal with the devil leads to eventual loss, regret, and separation from God.

In Baptism, Christ found Himself to us. He made no deal; He acted out of Love. The Trust and Love that we owed to God He gave; He exchanged His riches for our Poverty. His Word, sealed by the blood of the Cross, offers strength in every temptation.

As we abide in Christ. His victorious Life over the wily foe continues to prevail for us. Just as He did when tempted. Christ continues to Faithfully Proclaim God's Word to confront the devilish deals for us."

"Lord Jesus, thank you for fulfilling the obligations of our sinful dealings. Thank you that your life free from sinful dealings is given us as our own."
Lutheran-Missouri Synod PorTals Prayer ASH WEDNESDAY, March 6, 2019

HISTORICAL FACT: The great German writer-philosopher in his long story of FAUST says he will have the devil's [Satan's] gift for a 23 year period before he would have to forfeit his Soul to the devil. I did the math and calculated that ADOLF HITLER held his demonic power also for 23 years 1922-1945! I wonder if HITLER knew this Faust story and time allotted Faust by the devil? Hitler rarely spoke of God or Jesus so he didn't break the Second Commandment "not to take God's name in vain". Hitler always spoke of PROVIDENCE leading him. This is beyond coincidence and though it sounds blasphemous to say was it God JESUS' PROVIDENCE or was it not? The German word FORSEHUNG means to "FORESEE" providence. God Almighty gave only His chosen Biblical Prophets the visions of HIS future HIS-tory. Throughout the Bible God JEHOVAH/YESHUA uses evil rulers to bring HIS-tory to HIS END-TIME.   AMEN

ARE THE IMPEACHMENT HEARINGS "DEMONIC"?

ASKDRBROWN Michael L. Brown Nov. 21, 2019

"In a recent interview with ERIC METAXAS, Rev. FRANKLIN GRAHAM [evangelist Billy Graham's son] stated that the constant attempts to undermine President TRUMP were "almost a demonic power," concurring with Metaxas that, "It is a spiritual battle."It Is Rev. Graham right, in which case the impeachment hearings would be the latest manifestation of this "demonic power"?

"As expected, the media has responded scornfully to this suggestion."

"Washington Post headline asks. "Who but a demon could impeach God's chosen one?"

"The article, by Dana Milbank, rightly notes that "if politics is a spiritual battle between God and demons from Hell, who cares what statistics from the Commerce Department say—or what any of the impeachment witnesses say?"

"Milbank continues, "On Fox News on Sunday, Energy Secretary RICK PERRY reported that he told Trump he was God's choice: 'I said, "Mr. President, I know there are people that say you said you were the chosen one and I said, 'You were.' "

"Milbank's question, "Who but a demon could vote to impeach God's chosen one?"

"Over at the ATLANTIC, the headline to the article by Peter Wehner asked, "Are Trump's Critics Demonically Possessed? Two of the president's prominent evangelical supporters are literally demonizing his opponents."

"As Wehner writes, "It isn't enough for Franklin Graham and Eric Metaxas, two prominent figures within the American evangelical movement, to lavish praise on President Trump.They have now decided they must try to demonize his his critics."

"At NEW YORK Magazine, the headline reads, "Christian Right Leaders Suggest Trump Critics Are Possessed by Demons."

"In the article, Ed Kilgore writes forcefully, "In Evangelical-speak, 'spiritual battle' or 'spiritual warfare' means a test of power between God and Satan (or his demonic minions), with human souls and the fate of all Creation in the balance. Describing one's opponents as on the wrong side of a 'spiritual battle' is simultaneously an expression of the most extreme hatred available to a Christian, and a rationalization for it on grounds that the object of demonic possession is not entirely responsible for becoming the devil's workshop (it's a variation on the old conservative Christian dodge of 'hating the sin but not the sinner' when it comes to, say, being gay)." Biblical? Gandhi quote.

"And he adds that Graham and Metaxas "are suggesting that the moral and spiritual superiority— nay, necessity—of Trump and his party are so resplendently obvious that only a turn to the darkest side imaginable can explain it."

"To be sure, I [Michael Brown] fully understand these critiques and concerns. And I recognize how this all sounds to a watching, often hostile world."

"And I agree that it's dangerous to label all opposition to Trump as demonic."

"Is Trump really "God's man" so that all who oppose him are of the devil?"

"Is the Republican Party of God and the Democrat Party of the devil?"

"Of course, some conservative Christians would respond by saying, "Just look at their platforms! That should answer your questions about who is of the Lord and who is devil.

"But in fact, Rev. Graham and Eric Metaxas were not talking about opposition to the Republican Party but rather to Donald Trump. There's quite a difference between the two, and it's unlikely that if someone other than Donald Trump had been elected president the opposition would be quite so fierce."

"Had it been a strong conservative like Ted Cruz who won the election. I believe that the opposition from the left would still be intense, not as intense as the opposition to Trump"

"Some of this is due to the fact that it he is a street fighter, constantly on the attack and engaging in a no-holds barred strategy. That certainly provokes more opposition."

"And of some of this has to do with his failings and shortcomings. He has been far from perfect as a leader, often playing fast and loose with the truth and sometimes reckless in his decision making."

"Is it "demonic" to criticize him fairly? Is it "demonic" to take issue with his policies? Is it "demonic" to be offended by some of his comments and actions?"

"So, again, I understand why the secular media takes issue with the Graham-Metaxas interview, and I share those concerns about demonizing all opposition to the president. It can make Christian supporters of Trump look bad and it can take voters' eyes off of relevant issues and put the emphasis on the unseen realm."

"At the same time, I fully understand what Graham-Metaxas were saying."

"As TUCKER CARLSON noted, "The Democrats have been talking about impeachment since the very day that President Trump was inaugurated." Trump must be ousted!"

"And, as I pointed out months ago, had Trump been a liberal politician, the left would be celebrating his success and his feistiness."

"Not only so, but some of the opposition to Trump has been demonic."

"For evidence of this, I point to the level of anti-Trump hatred in the women's marches, the clawing of the doors of the Supreme Court during the KAVANAUGH hearings, and the coalition of witches who regularly seek to hex the president. That sounds demonic."

"So, on the one hand, I believe that everyone needs to be guided by truth and righteousness, and when that means differing with Trump, we do so, with respect. That also means that we vote our conscience, rather than vote based on alleged demonic or divine activity."

"At the same time, if the ongoing attempts to remove a duly elected president are based on lies or exaggerations or misinformation spread by dishonest media and driven by partisan politics, then I would characterize those attempts as "demonic."

"LORD, BLESS MY ENEMY"—SAINT PATRICK

"Love your enemies and pray to those who persecute you." Matthew 5:44
Also read Matthew 5:38-48 + Psalm 51:10-13

"ST. PATRICK'S story is often forgotten in all the chatter surrounding the Holiday. Kidnapped from Britain by Irish raiders, he was made a lowly slave. Patrick escaped, but he felt compelled to return to Ireland. He forgave his enemies. Druids and chieftains who tried to kill him became his dear family in Christ. Patrick wrote that his life of Grace was the work of God alone.
We can learn from Christ and Christians throughout HIS-tory who have prayed for and embraced their enemies and persecutors, many of whom ended up becoming believers.
When we are reluctant to forgive, the Holy Spirit reminds us how God willingly forgave us when we were hostile to him. When we are reluctant to forgive, the Holy Spirit reminds us that God doesn't excuse sin. Rather, He put us sinners to death in Baptism and raised us up as a whole new Creation to be His sons and daughters—and He can do the same for our enemies.

Lord Jesus, save, bless, and raise up our enemies to become new creations of
Your Grace, just as You have done for us."   AMEN
Lutheran-Missouri Synod PorTals Prayer Sunday March 17, 2019 ST. PATRICK'S DAY

CELEBRATE ST. PATRICK'S DAY

The TORCHLIGHTERS Heroes of the Faith
"When most people think of St. PATRICK'S DAY, they think of shamrocks and leprechauns. However, the real St. Patrick was true hero of the faith. Patrick grew up in a well-to-do Christian family, and when he was only 16 years old, he was kidnapped and taken to the shores of Ireland

only to be sold as a slave. It was during his six-year enslavement that he was drawn to Christ, praying daily for his freedom."

"After escaping and returning home, Patrick began to prepare for the ministry in his homeland of Great Britain. But God had other plans and led Patrick to return to Ireland where he preached the saving message of Jesus Christ to the pagans who had once enslaved him."

AN IRISH BLESSING

I expect to pass through this world but once. Any good thing, therefore, I can do, or any kindness that I can show to any fellow creature, let me do it now; let me not defer or neglect it, for I shall not pass this way again.
Life is short and we do not have much time to gladden the hearts of those who travel with us. So be swift to love, make haste to be kind, go in peace to love and serve the Lord.

NAZIS BOMBING OF DUBLIN, IRELAND IN WORLD WAR II

"The first bombing of Dublin in World War II occurred early on the morning of 2 January 1941, when German bombs were dropped on the Terenure area of south Dublin. This was followed, early on the following morning of 3 January 1941, by further German bombing of houses on Donore Terrace in the South Circular Road area of south Dublin. A number of people were injured, but no one was killed in these bombings. Later that year, on 31 May 1941, four German bombs fell in north Dublin, one damaging Arms an Uachtarain [the residence of the President of Ireland] but with the greatest impact in the North Strand area, killing 28 people.   Wikipedia

The Nature and Destiny of Man

"REINHOLD NIEBUHR is probably the most influential contemporary American theologian of our century. A graduate of YALE DIVINITY School in 1928, he joined the faculty of UNION THEOLOGICAL Seminary in New York as Professor of Christian Ethics, and remained there until he retired in 1960. His great work is THE NATURE AND DESTINY OF MAN 1941 and 1943, which gives the best statement of Niebuhrian new-orthodoxy. It is characteristic of Niebuhr's basic ethical and practical interest that he devotes his 'magnum opus' to the clarification of the problem of the nature and destiny of man, rather than to 'the Word of GOD' or 'church dogmatics'. His aim is to demonstrate 'that the two main emphases of Western culture, namely the sense of individuality and the sense of a meaningful history, were rooted in the faith of the Bible and had primarily Hebraic roots.'"
CONTEMPORARY PROTESTANT THOUGHT C. J. Curtis, The Brown Publishing Co. 1970 p 112-113
"Niebuhr declares that the biblical symbols of the CHRIST and his adversary, the anti-Christ, are symbols of the fact that both good and evil grow in history, and that evil has no separate history, but that a greater evil is always a corruption of a greater good." Greater freedom is a greater good, but also a greater opportunity for evil. Better and more education enlarges the possibilities of evil, which is the corruption of the enrichment and enhancement of life which education can bring.

"Therefore," Niebuhr observes, "every effort to equate evil purely with the ignorance of the mind and with the passions of the body is confusing and erroneous."

"The equation of evil with ignorance or uncontrolled passion permits modern man to falsify the reality and power of evil and to make light of it." Ibid p 114

"Modern man may think that he cannot believe in God or in the Christ because the scientific world-view has made such belief impossible. But the real reason for disbelief in the Christian message is that modern man's easy conscience would be sorely troubled if he shared the Christian view of the essential and inescapable sinfulness of human nature. Following ST. AUGUSTINE, Niebuhr sees man's basic sin in Pride. Human pride includes "the idolatrous pursuit of false securities and redemptions in life and history." Because of man's pride, he refuses to see some of the obvious facts of human history'"   Ibid   p 115

"A biblical understanding of man can help us to see the limitations of human knowledge and power. Niebuhr believes that the scriptural concept of man is truer to reality than any other, because it has acknowledged pride as man's ineradicable sin. "For this reason it is possible to make a truer analysis of human destiny upon the basis of a religious faith which has disavowed human pride in principle, though it must not be assumed that any particular Christian analysis will not exhibit in fact what it has disavowed in principle." Ibid   p 115

"The great practical value of a Christian understanding of the nature and destiny of man is, according to Niebuhr, that it frees man from the vain attempt to achieve a perfect life or a premature end of history. Christian faith understands the meaning of history, and therefore can accept the suffering and historical responsibility without claiming to possess the proud certainty of knowledge." Ibid   p 115

"As a new-orthodox theologian Niebuhr closes his analysis of the nature and destiny of man with a strong reliance upon Grace and Faith. He concludes: "Wisdom about our destiny is dependent upon a humble recognition of the limits of our knowledge and our power. Our most reliable understanding is the fruit of 'Grace' in which Faith completes our ignorance without pretending to possess its certainties as knowledge; and in which contrition mitigates our Pride without destroying our hope."   Ibid p 11

Remembering and Celebrating Heroes of Germany's Resistance

Bernard Holland NY Times April 6, 1992

"While the vast majority of Germans and Austrians embraced Hitler as the embodiment of long-dreamed of destinies, there were dissenters. Some came late in opposition, appalled not by original goals but by the self-destructive methodology employed. Others were the "Heroes of Conscience" celebrated at RIVERSIDE Church on Sunday evening.

Musicians drawn from orchestras around the world were assembled, and appropriately enough at a church and by a school (Union Theological Seminary) both built on ecumenism. Remembered in general were the members of the German Resistance and in particular DIETRICH BONHOEFFER and HANS von DOHNANYI. The first a theologian with ties to Union Seminary, who returned voluntarily to Germany in 1939 and was executed in prison. The other was active in the smuggling of Jews to safety and in the numerous attempts on Hitler's life. He, too, was executed.

CHRISTOPH von DOHNANYI—the son of Hans von Dohnanyi and nephew of Dietrich Bonhoeffer — conducted an orchestra largely assembled from his Cleveland Orchestra and from the New York Philharmonic but also represented by players from Britain, Israel and Germany as well as from other American ensembles. BILL MOYERS read from correspondence. Hermann Prey sang.

Gidon Kremer played the violin. The New York Choral Artists under Joseph Flummerfelt sang Schoenberg and Brahms.

It was a touching program played by masters. Mr. Kremer directed Arvo Part's "Fratres," embroidering its hushed, repetitive, choral-like phrase with solo descants. The chorus sang Schoenberg's relatively early "Freide auf Erde" [Freedom on Earth] from the rear choir loft and then joined Mr. Prey's narrations for "A Survivor From Warsaw." Schoenberg's wonder of aphoristic tone-painting.

Wrapped into the latter was BEETHOVEN's "Egmont" Overture followed by the SCHUBERT "Unfinished Symphony" and two moments from the BRAHMS Requiem: Mr. Prey sang "Death where is thy sting"; the chorus ended with "How lovely is thy dwelling place." Medals for musical and human achievement were presented to Mr. Dohnanyi and to Kurt Masur in absentia.

The familiar Schubert and Beethoven pieces received far from routine performances. Mr. Dohnanyi's rigorous musicality rendered everything clean, fresh, deeply serious and without sentimentality.

Witnessed by a large international audience, recorded for television and managed by musicians obviously moved by what they were doing, this was the kind of event that one approaches reverently but at the same time with great care.

First, let us not rewrite history simply for the sake of reconciliation. The message of the THIRD REICH was clear. We may, however, have ignored an important minority report, written by valiant Germans. "HEROES OF CONSCIENCE" addressed this wrong.

Secondly, we should be deeply suspicious about music as a moral force. The healing powers of this concert surrounded the music: in the juxtaposition of violinists from Tel Aviv and Dresden, in a program that placed Beethoven and Schubert next to a Jewish composer writing about the massacres of Warsaw, in an audience joined together in mutual and civilized respect.

Radio transcriptions tell us that near the end of the war, sublime performances were being given by the Berlin Philharmonic not far from where Bonhoeffer and his colleges were imprisoned, abused and ultimately killed. Photographs of these concerts show seas of SS uniforms, the colleagues of Bonhoeffer's tormentors if not themselves.

Do not believe for a moment that these men were not as transported by Beethoven and Schubert as we were on Sunday night. In the moral sense, pieces of great music are like clothes: made with beauty, graceful proportions and soul-moving effect, but capable of being worn by both good and evil."

In August 1991, I called the Niebuhr residence from a 5 cent phone booth in front of the old NORMAN ROCKWELL museum in Stockbridge, MA. Christopher Niebuhr answered and I told him about writing a book about Hitler trying to destroy Christianity and how his father was an inspiration to me as the first of the few outspoken pastors and theologians to write about this fact. He said, "He would like to discuss this with me but his mother was meeting with book publishers to publish her letters to my father Reinhold."

[This article was sent to me by Christopher Niebuhr who was invited to the Riverside Church concert by conductor Christoph von Dohnanyi. Christopher and I visited him at intermission. Christopher shook his hand and went back to his seat. I told him that he was Reinhold Niebuhr's son. He later contacted Christopher and sent him Riverside Church ticket which partly honored the conductor's father Hans who was executed for treason in the Hitler Col. Von Stauffenberg unsuccessful bomb assassination attempt on Adolf Hitler on July 20, 1944. He was married to one of DIETRICK BONHOEFFER's sisters. The concert also honored him as one of the martyrs of the German resistance also connected to the failed bomb attack, though not directly proven. Bonhoeffer had actually broadcast his Christian disapproval of Hitler on Berlin radio, the day he was elected, calling Hitler antichrist. The Gestapo controlled his radio broadcast and cut this final comment. Bonhoeffer was hanged about three weeks before World War II ended. The Lutheran church doesn't speak about Bonhoeffer possibly because he spoke of the failure of the German churches Reformed Lutheran and Catholic church had become a "tool" of the Nazi government. Bonhoeffer coined the terms "CHEAP GRACE" and "RELIGIONLESS" Christianity, detached from the restraints of the State, a Gospel church. In Germany, during Hitler's 12 Year Nazi German Reich, faithful Bible believing Christians stayed home and read their Bibles like my grandmother Susanna did as she recalled to me, "Hitler's picture and swastikas were placed by the altar." The WORLD BOOK encyclopedia in Bonhoeffer's short biography states that even atheists admire his bravery. Atheists liked his religionless idea, which CHRISTOPHER HITCHENS rightly condemns in his book "god is NOT GREAT". Hitchens praises Bonhoeffer!

Reinhold Niebuhr's son's Letter—Our Tanglewood Concert

Christopher Niebuhr, Reinhold Niebuhr's son, letter of April 23, 1992

Dear Clive:

Thank you for the tape about, a Jewish American soldier in Germany [Search for Truth Arthur Katz] and Indiana Jones. [Transcript of Steven Spielberg's TV show Indiana Jones meets Albert Schweitzer from his Indiana Jones Chronicles] I have recently been reading Schweitzer's book on Bach. Bach in Leipzig had concertos in German thus today that city is known for its orchestra not its Opera House. I spent many nights while in the U.S. Army [nearby Vaihingen army base 1957-58] in the Stuttgart Opera House listening to Handel and Mozart operas.

Christopher Dohnanyi told the President of Union Seminary that he had meet me that Friday night, and I was invited to the concert at Riverside Church on April 5th. It is supposed to be on National Public Radio, and cassettes should be made but not yet. [We meet Dohnanyi during his Tangelwood concert intermission. I remarked that the man he had just meet was Reinhold Niebuhr's son.]

[Christopher had told me during my phone call that the Cleveland Symphony conducted by Christoph von Dohnanyi would be at the nearby Tangelwood Concert Hall. Ten hours later I arrived at the concert and sat next to a man who was reading a book about Dietrich Bonhoeffer. I told him I had been told that the conductor is related to him. The family's were intermarried. The man replied, "Yes, I know that." I asked, "Are you Christopher Niebuhr?" He answered, "Yes, I am." Christopher passed in June 2019. I am looking forward to seeing him and his parents and will introduce them to my beloved parents. There were more than a thousand people at the concert many on the grass behind us. Providence? We have been close friends since then and have shared many personal stories. Before the concert I picked up my mother's Book of the Month Club copy of THE RISE AND FALL OF THE THIRD REICH which WILLIAM SHIRER had autographed. Oh What a Night! A FRANKI VALLIE Four Seasons song. Shirer lived in nearby Lenox. Shirer's Russian wife said he would leave his book autographed on the porch. His Austrian wife had passed away. Shirer's daughter Elisabeth, also my mother's name and Christopher's sister's name, lived near Christopher's home in Lee, MA. Christoper let me stay overnight in his house twice.]

"PS I was interested in your tape [ARTHUR KATZ "SEARCH FOR TRUTH"] on a Jew in Germany, as I served with many Jews in Stuttgart and there were two views, laughter when told that the post war Germany was our friend, but in awe when an Army general told about Rommel who was killed or poisoned at Hitler's orders for standing up for his troops. [His support for the July 20, 1944, Col. Claus von Stauffenberg failed bomb coup to kill Hitler.] The general who told us that HAROLD JOHNSON left the U.S. Army during the Vietnam war for the Boy Scouts."

Schweitzer came to America for the Goethe Festival at Aspen, Colorado sponsored by the University of Chicago. He had a weak heart, and the high altitude bothered him. He told my father [Reinhold] that tropics were better for him, but not for his wife's health. She and, her daughter [RENA] who spoke English, told my father that to sleep at night they had mouse traps, as Schweitzer could sleep through the African night, but not his wife." [Schweitzer would not allow the mice to be harmed because of his All Life ethic.]

Schweitzer and my father [Reinhold] both gave Gifford lectures at Edinburgh University.

[Later, I will tell the story of Arthur Katz the Jewish American soldier in Germany circa 1960 from his autobiography diary "BEN ISRAEL" (Son of Israel) paperback book given to me by my fellow worker at Woolco Graham Sager who was from Norwich, England, where my father's bomber airbase was in World War II. His step-father was Jewish and before his passing was becoming Christian. Katz book and his audio tape "Search for Truth" was providentially given to me by Christian friends when I began my manuscript research as a BORN AGAIN Christian. It was a powerful Judeo-Christian testimony and witness. Arthur Katz has U Tube audios which are powerful Jewish messianic Christian testimonies. This was during 1983, when I began researching about Hitler and the church. I remained Jewish until my son's Bar Mitzvah on Saturday Sabbath Nov. 10, 1990, Martin Luther's birthday! I had been secretly attending Christian church services New Life in Christ (Westminster) and United Methodist in Fredericksburg, VA, Reverend REGAN, who lives in my community and have meet, and assistant pastor Don Wilson, when I took my children to Beth Shalom "House of Peace" Temple Sunday school.]

PERSONAL STORY: I visited Vihingen Army base near Stuttgart where Christopher was stationed in the Army 10 years earlier. My sergeant at Bitburg had me deliver an envelop there about model rocketry. I then drove to Stuttgart and from a hilltop looked down on the city and the Mercedes Benz and Porsche auto factories. Recently I was told the hill was actually built with the rubble from Allied bombing.

SMALL WORLD PROVIDENTIAL STORY: Christopher told me his mother URSULA was British and was born in Southampton. His father REINHOLD and mother were married in the nearby WINCHESTER CATHEDRAL. A popular English pop song in 1967. Christopher told me they went to London on their honeymoon and meet visiting Gandhi from India. I asked Christopher who was more intelligent your father or your mother? He recalled without hesitation "My mother she could read Hebrew, my father could read Greek." His mother was a visiting theologian at his father's UNION THEOLGICAL Seminary in Manhattan. Her intellectual brilliance is alleged to have captured the aging bachelor Reinhold's affections. Christopher was born on September 11, 1934. Providence? I know four people born on SEPTEMBER 11, two have passed.

A coincidence. Do the math subtract 9 months.

Rev. Don Wilson, attended Presbyterian Union College in Richmond, in 1986, I attended his Sunday school class and we became friends discussing my research about Hitler planning to replace Christianity with National SOCIALISM NAZISM. In 1986, Don gave me his copies of Reinhold's two volumes of THE NATURE AND DESTINY OF MAN 1941, 1943, my birth year. I found these two of his 12 books very Biblically/Historical and enlightening.I later went to Don's Christmas services at Kilmarnock and Winchester. I believe he may have passed at Ghent, a Norfolk suburb, my hometown was Ghent, NY. I still have his books with the pages half underlined. His Volume II, HUMAN DESTINY is a treatise on PRIDE—BIBLICAL, CHURCH and HUMANKIND'S. I wonder if FBI Director JAMES COMEY has read this book? I was deeply offended when I heard that Comey had the Chutzpah/audacity to pridefully use REIHNOLD NIBUHR'S name as his secret FACEBOOK SITE. Christopher was one of my closest friends for 29 years. I had heard Comey on the news quoting Reihhold Niebuhr and in his book he quotes him. Wikipedia says he wrote his thesis at WILLIAM AND MARY university in Williamsburg, Virginia in 1982, about NIEBUHR and JERRY FALWELL'S MORAL MAJORITY and their civil religion. Niebuhr was "liberal", actually new-orthodox biblical ultra-conservative. Falwell was a conservative biblical evangelist and promoted a more JUDEO-CHRISTIAN biblical "Dominion theology." This is impossible in the United States because we have complete religious tolerance and have every religion and some 2,000+ denominations, sects and cults, including the Church of SATAN, Scientology and Wiccan/witches. These "churches" have all qualified for tax exemption through liberal Internal Revenue IRS qualifications. There are newspaper ADs with a phone number to begin your own church. Is this religious freedom? Or is this Satan's way to deceive Americans away from our FOUNDING FATHER'S Judeo-Christian biblical original documents of liberty.

PERSONAL HISTORICAL OBSERVATION: Christopher revealed to me that his father personally knew DIETRICH BONHOEFFER who attended his father's Union Seminary for a brief time and could have stayed. Bonhoeffer felt he would be a traitor to his devout Christian faith which his homeland Germany was destroying through its APOSTASY, Latin apostasia for defection, abandonment or renunciation of a religious or political belief. Bonhoeffer returned to Germany and carried his cross, was imprisoned for years and hanged a month before World War II ended. Christopher recalled that Bonhoeffer visited the famous Negro-American Abyssinian Baptist Church in nearby Harlem. Christopher said Bonhoeffer was spiritually moved by the African-American Gospel sermon and upbeat powerful choir. The pragmatic or dogmatic German Lutheran services pipe organ and beautiful choirs were traditionally powerful but not as spiritually uplifting as this black American church. I believe German Bonhoeffer saw in this church a formerly persecuted and enslaved people who had been freed by President ABRAHAM LINCOLN in America's tremendously bloody CIVIL WAR. Bonhoeffer on Jan. 30, 1933, on the eve of ADOLF HITLER'S election as Chancellor of the Third Reich, on RADIO BERLIN tried to warn that Hitler was an antichrist. The Gestapo was in the radio control room and shut the mike at that last moment. He had no way to foresee that his beloved Germany would end in complete destruction in history's most destructive war.

CHRISTOPHER NIEBUHR'S STORY: Christopher recalled that this African American church also influenced the Reverend BILLY GRAHAM and he decided to create a spiritual Gospel choir for his Decision stadium revivals.

REINHOLD NIEBUHR'S DOGMATIC PRAGMATISM: In BILLY GRAHAM'S autobiography JUST AS I AM (1973) he reveals how he wanted to meet with REINHOLD NIEBUHR who he respected as an important theologian. Niebuhr was a pragmatic German-American, a new-orthodox Biblical Lutheran. He was leery of big evangelical rallies, maybe recalling Hitler's fanatical pseudo-religious pagan Nuremberg rallies, which were the antithesis of Christianity flying a multitude of stigmatic TWISTED CROSS SWASTIKA flags. [Christopher recalled to me, "My father was upset not with Billy Graham, a devout Christian, but with his "Christian" followers who sent him death threat letters, after my father made a published statement that it would be prideful for America to say that GOD/JESUS is "on our side" against Communist Russia."] God doesn't choose sides but we do need to choose Him.

I was no fan of Communist Russia. In Amityville grade school during the Korean War we had nuclear air raid alerts where we hid under our desks. What were they thinking? Manhattan was 30 miles away, but Republic jet factory was 3 miles away. We had a saying: "ENNY MINNIE MINIE MO CATCH THE COMMIE BY THE TOE. SHOOT HIM DEAD KILL THAT DIRTY RED." As a pre-teenager I didn't think of this as un-Christian they the Chinese Communists were the enemy invading democratic Korea after Communist North Korea invaded South Korea without a declaration of war. It was a Civil war like divided Vietnam and the United States when Abraham Lincoln ordered the invasion of Virginia in the American WAR OF SECESSION Civil War. My family and I have lived in Virginia (Garrisonville, Stafford County) since July 4, 1977. I was told New York Union soldiers had been encamped in Garrisonville. My son was born in the old MARY

WASHINGTON hospital in Fredericksburg, VA, on November 10, 1977. My daughter graduated from MARY WASHINGTON college in 1997 with a degree in German. She taught German at Stafford High School, one year, and the new Colonial Forge High School, 7 years. My daughter was married in MARY WASHINGTON'S HOUSE garden. My family attended the Reformed Jewish Temple BETH SHALOM in Fredericksburg for 13 years. We left the Temple after my son's BAR MITZVAH on the Sabbath/Saturday November 10, 1990. I had also attended the United Methodist church and non-denominational New Life in Christ church all within 2-3 blocks from MARYE'S HEIGHTS SUNKEN ROAD where General AMBROSE BURNSIDE (known for his sideburns) ordered the disastrous attack in the Fredericksburg battle defeat on the Mary Washington University campus grounds. My son graduated VIRGINIA TECH in 2000.

LINCOLN HISTORY FACT: "When a pious minister told Lincoln he "Hoped the Lord is on our side," the president responded: "I am not at all concerned about that…but it is my constant anxiety and prayer that I and this nation should be on the LORD'S SIDE." In November 1863, Lincoln travelled to Gettysburg, Pennsylvania, to participate in the dedication of the cemetery established there for the thousands of soldiers who died during the recent battle. There he gave his celebrated speech, the GETTYSBURG ADDRESS, wherein he hoped that the nation shall, "UNDER GOD," have a new birth and freedom. The words, "under God," may not have been in his written transcript, but it is posted in some sources that he added them extemporaneously from the podium. According to scholars, he may have drawn the expression from GEORGE WASHINGTON'S hagiographer, PARSON WEEMS." Wikipedia

"In December 1863, Lincoln's Secretary of the Treasury decided on a new motto, "IN GOD WE TRUST," to be engraved on coins. Lincoln's involvement with this is unclear."

ORIGIN OF THE UNITED STATES NATIONAL MOTTO

"IN GOD WE TRUST, designated as the U.S. NATIONAL MOTTO by CONGRESS in 1956 [during President EISENHOWER'S administration], originated during the Civil War as an inscription for U.S. coins. On Nov. 13, 1861, the Rev. M.R. WATKINSON, of Ridleysville, Pennsylvania, wrote to Treasury secretary SALMON P. CHASE requesting "recognition of the Almighty God in some form on our coins." Chase ordered designs prepared with the inscription IN GOD WE TRUST and backed coinage legislation that authorized use of this slogan. The slogan first appeared on some U.S. coins in 1864 and specifically thereafter until 1938, after which which all U.S. coins bear the inscription. A joint resolution passed by the 84th U.S. Congress and was signed by Pres. DWIGHT D. EISENHOWER July 30, 1956, declared IN GOD WE TRUST the national motto of the United States." THE WORLD ALMANAC AND BOOK OF FACTS

PROVIDENTIAL BIBLICAL FACT: Jesus held up a Roman coin and proclaimed: "Render unto Caesar what is Caesar's." The Jewish Israelites had to pay Rome the taxes that they imposed on their entire Empire. Jesus was born in Bethlehem because of Caesar's decree that all citizens had to go to their birthplace for his TAX CENSUS. This decree fulfilled prophet MICAH'S proclamation that Israel's MESSIAH would "Be born in Bethlehem Ehprata" where David had been born fulfilling the unbroken family "begots" lineage from King DAVID. This story could be considered as materialistic/worldly by other religions beliefs and by agnostics and atheists. MARTIN LUTHER explained this paradox in his TWO KINGDOMS SERMON.

Christopher Niebuhr's Letter October 1, 1995

Dear Clive   Stockbridge, Massachusetts 0126

Thank you for sending me the SCHWEITZER material.

You know that Schweitzer had a cousin, CHARLES MUNCH who was conductor of the BOSTON SYMPHONY ORCHESTRA. Many miss program, as he had a BACH week. He also was a player of BERLIOZ, which was played on August 6, 1995 the BERLIOZ REQUIEM. That concert was interrupted by applause. The audience would not let the orchestra complete the three part AMEN at the end of the concer

My parents met Schweitzer when he came to ASPEN, Colorado for the 1949 GOETHE FESTIVAL there. He did not like it for his heart condition made life difficult in mountains, while his wife [Helene] had a hard time sleeping in the tropics. She told my father she would pay the houseboys or staff to kill the mouses, as they would gnaw at night, keeping her awake, and that [Albert] Schweitzer did not use poison against mice or spray against flies [and deadly mosquitoes]. That is supposedly why [Rhena] Miss Schweitzer the daughter prefers BACH as a memorial as opposed to tropical medicine, as she did not think much of the hospital. Miss Schweitzer married a doctor, and lived in Atlanta, [U.S. DISEASE CONTROL CENTER], and other American cities.

It is interesting that BONHOEFFER like SCHWEITZER would not work in the German church, but in LONDON and BARCELONA. It is like some of the Puritan clergy who preferred the Indians [Native Americans], and Blacks [Negro African-Americans] to the State church. Germany was until 1945, like Virginia until 1785 a state church [Anglican] Have your read about the Virginia Baptists, or even Presbyterians?

I listened to Beyers Naude in Nov 1974 in Chicago, while the hearings were going to nominate NELSON ROCKEFELLER for Vice President, describe that Lutherans in South Africa were freer than the Lutherans in Germany, as their church was based on Free will offerings. Bonhoeffer held his meetings at BARMAN, the site of the Mission Institute, as it was not owned by the German State Church, or as PAUL TILLICH referred to as the Prussian Church.

ASPEN was developed by Mr. and Mrs. Paepecke, as he was Chairman of the Board of the Container Corp of America, and also the President of the Board of the University of Chicago. Ski in the winter and a summer school of push-ups and classes in the summer. Mrs. Paepecke who died in August this year, was or is a sister of the US negotiator, Paul NITZE, who Prof. Hocking of Univ. of Chicago philosophy department told me was an Anglo translation of the German NIETZSCHE, the German philosopher.

As you know Schweitzer went to French Equatorial Africa during the First World War, when Alsace were supposed to fight for Germany.   Yours CHRISTOPHER

Christopher Niebuhr Letter December 20, 1995

Dear Clive   Stockbridge, Massachusetts 01262

Thank you for sending me the two books. I really am interested in the paperback, by [George] BAILEY on the GERMANS, as I believe he was the person I would read about Germany when I was in the US Army in STUTTGART VAIHINGEN, 7th Army Headquarters, I would take out all my magazines to the field, actually I was stationed at the Armored Division Barracks, where they recently left for BOSNIA.

Since I have picked up some BONHOEFFER material intrigued that Gill did not interview any surviving members of the Bonhoeffer family. He was GERHARD LEIBHOLZ as a Jewish lawyer living in London, while his wife, a twin [Sabine] of DIETRICH BONHOEFFER stated she lived with family in OXFORD, and that her husband meet the family as he was in the same Lutheran Confirmation class as HANS VON DOHNANYI, the father of the CLEVELAND SYMPHONY conductor [Christophe] Bonhoeffer conducted Mrs. Leibholz's fathers funeral as he was a non observant Jew, whose children were all confirmed as Lutherans. The problem is that the Nazis considered him Jewish, as his father was Jewish. BAILEY wrote for the REPORTER MAGAZINE which was a great magazine until it folded in the 1960s.

In a recent Holocaust History, it refers to the German Army Barracks in VAIHINGEN as a Concentration camp, as it held political prisoners, I have written to the Department of the Army to find out if during my 18 months in Germany [1957-58] I lived in a concentration camp recycled as a US Army barracks. [He graduated Harvard 1957.]

What bothers me from my reading of German History is that Prussian socialists liked Russian Communism, and Prussian Conservatives liked the WHITE RUSSIANS. I think that a major problem with Hitler's first alliance with Russia, 1939-1941, then fighting Russia, that it made the German Army rebellious, but it also made Churchill resistant to dealing with the German Army and the church, as the Prussian establishment, not realizing that Hitler as a Bavarian right winger did not get along with the Prussians [The German General Corps had many Prussians born in northeastern Germany Prussia.]

I find it fascinating today that the US Army is using the rail network developed by General VON MOLTKE in the 1860's for Prussian domination, and today tanks are taken by rail to Hungary, and the Corp of Engineers have constructed a pontoon bridge to Bosnia from Hungary.

My father [Reinhold] worked for President HENRY SLOANE COFFIN, a famous Presbyterian [Yale University] clergyman. His nephew WILLIAM COFFIN worked in US Army intelligence in MOSCOW during World War II, and was an escort to the BOLSHOI BALLET. He worked for the CIA in 1951-53, his brother in law, FRANKLIN LINDSAY, was an OSS officer attached to the TITO partisans [Yugoslavian National Socialist/Communist] during World War II. I have just finished his book BEACONS IN THE NIGHT. He blew up bridges on Vienna to Constantinople [Istanbul] rail line used by the Nazis. His dispatches have been cleared for publication after 50 years and are now published by Stanford University Press. My best for 1996   Yours Christopher

Amazing History Christopher Niebuhr, was my close friend for 27 years, from August 1991 until he passed June 1, 2018, suffering a massive heart attack, at a senior citizen home in LEE, Massachusetts. Born September 11, 1935. Name means Christ's offering.

I learned of his passing when I received a call from his close friend SETH KIRCHNER, whose mother was a UNITED CHURCH OF CHRIST pastor. Christopher, Seth and I had a luncheon together in Lee once. Seth was given my cell phone number by someone at the retirement home. I wasn't going to answer the call but saw the location was near Lee. Seth told me about Christopher's passing. I was stunned when he said. "This is Seth." I told him, "Christopher had told me you had passed?" Seth said, "My wife had passed." I gave him my condolences. Seth revealed, "Christopher enjoyed your friendship and phone calls and books." I was pleased to hear that because in 27 years I talked many hundreds of hours to Christopher, but always would get amazing PAUL HARVEY responses. Christopher was one of my many wonderful Christian friends. He knew our meeting at the Tanglewood Cleveland Symphony concert, 11 hours after he told me about the Bonhoeffer/Dohnanyi connection, was not by chance but was providential that I sat next to him. I believe soon I will be with Christopher in JESUS' HEAVENLY ETERNITY. I will want him to introduce me to his father REINHOLD, his mother URSULA. I want to introduce the Niebuhr's to my German mother Elisabeth and father Alexander and my German grandparents Karl and Susanna Frank and the many Saints I have written about in my Witness/Testimony book.

REINHOLD NIEBUHR: AS I REMEMBER

Christopher Niebuhr Chapter 5 Dr. Franklin Littlell book January 1996

CHRISTOPHER NIEBUHR

"Forty years ago, my father wrote and dedicated to me his book entitled, THE IRONY OF AMERICAN HISTORY. That book reflects his indebtedness to the works of the Danish Philosopher, SOREN KIERKEGAARD (1813-55), who wrote ON THE CONCEPT OF IRONY (1841), My father saw irony as an answer to the dialectic of Hegel and Marx."

"Two conferences of a fraternal organization have discussed and deserted the rescue of Danish Jews in October 1943." [The Holocaust Memorial museum displays one of the small boats used to take Jews to Sweden. A sign reveals that Christian King Christian wore a yellow star the Nazis required Jews to wear,]

"This year also is the 200th anniversary of the abolition of the slave trade by the Danish government. My father described how his father and others brought up in Lippe-Detmold - a Calvinist principality - looked to Holland for their religion, but to Denmark for their politics and cultural life. Oldenberg, a neighboring state, was ruled by a Danish king from 1667-1773. Thus, there was a strong Danish influence for someone like my grandfather Gustav Niebuhr, and after he studied Kierkegaard for my father."

"My father's first written comment on the Second World War was the article "SYNTHETIC BARBARISM," written for the September 9, 1939 issue of "The New Statesman and Nation". The Niebuhr family was in Britain at that time, as my father was giving the GIFFORD LECTURES at the University of Edinburgh." [Dr. ALBERT SCHWEITZER and Archbishop SODERBLOM also gave Gifford lecturers.]

"My father's first visit to Germany was in 1923. My father reported in the "Evangelical Herald". "The benevolent occupation of doughboys has been superseded by yer usual French severity. In Koln [Cologne] we feasted our eyes on the beautiful cathedral and attended a mass there on Sunday morning. A Dominican monk preached to 9,000 people, but meanwhile the [nearby] railroad station was crowded with hundreds of young people belonging to youth bands, so widely developed in Germany. They are sporadic evidence of the revolt of youth against the atmosphere of despair that has gripped their elders. Communing with nature they try to forget their troubles." (reprinted, YOUNG NIEBUHR by William Chrystal, St. Louis, 1977, p. 127).   p. 56

"After the war, my father was on a State Department tour of German education in 1946, and then spoke on German education as U.S. Delegate to the UNESCO Conference in Paris in 1949. He was especially interested in Berlin, a socialist city with a strong Evangelical tradition in religion. In Berlin, Bishop Dibelius, on 27 August 1946, told him that Russian police wanted his pastors to be informers. In 1948, when the West Berlin government had been separately established, my father was elected to the American Board of the Free University of Berlin, created so that Americans such as HENRY FORD and others, including corporations, could receive tax deductions for gifts to a democratic charity. The European Recovery Program under Paul Hoffman, former head of Studebaker, relied on both Detroit business and leaders to reestablish the West German automobile industry, with worker participation. The Union for Democratic Action, the educational arm of Americans for Democratic Action helped sponsor tours for German leaders to visit the United States, or attend graduate schools. One leader was surprised that the United States called itself a free market, after visiting the Washington headquarters of the Federal Trade Commission and Interstate Commerce Commission."

"In the 21 February 1942 issue of NATION my father wrote: "I have previously suggested that the problem of the relation of the Jews to our Western democratic world call for at least two different approaches. We must on one hand preserve and if possible extend the democratic standards of tolerance and of cultural and racial pluralism that allow Jews Lebensraum [living space] as a nation among the nations. We must on the other hand support more generously than in the past the legitimate aspiration of Jews for a homeland in which they will not simply be tolerated but which they will possess. The type of liberalism that fights for and with Jews on the first battle line but leaves them to fight alone on the second is informed but unrealistic universalism. If its presuppositions are fully analyzed, it will be discovered that they rest upon the hope that history is moving forward to a universal culture that will eliminate all particularities and every collective uniqueness, whether rooted in nature or history. History has perennially refuted that home...the Jews were the first, as they have been the chief victims of Nazi fury. Their rehabilitation, like the rehabilitation of every Nazi victim, requires something more than the status quo ante."   p. 57

"In 1967, my father was awarded an honorary degree from Hebrew University in Jerusalem, and was appointed to the Jerusalem Committee, and international committee to advise the Major of Jerusalem. He accepted the honorary degree in Stockbridge, Massachusetts in 1970 from President Harman of Hebrew University. Due to ill health he turned down the Jerusalem Committee assignment. Having read the ADAMS-JEFFERSON LETTERS {ed. Cappon, 1959, Chapel Hill, NC), he appreciated the anti-clericalism of our founding statesman and also that of those in other countries such as DAVID BEN GURION in Israel an U NU in Burma {Myanmar]. He favored a two-party system, which he believed lacking in Israel. [Like many democratic socialist nations in Europe Israel and its presidents need to form coalition parties governments.]
"He criticized the religious establishment and the labor union domination in Israel, as protected in the state, as in many other countries, newly-established after World War II."
"My father travelled on Sundays to preach at many college campuses throughout the country. I did not hear him as I attended Sunday school in New York City. I did travel to attend two college commencements where my father received honorary degrees, in 1944. He was awarded a degree at Harvard at a commencement crowd small because it was wartime. President CONANT asked me if I would like to come to Harvard. I asked him if he would still be president in eight years when I would be a freshman. He stated that he would. Conant resigned in the middle of my freshman year, appointed U.S. High Commissioner to West Germany."   Chris graduated 1957, served in army in Germany.
[REMEMBRANCE AND RECOLLECTION Dr. FRANKLIN LITELL Temple University]

The Stuttgart Declaration of German Churches War Guilt

The Stuttgarter Schuldbekenntnis, known in English as the STUTTGART DECLARATION OF GUILT was a declaration issued on October 19, 1945 by the COUNCIL OF THE EVANGELICAL CHURCH in Germany (Evangelischen Kirche in Deutschland or EKD), in which it confessed guilt for its inadequacies to the Nazis and the THIRD REICH.   Wikipedia
The declaration states in part:
"Through us infinite wrong was brought over many peoples and countries, that we often testified to in our communities, we express now in the name of the whole church: We did fight for long years in the name of Jesus Christ against the mentality that found its awful expression in the National Socialist regime of violence; but we accuse ourselves for not standing for our beliefs more courageously, for not praying more faithfully, for not believing more joyously, and for not loving more ardently.
The declaration makes no mention of any particular atrocities committed during the Third Reich or of the church's support for Hitler during the early years of the regime.

One of the initiators of the declaration was Pastor MARTIN NIEMOELLER.

History: After the EKD conference at Treysa achieved some administrative unity, critics still found a lack of contention in the church. Niemoeller stated, with some frustration, that "You should have seen this self-satisfied church at Treysa."

American representatives reporting from the Treysa conference voiced views similar to Niemoeller. Robert Murphy, a career diplomat in the U.S. State Department commented:

"There is little evidence that the German Protestant church repented Germany's war of aggression or the cruelties visited upon other people's and countries."

[A separate Roman Catholic Concordant with the German democratic government was also signed in July 1933, 6 months after Adolf Hitler was elected Chancellor of the THIRD REICH on January 30, 1933]

The declaration was prepared in response to church representatives from the Netherlands, Switzerland, France, Britain and the United States who came to Stuttgart, Germany to reestablish ties with the German Protestant church, based on a "relationship of trust." The representatives believed that any relationship would fall apart in the absence of a statement by the German churches, due to the hatred in their home countries toward Germany in 1945.

But the 11 members of the Council had differing on the moral responsibility of their churches for Nazi Germany. One prepared a draft laying blame on "our fellow citizens" in Germany, thus implicitly denying or diffusing the responsibility of the church. This language was stricken from the draft, and Niemoeller insisted on the language "Through us infinite wrong was brought over many people and countries."

Hans Asmussen, Martin Niemoeller and Wilhelm Niesen needed no prodding to express lament over their own and the church's failure to speak out loudly and clearly against Nazism. Nevertheless, the Stuttgart Declaration was not simply an act of conscience. Persistent pressure by foreign church leaders for recognition of the inadequate response to Nazism played a significant role.

REACTIONS: The Declaration was viewed buy many Germans as a further capitulation to the Allies and a betrayal of German interests, one signatory asked the foreign churchmen to refrain from publishing the Declaration, entirely contrary to the purpose of obtaining it in the first place. Various interpretations and arguments were raised by some members of the EKD Council to try to defend the criticisms raised against them by irate parishioners:

* That the Declaration was merely an internal church document that did not attempt to address political guilt for the war;
* That only the German leadership had to be ashamed; or
* That it was not traitorous to confess guilt.

Of the 11 signatories, only Niemoeller chose to publicize it: "For the next two years", he claimed, "I did nothing but preach the Declaration to people." This bold approach, along with his [9 year] internment at DACHAU, [concentration camp in Munich suburb] helped create his controversial reputation.

EFFECTS: Many Germans objected to the confession of guilt, on the ground that they had also suffered in the war, as a result of Allied wrongdoing. [particularly Soviet]

The dreadful misery of 1945-1946 held the Germans back from all remorse. Because—most people believed this—the occupation troops were responsible for the misery. "They're just as inhuman as we were", was how it was put. And with that everything was evened up.

Some Germans quickly drew comparisons to the "war guilt" clause of the Versailles Treaty, as the Declaration admitted that there was a "solidarity of guilt" among the German people for the endless suffering wrought by Germany. They feared that once again, the victors would use such logic to impose punishment upon Germany, as Versailles had widely been viewed after the conclusion of World War I.

Furthermore, was "solidarity of guilt" a code word for "collective guilt"—the notion by some of the more hawkish Allied spokesmen, that all Germans (except the active resistance) bore all responsibility for the Nazi crimes, whether or not they had personally pulled triggers or ejected gas pellets on children! The Declaration did not expressly stipulate collective guilt, but neither did it expressly adopt the more moderate doctrine and responsibility, like all things human, were generally matters of degree. Niesen, a former student of KARL BARTH and one of the signatories of the Declaration, concluded that there was a general unwillingness by the German people to accept responsibility for the Nazi rule as Hokenos puts it:

"The righteous intermingling of self-justification and self-pity was as important a factor in creating a hostile environment for a public confession as were postwar fears of another Versailles or Allied charges of collective guilt."

One German churchman reflected on his contacts with his Swiss church comrade as those were renewed after the war; they had remained in contact even during the war, but there were boundaries still to overcome after the war's end. His reflections are reve467ling, both for the revelation and articulation of those boundaries and his own post-war attitude of "helplessness" in the face of totalitarianism, his underlying premise that individual Germans could do nothing because of the obstacles imposed by the Nazi totalitarianism was simply too great, so the clergy had no choice but to collaborate.

The accusation [from the Swiss] was that we [the German churchmen] had survived…for them that was treachery. They couldn't understand that, under a totalitarian system, one has to make compromises…one has to have a certain flexibility…they couldn't understand any of this. [Eventually there was mutual understanding and]…I was elected by the Swiss delegates to the governing council…me a German!"…That moved me greatly…the bridge was truly there again."

Many Germans raised the practical objection that the Declaration would be interpreted by the Allies as an expression of collective guilt, which would in turn justify harsh treatment by the Allies in the postwar world. Most Protestants were willing to admit some degree of responsibility, provided that the Allies reciprocated and admitted their own wrongdoing.

"In letter after letter [to the signatories] the same cry of resentment [against the Allies] is heard. To most Germans the suffering [of defeat and postwar conditions] itself was punishment enough for whatever share of guilt Germans bore…since the Allies also committed war crimes, this fact should somehow lessen the gravity of the crimes committed by Germany."

Others, who saw the Declaration more in theological than in practical terms, recognized that confession is made before God and not before men, and that such "conditional confessions" were theologically wrong-headed and misunderstood the meaning of Christian Confession: As one Protestant rather wryly noted, neither the Allies nor the World Council of Churches "are our father confessor!"

Hokenos identifies three basic reasons that Germans were reluctant to confess wrongdoing:

* Many Germans had in fact supported the Nazis and were unrepentant. Their racist and nationalist mentality was intact, even heightened by the defeat which triggered feelings of anger and resentment.

* The nature and extent of the Nazi barbarities was difficult to comprehend, even for some of those who participated in them. Bystanders were reluctant to take responsibility for a campaign that was, in both quantitative and moral terms, nearly incomprehensible.

* Germans were suffering also and they naturally gave priority to their suffering. Wiki

"The Messianic Legacy" Hitler's AntiChrist Third Reich

An unusual source about Hitler and his messianic religion was written by the three men who wrote the Apostate book HOLY BLOOD, HOLY GRAIL (1983) which gave author DAN BROWN the idea for his fictional plot which he used in his international multi language mega best seller book THE DA VINCI CODE (2003). The book became a blockbuster film with actor TOM HANKS as the symbolist who connects clues which alleges JESUS and MARY MAGDALEN had a female child and a secret bloodline. Mary Magdalen was the first person to tell the Disciples that Jesus had RISEN from his sealed tomb. In the Bible she meets a man "gardener" and asks him if he knows where my master Jesus body is. JESUS speaks and Magdalen recognizes HIS voice and exclaims, "RABBONI" RABBI teacher NOT HUSBAND! She then tells the DISCIPLES.
PROVIDENTIAL FACT: The German and Italian editions of the book THE DA VINCI CODE are titled SACRILEGIOUS! AMEN
The English authors of the HOLY BLOOD, HOLY GRAIL took DAN BROWN to the HIGH COURT in Great Britain, but lost their plagiarism law suit in the British court.
In their second book the MESSIANIC LEGACY (1986) English authors MICHAEL BAIGENT, RICHARD LEIGH and HENRY LINCOLN historically reveal:

"In his perverse way, Hitler gave the German people a new sense
of meaning, conferring a NEW RELIGION upon them and thereby
redeeming them from uncertainty—from the 'relativity of perspective
verging on epistemological panic' cited above. In the process, ironically
and paradoxically, he gave the rest of the world a new sense of meaning as
well. Because of Hitler and the Third Reich, the WORLD made SENSE, if only
for a time. The First World War had been an INSANE WAR. There were no
real heroes or villains. Everyone was to blame, everyone wanted it and
no one wanted it; and once under way, the whole thing had a grim
juggernaut momentum of its own, which no one was able to control.
In contrast, the SECOND WORLD WAR MADE SENSE. Not only was
it a SANE WAR; it was perhaps the most sane war to have been fought in
modern HIStory. It was sane, so far as the Allied powers were concerned,
precisely because Germany had effectively incarnated in itself the burden of
humanity's collective madness. By taking upon its own shoulders mankind's
capability of horror, for outrage, for atrocity, for bestiality, Germany,
paradoxically, redeemed the rest of the Western world into sanity. It took
Auschwitz and Belsen to teach us the meaning of EVIL—not as an abstract
theological proposition, but as a concrete reality. It took Auschwitz and
Belsen to teach us the acts we were capable of, and to make us repudiate
them. Unlike the war of 1914-18, the war against the Third Reich became
a legitimate CRUSADE in the name of decency, humanity, civilization.
Because HITLER had been a FALSE PROPHET, Western society came to
distrust all prophets. Because the Third Reich had promulgated its own
warped absolutes, Western society came to distrust all absolutes.
Eventually, the distrust of absolutes would culminate, once again, in an
all-pervasive relativity of perspective. p 163-165 THE MESSIANIC LEGACY 1986

Quite an astute summation of the two worst wars in HIStory which almost destroyed Christianity! Christian nation against Christian nation. Later, I will discuss Japanese imperialism, Stalin's Communist Russia, Mussolini, originator of Roman Fascism and the failed Ottoman Empire and

Lawrence of Arabia who didn't support Britain and France occupation of the Middle East. I believe SATAN, who accuses Humankind before God, had a brief bloody victory over the PRIDEFUL and coveting nature of nationalistic alliances during these two world wars.

The JEHOVAH'S WITNESSES, a non trinitarian denomination, "believed SATAN was CAST TO EARTH in 1914!"   LEO ROSTEN AMERICA'S DENOMINATIONS 1965

ADOLF HITLER was a corporal in the trenches in France at that time bravely running messages and was almost killed several times. His Jewish officer awarded him twice the esteemed German Iron Cross medal for his valor. Hitler wore it at his rallies.

American author Historian BARBARA TUCHMAN's epic book GUNS OF AUGUST (1961) outlines the background of how the imperialistic rivalries of European royal families and their alliance escalated into the Great War. Ironically, the British, German, Austrian and Russian, king, kaiser, arch-duke and czar were blood relatives making the war incestuous! A providential war which killed 8,000,000 soldiers and civilians. America tried to stay out of the bloodbath in the trenches with its heavy artillery, machine guns and first use of poison gas. A generation later it is understandable why nations were pacifist not wanting to die again in Europe.

HISTORY FACT: French General and Field Marshal FERDINAND FOCH prophesied after the signing of the un-Christian retributive VERSAILLES ARMISTICE: "This is not peace. It is an Armistice for 20 years!" On Sept. 3, 1939, Hitler's Army invaded neutral Poland, which had a military treaty with France and Great Britain, which began World War II. World War I began Sept. 1,1914, ended Nov. 11, 1919, 20 years!   HIStory.

These two world wars took the Christian "religion" and faith to its lowest point since the end of ROMAN EMPIRE, DARK AGES, BLACK PLAGUE and the COUNTER REFORMATION THIRTY YEARS WAR in Germany in the 1600s. Today, the State financed Churches and magnificent Cathedrals of Europe are almost empty except for tourists! The citizens of Europe have placed their faith in a new god, and many of their liberal secular humanist socialist government "cradle to grave entitlement governments."

DER FUEHRER ROCK OPERA

Recorded FEBRUARY — AUGUST 1977 at Ruessel Studios Hamburg, Germany

FUHRER WANTED—1ST MAN: SITTING HER IN THE MARKET-PLACE
NOTHING'S GOING ON — LIFE IS FILLED WITH EMPTY DAYS
NOTHING'S GOING ON — WOMAN: I WONDER WHY I'M LIVING ON
GOT NO AIMS, GOT NO HOLD— WHAT'S LIFE MORE THAN HANGING AROUND
AND JUST GROWING OLD?
2ND MAN: IF I GET NO JOB TODAY — I'LL HAVE TO DECIDE
IF I EARN MY MONEY ON THE GOOD — OR ON THE EVIL SIDE
1ST MAN: WE ARE LONGING FOR HAPPINESS   [sadness lost HOPE]
BUT WHAT DO THE PAPERS SPREAD?   [Newspapers fears]
FEAR OF THE FUTURE, BOREDOM OF LIFE   [Fear of the future]
OUR WORLD SEEMS SO BAD!   [World is bad no good]
CROWD: OH HOW WE WANT A MAN TO LEAD US OUT OF MISERY!
OH HOW WE WANT A MAN TO LEAD US OUT OF MISERY!

HE SHOULD LEAD US TO A BETTER WORLD — AND NEVER GO ASTRAY!
HE SHOULD BRING US BREAD AND WORK — AND TURN OUR FEARS AWAY!
OH HOW WE WANT A MAN TO LEAD US OUT OF MISERY!
OH HOW WE WANT A MAN TO LEAD US OUT OF MISERY!
THE PACT   GOEBBELS: I'M SO GLAD WE'RE ALL TOGETHER
COME, DON'T LET US WAIT NO MORE— TAKE YOUR SEATS AROUND THE TABLE
TO LEARN WHAT THE FUTURE HAS IN STORE
HE WILL ALWAYS COME AT NIGHTFALL   [Hitler's torchlight rallies]
I FELL VIBRATIONS IN THE AIR — BEFORE WE START YOU'VE GOT TO PROMISE
TO KEEP THE SECRET WERE GONNA SHARE
ALL: WE ARE CALLING. — WE ARE CALLING
GOEBBELS: MASTER IF YOU HEAR US — GIVE US JUST A SIGN
MASTER IF YOU HEAR US — GIVE US A SIGN — MASTER IF YOU HEAR US
I GOT A NEW BODY FOR YOU — GIVE US JUST A SIGN
ALL: WE ARE CALLING US. WE ARE CALLING
ARE YOU THERE? ARE YOU THERE?
SATAN'S VOICE OUT OF HITLER — BUILD UP MY REICH IN GERMANY
WITH LIGHT-HAIRED PEOPLE PRAISING ME
I'LL LEAD YOU AND I'LL LET YOU KNOW —WHAT TO DO AND WHERE TO GO
HITLER: I GOT THE MESSAGE, MASTER — I GOT THE MESSAGE, MASTER
SATAN: BUT BEWARE OF ICE AND SNOW! — BUT BEWARE OF ICE AND SNOW!
GOEBBELS: LISTEN TO ME— LISTEN TO ME EVERYBODY.
LISTEN TO THE NEWS I'VE GOT: I'VE FOUND THAT MAN YOU CALLED FOR
AND HE'S THE ONLY ONE WITH THE ABILITY TO HELP US OUT OF OUR MISERY!
CROWD: HE MUST BRING US LAW AND ORDER!
HE MUST BRING US WORK AND BREAD!
GOEBBELS: HE WILL BRING YOU LAW AND ORDER
HE WILL BRING YOU WORK AND BREAD!
CROWD: HE MUST BRING US PEACE AND FREEDOM!
HE WILL BRING US PROSPERITY!
GOEBBELS: HE WILL BRING YOU PEACE AND FREEDOM,
HE WILL BRING YOU PROSPERITY! HE WILL BRING YOU PEACE AND FREEDOM.
HE WILL BRING YOU PROSPERITY! — HE WILL BRING YOU LAW AND ORDER.
HE WILL BRING YOU WORK AND BREAD!
CROWD: SHOW US THE MAN WHO WILL BRING US OUT OF MISERY!
SHOW US THE WAY OF MAKING LIFE EXCITING AND GAY!
SHOW US THE MAN, SHOW US ANOTHER WAY
OF MAKING LIFE EXCITING AND GAY!   HERE I AM
HITLER: HERE I AM I HEARD YOU CALL ME — HERE I AM THE MAN YOU NEED
TIMES ARE BAD BUT I CAN HELP YOU — IF YOU'D ONLY TRUST ME
HERE I AM, HERE I AM, TRUST IN ME! HERE I AM TRUST IN ME!
EVERYWHERE I FELL YOUR TROUBLES
IT HURTS SO MUCH I CAN HARDLY STAND
WANNA MAKE YOUR LIFE WORTH LIVING
FOLLOW ME AND BE MY FANS! — HERE I AM, HERE I AM, FOLLOW ME!
HERE I AM, HERE I AM, FOLLOW ME! — HERE I AM, HERE I AM!
LET ME BE YOUR LEADER! — GIVE ME FOUR YEARS, ONLY FOUR YEARS,
YOU WON'T RECOGNIZE THE NATION!   MAGIC MAN
MAN: NOW THE TIMES WILL BE A CHANGING

EVERYTHING'S GONNA BE ALL RIGHT
GOEBBELS: SIGN YOUR FUTURE TO THE LEADER
YOU'LL BE SLEEPING WELL TONIGHT
MAN: FORGET ABOUT YOUR DREARY FEELINGS
RISE YOUR HANDS AND MOVE OUR FEET
BAD THINGS WILL SOON BE DISAPPEARING
KEEP   ON   DANCING   IN   THE   STREET   :
MAN: HE'S GONNA BE MY FAVORITE STAR
WOMAN: I'LL GIVE HIM EVERYTHING HE WANTS
GOEBBELS: YES, HE IS THE ONE WE REALLY NEED
ALL: HIS ARMY OF FANS THAT'S WHAT WE ARE
CROWD: WHEN THIS MAGIC MAN IS SPEAKING
THERE'S A BREEZE OF MYSTERY — IN HIS EYES HE'S GOT THE POWER
TO MAKE A POINT IN HISTORY — NOW THE TIMES WILL BE CHANGING
EVERYTHING'S GONNA BE ALL RIGHT — CAST YOUR FUTURE TO THE FUEHRER
YOU'LL BE SLEEPING WELL TONIGHT
GOEBBELS: LOOK HERE TAKE THIS SYMBOL   [SWASTIKA]
WHICH YOU ALL KNOW VERY WELL! — LOOK HERE TAKE THIS SYMBOL
WHICH YOU ALL KNOW VERY WELL! — FIRST YOU MUST BELIEVE IN HIM!
GOEBBELS: AND I'M SURE THERE IS GOOD REASON
CROWD: WE GOT A GOOD REASON, YEAH!
GOEBBELS: YOU ARE THE ARYAN MASTER RACE!
CROWD: ARYAN MASTER RACE
GOEBBELS: HE WILL MAKE YOU PROUD AGAIN!
CROWD: WE MUST BE PROUD AGAIN, YEAH
GOEBBELS: HE WILL KEEP YOUR FATHERLAND TIDY
CROWD:
WE MUST KEEP OUR FATHERLAND TIDY!
WE MUST KEEP OUR FATHERLAND TIDY!
WE MUST KEEP OUR FATHERLAND TIDY!
WE MUST KEEP OUR FATHERLAND TIDY!
GOEBBELS: HE WILL MAKE YOUR ARMY STRONG
CROWD: WE'RE GONNA FOLIOW HIM. YEAH!
GOEBBELS: FIRST YOU MUST BELIEVE IN HIM
CROWD: WE'RE GONNA FOLLOW HIM, YEAH!
GOEBBELS: YOU ARE THE ARYAN MASTER RACE
CROWD: WE'RE GONNA FOLLOW HIM, YEAH!
GOEBBELS: HE WILL MAKE YOU PROUD AGAIN
CROWD: WE'RE GONNA FOLLOW HIM, YEAH!
GOEBBELS: HE WILL MAKE YOUR ARMY STRONG
CROWD: WE'RE GONNA FOLLOW HIM, YEAH!
INTERVIEW: EVA: [Eva Braun Hitler's secret mistress.]
MAY I HAVE SOME INFORMATION JUST WHAT MAKES YOU SEEM SO STRANGE?
ONCE YOU WERE A MAN LIKE MILLIONS, WHEN DID YOU BEGIN TO CHANGE?
CAN YOU TELL ME WHY THESE PEOPLE SCATTER FLOWERS IN YOUR WAY?
LET ME KNOW IF YOU BELIEVE IN ALL THOSE FOOLISH THINGS YOU SAY.
CROWD: OUR MORNING STAR IS RISING ALL THE SHADOWS DRIFT AWAY
EVA: WHAT'S THIS KIND OF FASCINATION MAKES THEM SILLY AS THEY ARE?
HOW LONG WILL THEY TAKE TO NOTICE? YOU ARE JUST A SELF-MADE STAR!

HITLER: EVERY SINGLE GENERATION WANTS TO HAVE ITS LEADING MAN
WHO APPEALS TO THEIR EMOTIONS I SHALL DO THE BEST I CAN!
CROWD: OUR MORNING STAR IS RISING ALL THE SHADOWS DRIFT AWAY
EVA: WHAT' S IT ALL ABOUT YOUR MAGIC? I ADMIT IT'S WORKING WELL!
DID YOU GET YOUR MIGHT FROM HEAVEN?
DID YOU GET YOUR MIGHT FROM HELL?
HITLER: LET ME ANSWER WITH A QUESTION: IF THEY MADE A STAR OF YOU
WOULD YOU MODESTLY RETIRE? I SHALL DO THE BEST I CAN!
CROWD: OUR MORNING STAR IS RISING ALL THE SHADOWS DRIFT AWAY!
BEWARE OF HIM WARNING MAN: BEWARE OF HIM! DID YOU SEE HIS EYES?
ALL THOSE IMPRESSIVE WORDS, PEOPLE, THOSE WORDS ARE
NOTHING ELSE BUT LIES! PEOPLE BEWARE OF HIM!
HE'S MIXING UP YOUR MINDS BEWARE OF WHAT HE SAYS!
PEOPLE, OUR WORLD IS STILL TOO YOUNG TO DIE!
WARNING MAN: WHAT HE REALLY WANTS IS BOUNDLESS MIGHT!
CROWD: LEAVE US ALONE, YOU'RE DRIVING US MAD!
WARNING MAN: DRIVING YOU MAD, OH YES PEOPLE BEWARE OF HIM!
HE'LL MAKE THE WORLD TURN FASTER!
1000 YEARS SEEM LIKE MINUTES THEN! [Hitler proclaimed 1,000 year Third Reich.]
PEOPLE, OUR WORLD IS STILL TOO YOUNG TO DIE! HE CAN'T BE BAD
GOEBBELS:
HEY! TAKE CARE OF WHAT YOU'RE SAYING!
HEY! TAKE CARE OF WHAT YOU'RE SAYING!
HEY! HAVE YOU HEARD OF THE GESTAPO?
HEY! HAVE YOU HEARD OF THE GESTAPO?
CROWD: HE CAN'T BE BAD! HE CAN'T BE BAD!
HE GAVE US THE SYMBOL OF THE SUN!   [Swastika has reversed arms]
WARNING MAN: KING OF THE WORLD
GOEBBELS: DID YOU HEAR THOSE PEOPLE CALL?
YOU CAN HOLD THEM IN YOUR HANDS THEY ARE EASILY INFLUENCED
I THINK YOU'LL UNDERSTAND!
HITLER: WHEN I WAS A LITTLE BOY
PLAYING COWBOYS AND INDIANS [Hitler loved Karl May's Cowboy/Indian novels]
I USED TO GET THE LEADING PART AND I KNEW ALREADY THEN
HITLER & GOEBBELS:
KING OF THE WORLD MY FRIEND THAT'S WHAT I'M GONNA BE ONE DAY
KING OF THE WORLD MY FRIEND THAT'S WHAT I'M GONNA BE ONE DAY
GOEBBELS: YOU'RE ALREADY THE GREATEST STAR
WITH A HUGE ARMY OF FANS HOW YOU'RE ABLE TO FULFILL THE WORK
WHICH YOU ONCE BEGAN!
HITLER & GOEBBELS: KING OF THE WORLD MY FRIEND
THAT'S WHAT I'M GONNA TO BE ONE DAY KING OF THE WORLD MY FRIEND
THAT'S WHAT I'M GONNA TO BE ONE DAY
HITLER: OH I LOVE THEM ADORING ME LOVE TO FEEL MY POWER GROW
IF I'D TOLD THEM TO ROB AND KILL THEY WOULDN'T HESITATE TO GO!
HITLER & GOEBBELS: KING OF THE WORLD MY FRIEND
THAT'S WHAT I'M GOING TO BE ONE DAY KING OF THE WORLD MY FRIEND
THAT'S WHAT I'M GOING TO BE ONE DAY   WHAT A MAN!
EVA: WHEN I'M LEANING MY HEAD AGAINST HIS SHOULDER

THEN I'M FEELING SO GLAD THE BAD TIMES ARE OVER.
GOT HIM INTO MY LIFE GOT HIM INTO MY HEART
WE'LL NEVER PART! WE'LL NEVER PART AGAIN!
WHEN I'M LEANING MY HEAD AGAINST HIS SHOULDER
SOMETIMES I GOT THE FEELING IT'S GROWING COLDER
THERE ARE THINGS IN THE AIR THAT I DIDN'T UNDERSTAND
OH WHAT A MAN! SOMETIMES I'M A BIT SCARED
BY THE RUN OF THE STORY, SOMETIMES I CANNOT SHARE
HIS GREAT LUST FOR GLORY. I'M AFRAID THAT HIS LOVE'S
GONNA TURN MY FATE. WHAT CAN I DO? NOW IT'S TOO LATE!
THE BURNING OF BOOKS
GOEBBELS: THE WORKS OF KARL MARX — CROWD: INTO THE FIRE
GOEBBELS: THE WRITINGS OF FREUD —   CROWD: INTO THE FIRE
GOEBBELS: WITH THEIR CONDEMNATION— CROWD: INTO THE FLAMES
GOEBBELS: ERICH MARIA REMARQUE.   CROWD: INTO THE FLAMES
                [pacifist book ALL QUIET ON THE WESTERN FRONT]
GOEBBELS: BURN THEIR POISONOUS LIES — CROWD: BURNING, BURNING
GOEBBELS: ALL UNDESIRABLE THOUGHTS — CROWD: BURNING, BURNING
GOEBBELS: THE BOOKS OF TUCHOLSKY —   CROWD: INTO THE FIRE
GOEBBELS: THE MIND OF KASTNER   CROWD: INTO THE FIRE [children's books]
GOEBBELS: LIES, ALL LIES
STALINGRAD SOLDIER: ICY WINDS BLOW ON THE FROZEN SNOW
I LOST MY TRACES LONG TIME AGO
I'D NEVER JOINED THEM IF I'D KNOWN BEFORE
THIS SO-CALLED BLITZKRIEG WOULD BE SUCH A LONG WAR [soldiers used meth]
DARK IS THE SKY AND THE SUN IS WEAK
GOT NO DIRECTION, I'M IN THE MOOD TO WEEP
MY GIRL IS DREAMING THAT I'M COMING HOME
BUT AS IT IS NOW, I'VE GOT TO LEAVE HER ALL ALONE
I AM SO HUNGRY, CANNOT EAT MY GUN
WHAT A COMFORT NOT TO BE THE ONLY ONE
MY GIRL SHOULD KNOW NO SNOW IS GONNA COVER ME
MAYBE TOMORROW I'M A SHADOW IN HER MEMORY
SOMEBODY TELL ME WHAT I'M FIGHTING FOR
WHY SHOULD I DIE HERE? THIS IS NOT MY WAR?
HITLER'S VOICE: I GIVE THE ORDERS AND YOU JUST OBEY!
SO KEEP ON FIGHTING, NEVER ASK ME WHY!
SOLDIER: DARK IS THE SKY AND THE SUN IS WEAK
I FEEL SO EMPTY, NO MORE TEARS TO WEEP
HITLER VOICE: THINK OF YOUR COUNTRY! OUR AIMS ARE HIGH!
YOU GOT THE DUTY JUST TO FIGHT AND DIE!
SOLDIER: DYING FOR SOMEONE WHO DOESN'T EVEN KNOW MY NAME
I'M JUST A NUMBER, ONE OF MILLIONS IN YOUR MORTAL GAME
ICY WINDS BLOW ON THE FROZEN SNOW
TINGEL-TANGEL REVUE-GIRL: [Cabaret club song]
THIS TIME IS MY TIME LET'S MAKE IT A HIGH TIME
THINGS ARE OK, SOLDIER IF YOU CAN PAY, SOLDIER!
I WON'T DENY I'M NOT SO SHY
FOR A LITTLE FEE, SOLDIER YOU TOUCH MY KNEE, SOLDIER!

IF YOU PAY SOME MORE, SOLDIER ENTER MY DOOR, SOLDIER!
I WON'T DENY! I'M NOT SO SHY!
PRIDE IS JUST A LUXURY THAT I CANNOT AFFORD
LET US HAVE SOME FUN TOGETHER FOR LIFETIME IS SO VERY SHORT!
BUY ME AND USE ME BUT NEVER REFUSE ME
DON'T BE ASHAMED, SOLDIER LIFE'S JUST A GAME, SOLDIER
DO NOT DENY! DON'T BE SO SHY
STALINGRAD IS LOST!
GOEBBELS: STOP THE SHOW! STALINGRAD IS LOST!
HITLER: NO, NO! IT'S NOT TRUE! WE SHALL NEVER LEAVE!
MY ARMIES NEVER RETREAT! WE SHALL WIN
HITLER: OH JOSEPH WE SHALL WIN THE GAME
I'M WAITING FOR THE TIME TO SHOW I'M VERY SURE WE'LL WIN THE WAR
SO WHAT'S THE REASON WHY I'M FEELING SO LOW?
OH DOCTOR PLEASE I NEED MY FIX YOU KNOW [Dr. Morell gave Hitler meth, oxy]
THE FLASH WILL CLEAR MY FRIGHTENED BRAIN
SO TAKE MY ARM AND LET IT FLOW
I PROMISE NOT TO DO IT AGAIN   [junkie in end used cocaine no drugs available]
BUT JUST FOR ONE MORE TIME YOU'VE GOT TO HELP ME
OUT OF HELL   AGAIN!   [Hitler no alcohol, cigarettes, a vegetarian.]
YOU KNOW I FEEL SO VERY BAD TONIGHT
I'M LOST I'M LOST AND FALLING DOWN
ALL MY FRIENDS BUT YOU HAVE GONE AWAY
SO PLEASE DON'T LEAVE ME ON THE GROUND
OH JOSEPH CAN'T YOU SEE MY PAIN
I FEEL MY BLOOD LIKE CRYSTAL LEAD   [drug addiction]
THE DEVIL'S GOT HIS WAY AGAIN SO COME AND TAKE MY ARM I BEG YOU SO
AND JUST FOR ONE MORE TIME YOU'VE GOT TO HELP ME OUT OF HELL AGAIN
TOTAL WAR: GOEBBELS: LISTEN ALL TO OUR FUEHRER'S CALL!
THINGS GO RIGHT AS LONG AS WE'RE TOGETHER!
LISTEN ALL TO OUR FUEHRER'S CALL!
IF NECESSARY WE SHALL FIGHT FOREVER! THE FUEHRER NEEDS YOU
HE NEEDS ALL OF YOU NOW YOU'VE GOT TO FOLLOW HIS CALL!
THE FUEHRER NEEDS YOU HE NEEDS ALL OF YOU NOW
YOU'VE GOT TO FOLLOW HIS CALL! DON'T BELIEVE WHAT SOME PEOPLE SAY
THEY TRY TO TELL THE WORLD THAT WE ARE TIRED
THAT'S A LIE AND WE SHALL PROVE IT NOW!
WE SHALL PROVE TO THE WORLD THAT THEY ARE LIARS!
THE FUEHRER NEEDS YOU HE NEEDS ALL OF YOU NOW
YOU'VE GOT TO FOLLOW HIS CALL! THE FUeHRER NEEDS YOU
HE NEEDS ALL OF YOU NOW YOU'VE GOTTA FOLLOW HIS CALL!
ANSWER ME IN AN HONEST WAY: ARE YOU READY FOR THE TOTAL WAR?
SO TAKE A GUN, THERE ARE ENOUGH FOR EVERYONE,   [No 2nd Amendment law]
LET'S DEFEAT THEM AS THEY'D NEVER BEEN BEFORE!
DO YOU WANT THE TOTAL WAR? AS IT HAS NEVER BEEN BEFORE!
CROWD: JAAAAAAAAAAAAAAAAAAAAAAAAAAAAAAAAAAAAAAAAA!
GOEBBELS: ICH FRAGE EUCH: [I ask you]
WOLLT IHR TOTALEN KRIEG?   [Do you want total war?]
WOLLT IHR IHN, WENN NOETIG,

65

TOTALER UND RADIKALER ALS WIR IHN UNS HEUTE   [Total radical today]
UBERHAUPT ERST VORSTELLEN KOENNEN?   [Speech is on U Tube]
THE LOOKING GLASS HITLER: IT'S LIKE A WAITING ROOM
WHERE HAVE THOSE PEOPLE GONE? WHY AM I LONESOME NOW?
WHY AM I LONESOME NOW? I SOLD   MY SOUL
I FEEL MY BLOOD WHAT HAVE THEY DONE TO ME?
OH HOW I TRIED IN VAIN TO BE MYSELF AGAIN
HOW CAN I CLEAR MY BRAIN? I WONDER WHY I SHOULDN'T DARE
TO LOOK INTO THAT MIRROR THERE
THERE! THERE! OVER IN THE CORNER!   IT'S HE!, IT'S HE!
HE'S COME FOR ME! [Satan the devil Goethe's Faust given 23 years-Hitler 1922-1945]
NIGHTMARE:
HITLER: NOW IT'S THE TIME, NOW IT'S THE SEASON
NOW I'M SURE YOU'VE COME FOR ME!   [SATAN]
BEFORE I DIE TELL ME THE REASON [Hitler's suicide Walpurgis Night 4-30, 1945.]
WHY YOU'VE BEEN PLAYING TRICKS ON ME
YOU SHOULD REMEMBER THAT YOU PROMISED   [Faust's 23-yr. pact with devil.]
TO MAKE A MIGHTY MAN OF ME   [12 year THIRD REICH 1933-1945]
MY THOUSAND YEARS ARE NOT OVER YET [Jesus millennium Rev. 20:1-5]
GIVE ME THE FINAL VICTORY!   [Allied Victory in Europe May 8, 1945]
GOEBBELS TO HITLER: EVERYTHING'S ALL RIGHT, YOU SEE MY FUEHRER?
CAN'T YOU SEE? ENDINGS COMING NEAR, CAN'T YOU SEE MY FUEHRER?
CAN'T YOU SEE? HITLER: NOW YOUR TAKING MY SOUL WITH LAUGHTER
FORGETTING WHAT WE ONCE ARRANGED [Hitler led Nazi party 1922-1945-23 yrs.]
YES, YOUR TAKING MY SOUL WITH LAUGHTER
TELL ME WHY OUR TREATY HAS CHANGED [Goethe Faust pact with devil 23 years]
VOICES: WHY DID YOU MURDER US? WHY DID YOU MURDER?
CAN'T YOU SEE THE SMOKE RISING FROM THE CHIMNEY?
WHY DID YOU MURDER US? WHY DID YOU MURDER?
CAN'T YOU SEE THE SMOKE, BUILDER OF THE CHIMNEY?
GOEBBELS: SHOW ME MY FUEHRER WHOM YOU TALK TO! [His demoniac angel]
YOUR MANNERS TAKE ME BY SURPRISE BEHAVE AS BRAVELY AS YOU USE TO
I NEVER SAW YOU SO UNWISE
HITLER: DEAD BODIES STANDING UP AGAINST ME
KEEP THEM AWAY, I'M SO AFRAID!   [Resurrection of Holocaust civilians]
YOU GAVE THE ORDERS, I OBEYED! VOICES: CAN'T YOU SEE
THE SMOKE RISING FROM THE CHIMNEY? CAN'T YOU SEE
THE SMOKE RISING FROM THE CHIMNEY? CAN'T YOU SEE?
THE SMOKE, BUILDER OF THE CHIMNEY? CAN'T YOU SEE?
HITLER: NOW YOU'RE TAKING MY SOUL WITH LAUGHTER
FORGETTING WHAT WE ONCE ARRANGED
YES, YOU'RE TAKING MY SOUL WITH LAUGHTER
TELL ME WHY OUR TREATY HAS CHANGED?   [Satan is the great deceiver]
WARNING MAN: YOUR NOBLE AIMS WERE JUST PRETENDED
DESTRUCTION IS WHAT YOU ENJOY   [SATAN'S hatred of God's Creation in Eden.]
YOUR AIMS ARE REACHED YOUR GAME HAS ENDED   [SATAN'S TIME IS SHORT.]
PEOPLE HAVE ALWAYS BEEN YOUR TOY [Satan Humankind's deceiver and accuser]
GOEBBELS: SHOW ME MY FUEHRER WHOM YOU TALK TO!   [SATAN]
YOUR MANNERS TAKE ME BY SURPRISE

BEHAVE AS BRAVELY AS YOU USE TO DON'T WANT TO SEE YOU SO UNWISE!
EVERYTHING'S ALL RIGHT, CAN'T YOU SEE MY FUEHRER? CAN'T YOU SEE?
ENDINGS COMING NEAR, CAN'T YOU SEE MY FUEHRER?   CAN'T YOU SEE?
HITLER: NOW YOU'RE TAKING MY SOUL WITH LAUGHTER [SATAN'S false bargain]
FORGETTING WHAT WE ONCE ARRANGED.   [Satan's false bargain.]
YES, YOU'RE TAKING MY SOUL WITH LAUGHTER
TELL ME WHY OUR TREATY HAS CHANGED?
BROWN CLOUDS WARNING MAN: WE DON'T KNOW THE WAY
BUT WE'RE LEAVING THIS LAND
WE'RE LEAVING THE PLACES WE LOVE   [Final Solution Holocaust]
OUR HOPES IN A SUITCASE YELLOW STARS ON OUR COATS
AND BROWN CLOUDS ARE HANGING ALL ABOVE OH FATHER LET US KNOW
WHY DO THEY HATE US SO?
WHAT HAVE WE DONE? TO DESERVE SUCH A FATE?
I WONDER WHEN THE OLD CURSE WILL BE GONE?
THEY SAY WE ARE DIFFERENT AND SO WE ARE BAD
THE ONLY DIFFERENCE IS: WE'RE NOT BLONDE!   [Nazi Aryan master race myth]
OH FATHER LET US KNOW WHY DO THEY HATE US SO?
COME BROTHERS AND SISTERS TAKE YOUR CHILDREN BY THE HAND
THERE'S NOT TOO MUCH TIME LEFT TO WAIT. DON'T WAIT TILL THAT DEVIL'S
RAISING HELL AGAINST YOU.
TOMORROW IT MAY BE TOO LATE! OH FATHER LET US KNOW
WHY DO THEY HATE US SO? DYING DAY   PRISONER:
IT IS COLD AND DARK OUTSIDE. DOGS ARE HOWLING THROUGH THE NIGHT
I SAW THE OLD DAY DYING IN THE WEST. THE SUN WAS MOVING DOWN BEHIND THE
SMOKE. CAN'T FORGET THE TROUBLE WE'VE SEEN
COME ON AND TELL US WHY?
OUR LORD HAS LEFT US HERE ALONE IN CONCENTRATION CAMPS
CAN'T HE SEE, UP IN THE SKY? THE GREY SMOKE RISING? AND ONE DAY
IT MIGHT BE YOU MY FRIEND GHOULS AND FIENDS IN UNIFORMS
COULD HUMAN BEINGS REALLY EVER BE SO CRUEL?
INHUMAN BEASTS ARE SHOWING ME
SHOWING ME THAT LUCIFER IS STILL ALIVE
I SAW THE OLD DAY DYING IN THE WEST
THE SUN WAS MOVING DOWN BEHIND THE SMOKE
CAN'T FORGET THE TROUBLE WE'VE SEEN
CAN'T FORGET THE TROUBLE WE'VE SEEN
GREY SMOKE IS EVERYWHERE
FIRE'S BURNING DOWN THE PILLARS OF OUR LIVES
GREY SMOKE IS IN MY SOUL
WONDER, IF YOU'LL REMEMBER ME ONE DAY MY FRIEND
BERLIN BERLIN — CONSPIRATORS:
BERLIN, BERLIN COME TO BERLIN
LET US PUT AND END TO HIM!
THEY MADE A GOD OF HIM   [Hitler Germany's FALSE MESSIAH]
THEY'RE GONNA FOLLOW HIM   [fellow Austrian MESSMER'S animal magnetism]
HE'S GOT THEM IN HIS HAND IF WE WOULD TRY WE'D TRY IN VAIN
TO MAKE THEM SEE THAT HE'S INSANE! [media supported Hitler's law/order, jobs]
WHAT KIND OF MAN IS HE? SO MANY MEN BELIEVE IN HIS DIVINITY.   [messiah]

BUT WHEN WE ASKED FOR HIS AIMS NO ONE WAS ABLE TO EXPLAIN
WE MUST NOT LET HIM WIN LET'S PUT AN END TO HIM
HE IS TOO DANGEROUS FOR HE BELIEVES IN HIS OWN WORDS
KILLING HIM MEANS TO   SAVE THE WORLD!   [Ten failed assassination attempts]
COME TO BERLIN! COME TO BERLIN! I'M ALIVE
HITLER: I'M ALIVE SEEMS A MIRACLE   [Hitler believed in providence]
I'M NOT HURT AT ALL   [failed bomb attack Col. Staufenberg July 10, 1944]
THEY TRIED TO KILL ME, TRIED TO MURDER ME
THEY COULDN'T KNOW THEY WERE MUCH TOO SMALL CAMPS
I'M ALIVE IT'S NO MIRACLE NO ONE'S ABLE TO STOP MY FIGHT
TRY TO KILL ME AND YOU WILL REALIZE:
I'M PROTECTED BY A GREATER MIGHT   [DIVINE PROVIDENCE?]
SUDDENLY I GOT THE FEELING
THAT I HAD TO LEAVE THAT PLACE   [Relocated from the bunker was too hot in July]
IT WAS A MATTER OF DIVINATION   [Providence?]
WHICH WAS MAKING ME ESCAPE THE BLAZE
I'M ALIVE NOW MY FIGHT GOES ON FOR GREATER GERMANY
EVERYBODY NOT ALIGNED WITH US MUST BE CONDEMNED TO AGONY
EVERY NIGHT I HEAR MY VOICES
TELLING ME THAT I'M DOING RIGHT [fight Communism German churches supported]
LET ME ASK YOU A SIMPLE QUESTION ARE YOU WILLING TO JOIN MY FIGHT?
HITLER: I TOOK POLAND GOEBBELS: CZECHOSLOVAKIA
HITLER: I HOLD DENMARK GOEBBELS: AND NORWAY TOO
HITLER: ON TO HOLLAND GOEBBELS: THEN CAME BELGIUM
HITLER: FRANCE SOON FELL TO ME GOEBBELS: NORTHWEST AFRICA
HITLER: YUGOSLAVIA AND GREECE WERE BRUSHED ASIDE
WHO COMES NEXT? I'LL SOON DECIDE
CROWD: HEIL FUEHRER WE SHALL FOLLOW YOU BE AT YOUR COMMAND
EVA: EVERY MORNING WHEN I GET UP MY FRIEND
I WONDER WHO HE IS TODAY
I'M SO AFRAID OF THE NEXT TIME WHEN HIS FACE WILL CHANGE
I LOVE THE MAN HE WAS WHEN WE MEET AT FIRST
BUT WHO IS HE TODAY?   [Eva is shown as being the antithesis of Mary Magdalen.]
EVERY TIME WHEN I LOOK INTO HIS EYES I'M SEARCHING FOR A SIGN OF LOVE
BUT ALL I SEE IS THAT HE IS LOST IN TIME OR SPACE[Hitler belief in Reincarnation]
HIS BODY'S STILL WITH ME BUT HIS MIND HAS GONE   [heavy drug use]
GONE TO A DIFFERENT PLACE   [meth, crack/speed, cocaine, oxycodone addiction]
EVERY NIGHT WHEN I GO TO REST MY FRIEND
I THINK OF ALL THE DAYS WE SHARED
AND IN MY DREAMS WE ARE TOGETHER ALL THE TIME
I'M GONNA TRY TO HELP HIM GETTING SANE AGAIN AND BE FOREVER MINE EVA: WAKE
UP FROM YOUR NIGHTMARE LET ME TRY TO CALM YOU DOWN
COME AND SEE THAT NO ONE IS AROUND! WAKE UP FROM YOUR NIGHTMARE
LET ME TRY TO CALM YOU DOWN
CLOSE YOUR, EYES, DON'T LISTEN TO THE SOUNDS!
WHEN YOU FACE THE FACT THAT YOU HAVE BEEN GUIDED WRONG
WE CAN ALWAYS GO TO WHERE WE ONCE CAME FROM
AND I SHALL STAY WITH YOU! IT'S SO VERY HARD TO SEE
AN EAGLE FALLING DOWN! I'M GONNA HELP YOU GET UP FROM THE GROUND

TOMORROW IS ANOTHER DAY THE SUN WILL RISE AGAIN
THE FRESHNESS OF THE DAWN WILL END YOUR PAIN!
WHEN YOU FACE THE FACT THAT YOU'VE BEEN GUIDED WRONG
WE CAN ALWAYS GO WHERE WE ONCE CAME FROM
AND I SHALL STAY WITH YOU!
PIED PIPER WARNING MAN: DAY BY DAY YOU JUST HANG AROUND
WAITING FOR THE GREAT EVENTS TO COME — LEAD YOURSELF
OUT OF YOUR WORKING DAYS YOU GOT HANDS AND YOU GOT FEET TO RUN
CROWD: NOW HE'S GONE, HE WON'T COME BACK AGAIN
NOW HE'S GONE AND WE NEED SOMEONE NEW
YES, WE NEED ANOTHER LEADING MAN
TO TELL US HOW TO LIVE AND WHAT TO DO   [Socialist Nazi Germany]
HOW TO LIVE AND WHAT TO DO, YEAH!
WARNING MAN: ANY PIED PIPER CAN MAKE YOU FOLLOW HIM
LIKE THE RATS IN THAT FAMOUS FAIRY TALE [Grandpa's grave 20 mi.from Hameln]
HISTORY'S PLAYING IT'S FAVORITE GAME AGAIN
EVERY TIME IT'S GONNA END THE SAME   [HISTORY DOES REPEAT ITSELF.]
CROWD: NOW HE'S GONE, HE WON'T COME BACK AGAIN
NOW HE'S GONE AND WE NEED SOMEONE NEW
YES WE NEED ANOTHER LEADING MAN   [The END-TIME ANTICHRIST?]
TO TELL US HOW TO LIVE AND WHAT TO DO
HOW TO LIVE AND WHAT TO DO, YEAH!
WARNING MAN: ANY PIED PIPER CAN MAKE YOU FOLLOW HIM
LIKE THE RATS IN THAT OLD FAIRY TALE.   HITLER'S SPIRIT:
I'M STILL ALIVE AND YOU WILL FOLLOW ME.   ANYTIME, ANYTIME I'D CALL!

PERSONAL EVALUATION: The truth of Hitler's ROCK OPERA and America today: Today, Hitler's name and name Nazis are falsely invoked against President Trump and Republicans by left-wing liberal Socialist Democrats and biased/prejudicial media using Fascist Nazi rhetoric. Iran's Islamofascist Shia leaders, Fascist Putin, Communist China, Communist Cuba, Communist Venezuela, Communist Nicaragua and Communist Korea's leaders love President Trump being called a Fascist. He is a Christian Constitutional Populist Nationalist American.These nations all are the failed enemies of true western Democracy and Capitalism and America's Judeo-Christian Constitutional Republic. God's 9th Commandment condemns those who bear false witness [lie, slander and gossip] against their neighbor.
HITLER ROCK OPERA—MUSIC BY—LOTHAR SIMS/WALTER QUINTUS
LYRICS BY—GISELA SIMS
THE SINGERS—ADOLF HITLER—NEIL LANDON—JOSEPH GOEBBELS—PETER FRENCH—EVA BRAUN—MARTI WEBB—SOLDIER & JEW & WARNING MAN—IAN CUSSICK—REVUE GIRL—INGEBORG THOMSEN and—PHIL BAUMGARDEN—GEORGE HAYWORTH—LYVIA YIM—IRIS MOORE—AUDREY MOTOUNG WILLIAMS—ADRIAN ASKEW—and KODALIS are—BACKSTREET CHOIR
THE ROCK MUSICIANS: GUITARS—KARL ALLAUT—BASS-BENNY BENDORF—DRUMS—BERTE ENGELS—KEYBOARDS—JEAN JACQUES KRAVETZ—ADRIAN ASKEW—PERCUSSION—OKKO BEKKER—TRUMPET—BOB LANESE—SAXOPHONE/FLUTES—HERB GELLER
PRODUCED BY WALTER QUINTAS/LOTHAR SIEMS
ENGINEERED BY WALTER QUINTAS/LOTHAR SIEMS

THROUGH A LOOKING GLASS, DARKLY

GENERAL GEORGE S. PATTON, JR.

"Through the trail of the ages, Midst the pomp and toll of war, have I fought and strove and perished countless times upon the star.

In the form of many people In all the panoplies of time have I seen the luring vision Of the Victory Maid, sublime.

I have battled for fresh Mammoth, I have warred for pastures new, I have listed to the whispers When the race trek instinct grew.

I have known the call to battle In each changeless changing shape From the high souled voice of conscience To the beastly lust for rape.

I have sinned and I have suffered, Played the hero and the knave; Fought for belly, shame, or country, And for each have found a grave.

I cannot name my battles For the visions are not clear, Yet, I see the twisted faces And I feel the rending spear."

PATTON AS ROMAN CENTURION AT JESUS CROSS

"PERHAPS I STABBED OUR SAVIOR IN HIS HELPLESS SIDE. Yet, I called his name in blessing when after times I died."

In the dimness of the shadows Where we hairy heathens warred, I can taste in thought the lifeblood; We used teeth before the sword.

While in later clearer vision I can sense the coppery sweat, Feel the pikes grow wet and slippery when our phalanx, CYRUS [Persian king] met.."

Hear the rattle of the harness Where the Persian darts bounced clear, See their chariots wheel in panic From the [Greek, Macedonian] Hoplites leveled spear.

See the goal grow monthly longer, Reaching for the walls of Tyre. Hear the crash of tons of granite, Smell the quenchless eastern fire.

Still more clearly as a Roman, can I see the Legion close. As the third rank moved in forward And the short sword found our foes.

Once again I feel the anguish Of that blistering treeless plain When the Parthian showered death bolts, And our discipline was in vain.

I remember all the suffering Of those arrows in my neck. Yet, I stabbed a grinning savage As I died upon my back.

Once again I smell the heat sparks When my Flemish plate gave way And the lance ripped through my entrails As on CRECY's field I lay.

In the windless, blinding stillness Of the glittering tropic sea I can see the bubbles rising Where we set the captives free.

Midst the spume of half a tempest I have heard the bulwarks go When the crashing, point blank round shot.

I have fought with gun and cutlass On the red and slippery deck With all Hell aflame within me And a rope around my neck.

And still later as a General have I galloped with Murat When we laughed at death and numbers Trusting in the Emperor's Star.

Till at last our star faded, And we shouted to our doom Where the sunken road of Ohein Closed us in its quivering gloom.

So but now with tanks A' clatter Have I waddled on the foe Belching death at twenty paces, By the star shell's ghastly glow.

SO AS THROUGH A GLASS, AND DARKLY THE AGE LONG STRIFE I SEE
WHERE I FOUGHT IN MANY GUISES, MANY NAMES, BUT ALWAYS ME.
AND I SEE IN MY BLINDNESS WHAT THE OBJECTS WERE I WROUGHT, BUT
AS GOD RULES O'ER OUR BICKERING IT WAS THROUGH HIS WILL I FOUGHT.

SO FOREVER IN THE FUTURE, SHALL I BATTLE AS OF YORE, DYING
TO BE BORN A FIGHTER, BUT TO DIE AGAIN, ONCE MORE."

PROVIDENTIAL STORY: The Roman Centurion GIAS CASSIUS LONGINUS was born east of the Black Forest in Germania. His cataracts were cured by Jesus shed blood.

IS GENERAL PATTON IN VALHALLA OR HEAVEN?

"Georgie [Patton], a crack hurdler, tripped during a race. An understanding George Patton [father] consoled his son with a reference to mythology. Once, reading RUDYARD KIPLING'S poem "THE DESTROYERS," father and son had come across the phrase "The choosers of the slain," which neither understood. In an essay George Patton had just read, THOMAS CARLYLE explained its meaning:
"It seems that in the NORSE MYTHOLOGY—that of our ancestors the VIKINGS—the warrior who died in battle were accounted the real heroes—above those who survived—and before each battle the VALKYRIE—or VALKYES chose those who were adjudged WORTHY OF DEATH—and these Valkyes were thus called "the choosers of the slain," as the slain were called and esteemed "the chosen".
"So in Life's battles you can find the real heroes among the apparently defeated. The honors which are bestowed upon the apparently successful ones—are most other prizes of accident and circumstance—but again and again in some sequestered walk of life—unknown and unnoticed by the multitude we meet and instinctively recognize the "Heroes of the Strife"—and the wise and true know when they meet them."   p 36-37
GENERAL PATTON A SOLDIER'S LIFE, Stanley P. Hirshon, Harper Collins Publishers 10 East 53rd St. New York, NY. 2002

MY VIKING HERITAGE: In my dozen books about General PATTON I checked the indexes and didn't see any reference to RICHARD WAGNER and his four TEUTONIC NORDIC OPERAS which highlight the VALKYRIE gods and how the brave slain warriors entered VALHALLA. Wagner's music was well known in World War II because ADOLF HITLER and the NAZIS and especially the SS spiritually adopted WAGNER'S music into their pseudo ARYAN MASTER RACE dogma. General Patton must have known that Hitler was a Wagner fanatic and his Operas were performed to uniformed SS soldiers many of whom would die and go to "VALHALLA"? I can't picture General Patton being in VALHALLA with his former brutal enemies. VALHALLA sounds like HELL/HADES to me.
PROVIDENTIAL APOLOGETIC FACT: I read in a biography on C.S. CLIVE LEWIS that when he was a child his mother read him mythological stories. Also, when he first heard Wagner's Ride of the VALKKRIES OPERA he was mesmerized by the music. Lewis became an atheist after his mother died in his childhood. He became a Christian apologist through his discussions with J.R. TOLKIEN and CHESTERTON at OXFORD University where they taught him Jesus' Gospel. C.S.

71

LEWIS became a great Christian Apologist. The NARNIA "fairytales" and his epic MERE CHRISTIANITY books.

I first heard Wagner when I was in college circa 1963, when I bought bandleader STAN KENTON's Wagner LP album and I heard the RIDE OF THE VALKYRIES. Kenton had the largest jazz orchestra, 5 saxophones, 5 trumpets, 5 trombones (2 bass or 1 tuba), 3 mellophoniums (French horns with trumpet keys), guitar, bass, drums, Kenton's piano. Kenton's arrangements were unique and are still the only Opera played by a big band.

WHAT IS A VALKYRIE? Norse god ODIN's 12 HANDMAIDEN'S who conducted the slain warriors of their choice from the battlefield to VALHALLA. Old NORSE "chooser of the slain".Two of Patton's relatives died in Virginia units in the War of Secession.

HOLLYWOOD PROVIDENTIAL CONNECTION: In the film PATTON (1970) General GEORGE PATTON portrayed by GORGE C. SCOTT after his defeat of Gen. ERVIN ROMMEL'S AFRICA CORPS army in Tunisia views an ancient battlefield. Patton tells his commander Gen. OMAR BRADLEY his account of how the CARTHAGINIAN soldiers meet the ROMAN LEGIONS, who victoriously defeated the Carthaginians, at this site in their homeland. General BRADLEY portrayed by great character actor KARL MALDEN listens skeptically to Patton's historical vision of the ancient battle. Patton believed in REINCARNATION, a false belief, that he had lived previous lives. As a child Patton had been read the historic stories of ALEXANDER THE GREAT, JULIUS CAESAR, HANNIBAL and NAPOLEON. The notorious Confederate calvary marauder JOHN MOSBY told him his personal CIVIL WAR stories of his brave raids into northern Virginia attacking Union forces. Patton was actually recalling these heroic childhood stories. Patton was considered STUPID because he couldn't read. He had DYSLEXIA, an unknown symptom, which was a reading dysfunction. Patton's affliction caused him to be a "GOAT" at WEST POINT, the bottom of the class. Patton's Virginia family lost two members in the WAR OF SECESSION/WAR OF NORTHERN AGGRESSION, one during General THOMAS PICKETT's courageous, overly zealous, futile CHARGE at GETTYSBURG and another at battle of THIRD WINCHESTER.

THE GHOST OF GENERAL PATTON'S FOREFATHER

I visited Colonel Patton's grave at Winchester,Virginia, with my friend Bill Reeve when two women approached with a Patton's ghost pamphlet. I have heard many stories of apparitions in my Wilderness battlefield neighborhood. General SEDGWICK's SECOND DAY WILDERNESS TRENCH is 52 paces behind my house. In 15 years, I have thankfully not experienced anything unusual. When my family took the Gettysburg bus tour, I was surprised to see GHOST SHOPS, I don't recall seeing in 1974. One evening waiting in the car, with my 9 year old granddaughter, I noticed a statue and people gathering for a tour. I was going to see what was happening. My granddaughter stopped me saying, "OPA, don't go it is JENNY WADE'S GHOST TOUR." Jenny Wade was the only female civilian death during the horrific battle of Gettysburg. I asked my granddaughter, "How do you know about this?" She said, "My 4th grade teacher told our class this story." I asked one of my knowledgable CIVIL WAR group members about this. He recalled, "There is a teacher that teaches a lot about the Civil War in our neighborhood the center of four famous CIVIL WAR battles."

HARRY POTTER'S GHOSTS AND CIVIL WAR GHOSTS

My granddaughter has read all the HARRY POTTER books since she was 8 years old and seen all the videos, and gone twice to the Harry Potter ride at UNIVERSAL/DISNEY in Orlando, Florida. Apparently, the "ghosts" are restless spirits from unburied soldiers after the battle of Chancellorsville whose bodies were discovered during the horrific battle of the WILDERNESS where fires burned the thick undergrowth uncovering skeletons. These bodies had not received a Christian burial. National Park Rangers have heard these stories and may have experienced them. They will not discuss this even if asked. I have been shown a photo of ORBS by a lady friend who lives next to the Culpeper CEDAR MOUNTAIN battlefield. After the 150th Wilderness, at night a man took me into the woods, and made a prayer to the spirits. He took photos which showed these white dot ORBS. SPIELBERG's POLTERGEIST showed "ghosts".

Why Appeasement?

"For any government deliberately to deny to their people what must be their plainest and simplest right [to live in peace and happiness without the nightmare of war] would be to betray their trust, and to call down upon their heads the condemnation of all mankind."
"I do not believe that such a government anywhere exists among civilized peoples. I am convinced that the aim of every statesman worthy of the name, to whatever country he belongs, must be the happiness of the people for whom and to whom he is responsible, and in that faith I am sure that a way can and will be found to free the world from the curse of armaments and the fears that give rise to them, and to open up a happier, and a wiser future for mankind."
Prime Minister NEVILLE CHAMBERLAIN, November 1937

A wonderful democratic, humanist speech from a good peace loving man who didn't want to repeat the horrors of the GREAT WAR, World War I. He as few others could envision the future sins of Hitler and the Nazis though they had seen his regimented NUREMBERG RALLY and its outright pagan SWASTIKA flags and the multitudes adoration of their "1,000 year Reich" messiah, demi-god, Caesar they hailed with outstretched right arms jubilantly and loudly chanting their mantra—HEIL HITLER!

"What was Chamberlain thinking? "His family had long been Unitarians, who, because they rejected the deity of Christ, were ostracized from semi-official Church of England channels. Yet it was that very affiliation that contributed strongly to the Chamberlain family's dedication to public service, both his father and older brother were prominent in politics. Government was the natural vocation for those raised in UNITARIAN tradition, with its belief in the universal "goodness of all men," growing out of a sense of duty to mankind and a deep seated belief that reasonable, fair-minded men could work together to solve any difficulty…If only he could keep the German issue in its proper perspective and not let the war-lovers in either country gain too much momentum." Charles Colson, KINGDOMS IN CONFLICT (William Morrow/Zondervan Publishing House, 1987) p 155-156 [The "PEACE IN OUR TIME" treaty signed in Munich 9-30-38.]

The other powerful and wealthy appeasement faction was the CLIVEDEN SET headed by Lord and Lady NANCY ASTOR, a wealthy Philadelphian, who became Britain's first women in the

HOUSE OF LORDS. At a party at their huge Thames River mansion CLIVEDEN they entertained CHARLES LINDBERGH, who 10 years earlier made the famous first solo non-stop flight in his single engine SPIRIT OF ST. LOUIS monoplane.

"He had spent several weeks in Germany, warmly welcomed by the Nazis, even given a medal, by the Nazis and had come away tremendously impressed. The democracies seemed to him tired and decadent; in Germany he found a virile masculinity and spirited commitment that resonated in his soul. He had also been impressed by the German air force; so much so that wherever he went he preached that no one could stand against it." [He overestimated the Luftwaffe's capabilities which were tactical not strategic.]

"After the terrible kidnapping and death of their son, the Lindberghs had fled America for England; today they were guests at Nancy Astor's Cliveden weekend...'I am afraid this is the beginning of the end for England.' Lindbergh said sternly. 'The old instincts are being summoned up for war. People are talking about 'dishonorable peace,' and so on. Nobody seems to realize that England is in no condition to fight a war.'"

"It's madness," Nancy Astor said in one of her wild, stabbing protests. 'War will destroy Western civilization! Europe will be destroyed! Then Communism will spread, for it always feeds on death like a vulture.'"   Ibid p 163

"Why appeasement? "First of all, there was a great revulsion in England over the senseless butchery of trench warfare in the First World War. The country had little stomach to fight again. Chamberlain himself had lost a cousin, perhaps his closest friend, in France. He never stopped grieving. A second factor was Chamberlain himself. He had grown up in a tightly-knit UNITARIAN family. They had rejected the Christian belief in man's innate sinfulness, preferring to place faith in the innate goodness and 'reasonableness' of man. Influential Britons of all backgrounds were infected by such thinking. Faith in the social sciences, in intellectual solutions to moral problems, had never been higher than in the thirties. The flourishing of CHRISTIAN SCIENCE within Nancy Astor's influential circle at CLIVEDEN was symptomatic; Christian Scientists believe that all evil is an illusion that it can be eliminated by the exercise of the mind. Chamberlain, who was close to many of the Cliveden group, lived among people to whom the harshness of human evil had ceased to seem real."

"Hitler gave Chamberlain more than adequate evidence that he was evil, unreasonable, and bent on war. Yet the prime minister could not, would not, see it...And finally, the church in England failed to provide an independent moral voice for the country. They to had a difficulty discerning EVIL except in 'outmoded' policies. Much of the clergy seized on the peace issue and promoted forums like the League of Nations with such indiscriminate fervor that they seemed to believe that God Himself spoke exclusively through international gatherings. Led by Bishop William Temple they put more faith in progressive politics and economics than in God. Churchmen were so enamored with the fledgling ecumenical movement that, to Bonhoeffer's disgust, they refused to censure the German church even after German "Christians" had taken control."   Ibid p 173

"The failure of both the state and the church contributed to the disaster that befell the world. Had they acted sooner to discharge their respective duties, the HOLOCAUST might well have been avoided. The roots of World War II were in a sense theological. In England and in Germany, the State and the Church failed to fulfill their God ordained mandates. And whenever that happens, evil triumphs!"

"Hitler was determined to exceed government's ordained and delegated role. For him the state was everything, and he was god. The Communists and the Jew, his hated targets, could offer little organized resistance, and no one spoke in their defense. In the face of Hitler's enormous popularity, all the trusted institutions of modern society utterly failed to resist. The trade unions, the Parliament, the political parties, the universities, the associations of medical doctors,

74

scientists, and intellectuals—all were completely under Hitler's power within six months. Only the church had the independence and the institutional power to stand between Hitler and absolute totalitarianism. Ibid   p 173-175

THE PACIFIST DILEMMA

"Pacifism was a strong element in American Protestant thinking after [The Great War] World War I. It drew its strength from several factors—the general disillusionment with the war and with the peace settlement, a reaffirmation of the New Testament emphasis on love, the traditional nonresistance doctrines of the historic peace churches, the liberal idea of human goodness, and the Marxist teaching about the nexus between capitalism and war. Pacifists were firm internationalists in their outlook, opposed to "militarism" in all its forms, and for the most part critical of capitalism and its accompanying materialism."   Ibid p 152
Richard V. Pierard THE WARS OF AMERICA CHRISTIAN VIEWS; William B. Eerdmans Publishing Co., Grand Rapids, Michigan 1981

The rise of National Socialism [Nazism], however, put them in a different position, particularly when Hitler's war machine rolled over one country after another. One pacifist REINHOLD NIEBUHR of UNION THEOLOGICAL SEMINARY, frankly acknowledged the problem when he pointed out that the imperial ambitions of Nazi Germany "represent a peril to every established value of a civilization which all Western nations share and of which we are all custodians." Christian Century, Dec. 18, 1940, p 1578

[Fellow associate and apartment neighbor] Theologian JOHN C. BENNETT admitted candidly "that the alternative to successful resistance to Germany is the extension of the darkest political tyranny imaginable over the whole of Europe with the prospect that the whole world will be threatened by the AXIS powers." Ibid., Dec. 4, 1940,   p 1506
"Nazism had dealt a severe blow to liberal humanistic pacifism, one from which it would never fully recover." Ibid   p 153

"Non pacifists such as Loraine Boettner, a conservative Presbyterian whose viewpoint on war accurately mirrored that of most evangelicals at the time, ridiculed the liberal pacifists for their short-sightedness and faulty theology, maintaining that their position could not cope with unprovoked aggression. In his opinion they failed to recognize that human nature is FALLEN, man is essentially selfish, and without forcible restraint there is no limit to the injustice he will commit. Pacifism is irresponsible and "PEACE AT ANY PRICE'" means certain tyranny. In these circumstances 'combat is not only sanctioned by God but [also] it is our duty to perform it with all available resources."
THE CHRISTIAN ATTITUDE TOWARD WAR, Eerdmans, 1940   p 73-74

NOTE: He also said: "True religion and true patriotism have always gone hand in hand, while unbelief, doubt, modernism, etc. have invariably been accompanied by socialism, communism, radicalism, and other enemies [Nazism] of free government." Ibid p 83-84
"A radical shift took place in the months between the Munich agreement and the fall of France in the thinking of "mainline" theologians, many of whom had been pacifists and even socialists during the 1930s. The most important "revisionism" came from the pen of REINHOLD NIEBUHR. In numerous essays he struck at the theological foundations of pacifism, arguing that it is impossible "perfectionism." Man is a sinner and lives in a world shot through with sin. Christians who live in

and benefit from a society in which coercive relationships are taken for granted have no right to introduce the uncompromising ethics of the Gospel into an issue like war. The Kingdom of God is not a human possibility. The cross as a pure act of sacrifice can occur only outside of History and to make it a normal for human behavior in a sinful world is illusory. The cross reveals what History ought to be, not what History is or can be. Within History people must settle for conflict and balance of power, because justice can only be observed by protecting each life and interest against all others. However,

> "Most of our liberal Protestantism has neatly disavowed all the profounder
> elements of the Gospel which reveal the tragic character of History and has
> made the Gospel identical with the truism that all men ought to be good
> and with that falsehood that goodness pays. The end of pure goodness,
> of perfect love is the cross." Christian Century Dec. 18, 1940 Ibid p 1580

"Further, pacifism has an element of impractical realism. It springs from "an unholy compound of gospel perfectionism and bourgeois utopianism," the later flowing from 18th century rationalism. This kind of pacifism is not content with martyrdom and the rejection of political responsibility. It tries to fashion "political alternatives to the tragic business of resisting tyranny and establishing justice by coercion." Ibid p 1580
"if one refuses to meet evil with evil, that is, tyranny with violent resistance, he becomes a party to the enslavement of nations and the suppression of freedom, thought and life."

Nazism "THE WAVE OF THE FUTURE"

"JOHN BENNETT further exposed the inadequacy of peace at any price pacifism by examining some of their current arguments. He said Nazism is not "the wave of the future," as many were contending, but rather a throwback to the remote past that has undone the results of previous revolutions. Moreover, there is no reason to believe that Germany will moderate its rule as its position in Europe becomes more secure. The opposite is more likely the case—tyranny will become even greater. Also inadequate is the view of many European Christians that Nazism is a judgment on the sins of their churches and SECULARIST DEMOCRACY, and that it may lead to a cleansing of Europe and the development of a more Christian culture. As Bennett put it, the alternative to secularist democracy is not necessarily some kind of Christian authoritarian society but a blatantly secularist tyranny. Furthermore, a church driven underground loses touch with its society and is unable to shape the mind of the community in a Christian fashion."   Ibid Dec. 4, 1940 Ibid p 156-157
[Professor Pierard a sociology professor at Indiana University] retorts: "It is unfair to lay the responsibility for the spread of totalitarian dictatorships at the feet of the liberal Protestants and secular pacifists in the Western democracies, and it is simply wrong to accuse them of cowardice in the face of mounting tyranny. But pacifists operated in a different world, and their ideas, although noble and admirable, were unworkable in the realities of the 1930s. They were unprepared to assume political responsibility and to support efforts in their countries to resist Axis aggression. They were undoubtably convinced the righteousness was on their side, but they did not and would not involve themselves in the struggle against tyranny."   Ibid p 155
"Therefore, doctrinaire pacifists constituted a source of weakness rather than strength in the Western democracies. Only when it was almost too late did many adherents realize its flaws and act accordingly to defend democracy, even if this required taking up arms. As REINHOLD

NIEBUHR wrote in the first issue of a new journal, CHRISTIANITY AND CRISIS, the organ of those theologians who understood the failing of pacifism:

> Nazi tyranny intends to annihilate the Jewish race, to subject the nations
> of Europe to the dominion of a "master" race, to extirpate [destroy completely]
> the Christian religion, to annul the liberties and the legal standards which
> are the priceless heritage of ages of Christian and humanistic culture, to
> make truth the prostitute of political power, to seek world domination through
> its satraps and allies, and generally to destroy the very fabric of western
> civilization. We do know what a Nazi victory would mean; and our first task
> must therefore be to prevent it."   Ibid p 158

CHRISTIANITY AND CRISIS "The Christian Faith and the World Crisis" Feb.10,1941

American Pastor gives Hitler's Nazis his Blessing

"The new order in Europe found many admirers in the United States, and Christians were numbered among their ranks. Gerald Winrod, a popular fundamentalist preacher from Kansas and candidate for the U.S. Senate in 1936, wrote in his paper "The Defender":

> Nazism and Fascism are patriotic and nationalistic; Communism is not
> Of the three forms of government, Nazism and Fascism are as far in
> advance of Bolshevism as the 20th century is from the Dark Ages.
> One stands for life life, happiness and prosperity; the other, death,
> misery and starvation.

UNDER COVER (New York: Dutton, 1943)   Ibid p 167

"Another prominent religious figure, FRANK BUCKMAN, the founder of MORAL REARMAMENT, returned from the OLYMPIC GAMES in Berlin and told a New York reporter that he "thanked heaven" for ADOLF HITLER, who built "a front line of defense against the Anti-Christ of Communism." NY WORLD-TELEGRAM, Aug. 26, 1936
"WILLIAM RANDOLPH HEARST, although not known for his deep spiritual insights, yet being a newspaper-man [owner-editor] who should have been more preceptive when dealing with political figures, was taken in just as effectively by Hitler. After meeting with the Fuehrer in 1934, Hearst reported that he "is certainly an extraordinary man...We estimate him too lightly in America." Hitler's "great policy, great achievement was to have saved Germany from Communism." "The Politics of Upheaval" Schlesinger." p 8 "Hearst promoted BILLY GRAHAM in his newspapers." Evangelist Pat Robertson

Billy Graham's Ministry and My Dad at ABC TV "Just as I Am" autobiography

"I had been invited to PARAMOUNT STUDIOS to have lunch with the company's president, Frank Freeman, whose wife was a deeply spiritual person. There I met [CECIL B.] DEMILLE; he was in preproduction for the remake of his [silent] 1923 classic, THE TEN COMMANDMENTS. Also at the lunch was ANTHONY QUINN, Barbara Stanwyck, BETTY HUTTON, and Bob Hunter, a

Paramount executive who was a committed Christian and treasurer of Hollywood's First Presbyterian Church."   p 175

"Walter and Fred arrived in New York on a Saturday to conclude the contract, and they found only one person in the [American Broadcasting Company] ABC offices, a junior executive. He informed them that the ABC board had just made a decision not to allow any more religious programming on the network.

"Walter and Fred protested strenuously: "You promised it. We've guaranteed this young man, BILLY GRAHAM, that he has a network. To change your minds now is very unfair to us. Get hold of the board."

"That's impossible," he said. "They're all playing golf."

"Well, get them on the golf course."

"I can't do that," he said, digging in his heels. "You'll have to wait till Monday."

"We are not coming back on Monday," they said firmly. "We'll sit here until this thing is resolved."

The 18TH GOLF HOLE and the Holy Spirit

Seeing their determination, the man finally reached one of the board members on the 18TH HOLE and explained the situation. The board's decision was reversed on the spot, and THE HOUR OF DECISION was saved. p 179 [The clubhouse no cell phones]

[After high school, he enrolled in BOB JONES college, but found the school stifling, and transferred to FLORIDA BIBLE INSTITUTE in Tampa. There he practiced sermonizing in a swamp, preaching to birds and alligators (St. Francis?) before tryouts with small churches. He still wasn't convinced he should be a preacher until a soul-searching late-night ramble on a golf course. "I finally gave in while pacing at midnight on the 18TH HOLE," he said. " 'All right, LORD,' I said. 'If you want me, you've got me.' "]

GOLF FACT: The 18th hole is the last hole at the end of this challenging Scottish game. Billy Graham reportedly meet and prayed with 12 American presidents. I believe they all played golf. Question: Will the Good Lord Jesus have a golf course available for them? The streets of gold of Heaven? aren't as useful as golf course greens, sand bunkers and water traps. The TRINITY GOD created the Earth and Universe [NICENE and APOSTLE's CREEDS] GENESIS in "SIX GOD DAYS". God created His humans he created in His image on the 6th day in His earthly/heavenly Garden of Eden.

PERSONAL FACT: I asked my golfer friend Brian Corbin why there isn't a 19th hole in golf? He laughed and retorted, "The 19th hole is the watering hole at the clubhouse barroom." He lived with his 100 year old father James, the Marine Corps sergeant whose platoon guarded the ENOLA GAY and BOCK'S CAR atomic bombers. His birthday August 7 after Hiroshima atomic bomb was dropped by the Enola Gay on August 6 and August 9, 1945 Nagasaki atomic bomb ends World War II.

Fredericksburg, Virginia Free Lance-Star Feb. 22, 2018
"The secret of my work is God. I would be nothing without Him."
GRAHAM REACHED MILLIONS WITH A SIMPLE MESSAGE
by Rachel Zoll AP RELIGION WRITER
Full Front page Graham portrait

PROVIDENTIAL DATES IN MY LIFE

The Free Lance-Star newspaper Fredericksburg, Virginia, Thursday February 22, 2018. My mother was born in Frankfurt am Main, district Hesse (Hessian) February 22, 1915.

The newspaper was located a block from the Virginia FREEDOM OF RELIGION memorial January 1777, on Washington Ave. across from MARY WASHINGTON's cemetery grave obelisk overlooking MARY WASHINGTON college, now university. It is next to the flat projecting rock, overlooking the future campus, where she devoutly prayed when her son George was barely surviving the winter at VALLEY FORGE, Pennsylvania. My Jewish daughter graduated there with a German degree in May 1997. My daughter was married in MARY WASHINGTON'S garden in 2005.

This memorial article was published on GEORGE WASHINGTON's birthday. Evangelist BILLY GRAHAM born in Charlotte, N. Carolina November 7, 1917

Donald Trump elected president	November 8, 2016
My son was born	November 8, 1977 Fredericksburg, VA.
My wedding	November 9, 1974 CRYSTAL NIGHT
	November 9, 1938 KRISTALLNACHT

Nazis failed Putsch March Munich jailed   November 9, 1923
Berlin Wall torn down by German civilians   November 9, 1989

Nazi persecution the night of my Jewish Orthodox wedding at HAAVATH ISRAEL in Midwood section of Brooklyn. The Nazis destroyed every synagogue in Germany and Austria. Brownshirts broke the glass windows of synagogues and businesses sounding like crystal. Thousands of innocent Jewish men were killed until November 10, 1938.

My son's Bar Mitzvah   November 10,1990   13th yr. Saturday Jewish Sabbath
Martin Luther's birthdate November 10,1483 Luther's parents baptized, christened baby Luther the next day and gave him name Martin November 11, 1458 in honor of founder of Chaplains St. Martin of Tours, France day   November 11, died Nov. 8, 387

The Great War World War I, ended   Armistice Day   November 11, 1918 11 AM the
11th month 11-11-11,1918.

Princess Diana and Prince Charles Reagan dinner	November 11, 1985
Princess Diana dances with Travolta at White House	November 8, 1985
My Jewish wedding Temple Havaath Israel Brooklyn	November 9, 1974
Amityville horror house murder my hometown	November 13, 1974
U.S. Marine Corps founded in Philadelphia	November 10, 1775

Semper Fidelis, Semper Fi   UUH RAH!

Martin Luther born	February	16,	1546
Rev. Graham passed on	February	21,	2018
My mother Elisabeth Francois Frank was born	February	22,	1915
Col. Tibetts pilot dropped first atomic bomb born.	February	23,	1915
George Washington was born Colony Virginia	February	22,	1732
American flag raised on Iwo Jima	February	23,	1945

Bishop Shabaz of my church born in Pakistan	November 8,	1938	Crystal Night
Hitler's Nazi failed Putsch Munich jailed 9 months	November 8-9	1923	
Bobby Bowden Seminoles coach born, Woodland	November. 8,	1929	
Tony Nathan biggest high school game Woodland	November 9,	1975	
Bart Millard Gospel country singer married	November 9,	2002	

My mother passed when I at Bitburg AB, Germany	September 30	1967
My brother Paul Thomas born in Lexington, KY	September 30	1945
My granddaughter born Fredericksburg, VA	September 30	2005
Her 1st cousin Benjamin born Oviedio, Florida	September 30	2005
I retired from Pep Boys Automotive after 16 years	September 30	2005
Bitburg AB, Germany closed end of Cold War	September 30	1994
PM Chamberlain/Hitler Munich "Peace Pact"	September 30	1938
Eliezer "Elie" Wiesel, Holocaust survivor was born	September 30	1928
Meryl Streep married sculptor Don Gummer	September 30	1978
Eric Stoltz "Memphis Belle" 1990 B-17 crewman	September 30	1961
Marion Cotillard "Allied" 2016 Brad Pitt's spy wife	September 30	1975
Victoria Tennant Winds of War, War Remembrance	September 30	1950

My Birthday Famous Babies

My birthday at St. Joseph's hospital Lexington, KY	May 4, 1943
George Clooney born at same St. Joseph's hospital	May 6, 1961
Audrey Hepburn born, starved in Holland in WW II	May 4, 1929
Hosni Mubarak, Egyptian president 1981-2011	May 4, 1928
Maynard Ferguson Canadian jazz trumpeter	May 4, 1928
Roberta Peters, American opera soprano NY Met	May 4, 1930
George Will political analyst ABC Nightline	May 4, 1941
Stella Parton, singer Dolly's sister born on my birthdate	May 4, 1943
Nickolas Ashford singer Ashford & Simpson birthdate	May 4, 1943
Mihail Chemikin Russian painter Moscow my birthdate	May 4, 1943
Randy Travis country singer	May 4. 1959
Ana Gasteyer actress Saturday Night Live	May 4, 1967
Horace Mann father American education public schools	May 4, 1796
Thomas Huxley English biologist comparative anatomy	May 4, 1825
Frederick Church landscape artist lived in my county	May 4, 1826
Alice Liddell English model for Alice in Wonderland	May 4, 1852
Aleksander Kerensky, Russian premier 1917 overthrown	May 4, 1881
Francis Spellman American Catholic Bishop/Cardinal	May 4, 1889
Margaret Thatcher first female PM United Kingdom.	May 4, 1979
Kent State Univ. 4 protestors killed	May 4, 1970
May 4th China protest German land given to Japan	May 4, 1919
Pope Alexander VI divides New World Spain/Portugal.	May. 4, 1493
Peter Minuet lands in New Netherland today Manhattan	May 4, 1626
Rhode Island first colony to renounce King George III.	May 4, 1776
Surrender of Alabama, Mississippi, Louisiana	May. 4, 1865
Reformers John Wycliffe, Jan Hus condemned as heretics.	May 4, 1415

11:11 (Numerology) Chance, Coincidence, Synchronicity Deja Vu, Providence, Predestination or Prophecy?

"Some numerologists believe that events linked to the time 11:11 appear more often than can be explained by CHANCE or COINCIDENCE. [URI GELLER "The 11:11 phenomenon" 2006. Web. 22 Dec. 2014. [Israeli psychic, illusionist, magician, psychokinesis, telepathy 40-year TV personality.] This belief is related to the concept of SYNCHRONICITY. Some authors claim that 11:11 signals a spirit presence. [SOLARA (1992). 11:11: Inside the Doorway. Charlottesville, VA: Star-Borne Unlimited.

The belief that the time 11:11 has mystical powers has been adopted by believers in NEW AGE philosophies. ["Do you see 11:11?] Spirit Guardians. Retrieved 2011-11-11.] However, skeptics say that Uri Geller's examples of 11:11 phenomena in world events are examples of post-hoc reasoning and confirmation bias." Wikipedia

Post-hoc Skeptic Report 8 October 2009 reveals Geller's web site has a list of things he connects with the number 11. He believes the number to be all-important." Confirmation bias: "The law of truly large numbers 2 December 2009 claims, "The law of truly large numbers says that with a large enough sample many odd coincidences are likely to happen."   Wikipedia

Each reader of my numbers must decide the connectivity if it is Providential in HIS-story. I always hear stories that you can't believe or trust Wikipedia because people put false information in it. This has been done in the past but malicious or incorrect content has been "controlled" verified today. As one of the four researcher/writers for THE WORLD ALMANAC AND BOOK OF FACTS for six years I know about Facts. We published over a million copies yearly and only a few typos appeared in America's greatest one volume reference book. I have a B. A. degree in History and research. I was the editor of the Bitburg AB, Germany newspaper in 1968, the commander's spokesperson. Remarkably the German lead Linotype keyboard typists printed well and the type page setters could remarkably layout a page upside down. I am astounded at the magnitude of the universal information on Wikipedia. Instead of four people there must be thousands contributing to their topics. My only Wikipedia problem is too much information and the HYPERLINKS are endless, It is not trivia but sometimes seems unbelievable what you can be connected to. Later, my very personal connection to the SIX DEGREES OF SEPARATION, the KEVIN BACON Hollywood connections.

"Significance in Dates" Many marriages took place throughout the world on November 11, 2011. 11-11-11. A voluntary act. My wedding was planned by my mother-in-law Helen Denker 7 months earlier November 9, 1974, 11-9. I had nothing to do with the arrangements and didn't know its Jewish HIS torical significance until the Temple BETH SHALOM, House of Peace, student rabbi told my wife, son and I about Chrystal Night before my son's Bat Mitzvah. My son was 13, and his BAR MITZVAH was on Saturday November 10, 1990, on the Sabbath. We left the Temple soon afterward. MARTIN LUTHER was born on November 10, 1483. I then started going to a Missouri Synod Lutheran Concordia church in Triangle, VA. I attended it, on the way to work, occasionally since I providentially first visited it on Pentecost Sunday in May 1989. I was confirmed Lutheran, age 15, in May 1958, at Emanuel Lutheran church in Hudson, NY, jointly with my brother age 12 1/2. I could not memorize confirmation creeds which my brother could. We soon went to Germany and my mother said she wanted both her sons confirmed before we went to Germany in July 1958.

"The Armistice that ended the fighting in western Europe of the First World War took effect at 11 a. m. Paris time on November 11, 1918, "the eleventh hour of the eleventh day of the eleventh month". (11-11-11-18)   HIS STORY

Billy Graham Preaches Gospel to America on ABC

"In mid-August we signed a contract for thirteen weeks with the American Broadcasting Company to go on their coast-to-coast network, with a target starting date during our upcoming Atlanta Crusade."   Ibid p 180

"In 1954 we extended THE HOUR OF DECISION to the NBC network as well, bringing the total to 800 stations; that did not include foreign and shortwave."

"NBC had a policy against selling time for religious broadcasting, but the network made an exception through the personal interest of NBC's founder and president, General DAVID SARNOFF. I [Graham] met him, seemingly by accident, (providence) in Hawaii.

"When we were on the ship returning us from Japan and Korea in early 1953, we met a Jewish businessman named Jack Lewis. He invited us to a party he was giving, during which a woman performed a hula dance. When she found out who I was, she apologized, fearing that she had offended me, I told her I had been to Hawaii before and knew that the hula was a part of their ancient culture. It turned out that she was the wife of the owner of Honolulu's morning newspaper. After our arrival in the islands, she invited me to a dinner party at their home. General Sarnoff and his wife were there, and afterward they offered to take me back to the hotel. On the way, the general asked, "Is there anything I can do for you?"

'Yes, sir." I could tell he was surprised at my quick answer. "I'd like to go on NBC with my radio program."

"I'll see what I can do," he said.

"Apparently true to his word, we soon were on NBC, every Sunday evening."

"Often we broadcast live from various places where we were holding Crusades, from the front lines during the Korean War to the Hollywood Bowl."   Ibid   p 180-181

Graham's Close Media Friend Paul Harvey

"PAUL HARVEY, the radio commentator, has probably been my best friend in the American media. He has always been very supportive of us and often kept his many listeners informed about our work. We have been guests to his home many times, with his delightful wife, Angel."
Ibid   p 636

"Some of those I have met in the media have become good friends."

"Sometimes people have questioned whether a minister of the Gospel should be on entertainment shows. When it was announced that I was going to appear on the LAUGH-IN — a television show that sometimes included sketches that were risqué or profane we received so many letters from our supporters that I had to draft a special response just to answer their concerns. "My sole purpose in accepting these invitations," I wrote, "is to witness for Christ in a totally secular environment. Very few Christians have this opportunity. It is important to keep contact with the millions of Americans that never darken the door of a church...It seems to me that this was the method of our Lord. He went among publicans and sinners."   Ibid   p 636-637

RADIO—THE HOUR OF DECISION

Graham Admirers Lutheran Radio Preacher Dr. Maier

"Some months before, in Boston, I heard over the radio that Dr, WALTER A. MAIER, the great Lutheran theologian and radio preacher from St. Louis, had died of a heart attack. I was so jolted in my hotel room and prayed that God might rise up someone to take his place on the radio. In those days radio was still king; television's impact was just beginning to be felt. There were only a few evangelical programs on national radio, and none seemed to have a wide audience among nonbelievers. Dr. Meier and CHARLES FULLER were virtually the only preachers on national radio at the time." Ibid   p 176-177

Dr. Maier's Son's Seminars at my local Grace Lutheran

I met Dr. Maier's son PAUL twice at two religious seminars at my sister church GRACE Lutheran-Missouri Synod in Woodbridge, Virginia. I bought his biography about his father's radio ministry and his historical books about JOSEPHUS and EUSEBIUS and one picture book of the Holy sites in Israel.

"We held rallies throughout West Germany, at the largest stadiums and arenas available in the cities of Frankfurt, Wiesbaden, Kaiserslautern, Mannheim, Stuttgart, Nurnberg, Darmstadt (where I had the privilege of meeting the great hero of the resistance to the Nazis, Lutheran pastor MARTIN NIEMOELLER), and Dortmund."   Ibid p 254

Graham Didn't Comprehend Neo-orthodox Theology

Reinhold Niebuhr Refuses to Meet Graham

"I wanted to keep abreast of theological thinking at mid-century, but brilliant writers such as KARL BARTH and REINHOLD NIEBUHR really made me struggle with concepts that had been ingrained in me from childhood. They were the pioneers in what came to be called new-orthodoxy. While they rejected old liberalism, the new meanings they put into some of the old theological terms confused me terribly. I never doubted the Gospel itself, or the deity of Christ on which it depended, but other major issues were called into question."   Ibid p 135
[Previously, I discussed this new-orthodoxy which was a reaction to the two apocalyptic un Christian world wars the liberal, pacifist, modern secular humanist political, printed and video medias had promoted as a new age religion.The German Nazis weren't the only people who believed that the Old Testament "mythical" judgments were relevant to anyone today but only the Israelites. I am a Judeo-Christian all the Bible.]
"Problems of a different kind sort of came from the opposition that arose over our plans for New York City. One source was the liberal wing of Christianity. The magazine THE CHRISTIAN CENTURY grumbled that "the BILLY GRAHAM campaign will spin along and an audience gladly captive to his own sensations is straining for the grand entrance whether or not the HOLY SPIRIT is in attendance."   Ibid p 300-301

83

Theologian/Pastor Niebuhr Billy Graham's Opponent?

"More thoughtful was the objection raised by one of the nation's leading liberal theologians, Dr. REINHOLD NIEBUHR of New York's UNION THEOLOGICAL SEMINARY. I appreciated his commitment to social concern but could not agree with his scorn of evangelism. In an article in LIFE magazine, he termed me "obviously sincere" but added that the message we preached was 'too simple in any age, but particularly so in a nuclear one with great morale perplexities…Graham offers Christian evangelism even less complicated than it has ever before provided.'"

"I let it be known that I wanted to meet Dr. Niebuhr. George Champion called him to see if he would see me, but he declined. Not used to giving up easily, George then called the chairman of the Union Theological Seminary. He simply refused to see me."   p 301

My Providential Meeting with Reinhold Niebuhr's Son

I providentially met Reinhold Niebuhr's son CHRISTOPHER NIEBUHR at a Tanglewood, MA, symphony concert in August 1997, by sitting next to him. He had told me about the concert on the phone 10 hours earlier My ticket's set was numbered. I told part of our story earlier. Christopher and I have stayed in phone contact and I have spent two nights at his home in Lee, Massachusetts. He was born September 11, 1934.

Pastor Graham's AWE of Meeting C.S. Lewis

"John Stott was very anxious for me to meet Professor Lewis (C.S. Clive Lewis) and went with me. Lewis was not as well known in the United States as he would become in later years, particularly after his death in 1963. But I had read SCREWTAPE, and Ruth would later read the CHRONICLES OF NARNIA series."

"We met in the dining room of his college (Oxford), St. MARY MAGDALENE's, and we talked for an hour or more. I was afraid I would be intimidated by him because of his brilliance, but he immediately put me at ease. I found him to be not only intelligent and witty but also gentle and gracious; he seemed genuinely interested in our meeting. "You know," he said as we parted, "you have many critics, but I have never met one of your critics who knows you personally."   Ibid   p 258

Clive C.S. Lewis was not my Namesake

CLIVE "C.S." LEWIS was an ATHEIST until TOLKEIN (Lord of the Rings books), MALCOLM MUGGERIDGE and CHARLES MACDONALD, Christian fairy tales writer, evangelized Lewis who became a great "APOLOGIST" convert to Jesus Christ. In the film SHADOWLANDS Academy Award winner Welsh actor Sir ANTHONY HOPKINS meets his future Jewish/Christian wife American Academy award winning actress DEBORAH WINGER Mrs. Gresham. While walking with her at OXFORD University she asks Lewis, "Why do you call yourself CS, [Charles Staples] isn't your name Clive?" [Sir ANTHONY HOPKINS, Lewis retorted that he didn't like the name CLIVE." I almost fell out of my movie theater seat when I heard that. My German mother named me Clive after silent film English actor CLIVE BROOK. My dad was Alexander Bruce, I am Clive Dennis, mom was Elisabeth Francois Frank ABCDEF. My mother liked the name CLIVE.

On July 27, 2019, I drove 21 miles, to the MT. PONY PACKARD THEATER LIBRARY OF CONGRESS National film archives library. Theater organist Matthew improvised the sound background for the silent movie. I viewed the black and white silent film HULU (1927) starring CLARA BOW, the precocious, pampered daughter of a Hawaiian plantation owner, who follows the advice of her uncle "to follow a simple and natural life and is considered a 'wild child' who wears pants and rides a horse." Hula, Clara Bow falls in love with the British engineer building a dam on her father's land, portrayed by English actor CLIVE BROOK his 56th film of 105 films. He was the "CLARK GABLE/ERROLL FLYNN/JOHN BARRYMORE/LESLIE HOWARD/GREGORY PECK and KIRK DOUGLAS" of Great Britain. Hula CLARA BOW immediately falls in love with his striking handsomeness and puts her fingers on his chin's cleft, like actor KIRK DOUGLAS "SPARTACUS" also has, 102 years old in 2019. HULA is on U TUBE has an involved plot Clive Brook's character was married and for their love had to convince his "gold digging" wife to divorce him.

CLIVE BROOK'S FILMS: THE RETURN OF SHERLOCK HOLMES (1929) shot at the ASTORIA STUDIOS in New York, was the first sound film to feature SHERLOCK HOLMES, portrayed by Clive Brook. There was also a silent version for old theaters. In 1932, he stared in CONAN DOYLE'S MASTER DETECTIVE SHERLOCK HOLMES. In the film THE FOUR FEATHERS (1929) Clive Brook is the soldier friend of American actor WILLIAM POWELL, who is considered a "coward" when he refuses to join his British unit going to the SUDAN to avenge LORD Gen. KITCHNER's beheading in the BATTLE OF KHARTOUM. Actor CHARLTON HESTON portrayed General Kitchner in the film KHARTOUM (1968). British actor Sir LAWRENCE OLIVIER, in dark face makeup, portrayed his opponent the Muslim messianic IMAN MADHI. Capt. WINSTON CHURCHILL, disliked by General Kitchner, is portrayed by actor SIMON WARD in the film YOUNG WINSTON (1969) in a victorious battle in the Sudan. Churchill's American mother JENNIE JEROME is portrayed by talented ACADEMY AWARD winning, Bronx born actress ANN BANCROFT. She was married to the hilarious Jewish American movie actor, producer, director MEL BROOKS, whose films were irreverent, not politically correct, and brilliantly mocked America's "latent" racial injustice through his characters like black actor CLEVON LITTLE, the black sheriff of a small Western town, who is called "racist" names when he enters the town on his horse. Talented African American dancer GREGORY HINES is hilarious in Brook's film HISTORY (1970).

PERSONAL SMALL WORLD STORY: I lived in an apartment, on huge sycamore tree lined JEROME AVENUE in the BRONX, which JENNIE JEROME's wealthy banker father built to YONKERS where he attended horse races, still held today. I lived there with my father from April 1969 to November 1974, when I was married and moved to an apartment at 100 Diplomat Dr. in MT. KISCO, New York. We lived across from the MACCOMB DAM PARK facing YANKEE STADIUM.

PERSONAL FACT: When REGIS PHILBIN autographed his book I said I played tennis in the park next to Yankee Stadium Regis said, "MACCOMB DAM park."

HISTORY FACT: JENNY JEROME was not only WINSTON CHURCHILL's mother she was related to GEORGE WASHINGTON through his mother Mary Ball's Virginia family.

SMALL WORLD CONNECTION: In the book JENNIE her Jerome family met the wealthy "new rich" Englishman OLIVER NORTH, who is the great grandfather to Marine Lt. Col. OLIVER LAURENCE NORTH, who I was on my six boy track team in high school in 1960. I knew him as Larry because his father was named Oliver. He served with General Patton during World War II, and was awarded the SILVER STAR and BRONZE STAR for combat valor. Lt. NORTH was awarded the SILVER STAR and BRONZE STAR and PURPLE HEART for valor as a Marine in the Vietnam conflict.

CLARA BOW was nicknamed "THE IT GIRL" personified the ROARING TWENTIES and is described as its leading "sex symbol." Bow appeared in 46 SILENT films and 11 TALKIES. She was named first box-office draw in 1928, 1929, and second box-office draw in 1927, 1930.

I like the name CLIVE it is famous though rare in America except for prolific author CLIVE CUSSLER, some 30 novels, CLIVE DAVIS, singer impresario, who promoted BARRY MANILOW, CHICAGO, BARBRA STREISAND, WHITNEY HOUSTON and many others. CLIVE BARNES, former NY Times theater critic, and CLIVE IRVING, who wrote a novel AXIS about early Nazis economic/political influence on Great Britain and a novel PROMISE about the creation of the new Nation of Israel which are in my book collection. CLIVE OWEN, a great British actor, CLIVE GRIFFIN, a British pop singer whose album featured "WHEN I FALL IN LOVE" a duet with unknown Canadian singer CELINE DION her first English hit song not in French.

CLIVE

ROOT—   Cliff
OLD ENGLISH—   from the cliff
EMOTIONAL—   a man of compassion, patience, and love
NATURAL —   he excels naturally in all he does
PERSONALITY — one who staying composed is important
CHARACTER —   when adversity comes, he tries again
MOTIVATION —   he likes things to be in order
MENTAL —   a most literary type
EXPRESSION — is good at discerning
PHYSICAL —   has a gleam in his eyes

A profile? for the name CLIVE. I think all the famous Clive's mentioned would agree they have these attributes or would like to have them. Famous Biblical characters have names given to them by GOD, JESUS/YESHUA means SAVIOR, which translate in HEBREW to their future providential and often dangerous missions through their Faith.

NO MERE CHRISTIAN

CLIVE LEWIS

"You must picture me alone…night after night, feeling, whenever my mind lifted even for a second from my work, the steady, unrelenting approach of Him whom I so earnestly desired not to meet. "That which I greatly feared had at last come upon me…I gave in, and admitted God was God, and knelt and prayed: perhaps, that night, the most dejected and reluctant convert in all England."

Thus CLIVE STAPLES [C.S.] LEWIS, known to millions of grateful readers as C.S. LEWIS, described his conversion. An expert in English literature, Lewis is best remembered for his lively and imaginative Christian works.

Children know him as the creator of NARNIA, the imaginary land entered through an old wardrobe, or closet. Adults may have met him as the genius behind THE SCREWTAPE LETTER, a series of make-believe letters from an important devil to a junior devil. Still others primarily think of Lewis as the author of MERE CHRISTIANITY, a profound work of practical theology

But it's not just his writings that intrigue modern Christians. Even the life story of C.S. Lewis generates enormous interest.

Since Lewis' death in 1963, thousands of scholars have written theses and dissertations about him. In 1965, a research center for scholars—the Marion E. Wade Center—opened at Wheaton College in Illinois.

Most recently, Hollywood released SHADOWLANDS. This compelling movie portrays the love and loss that came to Lewis late in his life.

RELUCTANT CONVERT

Much of the interest in Lewis lies in the unique story of his conversion, which he relates in his autobiography, SURPRISED BY JOY.

The autobiography is short, not because his life lacked luster, but because Lewis focused on his journey of faith. The purpose of SURPRISED FOR JOY is not so much to explain his life as to explain his CONVERSION TO CHRISTIANITY.

Lewis explained his conversion in terms of joy. He believed that joy is a taste of the heavenly.

Joy is what God gives us, often through simple things, but always intended to create in our hearts a longing for him.

Lewis did not discover the source of joy for years. In fact, He was an avowed atheist who lived and worked in an academic world hostile to Christianity.

He describes his conversion as occurring in two stages. First, to theism in 1929, and then to Christianity in 1931.

Many of Lewis' [Oxford University] colleagues were understandably shocked. The man who had been so staunch an atheist had now become a Christian. And not just a Christian, but one who insisted on sharing his faith though his writings.

BUREAUCRACY OF HELL

Lewis published THE SCREW-TAPE LETTERS in 1942. They appeared in serial form through "The Guardian", a weekly church newspaper, and met with immediate success.

Shortly afterward, the letters were printed in book form and have been in print ever since. The SCREW-TAPE LETTERS, a masterful use of imagination, propelled Lewis to worldwide fame.

In the story, Screw-tape is an important devil in the bureaucracy of HELL. His letter of advice to WORMWOOD, his nephew and a devil newly assigned to a "patient" on earth, form the book's structure.

In each letter, Screw-tape proposes some new strategy to be tried in an effort ————— to win the patients soul for Hell.

Through humor, Lewis takes the reader into the absurdities of human thinking. Each chapter, between three and five pages, covers a separate topic, always humorously.

For example, discussing prayer, faith and doubt. Screw-tape tells Wormwood not to "forget to use the 'Heads I win, tails you lose' argument. If the thing he prays for doesn't happen, then that is one more proof that petitionary prayers don't work; if it does happen, he will, of course, be able to see some of the physical causes which led up to it, and 'therefore it would have happened anyway," and thus a granted prayer becomes just as good a proof as a denied one that prayers are ineffective.

DEEPER TRUTHS

One of Lewis' most impressive works is his seven-part CHRONICLES OF NARNIA. This fantasy series for children is far more than a fantasy. It is a magical realm where they experience the central story of Christianity, but on their level.

The most important in the series is THE LION, THE WITCH AND THE WARDROBE, a book that appeals to the child in all of us. We experience the magic of life, the terror of sin, and the wonder of Christ's sacrifice through a child's eyes.

Another allegorical piece, THE GREAT DIVORCE, is considered by some to be Lewis' masterpiece.

The story is about a bus trip from Hell to Heaven—and back, for some of the passengers. Lewis blends perception, reason and imagination masterfully.

In the story, the narrator dreams he is in a cold and dingy city, but only later is it identified as hell. Catching the bus with hell's citizen's, the narrator watches their actions. The passengers, oblivious to their own displays of crude and revolting behavior, are acutely aware of their fellow passengers' shortcomings.

The bus leaves hell, flying high into the sky until it reaches the outskirt of heaven. To stay, each passenger must make a painful decision. For those who refuse to do so, choosing instead to return trip to hell, the bus waits.

None of this was intended to be a description of what happens after death. Instead, its purpose is to point out the consequences of decisions we make in life. THE GREAT DIVORCE is about the here and now, not the hereafter.

Bill Palmer THE PLAIN TRUTH

MERE CHRISTIANITY

Perhaps the best known of Lewis' works is MERE CHRISTIANITY. It is Christian apology, which is an intellectual defense of the faith

The Case for Christianity — MERE CHRISTIANITY

"Lewis spends most of his defense of the Christian faith on an argument from morality, a point which persuaded him from atheism to Christianity. He bases his case on a moral law, a "rule about right and wrong" commonly known to all human beings, citing the example of Nazism, both CHRISTIANS AND ATHEISTS believed that Adolf Hitler's actions were morally wrong. On a more mundane level, it is generally accepted that stealing is a violation of this moral law. [Nazi confiscation of Germany's Jewish property] Lewis argues that the moral law is like scientific laws or mathematics in that it was not contrived by humans. However, it is unlike scientific laws in that it can be broken or ignored, and it is known intuitively, rather than through experimentation. Lewis points out that earthly experience does not satisfy the human craving for "joy" and that only God could fit the bill; humans cannot know to yearn for something if it does not exist."

After providing reasons for his conversion to theism, Lewis goes over rival conceptions of God to Christianity. Pantheism, he argues is incoherent, and atheism too simple. Eventually he arrives at Jesus Christ, and invokes a well-known argument now known as Lewis's Trilema. Lewis, arguing that Jesus was claiming to be God was deliberately lying, or was not God but thought himself to be (which would make him delusional and likely insane). The book goes on to say that the latter two possibilities are not consistent with Jesus' character and it was most likely that he was being truthful."

Lewis claims that to understand Christianity, one must understand the moral law, which is the underlying structure of the Universe and is "hard as nails." Unless one grasps the dismay which comes from humanity's failure to keep moral law, one cannot understand the coming of Christ and his work. The eternal God who is the law's source takes primacy over the created Satan whose rebellion undergirds all evil. The death and resurrection of Christ is introduced as the only way in which our inadequate human attempts to redeem humanity's sins could be made adequate in God's eyes.

"God "became a man" in Christ, Lewis says, so that mankind could be "amalgamated with God's nature" and make full atonement possible. Lewis offers several analogies to explain his abstract concept: that of Jesus "paying the penalty" for a crime, "paying a debt", or helping humanity out of a hole. His main point, however, is that redemption is so incomprehensible that it cannot be fully appreciated, and he attempts to explain that the method by which God atones for the sins of humanity is not nearly as important as the fact that he does so."

CHRISTIAN BEHAVIOR—"The next third of the book explores the ETHICS resulting from Christian belief. He cites the five CARDINAL VIRTUES: PRUDENCE, JUSTICE, HOPE, FAITH, and CHARITY. Lewis also covers such topics as social relations and forgiveness, sexual ethics and the tenets of Christian marriage, and the relationship between morality and psychoanalysis. He also writes about the great sin PRIDE, which he argues to be the root cause of all evil and rebellion."

"His most important point is that Christianity mandates that one "love your neighbor as yourself." Even if one does not like oneself, one would still love oneself. Lewis calls this one of the great secrets: When one acts if he loves others, he will presently come to love them."

MERE CHRISTIANITY was adapted from a series of BBC radio talks made between 1941 and 1944, while Lewis was at OXFORD UNIVERSITY during the Second World War. It is considered a classic of Christian apologetics written in three pamphlets THE CASE FOR CHRISTIANITY (1942), CHRISTIAN BEHAVIOR (1943), and BEYOND PERSONALITY (1944). Lewis was invited to give the talks by James Welch, BBC Director of Religious Broadcasting, after he read his The Problem with Pain. Wikipedia

The book was published in 1952, one of history's most influential Christian books. Colson's conversion to Christianity resulted from his reading MERE CHRISTIANITY."

APOLOGETICS DEFINITION: "Reasoned arguments or writings in justification of something, typically a theory or something religious."   I pages dictionary

THESAURUS DEFINITION APOLOGETIC: "REGRETFUL, sorry, contrite, remorseful, rueful, penitent, conscious-stricken, compunctious, shamefaced, ashamed.   ANTONYM: UNREPENTANT

A LEWIS LIBRARY—C.S. LEWIS was a prolific writer, producing more than 40 books. Below are the descriptions of six of his more important Christian works not discussed in the main article. A GRIEF OBSERVED (1961). Written as a journal after the death of his wife, Joy; the emotional counterpart of THE PROBLEM WITH PAIN.

MIRACLES (1947). Argues that miracles are possible, using the ULTIMATE MIRACLE, THE INCARNATION.

OUT OF THE SILENT PLANET (1938). Theological science fiction dealing with the Fall, sin and atonement allegorically; the first, and considered the best, volume of his science-fiction trilogy, which also includes PERELANDRA (1943) and THAT HIDEOUS STRENGTH (1945).

THE ABOLITION OF MAN (1943). Draws from the great non-Christian religious writings to prove the existence of natural law; shows how the modern system of education abandoned its task of teaching values.

THE FOUR LOVES (1960). Discusses and distinguishes between four types of love: AFFECTION, FRIENDSHIP, EROS and CHARITY.
THE PROBLEM OF PAIN (1940). Examines the classic question of HOW A GOOD AND OMNIPOTENT GOD CAN ALLOW SUFFERING." Wikipedia
Lewis' 7-volume Chronicles of Narnia is both children's fantasy and Christian allegory.

C.S. LEWIS ON DEALING WITH CORONAVIRUS CRISIS

"Clive Staple Lewis (1898-1963) is considered to have been one of the greatest defenders of the Christian faith during the 20th Century. In 1948 he published an essay titled, "ON LIVING IN THE ATOMIC AGE." Although it was written 72 years ago, it is very relevant to the coronavirus pandemic that we are dealing with today. As you read the excerpt below, just substitute "corona virus" for "atomic bomb."

"In one way we think a great deal too much of the atomic bomb. 'How are we to live in the atomic age?" I am tempted to reply 'Why, as you would have lived in the 16th Century when the plague visited London…you are already living in an age of cancer, an age of paralysis [polio], an age of air raids, an age of railway and motor car accidents."
"In other words words, do not let us begin by exaggerating the novelty of our situation. Believe mom dear sir or madam, you and all whom you love were already sentenced to death before the atomic bomb was invented; and quite a high percentage of us are going to die in unpleasant ways. We had, indeed, one very great advantage over our ancestors — anesthetics, but we have that still. It is perfectly ridiculously to go about whimpering and drawing long faces, because the scientists have added one more chance of painful and premature death to a world which already bristled with such chances and in which death itself was not a chance at all, but a certainty."
"This is the first point to be made: and the first action to be taken is to pull ourselves together. If we are all going to be destroyed by atomic bombs, let that bomb when it comes find us doing sensible and human things — praying, working, teaching, reading, listening to music, chatting to our friends — not huddled together like frightened sheep and thinking about atomic bombs.They may break our bodies (a microbe [virus] can do that) but they need not dominate our minds."
"The Bible says that one of the reasons Jesus came to this earth was to free people from their bondage to the lifelong fear of death (Hebrews 2:15). Those of us who have put our faith in Jesus as our Lord and Savior should live and walk in that freedom."
"We should live with confidence and not in fear because we have hope — the promise of living forever in new glorified bodies in a new Jerusalem on a new earth. (Revelation 21:1-7)   THE CHRIST IN PROPHECY JOURNAL Lion and Lamb Ministries 3-26-2020

CORONAVIRUS CDC TRUE TIMELINE OF EPIDEMIC

A comment from my dad's World War II bomber unit FACEBOOK. "I was tired of hearing how Trump called the virus a hoax and "did nothing" until March. So I did research. Here's the real timeline of what happened (all of this before we had even 1 death in the US); 1/6 CDC issues travel advisory for Wuhan; 1/11 CDC tweets about corona related "pneumonia outbreak in China"; 1/13 WHO tweets that there is no evidence of human to human transmission; 1/17 CDC started doing health screenings at 3 airports of travelers from China; 1/21 first case of someone who traveled directly from Wuhan; 1/23 WHO again says no human to human transmission outside of China; 1/27 WHO raises alert level but is still saying China has it contained; 1/28 CDC states

"While CDC considers cover a serious situation and is taking preparedness measures, the immediate risk in the US is low."; 1/29 White House announces Coronavirus Task Force created.

Note — this despite the WHO downplaying the threat!;1/31 Trump bans travel to China; Media and multiple Democrats slam his decision calling it racist/xenophobic 2/5 Trump acquitted (impeachment); 2/5 Sen. Chuck Shumer in a tweet continues to call Trumps' travel ban from China "premature."; 2/7 White House's Coronavirius Task Force CTF gives press briefing.; 2/9 White House CTF meets with all governors regarding virus.; 2/12 CDC waiting for approval from Chinese for CDC team to travel to China.; 2/18 HHS announces partnership to develop a vaccine.; 2/21 Italy identifies its very first case in their country.; 2/21 CDC tweets that it is working with the States for preparedness; 2/24 Trump sent letter to Congress asking for $25 billion for virus effort.; 2/24 Nancy Pelosi made a stop in Chinatown San Francisco and encouraged people to "please come and visit and enjoy Chinatown."; 2/25 there is still no reported community spread in the United States! (per CDC tweet); 2/27 first community transmission in America; 2/27 Trump appoints Pence to coordinate efforts 2/29 FIRST reported Covid19 death in US.

It is helpful to look at the actual timeline. All of this happened before the 1st death in US.

7 Ways Satan has Gone to War during COVID-19

IBELIEVEcom Debbie McDaniel May 13, 2020

1 "He wants to consume us in doubt, fear and worry. He tries to deceive us into thinking we're all alone."
2 He tries to steal, kill, and destroy all that we hold dear. He's the master of destruction.
3 He tempts us to rely on ourselves and our own strength to get us through. He   disguises himself as an angel of light.
4 He is author of confusion. He breeds distrust and paranoia.
5 He tries to lead us into a downward spiral of depression and despair.
6 He causes sickness and disease.
7 He works hard to bring disunity and strife. He wants nothing more than to break up the body of Christ."

MARTIN LUTHER STAYS IN WITTENBERG DURING PLAGUE

"During the summer, the plague again struck Wittenberg. Many left the town as was the custom, to avoid contagion. On August 15, 1527, the entire university moved to Jena. Luther felt obligated to stay and care for the sick, Katie and their son Hans, who remained there. There is no question that Luther's faith is on display here, because he knew that remaining behind put him in physical danger, but he felt a responsibility to risk his life—and even the lives of his family—by remaining where he was and caring for the sick. God had called him, and he would answer God's call. The only thing he feared was not doing this. But during this time little Hanschen did get quite sick…This whole tragic scene [deaths of close friends] affected Luther powerfully, not least because Kathie was herself pregnant and due in December." p. 384-385 MARTIN LUTHER—THE MAN WHO

REDISCOVERED GOD AND CHANGED THE WORLD (2018) Eric Metaxas Viking 375 Hudson St. New York, NY

"It is believed that the twin agonies of Leo Kaiser's martyrdom and the plague deaths at the Black Cloister of Bugenhagen's sister Hanna, along with her child, were what led Luther to compose the hymn for which he is most famous, "Ein Feste Berg ist unsere Gott" (A MIGHTY FORTRESS IS OUR GOD) 1528. Luther composed not only the words but the melody too."   Ibid 386

PERSONAL STORY: I learned about the plague and Luther from the UTUBE video of my Lutheran Missouri Synod pastor on PALM SUNDAY 2020. There were only the mandatory 10 people present—Pastor James Knill, an elder, the organist/piano, choir Heidi the pastor's wife and Sarah, we share May 4th birthday, Christopher, usher pastor's son and four others. I looked in my Luther biographies and only found this story. I had been told by my mentor pastor professor Eric Gritsch of Gettysburg Seminary that Lutheran soldiers from Germany had marched to MIGHTY FORTRESS to aid anti Lutheran Catholic Vienna besieged by the Ottoman Muslim Turks.

Therefore, Luther's greatest hymn sung by many churches was not written against man's mortal enemies but against the plague which Luther calls mankind's Satanic foe.

"During this summer of Anfechtungen and plague, another believer would be martyred for his faith…Luther knew that for centuries no one had known the Bible nor what was in it. They had been a captive audience every week, and their own priests themselves knew nothing of the Bible or what was in it either. So the faith simply was not passed on in any measure. When Luther visited these villages and towns and saw the tremendous ignorance born of these dark ages, he was grieved, but his grief led him to write what is one of his greatest works, called THE LARGE CATECHISM. Published in 1529. It dealt with the basics of faith: the Ten Commandments, the Apostle' Creed, the Lord's Prayer, holy baptism, and the Eucharist (Communion). It was written in a question-and-answer form so that it could be easily taught, and Luther knew that it would aid many pastors who themselves were not acquainted with the basics of the faith and who therefore didn't know how to teach it."   Ibid 387-388

Hulk Hogan: God "Shut Down" Athletics, Musicians, Actors, Money—"Everything we Worship"

"Maybe we don't need a vaccine," legendary pro-wrestler Hulk Hogan writes, calling on the world to use its time of coronavirus-induced isolation to redirect its focus and worship Jesus, "the only thing that really matters."
"Just like he did with the plagues of Egypt, God has taken away everything we worship" — like athletes, entertainers and money. — Hogan wrote Monday April 7, 2020 in a Facebook post, including a photo leaning against a wall in prayer:

> "In three short months, just like He did with the plagues of Egypt
> God has taken away everything we worship. God says, 'you want
> to worship athletes, I will shut down the stadiums. You want to
> worship musicians, I will shut down Civic Centers. You want to
> worship actors, I will shut down theaters. You want to worship
> Money, I will shut down the economy and collapse the stock market.
> You don't want to go to church and worship Me, I will make it

Megyn Kelly Exposed One Truth About CNN That The Network Tried to Hide — Coronavirus

America Patriot Daily News Network April 8, 2020.

"Americans are beginning to ask about the coronavirus pandemic.

"The projectors and media hysteria that claimed hundreds of thousands of Americans would die in the coming weeks are falling apart.

"And to add another layer to this scandal, Megyn Kelly exposed one truth about CNN that the network tried to hide.

"The fake news media's hopes that record numbers of Americans would die from coronavirus are collapsing under the weight of reality.

"Fake news "reporters" carefully constructed a narrative built on the lies over the last several weeks that the coronavirus was an unstoppable silent killer that would lead to more American deaths than every war America fought in the 20th century."

"But it turns out the doomsayers were wrong.

"So now one fake news media is falling back on one of the old reliable smears — namely that Donald Trump is a liar."

"Former Fox News Channel anchor Megyn Kelly called out fake news CNN for turning their channel into an anti-Trump propaganda outfit by blurring the distinction between news and opinion hosts."

""CNN still pretends he is [they are] an objective new anchor (yeah, sure) while the MSM [main stream media] recoils in horror at the FOX, etc. Who do they think they're kidding?" Kelly asked.

"What set Kelly off was a monologue by Trump-hating liberal activist Don Lemon."

"Lemon ranted and raved about President Trump's daily press briefings."

"Without citing any evidence, Lemon whined and complained that President Trump routinely 'lied' to the public."

"Lemon compared himself to Howard Beale, the lead character in the movie "Network" where, as the anchor for a TV newscast, Beale told everyone to get mad as hell and say you aren't going to take it anymore."

"I have to be honest with you. For the last couple of weeks, when I walk into this building and I get in front of a camera, I swear I feel like I'm in the movie NETWORK. I feel like Howard Beale. Americans are mad as hell. What are you going to — how much can Americans take?" Lemon whined.

"Every single day berating people, lying, "Lemon added. "How much more. — How many people have to die."

"Americans, are you mad as hell? How much more are you going to take?' Lemon asked in conclusion."

"At Fox News — where Kelly became a star — the network differentiated between "straight news hosts" like Chris Wallace, Tucker Carlson and Laura Ingraham."

"CNN makes no such distinction."

"Trump-hating liberal activists like Jake Tapper, Chris Cuomo, Don Lemon and Anderson Cooper are presented as objective journalists even though their shows are commercials for the Democrat Party and group therapy sessions for liberals to scream and gnash their teeth about [President] Donald Trump."

"CNN tried to obscure this fact for years."

"But Megan Kelly called them out for the ultimate act of fake news in presenting Democrat Party activists as journalists."

MEDIA HYPOCRISY: Megyn Kelly had a NBC TV morning show and spoke about black face on a Halloween show. She was fired. My Governor Northam wore racist black face as "Coonman" with a hooded "KKK" college skit friend Yearbook photo at a Virginia medical college. He kept his job as Virginia's Democrat governor. This photo appeared the day after the doctor explained on TV how a mother could deliver a baby and the mother and doctor could decide if the baby should live. That is infanticide murder.

Obama Would have Botched the Coronavirus Response

"Many in the media are attempting to claim that the Obama administration would have handled the Coronavirus better than the Trump administration, is this any way true? Here is why the Obama administration would have handled this a lot worse."

1 H1N1 Outbreak—"The H1N1 outbreak was the last major outbreak to hit the United States and while it didn't hit as hard as the COVID-19 it did due damage. The Obama administration was late in calling it a pandemic, while some might say that the Trump administration was late to declare it an emergency he was not nearly as late as Obama.

2 FAILURE TO RESTOCK — "The Obama administration had a hand to play in this epidemic and that was preparing the next administration for a disaster just like the COVID-19 Pandemic. The Obama Administration failed to restock N95 masks after they had used them during the H1N1 outbreak, It was fine using them, that is what they are there for but you have to restock these vital supplies."

3 WHITE HOUSE PANDEMIC OFFICE—"Obama shut down the White House Pandemic Office in 2009. As a consequence of this, his administration was unprepared for the H1N1 virus and the Ebola virus that came soon after. Obama was short-sighted and moved to reopen the office after the Ebola outbreak."

4 VACCINE SHORTAGES—"The Obama Administration is documented to have made many promises they couldn't keep, one promise cost American lives. The Obama Administration claimed they would have 160 million vaccines for H1N1 before the flu season hit and they fell short, they were only able to get 30 million."

5 OBAMA CUT NIH FUNDING —"Government spending is out of control but there are some areas that really need the funding, one such organization was the National Institute of Health. Obama cut funding to the organization and this left the nation unprepared for the Coronavirus."

6 LACK OF TRAVEL BANS —"The Trump administration was met with protests after announcing that it would implement travel bans for countries affected by the Coronavirus, this move saved countless lives and gave America a good footing in the fight against the Coronavirus. Barack Obama would never have implemented Travel bans, not only is Obama an open borders politician his inaction on this front during the H1N1 virus serves as evidence to this conclusion as well."

7 WEAK ON CHINA — "Too often in public and private life do we fail to tell others no, it is time the United States begins to say no to China. For years the Obama administration bowed to China, a nation known globally for its abuse of Human rights and poor standards on several fronts. Trump began the process of moving America off of Chinese manufacturing with the Trade War, the hoarding of supplies by China has been met with fire and fury from the President, does anyone honestly believe that Obama would be during the same?"   Trump Train News April 9, 2020

Great Britain's Great Moat the English Channel

Clive is an Anglo Saxon name for cliff. In June 1958, I took my new SAAB 99 EMS to England on the last evening Hovercraft ferry from Calais to Dover, England. It was dark when we landed after 9:00 P.M. but I still recall seeing the famous White Cliffs of Dover. I remember it was a very choppy waves Hovercraft ride. As a child my mother had told me in January 1935, on the ocean liner from Hamburg to America she got seasick in the English Channel. She probably landed at the port of Southampton. I have been told that the Hovercraft service has been discontinued and also the Calais ferry boat. They built a tunnel highway under the English Channel several years ago. I took the Hovercraft because I had just seen James Bond use it in the movie DIAMONDS ARE FOREVER.

British actor ROGER MOORE had a Triumph Stag the least exciting car he ever drove. At the 1973 New York auto show I visited the Triumph car display and told the salesman I have ordered a European delivery SAAB with a Triumph designed engine. He showed me the Triumph Stag V-8 engine they had on display and told me that it was two SAAB 2.0 liter engines joined together, it was rated at 145 HP. My 1973 new fuel injected SAAB 99 EMS was rated at 110 HP which was the second most powerful four cylinder engine sold in U.S. next to turbo BMW 2002 which had a 135 HP fuel injected engine.

Unbroken's Berlin Olympic War Hero is BORN AGAIN

"But as the eighth week approached in Los Angeles, we all knew that the end had to come. Not that the blessings were diminishing. It was then that LOUIS ZAMPERINI was converted. He was the U.S. track star who pulled a flag bearing the Nazi swastika down from the Reichstag? during the 1936 BERLIN OLYMPIC games. Later, in the Second World War, he was shot down in the Pacific and drifted on a life raft for 47 days. He survived attacks by Japanese pilots who swooped down on him as target practice. Finally, the Japanese captured him and put him in prison for two years. Although he was a famous athlete and war hero, he came home feeling unhappy, disillusioned, and broken in spirit. (PTSD) One night he wondered into our tent with his wife and accepted Christ, and his life was transformed." Graham   Ibid   p 157

JAPANESE ROCK STAR PORTRAYS TORMENTOR IN UNBROKEN FILM

UNBROKEN MOVIE FACT: The Japanese actor who portrayed the brutal prison camp commander in the film UNBROKEN (2014) and tormented Zamperini is Japan's favorite rockstar MIYAVI. "Takamasa Ishihara is a Japanese guitarist, singer-songwriter, record producer and actor known for his finger-slapping style of playing guitar. Miyavi commented that as the movie was somewhat sensitive to the Japanese people, he had hesitated as to whether he should take the role. However, meeting with [director] ANGELINA JOLIE, and given the underlying theme of the story is FORGIVENESS, he wholeheartedly decided to accept it."   Wikipedia

"In 2013 Miyavi was nominated for the MTV European Music Award for Best Japanese Act, and at the MTV Video Music Wards Japan he won the Best Collaboration category with Yuksek. On March 14, 2009, Miyavi married Japanese-American singer MELODY. Melody was born in Honolulu, Hawaii on Feb. 24, 1982. My mother's birthday Feb. 22, 1915. They live in Los Angeles since 2014 during the release of his film UNBROKEN."

[Reverend Billy Graham passed on the first day of the Jewish Holy days of Purim.]

Five Ways to Pray at Purim Queen Esther's Prayer

Messianic Jews Going Before God at Purim
The Jewish Voice 2018

"Purim is one of the most joyous of holidays in the Jewish year - and with good reason. God saved the Jewish people from destruction as a result of an evil plot hatched against them. He elevated a Jewish maiden to the position of queen to be in the right place at the right time to plead for her people. God saved them and turned the tables on the man who sought to annihilate them."

"But before the rescue, Queen Esther spent three days in deep prayer. She also fasted. She called on her handmaids, and indeed all of Israel, to fast and pray with her. She was planning to go to the king unbidden, something strictly against protocol. If the king was displeased, it could result in her death - and would certainly leave the Jewish people unprotected against the plan to kill them."
"So Esther prayed."

"Before the rejoicing of Purim, many Jewish worshippers and Messianic (Christian) Jews go before the Lord in memory of Esther's brave faith and dedication before God. The Fast of Esther usually takes place the day before Purim begins."
"Whether or not you fast, here are five ways you can pray at Purim."

1 THE NATION OF ISRAEL

"What could be more fitting at Purim than praying for the nation of Israel? Today, it is not one man's plot, but hatred, violence, and prejudice from many fronts assails Israel. Here are just a few ways Messianic Jews and others can pray for Israel."

* Wisdom for Prime Minister Benjamin Netanyahu and Israel's Knesset (ruling body)
* An end to Palestinian and Arab incitement to violence against Israel. - this is waged through the media, on social media, in schools and public messages from leaders, and on the street.
* An end to United Nations bias against Israel and the permanent agenda item number 7 of the UN Human Rights Council which mandates that at every meeting, the council address Israel.

2 JEWISH PEOPLE TO KNOW THEIR PROPHESIED MESSIAH

"Ever more important than earthly peace is the eternal peace, and both Old and New Covenant Scriptures reveal that can come through the Messiah. As Messianic Jews, we pray for the Jewish people to come to know Him. We also pray:
* For the blinders to come off their eyes so they will see Yeshua (Jesus) for who He is. Israel's Messiah
* That they develop an insatiable curiosity about Messianic prophecies, particularly Isaiah 53
* That God will send loving bold, and biblically knowledgeable Believers into divine encounters with Jewish people throughout the world "for such a time as this" to share the Gospel with them.

3 BELIEVERS FROM ALL NATIONS TO FIND JOY AND GIVE THANKS

"Purim is a time of rejoicing, so let's fill our hearts and our prayers with thanksgiving, joy and praise. Please pray for:

* God's divine protection of Israel, and His protection over you in your daily life
* God's Word - living and active in His communication to us, to help us know Him more
* Us as Messianic Jews. We are blessed to see the Jewish roots of faith in Yeshua and how God has tied Old and New Testaments together into His one plan of redemption
* God's amazing involvement in our lives - that he will orchestrate details, events and people to work together for His purposes and our good

4 PEOPLE TO SEE THE WORK OF THE LORD AT EVERY TURN

"Though the name of God is not mentioned in the book of Esther. He is there at every turn. He is present and working to accomplish His purposes. Purim offers the opportunity to reflect on God's presence and power in our lives, and to pursue seeing Him more clearly, even in times when He seems hidden. Pray for:

* Eyes to look for, find and meet God in every situation.
* A hunger to trust Him more, to trust His goodness even when it can seem "hidden" in certain circumstances or for a time
* His powerful work "behind the scenes" in your life and in the hearts of people you know and meet

5 THE DESPERATE AND HOPELESS TO FIND HOPE IN THE LORD

"The Jewish people of Esther's day were in a desperate situation. An irrevocable decree assigned a specific day when citizens of Persia were going to raid the Jewish population and receive payment for every Jew they killed. All seemed hopeless unless Queen Esther would reveal herself as Jewish to the king and intercede for the Jewish people. But first, she interceded fervently to God to deliver her and her people from their dire situation. Purim is a good time for Messianic Jews to remember that there are those around us who nay feel desperate and hopeless, and to pray that they find the only true source of hope and peace. Yeshua the Messiah Himself. Pray:

* That those who do not know Him will call out to God in sincerity and humility, believing in Yeshua as our only rescue unto eternal life
* For those to know God's love, peace and hope in the midst of their situation
* That they will experience God's nearness and comfort, strength and power as they trust and rest in Him

May your time with the Lord be blessed as you join Messianic Jews around the world in this Purim season of prayer and rejoicing.

IS GOD FINISHED WITH ISRAEL?

Dr. Michael Brown May 15, 2018

"Is God finished with Israel? Is He done with the Jewish people as a people? Heaven forbid. All the Scripture and history shouts a loud "No" to this question.

Paul addressed this directly, asking, "So I ask, did they [speaking of the Jewish people as a whole] stumble in order that they might fall? By no means!" (Romans 11:11). Or, in the words of the King James Version, "God forbid."

So, despite Israel's rejection of Jesus as Messiah Israel has not fallen beyond the point of recovery. Rather, as Paul writes in Romans 9:4 (speaking, again, of non-believing Jews), "They are Israelites, and to them belong the adoption, the glory, the covenants, the giving of the law, the worship, and the promises."

As written in Jeremiah 31:35-37, "This says the fixed order of the moon and the stars for light by night, who stirs up the sea so that its waves roar — the Lord of hosts is his name: 'If this fixed order departs from before me, declares the Lord, then shall the offspring of Israel cease from being a nation before me forever.' Thus says the Lord: 'If the heavens above can be measured, and the foundations of the earth below can be explored, then I will cast off all the offspring of Israel for all they have done says Lord."

The Jewish People's Survival

That's why the Jewish people still exist today: We have been miraculously preserved by God, not because of goodness, but because of His goodness. Thank God that He keeps His promises! Thank God for His grace and mercy and long suffering! (To all of my non-Jewish, Jesus-loving friends, remember: The Church does not have a monopoly on grace.) What about the fact that the vast majority of Jews do not believe in Jesus? What about the fact that some militantly oppose faith in Jesus?"

That is tragic, and that is why Paul mourned in Romans 9:1-3. Jews without Jesus are lost, just as Gentiles without Jesus are lost (see Romans 2:6-11)

Yet, despite my people's rejection of our Messiah, we remain loved and chosen by God. As Paul stated so clearly, "As regards the Gospel, they are enemies for your sake. But as regards election, they are beloved for the sake of their forefathers. For the gifts and the calling of God are irrevocable." (Romans 11:28-29)

Some would argue that when Paul said "Israel" in these verses, he meant only the believing remnant, the Israel within Israel, Jews who believe in Jesus (see Romans 9:6-8), But to argue for this is to do violence to the Word of God.

First, after making this point about Israel within Israel (the believing remnant) in Romans 9:6. Paul used the word "Israel" 10 more times, culminating in Romans 11:26. In every case, he meant the nation as a whole, not just the believing remnant."

Second, the New Testament scholar F. F, Bruce pointed out in his commentary to Romans 11:26, "...it is impossible to entertain an exegesis which takes 'Israel' here in a different sense from 'Israel' in v 25 ('blindness in part is happened to Israel')." In other words, the Israel that has been temporarily blinded is the Israel that will be saved."

As Bruce explained, "Temporarily alienated for the advantage of the Gentiles, they are eternally the object of God's electing love because His promises, once made to the patriarchs, will never be revoked."

Jesus Prophecy of Future Regeneration of 12 Jewish Tribes

That's why Jesus spoke about the time of future "regeneration," with the twelve 12 tribes of Israel playing a central role (Matthews 19:28)

That's why Peter spoke about the time of the restoration of all things, in accordance with the words of the Old Testament prophets (see Acts 3:10-21)

And what did those prophets speak about? They spoke of the time when the Messiah would reign from Jerusalem, when Israel would be exalted, and when the nations would stream to Jerusalem to learn from Israel's God (see, for example, Isaiah 2:1-4)

The idea that a New Testament writer could reverse all these promises with a single stroke of his pen - as some claim Paul or others did - is to deny the inspiration and authority of the Old Testament. After all, Jesus the Messiah came to fulfill the Hebrew Scriptures, not abolish them (see Matthews 5:17-20). He came to confirm the promises of the patriarchs, not cancel them (see Romans 15:8-9)

And, as Paul also wrote, the Sinai covenant, which came 430 years after the promises to Abraham, cannot annul those promises (Galatians 3:17-18); this includes the promises to the Land of Israel; (see also Psalm 105:7-11)

That alone explains the history of the Jewish people. Without a homeland for many centuries, scattered around the earth, yet preserved through generations of unspeakable suffering only to be regathered to our ancient homeland. Nothing even remotely close to this has happened to any other people. It is only because of the Lord.

And so, both history and Scripture demolish the idea that God is finished with Israel. Not a chance!"

Today is Israel's 70th Anniversary May 14, 2018

The number 70 is composed of seven tens. The number 7 means Divine Perfection, the number 10 means completeness of an entire cycle with GOD.

President Donald Trump Meeting with Prime Minister Bibi Natanyahu in the Rose Garden for a Peace Solution with the Palestinian People

The Times of Israel (TOI) Staff Jan. 28, 2020   [My dad born Jan. 28, 1919]

Q "Do you expect Prime Minister NETANYAHU to implement the plan right away in the coming six weeks?"

President Trump: "We, I think he's [Bibi] is here for a reason. And, hopefully, that it will be a "yes" and peace in the Middle East has been long sought for many, many, many years and decades and centuries. And this is an opportunity; we'll see what happens. Whatever it is, it is. But he's here for a reason."

Q "Would you give a green light for annexation of the Jordan Valley within the coming months?"

Trump: "We're going to see. We're going to announce tomorrow at 12 o'clock. We're going to show a plan that's been worked on by everybody, and we'll see whether or not it catches hold. If it does, that'd be great. And if [it] doesn't, we can live with it, too. But I think it might have a chance."

Q "Do you expect Benny Gantz [foriegn minister] to agree to the plan?"

Trump: "Do I expect what?"

Q "Benny Gantz."

Trump: "He is coming here today. He'll be here also. And, as you know, they are two good competitors. They're fighting it out."

"I've been waiting now— this is his [Netanyahu] third election. We keep waiting, and waiting, and waiting. So, let's go. What kind of system is that? That's a very strange system you have over there. Wouldn't you say that? [Parliamentary multi-party coalition government.] Because we have been. We've been waiting — we've been talking about this for months and we keep waiting for the election. That system has to be looked at."

Q "But what about the allegations that this is an interference with internal politics to Israel? The fact that —"

Trump: "Well, I think what's happening is — one of the reasons that Mr. Gantz is here is for that reason. He's coming, too. So I'm going to speak to him right after this."

Q "What is your message to the residents of Judea and Samaria at this point?"

PM Netanyahu: "May I—say something?"

Q "Yeah.

PM: "I think — first of all, I'm very honored to be here with you—"

Trump: "Thank you. it's my honor."

PM: "—here today, Mr. President. And I look forward to making history with you tomorrow. And I think we'll talk about the plan; I'll talk about the plan — of vision and peace, which is historic — the President has put forward tomorrow."

"Today, I just want to say two words: Thank you. Thank you for everything you've done for Israel, everything you've done for Israel — for recognizing Jerusalem as Israel's capital; for moving your embassy there; for recognizing our sovereignty in the Golan Heights; for recognizing our rights in Judea and Samaria, the heartland of our biblical homeland; for the unprecedented security and intelligence cooperation between our two countries. I think, Mr. President, that the list of your support for Israel, the things you've done for Israel since you've become President, is very long. But the bottom line is short: You have made our alliance stronger than ever. And I look forward, in the coming years, to make it even stronger with an historic defense treaty that will anchor our alliance for generations."

"One last thing — one last thing, which I think is important: This is INTERNATIONAL HOLOCAUST REMEMBRANCE DAY. [My dad's birthday Jan. 28, 1919] And on this day, I'm proud to stand here, as the Prime Minister of the one and only Jewish State, and thank you for confronting the most anti-Semitic regime on the planet. When you came into office, IRAN was on the march. Because of your leadership, Iran is now on the run."   [Iran was Queen Esther's Persia renamed in 1935]

"You've withdrawn from the dangerous nuclear— the nuclear deal. You slapped on tremendous sanctions. You have — two weeks ago, you've taken out the most dangerous terrorist on the planet. All those who seek peace, all those who want to fight terrorism should thank you, Mr. President, for your bold decisions and your bold actions. And on behalf of the State of Israel, I want to thank you for everything you've done for Israel, for confronting Iran, and for your extraordinary decisions, your leadership."

"That's the end of my speech."

Q "President Trump, last time, I asked you if you were for a two-state solution. Are you going to say, tomorrow, "two-state and a Palestinian State"?

Trump: "You're going to see very, very quickly. We're going to release a plan tomorrow at 10 o'clock. You're going to see for yourself."

FASCIST Tendencies in America

"Another significant factor was the attraction that Fascism had for many Americans during the depression years. Several disturbing elements were evident in the native variety of the ideology that had carried MUSSOLINI and HITLER to power. Anti-semitism pervaded the outlook of most far-rightists, and even a responsible person, automotive manufacturer HENRY FORD, carried on a campaign against the Jews [international bankers] in the 1920s. Although he later repented of these excesses. Ford did accept a medal from Hitler on his 75th birthday in 1938. [CHARLES LINDBERGH also received this medal from Hitler after German Air Marshal HERMAN GOERING revealed new secret Luftwaffe fighters and bombers which he flew. He returned to America and told America's Air Corps chief Gen. "Hap" ARNOLD that the Nazis had aircraft far superior to America's.] Populist demagogues such as Senator HUEY LONG [Louisiana] with his "share the wealth" had extensive followings among the discontented. A Roman Catholic radio preacher in Michigan, Father CHARLES COUGHLIN, stirred millions of listeners by attacking plutocracy [wealthy ruling class], Communism, and the NEW DEAL [socialism]. He openly referred to Nazism and Italian Fascism as a "defense mechanism" against Communism [Stalin's atheist Soviet Union totalitarian government] and labeled HITLER, MUSSOLINI, and FRANCO [Spanish dictator] as "patriots rising to a challenge." Fascism "was and is Europe's answer to Russian Communism's threat of world revolution, and it is the bulwark against long active agencies of destruction." He subtly linked anti-Semitism with anticommunism by suggesting that the Jews were persecuted because of their association with Communism and their lack of patriotism."
CATHOLIC WORLD "American Catholics and Anti-Semitism in the 1930s" David O'Brien February 1967   Ibid p 204
"There was no lack of Fascist-style groups on American soil, the KU KLUX KLAN [KKK], the most famous of all the hate organizations, whose program in the 1920s had primarily been anti-Catholicism, declined somewhat in importance in the 1930s. Ibid 156
Among the most notorious was the German American BUND, headed by FRITZ KUHN, a German war veteran [WW I] who emigrated to the United States in 1926. It was virulently anti-Semitic, maintaining a private army of storm troopers, and supported the policies of the Hitler regime." Ibid p 157
"When war broke out in Europe, the influence of the Fascist spokesman rapidly waned. Many of them, however, were active in the isolationist AMERICA FIRST COMMITTEE, a reasonably respectable group formed in 1940."   Ibid   p 157
[Charles Lindbergh was the group's most vocal member. After Pearl Harbor Lindbergh was able to serve in the Pacific and helped increase the range of the twin engine Lockheed P-38 Lightening fighter flown by BONG and MCGUIRE America's top two fighter aces. Lindbergh against orders flew several combat missions not in uniform. This was against the Geneva Convention rules. If captured by the Japanese he would have been a famous prize like 1936 BERLIN OLYMPIC's LOUIE ZAMPERINI, the runner admired by Hitler for his final burst of speed as shown in director ANGELA JOLIE's film UNBROKEN a story of great suffering, endurance and forgiveness. Lindbergh could have been beheaded.]
Lindbergh was later a consultant at EDSAL FORD's new huge Willow Run Ypsilanti, Michigan B-24 Liberator bomber factory. The factory's radical new innovative ideas and technology built the large 110 foot wingspan bomber in an unprecedented record 55 minutes! About 6,000 B-24 bombers were built in the plant. When I first learned this I disbelieved it, there is a video. As a

child I built a one foot REVELL plastic B-24 model which I believe took longer than an hour to glue not thousands of rivets.

Great Britain and the Commonwealth of Nations Prime Minister Winston S. Churchill   Speaks to the Joint Session of the United States of America Congress in Washington, District of Columbia December 26, 1941 Anno Domini

"Members of the Senate and of the House of Representatives of the United States, I feel greatly honored that you should have thus invited me to enter the United States Senate Chamber and address the representatives of both branches of Congress. The fact that my American forebears have for so many generations played their part in the life of the United States, and that here I am, an Englishman, welcomed in your midst, makes this experience one of the most moving and thrilling of my life, which is already long and has not been entirely uneventful. [LAUGHTER] I wish indeed that my mother, whose memory I cherish, across the vale of years, could have been here to see. By the way, I cannot reflecting that if my father had been American and my mother British instead of the other way around, I might have got here on my own, in that case this would not have been the first time you would have heard my voice. In that case I should not have needed an invitation. But if I had it is hardly likely that it would have been unanimous. So perhaps things are better as they are. [Congressional laughter]

I may confess, however, that I do not feel like a fish out of water in a legislative assembly where English is spoken. I am a child of the House of Commons. I was brought up in my father's house to believe in democracy. "TRUST THE PEOPLE." That was the message. I used to see him cheered at the meetings and in the streets by crowds of workingmen way back in those aristocratic Victorian days when as [Jewish Prime Minister] Disraeli said "The world was for the few, and for the very few."

GETTYSBURG IDEAL: GOVERNMENT OF THE PEOPLE, BY THE PEOPLE, FOR THE PEOPLE

Therefore, I have been in full harmony all my life with the tides which have flowed on sides of the Atlantic against privilege and monopoly and I have steered confidently towards the GETTYSBURG IDEAL OF GOVERNMENT OF THE PEOPLE, BY THE PEOPLE, FOR THE PEOPLE.   [LONG LOUD APPLAUSE]

SERVANTS OF THE STATE—ASHAMED TO BE ITS MASTERS

I owe my advancement entirely to the House of Commons, whose servant I am. In my country as in yours public men are proud to be the SERVANTS OF THE STATE and would be ASHAMED TO BE ITS MASTERS. The House of Commons, if they thought the people wanted it, could, be a SIMPLE VOTE, REMOVE ME FROM OFFICE. But I am not worrying about it at all. [NERVOUS LAUGHTER]

As a matter of fact I am sure they will approve very highly of my journey here, for which I obtained the King's permission, in order to meet the President of the United States [Franklin D. Roosevelt] and to arrange with him for all that mapping out of our military plans and for all those intimate meetings of the high officers of the armed services in both countries which are indispensable for the successful prosecution of the war.

I should like to say first of all how much I have been impressed and encouraged by the breath of view and sense or proportion which I have found in all quarters over here to which I have had access. Anyone who did not understand the size and solidarity of the foundations of the United States, might easily have expected to find and excited, disturbed, self-centered atmosphere, with all minds fixed upon the novel, startling, and painful episodes of sudden war as they hit America. After all, the United States have been attacked and set upon by three most powerfully armed dictator states, the greatest military power in Europe, the greatest military power in Asia Japan, Germany and Italy have all declared and are making war upon you, and the quarrel is opened which can only end in their overthrow or yours.   [Applause]

But here in Washington in these memorable days I have found an Olympian fortitude which, far from being based upon complacency, is only the mask of an inflexible purpose and the proof of a sure, well-grounded confidence in the final outcome. We in Britain had the same feeling in our darkest days. We too were sure that in the end all would be well.   [Applause]

You do not, I am certain, underrate the severity of the ordeal to which you and we have still to be subjected. The forces ranged against us are enormous. They are bitter, they are ruthless. The wicked men and their factions, who have launched their peoples on the path of war and conquest, know that they will be called to terrible account if they cannot beat down by force of arms the peoples they have assailed. They will stop at nothing. They have a vast accumulation of war weapons of all kinds. They have highly trained and disciplined armies, navies and air services. They have plans and designs which have long been contrived and matured. They will stop at nothing that violence or treachery can suggest.

It is quite true that on our side our resources in manpower and materials are far greater than theirs. But only a portion of your resources are as yet mobilized and developed, and we both of us have much to learn in the CRUEL ART OF WAR. We have therefore without doubt a time of tribulation before us. In this same time, some ground will be lost which it will be hard and costly to regain. Many disappointments and unpleasant surprises await us. Many of them will afflict us before the full marshaling of our latent and total power can be accomplished.

ALLIED YOUTH TAUGHT THAT WAR IS EVIL
AXIS YOUTH TAUGHT AGGRESSIVE WAR NOBLE

For the best part of twenty years the youth of Britain and America have been TAUGHT THAT WAR IS EVIL, which is true, and THAT IT WOULD NEVER COME AGAIN, which has been PROVED FALSE. For the best part of twenty years, the youth of Germany, of Japan and Italy, have been TAUGHT THAT AGGRESSIVE WAR IS THE NOBLEST DUTY of the citizen and that it should be begun as soon as the necessary weapons and organization have been made. We have performed the duties and tasks of peace. They have plotted and planned for war. This naturally has placed us, in Britain, and now places you in the United States at a disadvantage which only time, courage and untiring exertion can correct.

We have indeed to be thankful that so much time has been granted to us. If Germany had tried to invade the British Isles after the French collapse in June, 1940, and if Japan had declared war on the British Empire and the United States at about the same date, no one can say what disasters and agonies might not have been our lot. But now, at the end of December, 1941, our transformation from easy-going peace to total war efficiency has made very great progress.

The broad flow of munitions in Great Britain has already begun. Immense strides have been made in the conversion of American industry to military purposes. And now that the United States is at war, it is possible for orders to be given every day which in a year or eighteen months hence will produce results in war power beyond anything which has been seen or foreseen in the dictator states.   [Applause]

Provided that every effort is made, that nothing is kept back, that the whole manpower, brain power, virility, valor and civic virtue of the English-speaking world, with all its galaxy of loyalty, friendly or associate communities and states-provided that is bent unremittingly to the simple but supreme task, I think it would be reasonable to hope that the end of 1942 will see us quite definitely in a better position than we are now. And that the year 1943 will enable us to assume the initiative upon an ample scale.   [Applause]

MASTERS OF OUR FATE

Some people   may be startled or   momentarily depressed when, like your president,
I speak of a long and hard war. Our peoples would rather know the truth, somber through it may be. And after all, when we are doing the noblest work in the world, not only defending our hearths and homes, but the cause of freedom in every land, the question of whether deliverance comes in 1942 or 1943 or 1944, falls into its proper place in the grand proportions of human history. Sure I am that this day, now, we are the MASTERS OF OUR FATE. That the task which has been set for us is not above our strength. That its pangs and toils are not beyond our endurance. As long as we have FAITH IN OUR CAUSE, and an unconquerable willpower, SALVATION WILL NOT BE DENIED US. In the words of the Psalmist: "HE SHALL NOT BE AFRAID OF EVIL TIDINGS. HIS HEART IS FIXED, TRUSTING IN THE LORD!"   [Loud Applause]

Not all the tidings will be evil. On the contrary, mighty strokes of war have already been dealt against the enemy-the glorious defense of their native soil by the Russian armies and people; wounds have been inflicted upon the Nazi tyranny and system which have bitten deep and will fester and inflame not only in the Nazi body but in the Nazi mind.[LONG LOUD APPLAUSE]. The boastful Mussolini has crumpled already. He is now but a lackey and a serf, the merest utensil of his master's will. He has inflicted great suffering and wrong upon his own industrious people. He has been stripped of all his African empire. Abyssinia [Ethiopia] has been liberated. Our Armies of the East, which were so weak and ill-equipped at the moment of French desertion, now control all the regions from Teheran to Benghazi [Libya], and from Aleppo [Syria] and Cyprus to the sources of the Nile.   [Long Applause]

For many months we devoted ourselves to preparing to take the offensive in Libya. The very considerable battle which has been proceeding there the last six weeks in the desert, has been most fiercely fought on both sides. Owing to the difficulties of supply upon the desert flank, we were never able to bring numerically equal forces to bear upon the enemy. Therefore, we had to rely upon superiority in the numbers and qualities of tanks and aircraft, British and American. For the first time, aided by these-for the first time we have fought the enemy with equal weapons. For the first time we have made the Hun feel the sharp edge of those tools with which he has enslaved Europe. The armed forces of the enemy in Cyrenaica [Libya] amounted to about 150,000 men, of whom a third were Germans. General Auchinleck set out to destroy totally that armed force, and I have every reason to believe that his aim will be fully accomplished, I am so glad to be able to place before you, members of the Senate, House of Representatives, at this moment when you are entering the war, the proof that with proper weapons and proper organization, we are able to beat the life out of the savage NAZS.   [Applause].

What Hitlerism is suffering in Libya is only a sample and a foretaste of what we have got to give him and his accomplices wherever this war should lead us in the Globe.

There are good tidings also from blue water. The lifeline of supplies which joins our two nations across the ocean, without which all would fail, that lifeline is flowing steadily and freely in spite of all that the enemy can do. It is a fact that the British Empire, which many thought eighteen months ago was broken and ruined, is now incomparably stronger with every month.   [Applause]

AMERICA UNITED AS NEVER BEFORE

Lastly, if you will forgive me for saying it, to me the best tidings of all the UNITED STATES, UNITED AS NEVER BEFORE, has DRAWN THE SWORD FOR FREEDOM and cast away the scabbard.   [LONG LOUD APPLAUSE]

All these tremendous facts have led the subjugated peoples of Europe to lift up their heads again in hope. They have put aside forever the shameful temptation of resigning themselves to the conqueror's will. Hope has returned to the hearts of scores of millions of men and women, and with the hope there burns the flame of anger against the brutal, corrupt invader. And still more fiercely burn the fires of hatred and contempt for the filthy QUISLINGS whom he had suborned. [Applause]
[Norwegian leader who supported Nazis whose name is synonymous in the English language for being a traitor to your country.]
In a dozen famous ancient states, now prostrate under the Nazi yoke, the masses of the people, all classes and creeds, await the hour of liberation when they too will once again be able to play their part and strike their blows like men. That hour will strike. And its solemn peal will proclaim that night is past and that the dawn has come.[Applause]
The onslaught upon us, so long and so secretly planned by Japan, has presented both our countries with grievous problems for which we could not be fully prepared. If people ask me, as they have a right to ask me in England, "Why is it that you have not got an ample equipment of modern aircraft and army weapons of all kinds in Malaya and in the East Indies?" I can only point to the victory General Auchinleck has gained in the Libyan campaign. Had we diverted and dispersed our gradually growing resources between Libya and Malaya, we should have been found wanting in both theaters.
If the United States was found at a disadvantage at various points in the Pacific Ocean, we know well that that is to no small extent because of the aid which you have been giving to us in munitions for the defense of the British Isles and for the Libyan campaign, and above all because of your help in the Battle of the Atlantic, upon which all depends and which has in consequences been successfully and prosperously maintained.
Of course, it would have been much better, I freely admit, if we had enough resources of all kinds to be at full strength at all threatened points. But considering how slowly and reluctantly we brought ourselves to large scale preparations, and how long these preparations take, we had no right to expect to be in such a fortunate position.
The choice of how to dispose of our hitherto limited resources had to be made by Britain in time of war, and by the United States in time of peace. And I believe that history will pronounce that upon the whole, and it is upon the whole that these matters must be judged, that the choice made was right. Now that we are together, now that we are linked in a righteous comrade-ship of arms, now that our two considerable nations, each in perfect unity, have joined all their life-energies in a common resolve-a new scene opens upon which a steady light will glow and brighten. [Applause]
Many people have been astonished that Japan should in a single day have plunged into war against the United States and the British Empire. We all wonder why, if this dark design with its laborious and intricate preparations had been so long filling their secret minds, they did not choose our moment of weakness eighteen months ago. Viewed quite dispassionately, in spite of the losses we have suffered and the further punishment we shall have to take, it certainly appears an

irrational act. It is of course only prudent to assume that they have made very careful calculations and think they see their way through. Nevertheless, there may be another explanation.

WHAT KIND OF PEOPLE DO THEY THINK WE ARE?

We know that for many years past the policy of Japan has been dominated by secret societies of subalterns and junior officers of the army and the navy, who have enforced their will upon successive Japanese cabinets and parliaments by assassination of any Japanese statesman who opposed or who did not sufficiently further their aggressive policy. It may be that these societies, dazzled and dizzied with their own schemes of aggression and the prospect of early victories, have forced their country-against its better judgment-into war.They have embarked upon a very considerable undertaking.

After the outrages they have committed upon us at Pearl Harbor, in the Pacific Islands, in the Philippines, in Malaya and the Dutch East Indies, they must now know that the stakes for which they have decided to play are mortal. When we look at the resources of the United States and the British Empire compared to those of Japan; when we remember those in China, which have so long valiantly withstood invasion and tyranny and when also we observe the Russian menace which hangs over Japan-it becomes still more difficult to reconcile Japanese action with prudence or even with sanity. What kind of a people do they think we are? Is it possible that they do not realize that we shall never cease to persevere against them until they have been taught a lesson which they and the world will never forget?   [Loud applause]

Members of the Senate, and members of the House of Representatives, I will turn for one moment more from the turmoil and convulsions of the present to the broader spaces of the future. Here we are together, facing a group of mighty foes who seek our ruin. Here we are together, defending all that to free men is dear. Twice in a single generation the catastrophe of world war has fallen upon us. Twice in our lifetime has the long arm of fate reached out across the oceans to bring the United States into the forefront of the battle.   [Loud applause]

If we had kept together after the last war, if we had taken common measures for our safety, this renewal of the curse need never have fallen upon us. Do we not owe it to ourselves, to our children, to tormented mankind, to make sure that these catastrophes do not engulf us for the third time?

It has been proved that pestilences may break out in the Old World which carry their destructive ravages into the New World, from which, once they are afoot, the New World can not escape. Duty and prudence alike command first that the germ-centers of hatred and revenge should be constantly and vigilantly served and treated in good time, and that an adequate organization should be set up to make sure that the pestilence can be controlled at its earliest beginnings, before it spreads and rages throughout the world.

Five or six years ago it would have been easy, without shedding a drop of blood, for the United States and Great Britain to have insisted on the fulfillment of the disarmament clauses of the treaties which Germany signed after the Great War. And that also would have been the opportunity for assuring to the Germans those materials-those raw materials-which we declared in the Atlantic Charter should not be denied to any nation, victor or vanquished. The chance has passed, it is gone. Prodigious hammer-strokes have been needed to bring us together today.

WE WILL WALK IN MAJESTY AND IN JUSTICE AND IN PEACE AGAIN

If you will allow me to use other language, I will say that he must indeed have a blind soul who cannot see that some great purpose and design is being worked out here below of which we have the honor to be the faithful servants. it is not given to us to peer into the mysteries of the future. Still, I avow my hope and faith, sure and inviolate, that in the days to come the British and American peoples will, for their own safety and for the good of all, WALK TOGETHER IN MAJESTY, IN JUSTICE AND IN PEACE." [Applause]

NATIONAL CHURCHILL MUSEUM

Watch the speech on U Tube. It has many moments of applause. It also highlights Prime Minister Churchill's smoker's cough from Cuban cigars.

SECRET FACT: Allegedly, when Churchill was sick or out of the country three of his radio broadcasts were impersonated by actor NORMAN SHELLEY who was the radio voice of the WINNIE-THE-POOH bear! The Winnie-the-Pooh radio character gave British children joy during the darkest days of the Battle of Britain bombing raids by the Nazi Luftwaffe.

Hitler's radio propaganda speeches reached the psyche of millions of Germans motivating their patriotism and pride after the retributive Versailles Treaty by the understandably vengeful Great Britain and France after the horrific Great War casualties. Where was Christian forgiveness? Jesus Gospel proclaims: 'Love thy enemies and do not hate." Why? Hatred hardens your hearth, a victory for Satan.

President Franklin D. Roosevelt gave many radio "FIRESIDE CHATS" which were patriotic and morale building stories especially in the early dark days after Pearl Harbor and initial defeats and surrenders. Roosevelt would highlight our victories. This was before television and 7/24 cable news. Sometimes he would SCOOP newspapers.

Churchill's Christmas Message to Americans

December 24, 1941

"I spend this anniversary and festival far from my country, far from my family, yet I cannot truthfully say that I feel far from home. Whether it be ties of blood on my mother's side, or the friendship I have developed here over many years of active life, or the commanding sentiment of comradeship in the common cause of great peoples who speak the same language, who kneel at the same altars and, to a very large extent, pursue the same ideals, I cannot feel myself a stranger here in the centre and at the summit of the United States. I feel a sense of unity and fraternal association which, added to the kindness of your welcome, convinces me that I have a right to sit at your fireside and share your Christmas joys.

This a strange Christmas Eve. Almost the whole world is locked in deadly struggle, and, with the most terrible weapons which science can devise, the nations advance upon each other. Ill would it be for us this Christmastide if we were not sure that no greed for the land or wealth of any other people, no vulgar ambition, no morbid lust for material gain at the expense of others, had led us to the field. Here, in the midst of war, raging and roaring over all the lands and seas, creeping nearer to our hearts and homes, here, amid all the tumult, we have tonight the peace of the spirit in each cottage home and in every generous heart. Therefore we may cast aside for this night at least the cares and dangers which beset us, and make for the children an evening of happiness in a world of storm. Here, then, for one night only, each home throughout the English-speaking world should be a brightly-lighted island of happiness and peace.

Let the children have their night of fun and laughter. Let the gifts of Father Christmas delight their play. Let us grown-ups share to the full in their unstinted pleasures before we turn again to the stern task and formidable years that lie before us, resolved that, by our sacrifice and daring, the same children shall not be robbed of the inheritance or denied their right to live in a free and decent world.
And so, in God's mercy, a happy Christmas to you all."

Churchill made Honorary Citizen of the United States

WHEREAS Sir Winston Churchill, a son of America though a subject of Britain, has been throughout his life a firm and steadfast friend of the American people and the American nation; and
WHEREAS he has freely offered his hand and his faith in days of adversity as well as triumph; and
WHEREAS his bravery, charity and valor, both in war and in peace, have been a flame of inspiration in freedom's darkest hour; and
WHEREAS his life has shown that no adversary can overcome, and no feat can deter, free men in the defense of their freedom; and
WHEREAS he has by his art as an historian and his judgment as a statesman made th past the servant of the future;

NOW, THEREFORE, I JOHN F. KENNEDY, President of the United States of America, under the authority contained in an Act of the 88th Congress, do hereby declare Sir Winston Churchill an honorary citizen of the United States of America.
IN WITNESS WHEREOF, I have here unto set my hand and caused the Seal of the United States of America to be affixed.
DONE at the City of Washington this ninth day of April, in the year of our Lord nineteen hundred and sixty-three, and the Independence of the United States of America the one hundred and eighty-seventh.

JOHN FITZGERALD KENNEDY   The White House, Washington, D.C., April 9, 1963
President John F. Kennedy said:

"We meet in honor a man whose honor requires no meeting - for he is the most honored man to walk the stage of human history in the time in which we live. Whenever and wherever tyranny threatened, he has always championed liberty. Facing firmly toward the future, he has never forgotten the past. Serving six monarchs of his native Great Britain, he has served all men's freedom and dignity. In the dark days and darker nights when Britain stood alone - and most men save Englishmen despaired of England's life - he mobilized the English language and sent it into battle. The incandescent quality of his words illuminated the courage of his countrymen. Given unlimited power by his citizens, he was ever vigilant to protect their rights. Indifferent himself to danger, he wept over the sorrows of others. A child of the House of Commons, he became in time its father. Accustomed to the hardships of battle, he has no distaste for pleasure. Now his stately Ship of Life. having weathered the severest storms of a troubled century, is anchored in tranquil waters, proof that COURAGE AND FAITH and the zest for FREEDOM are truly indestructible. The record of his triumphant passage will inspire free hearts for all time.

By adding his name to our rolls, we mean to honor him-but his acceptance honors us far more. For no statement or proclamation can enrich his name — the name Sir Winston Churchill is already legend."

Churchill's Son Accepts His Father's Honorary Award

Sir Winston's reply read by his son Randolph on the 9th April at the White House.

Mr. President, I have been informed by Mr. David Bruce that it is your intention to sign a Bill conferring upon me Honorary Citizenship of the United States. I have received many kindnesses from the United States of America, but the honor which you now accord me is without parallel. I accept it with deep gratitude and affection. I am also most sensible of the warm-hearted action of the individual States who accorded me the great compliment of their own honorary citizenships as a prelude to this Act of Congress. It is a remarkable comment on our affairs that the former Prime Minister of a great sovereign state should thus be received as an honorary citizen of another. I say "great sovereign state" with design and emphasis, for I reject the view that Britain and the Commonwealth should now be relegated to tame and minor role in the world. Our past is the key to our future, which I firmly trust and believe will be no less fertile and glorious.

CHURCHILL BORN HALF AMERICAN HIS MOTHER

"Let no man underrate our energies, our potentialities and our abiding power for good.

I am as you know, half American by blood, and the story of my association with this mighty and benevolent nation goes back nearly ninety years to the day of my father's marriage. In this century of storm and tragedy I contemplate with high satisfaction the constant factor of the interwoven and upward progress of our peoples. Our comradeship and our brotherhood in war were unexampled. We stood together, and because of that fact the free world now stands. Nor has our partnership any exclusive nature: the Atlantic community is a dream that can well be fulfilled to the detriment of none and to the enduring benefit and honor of the great democracies."   Winston Churchill

THEME OF UNITY ENGLISH-SPEAKING PEOPLES

Mr. President, your action illuminates the theme of unity of the English-speaking peoples, to which I have devoted a large part of my life. I would ask to accept yourself, and to convey to both Houses of Congress, and through them to the American people, my solemn and heartfelt thanks for the unique distinction, which will always be proudly remembered by my descendants."

Churchill's IRON CURTAIN Speech

Westminster College Fulton, Missouri March 5, 1946

"From Stettin [East Germany] in the Baltic to Trieste in the Adriatic an "Iron Curtain" has descended across the continent. Behind that line lie all the capitals of the ancient states of Central and Eastern Europe. Warsaw, Berlin, Prague, Vienna, Budapest, Belgrade, Bucharest and Sofia; all these famous cities and the populations around them lie in what I must call the Soviet [Union] sphere, and all are subject, in one form or another, not only to Soviet influence but to a very high and in some cases increasing measure of control from Moscow."

"Churchill's geographical description of the Iron Curtain was ambiguous as to which side of the Iron Curtain the Soviet occupation zones of Germany and Austria were on — Churchill described Berlin and Vienna, then divided into American, British, French and Soviet occupation zones but also surrounded by their countries' respective Soviet zones, as being "in the Soviet sphere." But Churchill also defined the Baltic terminus of the Iron Curtain as being Stettin, which is on the Oder-Neisse Line, thus implying the Iron Curtain to run along the revised Polish-German border as opposed to the border between the British and Soviet occupation zones in Germany. Had Churchill wanted to imply the Soviet Zone in Germany to be the eastern side of the Iron Curtain, he should have named Luebeck in place of Stettin. In any event, at the time of Churchill's speech the re-establishment of Austrian and German states with the latter encompassing Germany's pre-1938 territories west of the Oder-Neisse line was assured to be part of an inevitable final peace settlement."

Western Public Still Saw Russians As Our Allies

"Much of the Western public still regarded the Soviet Union as a close ally in the context of the recent defeat of Nazi Germany and of Japan. Although not well received at the time, the phrase iron curtain gained popularity as a shorthand reference to the division of Europe as the Cold War strengthened. The Iron Curtain served to keep people in and information out, and people throughout the West eventually came to accept and use the metaphor."   Wikipedia

"Churchill's "SINEWS OF PEACE" address was to strongly criticize the Soviet Union's exclusive and secretive tension policies along with the Eastern Europe's state form, Police State (Polizeistaat). He expressed the Allied Nations' distrust of the Soviet Union after World War II. In the same year September, US-Soviet Union cooperation line collapsed due to the disavowal of the Soviet Union's opinion on the German problem in the Stuttgart Council, and then followed the U. S. President Harry S Truman's announcement of enactment of hard anti-Soviet Union, anticommunism line policy. Since then, this phrase became popular and was widely used as anti-Soviet Union propaganda term in the Western countries."   Wikipedia

"In addition, Churchill mentioned in his speech that regions under the Soviet Union's control were expanding their leverage and power without any restriction. He asserted that in order to put a brake on this ongoing phenomenon, the commanding force of the strong unity between the UK and the U.S. was necessary."   Wikipedia

"Stalin took note of Churchill's speech and responded in Pravda [newspaper "Truth"] soon afterward. He accused Churchill of warmongering, and defended Soviet "friendship" with Eastern European states as a necessary safeguard against another invasion. He further accused Churchill of hoping to install right-wing governments in eastern Europe with the goal of agitating those states against the Soviet Union."   Wiki

The Soviet Union annexed; Estonia, Latvia and Lithuania as Soviet Socialist Republics within the Union of Soviet Socialists Republics. Germany effectively gave Moscow a free hand in much of these territories in the Molotov-Ribbentrop Pact of August 23, 1939

The Nazis and Soviet Union invaded Poland on Sept. 1, 1939, and divided along the Oder River as agreed. Eastern Poland was annexed into the Ukrainian and Byelorussian SSRs, part of eastern Finland became the Karelo-Finnish SSR, northern Romania became the Moldavian SSR, Kalingrad Oblast the northern part of East Prussia was annexed in 1945. Between 1945 and 1949 the Soviets converted the following areas into Soviet satellite states: German Democratic Republic, People's Republic of Bulgaria, Hungarian People's Republic, Czechoslovak Socialist Republic, People's Republic of Romania, People's Socialist Republic of Albania (which re-aligned itself in the 1960s away from the Soviet Union and towards the [Maoist] People's Republic of China.)"   Wikipedia

Soviet-installed governments ruled the Eastern Bloc countries, with the exception of the Socialist Federal Republic of Yugoslavia, which returned its full independence. [Marshal Tito, Joseph Broz, was its dictator who keep its unity. Today, Yugoslavia has separated into its Great War, World War I, countries after Eastern Orthodox and Muslim conflict which date to the medieval conflicts with the Ottoman Empire Turkish conquests and atrocities. Vlad the Impaler was an equally brutal and ruthless opponent. The last Dracula Hollywood film depicts how his father gives him to the Muslims as a tribute?]

[Yugoslavia had the largest per cent of its population killed in World War II. The Communists fought the Royalists under Mikalovich and also fought the Nazis. The only non Aryan (Nordic) SS unit was comprised of Bosnian Muslim mountain soldiers.

The Marshall Plan Rebuilds War Devastated Europe

"In a 5 June 1947 speech, [General George Marshall as Secretary of State] announced a comprehensive program of American assistance to all European countries wanting to participate, including the Soviet Union and those of Eastern Europe, called the Marshall Plan. Stalin opposed the Marshall Plan. He built up the Eastern Bloc protective belt of Soviet controlled nations on the Western border, and wanted to maintain this buffer zone of states combined with a weakened Germany under Soviet control. Fearing American political, cultural and economic penetration., Stalin eventually forbade Eastern bloc countries of the newly formed Cominform from accepting Marshall Plan aid. In Czechoslovakia, that required a Soviet-backed Czechoslovak coup d'etat of 1948, the brutality of which shocked Western powers more than any event so far and set in a motion a brief scare that war would occur and swept away the last vestiges of opposition to the Marshall Plan in the United States Congress.   Wikipedia

Stalin's Treaty with Hitler a Bargain of Two Devils

"Relations further deteriorated when, in January 1948, the U.S. State Department also published a collection of documents titled nazi-SOVIET RELATIONS, 1939 - 1941: Documents from the Archives of the German Foreign office, which contained documents recovered from the foreign Office of Nazi Germany revealing Soviet conversations with Germany regarding the Molotov-Ribbentrop Pact, including its secret protocol dividing eastern Europe, the 1939 German-Soviet commercial agreement, and discussions of the Soviet Union potentially becoming the FOURTH

AXIS POWER. In response, one month later, the Soviet Union published falsifiers of History, a Stalin-edited and partially rewritten book attacking the West. Wikipedia

HOLLYWOOD CONNECTION: In the movie THE WAY WE WERE (1974) BARBRA STEISAND, a Communist protestor, at UNION COLLEGE in Schenectady is disturbed when she learns Communist STALIN has made a peace pact with Fascist HITLER. ROBERT REDFORD was Barbra's husband. My fiancé and I saw the movie twice.
PERSONAL STORY: Union College is where I took my college SAT test in 1959 in Schenectady, is also a sister city to my Dutch relatives home Nijkerk, Holland. My dad went to 8th AF meetings at Schenectady airport and met in a "GE" building where they built some of the equipment for his H2X top secret bombing radar. One of the Memphis Belle crewman attended their meetings. My dad also worked on Proctor theater organ.

HITLER, STALIN, AND THE PACT FROM HELL

THE DEVILS' ALLIANCE—HITLER'S PACT WITH STALIN 1939-1941
Roger Moorhouse Historical Book Club review

"History remembers the SOVIETS and the NAZIS as bitter enemies, yet for nearly a third of World War II's timespan, HITLER and STALIN Germans and Soviets stood as partners. In the 'Devils' Alliance," Roger Moorhouse explores the causes and staggering impact of the Nazi-Soviet non-aggression   treaty."
"Together, the Germans and Soviets quickly conquered and divided central and eastern Europe, and the human cost was staggering. Fortunately for the Allies, the partnership soured, resulting in the surprise June 1941 German invasion of the Soviet Union—but ironically it made possible a far more bloody and protracted war than would have otherwise been conceivable. The Devil's Alliance is the most authoritative history of World War II's most nefarious collaboration."
"Though it ended in 1941, the pact would have a curious afterlife. Torn up by the Nazis and excused by the Soviets as a strategic necessity, its effects persisted long after its death. Indeed, the map of eastern and central Europe that we see today is largely its product: the boundaries hastily drawn by RIBBENTROP and MOLOTOV have proved remarkably durable. More immediately, two generations of LITHUANIANS, LATVIANS and ESTONIANS would endure life within the hated USSR, and bitter memories of the Soviet annexation and occupation of 1940-41 would fuel post-war resistance movements. Poetically, it would be the protests in the Baltic states on the 50th anniversary of the pact's signature in 1989 that would precede the USSR's dissolution.
"With the Devil's Alliance Roger Moorhouse has achieved what historians dream of. He has taken a negative facet of Second World War history—the unnatural and short-lived "marriage" between Europe's worst 20th century tyrants, Hitler and Stalin—and demonstrated that it was one of that century's crucial defining events."
ROGER MOORHOUSE—is the award-winning author of BERLIN AT WAR and KILLING HITLER: THE PLOTS, THE ASSASSINS, and the DICTATOR WHO CHEATED DEATH.

The Berlin Airlift Saves Germany Defeats Stalin

"After the Marshall plan, the introduction of a new currency to Western Germany to replace the debased Reichsmark and massive electoral losses for communist parties, in June 1948, the Soviet Union cut off surface road access to Berlin, initiating the BERLIN BLOCKADE, which cut off all non-Soviet food, water and other supplies for the citizens of the non-Soviet sectors of Berlin.

Because Berlin was located within the Soviet-occupied zone of Germany, the only available methods of supplying the city were three limited air corridors. A massive aerial supply campaign was initiated by the United State, Britain, France and other countries, the success of which caused the Soviets to lift their blockade in May 1949."   Wikipedia

The Bible on When War is Justifiable, Part 2

Capitol Ministries Ralph Drollinger founder-president May 15, 2018

"It raises the question that as our culture quickly jettisons its Judeo-Christian bases, will we continue to be informed and guided by The Just War Theory and The Four Principles of Fighting A War? You are leading the United States at a time when the world is filled with violence, aggression and conflict, and some nations are even attacking their own innocent civilian citizens. As you make decisions about when to engage in conflict or war, learning what Scripture has to say about the principles of war is critically important."

WE DISCOVERED IN THE FIRST BIBLE STUDY ON WAR THAT GOD IS
NOT NECESSARILY OPPOSED TO WAR RATHER, THE QUESTION
ONE SHOULD BE ASKING IS:
WHEN IS WAR JUSTIFIED?
THE MOTIVE OF WAR SHOULD ALWAYS BE THE DESIRE FOR
RESTORATION NOT ANNIHILATION

"This is similar in principle to what we as parents have in view when we punish our children—an oft necessity in a fallen world."

"In summary, these are the four biblically based inviolate and measured principles for fighting a war that is at first justifiable. Fortunately and historically, American culture of war has largely been informed by these principles and our nation has emulated these values in its use of force. However, we should not assume that will always be the case. As our culture is bent on jettisoning its Judeo-Christian bases, it is reasonable to expect that we will not continue to be informed and guided by The Just War Theory and The Four Principles of Fighting A War. Ideology and outward actions are intrinsically intertwined; one follows the other. Accordingly, teaching what Scripture has to say about these principles to lawmaker's is critically important."

THE PACIFIST POSITION

"A minority view opposed to the Just War Theory is Military Pacifism. This view believes it is always wrong to use military force and that believers should claim a conscientious objection if drafted into the military. Pacifists believe that violence is always wrong."

[Read my personal story about Private Desmond Doss the first conscientious objector to be awarded the Presidential Medal of Honor for his incredibly brave rescue under fire of 75 wounded soldiers as an unarmed medic.]

SUMMARY

"Secular Humanists, who believe man is basically good, have a resulting ideological problem with war. They believe all problems can be solved intelligently by appealing to reason. The Christian worldwide stands in sharp contradiction: man is fallen and has a propensity toward evil. It follows that war is necessary at times: God sends His people to war in Scripture. If God advocates war at times, it follows that He insists on the guidelines outlined in this study for the justification of going to war and fighting a war. It follows too that the pacifist and noninterventionist viewpoints are biblically unfounded, and portray a theological naïveté relative to the grave and serious ongoing implications of the FALL"

The Bible on When War is Justifiable, Part 1

Capitol Ministries founder-president Ralph Drollinger May 8, 2018
Victory in Europe VE DAY May 8, 1945

"If Jesus calls us to be "peacemakers" then how could a Christian Cabinet member or Congressman support the idea of going to war?
"The short answer is this: "Blessed are the peacemakers" is one of Jesus' beatitudes relative to how believers ought to conduct their personal lives (Matthew 5;9). But there is a distinction to be made between Jesus' instruction regarding personal behavior and the responsibilities He sets forth relative to His ordination of the institution of government (Romans 13:1-8 and 1 Peter 2:13-14) that Christian members are called to serve."

WHEN IS GOING TO WAR JUSTIFIABLE IN GOD'S EYES?

"Certainly the ancient practice of conquest and plundering another nation for the sake of gaining their wealth and new slaves is not a justifiable cause for war. So then what is? What are the specific earmarks that can help us to ascertain the justifiable and unjustifiable use of war in the eyes of God?"

SUMMARY OF THE JUST WAR THEORY
"Winston Churchill, when faced with the inevitability of engaging Nazi Germany worked through and fulfilled all the above criteria with Parliament. In entering the war, he personally emulated this ensuing right spirit and resolve—what necessarily must follow when justifiably and righteously a nation enters a war. In his address to Parliament in 1940 he said,
"Let us therefore brace ourselves to do our duty, and so bear ourselves that, if the British Commonwealth and its Empire lasts for a thousand years, men will still say, "This was their finest hour." And what is our aim?…Victory, victory at all costs, victory in spite of all terror, victory, however long and hard the road may be; for without victory, there is no survival."
"Churchill serves as an executive model for properly leading a nation into war. When war is justified and righteous, a country's leadership should never enter into it with "low testosterone." It is an all or nothing commitment of the totality of the nation in its decisive quest for all out victory as quickly as possible!"

Five Wrong Views Part 3: All Governments are Evil and Demonic

Ralph Drollinger founder-president Capitol Ministries July 17, 2018

PACIFISM IS NOWHERE TAUGHT IN THE BIBLE

"The world is fallen, mankind is depraved, and sin is rampant (especially when government enforcement is weak). Strong police forces and militaries are necessary as a result. Such fosters civility. Importantly, this next point will help to institutionally contextualize the aforementioned passages."

SUMMARY

"The "All Governments are Evil" understanding of the State encourages believers to oppose the use of governmental force to quell evil. This is antithetical to the Bible's clear teaching in Romans 13 and 1 Peter 2 wherein Government wields God's authority to use the sword with justice. The picture of Neville Chamberlain investing endless hours negotiating with Hitler comes to mind, as well as a defenseless Dalai Lama in the hands of an aggressive China. Do not our present-day problems with North Korea and Iran stem from an encroaching pacifism in need of immediate correction? We must think biblically here. No longer should we tolerate unbiblical pacifist thinking. One shudders to think what would happen worldwide if America continued in a pacifist direction.

Five Wrong Views Part 5: Understanding the Separation of Church and State

Capitol Ministries founder-president Ralph Drollinger July 31, 2018

"The Bible clearly teaches that today, there is to be an institutional separation and State. To think otherwise is to believe in a theocratic or sacerdotal form of Government. What the Bible does not teach—and what the secularist would like to say the U.S. Constitution supports—is an influential separation of Church and State. Clearly, however, such thinking is not supported in the Constitution or the Scriptures."

"Render unto Caesar" represents one of the biblical passages that supports the idea of institutional separation. Let us examine this more closely from a historical perspective."

"As primitive Christianity began as recorded in the book of Acts, the separation of the Church from the State of Rome clearly existed. It was not until the fourth century A.D., when Constantine co-opted Christianity as the State religion (in an attempt to unify the vast and diverse Roman Empire), that the clearly, previously existing, separation between the two institutions disappeared. Tragically, this lack of separation occurs even during the Post-Reformation period. LUTHER, ZWINGLI and CALVIN practiced a sacerdotal societal structure, versus a composite one per the clear teaching of the NT (cf. Matthew 20:20-22). Romans 13:1-8;1 Peter 2:13-14). In that much of the reformer's emphasis on doctrinal correction of heresy related to soteriology (the doctrine of Salvation) no surgical exercise was performed relative to the aberrant earlier wedding of Church and State."

"NO TIME To Go WOBBLY!"

Dr. James Dobson's Family Talk August 2018 Newsletter

"I would like to tell you about an experience Shirley and I had while visiting the cultural centers of Europe about 20 years ago. One of the cities we toured was Berlin, Germany. I have been fascinated since I was a child with World War II and what made the adults around me so fearful. I have wondered in the ensuing years how highly educated and intelligent Germans could have been so corrupted and deceived by the propaganda that lay the foundation for tyranny. It is still difficult to comprehend how so many Christian churches with their good people fell prey to the lies screamed by ADOLF HITLER and his evil cohorts. Even before he revealed his murderous intentions, they stood with their arms and hands extended, cheering rabidly for a man who was to become one of the most ruthless dictators in world history."

A WALK INTO HITLER'S HISTORY OF HATRED

"I searched for an understanding of the processes that led to torchlight parades, book burning, racial hatred, mass killings of Jews, Gypsies, Poles, homosexuals, and pitifully disabled and mentally ill people. While most Germans didn't know about the extermination camps, the majority favored his preparations for war. Many books have been written on that subject, but I needed to see it for myself. I found an explanation, at least partially, on the streets of Berlin."

WORLD WAR II HISTORY TOUR OF BERLIN

"One morning, I paid a small fee to be included in a "walk-about" tour of the important buildings and sites from the Nazi era. An articulate professor led our group and recounted what happened before and during the war. I was taking notes furiously as he spoke. First, we stood outside HERMAN GORING's headquarters. He was second in command after Hitler. Then we walked past GOEBBEL's propaganda ministry from which he spread lies and "fake news" during the 1930s and 1940s. Our group then stopped outside GESTAPO headquarters where so many people were tortured and murdered for daring to oppose the regime. Demons seemed to leer from the windows and rooftops. The tour ended at the parking lot that now sits over the bunker where Hitler spent his last days and eventually committed suicide with his wife of less than 40 hours, EVA BRAUN. Most of the city was demolished by Allied bombing, but these historic locations remain intact because they were reinforced by steel and concrete."

"The tour lasted two hours, during which I learned how the Nazis managed to enslave the German people and then molded them into a force that devastated and conquered almost every country of Europe. Millions of people around the world held their breath as destiny hung in the balance."

"Our Republic and Its Press Will Rise and Fall Together." Joseph Pulitzer

'What the professor told us remains in my memory today. He said the Nazi success was made possible by one primary factor. It was their complete and utter control of the means of communication. There was no Internet or television at the time, of course, but what did exist reached every dimension of the nation. Radio was highly effective in those days, as were newspapers, films, speeches, books and magazines, posters, rallies, and yes, public schools and universities. Every word spoken in Germany was scrutinized, and those who rejected Nazi lies publicly were often murdered or sent to concentration camps from which most didn't return. Terror was the stock and trade of the Gestapo. It was a common occurrence for secret police to knock on the doors of anyone who didn't conform to the party line. An offender would be dragged outside and shot, leaving terrifying images and warnings for the neighbors to see. It told them what would happen if they also got out of line. Even children were urged to report the activities and private conversations of their parents who talked at home about their opposition to the gangsters in government. They were tortured or murdered too. What a ghastly period in human history."

"Speaking of children, one of the most wretched elements of the dictatorship was the complete domination of public schools. Parents had no influence on how their boys and girls were educated. In fact, all schools became training centers for Nazi propaganda. The boys were prepared for war, and girls in their mid-teens were actually sent to camps where they were expected to get pregnant from sexual contact with nearby boys. Babies born out of wedlock from these encounters became wards of the state to replace men likely to be killed in action." [Read my Nazis LEBENSBORN program]"

"Here's how Adolf Hitler viewed public school. He said, "Your child belongs to us already…what are you? You will pass on. Your descendants, however, now stand in the new camp in a short time, they will know nothing but this new community." Later, as war approached, Hitler said, "This new Reich will give its youth to no one.""

"If you want to know more about this tragic era, read THE RISE AND FALL OF THE THIRD REICH, by WILLIAM SHIRER."

WHY AM I RECALLING THESE BITTER MEMORIES?

"This historical account is relevant today because America and other Western nations have for decades been losing their God-given rights that define us as a free people. We are not experiencing Nazi-like tyranny yet, but we are steadily being expected to think, speak, write, and act in a prescribed manner in conformity with what is now called "political correctness." The mainstream media has become a tool to influence elections and spread this belief system. Sadly, the rights handed down to us by our forefathers more than 200 years ago are gradually being overridden, ignored, contradicted, or disregarded by the courts and legislatures. Alas, we are less free now than we were even five years ago."

"As I hope you learned in school, although it is unlikely, the principles on which our freedom was built are spelled out in the first ten amendments to our Constitution. They are called the BILL OF RIGHTS. The first among them addresses the most important guarantee. It promises religious liberty and include these words: "Congress shall make no law respecting the establishment of religion or prohibiting the free exercise thereof." Despite what you may have heard, nothing within the Constitution mentions the separation of church and state. To paraphrase the First Amendment, it not only offers an ironclad guarantee that we will enjoy freedom of religion, but also promises freedom of speech, a free press, protects the rights of the people to ASSEMBLE PEACEFULLY and to PETITION the government when citizens are aggrieved. These rights are fundamental for a liberated people."

"The other nine amendments within the Bill of Rights enumerate additional assurances to the people that their government will have restricted authority over them. ALEXANDER HAMILTON wrote the FEDERALIST PAPER 84 that the Constitution tells Congress what limited powers it has to make law, and the Bill of Rights reiterates to Congress what powers it does not have to infringe on our rights."

"Reflecting this affirmation, ABRAHAM LINCOLN said in his GETTYSBURG ADDRESS that ours is a government "OF THE PEOPLE, BY THE PEOPLE, AND FOR THE PEOPLE." These assurances are precious to us today, and I thank God for the dedicated men who inspired and fought for them. We dare not be officious justices, judges, legislators, or politicians take even one of them away from us. But some liberals today are diligently trying to do just that. We must stop them, but how? Our rights are being trampled every day. The only way to defend our liberties is at the ballot box."

"Unfortunately, more than half of Americans, including the majority of Christians, don't even bother to vote. Shame on them all. Don't they know that tyranny for us and our children is only one generation, or even one election, away? We must vote, vote, vote to elect leaders who defend what has been purchased with the blood of patriots who died to protect our liberty. We owe it to the memory of their sacrifice to preserve what they did for us. We must not fritter it away on our watch. If any politician tells you he will "fundamentally change" this nation, what he means is that he plans to undermine our Constitution and take away our heritage of freedom. Run from him or her."

"Let me illustrate what can happen in a country that doesn't respect basic human rights as they have been understood historically. The Parliament of Canada, our neighbor to the north, passed an act into law on June 19, 2017. It is called the Transgender Rights Bill, and it imposed jail time and fines on anyone who uses inappropriate pronouns with regard to gender identity, gender expression, race, national or ethnic origin, color, religion, age, sex, sexual orientation, marital status, family status, genetic characteristics, disability or conviction of an offense for which a pardon has been granted. Forget laws protecting freedom of speech. Violations of this act are considered to be hate crimes in Canada's Criminal Code. Its passage has been lauded by Prime Minister Justin Trudeau as "another step toward equality." No! It is a step toward tyranny for our Canadian friends."

"So much for free speech and thought. How about here in America? In my lifetime. I have witnessed the steady erosion of the principles that made this country great. Here are a few examples of what the judiciary that became the law of the land has done, or attempted to do, in this great land of the free."

"The Ninth Circuit Court of Appeals in California has done more to unhinge liberty than any other court. Some call it "The Ninth Circus." In 2015, for example, it upheld an outrageous legislative measure that forced profile clinics, which are dedicated to the sanctity of human life, to promote abortions with their patients, and to place posters on the walls telling them where they can go to kill their babies. That became the law of the land in 9 Western states for 12 months."

"Thanks to President Trump's nomination and the Senate's subsequent confirmation of Neil Gorsuch to the Supreme Court, that ruling was overturned this past June by a vote of 5 to 4. How close the Court came to decimating freedom of speech in those clinics. So many other critical issues related to the Bill of Rights have been decided by a vote."

"Here's another in Obergefell v Hodges, 2015, the Supreme Court redefined marriage as it had been protected in law and celebrated internationally for more than 5,000 years. The decision was 5 to 4, and it eliminated the exclusivity of marriage between a man and a woman in 31 states. Five Justices imposed that cultural earthquake on America. Let me describe that ruling in another way, The laws protecting traditional marriage in 31 states had recently gone to their polling places and voted to define marriage as being exclusively between one man and one woman. By a single vote, an arrogant, imperious, unelected Justice and four colleagues on the Supreme Court overrode the will of the people and swept away collective decisions of the populous."

"These five unelected and imperious Justices imposed a cultural disaster on America. Some court-watchers say it was tantamount to the ROE v WADE decision in 1973, because it helped to undermine the institution of marriage. The family will never be the same. Lincoln's words at Gettysburg became hollow. Whatever happened to the promise that ours is a government of, by, and for the people? What hubris those pious Justices demonstrated with their votes."

"In my opinion, this next example stands as one of the most outrageous assaults on parental rights in American history. Children attending Mesquite Elementary School in Palmdale, California, came home one afternoon and told their parents what had happened to them in class. It was a shocker. One of the their teachers, with administrative approval, sat for hours with students, aged seven to ten, to ensure that each of them completed 79 items on a questionnaire. The kids, barely out of babyhood, were required to respond to highly personal questions about their private thoughts, including 10 items about their sexuality. Permission was neither requested nor discussed with parents. The children were asked about such topics as frequency of thinking about having sex, and thinking about touching other peoples' private parts, among many others."

"The parents were incensed, (wouldn't you be?) and filed suit in both federal and district courts against the school district for invading their children's privacy and the parents' rights to control the upbringing of their children. They were desperately trying to defend the innocence of their children, but to no avail.

The courts ruled that there is no fundamental right of parents to be the exclusive provider of information regarding sexuality or education of their children. Both the district and federal courts dismissed the case. One of them asserted that parents have to determine what their sons and daughters will be exposed to while enrolled in California's public schools."

"When the parents appealed their case it went (where else?) to the Ninth Circuit Court of Appeals in California. You can guess what happened there. The Judges upheld the lower court ruling in favor of the school district and concluded that education is not merely about teaching reading, writing, and arithmetic. Education, they said, serves higher civil and social functions, including the rearing of children into healthy and responsible adults. In other words. "Parents, get lost."

"I screamed to the high heavens when this ruling came down, but most residents in California yawned and accepted the invasion with a whisper. What a tragedy. I can envision the founding fathers rolling in their graves, and if they were alive today, thinking. "Is this what we fought the American Revolution for?"

"Time and space will not permit me to cite similar horrendous rulings from unelected and imperious judges. Instead, I am excited to end my letter with some encouraging news. For the first time since the courts began to run things in the 1960s, the judiciary is changing dramatically. It is true. Some good things are starting to happen."

"In June, the Court overturned a ruling against Jack Phillips, whose beliefs would not allow him to bake a wedding cake for homosexual activists. That assault on religious liberty failed by a 5 to 4 decision."

"You can understand why the far left is in a state of panic today. It is looking for anything on which to hang its opposition to Judge Kavanaugh. One of their criticisms is that while in college, he put ketchup on his pizza. Are you kidding me? Does anyone else see the evidences of desperation here?"

"So far, President Donald Trump has nominated 44 judges who have been confirmed to the bench, and there are many others (88) in the pipeline. There is hope for additional conservative and common-sense decisions to be handed down in the future. This is a matter for sincere prayer among those of us who longed for relief from judicial tyranny." "The newly established Dr. James Dobson Family Institute, which consists of Family Talk, the Policy Center, the Education Center, and the Digital Library, is working hard to defend righteousness and family values on the home front. We will continue to speak for those of you who agree. Ours can be a lonely vigil unless defenders of the Constitution, and particularly conservative Christians, stand shoulder to shoulder with us in this struggle. We and other conservative organizations are winning in the public square. This is no time to go wobbly."   James Dobson, PH.D —Founder and President Family

The Heart and Conscience Has Room Only for God

Missouri Synod Lutheran Witness Magazine
Congressional Hearing Testimony about Obamacare Abortion medication

On Feb. 16, 2012, the Rev. MATTHEW C. HARRISON, president of the LUTHERAN CHURCH— MISSOURI SYNOD was one of several witnesses to give testimony during the House Committee on Oversight and Governmental Reform's hearing:

LINES CROSSED: OF CHURCH AND STATE. HAS THE OBAMA ADMINISTRATION TRAMPLED ON FREEDOM AND RELIGION AND FREEDOM OF CONSCIENCE?

CHAIRMAN ISSA. I will note for the record that the witness swore or affirmed, depending on their faith. With that we go to Reverend Harrison.

US Congress Statement by Reverend Dr. Matthew C. Harrison

"Thank you, Mr. Chairman, it's a pleasure to be here. The Lutheran Church—Missouri Synod is a body of some 6,200 congregations and 2,300,000 members across the U.S. We don't distribute voter's lists. We don't have a Washington office. We are studiously non-partisan, so much so that we're often criticized for being quietistic.

I'd rather not be here, frankly our task is to proclaim, in the words of the blessed apostle St. John, the blood of Jesus Christ, God's Son, cleanses us from all our sin. And we care for the needy. We haven't the slightest intent to Christianize the government. MARTIN LUTHER famously quipped one time, "I'd rather have a smart Turk than a stupid Christian govern me!"

We confess that there are two realms, the church and the state. They shouldn't be mixed—the Church is governed by the Word of God, the State by natural law and reason, the Constitution. We have 1,300 early childhood centers, 10 colleges and universities, we are a machine which produces good citizens for this country and at tremendous personal cost.

We have the nation's only historic black Lutheran college in CONCORDIA SELMA. Many of our people [who are alive today] walked with DR. KING 50 years ago on the march from Selma to Montgomery. We put the first million dollars and have continued to provide finance for African Americans.

I'm here to express our deepest distress over the HHS provisions. We are religiously opposed to supporting abortion-causing drugs. That is, in part, why we maintain our own health plan. While we are grandfathered under the very narrow provisions of HHS policy, we are deeply concerned that our consciences may soon be martyred by a few strokes of the keyboard as this administration moves us all into a single-payer system. Our direct experience in the HOSANNA TABOR case with one of our congregations gives us no comfort that this administration will be concerned to guard our free-exercise of rights. We self-insure 50,000 people. We do it well, our workers make an average of $43,000 a year, 17,000 teachers make less, on average, Our health plan was preparing to take significant cost-saving measures, to be passed on to our workers, just as this health care legislation was passed. We elected not to make those changes, incur great cost, lest we fall out of the narrow provisions required under the grandfather clause. While we are opposed in principle, not to all forms of birth control, but only abortion-causing drugs, we stand with our friends in the Catholic Church and all others, Christians and non-Christians, under the free-exercise and conscience provisions of the United States Constitution.

Religious people determine what violates their consciences, not the federal government. The conscience is a sacred thing. Our church exists because overzealous governments in northern Europe made decisions which trampled the religious convictions of our forebears. I have ancestors who served in the Revolutionary War. I have ancestors who were in the Lewis and Clark expedition. I have ancestors in the War of 1812, who fought for the North in the Civil War. My 88 year old father-in-law has recounted to me, in tears many times, the horrors of the Battle of the Bulge. In fact BUD DAY, the most highly decorated veteran alive, is a member of the Lutheran Church-MS.

We fought for a free country in this country, and we won't give up without a fight. To paraphrase MARTIN LUTHER, the heart and conscience has room only for GOD, not for God and the Federal government. The bed is too narrow, the blanket is too short. We must obey God rather than men, and we will. Please get the federal government, Mr. Chairman, OUT OF OUR CONSCIENCES. Thank you."

CHAIRMAN ISSA. Thank you.   [Please view it on U Tube.]

Feb. 16, 2012

Chairman ISSA, Ranking Member Cummings, and other members of the committee:

"Thank you for your public service to our nation, and thank you for the opportunity to share our church's concerns regarding the recent federal mandate.

The Lutheran Church—Missouri Synod is apprehensive. Our church's history is rooted in religious liberty. Our Lutheran forefathers left Europe seeking religious freedom in America, and since their arrival in 1837, Missouri Synod Lutherans have rigorously guarded these beliefs and practices. We are unconditionally committed to preserving the essential teachings of our faith, to guard our religious rights, and to act as conscience dictates as informed by faith.

The recent federal mandate has prompted our church to voice public concern about federal intervention into religious beliefs and practices. Specifically, we object to the use of drugs and procedures used to take lives of unborn children. We oppose this mandate since it requires religious organizations to pay for and otherwise facilitate the use of such drugs by their employees—a requirement that violates our stand on the biblical teaching of the sanctity of life, which is a matter of faith and conscience.

Furthermore, we believe and teach that freedom of religion extends beyond mere houses of worship. We must be able to exercise our faith in the public square and, in response to Christ's call, demonstrate His mercy through our love and compassion for all people according to the clear teaching of Holy Scripture.

We deem this recent government mandate as an infringement upon the beliefs and practices of various religious communities. Therefore, we voice our public objections in solidarity with those who cherish their religious liberties. The decision by the U.S. Department of Health and Human Services to require virtually all health plans to comply with this mandate will have the effect of forcing many religious organizations to choose between following the letter of the law or operating within the framework of their religious tenets. We add our voice to the long list of those who have championed their God-given right to freely exercise their religious beliefs according to the dictates of their faith, and to provide compassionate care and clear Christian witness to society's most vulnerable, without government encroachment."

HISTORY FACT: The whole 178 page Congressional testimony is on the Internet. Members of the Catholic, Baptist, Jewish and Eastern Orthodox faiths also testified for the sanctity of life and how this was a violation of their faiths religious beliefs! Hitler's Germany and Stalin's Soviet Union and many other totalitarian governments today have enacted laws against religious and civil rights except for the elite oligarchs.

QUESTION? Where were Muslims and Mormons? A German "Aryan" blonde woman beheaded for abortion. Muslims and Mormons have large families no abortions.

PERSONAL STORY: My German mother Elisabeth Frank was a blonde Lutheran and saw how her most cultured nation became ruled by unChristian thugs who burned books and people in her hometown Frankfurt. This had been done before in Germany but the history books tried to erase these unChristian, or any other religions, sins. Today, after Charlottesville because of two evil groups a few neo-Nazis and KKK and a few ANTIFA, antifascist Communists thugs there was no "freedom of speech"! My mother told me as a child see saw the Nazis fighting atheist Communists in the streets of her hometown Frankfurt. She knew neither sides violence was right or good. The church looked at the Nazis as bringing "law and order" to Germany. That is an OXYMORON! The

Nazis majority won over the atheist Communists. Then the German people accepted an Apostate Christianity which is a greater Christian SIN OF NATIONAL PRIDE, over Jesus Word, than being an atheist non believer. Jesus was asked by His Disciples when He would return? He prophesied: I will return when the world follows false Christs and Messiahs and through Apostasy His church divides and brother will fight brother!" That is a paraphrase, but I have not heard that sermon in the thousands of "good" sermons I have heard in many denominations. I have written how the "tolerant" liberal secular humanist churches in Europe became Apostate and didn't believe in Jesus' Almighty judgment and in two Christian World Wars Europe was decimated. Previously, the Romans, northern pagans, Attila the Hun, the Mongols, the Black Plague, the Counter Reformation wars, mini ice age 1600-1800, and the Muslims in 732 AD and Ottoman Turks in the 1500s also almost succeeded in destroying Christianity. Europe will be Muslim in 50 years because they don't believe in abortion! In Genesis the Creator said, "Go forth and multiply!" Jehovah promised Abraham's children would be as numerous as the sands!" The Muslims believe in Genesis man's Creation and they know they are Abraham's descendants through Ishmael. Islam is tied for second largest religion with Hindu-Buddhism. So God was right.

I watched the whole Charlottesville TV event. I blame the media, the police for allowing men with black masks, like ISIS, to conceal their identity allowing violence. Governor McAuliffe made an interesting statement how demonstrators on both sides were 90% outsiders. The police should not have allowed any type of weapon or shield or spray. The FIRST AMENDMENT allows PEACEABLE ASSEMBLY and freedom of speech. The mayor said that the police department is independent from him. He is not a policeman, but is responsible for law and order. This turned into a national scandal, and internationall incident like ISIS. I consider both sides equal to external terrorists. I think this is an FBI case because of so many people crossing state borders. Haven't heard that maybe they are too busy? I know good people in the FBI and they aren't happy with the bad press about the Bureau. I personally think this was not incompetence but was a setup! The left wing media needed something to show how they are for freedom and civil rights. They were also looking for something to hold against President Trump. Governor MacAuliffe is a very close friend to the Clinton's. I think Hillary has been very quiet about this incident but must be happy with her news friends who can't believe she lost the election. The "Fake news" attacked President Trump for not saying something immediately! He was busy being President at his home signing a legislative bill for extending veterans benefits and allowing, them to go to civilian hospitals if needed for six month. I learned that on the Internet! TV news was to busy with action seens, that's their business to keep the viewers tuned in for commercials. Show me the money. My dad was an ABC TV Master Control room engineer from 1949-1983, 34 years. My dad saw history first hand and sent it nationwide. He meet many famous people who would visit the Control room with ABC's president Leonard Goldenson. After he retired my dad told me something I never forgot that statement but now really understand it. He said son, "I was a prostitute for 34 years!" Today, he would pull the plug on many of the shows. YOUR FIRED! HAPPY DAYS, MORK AND MINDY, DICK CAVETT, MONDAY NIGHT FOOTBALL with FRANK GIFFORD and HOWIE COSELL, ROONE ARLEDGE ABC SPORTS and THE OLYMPICS, THE LONE RANGER, SUPERMAN, WYATT EARP and the great DICK CLARK's AMERICAN BANDSTAND!

President Trump had to see the videos and make an analytical national comment. He detested the un American acts of the neo-Nazis, KKK and the new ANTIFA, Leninist anarchists. Why he didn't say Communists and relate that this is what happened in Germany and got Hitler elected. What would the left wing liberal media say about that? When President Trump read his press statement to a rally he didn't explain what he meant by there were some good people on both sides. The media didn't want to hear from the rational good Americans many of whom were probably local people. Sadly, the rally was to be in front of Gen. ROBERT E. LEE's statue on his horse Traveller. Lee didn't want statues and wanted Americans to heal after the worst war America ever fought, a CIVIL WAR or as some in Virginia say correctly the WAR OF NORTHERN AGGRESSION. I have lived in Stafford, VA, since July 4, 1977, which was occupied by Union soldiers during most of the war. My grandfather from Calais, ME, voted for ABRAHAM LINCOLN twice. His 12th Maine Regiment occupied New Orleans but he contracted typhoid and malaria at Ship Island, MS, in April 1962, and was sent to Boston. In May 1862, he had a relapse in Massachusetts General hospital. The doctors told a nurse to take him to the morgue. She saw his toe twitch! He was 79, when my father was born in 1919. His wife from Eastport was 38. He passed in 1934, age 94.

HISTORY FACTS: Now they want to take all statues down, remove names and even are threatening many of our greatest Founding Fathers, Presidents, Columbus and someone painted Lincoln, a KKK? Author George Santayana prophesied: "Those who forget History are condemned to Repeat it! News media? Also, in his 1948 fictional book 1984, author GEORGE ORWELL, a former "Communist", portrayed his main character Winston as working in the Ministry of "Truth" where he burned news stories of former political leaders who were considered traitors. Millions of dollars will be spent in revisionist History which could be spent on helping the needy. "So it Goes!" Vonnegut.

The Cost of a Conscience as an American Citizen

By Mark Hofman "Lutheran Witness-Missouri Synod" April 2012

"The cost of conscience can be heavy. Bound together by the Word of God, the church pays a heavy cost when we exercise our rights as citizens of the United States. 'We must, indeed, all hang together.' Benjamin Franklin once quipped while debating the potential cost of gaining freedom, 'or most assuredly we shall all hang separately!'

At the core, there is a cost to send out exceptionally well informed pastors, teachers and other church workers. We work together as a Synod to sustain two world class seminaries that publicly proclaim Jesus Christ as the Savior of mankind, the Good News that informs and gives purpose to our life together in this world and the next.

There is a cost to forming good citizens who 'Love the Lord your God with all your heart and with all your soul and with all your mind." (Matt. 22:37). At no small cost, in our life together as a Synod, we operate thousands of schools and nearly a dozen colleges and universities who help parents 'train up a child in the way he should go' (Prov. 22:6).We also sustain congregational, district, campus and Synod youth ministries. Graduates of these institutions are actively involved in the witness, mercy and life together of the church, even as they flourish as good citizens of the land.

There is a cost for bold acts of Christian mercy. Following the wake of natural disasters, we feed and clothe, provide shelter and counseling. We comfort the grieving, restore the hopeless, offer true compassion and share the saving Gospel with those who are suffering the harshest realities of a fallen world.

There is a cost to the Synod for having a dedicated Life Ministries focus and staff who advocate for the sanctity of human life from conception to the final breath. Together as a Synod, we speak with one voice on behalf of those who cannot speak for themselves, those who bear the ultimate cost if we remain silent.

There is even a cost to defend our rights as a religious community under the First Amendment of our nation's Constitution. Recently we witnessed our Synod's president enter the realm of the government and do just that. He stated that our consciences obey God rather than men (Acts 5:29), because our hearts 'bed is too narrow' for both God and the government. (Isaiah 28:20)

"Why Do We Have Such A Problem with Righteousness?"

Pastor Dr. James R. Knill Concordia Lutheran Church-Missouri Synod May 1, 2018

"When you think of righteousness, you tend to think of something we do, a quality we earn. In the civil realm that's true. We know about the righteous behavior of the person who will stand up for the truth, no matter what—of someone who takes up the cause of the downtrodden when they are oppressed. The righteous one gains standing in the community, because he or she is clearly a good person (even though we all know, "No on is perfect.")

"People generally like to think that's the way it is in our relationship with God. We do good things. We show we are righteous. God will be pleased with us, and He will take us to heaven, because we have shown we are righteous. What's the problem?"

"The problem is, we are all sinners, no matter how good our behavior is. Jesus said, "You therefore must be perfect, even as your heavenly Father is perfect (Matthew 5:48). "Whoever breaks one commandment is guilty of all." Adam and Eve were expelled from the Garden of Eden for one sin, for breaking one commandment, and all their descendants bear that taint to this day."

"Who, then, is truly righteous? Who can stand justified before God? Who can prove to God he or she is worthy of heaven? The answer is no one. And here's where the problem with righteousness exists. We are not righteous or justified by what we have done; we are declared righteous by God through the faith that believes Jesus Christ paid for ALL our sins, and so we are left sin-less before God. The righteousness we have is purely and totally a gift from God, for Christ's sake. We earn none of it."

"'But the problem continues. The "natural man" wants to prove he or she can at least do something to earn God's favor and gain salvation."

"The Lutheran Reformers professed a simple statement on justification when they stood before the Emperor and representatives of the Church of Rome in Augsburg, Germany, 1530:

> "It is taught among us that we cannot obtain forgiveness of sin and
> righteousness before God by our own merits, works, or satisfactions,
> but that we receive forgiveness of sin and became righteous before
> God by grace, for Christ's sake, through faith, when we believe that
> Christ suffered for us and that for his sake our sin is forgiven and
> righteousness an eternal life are given to us. For God will regard and
> reckon our faith as righteousness, as Paul says in Romans 3:21, 26
> and 4:5." [Augsburg Confession, Article IV, p. 30, Tappert edition.]

"The Roman Church rejected this article, insisting that God's grace makes our works worthy of eternal life [Roman Confutation, Part 1, Article IV]. The Reformers' response, written by Philip Melanchthon, used 61 pages to expand on the paragraph above, pointing out, among many other things, that to give any measure of credit to human activity leading to salvation denies the fully satisfactory work of Christ and is in fact an insult to Him and His sacrifice [Augsburg Confession, Article IV, p. 127, Tappert edition].

"Melanchthon pointed out that no work is a truly good work apart from faith. He also made it clear that works done in faith by believers do receive rewards from God. But those works do not earn salvation. That is completely a work of Christ and totally satisfying to God. We can add nothing to it. It is a GIFT, fully, solely and completely."

"So, you see there is a problem with righteousness. Our old nature wants to assume at least some credit for our saved status from God. That misbelief survives, not only in worldly thinking, but even in some churches that claim to teach Christian belief accurately. The truth is, believers are righteous, and it's completely a gift, received through faith, without any works on our part."

"May this little piece help provide a solution for what does not need in any way to be a problem with righteousness."

"Joining you in thanks and praise to God for His free, full, and unmerited gift of salvation through faith."   Pastor Knill   [My pastor since Pentecost Sunday May 1989]

INDIANA JONES Meets DR. SCHWEITZER

Retrieved from STEVEN SPIELBERG'S INDIANA JONES CHRONICLES TV series. Indiana Jones is visiting Dr. Schweitzer in Gabon French Equatorial Africa circa 1916.
        J is for Indiana Jones and S is for Dr. Albert Schweitzer's dialogue.

J What's a man like you doing in the back side of Creation?
S Running a hospital because it is needed!
J But it is so hopeless, to leave Europe, a man of your talents.
S Must apply them in the service of Humanity. God gives us talent for that very purpose.
   To use them is the greatest thing.
J What can you accomplish?
S Like gathering pebbles.

[They play the piano together, first Chopsticks than Ragtime Jazz. Schweitzer's   Jewish wife Helene, daughter of a Strasbourg University professor, watches along with his beloved pet pelican Parsifal who flaps his wings and squawks. Schweitzer was a renowned JOHANN SEBASTIAN BACH hymn cathedral organist.]

S Civilization is collapsing all around us!
J Because of the war?   [The Great War, World War I In Europe}
S No, the war is not the cause merely a symptom. Would it ever occur to you to enter a
    stranger's home and kill everyone who lived there and seize the house as your own?
J Of course not, it would be wrong!
S Why? Your heart tells you this. But governments decide to invade the strangers home
    and commit murder, millions of men as moral and ethical as you [Jones] flock to the
    task even at the cost of their own lives. Why?
J It's not the same thing.
S But something you have been taught to believe, society doesn't want   thinking men,
    nor governments or religions, not even in the stars themselves! Can you look into this
    man's face (African patient's smiling face) and tell me why I came to Africa? (Seated
    around a campfire) The thankful chief asks about the GREAT WAR in Europe. How
    many men have been killed? As many as three?
Schweitzer says, Yes. As many as 10? Yes, as many as 10. The chief says, such a cost
of life. Why don't the Chiefs meet and palaver? How can your tribes afford to pay for so many
dead men?
J What do you mean pay?
S Here when two tribes go to war each side pays compensation for the men that are
    killed.
J They place a currency value on human life, it's BARBARIC!
S At least they place some value on life which is more than I can say of my fellow
    Europeans. If you wish to compare barbarities, my brother writes often of the war,
    most recently he tells of a French effort to capture a German position at Lingenkopf
    which is a nearby mountain. The French sent wave after wave up the slopes to be
    slaughtered. By the time the French generals called of the offensive they had lost

30,000 men. These people   can't comprehend 10 men killed, so how do   I explain
30,000 men lying in heaps on the slopes of Lingenkopf the results of a morning battle?
or the 7 or 8,000,000 killed in the war so far.
The chief says,"The Europeans must be very rich to kill 10 men in battle.
[Cruising down the Ogoowe River in French Equatorial Africa, Gabon]

DR. Schweitzer's REVERENCE FOR ALL LIFE ETHIC "Ehrfurcht vor dem Leben"

S It was on this very river on a trip such as this that my thoughts drifted into a
contemplation so deep that I sank into my own Heart and Mind and in that harmony
of thoughts there leapt unbidden into my mind a phrase "Reverence for Life".
Everything I am or shall ever be stems from it and leads back to it.
J But what does it mean?
S You value your life, you want to continue to live?
J Of course!
S That's the most fundamental trait of awareness. One you can share with all living
creatures. A desire for further life a thinking man looks into the Heart and recognizes
this truth. I'm a life which wills to live in the midst of life which wills to live. Look around
you soldier [Jones in uniform] LIFE is everywhere, the creeks (alligator dives into the
water) it flys (egrets fly up) it rises as the biggest cathedral, but most of all it wills to
live and go on living! The thinking man gives every life the same Reverence that he
gives his own.
J But sometimes taking a Life is inevitable, to eat I have to hunt, to survive a leopard's
attack I have to shoot it.   [Dr. Schweitzer became a vegetarian.]
S If you want guidelines you've come to the wrong place. Reverence is a state of Mind,
not a set of rules. All it requires is everything be done in deep awareness. GOOD is
whatever LIFE is! Evil is whatever destroys it. From there you make your decisions.

At night they return to the hospital and are challenged by a French gunboat.   His wife
Helene says, "We are no longer welcome here in French territory." The French commander barks,
"All German nationals are to be deported to Europe by order of Minister Clemenceau!" [Schweitzer
was born and lived in the French province of Alsace which was annexed to Germany after the
Franco-Prussian War, 1871. [He was bilingual]
S We have been here four years even since before the war began.
Officer "I have orders to escort you to a French garrison."
S As a prisoner of war?
Officer "Call it what you like."
J This man is doing nothing here but treating the sick!
Officer "He is a German. Our orders are very specific. You may take up the matter with
my superiors. You should understand, I am a soldier like you."
J You are a petty bureaucrat!
(Officer slaps Indiana Jones who is American) Jones leaps at the French officer and is taken into
custody.
J What about them? (pointing to the African patients) The sick and the suffering. What's
going to happen to them?   (camera shows natives going into the jungle)

Helene says, "They will go back to dying!" Dr. Schweitzer with his arm around his wife leaves on the riverboat watched by his African assistant. (last shot shows piano with window blowing open and sheet music blowing away in the wind)

AT PORT SIDE

J I wanted to say goodbye. "Helene, it was a pleasure meeting you both." (Jones   kisses her hand) I tried talking to them they wouldn't listen.
S So it goes and are you well?
J Until I meet you I thought I was becoming a person I could respect. Now, I'm not so
   sure. I feel sick in my Soul.
S That's a disease even I can't treat, I'm afraid it's up to you to heal yourself.
J I don't know where to start?
S You already have soldier. (on boat launch) Jones: "I'll always think of you both with
   that floating arsenal ripe with the promise of death, but we used it to save life.
   Nichts war? (Not true?) Jones says in German.
S A little subversive is good for the Soul.
In an American hospital an elderly Indiana Jones finishes his story of his meeting with Dr. Albert Schweitzer and tells a black doctor Schweitzer's words:

"Sometimes our light goes out, but is blown again into a flame by an encounter with another human being. Each of us owes the deepest thanks to those who have rekindled this inner light." The ALBERT SCHWEITZER HOUSE was in Great Barrington, Massachusetts about 20 miles from my home in Ghent/Harlemville, New York. I have a VHS video tape about his life. His granddaughter Christina says her grandfather was in a great state of depression after he and his wife Helene's internment during World War I. He said he felt lost, "Like a penny that had rolled under a carpet." She said, Archbishop Soederblom invited him to Uppsala University where their great Lutheran Christian faiths temporarily restored his hope for Christian humanity. However, as I have said Hitler destroyed that hope. After his short recuperation he returned to his African hospital until his passing Sept. 3, 1965. Providentially, I was at the Bronx Zoo that day near my father's apartment.

CASALS DEDICATES SCHWEITZER LIBRARY

McCandlish Phillips New York Times June 28, 1971
"GREAT BARRINGTON, Mass. June 27—A living legend came here today to pay honor to a legend of the recent past. Pablo Casals, the 91-year-old cellist, came to a bright red barn in the Berkshire hills to dedicate the ALBERT SCHWEITZER library, an annex to the Albert Schweitzer Friendship House established here in 1967 by Mrs, ERICA ANDERSON, who had portrayed the life of the renowned medical missionary in photographs and films before he died at 90."
"Mrs. Anderson visited Africa in 1950, intending to make a film of Dr. Schweitzer, but stayed on to become "HIS GIRL FRIDAY." "Make a path for the maestro," the ebullient hostess cried to her guests, who had parked their cars by the score in a field of her 41-acre farm property on Hurlburt Road. Fewer than 100 guests out of the 460 who came crowded into the barn and many pressed near   to   the   barn   door."
HOSTESS DRAWS LAUGHTER

"Facing the overflow, Mrs. Anderson drew laughter by demanding, "Are you people happy, outside here, or are you all now my enemies?" There was a ripple of applause, then silence, as Mr. Casals emerged from the white frame farmhouse opposite the barn, shielding his face and bald head from the sun with his Panama hat. An umbrella was held over him as he walked slowly to the barn —a short, roundish figure in a crisp blue suit, blue shirt and blue tie." "I would like the maestro to dedicate this library by saying a few words, or by playing — whichever you like," Mrs. Anderson said, setting an informal and exuberant style by which she would guide the two-hour dedication ceremony. "Casals, who flew here from Mexico, had never seen Mrs. Anderson's documentary film on his friend, Dr. Schweitzer, until this morning at a private showing of the French version in the barn. Mrs. Anderson won an ACADEMY AWARD for that film in 1959. Before he saw it, Casals remarked, "I don't know any better dedication than to play BACH." He went to the Steinway grand piano and played a short piece."

"Now it was afternoon and the question was, which instrument would the aged conductor, composer and cellist choose—the microphone or the piano? He walked to the piano but stopped just short, turned and faced the microphone, with his back resting on the edge of the piano. A television camera poked in through an open window. He did not think that the whole world had come to appreciate Dr, Schweitzer, "but it will come," Casals said, his voice said not much beyond a whisper. Dr. Schweitzer had written books, "but the books are forgotten in a very short time."

JESUS IS THE WORD THAT COUNTS

"His voice grew momentarily loud, "Jesus Christ has not written a book," he declared. "Is the WORD THAT COUNTS." Of his relationship to Schweitzer the musician, Casals said: "I owe to him — I can't say that I owe to him my enthusiasm, my devotion, my admiration for Bach — but I can say that his conversation and his playing of Bach have inspired me certainly."

"When I play Bach I remember him. He is with me."

SCHWEITZER GOES TO AFRICA TO SERVE HUMANKIND

"The old man — Casals made his professional debut in Paris in 1899 and his New York debut in 1904 — expressed a desire that Dr. Schweitzer's work be "remembered for centuries and centuries." "Albert Schweitzer abandoned brilliant prospects as a Biblical scholar, educator, preacher and concert organist in Europe to take up medicine at the age of 30 and then to establish a primitive hospital in the steaming jungle, a few miles from the Equator, at Lambarene on the Ogooue River. It was French Equatorial Africa then, now Gabon."

"It seemed to me a matter of course that we should all take our share of the burden of pain that falls upon the world," the missionary once said. He built much of his extensive hospital village with his own hands."

"Ehrfucht vor dem Leben—REVERENCE FOR LIFE" was the essence of his philosophy."

"Dr. Schweitzer's daughter, Rhena, was here with her husband, Dr. David C. Miller, who had been physician to Dr. Schweitzer at the end of his life. He died on Sept. 4, 1963.

"The library, wing added to what Mrs. Miller remembered as "this tumbling house "everything written by Schweitzer, miles of film, 37,000 pictures".

"Norman Cousins, editor of the "Saturday Review, Dr. Elizabeth Hall, founder of [nearby] Simons Rock College here, and Dr. Miller were among the speakers."

ABORTION AND REVERENCE FOR ALL GOD'S CREATURES

"Dr. Miller spoke of "Birth control and death control," in such measures as ABORTION, and reflected on the difficulty of applying "reverence for life" to practices urged upon society by the prospect of overpopulation."

"He quoted Schweitzer: "I am life that wills to live in the midst of life to the midst of life that wills to live. Except for green trees, which can synthesize their own food, all the rest of us are either predators or parasites," he said. Dr. Miller said he thought that man, with his landscape-blighting technology, was easily the greatest parasite in nature."

"Mr. Cousins referred to the severe criticisms made of sanitary conditions at the jungle hospital by JOHN GUNTHER, the late writer." [In his INSIDE AFRICA book.] "It seems to me that John Gunther, in getting inside of things, got inside of something he didn't understand," the editor said. "Certainly he didn't get inside Albert Schweitzer."

"Dr, Schweitzer didn't go to Africa to build a gleaming, marbled, white-walled, white sheeted hospital. There were many hospitals like that in Africa—empty. They had everything but the people."

"Lili Kraus, a concert pianist for more than 40 years, who had played for Dr. Schweitzer and Lambarene, closed the dedication with Mozart's "Fantasia" Sonata, which Casals listened at times with his hand cupped behind his right ear. A bird chirped one high note into her performance, discordant with her music but in HARMONY WITH NATURE."

"Mrs Anderson, who established this memorial on $10,000 left to her by Dr. Schweitzer, had the final word: "The library is open. Refreshments are this way," she said, flinging her left arm out. "The library is that way," she said, flinging out her other arm."

PERSONAL STORY: Read how my dad providentially meet Erica Anderson shortly after my mother's passing in September 1967. The last book my mother read was her large picture book SCHWEITZER ALBUM. My mother would have loved her for her Schweitzer book showing his reverence for all animals. Erica was a Jewish refugee from Vienna. My mother could have spoken to her in German if she desired and would have supported her financially and physically. We lived about 20 miles away and I had a chance to visit her often because my grandmother was in a nursing home nearby. My father said Erica and her Dr. Schweitzer's book literally became my father's Bible and inspiration. I met Erica after my mother's funeral in October 1967 She gave me the name of the pastor at the Gunsbach church in Alsace, France. I meet him on June 4, 1968, the day Senator Robert Kennedy was assassinated. A providential day in my life.]

SEEING DEATH, SEEING LIFE

"It had been revealed to him by the holy spirit that he
would not see death before he had been seen the Lord's Christ." Luke 2:26

"SIMEON was going to die. But he had a sure promise of the Lord to cling to; he would see the MESSIAH before his last day. Before Simeon saw death, he would see life in the flesh. This promise of God gave purpose and meaning to Simeon's life, even in his old age. He lived for the coming of the Christ, eagerly anticipating it. With Spirit-worked faith, he waited on the Lord, seeking him in his house, until finally he held the infant JESUS in his arms and said, "Lord, now You are letting your servant depart in peace." (verse 29)."

"Whether our death is in the near or distant future, we, too, live in anticIpation of Christ's coming. We have the sure promise of His Word to cling to, the resurrection of the body and the life everlasting. This is what we have to live toward. And in the Holy Supper, the Spirit leads us to

Jesus. We behold Christ by faith as we receive HIS TRUE BODY AND BLOOD for our FORGIVENESS. This is why we sing Simeon's song after HOLY COMMUNION. For our eyes have seen salvation."

Lord, grant me strength of faith to wait for You. Amen
PorTals of Prayer Sunday Dec. 29, 2019 Read Luke 2:25-40 + Psalm 27

HE WAS BORN THAT WE MAY BE ADOPTED

"God sent forth His Son, born of women, born under the law
to redeem those who were under the law, so that we might
receive adoption as sons." Galatians 4:4-5

"PAUL refers to all Christians, both men and women, as those who "receive adoption as sons." Why would he speak that way? The answer is in how our adoption into God's household happened. A few verses earlier, the apostle wrote, "In Christ Jesus you are all sons of God, through faith" (Galatians 3:26). Baptized into the Son of God, we ourselves are counted as sons of God for His sake. Robed in His righteousness, we are little Christs. By Grace, the Father gives us the same standing as Jesus Himself."

"This is why Jesus was born of woman and placed under the Law: to redeem us who by nature were children of wrath, slaves to the false spiritualities of the world. Only through Him can we come to the Father as dear children. By fulfilling all the requirements of the Law for us, Jesus rescued us from our sin and unbelief and made us candidates for adoption. Now the Father looks upon us in Christ and says, "I claim you as family; I love you, and I want you to be with Me in My household forever. Welcome home.""

Father, grant me not to give way to my fear but confidently to hope in restoring mercy. Amen
PorTals of Prayer Dec. 30, 2019   Read Galatians 4:1-7 + Psalm 80

JESUS PREDESTINATION OF ISRAEL AS A NATION The LAST JUBILEE 2017

Rabbi Ben Samuel HIS-tory Predestination Prophecies
For a period of 70 years GOD has not allowed mercy upon Israel and especially   Jerusalem. The BABYLONIAN CAPTIVITY was 70 years.

Nations who "help" Israel, but with Evil Intentions:

"And the LORD answered the ANGEL who talked to me, with good and comforting
words. So the ANGEL who spoke with me said to me, "Proclaim, saying, "Thus
says the LORD OF HOSTS: 'I am zealous for Jerusalem and for ZION with great
zeal. I am exceedingly angry with the nations at ease for I was a little angry.
And they helped but with evil intent." Zechariah 1:13-1

Now here we see the anger which God has against the nations who have "used" ISRAEL. Does this sound like AMERICA or other western "Christian" nations today? And they 'helped' but with evil intent! The PROPHECY about a rebuilt Temple.

"Therefore thus says the LORD: 'I am returning to Jerusalem with mercy, My house shall be built in it.' says the LORD OF HOSTS. "And a surveyor's line shall be stretched out over Jerusalem." Zechariah 1:16

Also Prophetically

"Then I was given a reed like a measuring rod. And the ANGEL stood, saying, "Rise and measure the TEMPLE of GOD, the altar, and those who worship there." Revelation 11:1

The Prophecy of Rabbi Judah ben Samuel head Talmudic scholar in Germany.
Just before he died in the year 1217, the rabbi Prophesied that the Ottoman Turks would rule over the Holy City of Jerusalem for 8 Jubilees! That is 400 years (8 x 50)
Three hundred (300) years later in Germany MARTIN LUTHER posted his 95 THESIS, talking points, on the Wittenberg church's door on All Saints Eve (Halloween) October 30, 1517! God's Providence? This year 2017 is the 500th Anniversary of LUTHER's PROTESTANT REFORMATION. In 1917, the Ottoman Turkish army surrendered JERUSALEM to British GENERAL ALLENBY on the first day of Hanukkah, the Festival of 7 Days of miraculous candlelight, after the 400 years prophesied by Rabbi Samuel in 1217! PROVIDENCE or HIS-tory? Rabbi Samuel further proclaimed that after the 8 Jubilees, the 9th Jubilee would have Jerusalem being a no-man's land, which it was from 1917 to 1967 until the 6 DAY WAR! On the 7th DAY they rested. That day was June 6, 1967. [The Normandy invasion was on June 6,1944, providentially decided because of coming adverse weather conditions.]
Rabbi Samuel Prophetically concluded: "In the 10th Jubilee JERUSALEM would be controlled by Israel, and then the Messianic END-TIMES would begin in the year 2017!"
This was revealed to the Rabbi in the Old Testament Divine Prophecies. This is not Nostradamus "viewing" the Future through sorcery. The Rabbi died in 1217, 800 years before the "return" of Israel's Messiah who has been longed for 2,000 years. If you read all the Holy Bible you will see the Messiah will be JESUS SECOND COMING!
Another HIStorical Fact: There is a connection between August 1914 and December 1917 (3 1/2 year period).
The beginning of the Great War, World War I, was on the 9th of AV (August 1) 1914 when Russia and Germany entered the war establishing the plurality of the nations involved in the war. The 9th of AV is the most Prophetic dreaded day in Jewish HIStory! The 9th of AV is the day that the two Jerusalem Temples were destroyed 567 years apart on the same Lunar calendar day.
In 1917, all nations that were involved in the war became involved when America joined the war. In December, on the first day of Hanukkah, 1917, British General ALLENBY entered Jerusalem, without firing a shot, and established it for Israel, taking it from the Ottoman Turks.

There are 1,260 days between the 9th of AV (August 1) 1914, and Hanukkah (Kislev 26) 1917. This timing of 3 1/2 years is the same time for JACOB'S TROUBLE, and the entry of the MESSIAH into JERUSALEM.
100 years is the limit of a generation found in the BIBLE (and defined by ABRAHAM'S 4 generations of a total of 400 years. Is this a coincidence that the Rabbi's Prophesy of 400 years also ends in 1917. 1517 + 400 (Ottoman rule) = 1917: 1917 + 100 years (limit to a generation) = 2017

Summary of Rabbi Ben Samuel's Prophecy

1517 Ottoman rule of JERUSALEM begins and will last for 400 years
1914 World War I starts on 9th of AV August 1 [9th of AV also Temples destruction date].
1917 Ottoman rule ends on Hanukkah December General Allenby takes Jerusalem,
    3 1/2 years after Great War starts, end of 8 Jubilees, 400 years, for Israel
1917-1967 9th Jubilee, 50 years, for ISRAEL, ends Jerusalem as no-man's land.
1967-2017 10th Jubilee, 50 years, for ISRAEL, Jerusalem is controlled by Israel
2016, President Barack Hussein Obama II wants to give Jerusalem to Palestinians.
2017, 11th Jubilee, 50 years, for Israel, Messianic Age will begin when Yeshua returns!
70 years conclusion of the Prophecy of ZECHARIAH.
"Then the ANGEL OF THE LORD answered and said, 'O LORD OF HOSTS, how long will you not have mercy on Jerusalem and on the cities of Judah, against which You were angry these 70 years?' "

1948 - rebirth of ISRAEL in 1948 (involving the replanting of the Myrtle trees used for wood by the Ottomans) The Turks taxed trees which Jews cut down. Israel a Wilderness
+70 years that God has been angry with Jerusalem and the cities of ISRAEL (Judah)

WE ARRIVE AT THE YEAR 2017

As a B.A. degree Historian I only learned the recorded events that had happened in the ancient past long after the daily news event. There are few colleges, including biblical, that teach PREDESTINATION HIS-tory. Read the WIKIPEDIA article about Irish monk MALACHY who envisioned the 112 "names and deeds" of future Roman Catholic popes for 800 years ending with the current POPE FRANCIS, the only JESUIT POPE in HIStory! Much of his PROPHECY can be debated, however, the names and profiles appear to be a Predestination of Apocalyptic future events.

The description of Pope PIUS XI, who died [murdered?] in 1939, just before his planned speech Encyclical against Fascism, racism and antisemitism to the VATICAN COUNCIL OF CARDINALS! The book THE POPE'S LAST CRUSADE (2014) is a tribute to this bravest Pope. Pope PIUS XII, PACELLI his papal secretary was "elected" as pope and passed in October 1958. He was archbishop of Munich when Hitler and his Nazi party were fighting the atheist Communists for power in the streets of Munich. He has been called "HITLER'S POPE" because of his silence regarding German Nazi and Italian Fascism's Apostasy, un-Christian beliefs and deeds. His motivation was caused by his fierce opposition to STALIN's Communist atheist persecution of Catholics in Russia. He viewed Hitler as their savior after his initially victorious invasion of Russia in June 1941.
PERSONAL CONNECTION: My friend CHRISTOPHER NIEBUHR told me he sat with this American Jesuit priest on the train from New York City to Harvard where he was going to his reunion class circa 1957. Christopher, pastor-theologian REINHOLD's son was also returning to Harvard. He recalled, "We discussed the German church during Chancellor BISMARCK'S rule." The Jesuit priest had taught Negro children in St, Mary's County, Maryland. He had written a book on American Civil Rights and was called to the Vatican by Pope Pius XI to draft an encyclical against Fascism, racism and anti-semitism which was intentionally delayed and then Pope Pius XI passed away.

These historical events are not coincidences or chance. There are powerful Satanic forces in very high places. It can only be Almighty God JEHOVAH/JESUS COSMIC DIVINE PLAN revealed through HIS Prophets, Kings, the Patriarchs/Matriarchs and Disciples/Apostles culminating in JESUS CRUCIFIXION and RESURRECTION. HIStory may be pre-ordained but we all have Freedom to have FAITH in JESUS and believe in JESUS and his unparalleled suffering for all Humankind's SINS for believers salvation and eternal life with HIM and our loved ones.

DO YOU KNOW THE ANSWERS TO THESE IMPORTANT QUESTIONS ABOUT ISRAEL?

The Destiny of the Church and the World Depends on What Happens in Israel
You Need to Know what the Bible Says About Israel's Role in the Last Days!

1 Does the 45TH BIRTHDAY of Israel mean it's closing time?

2 Why have Jews, who constitute one half of one percent of the population, receive twelve percent of the NOBEL PEACE PRIZES?

3 Where did the terms "Hebrew," "Israel," and "Jew" originate?

4 What are Israel's five covenants and why were they given?

5 Who owns the land—Jews or Arabs?

6 What caused numerous anti-Semitic holocausts from Titus, A.D. 70 to Hitler, 1943?

7 Was Christopher Columbus looking for a haven for Jews?

8 Why are 75 per cent of American Jews of Russian origin?

9 Why did Russia's Joseph Stalin compete with Germany's Hitler for Jewish lives?

10 What part did these men play in Israel's History? Stalin * Herman Goring * Rudolf Hess * Joseph Goebbels * Heinrich Himmler * Chaim Weizman * David Ben Gurion * Ariel Sharon * Theodore Herzl * Alfred Dreyfus * David Green * Franklin Roosevelt *Harry Truman * General Allenby

11 What miracle occurred in 1917 to change history and signal Christ's return?

12 What were the five stages Nazis used to eliminate Jews?

13 What was Hitler's Final Solution?

14 How were Germany's Christians duped and deluded?

15 Could a Jewish Holocaust happen in America?

16 Is Hitler's Holocaust—the murder of six million Jews—a hoax?

17 What hate literature did Henry Ford, of the Ford Motor Company write? Did Hitler use it in his book. Who is presently propagating this trash?

18 Did Hitler claim to be a Christian?

19 In 1669, who predicted Israel's return to their land as the beginning of the end

20 What American President did the most for Israel?

21 What great sign happened after 2,553 years ago?

22 How long is a generation?

23 In 1935, what famous Rabbi predicted Desert Storm, and where did his prophecy fit into End-Time events?

24 Is any other book of the Bible needed besides Daniel, to prove it's closing time? If not—why?

25 Will Iraq be a major player at Armageddon? What about Iran?

26 Are there black Jews?

27 Which nation produces the final tribe returning to Israel? Is it happening?

28 What part does the European Community play in latter-day events for Israel?

29 What will the Antichrist's peace pact with Israel involve?

30 Could the peace program occur in one day? If yes—why?
31 Will Brussels and Jerusalem both be capitols of the New World Order?
32 What important historical fact occurred 1,600 years before the birth of Mohammed?
33 What land was originally promised to Israel by Abraham, and what areas and nations does it cover today?
34 Why are Nazism and Fascism rising again in Germany—and where will it end?
35 Graffiti on the walls of what nation states,: "Jews to the ovens," "Jews to soap," and "We missed you the first time but not again"?
36 Is the United Nations hypocritical?
37 Are the Jews also God's elect?
38 Will animal sacrifices again be offered in the Jewish Temple?
39 Is the 1,000-year reign of Christ literal or symbolic?
40 What is the abomination of desolation or the abomination that makes the Temple desolate?
41 Could there be two temples erected soon?
42 What preparations are now in progress for Temple service?
43 Will Christians be on earth to see the third Temple?
44 How near are the Jews to discovering the red heifer to be used for sacrifice?
45 How many priests does Rabbi Kahane have ready for immediate Temple service?
46 What is the goal of the Muslim brotherhood?
47 What is Iran's goal for Israel, described as "the cancerous tumor"?
48 Why could Iraq be the gateway to Armageddon at any moment?
49 What's the significance of Turkey's 15 dams presently under construction?
50 Is Israel looking for her Messiah by A.D. 2000?   [Dr, Jack Van Empe ministry]

My Mother's Letter from President Dwight Eisenhower DDE Hotel Commodore New York, NY December 27, 1952 Dear Mrs. Louden:

Mrs. Eisenhower and I were deeply touched by the kindly thought of your letter and by the deep concern for our country that inspired you to write to us. I assure you that so far as lies in our power, we shall work for peace and understanding in the world. We are delighted to know that you fit so well into our country's life and that you are so devoted to it.
Sincerely,   Dwight D. Eisenhower
P.S.: Thank you for sending us the picture of your interesting family. Your youngsters are indeed healthy and fine looking young Americans.

DE

Mrs. Alexander B. Louden
96 Park Avenue   Amityville, NY
President elect Eisenhower then flew to South Korea to begin his   Peace talks to end the Korean Civil War conflict.
I called President Eisenhower's historical library in Abilene, Kansas. They were unable to find a copy of my mother's letter. I imagine my mother wrote the President elect about leaving Hitler's Germany in January 1935, and becoming an illegal alien for 5 years. My mother would have thanked him for his victory and freeing her parents in Germany.

Pres. Eisenhower's Address to Transylvania College

Pres. DWIGHT DAVID EISENHOWER, 34th president of the United States: 1953-1961

My father Alexander Bruce Louden attended TRANSYLVANIA COLLEGE in Lexington, Ky from 1939, graduating in June 1942 with a degree in History/Political Science and Psychology. My father graduated from Amityville High School in 1938 on Long Island in June 1938, and attended recently opened, 1935, HOFSTRA COLLEGE in 1938 living at home. His high school friend Franklin Quick Smith "Bunkie" convinced my father to transfer to Transylvania College. My dad owned a 1938 stick shift Chevrolet Coupe. It must have been a three day drive. My dad showed me a photo of Bunkie soloing in a Piper Cub at Blue Grass airport in Lexington. I have told his amazingly brave and tragic story as one of America's highly decorated combat pilots. He survived 100 night missions in Korea as a B-26 Invader bomber pilot who received a SILVER STAR and two DISTINGUISHED FLYING CROSSES. I know this because I have visited his grave at ARLINGTON CEMETERY in the old section. I remember him lifting me up as a child and I remember his colorful ribbons and touched the leaf on his shoulder a Major or Lt. Colonel. After graduating my father, went according to my May 4, 1943 original birth certificate father's occupation, Lexington Avon depot Canadian radio later named Bluegrass. My dad told me Canadian radio was secret radar invented by Canadian engineer Sir Robert WATSON-WATT. My birth certificate also says my mother Elisabeth Frank, housewife, born Frankfort, Germany not Frankfort, the capitol of Kentucky. My dad's left handed analytic aptitude qualified him to go to the highly selective top secret new bombing radar tech school at BOCA RATON AB, Florida. In high school he didn't do well in algebra and was told he wouldn't do well in Geometry. He got a 99% on the New York state Regents exam. So it Goes.

I passed two years of algebra tutored the second year did well. Got an A in algebra in freshman year college. Never used it. My dad also said in college he took calculus and sometimes would go to sleep and the next morning could answer the problem! I asked my father about the security issue of his wife, my mother, being born in an enemy country,, Hitler's Nazi Germany. He said he had to get a security clearance "vetted" to go to the Avon secret tech school   and told an Army Captain how and why his wife left Hitler's Germany in January 1935, on a 6 month tourist visa and was illegal for 6 years until they married in August 1941. My dad recalled, "The captain retorted, "My mother was probably less a security risk than some American citizens!" My mother's story is a Testimony and Witness to what that patriotic American officer understood. I believe that officer may have had ancestors who immigrated to America because of intolerance and persecution in their homeland, His relatives may have even been Jewish?

President Eisenhower's speech was give at a time when I was in 6th grade in Amityville three miles from Republic Aircraft and 6 miles from Grumman Aircraft whose factories were building many of America's Air Force and Navy jet fighter bombers which had been used against the Chinese Communist "volunteer" soldiers a year earlier in Korea. Republic's jets were also NATO's main tactical fighters at that time. I remember having atomic bomb drills at school where students took "shelter" under their desks. Seriously?

President Eisenhower, as a 5 star general, who led the Allied Armies to victory in Europe destroying Hitler's Nazi armies in Western Europe. He wrote his memoir CRUSADE IN EUROPE (1948). I left BITBURG AIR BASE on March 28, 1969, and noticed the HQ flag was at half mast. I asked an airman who died? The airman replied, "President Eisenhower!" Providence? Then I boarded the Air Force bus which took me to Rhein Main Air Base, the south side of Frankfurt International airport now closed. My last days in Germany were in my mother's beautiful hometown Frankfurt am Main. My mother and I visited Frankfurt when I was 15 in August 1958. The city was still in rubble from bombing in World War II. In 1966, I didn't see any bombing damage anywhere and I traveled all over Germany. However, interestingly, a building behind the German printing plant where we published the Bitburg AB Skyblazer newspaper, had what looked like bricks damaged by bullets! Patton's Army had a tough battle in Trier which was his proudest battle and historically had been Rome's northern capital under Emperor Constantine in the 4th Century and was the oldest city in Germany and had the Roman Gate the Porta Nigra, Black Gate, which Patton proudly marched through.

PUBLISHING FACT: REGNERY publishing uses the Porta Nigra as its logo.

It was on the same street as the Skyblazer newspaper Catholic Paulinus printing plant on KARL MARX STASSE. I think General Patton knew this HIStorical fact and after Hitler Patton hated Stalin and his Communist nation as much as he hated the Nazis. In the movie Patton this is made clear and he is relieved as commander in Germany. His controversial non military accidental death silences Patton. RIP In June 1998, I took my daughter to the Hamm military cemetery in Luxembourg, where his grave cross is at the head of thousands of his fellow soldiers. My Jewish daughter had just taught her first year German at Stafford High School. There is a display there honoring two Olympic Gold Medal alumni who she had swum with on the Quantico Dolphins swim team. In two Olympics Jeff Rouse won 1 Gold and one Silver medal for backstroke at Barcelona, and Gold at Atlanta. Mark Lenzi won Gold for his Hi Dive at Barcelona, and Bronze at Atlanta Olympics. His coach talked him into competing and he only practiced 6 months!

Pres. Eisenhower's Patriotic God Fearing Speech Reprinted from the American Presidency project speech April 23, 1954 at TRANSYLVANIA COLLEGE, Lexington, Kentucky

Pres. ROSE, Senator Cooper, Dr. Thomas, members and friends of this great college:

"It is my unique privilege and honor to bring to this gathering a salute from the national Government on the 175th anniversary of the founding of this institution. This honor that I feel does not find its source merely in an age which by American standards is truly venerable. It comes from many things, that this institution is a member of that great body of institutions that has two great dedications; the preservation, the enrichment, and the dissemination of knowledge; and the propagation and increase of that faith in the dignity of man, in the capacity of man the cornerstone of our free government system.

If you will pardon me for referring to Dr. Thomas' address, and particularly allow me first to say that I am overwhelmed by the over generosity of his concluding remarks with respect to myself, I would want to make this point: it is indeed refreshing to have a distinguished scientist stand in front of a body of educated people and publicly proclaim that the spiritual values of America are its true values, transcending all of the intellectual and scientific and political and material progress we have made.

Now, what exactly do we mean by these spiritual values? We mean, I think, those characteristics of man that we call ennobling in their effort upon him—courage—imagination—a sense of decency, of justice, and of right. The faculty of being ready to admit that the limit placed upon our personal rights is that we do not transgress upon similar rights of others. All of which, in a very real sense, is a translation into a political system of a deeply-felt religious faith.

Our forefathers acknowledged this when they wrote, in their first great document: "We hold that all men are endowed by their Creator with certain rights." They did not hold that these rights were yours and ours today because we are born here, because of our height, or weight, or any other characteristic physical or geographical in character, but because you were a child of the Creator. They acknowledged that, in attempting to explain our Government to the world, which they stated in the DECLARATION OF INDEPENDENCE, that that is what they were trying to do. They said, MAN is endowed by his Creator with certain rights.

Now, Transylvania, it seems to me, shows certain of these spiritual qualities in its very founding. To come out to this country 175 years ago—and I have been doing some mental arithmetic, sitting here in my seat on the platform—I think that adds up to 1779, and if I am wrong I am sure I will be corrected by those present—but that was 2 years before Yorktown, that was 4 years before the treaty of peace with Britain, that was 8 years before the meeting of our Constitutional Convention.   [Founded in 1780]

Ladies and gentlemen, it is almost overpowering to think that someone at that time, coming west of these Alleghenies, and before we even were a nation, before the War of Independence had successfully concluded, was establishing, here an institution to disseminate knowledge and to propagate and to promote and to sustain these great spiritual values that are at the heart of our system.

It seems to me that everybody who in the past has graduated from this institution, who today is privileged to serve in it, or to be here as a student, has a great heritage and tradition and understanding that cannot fail to enrich his life as long as he shall live.

One of the great figures identified with the school is, of course, HENRY CLAY, a man of great courage and forthrightness, and who preached reason as opposed to emotionalism, who strove to get people to use the faculties with which they were endowed, to help solve the problems of the day, and not give way to mere prejudice.

"GOVERNMENT IS A TRUST" HENRY CLAY LOCAL ALUMNI

About 125 years ago he said, once, "GOVERNMENT IS A TRUST. The officers of government are trustees. And both the trust and the trustees were created for the benefit of the people." That statement of his is not only accurate today, but he summed up in one single sentence, it seems to me, all the great reasons why it is necessary that Americans today stand shoulder to shoulder in defense of values that brought about the founding of this College, and the establishment of this country, as against an institution, a doctrine which states government exists to direct people, and people are mere pawns of government, although they clothe their purpose in their rather euphemistic slogan, "A DICTATORSHIP OF THE PROLETARIAT!" It is still dictatorship, and the exact ANTITHESIS of the definition given us by CLAY.

Now the point I want to make, again I refer to the address of Dr. Thomas, when he talked about the terrifying power of the ATOM BOMB and the HYDROGEN BOMB. But let us remember this: in a democracy, there is only one truly great force, an overwhelming public opinion.

WOODROW WILSON put it this way: "The highest form of efficiency," he said, "is the spontaneous cooperation of a free people." If you consider the force that can be generated by the vast majority of 160,000,000 people, with the highest level of education in the world, with the greatest material prosperity and productivity, and with the greatest understanding in the hearts of what freedom and dignity of man means. If you will try to get some conception of what that force can be, my friends, you will realize that they can conquer the atom bomb and the hydrogen bomb, or anything in this world to which they set their minds and hearts.

Now, great power can be used for good or evil. As Dr. Thomas explained, the atom bomb and the scientist's laboratory may produce the force that spells destruction for a city. But it can also produce, or they can produce, things of vast benefit for all human kind, to make life richer and happier.

Now, so can public opinion, if not based upon fact—fact as seen in its proper perspective—then it can go wrong. So again I think it is—we can repeat, the function of such an institution as this is the place the facts before us in proper perspective, then to relate those facts and that perspective to the faith by which we live. Out of these two things will grow this public opinion that will insure the safety and security of America.

In the kind of understanding, in the kind of power of which I speak, then we would understand that no nation can live alone today. Just as so many others are dependent upon the products of our laboratories, our factories and our farms, so are we very definitely dependent upon many of the materials that we use.
All of the original, atomic bombs, for example, were made of material brought almost exclusively from central Africa. But tin and tungsten and rubber and platinum and many other items used in our daily lives, we do not produce.

We cannot live alone. Understanding of these facts, and again our dedication to FREEDOM AND LIBERTY, are bound together, and they begin to emerge into policy as it happens. The words "Dien Bien Phu" are no longer just a funny-sounding name, to be dismissed from the breakfast conversation because we don't know where it is, or what it means. We begin to understand that in a far-off corner of the globe in an agony of conflict, where no matter how it starts, has become again a testing ground between dictatorship and freedom, desire on the one side to give a people the right to live as they shall choose, and on the other side to dominate them and make them mere additional pawns in the machinations of a power-hungry group in Kremlin and in China.

JEFFERSON DAVIS AN ALUMNUS—LINCOLN VISITED HERE

And then we begin to understand why the special conflict is of such importance to us. When we begin to picture the possibility of more hundreds of millions, starting with this neck in the bottle in INDOCHINA, spread over all Southeast Asia and through the great island of the Pacific, then begin to get an understanding of what your representatives in international conferences are striving to preserve for you: basically the same freedom that your Founders brought to the spot. That LINCOLN came here and talked about. That JEFFERSON DAVIS and others imbibed here. Understanding of the facts, coupled with the FAITH IN AMERICA—THE SPIRITUAL FAITH THAT ALL THINGS ARE POSSIBLE TO US, if we UNITE behind them, and they are decent and right.

I should like to make clear, before I say goodbye, that when I talk about united, I do not mean united behind special labels or behind the political doctrines of any particular figure. I am not talking about the details of taxes, which none of us likes. I am not talking about anything that must be argued out freely in our public forums, if we are to reach democratic answers. I am talking about the basic ideals of America. In fact, the kind of thing that, when you stop to think, would be the richest heritage we could pass on to our own children—and I am old enough to talk in terms of grand-children: A FAITH IN THIS COUNTRY, AND IN OUR GOD, in themselves, that they may proceed down the road of time, doing all the more than all these past great figures that we today revere, respect, and salute, have done for us.

For the very great courtesy you have paid me in the invitation to appear before you, my profound thanks, through you, I could extend my thanks, also, to every person who gave me a smile on the streets of this city [Lexington], and in the sections I traveled today, I would be grateful indeed."
NOTE: The President spoke at 4:35 P.M. His opening words referred to DR. FRANK ROSE, President of Transylvania College, JOHN SHERMAN COOPER, U.S. Senator from Kentucky, and DR. CHARLES ALLEN THOMAS, Pres. of Monsanto Chemical.

THE EISENHOWER INTERSTATE SYSTEM THE HISTORY BEHIND THE STORY

MOTOR TREND September 2019 70th Anniversary issue

"In June 1956, President DWIGHT D. EISENHOWER signed a landmark piece of legislation he'd been championing for years. THE FEDERAL AID HIGHWAY ACT of 1956, more commonly know as the NATIONAL INTERSTATE AND DEFENSE HIGHWAYS ACT, authorized $25 billion (more than $235 billion in today's money) for the construction of 41,000 miles of interstates over 10 years.

"Popular lore tells us of GENERAL EISENHOWER'S interest of the strategic value of Germany's autobahn during the war and his desire to replicate it at home. But the history is much longer than that. In fact, it predates World War II and World War I. It does not, however, predate Eisenhower.

"As popular interest in the automobile ignited in the early 1900s, Congress recognized the need for better roads for both strategic and commercial reasons, and it permanently established the OFFICE OF PUBLIC ROADS under the DEPARTMENT OF AGRICULTURE in 1905 (now the FEDERAL HIGHWAY ADMINISTRATION under the DEPARTMENT OF TRANSPORTATION). The Office of Public Roads released its first proposal for 12 transcontinental highways in 1911 based on the submissions from "GOOD ROADS" organizations around the country.

"CARL FISHER, the founder of the INDIANAPOLIS MOTOR SPEEDWAY is believed to be the first owner of an automobile dealership in this country, conceived and launched a fundraising campaign to build the LINCOLN HIGHWAY (later ROUTE 30) from TIMES SQUARE in NEW YORK CITY to LINCOLN PARK in SAN FRANCISCO in 1912. He officially dedicated the highway in October 1913.

"It wasn't until 1916 that Congress opened its checkbook with the FEDERAL AID ROAD ACT, signed by WOODROW WILSON to build rural postal roads. Little actual work was done before the U.S. entered World War I, sapping resources and labor.

"After World War I, then—Brevet Lt. Col. Eisenhower participated in the first-ever military transcontinental convoy in the summer of 1919. More than 80 Army trucks and other vehicles trundled down the Lincoln Highway, covering 3,251 miles in 61 DAYS—an average of just 53 miles per day—in a test of military mobility (or immobility) in the event of an invasion. Eisenhower would later credit that experience, as well as lessons learned in Germany in World War II, for his desire to build America's Interstate System."

"The Federal Highway Act of 1921, replacing the expiring 1916 act, both increased funding for highway construction and resolved a number of technical and legal issues in the earlier act. It was the PERSHING MAP, commissioned by the BUREAU OF PUBLIC ROADS and overseen by Army Gen. JOHN J. PERSHING in 1922, that laid the groundwork for a national highway system. The first topographic map of the United Sates, it included 78,000 miles of roads in three categories of priority with an emphasis on the coasts, transcontinental routes, and border crossings. Most of the routes recognized by Pershing's commission would become federal highways."

"The first formal standards for road signs would be adopted in 1926, along with the plan to officially number highways with a white shield. But it was the Depression-era NEW DEAL suite of job-creation programs that would get tens of thousands of highways actually built in the mid-to late 1930s, including the famous ROUTE 66.

"America's involvement in World War II would again spur a military incentive for road building. That's part of the reason the disconnected states of Alaska and Hawaii have "interstate" highways—to connect population centers with areas of industry and to promote national defense."

"The Federal-Aid Highway Act of 1944 authorized but didn't fund 40,000 miles of highways. Funding would not appear until the Federal Aid Highway Act of 1952, in a token amount. It was Eisenhower, upon taking office in 1953, who would finally kick-start the Interstate System."

"With the Federal-Aid Acts of 1954, 1956, 1958, and 1959, the Eisenhower Administration greatly increased federal funding for the interstate system and established the HIGHWAY TRUST FUND to build and maintain the new roads, funded primarily by a tax on gasoline.   Scott Evans Motor Trend

HISTORY FACT: Tennessee Senator AL GORE Sr. proposed Bill for Interstate System.

PRESIDENT EISENHOWER'S FAREWELL ADDRESS

Televised address January 17, 1961
"Eisenhower served as a president for two full terms from January 1953 through January 1961, and was the first president to be TERM-LIMITED from seeking re-election again. He had overseen a period of considerable economic expansion, even as the COLD WAR deepened. Three of his national budgets had been balanced, but spending pressures mounted. The recent presidential election had resulted in the election of JOHN F. KENNEDY, and the oldest American president in a century was about to hand the reins of power to the youngest elected president."

"As early as 1959, Eisenhower began working with his brother MILTON EISENHOWER and his speechwriters, including the chief speechwriter MALCOLM MOOS, to develop his final statement as he left public life. It went through at least 21 drafts. The speech was "A SOLEMN MOMENT IN A DECIDEDLY UNSOLEMN TIME", warning a nation "Giddy with prosperity infatuated with youth and glamour, and aiming increasingly for the easy life."

"DON'T PLUNDER THE RESOURCES OF OUR GRANDCHILDREN"
"As we peer into society's future, we—you and I, and our government—
must avoid the impulse to live only for today, plundering for our own ease
and convenience the precious resources of tomorrow. We cannot mortgage
the material assets of our grandchildren without risking the loss of their
political and spiritual heritage. We want democracy to survive for all
generations to come, not to become the insolvent phantom of tomorrow.

"MILITARY-INDUSTRIAL COMPLEX"

"Despite his military background and being the only general to be elected president in the 20th century, he warned the nation with regard to the corrupting influence of what he describes as the "MILITARY-INDUSTRIAL COMPLEX".

"Until the latest of our world conflicts, the United States had no armaments industry. American makers of plowshares could, with time and as required, make swords as well. But we can no longer risk emergency improvisation of national defense. We have been compelled to create a permanent armaments industry of vast proportions. Added to this, three and a half million men and women are directly engaged in the defense establishment. We annually spend on military security alone more than the net income of all United States corporations.

Now this conjunction of an immense military establishment and a large arms industry is new in the American experience. The total influence— economic, political, even spiritual—is felt in every city, every Statehouse, every office of the Federal government. We recognize the imperative need for this development. Yet, we must not fail to comprehend its grave implications. Our toil, resources, and livelihood are all involved. So is the very structure of our society.

In the councils of government, we must guard against the acquisition of unwarranted influence, whether sought or unsought, by the military-industrial complex. The potential for the disastrous rise of misplaced power exists and will persist. We must never let the weight of this combination endanger our liberties or democratic processes. We should take nothing for granted. Only an alert and knowledgeable citizenry can compel the proper meshing of the huge industrial and military machinery of defense with our peaceful methods and goals, so that security and liberty may prosper together."

"He also expressed his concomitant concern for corruption of the scientific process as part of this centralization of funding in the Federal government, and vice-verse."

Akin to, and largely responsible for the sweeping changes in our industrial-military posture, has been the technological revolution during recent decades.

In this revolution, research has become central, it also becomes more formalized, complex, and costly. A steadily increasing share is conducted for, by, or at the direction of, the Federal government. The prospect of domination of the nation's scholars by Federal employment, project allocation, and the power of money is ever present and is gravely to be regarded.

Yet in holding scientific discovery in respect, as we should, we must also be alert to the equal and opposite danger that public policy could itself become the captive of a scientific-technological elite.

LEGACY

"Although it was much broader, Eisenhower's speech is remembered primarily for its reference to the military-industrial complex. The phrase gained acceptance during the VIETNAM WAR era and 21st-century commentators have expressed the opinion that a number of the fear's raised in his speech have come true. The speech has been adapted as an oratory for orchestra and orator.

The speech was depicted in the opening of the 1991 film JFK. Every episode title in the third season of ORPHAN BLACK was taken from the speech."   Wikipedia

"ORPHAN BLACK is a Canadian science fiction thriller television series."   Wikipedia

Dr. Frank Rose of Transylvania Confronts Racism

New York Times February 4, 1991 obituary Peter Flint

PERSONAL NOTE: FRANK ROSE attended TRANSYLVANIA COLLEGE in 1940, my dad was his classmate, Rose received an A.A. degree and then he transferred to the nearby LEXINGTON THEOLOGICAL seminary where he received a doctor of Divinity degree. Dr. Rose was later appointed president of Transylvania, the youngest president, 31, of a higher education institute in America. Transylvania College was founded in 1790, the first college west of the Appalachian Mountains.
"Frank Anthony Rose, the president of the University of Alabama from 1958 to 1969, the era when it was peacefully desegregated, died Friday at George Washington hospital in Washington, D. C., he was 70 years old and had homes in Washington [Alexandria] and Lexington, KY. He died of cancer and pneumonia, a family spokesman said.

Dr. Rose Gov. Wallace's and Pres. Kennedy's Mediator

'With tact and diplomacy, Dr. Rose acted as the middleman in the June 1963 confrontation between Gov. GEORGE C. WALLACE and the Justice Department of the KENNEDY administration. The university president who described himself as neither a segregationist nor an integrationist but a realist, had vowed to insure obedience to the laws and peace on campus.
So when the Alabama governor stood defiantly in front of a campus door and raised a hand against federalized troops, but stepped aside moments later, two black students were enrolled without further incident."

Raised Faculty Pay and Morale

"In his 11-year tenure at the university, Dr. Rose increased the faculty and its pay and morale, raised millions of dollars in research funds, tightened academic standards, expanded the graduate departments and helped build football teams that won national championships."

"Character is Not Built by a Losing Team!"

"A 6-foot-2-inch Mississippian, he excelled as an administrator, fund raiser and university spokesman rather than as an academician, and was popular with business leaders and politicians. When accused of stressing sports over scholarship, he replied simply, "Character is not built by a losing team!"   [CRIMSON TIDE Baer Bryant]
Dr. Rose left Alabama in 1969 for Washington, where he founded and headed a not-for-profit consulting concern, University Associates, clients that included black colleges."

Picked Cotton, Plowed Fields to Pay for Transylvania

"Frank Rose was born in Meridian, Miss., on Oct. 16, 1920, his father died when he was 10, and early on he picked cotton at 50 cents a day and later plowed fields and drove soft-drink trucks to earn money to go to Transylvania College in Lexington, Ky., where he earned bachelor's degrees in philosophy and divinity and was elected to Phi Beta Kappa. A college president at 31.

He taught at the college while preaching as an ordained minister in the Disciples of Christ. [Transylvania's affiliation] At the age of 31, he became president of Transylvania, serving for 7 years until he accepted the presidency of Alabama. He was awarded honorary doctorates by more than a dozen universities.

Over the years, Dr. Rose held many advisory posts with groups like the Salk Institute for Biological Studies; the White House committee on education and minority affairs, and governing boards of Georgetown University and its medical center, the Mount Sinai Center and the Christian Church Foundation."

Dad's Dr. Rose Story Governor Wallace's Visit to Alabama U

My dad told me when Governor Wallace planned to block the black girl and boy students from entering the University of Alabama classroom, President Rose had the grounds keepers pick up all loose stones and branches on campus so they couldn't be thrown by anti-Civil Rights and pro-Civil Rights protestors. Pres. JOHN KENNEDY had to federalize the Alabama National Guard, through his brother ROBERT, U.S. Attorney General. The POSSE COMMITATUS law forbids regular military personnel to be used in a domestic law enforcement event. This is done in Communist and Fascist and Islamic totalitarian countries. There was no violence but TV cameras showed protestors. My dad was an ABC Master Control room broadcast engineer in New York City showing the country and the world what was happening at his classmate's university. My dad knew this because he received the Transylvania alumni newsletter. President Dr. Frank Rose, an ordained minister, from Lexington Theological college, after receiving his degree at Transylvania college, did what he could as a Christian pacifist. I vaguely recall my dad told me that Dr. Rose told Governor Wallace, a Methodist, that admitting the Negro students wasn't a federal civil rights issue and told the politician Wallace: "This is Jesus' Gospel "Love thy neighbor as Jesus proclaimed that there is no longer slave or bondsman or woman in bondage in His kingdom!"

HISTORICAL FACT: Governor Wallace stood in the University of Alabama classroom doorway blocking the two Negro students protesting their entry then stepped aside. The female student was the sister of former Attorney General ERIC HOLDER's wife! ONLY IN AMERICA! Did our former mulatto Pres. BARACK OBAMA know this? He was elected to two presidential terms 8 years. ONLY IN AMERICA! What did he do to make America Great? I blame the Nobel committee giving newly elected President BARACK OBAMA the Peace prize for what? His appeasement policies and the United Nations, with Russia and China's Security Council vetoes have destroyed the world. The League of Nations gave us World War II. The Bible prophets and Jesus told us what is going to happen. Pastors preach only Jesus' Salvation in this EVIL sinful world.

In the book and movie FORREST GUMP author WINSTON GROOM has a scene where Gump portrayed by TOM HANKS interacts in the Wallace University of Alabama event. Gump also portrays the Alabama CRIMSON TIDE football player TRAMMELL, who receives an award from Pres. JOHN KENNEDY. Recently, I meet Winston Groom, who is about 3 months older than me, at a book lecture at MARY WASHINGTON university, my daughter's alma mater, about his wonderful historical book AVIATORS. At the book signing I gave him this story I wrote about Dr.

Rose. He said, "Dr. Rose was president at Alabama when I attended and a friend of mine dated his daughter."

President Obama, Eric Holder and the elected leaders of Baltimore, MD failures in the drug sellers death, not murder, by male and female black and white police officers became a national disgrace. The cell phone "evidence" should not have been released on TV news prejudicing the case. The phone should have been taken by law enforcement as evidence. Will this become a law? It should be turned over to a non political judge. The anti police rioting and looting of innocent stores occurred because the Baltimore police force were ordered to stand down. The results became the lead story for all national news medias and even international. The burning CVS PHARMACY, which was looted for opiate and PSE drugs, for CRACK cocaine was shown in the background of news videos. There was no police opposition! Insurance paid for rebuilding the CVS. Why rebuild in this depressed neighborhood? CVS serves and supplies the area's retired and poor minority people with their prescription medication through Medicare, Medicaid and other health plans. CVS has some 9,000 stores nationwide a leader in health care. A few years earlier CVS removed cigarettes a $1,000,000,000,000 annual loss which actually increased its stock market share value as a health provider. FUN FACT: This was the answer to a four-part question on the MILLIONAIRE TV show asking what CVS Pharmacy's stopped selling at a billion dollar loss. The taxpayers of Baltimore paid the deceased drug dealer's family millions of tax payer dollars. A precedent? So it Goes.

FRANK ROSE Biography

"The following biographical sketch was compiled at the time of induction into the Alabama Academy in 1969."   August 25, 1969.

"Dr. Frank A. Rose, former president of the University of Alabama, was a native of Meridian, Mississippi, and is recognized as one of the nation's leading educators.

Dr. Rose received his A.B. Degree from Transylvania College, his B.D. from Lexington Theological Seminary, and did graduate study at the University of London. His career in higher education began in 1945 when he became a professor of Philosophy at Transylvania College. He was named president of his alma mater Transylvania College in 1951, becoming the YOUNGEST COLLEGE PRESIDENT IN THE NATION. The University of Alabama called him as its president in 1958."

"During Dr. Rose's tenure at the university, enrollment on the main campus almost doubled, and enrollment on all campuses climbed to 20,000. The graduate school increased ten-folded, and the full-time faculty more than doubled. University assets of $50.6 million in 1958 climbed to $141 million, and the operating budget grew from $16.2 million to $60.3 million. Dr. Rose raised academic standards by recruiting highly-qualified faculty, raising entrance requirements for students, emphasizing program"s for scholars, and appealing to outstanding students.

Dr. Rose was elected in 1955 by the United States Junior Chamber of Commerce as one of the "Ten Outstanding Young Men of America." In 1960, he was elected to the South's Hall of Fame for the Living."

Dr. Rose was National President of Omicron Delta Kappa, a group that awarded him its Distinguished Service Key in 1966. He was 1968 Chairman of the Board of Visitors, United States Military Academy, West Point, and was 1968 Chairman of the Educational Advisory Committee of the Appalachian Regional Commission.

He was a member and former president of the Southern University Conference, Regional Chairman of the March of Dimes, Chairman of the American University Field Staff Program, and a member of the Executive Committee of the Southern Regional Education Board.

Dr. Rose served in 1959 as a Delegate to the Atlantic Congress of NATO for the United States Committee. He was a member of the National Citizen's Committee on Public Television, and a member of the Advisory Panel for ROTC Affairs, U.S. Army.

Dr. Rose held Honorary Degrees from the University of Cincinnati, the University of Alabama, Samford University, Transylvania College, Lynchburg College, St. Bernard College, and the University of the Americas in Mexico City."

Commissioner Happy Chandler Integrates Baseball

Another TRANSYLVANIA COLLEGE Lexington, Kentucky alumni who served JESUS CHRIST was ALBERT BENJAMIN "Happy' CHANDLER. The NATIONAL BASEBALL HALL OF FAME Website history cites that Mr. Chandler was elected to the Hall of Fame by the Veterans Committee: 1982   [Watch his U TUBE VIDEO of his speech]

Albert "Happy" Chandler became baseball commissioner in 1944. Albert Chandler guided baseball through 6 turbulent years. A former U.S. Senator and governor of Kentucky, the honest Chandler maintained the commissioner's office as a position of authority. He took swift action against players who left to play in the Mexican League an presided over the game when Brooklyn Dodgers' BRANCH RICKEY signed JACKIE ROBINSON in 1945 and integrated Major League baseball in 1947. Baseball commissioner KENESAW MOUNTAIN LANDIS passed in 1944. I am a friend of his cousin LINCOLN "Linc" LANDIS who gave me a copy of his GREEN LIGHT letter from Pres. FRANKLIN D. ROOSEVELT. It is on INTERNET. At the COOPERSTOWN BASEBALL museum in Cooperstown, NY, a guide took me to the 12-foot display of the letter and took my picture next to it. A great museum to America's first national sport.

HISTORY FACT: President FRANKLIN D. ROOSEVELT tried to appoint FBI director J. EDGAR HOOVER to be America's baseball commissioner! Hoover turned down the offer because he believed his job as FBI director was more important during World War II protecting America from our AXIS enemies. Hoover didn't want to be "thrown under the bus" and served under 7 American presidents until he passed away during his close friend President RICHARD M. NIXON's WATERGATE scandal. Assistant FBI director MARK FELT was passed over for FBI director he was "DEEP THROAT", the WOODWARD AND BERNSTEIN, WASHINGTON POST reporters WATERGATE "leaker" informant. This secret fact was revealed in Mark Felt"s obituary. Does HIStory repeat itself? Elected Pres. DONALD TRUMP's high level FBI treasonous collusion.

Chandler's Baseball Hall of Fame—Induction Speech

Cooperstown, New York August 1, 1982

"Thank you Mr. commissioner, Mr. president, Mr. Stack, Mr. Joe Cronin, chairman of the Veterans Committee, Mr. Fenney, the president of the National League, Mr. MacPhall, the president of the American League, members of the Hall of Fame, my partners in this ceremony Robbie and Hank and the fellow you just heard. Ladies and gentlemen I feel a bit like the mosquito that flew over the fence into the nudist camp. I hardly know where to start! (applause and laughter)

But I first want to express my gratitude to ALMIGHTY GOD for his kindness to me in letting me come in this day... Every now and then as I travel about the country, and I'm past my 84th birthday and at the end of this day I will have been the oldest man ever elected to the Baseball Hall of Fame.

I have so much to say and so little time to say it. There must be a sad note into the lives of all of us some rain must fall. And I'm missing today my dad, who stood with me on two occasions when I took the oath of office as Governor of the Commonwealth of Kentucky. And that never happened to anybody else in the lifetime of the people of the Commonwealth. I used to bring him to the World Series he was in his 80s and I thought that was old. I don't think so now. I introduced him to CONNIE MACK and to Mr. CLARK GRIFFIN, For the first time in his life he was speechless, he stood and shook his head and uttered no words. He said, 'Cornelius McGillicuddy". And then I introduced him to Clark Griffin and he thought of one more word. He said, "The old fox." But I'm certain he's standin' on the ramparts of Valhalla observing this scene that he knows about it and that within the hour his name will forever be enshrined in the Baseball Hall of Fame, the Veteran Committee, Mr. Cronin, and the record will show, to Major League baseball.

U TUBE VIDEO: Baseball commissioner Happy Chandler's Baseball Hall of Fame complete speech at Cooperstown, New York is on U Tube archive. The 82-year-old Kentuckian, former US Senator and Governor, reveals his humorous oratory charisma. It is well worth watching and listening to. In the audience is JACKIE ROBINSON's family and other famous African-American athletes.

Chandler and Rickey as Christians Integrate Baseball The Jackie Robinson Story —What Would Jesus Say?

I'd like to tell you briefly the JACKIE ROBINSON story because I know it better than anybody else, living or dead. For 24 years my predecessor would not let the black men play. Now that's the record. If you were black you were automatically disqualified. He went further than that wouldn't let them barnstorm together after the season was over. And I'm not going to be too harsh with him because he was doing what the owners wanted him to do and that was keep the game segregated. In January of 1947 the owners had a meeting at the WALDORF ASTORIA HOTEL in New York and I presided over the meeting. It was closed to the Press. They had anticipated that the Brooklyn team might want to bring JACKIE ROBINSON from Montreal to Brooklyn. They debated the Robinson issue for an hour and a half or two hours and than took a vote. I announced the vote 15 no's and 1 yes.

Well immediately after that meeting I had gone to the French hospital to see my friend BABE RUTH. I knew him quite well and he had been neglected, unfortunately. We got him up though and got him a job and gave him another chance and gave him a special day. The day we gave him a special day, it happened that I had suspended a fella that I had thought ought to be suspended. He wrote a book it wasn't required reading so I didn't read it, and it wasn't a best seller. But 73,000 people I think that must have been a record booed me at YANKEE STADIUM because of that decision. Well, I stood my ground and I looked them straight in the eye and then 50,000 cheered me and I never had much trouble after that.

But Mr. Ricky, you came along. I got a cabin on the backside of my place where I've made most of my important decisions in this life in its 50 years old. I used to invite my friend TY COBB and at the others rates were rights and he said, 'Skipper on these terms I'm gonna give you a generous share of my business.' Mr. Rickey came down to the cabin and we talked for about two hours about Jackie Robinson. And he said, commissioner, 'I can't do this unless I'm assured of your complete support," And I said, "I know that, Mr. Rickey, this 15 to 1 one vote was meant to be information for you and information for me." They did not want the black men to play and I said, I have said to Rick Roberts and John Holloway and others that I don't think it is quite fair to have these fellas fight at Okinawa, and Iwo Jima, and Tarawa and the other places and then be told when they come back home that they couldn't play the great American game, baseball, although

146

they were very talented. I told him I thought that was wrong. This statement must be taken as self serving because I'm not running for anything either. So I said to Mr. Rickey, I'm going to have to meet my maker someday and if he asks me why I didn't let this boy play, and I said it was because he was black. That might not be a satisfactory answer." I said, "You bring him in and I will approve of him, the transfer of his contract from Montreal to Brooklyn." And I did, and I was the only one that could have done it. And I said to Mr. Ricky. "If LANDIS [Kennesaw Mountain] was commissioner you wouldn't go to see him because he wouldn't let you."

And he said all had been said about the thing had already been said and he had nothing else to say about it. And you wouldn't even have asked him because it wouldn't have made any difference. And I said you bring him in and we monitored every game he played. They said, "How we gonna threat this fella? Just as any other ball player no better and no worse. Don't give him anything but don't take anything away from him." And we made the switch and there are those people. I wasn't taking any credit for it. I was doing what justice and mercy required me under the circumstances. And if I had it to do over again I'd do the same thing.
I am, as the commissioner said, more responsible for the players' pension fund than anybody living or dead. Tom Gallery called me immediately after I was elected to the Hall of Fame. He always called me Champ.

He said, "Champ we made the original television contract. The new owners had given themselves five years and they had also given themselves the right to quit in five years if they didn't like it. I didn't blame them for that, but they didn't know that I had gotten pensions for State police in Kentucky. And I was committed and another thing I saw what they didn't see. I saw GROVER CLEVELAND ALEXANDER [HOLLYWOOD FACT: A legendary pitcher who suffered with undiagnosed epilepsy, the media falsely reported as alcoholism. Alexander was portrayed compassionately by RONALD REAGAN. DORIS DAY was his faithful wife]. Alexander and Dazzy Vance playing with the HOUSE OF DAVID [a bearded Orthodox Jewish baseball team] in order to get enough money to temporarily live on. And I always thought it was a great pity that we had to permit that to go on, especially when those baseball men had made magnificent contributions to the game. And yet a great many of them in those days, except for baseball, couldn't do anything else…" [The Great Depression]

This is The Greatest Country on Earth

I stand a little straighter and shed a tear when the flag goes by. THIS IS THE GREATEST COUNTRY ON EARTH! Two weeks ago I joined the commissioner in Montreal when we took the game to the Canadian side for the first time in the history of baseball in this hemisphere…
Nearly 200 years of glorious History lie back of the people of this Republic. I support the President of the United States [REAGAN] and Miss NANCY. And one of the first messages I got came from him and from Mr. NIXON, one of our better presidents in our lifetime and I appreciate I don't mind, my God that's the way I feel about it…
Thank you and God bless you all."

[This speech is on U Tube a must see. Jackie Robinson's family with black athletes.]

Pres. Franklin Roosevelt Keeps Baseball during World War II

This letter was given to me by LINCOLN LANDIS, a member of the Lake of the Woods church and LOW Veterans club. His uncle was KENNESAW MOUNTAIN LANDIS, the American baseball commissioner in the 1930s and during World War II until he passed in 1944. After the undeclared attack on the U. S. navy's battleships by the Japanese Imperial naval aircraft at Pearl Harbor, Honolulu, Hawaii at 6:55 A.M. Sunday morning Dec. 7, 1941, he wrote Pres. Franklin D. Roosevelt asking him if America should stop playing baseball which was America's favorite sport on the radio.

President Roosevelt's "Green Light" Letter

January 15, 1942

My Dear Judge: [KENESAW LINCOLN LANDIS]
Thank you for yours of January fourteenth. As you will, of course, realize the final decision about the baseball season must rest with you and the Baseball Club owners—so what I am going to say is solely a personal and not an official point of view.
I honestly feel it would be best for the country to keep baseball going. There will be fewer people unemployed and everybody will work longer hours and harder than ever.
And that means that they ought to have a chance for recreation and for taking their minds off their work even more than before.
Baseball provides a recreation which does not last over two hours or two and a half, and which can be got for very little cost. And, incidentally, I hope that night games be extended because it gives the opportunity to the day shift to see a game occasionally.
As for players themselves, I know you agree with me that individual players who are of active military or naval age should go, without question, into the services. Even if the actual quality of the teams is lowered by the greater use of older players, this will not dampen the popularity of the sport. Of course, if any individual has some particular aptitude in a trade or profession, he ought to serve the government. That, however, is a matter which I know you can handle with complete justice.
Here is another way of looking at it — if 300 teams use 5,000 or 6,000 players, these players are a definite recreational asset to at least 20,000,000 of their fellow citizens — and that in my judgment is thoroughly worth while.

> With every best wish,
> very sincerely yours,   signed Franklin D. Roosevelt

Baseball was the only national sport at this time! This was before television. Radio broadcast baseball games with announcers who could make you "see" the game.

PERSONAL STORY: LINCOLN "Linc" LANDIS told me when he was 8 he sat with his uncle Commissioner Landis at the legendary "CALLED PITCH" World Series game when BABE RUTH, of the New York YANKEES was heckled by the CHICAGO CUBS fans after contesting two "strike" pitches. BABE RUTH then legendarily pointed his bat in the direction he would hit the ball and hit the "best home run of my life!" I recorded the radio broadcast audio of Ruth's after game interview, at the BASEBALL HALL OF FAME at Cooperstown, NY, retelling that famous moment. President elect Franklin Roosevelt was there rooting for the Yankees. His family home was at Hyde Park, NY, and he had been New York's governor.

Lincoln Landis was a graduate of the WEST POINT class of 1945, the short 3 year term. He spoke to our Veteran's Club about graduating from West Point and being sent to Germany and was stationed along the forest in the Hartz mountains before the Russians and East Germans built a fence and guard towers. He spoke Russian and talked with our former allies and said the enlisted men were still friendly. In East Berlin he was jailed for a brief period. He was later a WHITE HOUSE consultant for Pres. HARRY S TRUMAN and Pres. DWIGHT D. EISENHOWER.

One day I asked Linc if he ever saw the Skyblazers F-84 jet team from Furstenfeldbrueck fly at an airshow. He said he had. I told him my commander at Bitburg AB, Germany in 1967-68 Col. Charles "Bill" Patillo flew in the Skyblazers as wingmen with his twin brother. Link then replied, "My son is married to his brother's daughter." Small World? I asked Linc about his uncle's name Kennesaw Mountain which was General WILLIAM SHERMAN's worst battle near Atlanta. He said his grandfather was a surgeon at that battle. He said he was hit by an unexploded cannon ball which broke his leg! He sat against a tree and told another surgeon to get away from him saying, "I don't want you to cut off my leg!" Sherman ordered one charge up the mountain which was disastrous. He did not order another attack unlike Gen. AMBROSE BURNSIDE, who ordered seven units to attack little Marye's hill in Fredericksburg which had a sunken road and stone wall impenetrable defense. It is probably the deadliest single area in American History. In Georgian TED TURNER's movie GETTSYBURG (2000) Gen. WINFRID HANCOCK's and Col. JOSHUA CHAMBERLAIN's unit's at Cemetery Ridge shout "Fredericksburg" after defeating General PICKETT's Virginia Corps suicidal charge 7 months after their unit's disastrous attack at Marye's Heights.

MOM "I WANTED TO MEET TONTO!"

When I was 13, in September 1956, my mother took me to a movie premiere at the local COMMUNITY theater in Hudson, New York. The film WALK THE PROUD LAND was based on the true story of a local man a Christian Indian agent sent in 1874, to Apache Indian territory where the legendary GERONIMO, actor JAY SILVERHEELS, was rebellious. President Ulysses S. Grant, because of government officials and the U. S. Army's mistreatment, of Native Americans ordered the government to send only Christian, not abusive, corrupt government bureaucratic agents to "try a new approach to peace with the Apaches based on respect for autonomy rather than submission to the Army." Indian agent JOHN CLUM, was born at nearby Claverack, New York, where my High School Ockawamick Central, K-12, now Taconic Hills is located. He attended the DUTCH REFORMED Church in Claverack which my high school Facebook revealed celebrated its 300th anniversary in 2016.

GERMAN KARL MAY FAMOUS NATIVE AMERICAN NOVELIST

Why were American occupation soldiers greeted in friendship by German children wearing American Indian headdress and with bows and arrows and tomahawks? German author KARL MAY, who never saw a Native American Indian, wrote dozens of "dime" novels about American Indians and Cowboys. ADOLF HITLER was so inspired by May's writing that he passed out his novels among his Great War, World War I trench mate Bavarian unit German soldiers. Hitler was a fan of the American Indian "noble savage" whose homeland hunting grounds were occupied by the repressive white man.

Wikipedia recalls, "For the novels set in America, May created the character of WINNETOU, the wise chief of the APACHES [Geronimo?] and OLD SHATTERHAND, Winnetou's white blood brother. May had not visited the places he described, but he compensated successfully for this lack of direct experience through a combination of creativity, imagination, and documentary sources including maps, travel accounts and guide books, as well as anthropological and linguistic studies. The work of writers such as JAMES FENIMORE COOPER, Gabriel Ferry, Friedrich Gerstaecker, Baldouin Moellhausen and Mayne Reid allegedly served as his models."

Wikipedia asserts, "Non-dogmatic Christian values play an important role in May's works. Some of the characters are described as being of German, particularly Saxon, origins. Characters described as Native Americans are usually portrayed as innocent victims of white law-breakers."

Wikipedia cites, "In a letter to a young Jew who intended to become Christian after reading May's books, May advised him first to understand his own religion, which he described as holy and exalted, until he was experienced enough to choose."

My Austrian mentor Professor Pastor ERIC GRITSCH of Gettysburg Lutheran Seminary told me Hitler suppressed the reading of Karl May's American novels during the war and abolished the military Chaplaincy with the Luftwaffe being the last to have chaplains.

"Wikipedia recalls, "Adolf Hitler was an admirer, who noted in MEIN KAMPF that the novels of KARL MAY "overwhelmed" him as a boy going as far as to ensure "a noticeable decline" in his school grades. According to an anonymous friend, Hitler allegedly attended the lecture given by May in Vienna in March 1912 and was enthusiastic about the event. Ironically, the lecture was an appeal for peace, also heard by later NOBEL PEACE Prize laureate BERTHA von SUTTNER. Hitler allegedly later recommended May's books to his generals and had special editions distributed to soldiers at the front, praising Winnetou [Geronimo?] as an example of "tactical finesse and circumspection." ALBERT SPEER, Nazi Armaments minister, recalled, "When faced by seemingly hopeless situations, he [Hitler] would still reach for these [May] stories," because "they gave him courage like works of philosophy for others or the Bible for elderly people." German writer KLAUS MANN considered May as a "mentor" for Hitler. However, "In his admiration, Hitler ignored May's Christian and humanitarian approach and views completely, not mentioning his sympathetic description of the Jews and other persons of non-Northern European ancestry." Wikipedia

"The fate of Native Americans in the United States was used during the world wars for anti-American propaganda. The National Socialists in particular tried to use May's popularity and his work for their purposes." (Tales of The Grand Teutons: Karl May Among the Indians The New York Times, 4 January 1987)

Karl May was born February 25, 1842 in the Kingdom of Saxony on the northwestern border of Czechoslovakia. My mother's birthday February 22, 1915 in Frankfurt, Hesse.

KARL MAY AND HOLLYWOOD

"From 1962 to 1968, a series of May films were made. While most of the 17 movies of this series were WILD WEST movies. American actor LEX BARKER portrayed Old Shatterhand, PIERRE BRICE portrayed Winnetou and American actor STEWART GRANGER portrayed Old Surehand. The film score by Martin Boettcher was filmed in Yugoslavia. East German director Christophe von SYBERBERG filmed a German TV documentary about Karl May. Wikipedia

Wikipedia lists many pages of May's prolific other works including the Middle East. One unique one: "May's poem AVE MARIA (1896) was set to music in at least 19 versions."

HOLLYWOOD TRIVIA: Lex Barker was married to actresses ARLENE DAHL and LANA TURNER. He was born in Rye, Westchester County, New York on May 8, 1919 [my birthday May 4, 1943] Victory in Europe Day May 8, 1945. My mom lived on Milton Rd. Rye before moving to Amityville. Barbara Bush was born in Rye, NY. Barker passed on May 11, 1973, and was engaged to his to be 6th wife TV actress KAREN KONDAZIAN at the time of his passing. Her birthday in Newton, Massachusetts was January 27, 1950. My dad's birthday January 28, 1919 in Amityville, NY. Her Wikipedia site shows author OF CAT ON A HOT TIN ROOF TENNESSEE WILLIAMS kissing her on the mouth and Italian opera singer LUCIANO PAVOROTTI, THE THREE TENORS, kissing her on the left cheek on the set of YES, GIORGIO (1982) in which she acted.

Barker had a short but compelling role as Swedish actress ANITA EKBERG'S fiancé in FREDERICO FELLINI'S LA DOLCE VITA (1960). In February 1941, Barker enlisted in the U.S. Army achieving the rank of major. He was wounded in the head and leg fighting in Sicily, Italy (1943) during World War II, and received two Purple Heart awards. In the World War II film AWAY ALL BOATS (1956) he portrayed Commander Quigley.

Ekberg was born September 29, 1931 in Malmo, Sweden. My mother passed September 30, 1967, my brother, and granddaughter and cousin were born on September 30, 1945, and same day September 30, 2005, in Virginia and Florida.
Lex Barker may be best known for his role in TARZAN'S MAGIC FOUNTAIN (1949) Barker became the 10th official TARZAN of the movies. His blond, handsome, and intelligent appearance, as well as his 6'4" frame helped make him popular in the role [Olympic gold medal swimmer] Austrian born JOHNNY WEISSMULLER had made his own for 16 years. Barker made three more Tarzan action films.
Barker made a Western with another tall actor 6' 2 1/2" RANDOLPH SCOTT in THUNDER OVER THE PLAINS (1953). Scott was born in my Orange County, Virginia on January 23, 1898. My dad was born January 28, 1919. Scott was married to the heiress MARION DUPONT 1936-1939 and lived at MONPELIER, the former home and estate of President JAMES MADISON, 4th President of the United States and the Father of the Constitution. Scott served as a 2nd lieutenant in France during World War I, as a field artillery officer and learned horsemanship. He had attended the elite Orange County WOODBERRY FORREST School founded in 1889. Famous Alumni: Marvin Bush, youngest son of President GEORGE H. W. BUSH and brother of President George W, Bush; JAMES MCMURTRY, singer-songwriter LONESOME DOVE; JOHNNY MERCER, prolific standard songwriter; BETO O'ROURKE, 1991, former U.S. Texas Congressman; J. SARGEANT REYNOLDS, former U.S. Senator and Lt. Gov. of Virginia; and Julius Lewis, Jr. former mayor of Savannah, Georgia, 8TH AAF birthplace.
Wikipedia notes, "In 1966 Lewis became the first Republican mayor of a Georgia city since RECONSTRUCTION." Supreme Court Justice THOMAS was born in Savannah as was mayor Lewis. So it Goes.

Hollywood's Best American Indian Movie a Flop?

The movie script is based on a book APACHE AGENT: THE STORY OF JOHN P. CLUM written by his son Woodworth Clum. The film's location is San Carlos, Arizona, but was filmed in CinemaScope Technicolor at Hollywood's Old Tuscon site in Tuscon, Arizona.
The film's director JESSE HIBBS attended the University of Southern California (USC), where he was the captain of USC's first national championship team, in 1928. He was an ALL-AMERICAN tackle for the TROJANS in 1927 and 1928. Among his 1926 teammates was Marion Morrison,

151

later known as JOHN WAYNE. The year before WALK THE PROUD LAND in September 1955, Hibbs directed the movie TO HELL AND BACK based on AUDIE MURPHY's 1949 autobiography. Murphy was America's most decorated combat soldier in World War II. I visited Murphy's airplane crash site on Brush Mt., within sight of Roanoke, Virginia airport. Wikipedia shows Audie Murphy's memorial site which has 'only American flag' flying 24 hours without lighting on this mountain top.

I Meet Audie Murphy Most Decorated American Soldier

AUDIE MURPHY starred as Clum who would as part of the script quote from the Bible.

SPECIAL ATTRACTION: MISS AMERICA 1956, SHARON RITCHIE Miss Colorado also attended the premiere. She was crowned at the Boardwalk Hall in Atlantic City, New Jersey on September 10, 1955. As she was crowned by the former Miss America LEE ANN MERIWETHER, Miss California. The master of ceremonies BERT PARKS sang the song "THERE SHE IS, MISS AMERICA" for the first time. The pageant was televised nationally on ABC. My father was the senior broadcast engineer in ABC's Master Control room. I told my mother she was prettier than Miss America.

HISTORICAL FACT: Meriwether was crowned Miss America on the first live nationally televised broadcast of the competition on ABC TV on September 11, 1954. She later co-starred on the TV series BARNABY JONES, filmed in Wilmington, North Carolina, a popular movie and TV site, she portrayed RUTH MARTIN on the daytime soap opera ALL MY CHILDREN which also featured KELLY RIPA and her husband MARK COUNSELOS and the legendary ERICA KANE, SUSAN LUCCI. The record, 41-year "soap opera" 1970-2011 was an ABC TV production which my father put on the air from the Master Control room except in his final years in the new computerized TV control room switching to the late night shift before retiring in 1983.

FUN FACT: Meriwether portrayed CATWOMAN in the film version of BATMAN in 1966, the earliest big screen DC COMIC book ACTION HEROES film. These films today are immensely popular greatly aided by computer CGI technology.

"Walk the Proud Land" Actors

The great character Academy Award actress ANN BANCROFT, Bronx born Italian, great comedian MEL BROOKS wife, portrayed an Indian widow, made his housekeeper and falls in love with Clum, knowing he is an engaged man, his fiancé soon arrives. Clum's wife was actress PAT CROWLEY who later did many favorite TV shows. Her husband was an agent for ELVIS PRESLEY, JOHNNY CARSON and TOM BROKAW.

Actor CHARLES DRAKE is Clum's assistant a retired calvary sergeant who trains the Apache Indian police. Drake acted in several JAMES STEWART films WINCHESTER '73, about the inventor of the famous lever-action rifle, HARVEY, Stewart's imaginary rabbit friend film, both in 1950, THE GLENN MILLER STORY, 1954. Drake also appeared in other Western films with AUDIE MURPHY: GUNSMOKE, Audie a hired gun,1953, NO NAME ON THE BULLET, Audie an infamous very young hired gunman,1959. Drake also appeared with him as a close friend combat soldier in Murphy's TO HELL AND BACK about his combat in Italy and France in World War II. Drake is killed by German machine gun fire.

My Dad and the LONE RANGER

GERONIMO was portrayed by the most famous Native American actor JAY SILVERHEELS, born Harold Smith in SIX NATIONS OF THE GRAND RIVER FIRST NATION, Indian Reserve, Hagersville, Ontario, Canada on May 26,1912. He is best known for his 8 years portraying TONTO, the LONE RANGER's partner, on ABC TV's first true "hit". He helped bring justice to the Wild West. HI HO SILVER! The WILLIAM TELL OVERTURE played at the end of the show, became the most famous classical tune in history! My dad was an ABC Master Control engineer who connected the Lone Ranger to all America from the beginning. Jay Silverheels as Tonto was in 217 episodes; 1949-1957.

Lone Ranger Makes Famous TV Stars We All Loved

Many later famous actors were featured on the episodes: MICHAEL ANSARA, who also played Indian roles was husband of BARBARA EDEN "JEANNIE" with LARRY HAGMAN, JR of DALLAS, son of singer/actress MARY MARTIN; JAMES ARNESS, GUNSMOKE; PHYLLIS COATES, Lois Lane in the first SUPERMAN movie, 1951, and 26 episodes of ADVENTURES OF SUPERMAN, receiving equal billing at Superman GEORGE REEVES request. It was also an ABC TV popular series. She had a powerful "damsel in distress" scream which was effective in summoning Superman's assistance. George Reeves was a superman. Actor BEN AFLECK portrayed Reeves biography in a recent film. As a child I could not relate to Superman's death, a "suicide"? So Sad. Recently, Afleck portrayed BATMAN in BATMAN v SUPERMAN: DAWN OF JUSTICE which introduced the new WONDER WOMAN, GAL GIDOT. "At age 18, in 2004 she won the Miss Israel beauty pageant. Her maternal grandparents were HOLOCAUST survivors. At 20, she served two years as an enlisted soldier in the Israeli Defence Forces, serving as a combat trainer. Regarding this requirement about her time in the army she replied: "You give two or three years, and it is not about you. You learn discipline and respect." She was born in Petah Tikva, Israel Apr. 30, 1985. Her hometown was founded in 1878, by orthodox Jews and received financial aid from Baron EDMOND de ROTHCHILD, to drain the swamp, long before the post World War I BALFOUR declaration. The town's name was chosen by its founders from the prophecy in Hosea 2:15 proclaiming: "And I will give her vineyards from thence, and the Valley of Achor for an opening of hope: and she shall sing there, as in the days of her youth, and as in the day when she came up out of the land of Egypt." The city is Israel's hi-tech center the headquarters for IBM, INTEL, ORACLE, ECI Telecom and Alcatel-Lucent and the largest data center in Israel." Wikipedia. A vital city in Israel's economy and defense.
Another Lone Ranger show actress was MARION ROSS, best known for her 1974-1984 ABC TV role on HAPPY DAYS, as RON HOWARD's mother. My father retired from ABC Master control room in 1983, the senior technician, 34 years since it opened in 1949. Ross was born Oct. 25, 1928, age 88! My wife went into labor during the middle of a Happy Days show. My daughter was born in the MT. KISCO, NY Northern Westchester hospital December 24, 1975 morning. CHRISTOPHER REEVE, the second movie film SUPERMAN passed in the same hospital, he lived in adjoining Bedford Village. Reeve had his tragic paralyzing accident at nearby Culpeper VA, during a hazardous steeplechase horse show about 20 miles from my home. In October 1949, BRUCE JENNER was born in the same hospital. His family moved to nearby Newtown, Connecticut where he went to high school and learned sports. In the 1972, WORLD OLYMPICS in Montreal, Canada, he was awarded the GOLD medal in the demanding DECATHLON 10 events which has been dropped. Another actress was MARJORIE LORD who portrayed DANNY THOMAS wife for 8 TV seasons on MAKE ROOM FOR DADDY. Thomas founded the ST. JUDE

CHILDREN's hospital in Memphis which gives free care to needy families. RIP Lebanese American Danny Thomas. His daughter MARLO THOMAS is married to PHIL DONAHUE, former TV talk show host.

Jay Silverheels Path to Hollywood

"Silverheels was one of 11 children of a MOHAWK tribal chief, a Canadian military officer Major George Smith. Jay played indoor lacrosse as Harry Smith with the "Iroquois" of Rochester, NY in the 1930s. Living in Buffalo, NY, he placed second in the Middleweight class of the GOLDEN GLOVES boxing tournament in 1938. In 1937, while his team played lacrosse in Los Angeles, Silverheels impressed the beloved comedian JOE E. BROWN with his athleticism. Brown encouraged him to do a screen test leading to his career as an extra and stunt man. [Brown's only child, a pilot, was killed in an A-20 bomber near its Douglas aircraft factory in Los Angeles.] He later took a screen name Jay Smith Silverheels an uncle dubbed him with for his running style."
Of course, he was typecast racially as an Indian, Native American. Hollywood from the black and white silents in the 1920s through the big screen color movies of the 1950s produced hundreds of COWBOY AND INDIAN films. This guaranteed him numerous roles and because of his skill he received roles as some historical Indians. Ironically, some major Indian roles were also performed by famous Latino and even some Jewish American actors.This was because of the movie studio "star" actor-actress contract agreements.
Silverheels was featured, sometimes uncredited, not unusual for new actors, in big movies such as TYRONE POWERS CAPTAIN FROM CASTILE, as a runaway Aztec Spanish slave, 1947. It was his film debut along with a new starlet JEAN PETERS, who later married HOWARD HUGHES. KEY LARGO, with HUMPHREY BOGART, 1948; LUST FOR GOLD, GLENN FORD,1949; BROKEN ARROW, as Geronimo, with JAMES STEWART, 1950; THE PATHFINDER, as Chief Chingachgook the last of the Mohicans, 1952. WAR ARROW with MAUREEN O'HARA, 1954; THE BLACK DAKOTAS, he leads a justly vengeful Sioux war party, 1954, the heroine is actress WANDA HENDRIX, Audie Murphy's first wife 1949-1950, who introduced him to Hollywood. They divorced because of his violent war nightmares, PTSD. A man in my church who was in Murphy's unit told me he read that after the war Murphy slept with a gun under his pillow.
Wikipedia lists Jay Silverheels numerous movies and TV shows. He received a Star on the Hollywood Walk of Fame at 6538 Hollywood Blvd. I believe he is the only Native American to be so honored.
FUN FACT: "Jay raised, bred and raced Standard bred horses. A reporter asked him if he would race his famous paint horse Scout in a race. Jay laughed at the idea retorting, "Heck, I can outrun Scout!"   Wikipedia
In the movie WALK THE PROUD LAND Indian agent John Clum Audie Murphy uses his small Indian police force and using a Gideon Bible story he places some in the hills and has them fire their rifles and the echoes sound like a larger force. Geronimo, Jay Silverheels is tricked and surrenders. Wikipedia reveals that Clum had a larger force but he did surrender peaceably.

The Day I Met America's Most Decorated Soldier

THE REST OF THE STORY: At the end of the film my blonde German Lutheran refugee mother, from January 1935, told me to shake Audie Murphy's hand after telling me he is a brave American patriot. I had just turned 13, I didn't know that the Presidential Medal of Honor was only given to

154

America's bravest soldiers. As a young child I had a plastic carbine like he used in World War II, and would play soldiers in the woods in Amityville, Long Island, bordering the Massapequa woods, two streets west. I was stunned at the beginning of the 19xx movie BORN ON THE FOURTH OF JULY to see the name Massapequa shown in the woods screen scene where RON KOVIC was born. TOM CRUISE portrayed Kovic a US Marine, who accidentally kills a fellow Marine, is wounded and becomes a paraplegic pacifist. Cruise should have won the best actor Academy Award. His birthday in Syracuse, NY is July 3. Syracuse is also the birthplace of actor RICHARD GERE and TV commentator and morning show host MEGHN KELLY. Welsh actor DANIEL DAY LEWIS won for MY LEFT FOOT.

Mom "Where was Tonto?"

On the 14 mile drive to our home I told my mother I wanted to see Tonto! Tonto was in my living room for 8 years thanks to my father in the ABC Master control room. I don't know the reason Jay Silverheels wasn't there. Maybe he was making another film? His role as Geronimo was the highlight of the show and usually a main character is required to attend a premier as part of their Hollywood contract. Maybe he didn't come to the premiere from California because he was a proud native American?

Why the Movie Failed

Another possible factor according to Wikipedia Reception: "The film was not a success at the box office, something attributed to the fact that Murphy played a PACIFIST rather than an ACTION hero." U TUBE has this great video duration 1:24:35 minutes.

My mother took me to an endless number of cowboy and Indian movies. I considered this movie a welcome change from the excessively violent Hollywood portrayals. THEY DIED WITH THEIR BOOTS ON movie with dashing actor ERROL FLYNN portraying Col. GEORGE CUSTER, a brave and effective calvary general in many of the battles during the American Civil War of Secession, zealously rides his calvary to their death. The Sioux under CRAZY HORSE and chief SITTING BULL were fighting for their sacred land where some gold had been discovered? An historical fact everyone knew, no surprise Hollywood ending it was Custer's last stand along with his Medal of Honor winning brother who the Indians admired for his bravery.

Sadly, "Walk the Proud Land" failure ended Audie Murphy's plans to make his dream project, a biopic of painter CHARLES MARION RUSSELL. Russell painted hundreds of water colors of cowboys and Indians. Wikipedia shows several of his historical photograph like paintings. He did a painting of the Indians peaceably discovering LEWIS AND CLARK and THE CUSTER FIGHT from the point of view of his Indian opponents. His paintings are similar to what JOHN AUDUBON did in his paintings book the BIRDS OF AMERICA. Hollywood's best film about an artist was LUST FOR LIFE, one of actor KIRK DOUGLAS most difficult roles. It is alleged that after seeing his portrayal of the brilliant but mentally disturbed VINCENT VAN GOGH, John Wayne rebuked him for his role which ends in Van Gogh's suicide. That is what actors do "DUKE". Wayne's worst film was THE CONQUEROR where he portrayed GENGHIS KHAN. Yes, he and the Mongolians rode horses well. TV had a show about how many people in that film died from cancer because of atomic bomb tests in the Nevada desert where it was filmed. Cigarettes weren't blamed for cancer then but also were a cause.

Murphy's Chancellorsville Battle "Red Badge of Courage"

Audie Murphy also starred in the "coward turned hero" movie THE RED BADGE OF COURAGE an account of the local battle of Chancellorsville given to author STEPHEN CRANE by surviving veterans. Gen. THOMAS "Stonewall" JACKSON's famous surprise "12 mile flanking march" defeat of General JOSEPH HOOKER's much larger Union army. Jackson is wounded accidentally by Confederate soldiers because of his zealous "scouting" advance into the dense Wilderness forest in the dark. His left arm is amputated, and he soon passes from pneumonia while in bed recovering. His surgeon was Dr. HUNTER HOLMES McGUIRE. The large Veterans hospital in south Richmond, VA is named in his honor. Gen. ROBERT E. LEE laments, "I have lost my right arm!" The victory encourages Lee to take his army of Virginia about 115 miles north where he is meet by Union forces at GETTYSBURG, PA, July 1-3, 1863, where Lee's army suffers its greatest casualties. McGuire also founded Richmond Virginia Commonwealth hospital where America's first heart transplant was performed. McGuire hospital performs heart operations for veterans in the northeast. It also does many prosthetic operations. I had my broken left elbow repaired there by Dr. JEB STUART. I told him the story of Dr. McGuire and General Jackson's left arm amputation. He said, "Don't worry."

I just watched the black and white "Red Badge of Courage" (1951) on U TUBE, 1 hr. 46 min. I don't recall ever seeing it. It is incorrect showing the first Confederate attack being repulsed, then the second attack shows Union soldiers fleeing including Murphy going "AWOL" because of his overwhelming and understandable fear. The last battle scene shows the Union winning the battle with one captured Confederate soldier "complementing" Murphy's bravery. Murphy knew the scene was not bravery but Hollywood foolishness that would have killed him in combat. However, the book doesn't name the battle as Chancellorsville. My granddaughter when in 4th grade has a children's edition with many drawings which aren't graphic but realistic. The book was finally printed in 1895, just before his death on June 5, 1900, it is considered a classic. He died of tuberculosis, age 28, in a sanatorium in Badenweiler, in the German Black Forest. In July 1902, the great Russian writer ANTON CHEKOV passed there also.

During his final years Crane became a war correspondent in the Greco-Turkish war, 1897. He was accompanied there by CORA TAYLOR, whom he had meet in Florida, and knew Crane was renowned for his book Red Badge of Courage, but maybe also for his other book MAGGIE A GIRL OF THE STREETS which she could relate to through her Jacksonville, Florida "business". Read her wikipedia entry a soap opera script? She is recognized as the first woman war correspondent, she later lived in England as his common-law wife, taking his name from 1896-1900.

Her actual husband was a British Army captain whose father was Commander in Chief of India for QUEEN VICTORIA. When he was assigned to India she stayed in England as an "Empire widow". In England she was in the same upper society circle as fellow American JENNIE JEROME, a New York City socialite, who married Lord Randolph Churchill and was Winston Churchill's mother. The Crane's were befriended by two of Britain's greatest writers H. G. Wells and Joseph Conrad, a brilliant Polish-English writer." Wikipedia

HUMOROUS HISTORICAL FACT: On December 26, 1941, WINSTON CHURCHILL addressed a joint session of the whole American Congress, the first foreigner to do so. PROVIDENTIALLY, this was three weeks after America's most disastrous day PEARL HARBOR. Churchill's great rhetoric and humor were the catalyst needed by a shocked American nation on the day after Christmas. His address was broadcast nationally on the radio. It is on U TUBE and its message is still a motivation against world tyranny. He presented a realistic picture of the free world's dangerous situation against the Fascist totalitarian AXIS powers Germany, Japan and Italy. The British Commonwealth had been alone since France fell in June 1940, 17 months earlier. He used his American heritage as a political uniting sense of humor. He recalled, "If my father had been American rather than my mother I may have gotten here by myself! But, maybe that may not have happened at all!" His political statement brought laughter and great applause for awhile. Then he got serious but optimistic. He recalled the Great War and the resources America possessed but realistically said it will take time and great effort.

Mauldin WW II Cartoonist with Murphy in Badge of Courage

In the film Murphy's closest friend is BILL MAULDIN, an American combat soldier editorial cartoonist who won two PULITZER PRIZES and was awarded the military LEGION OF MERIT medal. "Mauldin was born in a mountain top village in New Mexico, his father was an artilleryman in World War I, and his paternal grandfather was a civilian calvary scout in the APACHE WARS. Mauldin joined the 45th Infantry Division of the US Army part of the Oklahoma Army National Guard. The unit traced their lineage from frontier militias that operated in the Southwestern United States throughout the late 1800s. The unit became the first National Guard unit activated in World War II in 1941. The unit began basic training at Ft. Sill, Oklahoma, then Ft. Devens, Massachusetts for amphibious assault training, then Pine Camp, New York for winter warfare training, hampered badly by poor weather, unfamiliar to the unit's desert inhabitants. In January it received its final combat training at Fort Pickett, Virginia. They first fought in the amphibious landing in Sicily, Salerno, amphibious landing at disastrous Anzio, Monte Cassino, Rome-Arno River in Italy, then southern France, Alsace-Ardennes Mountains and central Germany. In the Korean War the unit with many Latino Americans fought the Chinese People's Volunteer Army in fierce battles at Old Baldie hill alongside Colombian soldiers and at Eeerie Hill alongside Filipino soldiers." Wikipedia. The unit in both wars fought in the most mountainous and coldest weather of any American unit the frozen CHOSIN RESERVOIR in Korea and the war in Afghanistan's high mountains since 2001. See the movie-video 12 STRONG (2017) one of the greatest true historic military action films. It is realistically directed by RIDLEY SCOTT.   Wikipedia

Mauldin's Cartoons Anger His Commander General Patton

"During July 1943, Mauldin was a sergeant in the Sicily invasion as a cartoonist for STARS AND STRIPES, the American soldiers' newspaper and the 45th Division News then transferred to the Stripes in February 1944. Given a jeep he roamed the front line drawing his popular cartoons which the War Office allowed to be syndicated to newspapers, because they helped publicize the ground forces and also showed the grim side of the war, which helped show that victory would not be easy. His images—which often parodied the Army's spit-shine and obedience-to-orders-without-question policy—offended some officers.

PATTON THREATENS MAULDIN WITH JAIL

One of his cartoon's ridiculed Gen. GEORGE PATTON's decree that all soldiers be clean-shaven at all times, even in combat, Patton called Mauldin an "unpatriotic anarchist" and threatened to "throw [his] ass in jail" and ban the "Stars and Stripes" from his THIRD ARMY jurisdiction. Gen.

Dwight Eisenhower, Patton's superior, told Patton to leave Mauldin alone, he felt the cartoons gave the soldiers an outlet for their frustrations. "Stars and Stripes" is the soldiers' paper," he told Patton, "and we won't interfere." [Note: It is hard and painful, to shave with cold water from your helmet shown in some war films. However, there is a health aspect bandaging a head/neck wound. Bomber, fighter airmen shaved so their oxygen masks fit snugly.]

Generals Jackson, Patton, Marshall and Eisenhower

In a 1989 interview, Mauldin said, "I always admired Patton. Oh, sure, the stupid bastard was crazy. He was insane. He thought he was living in the Dark Ages.

[HISTORICAL NOTE: In the 1970 film PATTON portrayed by GEORGE C. SCOTT, born in Wise, VA, on the Kentucky border, with Gen. OMAR BRADLEY, after defeating ROMMEL'S Africa Corps, historically relives "reincarnation" the defeat of the CARTHAGINIAN army by the Roman legions at an historical site in Tunisia their homeland. Bradley portrayed by character actor KARL MALDEN bewilderedly listens to Patton's "History" story. Patton was a goat, last in his West Point class, because of his undiagnosed DYSLEXIA reading disability. As a child Patton's parents read him the historical stories about Alexander the Great, the Roman Caesar's, Napoleon and Rommel's tank memoir. Therefore, Patton was recalling childhood stories?

He learned about his favorite hero THOMAS "Stonewall" JACKSON when he attended, for a year, the VIRGINIA MILITARY INSTITUTE, VMI, in Lexington, Virginia, where Jackson taught, but had to go to WEST POINT for promotions. He didn't worry about the low pay because his and his wife's family made them the richest couple in the military. Gen. DWIGHT EISENHOWER, was son of a poor farm family in Kansas, received the epitaph "Swedish Jew" in his West Point year book, because of his frugality. Hitler must have know he wasn't Jewish. Actually, his name Eisenhower, in German means iron hewer, hauer is the German spelling, like a blacksmith. This is actually a Wagnerian analogy because in Wagner's Opera DAS RHEINGOLD there are dwarfs in the Underworld beating gold like blacksmiths. Hitler was obsessed with Wagner's Teutonic Nordic operas.

C.S. LEWIS MESMERIZED BY WAGNER OPERA

Ironically, C.S. CLIVE LEWIS was also captivated when he first heard Wagner's music. Lewis' departed mother read him many of the mythological stories about the Greek "mythological" demigod half human creatures satyrs which he depicts in his children's novels shown in three films. "IKE" was promoted faster than any general in US History. As a Lt. Colonel in 1940, "war games" Eisenhower's winning battle plan, Colonel Patton also participated, at Ft. POLK, Louisiana, impressed Army chief-of-staff Gen. GEORGE MARSHALL, a VMI graduate.
A Republican in a Democrat part of Pennsylvania he couldn't get a needed congressional appointment to WEST POINT! As Chief of Staff he led America's 16,500,000 military forces! Eisenhower had a brilliant organizational mind and was an excellent contract bridge player. Usually, military tacticians were chess players. RICHARD NIXON served as a Navy Lt. Commander supply officer in the Pacific during World War II. He was a skilled poker player. He had a poker face no "tell"? He was ready to make peace with Russia and China, therefore also Korea?, but WATERGATE ended his diplomacy! SOUND LIKE TRUMP'S DILEMMA?

GEN. EISENHOWER'S SECRET TO HIS MILITARY GENIUS BRIDGE—NOT CHESS—IS ULTIMATE WAR GAME

WALL STREET JOURNAL—OPINION by Michael Ledeen May 17, 2015

"There's a reason why Eisenhower and his generals were passionate about this most cerebral pastime.

"On the night of Nov. 7, 1942, [my son's birthday Nov. 8, 1977] as Allied forces in OPERATION TORCH headed for the North African coast, commanding Gen. Dwight Eisenhower waited anxiously. It was foggy, and news of the invasion was slow to arrive. To pass the time, IKE and three associates played bridge.

The game was an important part of Ike's life—throughout the war, in the White House and in retirement. In those years many American leaders were passionate bridge players: One of the men at Eisenhower's table that night was Gen. ALFRED GRUENTHER, later NATO commander and for many years president of the WORLD BRIDGE FEDERATION, Secretary of State JOHN FOSTER DULLES bragged about his mastery of the game, and his department long conducted a world-wide bridge tournament in embassies and consulates.

You'll hear that CHESS IS THE ULTIMATE MODEL FOR GEOPOLITICS, INDEED FOR WAR ITSELF. In the 1963 hit movie FROM RUSSIA WITH LOVE, JAMES BOND [SEAN CONNERY] is menaced by the brilliant Soviet chess master Tov Kronsteen (clearly modeled on BORIS SPASSKY).

But Eisenhower knew better. No board game can replicate the conditions of the battlefield or maneuvers of geo-strategy, for one simple reason. All of the pieces are visible on the table. Card games are better models because vital information is always concealed by the "fog of war" and the deception of opponents. Most of the time a bridge player sees only one-quarter of the cards, and some of the information he might gather from them is false.

Bridge is largely about communication, and every message a player sends— by bidding or playing a significant card—is broadcast to the player's partner and his opponents. Frequently a player will have to decide whether he would rather TELL THE TRUTH TO HIS PARTNER (thereby informing his opponents) or deceive the enemy (thus running the risk of seriously fooling his ally across the table).

Nothing like this exists in even the greatest board games. They permit some feints, to be sure, but not outright lies. GREAT BRIDGE PLAYERS are GREAT LIARS—as are BRILLIANT MILITARY LEADERS and DIPLOMATS and POLITICIANS. To take the most celebrated recent example, DENG XIAOPING, the man who transformed modern China, was an avid bridge player who had a private railroad car for his games.

The DIFFICULTY OF WEIGHING TRUTH AND LIES is one REASON that COMPUTERS DON'T WIN AT BRIDGE, whereas at the highest level of CHESS they DO VERY WELL. IBM DEEP BLUE defeated grandmaster GARRY KASPAROV in a six-game match in 1997, but BRIDGE IS SIMPLY TOO TOUGH FOR THE MACHINES.

Bridge may also be too tough for contemporary Americans. The bridge playing population is shrinking and aging. In Eisenhower's time, close to half of American families had at least one active bridge player, as of 10 years ago, a mere three million played at least once a week, and their average age was 51. Kibitz at a national bridge championship or a local club and you'll be impressed by the white hair and number of wheel chairs and oxygen tanks.

Another measure: When OPERATION TORCH landed, there were several bridge books on the best-seller list. Nowadays bridge books are printed in small numbers by specialized publishers.

The shrinking population of American bridge players goes hand in hand with other evidence of DECLINING MENTAL DISCIPLINE, including SHORTENING ATTENTION SPANS and

DECREASES IN BOOK READERSHIP. You can't be a WINNING CARD PLAYER UNLESS YOU CAN CONCENTRATE FOR SEVERAL HOURS, and mastery of the game takes years. Neither is bridge a solo activity; you need a partner with whom you must reach very detailed agreements about myriad situations. All this is GOOD FOR THE MIND. BRIDGE PROVIDES STIMULATION that can help players RETAIN THEIR MENTAL TOUGHNESS and stave off DEMENTIA.

It might be helpful to introduce bridge and competition to high schools and colleges, as has been done with chess. Bridge lovers like BILL GATES and WARREN BUFFETT would surely approve and could sponsor programs and tournaments for young players, with suitable rewards.

It's no accident that the GREATEST THINKER OF MODERN TIMES, NICCOLO MACHIAVELLI, was a card player, nor that his masterpiece, "THE PRINCE," REMAINS ESSENTIAL READING FOR OUR special forces officers. A prince, Machiavelli wrote, should be "faithful to his word, guileless" but "his disposition should be such that, if he needs to be the opposite, he knows how." That's A LESSON YOU CAN ONLY LEARN FROM KINGS AND JACKS, not kings and rooks."

(Mr. Ledeen, a freedom scholar at the Foundation for the Defense of Democracies, is a BRIDGE LIFE MASTER and the former coach of the ISRAELI National bridge team.)

Eisenhower's Other Title: Bridge Player in Chief

By Phillip Alder the New York Times Jan. 18, 2009

"Tuesday sees the inauguration of BARACK OBAMA as the 44th president of the United States. Bridge does not have a great history in the White House. The outgoing president, GEORGE W. BUSH, does not play, and his father, when asked if he played, replied: Bridge! The last time I played bridge was in 1950." BARBARA BUSH used to be a keen player, but has not competed in many years.

QUEEN ELIZABETH II does not play, preferring racing demon, complicated games of solitaire and six-deck bezique. The only British monarch known to have played was EDWARD VII. Other world leaders who played include DENG XIAOPING of China, who was very enthusiastic and often partnered WAN LI, once the chairman of the National People's Congress; WINSTON CHURCHILL and HERBERT ASQUITH, two British prime ministers who sensibly stuck to their day jobs.

Two famous Indians could play, MOHANDAS GANDHI learned bridge when studying in England. Karma, he observed, is like a bridge deal. Dharma corresponds to how the deal is played, and skill affects the outcome. NEHRU was an accomplished player.

Obama will be famous in his own way, but not as the best presidential bridge player, That honor belongs to DWIGHT EISENHOWER, who held Saturday-night games at the WHITE HOUSE. Regular players included FRED VINSON, CHIEF JUSTICE of the United States, and HAROLD TALBOTT, secretary of the Air Force. In the diagrammed deal, North was OSWALD JACOBY, one of the greatest players of all time.

The auction was straightforward: an opening bid, a strong jump-shift, support, Blackwood, one ace, slam.

After Vinson (West) led the diamond three and the dummy had been tabled, Eisenhower (South) saw that he would lose one diamond trick and that he could avoid the club finesse if he could establish a third heart trick with the diamond ace, South unblocked his king to give himself another dummy entry in case the trumps broke badly...Eisenhower won with his club ace, drew trumps and played on hearts, using dummy's diamond honors as entries. His club queen was eventually discarded on the heart jack."

160

[I will never be a BRIDGE card player this is all Greek to me. I won't ever be a tactical general either. At Bitburg AB in 1968, I was the editor of the airbase SKYBLAZER newspaper as a three stripe A1C, today senior airman, but called a Buck sergeant then. My commander was Col. CHARLES "Buck" PATILLO, who with his twin brother "Bill" PATILLO, were wingmen of the first Air Force THUNDERBIRDS precision jet team. They previously were wingmen with the SKYBLAZER jet demonstration team flying airshows in Europe in Republic F-84 Thunderjets which were built 3 miles from my house in Amityville, Long Island. They were stationed at FURSTENFELDBRUECK with the 36th Tactical Fighter Group which was relocated to the newly built Bitburg AB in January 1953. Colonel Patillo was my CO of the 36th Tactical Fighter Wing 1967-1968. After, an F-4D Phantom II crew chief was killed in an auto accident Colonel Patillo ordered/requested that as editor of the SKYBLAZER I promote auto safety through newspaper articles. When I was discharged from the Air Force at MCGUIRE AFB, New Jersey, in April 1969. I was told to review my Air Force file. I was pleased to see that Colonel Patillo wrote a commendation letter for my auto safety news stories. I have found my initial long FRONT PAGE article which I have included as part of my testimony. Lt. Gen. Charles Patillo passed in May 2019, age 95. He lived about five miles from my home and a few years ago I had a chance to meet him. He remembered me his 3 stripe airman. I had wanted to be a pilot like my dad had wanted in World War II. The Good Lord gave me the right Air Force position INFORMATION Specialist AFSC 72150 Air Force journalist. My personal, historical Witness/Testimony will proclaim:
"THE PEN IS MIGHTIER THAN THE SWORD!" Lord Acton

How was the Phrase "TRUMP CARD" Originated?

Christopher Burke, Citizen Baby Boomer—Quora Nov. 17, 2016

"In some card games, including Bridge, one of the suits is designated as the "TRUMP" suit. For the duration of the game, EVEN THE LOWEST CARD OF the "TRUMP" SUIT BEATS ANY CARD, NO MATTER HOW STRONG, OF ANY OTHER SUIT.
Also in these games, people don't see all of each others cards; they don't know for sure who has what cards.
Thus a "TRUMP CARD" REFERS TO A KIND OF SECRET WEAPON that, WHEN USED, MAKES WINNING VERY LIKELY. UNLESS YOUR OPPONENT USES A STRONGER "TRUMP CARD" TO BEAT IT.
The term originates from the same word as "TRIUMPH" and is centuries old."

[Pres.] TRUMP'S SUCCESS 'deranges' BRIDGE PLAYERS, Shedding Light on Biomedical Studies

By Sharon Begley STAT June 24, 2016

"The prospect of DONALD TRUMP becoming president is unconsciously affecting bridge players so muCh that they become "subtly deranged," researchers reported on Friday, with players succeeding with "NO TRUMP" games more often than before the real estate developer entered politics.
The study is real. The researchers are respected statisticians. The meeting where they presented the discovery is legitimate. The "NO TRUMP EFFECT" is bogus.

161

Statisticians analyzed data from the bridge tournaments to see if Trump's march to the WHITE HOUSE has "irrationally changed the behavior" of elite players.

The researchers adhered to good scientific practice by starting with a hypothesis—namely, that the idea of a President Trump would make bridge players (whom they believe to lean Democratic, or why would a liberal super PAC be called American Bridge?) unconsciously try harder to win their no trump bids. The bidders would unconsciously focus and strategize more intently, and their opponents would also be so unconsciously "DERANGED" at the possibility of a no trump bid failing that they don't put up much of a fight.

Data supported that hypothesis. "Back in 1999, one could afford to be nonchalant about declaring no trump since the decision to do so had no overt political implications," the researchers wrote. But "In 2015, if you're going to state the word "TRUMP" aloud, you need extra confidence that you can succeed, therefore inoculating yourself against a charge of political bias."

What Really Happened at Watergate? Tape on DNC Door?

The Watergate burglars put a piece of masking tape on the Democratic National Committee office door which was found by a guard removed the tape and on making his rounds the tape reappeared on the door again? The Negro security guard saw this, and called the DC police. HISTORY! In July 1973, at closing WESTOVER AFB SAC B-52 base near Springfield, MA, my born in Scotland in 1942, Air Force friend IAN, who worked with covert ops at HQ 17th AF Ramstein AB, SAC, DIA, Iran, Turkey, told me Nixon was SET UP by the Cuban DNC headquarter burglars! They were anti-Castro refugees opposed to President RICHARD NIXON and HENRY KISSINGER, Secretary of State, meeting the Chinese Communists and Stalinist Russians who were aiding FIDEL CASTRO's brutal Communist government in their homeland!

The film THE POST ends with the African-American night guard pointing his flash light at the DNC office door and he views a lot of masking tape on its lock. He calls the DC Police not FORREST GUMP's TOM HANKS. Hollywood FAKE HISTORY. Liberals must have loved that ending. The security guard removed a piece of tape then later saw tape again, called police. Wikipedia. I met GORDON LIDDY and told him my Air Force friend's story and asked him about the tape on the door. LIDDY retorted, "The cleaning ladies put the tape on door!" HE LIED! He knew the truth and went to jail. SO IT GOES!

President NIXON and WOODWARD and BERNSTEIN didn't know this? I guarantee you Russia's KGB spies and their East Germany agent Lt. Col. VLADIMIR PUTIN knew this. What did the FBI and the CIA know? This isn't difficult to connect. PERRY MASON or INSPECTOR CLOSEAU, the bumbling English actor PETER SELLERS. My favorite sleuth was the beloved TV detective COLOMBO, PETER FALK, who used the FACTS and always got his man. Justice. He was born in Ossining, NY where SING SING prison is located. Check his many films on Wikipedia.

BERNSTEIN on CNN called President TRUMP "PUTIN'S PAWN." PUTIN LOVES America's left wing socialist/fascist progressive "news" media. Trump is rebuilding our military and checking Putin's attempt to MAKE RUSSIA GREAT AGAIN. Only FOX NEWS admits Trump is making AMERICA GREAT AGAIN and destroying the Democrat Party which is imploding with its left wing socialist promises which have failed in Europe and everywhere else. The Golden goose has died! SHOW ME MY OWN MONEY!

Woodward has written book FEAR about President Trump. He will be reelected! MAGA!

DEEP THROAT was a disgruntled FBI agent MARK FELT, only revealed after his death. Does HIStory REPEAT ITSELF? Watch SEAN HANNITY, a "commentator", on FOX news. He has FOX lawyers which have without a doubt verified the political sedition/treason of top FBI officials, Justice Department, CIA, Defense Intelligence Agency?, NSA?, State Department, presidential candidate HILLARY CLINTON, UN secretary, and possibly the man at the top Pres. BARACK OBAMA, "the Buck stops here" and VP JOSEPH BIDEN and their "Russian collusion" trying to guarantee Hillary Clinton's "entitled" election. Culpable deniability?

Communist BERNIE SANDERS was actually defeating Hillary until the Democratic National Committee rigged it, super delegates. Then the first Assange EMAILS were released proving this and DNC chairman DEBBIE WASSERMAN SHULTZ, my son's Broward County representative, was fired at the DNC convention. Now, they are trying to remove President Trump. A banana republic junta/coup? The FOX news reporters/lawyers have all written detailed books about their corruption. A liberal media woman pundit referred to fired assistant FBI director McCabe as a "departed" agent. They promote dishonorable books which are best sellers bought by ignorant Trump haters.

America's Media Hates Trump more than Nixon! A Disgrace

Watergate did not affect any American's life. Nixon had received an unprecedented 62 per cent of the vote and 49 states! Because he "LIED" to Congress and his secretary "accidentally" erased 18 minutes of tape he resigned rather than be impeached. Was President RICHARD NIXON treasonous? Only hateful Democrats believe that. The Democratic party is destroying itself because they know time is running out. Their obstructing Republican congressmen from obtaining information is attempting to protect guilty Democrats by passing the statue of legal prosecution date. Democrats believe Clinton should be president because she received 3,000,000? more votes than President Trump. President DONALD TRUMP received more electoral votes than any political pundit left or right thought possible.The self righteous LIBERAL MEDIA was literally in SHOCK at 2:23 AM when Pennsylvania, where they "cling to their guns and Bibles and dislike others who are different than them", cast its vote for Trump.Then "rust belt" states West Virginia, Ohio, Michigan and liberal Wisconsin gave him 322 electoral votes more than the "impossible to get" 271 needed to become president. Pres. JIMMIE CARTER received 272 electoral votes against Pres. GERALD FORD in 1976.

Is CIA DIRECTOR John Brennan a PAID LIAR on CNN?

Wikipedia recalls, "Brennan applied to the CIA in 1980. During his application he admitted during the lie-detector test that he had voted for the Communist Party candidate four years earlier [1976]. To his surprise, he was still accepted; he later said that he finds it heartening that the CIA valued freedom of speech." Tal Kopan "Polygraph panic: CIA director fretted his vote for a communist." CNN September 15, 2016.

PERSONAL CONNECTION: In the summer of 1982, I took a headquarters CIA lie detector test to become a courier. The African American lie detector agent asked many simple questions. He read a list of organizations and associations and asked if I belonged to any of them. I had never heard of any of them and told him. The final question was "Is there any question you would like to discuss with me." I asked him. "Is the Beethoven Association communist or Nazis." He said it is a communist group. I asked if any of the other groups were Nazis. He retorted, "No." I told him my Lutheran mother left Hitler's Germany in January 1935, and was an illegal alien for five years until she married my father in August 1940. I said the CIA should include fascist/Nazi organizations. I didn't get the job to be a courier who carries CIA documents handcuffed

Former Senior CIA Officer Urges Reform of US Intelligence

American Action News April 20, 2020

"One retired 25-year CIA officer is leading the fight to fix and reform US intelligence. Brad Johnson spent his entire CIA career fighting America's enemies in the shadows, but after retiring he has a new mission—to depoliticize, rebuild and reform US intelligence. To fulfill his new mission, Johnson—who retired as a Senior Operations Officer with the CIA's Dir. of Operations founded Americans for Intelligence Reform."

"Sadly, the intelligence community has been politicized, and damaged, but not necessarily by the current [Trump] administration. Johnson explains that the CIA's so-called "modernization" plan implemented under the Obama administration by former director JOHN BRENNAN is a case in point. Brennan's imaging plan did not receive the attention it should have from the CIA's congressional overseers, or the media. As Johnson states, the Brennan plan "systematically dismantled and destroyed the CIA's operations division—the heart of the agent's central mission of using people to steal vital secrets around the world.""

"Johnson adds, Many of us who devoted our lives to the clandestine service as CIA operations officers were stunned to hear Mr. Brennan announced that based on his "modernization plan, he no longer regards the CIA as being an espionage business. 'We don't steal secrets,' Mr. Brennan astonishingly stated in an interview with NPR. As Johnson describes it to AM:

> The Brennan plan instead called for other nations' intelligence services to provide the CIA with spies as intelligence collectors. Real espionage is the direct recruitment of spies or reporting sources who steal information from other countries or organizations such as terrorists. An important feature of this process is that no one should know that our spies are stealing the information. Keeping the operations clandestine is fundamental to the credibility and reliability of the information. When another intelligence service selects spies for the CIA, the information provided could easily be mixed with damaging disinformation and we have no way to be sure of who else is aware we are receiving the information.

"This plan fundamentally alters and undermines the US intelligence mission, and according to Johnson, "combined with other factors makes the IC (intelligence community] fundamentally unreliable and marginalized when they are so desperately needed for our National Security."

PERSONAL ANALYSIS: CHRISTOPHER STEELE, a former British MI6, secret service, was a DONALD TRUMP hater. His phony dossier about presidential candidate Donald Trump and his Russian collusion cost American taxpayers $32,000,000 MUELLER investigation which distracted the CIA and FBI from more important United States security matters. Steele was born in British ADEN, today's YEMEN. Why would a British

Secret service agent be against an American presidential candidate?

I believe Steele was against BREXIT which candidate Trump proclaimed was a patriotic move for British citizens to separate from the European Common Market. Steele is likely a globalist like the liberal American Democrats who tried to remove President Trump in a hate Trump media blitz. A national disgrace, the left wing globalist media and politicians propagate for their economic gain with foreign companies. Wake up America

"A Republic if We Can Keep it!" Benjamin Franklin

Democrats claim America is a democracy and this isn't fair because of the popular vote. The FOUNDING FATHERS put the electoral college in the Constitution to actually protect states' rights. Hillary Clinton only got the vote of the three West Coast states, New England, New York, New Jersey, Illinois, Maryland and northern Virginia. That is not the UNITED STATES OF AMERICA.

Politicians just want to stay in POWER using their "bases". TERM LIMITS.
After, the new American Constitution was ratified it is a maxim that a women asked BENJAMIN FRANKLIN "Mr. Franklin what type of government do we now have?" Franklin retorted, "A REPUBLIC IF WE CAN KEEP IT!" America doesn't have royalty kings or queen's. However, we have had had family presidents: father, son, grandson or cousin presidents: JOHN and QUINCY ADAMS; WILLIAM HENRY HARRISON and BENJAMIN HARRISON; THEODORE and FRANKLIN ROOSEVELT; JOHN KENNEDY and almost ROBERT KENNEDY; GEORGE H.W. BUSH and GEORGE W. BUSH and BILL and almost HILLARY CLINTON.

I listen to the hateful exaggerated "progressive leftist" politicians and the mostly liberal "tolerant" news media and Hollywood attacks on a legally elected President DONALD TRUMP unrepentantly covering up or minimizing what appears to be undemocratic, un American acts of high level unelected officials with great power who are sworn to protect Americans including President DONALD J. TRUMP America's legally elected leader. I think of Hitler/Stalin. My mother met Eleanor Roosevelt in 1955. Read her letter from president elect Eisenhower Dec. 27,1952, for peace during the Korean War.

I well remember the longtime incredibly negative, biased and prejudicial media dislike of Richard Nixon even after his landslide presidential victory. After my discharge from the U.S. Air Force I visited my dad in the ABC Master Control room where he was the senior engineer. I recall the ABC news that night was very controversial because it regarded the American media's criticism of President Nixon. Vice President SPIRO AGNEW appeared on TV and spoke his detested alliterative rhetoric rebuking the media as: "Nattering nabobs of negativity." I understood Agnew's message which few viewers did.

THE FOURTH ESTATE'S PROPAGANDA

THE "FOURTH ESTATE" the media (Press, TV, Radio, Cable and now Internet) are supposed to serve as a means to inform citizens of national and international political events. It is to be a "watch dog" not an "attack dog" like it has become today. The news is polarized with left wing progressive socialist bias and right wing conservative bias and even prejudice which is dividing and polarizing Americans. Only the Vietnam War and Civil Rights protests rightfully caused a greater popular division in the media. This allows our enemies who have repressive and totalitarian governments to show Americans as divided which we really aren't.

Defense Information School of Journalism Ft. Slocum

I attended this school on the Long Island Sound for 10 weeks July to September 1965. its last class. Three future vice presidents attended there DANIEL QUAYLE, WALTER MONDALE and AL GORE. ANDRIAN CRONAUER, radio broadcaster in GOOD MORNING VIETNAM attended there a year earlier. He said ROBIN WILLIAMS portrayed some events which would not have been tolerated according to the rules manual. TIGER WOODS father also graduated at Ft. Slocum. The most famous person there who attended the additional two week radio-TV course was PAT SAJACK.

The FIVE Ws of Journalism the Lead Paragraph

"This is the FIRST RULE of journalism in newspaper, magazine writing or TV and radio stories. [It is loosely applied to in TWITTER, BLOGS and EMAILS]. The Five Ws are questions whose answers are considered basic information gathering or problem solving. They are often mentioned in journalism (news style), research and police investigations. They constitute a formula for getting the complete story on a subject. According to the principle of the Five Ws, a report can only be considered complete if it answers these questions starting with an interrogative or question word sometimes called WH-WORDS, because in English most of them start with WH. They may be used in both direct questions or in indirect questions."   Wikipedia
*WHO *WHAT *WHEN * WHERE *WHY
"Some authors add a sixth question, HOW, to the list. *How did it happen?
Each question should have a factual answer—facts necessary to include for a report to be considered complete. Importantly, none of these questions can be answered with a simple "YES" or "NO".   Wikipedia
"The Five Ws and How were long attributed to Hermagoras of Temnos, an ancient Greek rhetorician of the Rhodian school and teacher of rhetoric in Rome in the 1st century BC.
Some attribute the Five Ws earlier to the great Greek philosopher ARISTOTLE, ALEXANDER THE GREAT's tutor, in his Nicomachean Ethics as the source of the elements of circumstance or Septem Circumstantiae. Catholic theologian THOMAS AQUINAS acknowledged Aristotle as the originator of the elements of circumstances, providing a detailed commentary on Aristotle's system in his "Treatise on Human Acts". He examines the concept of Aristotle's voluntary and involuntary actions in his SUMMA THEOLOGIA as well as a further set of questions about the elements of circumstance."
"Aristotle wrote: "For in acts we must take note of WHO did it, by what aids or instruments he did it (WITH), WHAT he did, WHERE he did it, WHY he did it, HOW and WHEN he did it."   Wikipedia
"For Aristotle, the elements are used in order to distinguish voluntary or involuntary action."
"These elements of or circumstances are used by Aristotle as a framework to describe and evaluate moral action in terms of What was/should be done, Who did it, How it was done, Where it happened, and most importantly for what reason (Why), and so on for all the other elements." Wikipedia
"In the POLITICS, Aristotle illustrates why the elements are important in terms of human (moral) action stating: "I mean, for instance a particular circumstance or movement or action). How could we advise the Athenians whether they should go to war or not, if we did not know their strength (How much), whether it was naval or military or both (What kind), and how great it is (How many), what their revenues amount to (With), Who their friends and enemies are (Who), what wars, too they have waged (What), and with what success; and so on."   Wikipedia
"By 1917, the "Five Ws" were being taught in high-school journalism classes, and by 1940, the tendency of journalists to address all of the "Five Ws" within the lead paragraph of an article was being characterized as old-fashioned and fallacious:
"The old-fashioned lead of the five Ws and the H, crystallized largely by Pulitzer's "new journalism" and sanctified by the schools, is widely giving way to the much more supple and interesting feature

lead, even on straight news stories." "Trends in Newspaper Content" Annals of the American Academy of Political and Social Science, Frank Mott

PERSONAL STORY: I was the Historical/Political editor at the World Almanac and Book of Facts 1969-1975. The World Almanac was created by JOSEPH PULITZER, editor of the St. Louis Dispatch in 1868 as a "compendium of universal knowledge." Today, it is still the most comprehensive and respected one volume reference book in the world.

Pulitzer, a Jewish immigrant from the Austro-Hungarian Empire. served as a Union cavalry officer during the American Civil War of Secession. Pulitzer founded the America's first school of Journalism at Missouri University.

HOLLYWOOD FACT: Actor BRAD PITT was one semester short of getting a journalism degree at the University of Missouri but decided to go to Hollywood instead.

The PULITZER PRIZE is journalism's version of the NOBEL PRIZE or ACADEMY AWARD. Today, these esteemed awards have become "modern secularly progressive liberal" rejecting the traditional American biblically conservative constitutional beliefs.

PULITZER'S PROPHECY: Joseph Pulitzer's 1948, 3 cent commemorative postage stamp features his image with his prophetic words: "OUR REPUBLIC AND ITS PRESS WILL RISE AND FALL TOGETHER."   Today, this would include electronic media.

THE 2016 ELECTION AND THE DEMISE OF JOURNALISTIC STANDARDS

Michael Goodwin The NEW YORK POST speech April 20, 2017
Hillsdale College, MI National Leadership Conference Atlanta, Georgia

"I have been a journalist for a long time. Long enough to know that it wasn't always like this. There was a time not so long ago when journalists were trusted and admired. We were generally seen as trying to report the news in a fair and straight forward manner. Today, all that has changed, for that, we can blame the 2016 election or, more accurately, how some news organizations chose how to cover it. Among the many firsts, last year's election gave us the gobsmacking revelation that most of the mainstream media puts both thumbs on the scale — most of what you read, watch, and listen to is distorted by intentional bias and hostility. I never seen anything like it. Not even close."

"It's not exactly breaking news that most journalists LEAN LEFT. I used to do that myself, I grew up at THE NEW YORK TIMES, so I'm familiar with the species. For most of the media, bias grew out of the social revolution of the 1960s and '70s. Fueled by the Civil Rights and antiVietnam war movements, the media jumped on the anti-authority bandwagon writ large. The deal was sealed with WATERGATE, when JOURNALISM WAS VIEWED AS MORE TRUSTED THAN GOVERNMENT— and FAR MORE EXCITING AND GLAMOROUS. Think ROBERT REDFORD in ALL THE PRESIDENT'S MEN. [INVESTIGATIVE JOURNALISM through a disgruntled top FBI agent leaker MARK FELT "DEEP THROAT"]. Ever since, young people became journalists because they wanted to be the next WOODWARD and BERNSTEIN, find a DEEP THROAT, and BRING DOWN A PRESIDENT. [That has been attempted on President TRUMP through corrupt high-level FBI appointees, heads of Intelligence agencies and Justice Department self-righteously presenting seditious false information on TV news or through hundreds of "leaks" to biased media like CNN and MSNBC, whose top executives order their "news persons" to emphasize only "news" critical to President Trump's presidency because it has created the best American economy in 50 years. These news persons have become wealthy as long as they keep their Trump hating viewers "tuned in" so they don't lose their expensive advertising ads. Their news is scripted from higher up so they all use "parrot" talking points repeating the same catch phrase like "bombshell news." [It is truly biased FAKE HATE NEWS.]

"Of course, most of them only wanted to BRING DOWN A REPUBLICAN PRESIDENT."

"During the years I spent teaching at the Columbia University of Journalism, I often found myself telling my students that the job of the reporter was "TO COMFORT THE AFFLICTED AND AFFLICT THE COMFORTABLE." I'm not even sure where I first heard that line, but it still captures the way most journalists think about what they do. Translate the first part of that compassionate-sounding idea into the daily decisions about what it makes news, and it is easy to fall into the habit of thinking that every person afflicted by something is entitled to help. Or, as liberals like to say, Government is what we do together." From there, it's a short drive to the conclusion that every problem has a government solution."

"The rest of the journalistic ethos — "afflict the comfortable" — leads to the knee-jerk support of endless taxation. Somebody has to pay for that government intervention the media loves to demand. In the same vein, and for the same reason, the average reporter will support every conceivable regulation as a way to equalize conditions for the poor. He will give sympathy coverage to groups like OCCUPY WALL STREET and BLACK LIVES MATTER."

A NEW DIMENSION

"I knew all of this about the media mindset going into the 2016 presidential campaign. But I was still shocked at what happened. This was not naive liberalism run amok. This was a whole new approach to politics. No one in modern times has seen anything like it. As with grief, there were several stages. In the beginning, Donald Trump's candidacy was treated as an outlandish publicity stunt, as though he isn't a serious candidate and should be treated as a circus act. But television executives suddenly made a surprising discovery: The more they put Trump on the air, the higher their ratings climbed. Ratings are money. So news shows started devoting hours and hours simply to pointing the cameras at Trump and letting them run."

"As his rallies grew, the coverage grew, which made an odd dynamic. The candidate nobody in the media took seriously was attracting the most people to his events and getting the most news coverage. Newspapers got in the game too. Trump, unlike most of his opponents, was always available to the press, and could be counted on to say something outrageous or controversial that made   a   headline."

"Despite the mockery of journalists and late-night comics, something extraordinary was happening. Trump was dominating a campaign none of the smart money thought he could win. And then, the crowded Republican field began to thin and Trump kept racking up primary and caucus victories did the media's tone grow more serious."

"One study estimated that Trump had received so much airtime that if he had to buy it, the price would have been $2,000,000,000 [billion]. [HILLARY CLINTON spent about a billion dollars of Democratic Party and liberal wealthy elitist funds.] The realization that they had helped Trump's rise seemed to make many executives, producers, and journalists furious. By the time he secured the nomination and the general election rolled around, they were gunning for him. Only two people now had a chance to be president, and the overwhelming media consensus was that it could not be Donald Trump. They would make sure of that. The coverage of him grew so vicious and one-sided that last August I wrote a column on the unprecedented bias. Under the headline "AMERICAN JOURNALISM IS COLLAPSING BEFORE OUR EYES," I wrote that the so-called cream of the media crop was "engaged in a naked display of partisanship" " designed to bury Trump   and   elect   HILLARY   CLINTON."

"The evidence was on the front page, the back page, the culture pages, even the sports page. It was at the top of the broadcast and at the bottom of the broadcast. Day in, day out, in every media market in America, Trump was savaged like no other candidate in memory. We were watching the total collapse of standards, with fairness and balance tossed overboard. Every story was an opinion masquerading as news. and every opinion ran in the same direction — toward Clinton and away from Trump."

"For the most part, I blame The New York Times and The Washington Post for causing the breakdown. The two leading liberal newspapers were trying to top each other in their demonization of Trump and his supporters. They set the tone, and most of the rest of the media followed like lemmings."

"On one-level, tougher scrutiny of Trump was clearly defensible. He had a controversial career and lifestyle, and he was seeking the presidency as his first job in government. He also provided lots of fuel with some of his outrageous words and deeds during the campaign. But from the beginning there was also a second element to the lopsided coverage. The New York Times had not endorsed a Republican for president since DWIGHT EISENHOWER in 1956, [60 years] meaning it would support a dead raccoon if it had a "D" after his name. Think of it — GEORGE MCGOVERN OVER RICHARD NIXON? JIMMY CARTER OVER RONALD REAGAN? WALTER MONDALE OVER REAGAN? Any Democrat would do. And The Washington Post, which only started making editorial endorsements in the 1970s, HAS NEVER ONCE ENDORSED A REPUBLICAN CANDIDATE."

"But again, I want to emphasize that 2016 had those predictable elements plus a whole new dimension. This time, the papers dropped the pretense of fairness and jumped headlong into the task for one candidate over the other. The Times media began a story this way:

> If you're a working journalist and you believe that Donald J. Trump
> is a DEMAGOGUE playing to the NATION'S WORST RACIST and
> NATIONALIST TENDENCIES, that he cozies up to anti-American
> dictators and that he would be dangerous with control of the
> United States nuclear codes, how the heck are you supposed
> to cover him?

"I read that paragraph and I thought to myself, well, that's actually an easy question. If you feel that way about Trump, normal journalistic ethics would dictate that you shouldn't be covering him. You cannot be fair. And you shouldn't be covering HILLARY CLINTON either, because you've ALREADY DECIDED WHO SHOULD BE PRESIDENT. [Hillary Clinton actually roped off reporters from her so they couldn't ask her questions.] Go cover sports or entertainment. Yet The Times media reporter rationalized the obvious bias he had just acknowledged, citing the view that Clinton was "normal" and Trump was not."

"I found the whole concept appalling. What happened to fairness? What happened to standards? I'll tell you what happened to them. The Times top editor, Dean Baquet, eliminated them. In an interview last October within the Nieman Foundation for Journalism at Harvard, Baquet admitted that the piece by his media reporter had nailed his own thinking. Trump "challenged our language," he said, and Trump "WILL HAVE CHANGED JOURNALISM." Of the daily struggle for fairness, Baquet had this to say: "I think that Trump has ended that struggle…We now say stuff. We fact check him. We write it more powerfully that [what he says is] false."

"Baquet was being too modest. Trump was challenging, sure, but it was Baquet who changed journalism. He's the one who decided that the standards of fairness and nonpartisanship could be abandoned without consequence."

"With that decision, Baquet also changed the basic news story formula. To the age-old elements of WHO, WHAT, WHEN, WHERE, and WHY, he aded the reporter's opinion. Now the floodgates were open, and virtually every so-called news article reflected a clear bias against Trump. Stories, photos, headlines, placement in the paper — all the tools that writers and editors have — were summoned to battle. The goal was to pick the next President."

"Thus began the spate of stories, which continues today, in which The Times routinely calls True a liar in its news pages and headlines. Again, the contrast with the past is striking. The Times never called Barack Obama a liar, despite such obvious opportunities as "YOU CAN KEEP YOUR DOCTOR" and "THE BENGHAZI ATTACK WAS CAUSED BY AN INTERNET VIDEO." [To disagree with president OBAMA'S policies would have been called RACIST losing readers and advertising revenue for a bankrupt newspaper bought cheaply by a socialist liberal.]

"Indeed, The Times and The Washington Post, along with most of the WHITE HOUSE PRESS CORPS, spent 8 years cheerleading the [GLOBALIST] OBAMA administration, seeing not a smidgen of CORRUPTION AND DISHONESTY. They have been tougher on HILLARY CLINTON during her long career. But still they never called her a liar, despite such doozies as "I SET UP MY OWN COMPUTER SERVER SO I WOULD ONLY NEED ONE DEVICE," "I TURNED OVER ALL THE GOVERNMENT EMAILS," and "I NEVER SENT OR RECEIVED CLASSIFIED EMAILS." All those were a lie, but not to the national media. Only statements by Trump were fair game."

"As we know now, most of the media missed Trump's appeal to millions upon millions of Americans." [63 million/Clinton 65 million] The prejudice against him blinded those news organizations to what was happening in the country. Even more incredibly, I believe the bias and hostility directed at Trump backfired. [Hillary Clinton called "half the Trump voters DEPLORABLE." Final vote was 51% Democrat 49% Republican — State electoral votes needed 270, Trump got 302 to 238]

"The feeling that the election was, in part, a referendum on the media, gave some voters the incentive to vote for Trump. A vote for him was a lot against the media and Washington. Not incidentally, Trump used that sentiment to his advantage, often reviving up his crowds with attacks on reporters. He still does."

"If I haven't made it clear, let me do so now. The behavior of much of the media, but especially The New York Times, was a disgrace. I don't believe it ever will recover THE PUBLIC TRUST it squandered."

"The Times' previous reputation for having the highest standards was legitimate. Those standards were developed over decades TO FORCE REPORTERS AND EDITORS TO BE FAIR AND GAIN THE PUBLIC TRUST. The commitment to FAIRNESS made The New York Times the flagship of America journalism. But standards are like laws in the sense that they are made to guide your behavior in good times and in bad. Consistent adherence to them was the source of the Times' credibility. And eliminating them has made the paper less than ordinary. Its only standards are of double standards."

"I say this with great sadness. I was blessed to grow up The Times, getting a clerical job right out of college and working for a decade. It was the formative experience of my career where I learned most of what I know about reporting and writing. Alas, it was a different newspaper then. Abe Rosenthal was the editor in those days, and long before we'd heard the phrase "zero tolerance," that's what Abe practiced toward conflicts of interest and reporters opinions. He set the rules and everybody knew it."

"Here is a true story about how Abe Rosenthal resolved a conflict of interest. A young woman was hired by The Times from one of the Philadelphia newspapers. But soon after she arrived in New York, a story broke in Philly that she had a romantic affair with a political figure she had covered, and that she accepted a fur coat and other expensive gifts from him. When he saw the story Abe called the woman into his office and asked her if it was true. When she said yes, he told her to clean out her desk— that she was finished at The Times and would never work there again. As word spread through the newsroom, some reporters took the woman's side and rushed in to tell Abe that he was too harsh. He listened for about 30 seconds, raised his hand for silence, and said (this is slightly bowdlerized): "I don't care if you have a romantic affair with an elephant on your personal time, but then you can't cover the circus for the paper." Case closed! The conflict of interest policy was clear, absolute, and unforgettable."

"As for reporters' opinions, Abe had a similar approach. He didn't want them in the news pages. [Like Sergeant JOE FRIDAY on the TV series DRAGNET "NOTHING BUT THE FACTS MAM!"] And if you put them in, he took them out. They belonged in the opinion pages only, which were managed separately. Abe said he knew reporters tended to lean left and find ways to sneak their views into stories. So he saw his job as steering the paper slightly to the right. "That way," he said, "the paper would end up in the middle." he was well known for his attitude, which he summed up as "keeping the paper straight." Like most people, I thought this was a joke. But after I related this in a column last year, his widow contacted me and said it wasn't a joke—that, in fact, Abe's tombstone reads, "He kept the paper straight." She sent me a picture to prove it. I published that picture of his tombstone alongside a column where I excoriated the Times for its election coverage." Sadly, The Times' high standards were buried with Abe"

LOOKING TO THE FUTURE

"Which brings us to the crucial questions. Can the American media be fixed? And is there anything that we as individuals can do to make a difference? The short answer to the first question is, "no it can't be fixed." The 2016 election was the media's Humpty Dumpty moment. It fell off the Wall, shattered into a million pieces and can't be be put back together again. In case there is any doubt, 2017 is confirming that the standards are still dead. The orgy of visceral Trump bashing continues unabated."

"But the future of journalism isn't all gloom and doom. In fact, if we accept the new reality of widespread bias and seize the potential it offers, there is room for optimism. Consider this — the election showed the country is roughly divided 50-50 between people who will vote for a Democrat and who will vote for a Republican. But our national media is more like 80-20 in favor of Democrats. While the media, in theory, broadly reflect the public, it doesn't. Too much of the media acts like a special interest group. Detached from the greater good, it exists to promote its own interest and the political party with which it is aligned."

"Ronald Reagan's optimism is often expressed in a story that is surely APOCRYPHAL, but irresistible. He is said to have come across a barn full of horse manure and remarked cheerfully that there must be a pony in it somewhere. I suggest we look at the media landscape in a similar fashion. The mismatch between the mainstream media and the public's sensibilities means there is a vast untapped market for news and views that are now not represented. To realize that potential we only need three ingredients, and we already have them: First, free speech, Second, Capitalism and the free market; and the Third ingredient is you, the consumers of the news.'

"FREE SPEECH IS UNDER ASSAULT, most obviously on many college campuses, but also in the MEDIA, which presents a conformist view to its audience and get a politically segregated audience in return. Look at the letters section in The New York Times — virtually every reader who writes in agrees with the opinions of the paper. This isn't a miracle; it's a bubble. Liberals use to love to say, "I DON'T AGREE WITH YOUR OPINION, BUT I WOULD FIGHT TO THE DEATH TO LET YOU SAY IT. "You don't hear [read] that anymore from the left. NOW THEY WANT TO SHUT YOU UP IF YOU DON'T AGREE. And they are having some success."

"But there is a countervailing force. Look at what happened this winter when the Left organized boycotts of department stores that carried IVANKA TRUMP'S clothing and jewelry. NORDSTROM folded like a cheap suit, but Trump's supporters rallied on the social media and Ivanka's company had its best month ever. This is the model I have in mind for the media. It is similar How Fox News got started. RUPERT MURDOCH thought there was an untapped market for a more fair and balanced news channel, and he recruited ROGER AILES to start it more than 20 years ago. Ailes found a niche market alright — half the country!"

"Incredible advances in technology are on the side of free speech. The explosion of choices make it impossible to silence all dissent and gain a monopoly, though Facebook and Google are trying." [FACEBOOK and GOOGLE have in the summer of 2019, testified before Congress about their ALGORITHMS being used to block Conservative/Republican commentary and being biased supporting Liberal and Socialist/Democrat commentaries.]

"As for the necessity of preserving capitalism, look around the world. Nations without economic liberty have little or no dissent. That's not a coincidence. In this, I am reminded of an enduring image from the OCCUPY WALL STREET movement. That movement was a pestilence, egged on by President OBAMA and others who view other people's wealth as a crime against the common good. This attitude was on vivid display as the protestors held up their — iPhones —to demand the end of capitalism. As I wrote at the time, did they believe STEVE JOBS made each and every APPLE product one at a time in his garage? Did they not have a clue about how capital markets make life better for more people than any other system known to man? They had no clue. And neither do many government officials, who think they can kill the Golden Goose and still get golden eggs." [A very appropriate term I have also long equated to the decadence of COMMUNISM/FASCIST-SOCIALISM. In the Air Force I graduated from the Defense School of Journalism last class at Ft Slocum, NY. I was the editor of the Bitburg AB, Germany SKYBLAZER newspaper in 1968. I was History/Government editor researcher-writer at THE WORLD ALMANAC and BOOK OF FACTS 1969-1975. Journalists primary job is dealing with facts and conveying them to their readers in an accurate truthful way with no biased opinion. In the U.S. Air Force as editor I was the Wing and base commanders and all officers and airmen's spokesman. Factual inaccuracy or biased opinion could cause conflict at Bitburg Air Base which was the most strategic COLD WAR location in Europe 1966-1969. I could have been demoted "busted" or even imprisoned. Read my story of how I providentially reported DR. MARTIN LUTHER KING'S assassination by using the HQ flag at half mast. I was on mess hall check when an African American airmen told me about the assassination.]

"Which brings me to the THIRD necessary ingredient to determining where we go from here, IT'S YOU. I urge YOU to support the media you like. As the great writer and thinker Midge Decter once put it, "You have to join the side you're on." It's no secret that newspapers and magazines are losing readers and money and shedding staff. Some of them are good newspapers. Some of them are good magazines. There are so wonderful, thoughtful, small publications and websites that exist on a shoestring. Don't let them die. Subscribe or contribute to those you enjoy. Give subscriptions to friends. An expanded media landscape that better reflects the diversity of public preferences would, in time, help create a more level political and cultural arena."

SOVIET JOURNAL FINDS AMERICAN PRESS LACKING

New York Times James F. Clarity September 22, 1969
"In Judging 19 Papers, It Calls Several Bourgeois and Most
Bourgeois and Most Heavy With Advertising."

"MOSCOW, Sept. 21 — ZHURNALIST, the organ of the Soviet Union of Journalists, has assessed "the most important" American daily newspapers and found them generally unprogressive, heavy with profitable advertising and ties to special interest groups." "In its current issue, the monthly magazine characterized several of the 19 papers appraised as bourgeois, one of the favorite pejoratives of the Soviet press." "Only the DAILY WORLD, the paper of the American Communist party, and the PEOPLE'S WORLD, published in San Francisco, were accorded what could be considered unqualified praise."

"The magazine said that "despite the large quantity of pages" in the American papers, "on the average two-thirds of their space is devoted to advertising." The papers, Zhurnalist reported, derive more income from advertising than from paid circulation. Zhurnalist gave the following descriptions of "the most important organs of the press" in the United States."

BALTIMORE SUN—"Closely tied to financial circles."

CHICAGO SUN-TIMES —"Reflects the views of the liberal bourgeoisie."

CHICAGO TRIBUNE—"Of philistine character. Pursues the policy of conservative circles of the monopolistic bourgeoisie of the Middle West."

DAILY WORLD—"Carries on a persistent struggle for the protection of the rights of American workers."

DES MOINES REGISTER—"Adheres to moderate views."

DENVER POST—"Reputedly independent. Supports liberal bourgeoisie circles."

JOURNAL OF COMMERCE—"Influential organ of business circles."

CHRISTIAN SCIENCE MONITOR—"Formally a religious newspaper, in fact a general political publication. Reflects the views of the big bourgeoisie."

LOS ANGELES TIMES—"Takes conservative positions."

DAILY NEWS (of New York)—"A philistine newspaper. Reflects the attitudes of extreme reactionary circles."

NEW YORK POST—"Reportedly independent. In fact supports the policies of the Democrat party."

NEW YORK TIMES—"Influential newspaper, closely tied to big monopolistic capital."

PEOPLE'S WORLD—"Progressive daily newspaper published in San Francisco."

SAN FRANCISCO CHRONICLE—"Reflects the views of the big bourgeoisie."

ST. LOUIS POST-DISPATCH —"Reputedly independent. Sometimes advances criticism of particular aspects of government policy."

WALL STREET JOURNAL—"Organ of business circles. Adheres to rightest views."

WASHINGTON DAILY NEWS—"Has philistine character. Lends support to reactionary circles."

WASHINGTON EVENING STAR—"Reflects the views of the big industry and the financial bourgeoisie."

WASHINGTON POST—"Reputedly independent. Supports the liberal wing of the major bourgeoisie."

"In addition, Zhurnalist said that in America, "the progressive press feels constant pressure from the ruling circles of the U.S. and finds itself in a difficult material position."

"The Soviet magazine is published jointly by PRAVDA [TRUTH], THE Communist party daily newspaper, and the Union of Journalists. Its slogan is:

"WORKERS OF THE WORLD UNITE."

[This article is 50 years old and many of these newspapers folded or have new ownership and may vary in their current political views. Today, most newspapers are liberal not conservative. Newspapers are dependent on advertising to survive and circulation has dropped because of television cable news and the Internet.]

PERSONAL STORY: In the Bronx, across from Yankee Stadium, in 1972, I played tennis with a Jewish man who was a Linotype typesetter for the JEWISH FORWARD published for New York City's large Jewish population.

"UNFREEDOM OF THE PRESS"   Mark Levin

I have just read Mark Levin's brand new best selling book UNFREEDOM OF THE PRESS (2019) about how the press has been historically used and abused by many presidents. Illegally obtained spied information has been obtained from the IRS, FBI and CIA since the presidency of FRANKLIN ROOSEVELT. Levin highlights how illegal spying and leaking to the media false information has reached its pinnacle during DONALD TRUMP's pre-election and during his presidency which is treasonous. He reveals how the anti-Trump socialist media and Congressional socialist Democrat's have refused to admit this publicly. Only FOX news has reported and written several books about how the FBI and top intelligence Obama administration officials willingly colluded to remove President Trump who they believed was not fit to be America's president. Democracy would have made HILLARY CLINTON president with some 2,000,000 more popular votes mostly in Democrat entitlement California. The Republic of America FOUNDING FATHERS added to the Constitution a unique idea the ELECTORAL COLLEGE which gives small states a voice over the larger populous states. This does not allow the liberal California, New York, Illinois and northeastern states populations to dominate the American government. The media and Democrat party all said Donald Trump could never get 270 electoral votes. He got 302. Many "democracy" socialist Democrats want to repeal the electoral college as unconstitutional. The Democrat party wants to start another Civil War which they started in 1861, when Democrats voted to secede from the Union to protect their Constitutional "states rights" because they believed slavery would be abolished.

In June 2019, Attorney General WILLIAM BARR, Inspector General JOHN HOROWITZ and Connecticut District judge JOHN DURHAM will reveal the FBI involvement behind the MUELLER investigation of candidate and President Donald Trump. Durham had investigated Mueller's WHITEY BOLGER FBI corrupt mob infiltration in Boston. The Hollywood film the DEPARTED is loosely based on this event which kills many famous actors. Bolger was an FBI 10 Most Wanted, only recently being captured. He was killed in prison soon afterward. Case closed? A Hollywood movie.

FAKE NEWS: "THIS IS CNN THE MOST TRUSTED NAME IN NEWS." actor JAMES EARL JONES aka DARTH VADER. A great actor in many films with a basso-profundo voice. Jones narrated the very accurate 25 minute historic FREDERICKSBURG Civil War battlefield park video depicting the horrific defeat of the Union Army in December 1862. It highlights how this city, George Washington's boyhood home, was destroyed by Union army cannon fire. My family moved to nearby Stafford on July 4, 1977. My son was born in the old Mary Washington hospital Nov. 8, 1977. My granddaughter was born in the new Mary Washington hospital Sept. 30, 2005. My daughter was married in the garden of Mary Washington's house, Washington's mother, in Fredericksburg. My daughter graduated from Mary Washington college in 1997, with a degree in German. She became a high school German teacher in Stafford, Virginia. My family attended services at Beth Shalom, House of Peace, reformed Jewish temple in Fredericksburg three blocks from Marye's Heights Sunken Road. Seven Union assaults failed there. This is one of America's bloodiest locations.

I have attended the Fredericksburg cemetery Memorial Day evening ceremony with thousands of candles several times. There are some 16,000 American soldiers buried there the majority in unmarked graves. The national park rangers give tours and dozens of Boy Scouts place the candles around the marked graves and on the Sunken Road today a park pathway. Battlefields Chancellorsville, The Wilderness and Spotsylvania Courthouse surrounding Fredericksburg are historically America's most tragic area.

SHAPING THE NEWS

"Many readers perceive the news with their own prejudices and therefore find nothing fair that does not agree with their own views."

"The principle objections against the media are as follows:

"1 Slanting or bias in news stories 2 Inaccuracy 3 One-sided editorial policy 4 Sensationalism 5 Overplaying crime news 6 Not enough local news 7 Not enough national and foreign news 8 Too much bad news." p 81-82

SHAPING THE NEWS —How the Media Function in Today's World M.L, Stein Washington Square Press 1974

PRESS FUNCTIONS—"1 Does the press transmit its views and ignore others? 2 Is the press influenced by advertisers? 3 Does the press forsake the significant for the trivial? 4 Does the press resist social change? 5 Does the press invade privacy?"   Ibid p 178

CABLE NEWS—"The cable TV has received a White House blessing and a promise from President RICHARD NIXON that the government will help it receive its full potential in the communications field. In a message to the 22nd annual convention of the National Cable Television Association in 1973, the President warmed the hearts of delegates by saying that cable TV "with its abundant channel capacity can greatly expand the diversity of programming. With the opening of additional cable channels to local groups, programs can be more responsive to the needs of the community." The next few years should be interesting ones in the broadcast industry for viewers." Ibid 79

Teenager Patton Hears Personal Civil War Stories

As a child in California Patton learned about his Virginia Confederate relatives killed at PICKETT's CHARGE at GETTYSBURG and the battle of THIRD WINCHESTER, in Virginia where Colonel Patton is buried. I have visited his grave and two ladies came up and showed me Patton's ghost pamphlet. I have heard spirit stories because I live in the Wilderness battlefield. Gettysburg has a ghost tour for JENNY WADE, the only civilian killed in the battle. There are several ghost tourist stores. The "GREY GHOST" JOHN MOSBY lived in California and told Patton his personal stories about his cavalry raids in Union Army occupied northern Virginia from Warrenton to Fairfax where he captured a Union general in bed.

BILL MAULDIN'S DISLIKE OF GENERAL PATTON

Mauldin said, "Soldiers were peasants to him. I didn't like that attitude, but I certainly respected his theories and the techniques he used to get his men out of their foxholes."

[Patton's soldiers mostly were proud of the Third Army's blitzkrieg of the THIRD REICH. Though suffering high casualties his soldiers overwhelmed their opponents quickly and decisively. Patton relied on the 9th Air Force's close air support of its Republic P-47 Thunderbolts and twin engine Martin B-26 Marauder bombers attacking ahead and protecting his extended flanks. He made a whiskey pact with General Weyland,9th AAF]

Mauldin also lamented: "I'm convinced that the infantry as a group in the Army gives more and gets less than anyone else." Wikipedia

Mauldin wrote 9 books, four were made into films from 1941-1985. He had 6 sons and one daughter. In March 2010, the US Post Office printed a .44 cent commemorative postage stamp of Bill Mauldin depicting him with his legendary dog faced GI's "Willie and Joe". Mauldin was buried in ARLINGTON NATIONAL CEMETERY on Jan. 29, 2003. Wikipedia My father was born on January 28, 1919, the same day as Francis Gabreski. He was the top ace in the 8th Air Force during World War II, and a jet ace in the Korean War. Gabreski and my father were both in the 8th Air Force. Gabreski flew a Republic P-47C Thunderbolt which was built three miles north of my father's birthplace/hometown Amityville. Suffolk County AFB east of Amityville was renamed Gabreski AFB

When stationed in Germany I sent articles to the Stars and Stripes and once visited it in Darmstadt, north of Heidelberg.

The Native American Thunderbird Division

The 45th Division unit shoulder sleeve insignia was the American Indian, Native American THUNDERBIRD, a Native American symbol of their historic contact with the Heavens. The History Channel had an interesting show revealing ancient Native American History and its relationship to the stars. Providentially, the Old Testament also talks about the Pleiades, 7 sisters, star system in Isaiah, one of the greatest prophets. It is in the Constellation TAURUS which is my astrological birth sign. Actress Shirley MacLaine and Adolf Hitler were both born at the end of April the beginning of the Taurus month astronomical cycle of May which is alleged to create a "messianic" character? Orion's Belt stars are also in the Old Testament and also Greek god "mythology"!

IRONIC HISTORY FACT: "The division's original shoulder sleeve insignia, approved in August 1924, featured a SWASTIKA, a common Native American symbol, as a tribute to the Southwestern United States which had a large population of Native Americans. However, with the rise of the NAZI party in Germany, with its infamous swastika symbol, the 45th Division stopped using the insignia. New designs were submitted and a Carnegie, Oklahoma native Woody Big Bow proposed the THUNDERBIRD emblem which was approved in 1939." Wikipedia

ORIGIN OF SWASTIKA: The Finnish Air Force used the swastika symbol on the side of its aircraft in the 1920s and during its short war with Stalin's Russia in 1939, then allied itself with the Third Reich. It was also a Viking symbol revived by Swedish Count Rosen circa 1920s. Check Wikipedia. The India HINDU's use a religious swastika "SUN SIGN" but its arms are clockwise facing in the opposite direction. Actress SHIRLEY MACLAINE used a circled Hindu reversed swastika "sun sign" symbol in her chapter beginnings in her best-selling NEW AGE book OUT ON A LIMB.

My Personal Connection to the Air Force Thunderbirds

AIR FORCE JET TEAM FORMED: "The United States Air Force's official jet demonstration team was activated at Luke AFB, Arizona on May 25, 1953. The unit adopted the name THUNDERBIRDS, influenced by the strong Native American culture in the locality. World War II P-51 Mustang pilots twin brothers Bill and Buck Patillo were selected and flew as left and right wingmen, respectively. The Patillos, both captains, were ideal choices as both had flown with a

demonstration team [THE SKYBLAZERS at Furstenfeldbrueck AB] Germany for three years."
Thunderbirds Internet Homepage

PERSONAL STORY: Col. CHARLES "Bill" PATILLO was my commanding officer of the 36th Tactical Fighter Wing at Bitburg AB, Germany from 1967-1968. I was the SKYBLAZER airbase newspaper editor in 1968, and as a "house organ" I served as his spokesman. The Skyblazer was named for the first American jet team, part of the 36th Tactical Fighter Group, where he and his twin brother had flown Republic F-84 Thunderjets 1949-1952, at Furstenfeldbrueck AB near Munich, Germany.

Their commander had been Col. ROBERT SCOTT, who wrote GOD IS MY CO-PILOT, about his flying for the pre World War II, FLYING TIGERS, American volunteer pilots, who shot down many Japanese bombers and fighter aircraft in China. Scott was the first Wing commander, 36th Fighter Wing, at the newly built Bitburg AB, and landed flying his Republic F-84 Thunderjet, with a roaring Tiger emblem painted on its nose in January 1953. Bitburg was located 10 miles from the Luxembourg border for "safety". Bitburg was the first airbase in Europe to receive the newest jet fighter bombers. In 1960, it received the first Republic F-105 Thunderchief supersonic low level nuclear fighter bombers. In Vietnam it dropped more bombs than any aircraft. Many of Bitburg's Thunderchief pilots were highly decorated and some died in combat or were shot down and were prisoners.

Colonel Patillo was assigned to UBON RTAB, in Thailand taking command from famous mustached MIG killer pilot Col. ROBIN OLDS, who had been stationed in Great Britain on a Royal Air Force airbase. As a Brigadier General Olds became commandant of the Air Force Academy. Bitburg was the first American airbase to receive the upgraded new McDonnell F-4D Phantom II. A few of our jets were kept on 5-minute nuclear readiness!

My first assignment at Bitburg's Information Office in October 1966, was to go to the flight line and see a maintenance sergeant to write a story about the new Phantom jets maintenance Phase Inspection program. The Phantom was a US Navy aircraft. The program was used aboard aircraft carriers rather than periodic inspections, which disabled aircraft for a longer period not acceptable on an aircraft carrier during active combat during the Vietnam War. It used a scheduled manual checking systems separately unless there was a mechanical/electrical problem detected which needed immediate repairs. This system was also used by the Strategic Air Command (SAC) on its six and eight jet engine large bombers. Civilian airlines also use the Phase System which meant less down-time maintenance and more flight time. The system was effective and new technology helped.

PERSONAL STORY: In May 1958, visiting our former hometown Amityville, Long Island I asked my father lets go by the nearby Republic aircraft factory, 3 miles north, to see what is going on. Remarkably, it was the day the Republic factory had its first Open House for the new F-105 Thunderchief. The largest single engine jet fighter bomber in the US Air Force, a sign stated it was a supersonic nuclear low level fighter bomber with an internal bomb bay. I told my father we will never use this jet. I had just had my 15th birthday. In Vietnam it dropped 3,500,000 tons of iron bombs! My dad's World War II EIGHT ARMY AIR FORCE dropped about 700,000 tons of bombs in Europe. His unit's B-24 Liberators dropped 12,000 tons of bombs in 212 missions about 5,500 sorties. My dad was a top secret radar bombing technician and his 467th BG was rated as the most accurate of the 41 heavy bomb groups.

Regrettably, I arrived at Bitburg six months after all the Thunderchiefs returned to America and than all were sent to TAKHLI and KORAT airbases in Thailand from which they bombed North Vietnam on extremely dangerous missions. The F-105 in SEA camouflage paint at the Dulles Air Museum was at Bitburg and the one on a pedestal at the Air Force Academy was also at Bitburg.

I would have liked to have done a Skyblazer newspaper story on the last Thunderchief leaving Bitburg and related it to my childhood story of being at its first public display near my hometown.

The Air Force Thunderbirds Connection to My Church

SMALL WORLD STORY: Colonel CHARLES "Bill" PATILLO, my CO of the 36th Tactical Fighter Wing at Bitburg AB, Germany, in 1968, bought a Hallmark card from me where I work and I recognized him. I told him I was Sergeant Louden editor of the Skyblazer newspaper. He remembered me a Buck sergeant. He is a retired Lieutenant General, 3 star, living in nearby Fawn Lake. His grandson, in Sept. 2018, said he is 95.

REALLY SMALL WORLD STORY: LINCOLN "Linc" LANDIS in my neighborhood Lake of the Woods Bible church spoke to our Veterans group about going to Germany after graduating from the short three-year West Point class of 1945. He speaks Russian. One day in church I asked Link if he ever saw the SKYBLAZER jet team fly when he was in Germany? I told him one of the SKYBLAZERS team Colonel Charles Patillo was my CO at Bitburg AB in 1968. He surprised me when he said he had seen them at an airshow and told me, "'My son is married to his twin brother Buck's daughter." He passed 2016.

TV's Red Badge of Courage

In 1974, CBS TV televised the RED BADGE OF COURAGE featuring RICHARD THOMAS in Audie Murphy's role: "A young man who enthusiastically joins the Union Army thirsting to find glory and honor, but his first battle opens his eyes to the reality of how inglorious and dishonorable war really is." IMDb Thomas is best known for his role as "JOHN-BOY" in CBS TV's beloved series THE WALTON's based on a rural Virginia family meeting the demands of the GREAT DEPRESSION and World War II. It was filmed in SCHUYLER, Virginia, 25 miles due south of Charlottesville. The house is today a tourist attraction. It is the birthplace of EARL HAMMER, Jr., the shows creator based on his novel SPENCER's MOUNTAIN, made into a movie featuring HENRY FONDA and MAUREEN O'HARA in 1963.
HISTORICAL FACT: Schuyler had 8 soapstone quarries. The mineral is used for kitchen counter tops and sinks. Some Native American tribes have made bowls and cooking slabs for centuries out of soapstone.

Claverack College is Clum's and Crane's Alma Mater

SMALL WORLD FACT: JOHN CLUM and STEPHEN CRANE both attended Claverack College, a quasi-military school 1779-1902, formerly located over the hill from my high school. MARTIN VAN BUREN also attended it before he became America's 8th president. the only non English president. He also spoke Dutch. His home LINDENWALD was only a few miles north of the school in KINDERHOOK. His 1836, election rally slogan was "O. K. with Van Buren", the derivation of today's world famous slogan OK, which stood for Old Kinderhook. Ironically, his administration suffered America's first Wall Street economic panic. Wikipedia Claverack College shows photo of Stephen Crane in uniform, age 17. He recalled his time at Claverack College as "The happiest period of my life although I was not aware of it."

AMAZING HISTORY FACT: A young girl revealed that all American presidents, except Van BUREN are related to one English King! It was King JOHN, who nobleman forced to sign the MAGNA CARTA in 1215, limiting the King's powers. Hollywood has portrayed this king who was ROBIN HOOD's foe who returned the tax money to the poor. Ironically, America's presidents are in the bloodline of a notorious taxation king! Providence? I believe President DONALD TUMP is not in King John's bloodline. His mother was born in Scotland and his father is of German heritage. He has CUT TAXES!

Planned Parenthood's Sanger Attended Claverack College

Another famous, or maybe infamous, alumni at Claverack College's, Hudson Institute for women was MARGARET SANGER, "women's rights" founder of Planned Parenthood. My father sent me a remarkable article from the local Hudson, NY, Register Star newspaper about this woman. HILLARY CLINTON during her failed 2016 presidential campaign "identified" with Sanger claiming her as a "HERO" to get women's votes. The article explains Sanger's life's motivation, which I found so understandable, but shockingly wrong. She was born in Corning, NY, the glass making city, to a large family. She was one of the youngest children and her family couldn't afford new clothing for her. She wore "hand me down" clothes to school which, of course, didn't fit properly. This is not unusual or a sin. One of her teacher's criticized her clothing in front of her classmates, "bullying"? Most boys probably wouldn't care about their clothes but girls cry. She told her siblings, not her parents, who she knew did their best. Her brothers and sisters got jobs and with their money sent her to Claverack College. Wikipedia and google tell her impact on the world. She married a doctor and she was "qualified" in health. The Internet has statements, and even a video, by her that are undeniably racist anti Negro Americans and even against poor whites advocating not only birth control but also illegal abortion in the pre-World War II world. Some of her ideas were used by the Nazis when in the beginning of Hitler's regime 400,000 mentally ill, alcoholics, congenitally disabled, prostitutes and homosexuals were killed with carbon monoxide, euthanized or sterilized. The church and the German people put a stop to this "legalized" murder until World War II began.

Another article my dad sent me from an Albany, NY newspaper about Margaret Kingman who lived near Pittsfield, MA, who I had a chance to talk to briefly. She was in early Nazi Germany and as a pilot was able to do photo mapping and actually knew Dr. Karl Haushofer, who was a Geopolitical professor at the University of Munich, whose avid student RUDOLF HESS, was Hitler's close friend. Hitler later appointed him deputy fuehrer, VP. Haushofer gave Hitler his Germany's future LEBENSRAUM, living space, conquest theory. Poland's "re-conquest" was written in Hitler's MEIN KAMPF book.
The newspaper cited that Mrs. Kingman sailed to Europe accompanied with Margaret Sanger. She stated, the Nazis would not allow Sanger into Germany because of her Planned Parenthood ideas. Hitler and the Nazis "Aryan" Nordic policy was for women to have as many children as possible to occupy the new lands they would soon conquer. She said Stalin's Soviet Union did not welcome them either. Though Sanger was well known she was overlooked because CHARLIE CHAPLIN was aboard the ocean liner.

Clum Biography and Religious Reason made Indian Agent

"John P. Clum was born in Claverack, NY on September 1, 1851. He attended his local CLAVERACK COLLEGE, a military academy. He attended services at the local Dutch Reformed church built in 1616 is still open. In 1870, he attended RUTGERS college in New Jersey got a classical education Latin, Greek, algebra, natural history and rhetoric. He was on the football team, but didn't play on the first intercollegiate game between Rutgers and Princeton on Nov. 6, 1869, but played on the second game in 1870." Wiki

"Clum joined the US Army Signal Corps in 1871, and was sent to Santa Fe, New Mexico, where he became a weather observer sergeant. President U. S. Grant established the San Carlos Reservation in 1872. After an investigation of political abuses within the Office of Indian Affairs, the government gave Protestant religious groups the responsibility for managing the Indian reservations. The DUTCH REFORMED church was given charge of the Reservation. They sought a candidate at Rutgers to run the reservation and were connected with Clum. Clum knew Indian agents were being replaced because some were profiting by selling government-supplied food and clothing allocated to the American Indians. The Indian agent office became very political with military commanders and civilian agents competing for control over Indian reservations and the appropriated money to the determent of the needy Native Americans. The Apache tribe were at San Carlos and suffered the most with some soldiers including some of their officers brutally torturing and killing them for sport." Wiki

The movie WALK THE PROUD LAND didn't show that. "On his second day on the reservation August 5, 1874, Apache scouts presented him with the severed head of Cochinay, a TONTO Apache renegade they had tracked down and killed. Clum inherited a legacy of violence and mayhem, and a military presence which showed both animosity toward the Indians and disdain for the civilian Indian agents. [John P. Clum—The Early Years] To the distant politicians in Washington, D.C., all Indians were alike. They did not give consideration to the different tribes, cultures, customs and language. They also ignored prior political differences and military alliances. They tried to apply a "one-size-fits-all" strategy to deal with the "Indian problem." Wikipedia

"Clum treated the Indians as friends, established the first Indian Tribal Police and a Tribal Court, forming a system of Indian self-rule. The Army disliked Clum's actions, as it prevented them from raking off part of the funds passing through the reservation. Clum tired of the Army's constant meddling in his management of the reservation and the lack of support from the Indian Bureau, the very people who a short time previously had sought him out specifically as a man who would make a good agent." [John Clum-The Spell of the West]

"GERONIMO was defiant. Clum hid 100 of his Apache police in the commissary building at Oje Caliente and on Apr. 21, 1877, they surprised Geronimo, seizing his rifle and throwing him in shackles. Clum's success gave the US Army a black eye; it was the only time Geronimo was captured at gunpoint without a shot being fired on either side." Wikipedia.   ["Walk the Proud Land" film showed a small group "tricking" Geronimo.]

"Clum's feuds with the military escalated. Faced with superior officers who strongly disagreed with his methods, dogged by an uncaring Indian Bureau administration and under constant harassment by the Army, Clum was frustrated. He resigned at noon July 1, 1877, nearly three years after he had arrived. His successor freed Geronimo and his men, leading to 15 years of bloodshed and Indian wars until Geronimo was recaptured by General Miles on Sept. 4, 1886, finally ending the Indian wars." Wikipedia

"Throughout his life, Clum believed that his work among the Apache was the finest and noblest work that he had ever done." [John Clum-The Early Years]

John Clum Sheriff Wyatt Earp's Friend at Tombstone

Clum and his wife moved to Florence, Arizona Territory and bought a weekly paper, The Arizona Citizen, he moved from Tucson. For two years he published editorials criticizing "the Army of Arizona and the political double-crossers in Washington." Following the great silver strike in TOMBSTONE, in 1877, Clum moved to Tombstone and began publication of THE TOMBSTONE EPITAPH on May 1, 1880. He helped organize a "Vigilance Committee" to end lawlessness in Tombstone, and his association with that group helped get him elected as Tombstone's first mayor under a new city charter. While mayor he became a lifelong friend of WYATT EARP and one of his greatest supporters.

Gunfight at the O.K. Corral

After the Gunfight at the O. K. Corral on October 26, 1881, the Earps suffered losses to their family. Clum's friendship with Earp and loyalty to his business leadership made him a target for outlaws and believed he was targeted during a stagecoach hold-up. Clum sold the Tombstone Epitaph which is a nationally distributed chronicle of the Old West.

Clum is featured in the 9 Hollywood Earp films which has featured many famous male actors. The 1957 film stared KIRK DOUGLAS, BURT LANCASTER and WHIT BISSELL as Clum. In 1946 MY DARLING CLEMENTINE starred HENRY FONDA. In 1994, WYATT EARP film starred KEVIN COSTNER, DENNIS QUAID, GENE HACKMAN and JIM CAVIEZEL. In 1967, the film HOUR OF THE GUN staring JAMES GARNER, JASON ROBARDS and ROBERT RYAN. In 1939 film FRONTIER MARSHAL starred RANDOLPH SCOTT and CESAR ROMERO. in 1971 DOC starred STACY KEACH as Doc Holliday and FAYE DUNAWAY as Kate Elder his Hungarian common-law wife.

All great classic westerns about an historic gunfight which lasted 8 minutes. The 1993 movie TOMBSTONE, however, may be the the best representation with an epic cast: KURT RUSSELL, VAL KILMER, CHARLTON HESTON, SAM ELLIOTT, BILL PAXTON, POWERS BOOTH, BILLY BOB THORNTON, JOHN CORBETT, HARRY CARY, JR., MICHAEL BIEHN, JASON PRIESTLY, THOMAS HAYDEN CHURCH, BILLY ZANE AND STEPHEN LANG portrayed Ike Clanton who with his brothers fight the Earp brothers. Lang is my favorite "bad guy" actor in AVATAR. His role as Gen. THOMAS "Stonewall" JACKSON in GODS AND GENERALS was one of the most powerful compassionate roles I have seen. I live 5 miles from where General Jackson was critically wounded. I have driven past his memorial where he was shot hundreds of times. CLUM was portrayed by well known actor TERRY O'QUINN.

The TOMBSTONE movie also had a strong female cast DANA DELANEY, PAULA MALCOMSON, DANA WHEELER-NICHOLSON, JOANNA PACULA and LISA COLLINS who portrays Morgan Earp, Bill Paxton's wife, her actual husband BILLY ZANE had a small role. He was KATE WINSLET's "bad guy" fiancé in the mega film TITANIC.

The gunfight was between 8 men who fired 30 bullets in 8 minutes.

One Wyatt Earp film THE LIFE AND LEGEND OF WYATT EARP was the first western television series written for adults, premiering four days before GUNSMOKE on September 6, 1955. The half-hour black-and-white program aired for 229 episodes on ABC TV from 1955 to 1961 featuring actor HUGH O'BRIAN as Wyatt Earp. Again my father was in the ABC Master Control room.

O'Brian used a fictitious "Buntline Special" pistol with a 12 inch barrel, which triggered a mild toy craze at the time the series aired. In the many Hollywood Western gun fight scenes a long 12 inch barrel would not have made a good quick draw weapon which would have been fatal.

I vaguely remember my father told me that it was alleged O'Brian doing a quick draw with real bullets shot or "almost'" shot himself in the foot.

Famous Actors from New Trier High School

Hugh Krampe (O'Brian) was born in Rochester, NY, in April 1925, the son of a US Marine Corps officer, as a child lived in Lancaster, PA, then attended New Trier High School in Winnetka, Illinois. Other famous New Trier actor students are; ANN-MARGRET, 1959; ADAM BALDWIN, 1980; RALPH BELLAMY, 1922; BRUCE DERN, 1954; CHARLTON HESTON, 1941; ROCK HUDSON, 1944; VIRGINIA MADSEN, 1979. Politicians: RAHM EMANUEL, 1977; DONALD RUMSFELD, 1950. Journalism: ANN COMPTON, 1965; STEPHEN MOORE, 1978; JOHN STOSSEL, 1965. FUN TRIVIA FACT: The movie MEAN GIRLS was based on New Trier high school? This film describes the cliques and bullying in high school. The lead actress was LINDSAY LOHAN also RACHAEL McADAMS AND SATURDAY NIGHT LIVE comedians AMY POEHLER, TINA FEY, ANA GASTEYER, and was AMANDA SEYFRIED's breakout role. She was the star of MAMMA MIA movie using Swedish pop group ABBA's complete hit list of songs, A fun movie and cast, MERYL STREEP, PIERCE BROSNAN, COLIN FIRTH, PETER SKARSGARD. Mean Girls was not a funny movie, maybe a warning.

O'Brian went to Kemper Military school, then U. of Cincinnati, a semester, in World War II enlisted in the US Marines, at age 17, he became the youngest Marine drill instructor.

SMALL WORLD CONNECTION: Other than my father's ABC connection to Hugh O'Brian I bought an ALBERT SCHWEITZER VHS tape at the ALBERT SCHWEITZER FRIENDSHIP HOUSE in Great Barrington, Massachusetts circa 1979. I was stunned at the end of the tape was the providential story of how O'Brian went to Africa to meet Dr. Schweitzer at his Equatorial African hospital. Dr. Schweitzer had never seen any of his films or TV Wyatt Earp shows. The anti nuclear atmospheric atomic bomb testing NOBEL PEACE PRIZE winning Lutheran pastor, theologian, doctor, author and renowned Bach concert organist told O'Brian how he left behind his fame in Europe to create his mission to aid poor African natives. He told O'Brian that his fellow intellectuals in Europe rebuked him telling him he would fail. Schweitzer inspired Hugh O'Brian to choose a new path to help others. O'Brian ended his successful Hollywood career.

Returning to America, O'Brian founded the HUGH O'BRIAN YOUTH LEADERSHIP FOUNDATION (HOBY), a non-profit youth leadership development for high school scholars which has sponsored over 435,000 students since he founded the program in 1958. HOBY sponsors 10,000 high school sophomores annually through its over 70 leadership programs in all 50 states and 20 countries.

The concept was inspired in 1958 by a 9 day visit O'Brian had with famed humanitarian Dr. Albert Schweitzer in Africa. Dr, Schweitzer believed "THE MOST IMPORTANT THING IN EDUCATION IS TO TEACH YOUNG PEOPLE TO THINK FOR THEMSELVES." Wikipedia

O'Brian's Legacy to America Wasn't as a Western Lawman Hugh O'Brian "The Freedom to Choose"

"I DO NOT BELIEVE WE ARE ALL BORN EQUAL. CREATED EQUAL in the EYES OF GOD, YES, but physical and emotional differences, parental guidelines, varying environments, being in the right place at the right time, all play a role in enhancing or limiting an individual's development." 'But I DO BELIEVE EVERY MAN AND WOMAN, if given the opportunity and encouragement to recognize their potential, regardless of background, has the freedom to choose in our world. Will an individual be a TAKER OR GIVER in life? Will that person be satisfied merely to exist or seek a meaningful purpose? Will he or she dare to dream the impossible dream? I believe every person is created as the steward of his or her own destiny with great power for a specific purpose, to share with others, through service, a reverence for life in a spirit of love."

North to ALASKA

Clum was sent by the US government to Alaska to create the new postal service and traveled some 8,000 miles by mule.

In the summer of 1900, Clum met his old friends Wyatt Earp and George Parsons, who wrote a diary about Virgil and Wyatt Earp. Wikipedia has a photo of him standing with Wyatt Earp in Nome, Alaska near the Arctic Circle. He became postmaster of Fairbanks until 1909. He then worked for the Southern Pacific Railroad giving hundreds of lectures promoting tourism. Clum passed away on May 2, 1932, age 80 in Los Angeles. My birthday was May 4, 1943, in Lexington, Kentucky.

SMALL WORLD STORY: I was at Virginia Beach rock and roll weekend actually jazz, and met a man wearing a T shirt saying Alaska. I asked him if he was a INUIT Indian. I told him Clum's story about being a Christian Indian agent who peaceably captured Geronimo, who knew Wyatt Earp in Tombstone and then organized Alaska's postal system. He didn't know these stories. He then told me, "I am related to Geronimo through my Mexican father." SMALL WORLD! So it Goes.

GERONIMO THE LAST NATIVE AMERICAN FREEDOM FIGHTER
The Geronimo Tribute Rifle—Saluting the Spirit of the Legendary Apache Warrior

"The Apache people hailed him as a hero. The U.S. army called him a renegade. The Mexican government considered him an enemy. His name was GERONIMO, and he was all of those things. For nearly four decades, Geronimo waged war in the American Southwest. First, he fought the Mexican military, fueled by vengeance for the death of his beloved wife, mother, and three young children. Later he would clash with the United States soldiers and settlers who were moving westward and establishing settlements along the Western Frontier. He led raids, rushed headlong into battle and became leader of the Apache resistance, establishing his reputation as a fearless brave warrior. He fought and kept on fighting, and with every victory, his legend grew. Many of his followers believed that he was a powerful shaman who could slow time and stop bullets.

The Geronimo myth grew so large that it almost devoured the man, but underneath all the stories and wild tails, there is the truth. Geronimo became a LEGEND BECAUSE HE FOUGHT FOR FREEDOM. His unwavering strength and courage came from a deep love for his family, his Native American heritage, and his homeland.

To honor the legendary Apache leader and his brave warriors who fought so gallantly to PROTECT THEIR FREEDOM AND HERITAGE, America Remembers proudly presents the Geronimo Tribute Rifle. For this Tribute, we selected the classic Model 1873 Rifle, arguably America's most famous western rifle. Widely considered to be "THE RIFLE THAT WON THE WEST," the Model '73 Rifle was a prized weapon on the frontier, combining lightweight utility and long-range power. The rugged lever-action was simple to operate and offered quick and plentiful firepower.

[James Stewart dedicated a film to this rifle. His film "WINCHESTER '73" is on display in the James Stewart museum in his hometown Indiana. Pennsylvania.]

GERONIMO—THE LAST RENEGADE

THE LAST RENEGADE—"Geronimo was a bold military leader who became a master of surprise attacks, stealth maneuvers and narrow escapes. Although he was never a chief, he possessed a special kind of power to lead people into battle. His reputation as a medicine man and a mystic helped convince others that he was invulnerable and all-seeing. By the late 1870s, most of the warriors of the Great Plains had stopped fighting. The Cheyenne and the Comanche surrendered to the U.S. Army, and Sioux legends CRAZY HORSE and SITTING BULL gave up their weapons. But Geronimo and his followers continued to fight to keep their lands and preserve their way of life.

Geronimo surrendered three times, but never cared for life on the reservation. After breaking out for the third time in 1885, he and his small band of CHIRICAHUA followers became the most wanted men, women, and children in North America. Geronimo and his followers were hunted by 5,000 U.S. soldiers and 3,000 Mexicans. The Apaches were able to elude both forces through the rugged Southwest backcountry for months, but by late August, the sweltering heat and relentless pursuit took its toll. On September 4, 1886, Geronimo surrendered to Gen. NELSON MILES at Skeleton Canyon, Arizona.

"In his later years, he cashed in on his celebrity by selling autographs and other items to tourists. Geronimo appeared in WORLD'S FAIRS and BUFFALO BILL'S WILD WEST SHOW. On March 4, 1905, he even took part in President THEODORE ROOSEVELT"S
inaugural parade in Washington, D.C.

"Perhaps the most remarkable fact about Geronimo is that he spent decades at war and survived every single battle. No soldier, bullet, arrow, knife or sword ever stopped him."

"The Geronimo Tribute Winchester rifle has 24-karat gold and nickel engraved artwork next to its lever. It recreates C.S. FLY's historic 1886 photograph Geronimo requested to be taken by Geronimo himself. Geronimo is on horseback wearing his famed bandana."

(AMERICA'S 1ST FREEDOM magazine April 2019 Advertisement page 5)

SMALL WORLD PERSONAL STORY: In December 2019 it was NATIVE AMERICAN INDIAN month. They had 5 tables set up to sell their handicrafts at the Veteran's Hospital in Richmond, VA. I told one Native American about when I meet World War II Medal of Honor soldier AUDIE MURPHY at a movie premier of WALK THE PROUD LAND where he portrayed the Indian agent who peacefully captured Geronimo. Clum was from little CLAVERACK where my Ockawamick, a Mahician Indian name, Central School was located. The man in Native American chief feather headdress retorted: "Native Americans don't like GERONIMO because he kept fighting for 20 years and promoted prolonged hatred of our people." I told him singer-actor WAYNE NEWTON was related to POCOHANTAS lived in Stafford, Virginia where Pocohantas' family POTAWAMIC tribe lived on the Potomac River. He said he was from Norfolk, he was in Stafford when he and his brother went to LAS VEGAS with a country pop music show. Singer BOBBY DARIN had a popular show in Vegas and told 17 year old Newton that he had a song which he thought would be good for him to sing. DANKE SCHOEN, Thank you pretty, by BERT KAEMPHERT became a big hit even in Germany. FRANK SINATRA soon had two big hits written by Kaempfert STRANGERS IN THE NIGHT and THE SUMMER WIND. I told him Geronimo was portrayed by JAY SILVERHEELS, who was TONTO on the ABC TV series when my father was ABC senior Master Control room engineer. I told him that I shook AUDIE MURPHY'S hand after the premier, but on the way home I told my mother I wanted to meet Tonto JAY SILVERHEELS. I was 13, in 1956. He then surprised me and took out his iphone and showed me a photo of him with Jay Silverheels son, who lives in an undisclosed location in North Carolina.

Hitler the Anti-semitic Austrian Catholic "Christian" MY NEW ORDER Hitler's Speeches 1922-1941

The following passages are from a very rare book my father bought in his 1941 senior year at Transylvania College in Lexington. Kentucky. MY NEW ORDER was published in August 1941, and is a compendium of all of ADOLF HITLER's speeches from April 4, 1922, ending with his Proclamation preceding launching his Operation Barbarossa blitzkrieg against Communist JOSEPH STALIN's Soviet Union on June 22, 1941. Hitler's undeclared attack broke his non-aggression Peace Pact with Stalin signed on August 23, 1939, one week before they jointly invaded Poland to repossess the land the Versailles Treaty took to recreate the nation of Poland. This epic 1,008 page compilation was edited by Raoul de Roussy de Sales and has lengthy reviews from newspapers with commentaries from top German, American, British and French newspapers. Some of the editorial critiques are providential. The Frankfurt Algemeine seemed to be the most insightful. My German grandmother came to America from Frankfurt in 1948, my mother was born in Frankfurt in 1915, had that newspaper sent to her. I never discussed newspapers and TV news was minimal in the 1950-1960s. The book also featured a calendar of the main historical events beginning with 1918.

My father married my German mother, an illegal alien 5 years since July 1935, 6-month visa expired, in August 1940, in his hometown Amityville, Long Island where she lived in the Dr.Titley House where [Sir] BENJAMIN BRITTEN, Britain's "Beethoven" also lived. An envelope to my dad from Titley at 123 LOUDEN Avenue is named for his father. His Mental, Drug and Alcohol Brunswick Knickerbocker hospital was at the other end of the street. My mother was a nanny for two psychiatrists not connected to his hospital. The 1940 US Census Rachel Titley, 5 and my mother is listed as German. She learned English there? I was born on May 4, 1943, in St. Joseph's [Jesus foster-father] Hospital in Lexington, Kentucky. GEORGE CLOONEY was born in St. Joseph on May 7, 1961!

Adolf Hitler and His Electronic Soapbox

The introduction by Raymond Gram Swing proclaims: "Hitler has been one of the most prolific orators of his time. He is a special kind of orator, not one of the classic school, but of a unique and modern category. It is oratory for the masses, and the masses were never accessible until the twentieth-century inventions made it possible for one man to be heard by millions. It is soapbox oratory heard in all corners of the nation, and at times in all corners of the world. Soapbox oratory is based on what an intellectual scorns as an emotional appeal to the baser passions. In the listener it stirs hatred and feeds self-vindication, and whether on paper it bears inspection for consistency, logic or soundness is immaterial...So the analysis of Hitler's oratory is the one revelation of Hitler's thought. Since his thought has engendered first a party, then a regime, and now a power which spreads over Europe and may reach out to dominate the world, the analyst must approach his oratory with keenest excitement of search."   p ix

"He comes to recognize, not the political plans, but the themes, like musical themes, that run through Hitler's output of words. Hitler is not only a philosophical Wagnerian, he composes his oratory with recourse to Wagnerian leitmotivs, which recur insistently, not as statements of political wisdom underlying his plans for government, but his detached concepts to be called upon for repeated reference and modulation."   p x

"He [the editor] will not attempt the question whether Hitler knowingly and from the outset willed to become the supreme leader of Germany and ultimately the ruler of the world, or whether he is a Man of Destiny...Only a first-rate political journalist is competent for such an editing task. The political journalist is imbued with a sense of history-in-the-making not to be expected of the historian. Indeed the true historian gathers his authority from the backward, not the contemporary look. Perspective and data are the handmaidens. The political journalist must labor without either. He must perceive in the present both the past and the future."   p xi

"That M. de Sales helped in the American edition of MEIN KAMPF adds to the logic of his selection to prepare this volume." He was the New York French political correspondent for the PARIS-SOIR newspaper. "His French roots are deep. In his veins flows the blood of St. Francis de Sales, who was made the patron saint of journalists by the late Pope." p xi

HISTORICAL FACT: Pope Pius XI was allegedly murdered before he could give an anti-Fascist, anti-racist, anti-semitic Encyclical address to the College of Cardinals in the Vatican. The 2013 book THE POPE'S LAST CRUSADE—How an American Jesuit Helped Pope Pius XI's Campaign to Stop Hitler by Peter Eisner, a Washington Post reporter, reveals the best kept secret of World War II. The Jesuit priest John LaFarge was a teacher in an African-American grade school in St. Mary's County, Maryland circa 1915. He had written a book against racism in the United States and was summoned by Pope Pius XI, to help draft his encyclical which would have been universally broadcast. He passed after a visit from the Vatican's head physician Dr. Petacci. Petacci's daughter was dictator BENITO MUSSOLINI's mistress. They were both captured at Lake Como fleeing to Switzerland and brutally killed by Communists.

SMALL WORLD FACT: I told my friend Christopher Niebuhr, theologian REINHOLD NIEBUHR's son, about this priest and how he was going to write Pope Pius XI anti-Fascist, anti-racist encyclical. Christopher said he meet him on a train from New York to Boston circa 1956. He said the Jesuit priest invited him to sit with him and said he was going to his Harvard reunion. Christopher said he was returning to Harvard to check out for the summer. They discussed the Evangelical church in Germany under Bismarck.

Hitler's Analysis of Jewish International Banking Collapse

Hitler's first recorded speech April 12, 1922 Munich, Germany

Germany was occupied by American, British and French soldiers to collect war debt reparations which were collapsing the Weimar Republic's economy which will soon have hyper-inflation. My mother was 8 years old when the German Mark collapsed in 1923. She told me her mother had to pay with a bushel basket full of marks.

Hitler proclaimed:

"And if we ask who was responsible for our misfortune, then we must inquire who profited by our collapse? And the answer to that question is that 'Banks and Stock Exchanges are more flourishing than ever before.' We are told that capitalism would be destroyed, and when we ventured to remind one or other of these, 'famous statesmen' and said 'Don't forget the Jews too have capital,' then the answer was: 'What are you worrying about? Capitalism as a whole will now be destroyed, the whole people will now be free. We are not fighting Jewish or Christian capitalism, we are fighting every capitalism: we are making the people completely free."   Ibid p 15

"'Christian capitalism' is already as good as destroyed, the International Jewish Stock Exchange capital gains in proportion as the other losses ground. It is only the International Stock Exchange and loan-capital, the so-called 'supra-state capital,' which has profited from the collapse of our economic life, 'the capital which receives its character from the single supra-state nation which is itself national to the core, which fancies itself to be above other nations and which already rules over them"   p 16

"Christian" Hitler Quotes Jesus Biblical "Hatred" of the Jews

"I would like here to appeal to a greater than I, Count Lerchenfeld. He said in the last session of the Landtag that his feeling 'as a man and as a Christian.' prevented him from being an Anti-Semite. I say: My feeling as a Christian points me to my Lord as Savior as a fighter. It points me to the man who once in loneliness, surrounded only by a few followers, recognized these Jews for what they were and summoned men to the fight against them and who, God's truth! was greatest not as sufferer but as a fighter. In boundless love as a Christian and as a man I read through the passage which tells us how the Lord at last rose in His might and seized the scourge to drive out of the Temple the brood of vipers and of adders. How terrific was His fight for the world against the Jewish poison. Today, after two thousand years, with deepest emotion I recognize more profoundly than ever before the fact that it was for this that He had shed His blood upon the Cross. As a Christian I have no duty to allow myself to be cheated, but I have the duty to be a fighter for truth and justice. And as a man I have the duty to see to it that human society does not suffer the same catastrophic collapse as did the civilization of the ancient world some two thousand years ago—a civilization which was driven to its ruin through this same Jewish people."   p 2

"For as a Christian I have a duty to my own people. And when I look on my people I see it work and work and toil and labor, and at the end of the week it has only for its wage wretchedness and misery. When I go out in the morning and see these men standing in their queues and look into their pinched faces, then I believe I would not be a Christian, but a very devil, if I felt no pity for them, if I did not, as did our Lord two thousand years ago, turn against those by whom today this poor people is plundered and exploited." 27

"Then indeed when Rome collapsed there were endless streams of new German bands flowing into the Empire from the North; but, if Germany collapses today, who is there to come after us? German blood upon this earth is on the way to gradual exhaustion unless we pull ourselves together and make us free!" Ibid   p 26

Adolf Hitler's Testimony in His Treason Trial

Defense speech before the Munich Court March 27, 1924

"When did the ruin of Germany begin? You know the watchword of the old German system in its foreign policy: it—ran—maintenance of world peace, economic conquest of the world. With both these principles one cannot govern a people. The maintenance of world peace cannot be the purpose and aim of the policy of a State. The increase and maintenance of a people—that alone can be the aim. If you are going to conquer the world by an economic policy, other peoples will not fail to see the danger."   Ibid 82

"What is the State? Today the State is an economic organization, an association of persons, for me, it would seem, for the sole purpose that all should co-operate in securing each others daily bread. The State, however, is not an economic organization, it is a 'volkic' organism. The purpose the aim of the State is to provide the people with its food-supply and with the position of power in the world which it is due. Germany occupies in Europe perhaps the most bitter situation in Europe of any people. Militarily, politically, and geographically it is surrounded by none but rivals: it can maintain itself only when it places a power-policy (Machtpolitic) ruthlessly on the foreground." Ibid p 82

"Two powers are in a position to determine the future development of Europe: England and France. England's aim remains eternally the same: to balkanize Europe and to establish a balance of power in Europe so that her position in the world will not be threatened. England is not on principle an enemy of Germany, it is the Power which seeks to gain the first place in Europe. The declared enemy of Germany is France. Just as England needs the balkanization of Europe, so France needs the balkanization of Germany in order to gain hegemony in Europe. After four and a half years of bitter struggle at last through the Revolution the scale of victory turned in favor of the coalition of the two Powers, with the following result: France was faced with the question: Was she to realize her eternal war-aim or not? That means: Could France destroy Germany and deprive it of all the sources whereby all its people was fed? Today France watches the ripening to fulfillment of her age-old plan: it matters not what Government will be at the helm in France: the supreme aim will remain—the annihilation of the Germans, THE EXTERMINATION OF TWENTY MILLION GERMANS, and the dissolution of Germany into two separate States..." Ibid   p 82-83

"The army which we have formed grows from day to day; from hour to hour it grows more rapidly. Even now I have the proud hope that one day the hour is coming when these untrained bands will become battalions, when the battalions will become regiments and the regiments divisions, when the old cockade will be reconciliation from the mire, when the old banners will once again wave before us: and then reconciliation will come in the eternal last Court of Judgment—the Court of God—before which we are ready to take our stand. Then from our bones, from our graves will sound the voice of that tribunal which alone has the right to sit in judgment upon us. For, gentlemen, it is not you who pronounce judgment upon us, it is the eternal Court of History which will make its pronouncement on the charge which is brought against us. The judgment you will pass, that I know. But that Court will not ask us...who as Germans have wished the best for their people and their Fatherland, who wished to fight and to die. You may declare us guilty a thousand times, but the Goddess who presides over the Eternal Court of History will with a smile tear in pieces the charge of the Public Prosecutor and the judgment of the Court: for she declares us guiltless."   Ibid p 83

Hitler invoked God [Jesus] as his armed insurrectionists justification for attempting to overthrow the Bavarian government. Bavaria was 100 per cent Catholic and was beginning to get infiltrated with Russian Communist agents trying to seize power.

Hitler was sentenced to 9 months prison where he had time to write his MEIN KAMPF autobiography which he dictated to his friend RUDOLF HESS who typed it on a Remington typewriter at Landsberg Prison near Munich. Hess became deputy fuehrer.

The World Press Bewildered Response to Hitler's Sentence

"'Plotting the overthrow of the Republic is not a hazardous occupation in Germany. If the practitioner of treason is a towering figure like Ludendorff, he is acquitted on the ground of 'innocent' complicity." New York Times   Ibid   p 84

[The Times did not realize the providence of corporal Hitler's oratory. The court and German people understood. General ERICH LUDENDORFF was the chief of staff of Germany under General PAUL von HINDENBERG. Ludendorff was a war criminal who initiated unrestricted submarine warfare which sunk the Lusitania ocean liner with American citizens killed. He brought Marxist VLADIMIR LENIN in an armored train to Russia to organize the Russian Revolution which succeeded in overthrowing CZAR NICHOLAS. The new Leninist Communist government made peace with Germany.]

FAMILY STORY: My mother's father Karl Frank was sent home after three years fighting on the Eastern Front. The war ended so he didn't fight on the Western Front. My mother was born on February 22, 1915, Washington's birthday, after he was sent to East Prussia to stop the Russian armies advance on nearby Berlin, Germany's capital. Ludendorff was my grandfather's head commander. My mother's middle name FRANCOIS was the name of the artillery general who destroyed the advancing Russian armies at the battles of TANNENBERG and MASURIAN LAKES. The Great War, World War I could have ended then. NO World War II, NO Communist Cold War, NO Israel.

"The trial has at any rate proved that to plot against the Constitution of the Reich is not considered a serious crime." London Times

"Not only from the judicial standpoint, but also from the point of view of national needs, the Munich verdict must be deeply regretted. For it means practically a verdict of not guilty, and an invitation to high treason." Germania (Catholic party organ) Berlin

"The verdict can only be explained on the basis of the principle that high treason, if born out of 'national' aspirations, is a venal minor crime. Nothing is more symptomatic than that of the court calls the minimum punishment of five years imprisonment, which dates from the pre-revolutionary period, 'a very considerable term.' Once upon a time high treason was a serious crime in Germany." Frankfurter Zeitung Ibid   p 84

"'Bankrupt Justice' "In full publicity, the bench of the Bavarian People's Court must be destroyed. For the verdict that was passed down today in the Infantry School in Munich, and which exceeded the direct expectations of skeptical critics, is tantamount to a declaration of the bankruptcy of Bavarian justice. It is a verdict without example in a time when so many errors of justice are being committed daily in political trials...Never before has a Court more openly denied the formation upon which it rests and upon which every modern state is built." Ernst Feder Berliner Tageblatt Ibid p 83-84

"This VERDICT can be criticized point by point. The crime is obvious: these men have attempted to seize power in Germany; they sought to corrupt the Reichswehr and march on Berlin." Le Temps Paris Ibid p 84

Hitler's Unlikely Mystical Appeal to the People

"The movement was now well underway; Hitler was established as a leader who could influence the masses. He was no longer the Chief of Propaganda but the Fuehrer of the Party. No one knew better than Hitler himself that his real power was his voice. To increase his effectiveness he took elocution lessons from a Munich actor called Basil." 4

"Hitler's speeches are no models of oratory. His German is sloppy and often full of grammatical errors. The sentences are long, full of cliches and bourgeois smugness. His voice is not pleasant and he often shouts himself hoarse. The substance of his speeches is usually confused and repetitious. especially in his early years, his method consisted in repeating and rehashing indefinitely the same theories, in hurling the same accusations at his opponents, and in drowning his audience under an avalanche of words. In no other country but Germany, where orators are rare, could Hitlerian eloquence be tolerated by an average audience, with an average taste and an average endurance."   Ibid   p 5

"But Hitler's appeal to the masses was undeniable, and from the earliest days, he showed that he had the gift and the power to stir the German people and to restore their self-confidence. His energy, his daring, his fanatical faith in his own mission was inspiring. To a country humiliated by defeat, impoverished by postwar inflation, and profoundly demoralized by the sense of its own weakness and impotence, Hitler spoke of hope for the future, of conquest, wealth and power. He told the Germans they had not lost the war, but had been betrayed, and that, provided they had faith in themselves and in him, all the glorious dreams of the past would come true—that they would be strong and proud again, and masters of the world."   Ibid p 5-6

"No one had told them that they were still a great people, that the sword was nobler than the plow, that they were innocent of all guilt, and they were right—right in the eyes of God, right in the eyes of History, always and absolutely right, merely because they were Germans. Hitler told his listeners that they belonged to a superior race, but also that they were victims. He told them that what was wrong with the war was not the war itself, but that they had lost it. He told them that the whole world was arrayed against them and wanted the destruction of Germany. He showed them that the Weimar Republic was allied with their enemies because it was a democracy, and therefore international and Jewish. He told them they had a mission: to regenerate Germany, and to achieve this end, they must be brutal, intolerant and ruthless. He preached violence and hatred to people whom anxiety and despair had made meek and spiritless. Small wonder that Hitler, the ex-soldier, who owned nothing, as he said himself, but a zinc plate with his name on it, should be hailed as savior when he exclaimed: "Our task is to give to the dictator when he comes a people that is ripe for him. German people, awake! It draws near today!"   Ibid   p 6

"The name of Wagner has often been mentioned in connection with Hitler, not only on account of his passionate admiration for that musician [composer] but because the world has sensed that there was a deep affinity between the conceptions of the two men…Hitler's method of presenting his ideas and of conveying impressions can indeed be compared to Wagner's use of musical themes, which through their recurrence and development serve to identify certain characters and certain concepts."   Ibid p 7-8

"The main difference between Wagner and Hitler, in this respect, is that whereas the former is an artist, the latter has no sense of proportion or construction…To make a point, he is bound neither by logic, nor plausibility, nor historic accuracy. His method is to assert as GOSPEL TRUTH both truths and lies and never to concede that he might possibly be in the wrong or even that a doubt could exist."   Ibid   p 8

"In his early days, Hitler made use of two fundamental themes: anti-Semitism and the denunciation of the Versailles Treaty. To make the Jew a scapegoat has always been an easy trick for a certain type of demagogue. The relative defenselessness of the Jewish minorities in each country has made them a convenient and safe target all through History. But in the case of Hitler, the Jew has been elevated, so to speak, to a degree of evilness which he has never attained before. In Hitler's conception of the world, the Jew becomes positively demonic and everything to which the qualification "Jewish" can be attached is automatically foul, destructive, and beyond redemption. The Jew has become the symbol of all impurity, and, by extension, all forms of impurity are more or less caused by the influence of the Jews." Ibid p 8

Hitler's Eternal Historical Sin and Evil of Antisemitism

"By arousing latent anti-Semitic prejudices in his followers and by denouncing as Jewish everything which opposed him, Hitler succeeded in giving to his doctrine a queer mystical unity. He created a new notion of Sin and Evil, a new rallying point for a modern crusade the aim of which is to destroy everything which he denounced as Jewish." Ibid p 8-9

Destroy Jewish Communism in Germany

"Communism and Bolshevism were of course the most obvious manifestations of "Jewish" corruption and he said he had no distinction between Marxism as a political and economic theory and its applications in Russia and elsewhere. To rid Germany of Bolshevism was indeed the first aim which Hitler proposed to his followers. He was later to amplify it and to propose a universal crusade against it to save civilization and Christianity." Ibid p 9 [Germany/Austria had a .5% Jewish population 500,000 mostly wealthy professional people. The Nazis and Communists were out of work Christians.]

"As an antithesis to the evilness of the Jews, Hitler opposed the purity, sanctity, and transcendental virtue of the Aryan or Nordic race. To establish the primacy of this "race,"
Hitler appealed to legends, superstitions, and vague beliefs which lay dormant in the soul of his German followers. Such mystic and barbaric ideas as the doctrine of "Blood and Soil," based on ancient cults were revived and somewhat modernized and bolstered up with dubious 'scientific' references.German science, pan-German teaching, and barbaric atavism were blended into one great revelation-the Hitlerian myth. Ibid p 9

Hitler's Three Promises to the German People

"The FIRST was that the Versailles Treaty was not only unfair but criminal. Its purpose, according to Hitler, was not to make peace but to destroy Germany or to keep her enslaved forever. Moreover, it was not the result of a defeat of the German armies. The German armies asserted Hitler, had never been defeated: they had been betrayed, stabbed in the back by Bolshevism, Jews and the "November criminals" (the Weimar Republic). The duty of the German people was therefore clear: they had to repair this monstrous injustice, and to do this nothing should stand in their way. Treaties, signatures, pledges, international contracts were nothing more than instruments of the oppression that Germany had the right to disregard and violate." Ibid p 10

"A SECOND point in Hitler's program was the reunion of all Germans into one community. This he justified on the principal of the right of self-determination—a principle established by Woodrow Wilson, but which, in the case of Germany, had been shamelessly violated." Ibid p 10   [Wilson's TEN POINTS at the Versailles Armistice.]

"The THIRD idea was that Germany should seek no alliance, except perhaps with Italy and England. England in Hitler's estimation, could be considered as a member of the Nordic race. As for Italy, her alliance should be sought, first of all because Mussolini had originated Fascism, and secondly because it would help destroy France, the eternal arch-enemy."   Ibid   p 10

MY NEW ORDER: Edited and commentary Raoul de Sales REYNAL AND HITCHCOCK New York copyright August 1941

Hooray for HOLLYWOOD

I have probably seen more Hollywood movies than anyone. My German mother was an avid movie fan and took me and my brother Paul to movies every Saturday in Huntington when we lived in Amityville, Long Island. I believe my first movie was BATHING BEAUTIES with red haired swimmer ESTHER WILLIAMS. I was a baby maybe 6 months old in a Tallahassee, FL movie theater on the way from Lexington, KY to Drew Army airfield, today's Tampa International airport, where my father was stationed. A controversial but popular song BABY ITS COLD OUTSIDE was featured. Christmas 2018, the song has been labeled "sexist" I have it sung by the talented "red haired" movie actress and singer ANN MARGRET who sang a duet with great New Orleans trumpeter AL HIRT and later with guitarist BRIAN SETZER, on his rocking Big Band's Christmas album. Setzer is from Massapequa next to my childhood home Amityville. His big band rocked playing LOUIS PRIMA's "Dirty Boogie" on the REGIS AND KATHIE LEE ABC TV morning show. It was also the home of actors Alec, Billy and Stephen Baldwin Alec Baldwin was born in Amityville in the same Brunswick Hospital my father was born in 1919. My dad's father built the Drug, Alcohol and Nervous Disorders hospital in the 1880s. Laudnum, morphine was a great addiction then from the many Union soldiers who had amputations to prevent their deaths from gangrene, It was recently demolished. Evangelist JIM BAKKER preached a sermon in Massapequa and then had an adulterous affair with JESSICA HAHN from nearby BABYLON. Jessica had to take the Sunrise Highway through Amityvillle to get there. He and his wife TAMMY were indicted for defrauding many of their church members. He went to jail. Civil War artist MORT KUNSTLER lived in Massapequa. I have 31 of his 'paintings' of battles in my local neighborhood, several autographed. My favorite is a large lithograph of Gen. THOMAS "Stonewall" JACKSON with little JANIE CORBIN next to the Christmas tree which is a beautiful scene in the movie GODS AND GENERALS (2002) directed by RON MAXWELL who also directed GETTYSBURG (1993). My friend Brian Corbin told me his father James, 100, is related to her! I also have the painting of General Jackson weeping after he is told little Janie has passed from scarlet fever. After Gen. AMBROSE BURNSIDE's larger Union Army is literally slaughtered at MARYE's HEIGHTS SUNKEN ROAD at FREDERICKSBURG, VA, on Dec. 12-13, 1862, Jackson is invited to spend the winter at the Moss Neck estate south of Fredericksburg in Caroline Co., where Janie lives. Her father is in the Confederate army elsewhere. The aggressively righteous Presbyterian General Jackson becomes a gentle surrogate father figure which he enjoys. NOTE: Little 8 year old Janie has a delightful southern accent the sweetest I have heard since living in Virginia since 1977. Actress LYDIA GRACE JORDAN is best known for her role as Alice in the 2008 film DOUBT. Wikipedia that movie and its cast nuns MERYL STREEP, AMY ADAMS and the great departed PHILIP SEYMOUR HOFFMAN, a priest. VIOLA DAVIS and AMY ADAMS were both nominated for an Academy Award for Best Supporting actress. Streep and Hoffman also were nominated for Academy Awards in DOUBT. Lydia Jordan had a New York accent which was easy because she was born in New York City. OH TO BE AN ACTOR.

Overly zealous Jackson rides beyond his lines in the moonlight and is shot by friendly fire and is severely wounded after his great surprise 12 mile stealth flanking march attack which defeats Union Gen. THOMAS HOOKER at the battle of CHANCELLORSVILLE May 2-5, 1863. Hooker was siting on the Chancellor family's porch which he was knocked off by a cannon ball fired from HAZEL RUN which today has 8 cannons on display. He was literally shell shocked. The house burned and is a popular Civil War site along Germanna Rt. 3 to Fredericksburg, with a cannon and a brick outline of the house's foundation. The Chancellor family had six daughters.

HISTORY FACT: Pres. ABRAHAM LINCOLN replaced timid generals GEORGE MCCLELLAN and AMBROSE BURNSIDE, who were defeated severely by Confederate Gen. ROBERT E. LEE, with Gen. JOSEPH HOOKER who was mistakenly called "Fighting Joe" because of a headline misprint. He also failed a potential victory on the second day of the Chancellorsville battle but may have suffered from shell shock?

HISTORY FACT: Woman "camp followers" of his army became known as "hookers"! Most of the women performed domestic services cooking and washing for the large Union Army, some provided close personal companionship.

General Jackson's amputated arm is buried at the ELWOOD HOUSE through the woods behind my house. A year later May 3-5, 1864, it became a Union Army HQ for Gen. WARREN in an even more brutal battle where I live in the WILDERNESS. Gen. ULYSSES GRANT, the new general of the Army of the Potomac had a tent about 1,000 feet behind my house. There are three historical signs in the woods. One says Grant could hear the battle a half mile away but the smoke from fires blocked visibility. It said he wore out his white gloves and nervously whittled wood and chewed on his cigars.

HISTORY FACT: The WILDERNESS battle was another defeat because Grant and General MEADE, victor at GETTYSBURG, couldn't deploy his superior forces because of the thick undergrowth in the woods. Years earlier around 1715, Governor Alexander Spotswood had Virginia's first German settlers cut and burn about 1,000 acres of forest timber for furnaces to make pig iron to send to Great Britain. This created a damaged environment which became the "WILDERNESS". Marine Gen. SMEDLEY BUTLER brought Marines from the new base at QUANTICO, VA, to practice combat here.

HISTORY FACT: The WILDERNESS was one of the most horrific battles in the Civil War because many of the wounded soldiers could not escape the forest fires and many are reported to have shot themselves to death rather than be burned alive! The Union soldiers knew this terrifying fact. Grant knew it also but was not going to retreat but continued his OVERLAND CAMPAIGN".His brave soldiers actually cheered his decision to continue to Richmond.Twelve miles down Brock Road was SPOTSYLVANIA COURTHOUSE where General Lee's Confederate soldiers were able to dig trenches and build log defenses. There they fought for 8 bloody days

HISTORY FACT: Lt. Gen. SEDGWICK's memorial cites how his aide told the general to take cover after a near miss shot. Foolishly he retorted. "They couldn't hit an elephant from that distance." He was shot in the eye by a sharp shooter with a telescopic sight Whitlock rifle at about 2,000 feet. The well liked general was the highest ranking Union officer killed during the Civil War. When I lived in the Bronx I drove on Sedgwick Avenue and didn't know this story, he was from Connecticut. i can see the 2nd day Wilderness Sedgwick trench from my house 22 paces in the National Park woods.

I have many favorite movies but I will highlight mostly the war movies that I can personally relate to. I have seen and have VHS and DVDs of almost every Air Force, Army and Navy war video for historical knowledge and acting realism.

HACKSAW RIDGE (Nov. 3, 2016) is the movie that took Hollywood 50 years to put on screen. It is the story of Medic PVT. DESMOND T. DOSS, the first conscientious objector, to receive America's highest combat award the Congressional Medal of Honor. He was a Seventh Day Adventist whose religious and personal life would not let him kill or even hold a weapon. Doss is portrayed humbly and compassionately by Anglo-American actor ANDREW GARFIELD in MEL GIBSON's almost too graphic battle scenes unfortunately it had to be rated R. It is the most gut wrenching and heart warming spiritual war film ever produced. BRAVEHEART and WE WERE SOLDIERS?

Private Doss' story was not unknown to me. I worked for THE WORLD ALMANAC AND BOOK OF FACTS 1969-1975 as historical/political/religious researcher/writer I also wrote 1,200 World Almanac Facts syndicated in 600 SCRIPPS HOWARD syndicated newspapers with an engraved sketch of the subject. One of my reference books was FAMOUS FIRST FACTS where I found Doss entered as the first conscientious objector to receive America's highest combat award. A former airman at Andrews AFB, I have photo of LBJ boarding Air Force One in September 1966, and was stationed at Bitburg AB, Germany, Europe's most strategic airbase near the infamous cemetery President REAGAN visited on my birthday in 1985. As editor of the Bitburg AB "Skyblazer" I interviewed Major BERNARD FISHER, the first Air Force Medal of Honor recipient in the Vietnam war who as a Lt. Colonel was assigned as a Convair F-102 delta jet interceptor 525th squadron commander. In 1956, when 13 years old, I had meet AUDIE MURPHY, the most decorated combat soldier during World War II. It was at the local movie premier of WALK THE PROUD LAND in which he portrayed a local man JOHN CLUM, an Indian agent who peacefully captured GERONIMO. At the Reading, PA, World War II air/army show I met Marine PVT LUCAS, the youngest Medal of Honor recipient. I met Marine Colonel WESLEY FOX who as a Captain received the Medal of Honor for his bravery in South Vietnam. I first met him as a customer at PEP BOYS. I saw his blue Medal of Honor ribbon with stars on his immaculate brown 1505 short sleeve uniform and mentioned that I had meet Major BERNARD FISHER. He said they both received their awards in the A SHAU VALLEY in South Vietnam. I later meet him at a Manassas airport airshow. I bought his autobiographical book RIFLEMAN which he signed and wished me well with my World War II book about my mother. He was born in nearby ASHBURN, VA, near Dulles airport. Colonel Fox is one of a dozen Marines featured in a video at the MARINE CORPS MUSEUM. So, I well understand the significance of this award even though I have never been near combat. I have the VHS/DVD of Audie Murphy's story TO HELL AND BACK. His Medal of Honor scene firing a machine gun from a burning tank was filmed in the summer.

HISTORY FACT: It was in December in snow in Alsace near Colmar, France. This is near ALBERT SCHWEITZER's birthplace KAYSERSBERG and home in GUNSBACH.

I wrote the WORLD ALMANAC FACT in 1971, and had no thought I would see Doss' story so dramatically portrayed on the big screen. I have driven by the Fredericksburg Seventh Day Adventist church hundreds of times. One day a couple of years ago I stopped by and talked to a lady who was a teacher there and mentioned that I had written a World Almanac Fact about Pvt. Desmond Doss, a 7th Day Adventist (SDA) which was sent to to 600 SCRIPPS HOWARD newspapers. She told me, "Pvt. DOSS was born in Lynchburg, Virginia."

The week before the movie I drove for the first time the 115 miles to Lynchburg to find out if there would be a premiere. I went in the library and was asking the librarian about the movie. A man behind me said, 'Take a seat my wife is related to him." He gave his wife's phone number. It was a week later when she told me her aunt was a relative of his. She was a Lynchburg native. I told her husband that I had met Audie Murphy at a movie premiere in Hudson, NY, when I was 13. I told him the man he portrayed was from Claverack where my high school was located. The man then said, "Ockawamick high school." I said, "Yes!" He went to ROE JAN high school in Hillsdale in my COLUMBIA county about 10 miles away. Small World.

I then drove 20 miles West to the D Day Memorial in BEDFORD, VA, and had an amazing tour. Then I drove 25 miles to Roanoke airport where I saw the B-24 Witchcraft, a replica from my dad's 467th BG 8th AAF unit in Norwich, England. at the airport. I mentioned to a man there that Audie Murphy's private aircraft crashed into a mountain near here. The man pointed across the runway and said it was there at Brush Mountain. The following week I went to the Thursday night premiere of HACKSAW RIDGE with maybe 50 people in his hometown theater? I think many more went on the weekend. The next day I drove around LIBERTY UNIVERSITY, JERRY FALWELL, JR. is the president. His father founded the MORAL MAJORITY during the time RONALD REAGAN was president. I bought some great religious historical books. I then drove to Brush Mt. on a beautiful crisp clear day. I had to ask directions several times there are no signs to Audie Murphy's crash site except where you turn into State Park. It is up a 3 mile one way gravel road on the side of the mountain. At the top of the mountain you park and walk 3/4 mile to Murphy's memorial. I sat on a bench across from a rock and granite memorial with an American flag waving in the wind day and night without a light. There is no electricity on this 4,100 ft. mountain ridge. It may be the only American flag flying in the dark? God bless AUDIE MURPHY and the United States of America.

I prayed and read a book of ROBERT E. LEE's prayers and wisdom which I had bought the previous day at the Lee Chapel burial site of Lee and his relatives at WASHINGTON AND LEE University next to the VIRGINIA MILITARY INSTITUTE VMI where THOMAS 'Stonewall' JACKSON taught and 5 Star Gen. GEORGE MARSHALL, WW II chief of staff graduated and GEORGE PATTON, Jr. attended for a year.

After visiting VMI, Jackson and Marshall's statues and Lee's resting place in the LEE CHAPEL at Washington College where he was president until his passing. I then drove to the Information center which is a block from Jackson's home where I took a tour of his house from which you can see VMI which he walked to when a professor there. I bought his own spiritual book and book of letters from his wife. His wife Anna was a Presbyterian minister's daughter. Jackson gave Bible study to Negro children in the LEXINGTON PRESBYTERIAN church, black adults were not allowed to have Bible study. "Come to me as a child." He is buried with his wife in cemetery a block away. I couldn't visit because I had to drive over BLUE RIDGE Mountains to get to HACKSAW RIDGE premiere. I arrived just before previews. What a historical day.

13 Rules For Radicals—Saul Alinsky

Thirteen Rules he originally praised LUCIFER as the "FIRST RADICAL"
1. Power is not only what you have but what the enemy thinks you have.
2. Never go outside the experience of your people.
3. Wherever possible go outside of the experience of the enemy.
4. Make the enemy live up to their own book of rules.
5. Ridicule is man's most potent weapon.
6. A good tactic is one that your people enjoy.
7. A tactic that drags on too long becomes a drag.
8. Keep the pressure on.
9. The threat is usually more terrifying than the thing itself.
10. The major premise for tactics is the development of operations that will maintain a constant pressure upon the opposition.
11. If you push a negative hard and deep enough it will break into its counter side.
12. The price of a successful attack is a constructive alternative.
13. Pick the target, freeze it, personalize it, and polarize it.

IT'S TIME TO SAY SOMETHING

Rev. Dr. James R. Knill pastor Concordia Lutheran Church-Missouri Synod
"In a recent article (PRINCIPLES, a publication of Christendom College, issue II), author David Corey identifies what he calls "the clash between traditional and progressive values that has been playing out not only in our political institutions, but also in every nook and cranny of our society." The traditional values he describes are pretty much aligned with Christian values (the sanctity of human life and marriage, etc.). "Progressive" values in large measure are the opposite."
I put "Progressive" in quotation marks, because the word in this context is a lie. It is the co-option of a good term to promote evil outcomes and to isolate, deem irrelevant, and even destroy those who oppose its values."

HOROWITZ WAS A COMMUNIST IN THE 1950S IS NOW A CONSTITUTIONALIST
DAVID HOROWITZ describes the adoption of the term, "PROGRESSIVE," for nefarious purposes by a 20th century political revolutionary, SAUL ALINSKY, in a 2009 booklet, THE ALINSKY MODEL. Alinsky's view was that current institutions need to be destroyed in order that a UTOPIAN REALM OF EQUALITY could emerge. He infiltrated the political system in order to develop a power base that would destroy the system. He accepted idealists, but told them idealistic causes didn't matter; only the amassing of power (supported by a reference to RULES FOR RADICALS, p. 113). Alinsky taught Progressives and other groups that self-interest (rather than the common good or loyalty to a standard "from above") is the only way to organize people. One of his basic maxims was to lie to opponents and disarm them by pretending to be what they are not.
To the extent these principles remain alive, the "Progressive" movement remains an enemy of what is TRUE and GOOD."

DON'T BELIEVE THE PROGRESSIVE LIE

My point in all this is to extend a warning not to believe the lie, or be taken by it, by a movement that calls itself "Progressive," or from wherever or whomever deceptive lies may come. SATAN is the AUTHOR OF LIES. Absolute truth exists. Truth is to be the maxim in all discourse, political or otherwise, Seek truth and support it, "Whatever is true, whatever is honorable, whatever is just, whatever is pure, whatever is lovely, whatever is commendable, if there is any excellence, if there is anything worthy of praise, think about these things" (Philippians 4:8).
Don't be duped. Be wise."   [My pastor since Pentecost Sunday May 1989]
FORGOTTEN FACT: Alinsky originally dedicated his book RULES FOR RADICALS to LUCIFER, the FIRST RADICAL, which he had to retract. Read Isaiah
HILLARY CLINTON'S thesis at Wellesley College was titled "Beyond Saul Alinsky". She was an ultra-conservative "Goldwater girl" for presidential candidate Republican Barry Goldwater. Her four year allegedly gay roommate at Wellesley made her Progressive.

MARXIST/COMMUNIST VLADIMIR LENIN PROPHESIED: "THE CAPITALISTS WILL SELL US THE ROPE WE HANG THEM WITH!"

"You never want a serious crisis to go to waste." Alinsky

"And what I mean by that [is] it is an opportunity to do things that you could not do before." Rahm Emanuel, former chief of staff for President BARACK OBAMA 2009-2010
Saul Alinsky, Rahm Emanuel and President Barak Obama were all Chicago Democrats.

"SAUL ALINSKY, the radical organizer and mentor of BARACK OBAMA and HILLARY CLINTON, used to ask his new followers why they wanted to become community organizers. They would respond with idealistic claims that they wanted to help the poor and oppressed. Then Alinsky would scream at them like a Marine Corps drill instructor, "No! You want TO ORGANIZE FOR POWER!" That's the way the SDS radicals the University of Texas approached the abortion issue—as a means of power, or, in MARGARET SANGER's words, to remake the world. As a writer in the 1960s radical SDS publication NEW LEFT NOTES put it, "The issue is never the issue. The issue is always the revolution."   p 84
DARK AGENDA—THE WAR TO DESTROY CHRISTIAN AMERICA D. Horowitz 2018

REPUBLICAN SENATOR SUSAN COLLIN'S CORONAVIRUS PROTEST

"Maine Senator Susan Collins, well known as a "moderate" Republican who often works with Democrats on a variety of issues cannot believe what is going on in the Senate and was dumbfounded when Democrat's tried to prevent her from speaking on the floor. Fortunately, they failed and what she had to say should be read by every America voter before the next election:

> I will tell you, Mr. President, I've had the honor to serve in this body for
> many years. Never, never have I seen Republicans and Democrats fail
> to come together when confronted with a crisis. We did so with the
> financial meltdown in 2008. Here we are facing an enemy that is
> invisible but equally devastating to the health of our people and to
> the health of our economy. And yet unbelievably the Democratic
> leader objected to my even being able to speak this morning.

ARE THERE 10?

"No, this is not about wondering if we have the maximum number of 10 in the church for a service during the COVID-19 pandemic. You'll see."

"i'm wondering if this time is an opportunity for this country — and yes, the world — to take stock of how it is living, of the choices it is making, over against even the laws of nature that remain in the conscience of humankind after the Fall. I'm wondering if this is a wake-up call God is giving us to seek Him, to see how we are doing, certainly under His will as expressed in the TEN COMMANDMENTS, but at minimum according to elementary natural law."

"The report card is not good. While in many places right now you can't go fishing or get a haircut, but getting an abortion is an "essential service," because, as one governor incredulously said in an interview, "it's a matter of life." Unrelated to the new corona virus, the governor of this Commonwealth [Virginia] said some time ago that a newborn baby could be left on a table while the mother decides whether or not the child should live. One or more news commentators, medical personnel, and professors/teachers have lost jobs for noting that gender is almost always an observable fact at birth. With respect to the Christian faith, through which God offers free salvation for all, public and private animosity is obvious. Samaritan's Purse, a Christian organization, recently was denied its offer to construct a 1,000 bed health facility in New York's Central Park to help with the city's overwhelming need for beds in this health crisis, reportedly because of its beliefs about gender. Catholic Social Services has been excluded from Philadelphia's foster program because of the agency's views on marriage. Virginia's governor [Northam] signed into law last month SB 868, a statute that defines churches as places of public accommodation, making most religious organizations, according to Virginia's Family Foundation, apparently (as the law is worded) not able to hold their employees to their core faith tenets on sexuality, marriage, and gender."

"Her's where the number 10 comes into play. When God told Abraham he was about to destroy Sodom because of its grave sin, the patriarch pleaded with God that he would spare the city for the sake of the righteous who lived there. (The "righteous" are those who believe in the true God.) Abraham began his plea for the city's reprieve if it could be found that 50 righteous people lived there. God agreed. Finally Abraham got down to the number 10. Would God save the city if there were 10 righteous living there? God agreed: "For the sake of 10 I will not destroy it." (Genesis 18:32). The city was destroyed. There were not 10. God rescued four, but even one of those turned back."

"Are there 10? Nations come and go, but this one has been special in many ways. Public affirmations of the blessings of God upon the land have been common, particularly in our past. Religious life has been supported, and even protected in our constitution. No, this is not the place where God will establish a reign on earth. It is not the "nesting place" for the Messiah, as was Israel, the only earthly nation given that special character, even though as a nation it rejected the Gift it produced. Countervailing forces took over, and societies, at least in their moral character, declined. The light of Christian influence seems to be dawning in Africa now, and some in Asia."

"What failed in these other places? And what seems to be failing in our nation? It could well be our version of a lack of "10." The number of righteous - believers - who are faithful to His revealed Word, who do not "look back" with longing at the moral decline and faithfulness of a society going under. Leaders that legislate evil. Churches that cave to expediency. A society that condones immoral living and even encourages it."

"Nineveh was also about to be destroyed for its evil (Job 1:2), but it repented when it learned of its impending doom, and it was spared for another century."

"Perhaps this current pandemic, with its vivid portrayal of our vulnerability is a wakeup call for our land. Or maybe especially for the "10," or less, that the faithful pray for the country, witness to the truth, and stand fast in God's Word. Let us cast off the works of darkness and put on the armor of light (Romans 13:12)."

"It's foolish to believe we know the mind of God, other than what He has revealed in His Word. Evil and wickedness are going to exist until Christ returns. We cannot presume upon His mercy, but we can pray for it."

"May there always be "10," or more."   Pastor James Knill   (my pastor since May 1989)

JEWISH FACT: In Judaism there are supposed to be 10 men for prayer a MINYAN.

FIFTH COLUMN TRAITORS

"A FIFTH COLUMN [5TH COLUMN] is any group of people who undermine a larger group from within, usually in favor of an enemy group or nation. The activities of a fifth column can be overt or clandestine. Forces gathered in secret can mobilize openly to assist an external attack. This term is also extended to organized actions by military personnel. Clandestine fifth column activities can involve acts of sabotage, disinformation, or espionage executed within defense lines by secret sympathizers with an external force."   Wikipedia

ORIGIN: "During the SIEGE OF MADRID in the SPANISH CIVIL WAR, NATIONALIST general Emilio Mola told a journalist in 1936 that as his four columns of troops approached Madrid, a "fifth column" (Spanish: Quinta columna) of supporters inside the city would support him and undermine the Republican government from within." Wiki

"The term was then widely used in Spain. ERNEST HEMINGWAY used it as the title of his only play, which he wrote in Madrid while the city was being bombarded, and published in 1938 in his book THE FIFTH COLUMN & FIRST FORTY-NINE STORIES."

"Though Mola's 1936 usage is widely regarded as the origin of the phrase, historian CHRISTOPHER CLARK quotes a February 1906 letter by Austrian military attache Joseph Pomiankowski using the phrase, "the fifth-column work of the [SERBIAN} RADICALS in peacetime, which systematically poisons the attitude of our SOUTH SLAV POPULATION and could, if the worst came to the worst, create very serious difficulties for our army." Wikipedia

HISTORICAL PROVIDENTIAL CONNECTION: In June 1914, GAVRILIO PRINCIP, a Bosnian/Serbian terrorist, assassinated the Austrian Archduke FRANZ FERDINAND and his wife in SARAJEVO, capital of Bosnia/Herzegovina. On Sept. 1, 1914, because of military alliances, Europe began the GREAT WAR, WORLD WAR I, "THE WAR TO END ALL WARS." Ferdinand was to become the heir to the Austrian throne of elderly Emperor FRANZ JOSEPH, a cousin of Germany's Kaiser WILLHELM II. September 1, was the 9TH OF AV, on the Jewish LUNAR CALENDAR. The two Jewish JERUSALEM TEMPLES were destroyed on the 9TH OF AV. PROVIDENCE?

PROPHETIC HISTORY: GEORGE ORWELL 1984

"Some writers, mindful of the origin of the phrase, use it only in reference to military operations rather than the broader and less well defined range of activities that sympathizers might engage in to support an anticipated attack."

SECOND WORLD WAR

"By the late 1930s, as American involvement in the war in Europe became more likely, the term "fifth column" was commonly used to warn of potential sedition and disloyalty within the borders of the United States. The fear of betrayal was heightened by the rapid FALL OF FRANCE in 1940, which some blamed on internal weakness and a pro-German "fifth column". A series of photos run in a June 1940 issue of LIFE magazine warned of "signs of Nazi Fifth Column Everywhere". In a speech to the HOUSE OF COMMONS that same month, Prime Minister WINSTON CHURCHILL reassured MPs that "Parliament has given us the powers to put down Fifth Column activities with a strong hand." In July 1940, TIME magazine referred to talk of a fifth column as a "national phenomenon". Wikipedia

"In August 1940, The New York Times mentioned "the first spasm of fear engendered by the success of fifth columns in less fortunate countries". One report identified participants in Nazi "fifth columns" as "partisans of authoritarian government everywhere," citing POLAND, CZECHOSLOVAKIA, NORWAY, and the NETHERLANDS. During the Nazi invasion of Norway, the head of the Norwegian Fascist party, VIDKUN QUISLING, proclaimed the formation of a new Fascist government in control of Norway, with himself as Prime Minister, by the end of the first day of fighting. The word "QUISLING" soon became a byword for "COLLABORATOR" or "TRAITOR". Wikipedia

PERSONAL PROVIDENTIAL STORY: I met a man who proudly told me and my father his Norwegian father was in QUISLING'S EXECUTION FIRING SQUAD! This occurred after a church service in the parking lot where he saw my Swedish SAAB 99 car.

"The New York Times on August 11, 1940 featured three editorial cartoons using the term. JOHN LANGDON-DAVIES, a British journalist who covered the Spanish Civil War, wrote an account called "The Fifth Column". In November 1940, Ralph Thomson, reviewing Harold Lavine's FIFTH COLUMN IN AMERICA, a study of Communist and Fascist groups in the United States, In the New York Times, questioned his choice of that title: "the phrase has been worked so hard that it no longer means much anymore."

Japanese Americans Unjustly Interned After Pearl Harbor

"Immediately following the Japanese ATTACK ON PEARL HARBOR, the U.S. Secretary of the Navy FRANK KNOX issued a statement that "the most effective Fifth Column work of the entire war was done in Hawaii with the exception of Norway." In a column published in the Washington Post, dated Feb. 12, 1942, the columnist WALTER LIPPMAN wrote of imminent danger from actions that might be taken by Japanese Americans. Titled "THE FIFTH COLUMN ON THE COAST," he wrote of possible attacks that could be made along the West Coast of America that would amplify damage inflicted by a potential attack by Japanese naval and air forces. Suspicion about an active fifth column on the coast lead to the forced internment of Japanese Americans."

"During the Japanese invasion of the Philippines, an article in the Pittsburgh Post-Gazette in December 1941 said the indigenous MORO MUSLIMS were "capable of dealing with Japanese and fifth columnists and invaders alike." Another in the Vancouver Sun in the following month described how the large population of Japanese immigrants welcomed the invasion: "the first assault on Davao was aided by numbers of fifth Columnists-residents of the town." Wikipedia

442nd JAPANESE REGIMENT AMERICAS'S MOST DECORATED UNIT

They received 21 Medals of Honor in Italy, France and Germany. One was Sen. Daniel Inouye. The unit also received 560 Silver Stars plus 28 secondary; 52 Distinguished Service Crosses; 4,000 Bronze Stars plus 1,200 secondary; 9,486 Purple Hearts.

TODAY ON TV: "The V TV shows, novels and comics about an alien invasion of earth. A group of aliens who are opposed to the the invasion, and who assist the human Resistance Movement are called The Fifth Column." Wikipedia

SECRETARY OF STATE MADELEINE ALBRIGHT: recalls, "German sympathizers in Czechoslovakia [where she lived] in the first years of World War II, does not use the phrase to describe their actions until she considered their possible response to a German invasion: "Many perhaps most of the Sudetens would have provided the enemy with a fifth column". Wikipedia

HISTORICAL FACT: After Germany's defeat in World War I, the Versailles Treaty German land and citizens became part of the new country of Czechoslovakia. The western area was Bohemia, the German area was Sudetenland. This was why Chancellor Hitler's and Prime Minister NEVILLE CHAMBERLAIN'S MUNICH AGREEMENT of September 30, 1938. Chamberlain returning to Great Britain waved the Munich Agreement in the air proclaiming: "Peace in our time." Shortly afterward the German Army "peacefully" occupied the rest of Czechoslovakia. This gave Hitler access to some vital minerals and industries needed for his future aggressive wartime needs.

ALCOHOLICS ANONYMOUS SERENITY PRAYER

God,
Grant me the Serenity
to Accept the things
I cannot change
The Courage
to change the things that I can
And the Wisdom
to know the difference.

"You do not need to be an alcoholic or drug user or suffer from a mental illness for this prayer to apply to you and you can change the Word God to a word that better suits your belief system. The prayer is just as effective if you are asking the Universe, the Goddess, or Allah.

This prayer works both ways. Serenity can bring us to a point of acceptance. Acceptance of circumstances and situations that can not be changed brings with it a serenity. Courage helps you change things that need changing, and changing things gives you courage. Knowing the difference brings you wisdom and wisdom helps you know the difference.

Surviving is not enough! There is a great deal of literature around that helps those who have lived through abuse to identify themselves as survivors. I would extend to say surviving is only the first step, recognizing your ability to survive is the second step, and moving on the third step.

It is right to stop and look back and recognize your survival skills, to see how you came through horrid situations, developed coping mechanisms to assist you along the way.

It is right to celebrate your survival mechanisms are but that is not as far as you can and should go, You need to go that one step further and move beyond mere survival.

When the ugly head of past pains rises up, it may make you suddenly feel old feelings over again. Recognize these old feelings as just that, old feelings that are attached to situations, that are now gone, over, finished. Acknowledge these feelings."

HOLLYWOOD FACT: The movie BILL W (2012) tells the story of ALCOHOLIC'S ANONYMOUS its founders Bill W, actor JAMES WOODS, and JAMES GARNER. bILL Wilson lived in Bedford Hills, NY the town next to my home in Mt. Kisco, NY.

His co-founder had gotten religious faith through the OXFORD GROUP and saved Bill.

12 STEPS PROGRAM OF ALCOHOLICS ANONYMOUS

1 We admitted we are powerless over alcohol—that our lives had become unmanageable.
2 Come to believe that a Power greater than ourselves could restore us to sanity.
3 Make a decision to turn our will and our lives over to the care of God as we understand Him.
4 Make a searching and fearless total inventory of ourselves.
5 Admitted to God to ourselves, and to one another human being the exact nature of our wrongs.
6 Were entirely ready to have God remove all these defects of character.
7 Humbly asked Him to remove our shortcomings.
8 Made a list of all persons we had harmed, and became willing to make amends to them all.
9 Make direct amends to such people whenever possible, except when to do so

would injure them or others.

10 Continued to take personal inventory and when we were wrong promptly admitted it.

11 Sought through prayer and meditation to improve our conscious contact with God as we understood Him, praying only for knowledge of His will for us and the power to carry that out.

12 Having had a spiritual awakening as the result of these Steps, we tried to carry this message to alcoholics, and to practice these principles in all our affairs.

PERSONAL STORY: In August 1991, at a Tanglewood concert by CHRIST0PH von DOHANAYI, conductor of the CLEVELAND SYMPHONY orchestra, I met CHRISTOPHER NIEBUHR, son of pastor, author and theological college administrator. I told my Lutheran pastor this and he said, "REINHOLD NIEBUHR wrote the SERENITY PRAYER for ALCOHOLICS ANONYMOUS." I had spoken to Christopher from a 5 cent phone booth in front of the NORMAN ROCKWELL painting museum in Stockbridge, Massachusetts. I told him about writing a book about Hitler trying to replace Christianity with national SOCIALISM, and that I had read that his father was one of the few pastors who knew Hitler was trying to destroy Christianity which he learned from German theologian PAUL TILLICH. Tillich was removed from his church and fled to America, where Reinhold Niebuhr's UNION COLLEGE SEMINARY made him a professor. Christopher told me his apartment was down the hall from his family's Riverside Drive apartment. Christopher said he would have liked to see me, he lived a block away, but a publisher was visiting his mother Ursula about her letter's to his father. She was a brilliant British theologian at the Union Seminary. Christopher said she could read Hebrew and his father could read Greek. I asked Chrisotpher, "Who was most intelligent your father or your mother?" Without hesitating Christopher retorted, "My mother." She was born in Southampton, England. Christopher said his parents were married in the nearby WINCHESTER CATHEDRAL and on their honeymoon visited London where they meet GANDHI.

I now reflect back to my Jewish daughter learning Hebrew and then she taught high school German for 9 years. SEHR SWEAR! VERY DIFFICULT. She has led seven high school student German trips to Germany and one with Latin class went to Rome and ST. PETER'S cathedral with her mother, a chaperone, and her brother. She also played the alto flute in the North Stafford high school orchestra and marching band.

Niebuhr collaborated with Pastor FOSDICK of the famous Riverside Church in New York City in initiating Alcoholics Anonymous.

ELIZABETH NIEBUHR, Reinhold's daughter wrote a book about the Serenity Prayer.

SMALL WORLD STORY: Christopher told me about a Tanglewood concert in August 1991, evening by CHRISTOPH VON DOHANAYI who was related to DIETRICH BONHOEFFER, his sister married his father, who was hanged for his "treason" in the Col. KLAUS von STAUFFENBERG bomb assassination attempt on Hitler.

I literally didn't have enough money to get back to Virginia but bought an inside ticket, to see and hear the orchestra better, than from the lawn. The concert was in Lenox, Massachusetts and I was able to find WILLIAM SHIRER's house, who wrote the epic THE RISE AND FALL OF THE THIRD REICH in 1960. I had to go to courthouse to find his address in land deeds records. It was across the street. I had my mother's BOOK OF THE MONTH club copy and met Shirer's second wife who was Russian. She said, "My husband is busy writing a book about TOLSTOY give me the book and he will autograph it and I will put it on the porch." I picked it up on the way to the nearby concert. I sat in my assigned seat next to a man who was reading a little book about Dietrick Bonhoeffer. I told the man, "I was told the conductor is related to Bonhoeffer." He responded saying, "I know that." I asked, "Are you Christopher Niebuhr?" He said, "YES!" We

202

shook hands and enjoyed a great concert by what some critics have called America's greatest symphony orchestra the CLEVELAND SYMPHONY.

At intermission we greeted the conductor. Christopher and I have been phone friends for 27 years and I spent two separate nights at his home in Lee, Massachusetts. Christopher passed in a care center in Lee, Massachusetts on June 1, 2018, of a massive heart attack, age 86. I am looking forward to meeting him and his father and mother and introducing them to my German mother Elisabeth and my father Alexander Bruce whose bombing unit was the most accurate unit in the 8th Air Force which destroyed HITLER'S SOCIALIST NAZIS THIRD REICH, I also want to meet my German grandmother Susanna and grandfather Karl Frank who were on Hitler's DEATH LIST for being old and unproductive.

GRACE IS FREE——BUT IT ISN'T CHEAP

"If you were a moviegoer in 1969, you may remember ARLO GUTHRIE singing his rendition of "AMAZING GRACE" in the movie ALICE'S RESTAURANT. The song became part of a religious revival among young people during those years.
PERSONAL STORY: The restaurant was located in Stockbridge, Massachusetts where Christopher Niebuhr lived. My mother's sponsors lived in nearby Housatonic.
This old family favorite was written in the 18th Century by JOHN NEWTON (1725-1807), a leader in Britain's Evangelical movement. It begins with these words:
"Amazing Grace how sweet the sound that saved a wretch like me! I once was lost but now am found, was blind but now I see."
"Yes, God is dispensing an amazing grace that saves wretches like you and me. Before God's Grace, were we lost, floundering in a world cut off from HIM. Through Grace God finds us and saves us from sin and eternal death."
"Yet most of the world has not heard about God's Grace. Others have heard about it, yet have misunderstood how it works."
"A friend of mine once wrote an article titled "I wish there was another word for Grace." He was addressing a dilemma. How do we make Grace relevant to people. who find the idea rather meaningless because of overuse and wrong use? Well, how much do you know about God's grace—and what does it mean to you?"

GRACE IN ROMANS

"The Greek word translated "Grace" in our English Bibles is charis. In the Greek world of Jesus and Paul, it meant any concrete favor or kindness given as an outright gift. Charis was also applied to divine favor of the gods toward Human Beings."
"Paul gave the word charis a meaning it did not have before. In his New Testament letters, Paul applied the word Grace to all. The gifts that God gives to us."Grace to all the gifts that God gives to us."
"Through these gifts, God sets about to renew us in His spiritual image. We call this renewal or rebirth being saved. In giving us His Grace, God is fulfilling a purpose he has nurtured from before the Creation of Humanity. (Genesis 1:26-27; 1 Peter 1:18-20)."
"The Apostle Paul explained why we need God's Grace, how it works and what it accomplishes, in a letter he wrote to the church of Rome."

"In other words, before God applies His Grace to Us, we are not yet what HE intends us to be, spiritually speaking. We are all sinners and under sin—given over to death (Romans 3:23; 6:23)."

"We live, said Paul, apart from God in a spiritually fallen world (Romans 5:12-14). Only his Grace can save us (verses 15-19)."

"Through Grace, God justifies us with himself—that is, makes us spiritually right—by erasing the penalty of sin (Romans 3:24). HE accomplishes this through the DEATH OF JESUS, who was God in Human flesh. (Romans 5:8-11)."

"Because of Grace, we are no longer accounted as sinners. We have become right with God, or righteous (Romans 4:20-24)."

"Under GRACE, our sinning human self is crucified, to use Paul's metaphor (Romans 6:6-7). Now, GOD can renew each of us as a new being—a kind of godly self. The result is that we can submit to the will to God."

"This change is possible only through the HOLY SPIRIT given us under Grace (Romans 5:5). This spirit applies the full work of Jesus Christ to us. Ultimately, grace results in the gift of ETERNAL LIFE, in all its fullness."

GRACE CANNOT BE EARNED

"God cannot give this precious grace in payment for human merit. Grace is just that—an unearned, unmerited gift from God.

"It is ABSOLUTELY FREE (Romans 3:24; 5:15). That is, we do not obtain God's grace because we do God's Will or live a pious of good life. We do God's Will because we first receive His Grace."

"Otherwise, Grace wouldn't be a gift, but wages paid for work done (Romans 4:4-5). So Grace, in that sense, comes to us without any cost."

"But because God's Grace is FREE does not mean it doesn't have a price. Grace, as it turns out, is the most expensive gift ever given. It's a gift that has no price but comes at great cost."

PASTOR DIETRICH BONHOEFFER'S CHRISTIAN GRACE

"That's what theologian and Lutheran pastor DIETRICH BONHOEFFER (1906-1945) discovered. He lived and taught in his Germany during the years of the Nazis regime, from 1933 to 1945."

"Bonhoeffer learned how costly God's Grace can be when the demands of Christ come into conflict with this world's ways."

"Because of his stand against the policies of the Nazi government, he was banned from teaching and pastoring. Bonhoeffer was imprisoned by the GESTAPO in 1943, and executed in the Nazi concentration camp at FLOSSENBURG on April 9, 1945."

"GOD'S FREE GRACE became extremely expensive for Bonhoeffer. It cost him his life."

"Bonhoeffer had to struggle to live a life of costly grace in a way most of us never have. He had to face the tough choice: What should he obey and follow—the will of Jesus Christ and God or the corrupt society around him?"

"Bonhoeffer wrote of this great struggle between costly and "cheap grace"—a term he coined—in THE COST OF DISCIPLESHIP, written between the years 1935 and 1937. The book deals with the tough choice disciples of Jesus face in a world hostile to what he stands for."

CHEAP GRACE

"Bonhoeffer had a lot to say about cheap grace. He said this is "grace sold on the market like cheapjacks' wares." a dealer's shoddy and inferior merchandise. It is "Grace without price, grace without cost!"

"Cheap grace, then, wrongly implies that Christ finished His work when he took our sins upon himself.. Since "the account has been paid in advance; and, because it has been paid, everything can be had for nothing," Bonhoeffer wrote."

"Cheap grace mistakenly suggests that we Christians need not be changed by becoming Christlike in submission to God's will. Therefore, cheap grace, said Bonhoeffer, is "The preaching of forgiveness without requiring repentance."

"Cheap Grace says a Christian need not "aspire to live a different life under grace from his old life under sin" Thus, the person molded by cheap grace is, by nature, no different than anybody else."

"Cheap Grace claims, "I can go sin as much as I like," wrote Bonhoeffer, "and rely on this grace to forgive me." Bonhoeffer's struggle to expose cheap grace was also a battle once fought in the early New Testament Church."

"The APOSTLE JUDE wrote about certain godless people who had secretly slipped into the apostolic Church. He said they "change the Grace of our God into a license for immorality and deny Jesus Christ our sovereign and Lord." (Jude 4). Such nominal Christians were using cheap grace as a cover up for evil. (1 Peter 2:16)."

"The APOSTLE PAUL wrestled with cheap grace as well. "Shall we sin because we are not under law but under grace?" he asked the church of Rome (Romans 6:15). "By no means!" was his unequivocal and decisive answer (same verse)."

"Earlier, Paul asked: "Shall we go on sinning so that Grace may increase? (verse 1). His answer? "By no means! We died to sin; how can we live it it any longer?" (verse 2)."

"WE DIED TO SIN"—that is why true grace is so costly. Only costly grace makes possible the death that sin demands. Costly Grace is applied in a two-fold way. It must take something away and then add something."

"Under Grace, we are cleansed of sin and our old, sinning self dies (minus). We are also given the Holy Spirit and the new self is born (plus). Both gifts make us new men and women."

"While these gifts are free, they exact a heavy price. That's because in both cases, for Grace to operate and save us, death must occur."

COSTLY GRACE

"When Christ cleanses us of sin, He dies for us. Bonhoeffer said Grace "is costly because it cost God His Life, and what that cost God much cannot be cheap for us."

"We are bought at a price: the life of God in Christ on the Cross. For it was He who gave himself for our sins as part of God's Grace toward us."

"But Grace can still be cheapened if we try to stop what Christ did for us on the cross. Christ continues to work in it now, Jesus does come, in our flesh as He did in his Incarnation (1 John 4:2; John 14:15-24)."

"But Jesus Christ can work in us only if we die, spiritually speaking. Thus, Grace will cost something else. Our Life."

"Earlier, we lauded to how the apostle Paul spoke of this cost of discipleship as spiritual death."

'We know that our old self was CRUCIFIED WITH HIM so that the body of sin might be done away with." he said (Romans 6:6)."

OUR CROSS

"Jesus also used a metaphor of pain and death when defining TRUE DISCIPLESHIP. He said those who would follow him must carry the Cross or burden that discipleship brings. (Luke 14:27)."

"Of course, our cross may not be the same size, nor the same shape, nor the same weight as that of another person's cross."

"We all have our own unique Cross to carry as individual disciples of Jesus Christ. But we must all bear a cross if we are to be disciples of costly Grace."

"Jesus said: "IF ANYONE WOULD COME AFTER ME, HE MUST DENY HIMSELF AND TAKE UP HIS CROSS DAILY AND FOLLOW ME. FOR WHOEVER WANTS TO SAVE HIS LIFE WILL LOSE IT, BUT WHOEVER LOSES HIS LIFE FOR ME WILL SAVE IT." (Luke 9:23-24)."

"Jesus is telling us not emphasizing the denying of things to ourselves. He was telling us we must deny ourselves. This is the ultimate cost of Grace."

"Will we try to save our lives by remaining what we are—sinful, human beings? If so, we will lose them. We will become the victims of cheap Grace."

"But we can take the road of costly grace, allowing Christ to dwell in us. We can be subservient to God's Will. Then we will save our lives by losing our own will."

"This is costly grace. However, it has its own gift of God, making it possible for us to be regenerated as his children."

"Paul urges Christians to give up the self, to embrace the costly and mind-renewing Grace: 'offer your bodies as living sacrifices Holy and pleasing to God —this is your spiritual act of worship.' " (Romans 12:1).

"Paul desired to travel this road of costly Grace to receive his spiritual prize."

"The apostle wrote: "I consider everything a loss compared to the surpassing greatness of knowing Christ Jesus my Lord, for whose sake I have lost all things. I consider them rubbish, that I may gain Christ. (Philippians 3:8)

PAYING THE PRICE

"What does it mean to grasp a costly grace? It is to use God's Spirit to crucify everything that tries to enslave us to sin. It is to crucify our own will and ways—anything to the mind of God in us."

"Those who belong to Christ Jesus have crucified the sinful nature with its passions and desires," Paul wrote (Galatians 5:24), They pay the supreme penalty—the death of self. They receive the supreme gift — a new Life."

"In Bonhoeffer's words: "Grace is costly because it calls us to follow, and is Grace because it calls us to follow Jesus Christ. It is costly because it costs a man his Life and it is Grace because it gives the man the only true Life."

"costly grace costs us our old life so that we may be given a new one in Christ. As Paul put it: "I have been crucified with Christ and I no longer live, but Christ lives in me." (Galatians 2:20). That is costly Grace in action."

PLAIN TRUTH Magazine   PAUL KROLL January 1995

COSTLY GRACE

THE LEGACY OF DIETRICH BONHOEFFER
BREAKPOINT with CHUCK COLSON

"Half a century ago, a Lutheran pastor named DIETRICH BONHOEFFER was involved in a plot to assassinate ADOLF HITLER — and was executed by the Nazis for treason."

"Astonishingly, a few weeks ago Bonhoeffer's reputation was resurrected when he was officially exonerated by a court in Berlin."

"But Bonhoeffer was more than a leader of the Resistance under the THIRD REICH. He was also a powerful voice for the Church."

"In his book, THE COST OF DISCIPLESHIP, Bonhoeffer paints a vivid picture of how to be true to the Christian faith under a hostile regime. Under persecution, Bonhoeffer discovered that even through God's Grace is freely given, it also extracts a high cost."

"It was costly grace that led Bonhoeffer to leave a safe haven in America and return to Nazi Germany so he could suffer with his fellow Germans."

"It was costly grace that led Bonhoeffer to continue teaching and preaching the word of God even though the Nazis tried to suppress his work."

"Costly grace led Bonhoeffer to stand against a turncoat church that mixed Nazi doctrine with Christian truth. Along with other faithful believers, Bonhoeffer signed the BARMEN DECLARATION, which boldly declared independence from the state and a co-opted church."

"Costly grace led Bonhoeffer to attempt to smuggle Jews out of Germany, even though it led to his arrest." [His twin sister Sabine married a Jewish judge and fled to Britain.]

"Costly grace led the young pastor to set aside his commitment to pacifism and join the assassination plot against Hitler — which finally led to his execution by the Nazis."

"Even in prison, Bonhoeffer's life shone with divine grace. He comforted other prisoners, who looked upon him as their chaplain. He wrote many moving letters that were later collected in a volume called LETTERS AND PAPERS FROM PRISON — a book I read during my own stay behind bars, finding strength and encouragement."

"On the morning of April 9, 1945 — less than a month before Hitler was defeated — Bonhoeffer knelt and prayed, and then followed his captors to the gallows, where he was hung as a traitor."

"Now, 51 years later, Bonhoeffer is finally receiving the official recognition to match the spiritual veneration he has inspired in so many believers."

"The late British journalist MALCOLM MUGGERIDGE wrote a tribute to Bonhoeffer in his book, THE THIRD TESTAMENT. Muggeridge wrote: "Looking back now across the years,...what lives on is the memory of a man who died not on behalf of Freedom or Democracy or a steadily rising Gross National Product {GNP], nor for any of the Twentieth century's counterfeit hopes or desires, but on behalf of a Cross on which another man died 2,000 years before."

"As on that previous occasion on GOLGOTHA," Muggeridge goes on, "so amidst the rubble of 'liberated' Europe, the only victor is the man who died. There can never be any other victory or any other hope."

"The lesson of Bonhoeffer's life and death is that God's grace is never cheap. It demands from us everything — even our lives. But in return it gives us a new life that transcends even the most oppressive political conditions."

"Like Bonhoeffer, we may at times be called traitors by an earthly regime, but our true citizenship is in heaven."   Transcript copyright 1996 Prison Fellowship

NO MATTER THE COST—PASTOR BONHOEFFER

THE PLAIN TRUTH MAGAZINE Paul Kroll January 1994

"Almost 50 years ago, German theologian and Lutheran pastor DIETRICH BONHOEFFER (1906-1945) was executed by the Nazi government. But his writings and life continue to exert a profound effect on Christians today.

Just last year, CHRISTIANITY TODAY magazine asked its readers to name books they felt had a significant impact on their Christian lives. Bonhoeffer's THE COST OF DISCIPLESHIP—finished in 1937—was among the top Five.

Bonhoeffer's continuing influence rests less on his formal theology than on his example and life experience. His influence on Christianity might have been limited had he not practiced what he preached."

Bonhoeffer was active in the world to which he preached. For this reason, theologian REINHOLD NIEBUHR said his life belonged to a modern acts of the Apostles.

Like other men and women of God before him, Bonhoeffer willingly suffered for the name of Jesus Christ. He was persecuted, imprisoned and then executed by a secular government.

Bonhoeffer's life illustrated his insistence that Christian Discipleship must be CHRIST-CENTERED—and that it requires often costly involvement with modern secular society.

His spiritual odyssey began soon after Jan. 30, 1933, the day that Adolf Hitler was installed as chancellor of Germany.

On July 23 of that year, the Lutheran General Church elections were held. The clergy and laymen who sided with Hitler gained 70 percent of the votes and occupied all the key church positions.

The GERMAN EVANGELICAL CHURCH was now controlled by Hitler's supporters. It called for a special German Christianity that included the Nazi ideology.

In effect, Bonhoeffer's church was now the REICH CHURCH. Its slogan was: "ONE PEOPLE, ONE REICH, ONE FUEHRER, ONE CHURCH." [An apostate heretical belief contrary to Jesus GREAT COMMISSION church for every nation.]

But a minority within the Church—including Bonhoeffer—remained opposed to Hitler. A SYNOD was soon formed by MARTIN NIEMOELLER (1892-1984), the symbolic figure of Protestant opposition to National Socialism in Germany.

Out of this came the PASTORS EMERGENCY LEAGUE—a group that originally numbered 2,000 pastors. The central figures in the Pastors Emergency League met at the BARMEN SYNOD in [June] 1934.

They issued a declaration enumerating the errors the Hitler regime had introduced into the church. Theologian KARL BARTH and BONHOEFFER framed the declaration.

One of the declaration's articles was an overt slap at Hitler's demand for personal allegiance. It stated: "WE REPUDIATE THE FALSE TEACHING THAT THERE ARE AREAS OF OUR LIFE IN WHICH WE BELONG NOT TO JESUS CHRIST BUT TO ANOTHER LORD." [referred to their leader Fuehrer ADOLF HITLER]

Thus, the CONFESSING CHURCH came into being in Germany, of which Bonhoeffer was a part. The Nazi regime, of course, was determined to stamp out this Christian witness against government.

In September 1937, HEINRICH HIMMLER'S SECRET POLICE launched a final assault on the Confessing Church. That destroyed the church as a viable organization.

Himmler's decree forbade all travel by pastors, and the convening of the church's assemblies. Its training centers were shut down. Hundreds of pastors were arrested and imprisoned, including Niemoeller. [Pastor Niemoeller was arrested and jailed in Berlin for reading in a church service a list of pastors names who the Nazis had illegally imprisoned. The Reich State church also stopped paying opposing pastors with government funds.]

Then, on Sept. 1, 1939, German troops invaded Poland. World War II had begun.

The Nazi government attacks on Bonhoeffer now became more personal. In March 1940, his secret instruction of pastors was discovered and halted by the Gestapo. Soon, Bonhoeffer was forbidden to preach, teach, publish or to live in Berlin.

On April 5, 1943, [My birthday May 4, 1943] Bonhoeffer was arrested by the Gestapo and taken directly to TEGEL PRISON in Berlin. Two years later, he was at the FLOSSENBURG Concentration camp.

With the first light of dawn on April 9, 1945, Bonhoeffer was taken to Flossenberg's courtyard. There he was led to the wooden gallows, taken up the platform and hanged.

His body was dumped into a wagon and taken to the crematorium.

In his death as in his life, Bonhoeffer had inspired many people. H. Fischer-Huellstrung, camp doctor at Flossenburg, was present during Bonhoeffer's final hours. He wrote:

"I saw Pastor Bonhoeffer…kneeling on the floor praying fervently to his God. I was most deeply moved by the way this lovable man prayed, so devout and so certain that God heard that prayer. At the place of execution, he again said a short prayer and then climbed the steps to the gallows, brave and composed…in the almost fifty years that I worked as a doctor, I have hardly ever seen a man die so entirely submissive to the WILL OF GOD." p 6 (I KNEW DIETRICH BONHOEFFER, edited by Wolf-Dieter Zimmermann and Ronald Gregor Smith, page 232

Trouble At Mill Unites Brothers, Body and Soul

The LONDON DAILY MAIL Mike Bygrave reports March 1986
(photo of actor David Soul and Pastor Daniel Solberg embracing his brother)

"DAVID SOUL, better known as Hutch in the television series STARSKY AND HUTCH, and his brother, Lutheran minister DANIEL SOLBERG, have become involved in a bitter labour dispute in the States which has cost David his second marriage and $250,000, and Daniel his job. The dispute follows the closure of 9 out of 10 steel mills in PITTSBURGH, Pennsylvania, leaving a quarter of a million people unemployed."

"DAVID SOUL is a famous Hollywood actor DANIEL SOLBERG is an infamous LUTHERAN pastor. Together, the SOUL BROTHERS (David shortened the family's Swedish name to SOUL when he became an actor} are involved in a bitter struggle in Pittsburgh, Pennsylvania OVER POVERTY, POWER and the POSITION OF THE CHURCH — a struggle which has cost Daniel his job and his freedom and David his second marriage and much of his money.

Says David Soul: "I CAN SIT HERE TELL YOU WHAT WE'RE DOING IS THE MOST IMPORTANT THING I'VE DONE IN MY LIFE."

"Then I can walk back into the hotel room where I'm living since my marriage broke up and think, but what about my family. There is great loneliness in this and great risk. Daniel has been jailed and is about to be defrocked; I've been fined and could go to jail. I've spent $250,000 of my money in the past two years. But my real conflict is, do I accommodate everything to save my marriage because there's nothing I want more than that? At the same time,   IT WOULD KILL ME TO STOP DOING what————
I KNOW WHAT IS RIGHT."

His younger brother Daniel says: "Because we're a widely separated family geographically, David and I weren't in close touch. There was always that bond of unspoken but strong love between us. Eighteen months ago I wrote David a letter trying to put on paper what I was doing and how I felt about it. When he read it, David decided to come to Pittsburgh to see for himself. He calls that his 'FATAL MISTAKE' "

What David Soul found in Pennsylvania was a real-life 'POWDER KEG' EVEN HOLLYWOOD COULDN'T HAVE INVENTED. The area once known AS AMERICA'S HEAVY-INDUSTRIAL HAS BECOME AN INDUSTRIAL WASTELAND. In a few short years, the US steel industry all but shut down, closing 9 out of 10 mills and throwing and estimated 250,000 people out of work. Since 'THE DOLE' [insurance] in America can only be claimed for about a year, their situation was then desperate."

In 1980, a group of local ministers formed a loose interdenominational network to address Pittsburgh's social problems. Dubbed the Denominational Ministry Strategy (DMS), and led by Lutherans like Daniel Solberg, the group was at first supported and funded by the church hierarchy. DMS hired a community organizer named Charles Honeywell and began a series of symbolic 'actions' directed primarily against MELLON BANK., the historic 'power behind Pittsburgh' and the giant US Steel. DMS activists put dead fish and a skunk in Mellon banks and threw pennies on the floor to disrupt business, much to the delight of local reporters and TV newsmen. They held press conferences and outdoor services denouncing Mellon and Pittsburgh's indifference to the unemployed and the devastating de-industrialization of the MON and OHIO Valleys.

While the DMS TACTICS WERE ALL NON-VIOLENT, they effectively split he Lutheran Church. Congregations turned on each other and on DMS pastors like Solberg and the Rev. DOUGLAS ROTH. The Lutheran synod cut off the funds for the DMS, fired Honeywell and Pastor PAUL HIMMELMAN, the bishop's liaison for the urban ministry, and dismissed the Revs SOLBERG and ROTH. When they refused to leave the churches, both men were arrested and jailed. Roth was defrocked: Solberg is part way through the disciplinary process which will lead to his defrocking."

SOUL'S CONNECTION TO BONHOEFFER's PERSECUTION

"Says David: "When I got Danny's letter I was doing research for a film I still plan to make on the life of DIETRICH BONHOEFFER, the German theologian who was executed for plotting to kill Hitler. What I found when I got to Pittsburgh WAS THE SAME SORT OF THING THAT WENT ON IN NAZI GERMANY. CRUSH THE UNIONS AND NEUTRALIZE THE CHURCH AND WHOEVER'S IN POWER CAN PRETTY WELL RUN THE SHOW."

SOUL began filming — and paying for filming — the story of the DMS. He has recently produced a 50-minute documentary called THE FIGHTING MINISTERS.

If the DMS ministers are still fighting. Charles Honeywell is the general who's making up the battle plan. A brick wall of a man, Honeywell is a veteran 'community organizer' (conservatives would probably call him an 'outside agitator'). A minister's son himself, Honeywell has forged radical pastors and dissident unionists in Pittsburgh into a unique coalition for social change, That alone is a remarkable achievement in a country where merely to call someone Socialist is to rule them out of public life. Honeywell doesn't call himself a Socialist and he says he has nothing against corporations making profits — as long as they don't do it at the expense of people."

"We're not saying they should put the steel industry back the way it was," says Honeywell. "What we're saying they should not put the steel industry back the way it was." says Honeywell. "What we're saying is, they have to give extended benefits to the people they've thrown out of work. We need federal government disaster money for the towns around Pittsburgh which are going bankrupt, and for job re-training when there is job at the other end. There are some particularly around Pittsburgh. "They turn around and accuse us of keeping new industry out of the area, scaring it off," says Honeywell. "We say, yes, that's true. The new industry we're scaring off is the $3.50-4 dollar-an-hour jobs. You can't keep a family on those wages. Opening dozen McdDonald's isn't the answer. It's significant that McDonald's is the 13th largest employer in Pittsburgh."

"To get their point across, Honeywell and the DMS have gone a very different route from Trade Unions or traditional protest movements. Says Honeywell: "Traditionally, protest movements are mass movements. You get 10,000 people in Central Park or Trafalgar Square for a Peace rally, they all go home and nothing changes."

"We're interested in the little church of 50 people — how can they get involved?"

We're not interested in activists and radicals. We find these Conservative, non-activist people, and we find if you rub 'em, they'll go to jail for you."

(Misquote: Should read "when people are rubbed the wrong way,
they will go to jail because of their values.")

"That's exactly what happened to 70-year old Wayne Cochrane, lay president of Roth's old congregation. When Roth was fired, Cochrane was one of eight supporters who barricaded themselves in the church for a week and went to jail for it."

[The London Daily Mail is Britain's Socialist worker's newspaper.]

MY CONVERSATIONS WITH HITLER—PASTOR NIEMOELLER

"The book "EYEWITNESS: HITLER" edited by ALLEN CHURCHILL relates this story of courageous Protestant clergyman. "Like so many Germans, MARTIN NIEMOELLER, U-Boat hero of World War I, first approved OF ADOLF HITLER. But the Fuehrer also turned out to be anti-religion. In 1941, when this article on early meetings with Hitler was smuggled out, the pastor had been in a concentration camp for four years because of opposition to the Nazis. He remained imprisoned until war's end."   (September 1941)

HITLER: "MORAL DECONSTRUCTIONISM OF GERMAN PEOPLE, STOP ATHEISM."

"PASTOR NIEMOELLER recalls, "I have met ADOLF HITLER exactly three times in my life. I met him for the first time in January, 1931, at the Kaiserhof Hotel in Berlin, where 70 Protestant clergymen had gathered to be addressed by him in explanation of his church program. Hitler said: 'I have asked you to come here because I want to persuade you that I—just as much as you— am working for a moral reconstruction of the German people. Since the last war Germany has been in need of more and better Christianity, more churches; and a stop must be put to atheism. What we need is a more profound inner faith in order to preserve ourselves as a people. I am a Catholic, but I am asking you to help me in my great task.' "

" 'Hitler than asked us to propose ways and means of cooperating with him. He promised us that as soon as he obtained power, the church would not only retain all its rights but would be entitled to greater support from the state, and would have control of the schools. In brief, there would be a better understanding between the government and the church than had been the case in the [liberal secularist] WEIMAR REPUBLIC. I must admit that we all had a very favorable impression from the modest way in which Hitler spoke, and I knew that from that time on he could count on the support of the majority of the Protestant clergy in Germany.' "

211

"CHRISTIANITY NEEDS HEROES OF THE LAST WAR"

"NIEMOELLER recalls, 'Immediately after the speech, Hitler walked up to me and said, 'I am pleased to see you here, Herr Kapitan-Lieutenant.' 'I am no longer an officer,' I said, 'I am a pastor now.' 'People like you,' he exclaimed, 'Who went straight from U-BOAT TO PULPIT, are exactly what the New Germany needs! Christianity needs the heroes of the last war.' " 'I was proud of his appreciation and really pinned all my hope on him [Hitler]. At that time we were certain that he would be the ruling party in Germany. I was charged by the United Protestant Church Association to ask Hitler certain definite questions in order to secure definite commitments. Present with him were GOERING, HESS, and ROSENBERG."

" 'I have come to you,' I said, 'Because the church frequently finds attacks directed against it in the Nazi papers, and because it is not always the Christian spirit that is found in the HITLER YOUTH and in the STORM TROOPERS. Furthermore, we find it hard to understand the many murders committed by the Storm Troopers.' "

PERSECUTION OF COMMUNISTS, JEWS, AND LIBERALS JUSTIFIED

" 'Murders?' Hitler shot back. 'How can you say murders?' 'What the Storm Troopers are doing is to purge Germany of the COMMUNISTS and MARXISTS, of JEWS and LIBERALS. This has NOTHING TO DO WITH MURDER. THIS IS SELF-DEFENSE.' "

" 'I shall never permit a member of my church to be molested!' "
" 'I shall never permit a member of my church to be molested!' "

" 'I said indignantly.' HITLER suddenly became soft and placating. 'Please, won't you see to it that they understand me? I have an enormous task ahead, the work of my life. The masses cannot always be feed with bread and sugar; they also need the whip. I have the toil and work, to struggle and organize, To crush this Republic which has nothing in store for Christianity because it's a JEW REPUBLIC. When I am CHANCELLOR AND FUEHRER, the church will live again, and live freely. I shall re-establish the cooperation between the government and the church, just as it used to be in the old Prussian state. The church will play the major role in the educational school system. I am not yet in a position to conclude any contracts. However, to you, as an officer, I give my solemn word of honor that I shall carry out all my promises.' "
"Niemoeller notes, 'I reported the results of my conversation to the church council, which considered everything satisfactory. But later events proved that they were as naive as we were blind. I trusted Hitler, and as HE BETRAYED ME just as he did THE REST OF THE WORLD WHICH LISTENED TO HIS PEACE UTTERANCES.' "

GOLDEN SWASTIKAS REPLACE CROSSES ON CHURCH TOWERS

"He continues, 'At the time of the last conversation I had with him before I was arrested, persecution of the church was at its peak. Crosses on the church towers had been replaced by GOLDEN SWASTIKAS; the Hitler Youth was educated in the spirit that not Jesus but Adolf Hitler was the true son of God. In the schools the Old Testament was decried as Jewish. Pogroms against the Jews were sweeping the country and our clergymen were being thrown into concentration camps. Gestapo officials were writing down every speech and priests were arrested even in their pulpits.' "

212

"He reveals, 'In this, our hour of greatest despair, I asked for an audience with Hitler, and it was on January 5, 1934, that I had my memorable talk with him. This time he was entirely different. I had to wait more than four hours at the Reich's Chancellery, and when he greeted me Hitler's manner was icy.' 'You desire to talk with me?' He began, 'standing like NAPOLEON with his arms crossed.' "

'Yes Mr. Chancellor,' I replied. 'I have come to you because I am worrying about the church.' 'What's the matter with you? Didn't I keep all my promises? Didn't I put REICHS-BISHOP MUELLER in charge? What are you complaining about?' "

'Never before,' I said, 'Did we have Protestant Bishops. Never was there any need for church ministries. You promised us equal rights, but you have made us only an instrument of the [Nazi] party.' "

"Hitler replied angrily, 'Why are you causing me such difficulties with this CONFESSIONAL CHURCH?' [Read the Barth/Niemoeller BARMAN CONFESSION OF FAITH] Hitler was becoming enraged.' "

"NAZISM IS DESTROYING THE CHURCH AND OUR FAITH"

" 'We don't want to cause you any difficulties, Mr. Chancellor,' I explained, 'But I am here as a representative of the Protestant faith. Your government has ordered measures that sooner or later will destroy our church and the fundamentals of our faith. We can't stand by idly while the government gives such orders. Didn't you promise us freedom of the church instead of its suppression?' "

" 'Now Hitler grew wild. He [Hitler] cried out like a madman.' 'You as an officer, have learned to obey! You have to obey! I alone determine what is and what is not Christian. I determine what the church has to do, I and I alone am the Fuehrer of this nation, The Lord has chosen me for this office and the people have called me!' "

" 'Not you, Herr Hitler, the Lord is my leader,' I replied. 'Only later did I learn that these words were responsible for ordering my arrest. But at the moment I tried to be a bit conciliatory. 'It is also my concern for the Reich that made me come to you.' I said."

HITLER REVEALS HIS PLAN OF WORLD CONQUEST

"Hitler was still shouting. 'You are concerned about the THIRD REICH? You had better leave that to me!' Hitler now betrayed his whole hatred and his true intentions: 'I thought of making the German church the most powerful in the world. I wanted to name German Bishops in all countries that I am going to conquer. I wanted a powerful church. I wanted to unite all religions and churches under the spirit of National Socialism. I thought of putting officers like you in charge. But you are all Jew-infested. Your Christianity, after all, is nothing but a stepchild of Jewry [Old Testament] grown soft and infested with these stupid humanitarian illusions.' " [Jesus Prince of Peace.]

HITLER THREATENS CHURCH WITH ANNIHILATION

"Hitler continued, 'If the Christian Church wants to fight me., I shall annihilate it as I have crushed and will crush all my other enemies. I don't mind walking over corpses so long as I reach my goal.

I need no Christianity. Whoever who won't obey me will be destroyed, and that goes for you too. You are a deserter, and you know that for desertion there is only one punishment — death!' "

" 'I HAVE ONLY DESERTED TO CHRISTIANITY,' I said vigorously.' 'To faith; and I am willing to take upon myself all the suffering it involves.' 'You will regret it!' These were HITLER'S LAST WORDS TO ME.' "

"KEEP THE FAITH!"

"Niemoeller concludes, 'During the years of my imprisonment I have never had any cause for regret. As long as I have my cell where I can pray, I am still happier than Hitler, the promise breaker and incorrigible liar!, who hardly dares to go out alone for fear that a bullet might hit him from behind.' "
'TO THE PEOPLE of the WORLD OVER I SEND THIS MESSAGE: KEEP THE FAITH!'
        EYEWITNESS: HITLER — Pastor Niemoeller ALLEN CHURCHILL

WHO WAS MARTIN NIEMOLLER?

Sybil Niemoeller von Sell, his wife
"One hundred and twenty years ago, the Swiss poet C.F. Meyer lets Ulrich von Hutton say about himself: "Ich bin keen ausgeklugelt Buch, ice bin ein Mensch mid seine Widerspruch." "I am not an intricately written book, I am a man with all his contradictions."
'Those words describe MARTIN NIEMOELLER to perfection. The man in the course of his long life was called anything and everything from turncoat to traitor, Communist, from prophet to hero and martyr. The last two names would make him cringe."
"My hero he became when I was eight years old."
"On a beautiful Sunday morning in June, a small girl was sent against her wishes to Sunday school in the little 900 year old village church of St. Anns in Dahlem, an edifice so solidly constructed with fieldstone that not even the 30-year war could accomplish its total destruction. Upon my return home I informed my parents that we had a new pastor. I had indeed met Martin Niemoeller's first at a children's service as a new pastor, who fascinated us with his tails as a submarine commander on a ship under the sea. My father wanted to know his name, but I decided to be difficult, since I had been made to go, so I told him that I neither knew nor cared."
"A man with no principles? He needed no principles. God's commandments were good enough for him."
"Straight sailing as a virtue, as proof of a stable character." Straight sailing is only possible if a vessel travels in still waters. Turbulence requires maneuvering and flexibility. Flexibility instead of stubbornness and tolerance instead of prejudice were the names of his game."
"He never tried to force his convictions or his beliefs on anyone. BILLY GRAHAM came to the house once and on his way out he turned around once more: "Pastor," he asked, 'What am I doing wrong?" And , he received the answer, "DO NOT TELL THE PEOPLE YOU MUST! RATHER ASK THEM WILL YOU ACCEPT JESUS CHRIST!" That was typical for a man who never tried to force his convictions on anybody, for whom the words hate and revenge were meaningless."
"Martin Niemoeller was a prophet the trouble with a prophet is that he is usually so far ahead of his time that even intelligent people cannot always follow him. He irritates them, for prophets seem irrational. Communism, 10 years ago, was already or him a thing of the past." "Communism," he proclaims at the end of a documentary. "What would Jesus say!" The real enemy of humanity was

MAMMON. Mammon consumes the whole man. And people cannot serve both mammon and God."

"When his adversaries ragout of slanderous names, their last resort was and still is, "anti-semitism" —a label, and, - in the Germanic tradition - everything and everyone has to have a label."

"Antisemitic" What else is new? Martin Niemoeller, and generations before him, was no exception in the Christian world into which he had been born. No question is easier to answer than the one. "Who was antisemite in Germany?" - and in other countries? The reply has to be "everybody!"

"Antisemitism, this mysterious and lethal disease - its cause unknown to this day, over hundred of years handed down from generation to generation - like Grandma's favorite cookie recipe had become a way of life, the church of Jesus Christ not excepted. The road to AUSCHWITZ was paved very carefully over many centuries: the CRUSADES, the SPANISH INQUISITION

"We remember Martin Luther's suggestions to throw the Jews into the street and to burn their houses of worship. Luther as a young man had been a supporter of the Jews until he realized they would not convert."

"Martin Niemoeller's background in this respect was not different from that of almost all other Christians, not only Lutherans. Too late he realized - so he admits and confesses - that he had been wrong with the rest, responsible with the rest for the HOLOCAUST. This is how he expressed it in a lecture, addressing students in HEIDELBERG in 1957:

> And the church and Christendom! In eagerness to involve themselves in
> nationalistic expressions, it became part of the anti-Jewish campaign
> begun already centuries ago, incapable and unwilling to fight antisemitism
> as it should have done. Those six million, therefore, are a heavy burden
> on Christendom and on the church and not on the Nazi party, the SS and
> the one mass murderer. Yes, the church bears the heaviest burden
> because it knew what it did when it did nothing. Antisemitism is the one
> acute threat to the church as a church. An antisemitic church would be -
> a contradiction in itself.

"Martin Niemoeller never found it beneath his dignity to publicly admit to his part in the guilt and to humbly beg forgiveness when he knew he had been wrong. He did so in big matters as well as in small ones, be it only for losing his terrific temper, which happened all too often and struck like lightening   out   of   the   clear   blue   sky."

"The subject of forgiveness became very acute around our President's [Reagan] visit to BITBURG [Military cemetery] when he saw fit to forgive evil that he had not suffered."   [Read my Bitburg Reagan visit letter-to-the editor May 1985.]

"SIMON WIESENTHAL, in his book, THE SUNFLOWER, deals with this specific problem. Who should, who can, who must forgive whom and for what: and who cannot?

In the second part of his book, he prints the opinions of over a dozen famous people on the subject. Here is Martin Niemoeller's reply:

"Injustice or pain inflicted on us personally, we can forgive. But evil done to others, we
  cannot forgive. Only those who suffered can do that and no one else in their stead."

GOD ALMIGHTY'S TEN COMMANDMENTS

God Almighty gave Moses TEN COMMANDMENTS which few live by. As ABC TV NIGHT LINE commentator TED KOPPEL once said the Ten Commandments are not the 10 SUGGESTIONS. My dad was senior ABC Master Control room engineer from the beginning in 1949 until he retired in 1983, at the age of 64. After retiring, on the phone my dad sadly retorted, "Clive I was a PROSTITUTE for 34 years!" SO SAD. I didn't respond to his comment. What could I say? You gave America so many great shows.

PROSTITUTE DEFINITION: A person typically a woman, who engages in sexual activity for payment. A person who misuses their talents or who sacrifices their self-respect for the sake of personal or financial gain: careerist political prostitutes.   TERM LIMITS.
PROSTITUTE THESAURUS: Call girl, whore, hooker, working girl, lady of the evening, street walker, member of the oldest profession, moll, escort, courtesan, joie de fille, hustler, ho; DATED—tart, scarlet woman, camp follower, harlot, woman of ill repute, wench, strumpet, cocette, trollop.   [My dad was not a prostitute.]
My dad was the senior ABC TV Master Control room broadcast engineer who at 4:00 connected DICK CLARK's AMERICAN BANDSTAND from its Philadelphia studio to the whole United States. He connected Americans to HAPPY DAYS, LAVERNE AND SHIRLEY, MORK AND MINDY, SUPERMAN, THE LONE RANGER, WYATT EARP, MONDAY NIGHT FOOTBALL (with FRANK GIFFORD and HOWIE COSSELL), ROONE ARLEDGE WIDE WORLD OF SPORTS, the OLYMPICS, PRESIDENTIAL ELECTION COVERAGE, children's shows XXXXXX XXXXX good news coverage before cable 24/7. TV was for entertainment not education like the HISTORY CHANNEL shows. The shows were G rated. I am happy my dad didn't have to work with today's television. He would have pulled the plug and walked out. It would have been like the film NETWORK when English actor PETER FINCH told his TV audience to open their windows and shout, "I AM MAD AS HELL AND I CAN'T TAKE IT ANYMORE!" His audience did what he said because they agreed that he was right. You can always change the channel.
Read what the Chicago community organizer Saul Alinsky, a far left socialist/communist rules for REVOLUTION are. This is not GOD's words but LUCIFER's the head angel in Heaven who decided he wanted to rule Heaven. God Almighty cast him and a third of his evil angel followers out of Heaven to Earth where he became Satan and they the demoniac. This is not a fairy tale. The great prophet ISAIAH writes Lucifer's story. Isaiah also wrote the story of the SUFFERING MESSIAH JESUS 53-54 who God the Father sent to Earth to take humankind's sins and free believers from Satan and the devil's lies.

FAKE, BIASED, PREJUDICIAL HATE NEWS

If you read Alinsky's 13 rules you realize these are not Judeo-Christian, Islamic or Hindu-Buddhist rules or laws It doesn't take much intelligence to see that they correlate to the left wing secular humanist "religious" atheist beliefs which claims to be tolerant and brotherly. This is the godless Marxist/Leninist ANTIFA "anti-fascist" belief which uses violent protest Revolution against capitalism, paying taxes and want "free" higher education, health care and guaranteed higher minimum wage. Communism and socialism has been failing around the world. It is simple economics. Capitalism and small business entrepreneurship creates jobs and through fair taxes pays for the national defense and many long paid for entitlements Social Security and Medicare, etc.

President BARACK HUSSEIN OBAMA II learned the Alinsky socialism when he was a community organizer in Chicago. He associated with many people who knew ALINSKY's CHICAGO PLAYBOOK. Where was the media? They were awed by Obama's "messianic" charisma and his well scripted teleprompter rhetoric about fundamentally changing America and its Constitution. When DONALD J. TRUMP was elected their shocked comments showed their prejudice, bias, ignorance and stupidity. Every comment is on record.Left wing media keeps calling President Trump Hitler, a Nazi, a Quisling etc. because it will get him more votes from evangelical, patriotic original Constitution, with Amendments, believing Americans. Even Nazi propaganda minister GOEBBELS knew you had to tell some truth or the intelligent German people wouldn't believe the lie. Are Americans any smarter? We will soon know.

Hollywood Has Screened Many Dystopian Movies

GEORGE ORWELL'S 1984 has been filmed twice and the tele screen spying is today in many American homes voluntarily? ANIMAL FARM is a short film about and equal society until the pigs decide to rule. Pigs are supposed to be one of the smartest animals. GEORGE CLOONEY owned a Vietnamese miniature pig so he probably knows. As a child I was shepherded by a border collie, the American Kennel club rates it as the smartest dog. On the Internet there is a female border collie which know 1,002 commands! In the film BABE, the pig, was a close friend to the smart border collie.

Orwell, a Communist, who went to Barcelona, Spain during the Spanish Civil War saw the Russian commissars living well as the workers and peasants died in the streets. He wrote 1984 and Animal Farm not as anti-Nazi but anti-Communist dystopias.

At a Mary Washington University GREAT LIVES book lecture on GEORGE ORWELL the author recalled that Orwell wanted to release 1984 in 1943-44, but there were publishing delays because of a "paper shortage" but it was actually censorship by the wartime British government because the Soviet Union was our ally.

BRAVE NEW WORLD—The Coming Dystopia?

There is one dystopian film which Hollywood has not made? BRAVE NEW WORLD by ALDOUS HUXLEY in 1932, tells about a drugged scientific and technological world which we are actually beginning to be voluntarily initiating.
"To deal with the confusion, power has been centralized and government control increased. It is probable that all the world's governments will be more or less completely totalitarian even before the harnessing of atomic energy, that they will be totalitarian during and after the harnessing seems almost certain. Only a large scale popular movement toward decentralization and self-help can arrest the present tendency toward STATISM. At present there is no sign that such a movement will take place. (Forward xi)
"In an advanced technology inefficiently is the sin against the Holy Ghost. A really efficient totalitarian state would be one in which an all-powerful executive of political bosses and their army of managers control a population of slaves who do not have to be coerced, because they love their servitude. To make them love it is the task assigned, in present-day totalitarian states, to ministries of propaganda, newspaper editors and school teachers."   (Forward xii)

"Chronic remorse, as all the moralists are agreed is a most undesirable sentiment. If you have behaved badly, repent, make what amends you can and address yourself to the task of behaving better the next time. The savage is offered only two alternatives, an insane life in utopia, or the life of a primitive in an Indian village, a life more human in some respect but in others hardly less queer and abnormal."   (Forward vii)

"There was a man named Cardinal Newman," He said, "a Cardinal," he said, He exclaimed parenthetically, "was a kind of arch-community-songster." He opened the book at the place marked by a slip of paper and began to read. "We are not our own anymore than what we possess is our own. WE DID NOT MAKE OURSELVES, WE ARE NOT OUR OWN MASTERS. We are GOD'S PROPERTY…"But as time goes on they as all men, will find…   p 157-8

BRAVE NEW WORLD Aldous Huxley Harper & Row New York 1932

INVICTUS POEM

Out of the night that covers me Black as a pit from pole to pole,
I thank whatever gods that be for my unconquerable soul.
In the fell clutch of circumstance, I have not winced nor cried aloud.
Under the bludgeoning of chance my head is bloody, but unbowed.
Beyond this place of wrath and tears looms but the Horror of the shade.
And yet the menace of the years finds, and shall find me, unafraid.
It matters not how straight the gate. How charged with punishment the scroll.
I am the master of my fate: I am the captain of my soul.

"IMPORTANCE: "When English poet William Henley was 16 years old, his left leg required amputation due to complications arising from tuberculosis. In August 1873, he traveled to Edinburgh to enlist the services of the distinguished surgeon JOSEPH LISTER, who was able to save Henley's remaining leg after multiple surgeries on his foot. While recovering in the infirmary, he was moved to write the versus that became INVICTUS. A memorable evocation of VICTORIAN STOICISM — the "STIFF UPPER LIP" of self-discipline and fortitude in adversity, which popular culture rendered into a British character trait — "Invictus" remains a cultural touchstone." Wikipedia

Wikipedia notes. 'The fourth stanza alludes to a parade from the King James Bible, Matthew 7:14: Because strait is the gate, and narrow is the way, which leaders unto life, and few there be that find it."

Wikipedia POSTERITY: C.S. [Clive] LEWIS, in Book Five, chapter III (The Self-Sufficiency of Vertue) of his early autobiographical work THE PILGRIMS REGRESS (1933) included a quote from the last two lines: "I cannot put myself under anyone's orders. I must be the captain of my soul and the master of my fate. But thank you for your offer." In the 1960 film SUNRISE AT CAMPOBELLO, the character Louis Howe, played by HUME CRONYN, recites the last two lines of the poem to FRANKLIN D. ROOSEVELT, played by RALPH BELLAMY. The recitation is at first light-hearted and partially in jest, but as it continues both men appear to realize the significance of the poem to Roosevelt's fight against his paralytic illness." [The polio shot ended epidemic.]

"In the 1942 film KINGS ROW, Parr's Mitchell, a psychiatrist played by ROBERT CUMMINGS, recites the first two stanzas of "Invictus" to his friend Drake McHugh, played by RONALD REAGAN, before revealing to Drake that his legs were unnecessarily amputated by a cruel doctor." [The doctor's daughter had a crush on Reagan who was known to have had previous "affairs" with other girls.]

"In the 1942 film CASABLANCA, Captain Renault, an official played by CLAUDE RAINES, recites the last two lines of the poem when talking to Rick Blaine, played by HUMPHREY BOGART, referring to his power in Casablanca. After delivering this line, he is called away by an aide to Gestapo officer Major Strasser."

"The INVICTUS GAMES: an international paralympic-style multi-sport event created by PRINCE HARRY in which wounded, injured armed service personnel and their associated veterans take part in sport, has featured the poem in its promotions. Prior to the inaugural games in London in 2014, entertainers including actor DANIEL CRAIG [James Bond] and actor TOM HARDY, and athletes." Wikipedia

Wikipedia HISTORICAL USES—"In a speech to the HOUSE OF COMMONS on 9 September 1941, WINSTON CHURCHILL paraphrased the last two lines of the poem stating "We are still masters of our fate. We still are captains of our soul."

"The poem read by US POWs in North Vietnamese prisons. JAMES STOCKDALE recalls being passed the last stanza, written with rat droppings on toilet paper, from fellow prisoner DAVID HATCHER."

PERSONAL STORY: So many courageous and beautiful stories. However, one story goes to the dark side. Wikipedia reveals, "The poem was chosen by OKLAHOMA CITY bomber TIMOTHY McVEIGH as his final statement before his execution."

My Air Force friend Johne Westfall, who was editor of the Ramstein AB RAMJET when I was editor of the Bitburg AB SKYBLAZER, told me on the phone he and his wife Susan were driving from Tulsa, Oklahoma to Oklahoma City for his birthday party. He said speeding rescue vehicles passed their car on the Oklahoma Turnpike. It was April 19, 1995, the day the Oklahoma City Federal building was destroyed by McVeigh's bomb killing 168 innocent people and many children in a day care, and injured 680 others. It remains the deadliest act of domestic terrorism in United States history.

The attack was on the second anniversary of the Waco siege ending in April 19, 1993, with allegedly 85 killed many were children killed in a massive internal explosion and fire. Hundreds of Alcohol, Tobacco and Firearms ATF agents and Federal Bureau of Investigation agents were involved in the February 28-April 19 standoff, with 4 ATF agents killed mainly on the roof and 16 wounded. The quasi-religious group believed in End-time prophecies but un-biblically armed themselves with legal AR-15 assault rifles. Judeo ChristianS are biblically passive unless threatened by Satanic enemies of the faith or democratic freedom like Hitler's Socialist Nazis or Japan's anti-Christian imperialism and Mussolini's militant Fascists.

McVeigh was also upset about the unjust RUBY Ridge 11-day siege by ATF, FBI and Federal U.S. Marshalls, August 21-31, 1992. These horrendous government acts occurred under an over zealous President BILL CLINTON and Attorney General JANET RENO administration. Violence is not justified against innocent people.

PROPHETIC SIGNIFICANCE? In the book THE BIBLE CODE there is an impossible to believe chapter from a 5 Hebrew character computer SKIP SEARCH. I read it in disbelief. I asked my Missouri Synod Lutheran pastor if he could read Hebrew he said he could read a little. He read the Hebrew letters down a column he said MURRAH. I said that is the name of the building in Oklahoma that was bombed. He then read Hebrew letters which intersected Murrah which said MVEIGH will destroy. This passage was from Exodus. Did GOD/JEHOVAH/JESUS know this event would happen about 4,000 years in the future? He is OMNIPOTENT, OMNISCIENT, OMNIPRESENT.

I told my pastor this is in the Old Testament where God is warning of Judah's destruction because of not obeying his commands. I showed this to my pastor on Sunday and said the Bible Code book was on a stack and fell on the floor and opened to this page. On Tuesday September 11, 2001, 9 days later terrorists destroyed the World Trade Center and crashed a jetliner into the PENTAGON, five sided military headquarters, cornerstone laid on September 11, 1940. Reverend Jerry Falwell was criticized for saying 9-11 was a judgment against America's pride. Bible enemies judge.

After the 9-11 Attack I drove to my church and I asked my pastor to pray with me at our communion altar. We knelt at the rail and prayed for America's innocent departed and for the future of America and the world.

HUXLEY'S "HERD-POISIONING" OF AMERICA'S MOB

"Groups are capable of being as moral and intelligent as the individuals who form them; a crowd is chaotic, has no purpose of its own and is capable of anything except intelligent action and realistic thinking. Assembled as a crowd, people lose their powers of reasoning, and their capacity for MORAL CHOICE. Their SUGGESTIBILITY IS INCREASED to the point where they CEASE TO HAVE ANY JUDGMENT OR WILL OF THEIR OWN. They become very excitable, they LOSE ALL SENSE OF INDIVIDUAL OR COLLECTIVE RESPONSIBILITY, they subject to SUDDEN ACCESSES OF RAGE, ENTHUSIASM and PANIC. In a word, a man in a crowd behaves as though he had swallowed a large dose of some powerful intoxicant. He is a victim of what I have called "HERD-POISONING." Like alcohol, herd-poisoning is an active extraverted drug. The crowd intoxicated individual ESCAPES FROM RESPONSIBILITY, INTELLIGENCE AND MORALITY into a kind of frantic ANIMAL MINDLESSNESS." P 42
BRAVE NEW WORLD REVISITED Aldous Huxley 1958 Harper & Row New York, NY
"During his long career as an agitator, HITLER had studied the effects of HERD-POISON and had learned how to exploit them for his own purposes. He had discovered that the orator can appeal to those "HIDDEN FORCES" which motivate men's actions, much more effectively than the writer. READING IS A PRIVATE NOT COLLECTIVE ACTIVITY. The writer speaks only to individuals, sitting by themselves in a state of normal sobriety. The ORATOR SPEAKS TO MASSES OF INDIVIDUALS, already primed with herd-poison. They are at his mercy and he can do what he wants with them,. As an orator. Hitler knew his business surprisingly well. He was able, in his own words, "to follow the lead of the great mass in such a way that from the living emotion of his hearers the apt word which he needed would be suggested to him and in its turn this would go straight to the heart of its hearers," OTTO STRASSER called him "a loud-speaker, proclaiming the most SECRET DESIRES, the least admirable instincts, the sufferings and personal revolts of a whole nation.   Ibid p 43
"HITLER wrote, "All EFFECTIVE PROPAGANDA must be confined to A FEW BARE NECESSITIES and then must be expressed in a few stereotypical formulas." These stereotyped formulas must be constantly REPEATED for "only constant repetition will finally succeed in IMPRINTING AN IDEA UPON THE MEMORY OF A CROWD,"   p 44
[CNN AND MSNBC top commentators all repeat a single misleading trigger word against President TRUMP making it sound like a truth.]
"MARXISM AND FASCISM, have the advantage of producing a great deal of SOCIAL ADHERENCE AMONG THEIR DISCIPLES....In Hitler's words, the propagandist should adopt " a systemically ONE-SIDED ATTITUDE towards every problem that has to be dealt with." He must NEVER ADMIT THAT HE MIGHT BE WRONG or that people with a DIFFERENT POINT OF VIEW might even be partially right. Opponents should not be argued with; they should be ATTACKED, SHOUTED DOWN, or, if they become too much of a nuisance, liquidated. "RIGHT is on the of the side of the active aggressor."45

"Under the Nazis enormous amounts of people were compelled to spend an enormous amount of time marching in serried ranks…Marching diverts men's thoughts. Marching KILLS THOUGHT. Marching makes and END TO INDIVIDUALITY. Marching is performed in order to accustom the people to be a MECHANICAL nation."   Ibid p 45-46

THE LAST MAN IN EUROPE—HE LOVED BIG BROTHER

THE FUTURIST magazine David Goodman December 1978

"In 1956, COLUMBIA STUDIOS produced a film version of GEORGE ORWELL'S 1984.
It starred EDMOND O'BRIEN as WINSTON SMITH, the main character of 1984, JAN STERLING as Julia, Smith's lover, and MICHAEL REDGRAVE as O'BRIEN, a leader of the THOUGHT POLICE who initially befriends Smith but later savagely betrays him.
The film relates the story of Winston Smith's rebellion from the dictatorial pressures of OCEANIA. At first, Winston is so fearful of discovery that he goes no further than keeping a diary, written in his kitchen to avoid the gaze of the TELE-SCREEN. But soon his defiance explodes into something much more deadly. He starts a love affair with one of his coworkers at the MINISTRY OF TRUTH, a girl named Julia, They meet surreptitiously—at isolated spots in the country, briefly at the cafeteria at lunch, and, most often, at the large public rallies where they can hide their movements in the crowd.
Together, Winston and Julia decide to approach O'Brien, who they believe to be a member of a conspiratorial organization called the BROTHERHOOD that is plotting to overthrow the government Oceania. O'Brien leads them on, inciting their hopes of rebellion, and providing Winston with a briefcase containing THE BOOK—an outlawed REVOLUTIONARY TRACT that details the TRUE NATURE OF THE SOCIETY in which they live. Winston rents a flat above a small store in the poor section of London and there he and Julia meet often to read the book and satisfy their love."

[Note: THE LAST MAN IN EUROPE is a title Orwell considered before deciding to call his last novel 1984. It is quite likely that Orwell took the date 1984 from JACK LONDON'S prediction in the 1905 IRON HEEL of when fascism could come to the U.S.]

HE LOVED BIG BROTHER

"During a rendezvous, in the flat that Winston rented, he and Julia look out the window at the common people, or proles, working and singing below. If there is hope in the world, Winston muses, it is with the proles. The party's reign cannot last forever. As Orwell describes Winston's thoughts: "The birds sang, the proles sang, the Party did not sing…you were the dead; theirs was the future. But you could share in that future if you kept alive the mind as they kept alive the body, and passed on the secret doctrine that two plus two make four."
" 'We are the dead.' he said.
" 'We are the dead,' echoed Julia dutifully.
" 'You are the dead,' said an iron voice behind them."
"Before they can move, the Thought Police are swarming through every entrance to their room. Escape is, as both knew all along, impossible. O'Brien enters the room, walks up to the large mirror above the fireplace, and breaks it. There, watching unbeknownst to them the whole time,

is a TELE-SCREEN. Both Winston and Julia are flogged—the first of many beatings—and led away."

"O'Brien has Winston taken to the MINISTRY OF LOVE, a tall, windowless building from which few return. But O'Brien does not want to kill Winston, at least not quite yet. He wants instead to reeducate him in the ways of the party, to make him 'sane' enough to realize that two plus two can equal five. [2+2=5] The physical and mental tortures O'Brien uses to make Winston see this truth are as horrifying as they are effective. But in his heart Winston holds out—he doesn't forsake Julia—and O'Brien is forced to turn to his ultimate form of torture in an attempt to break through Winston's final barrier." [O'Brien uses Winston's greatest fear a ravenous rat in his face.] Hollywood's scariest scene?

> "Not one of Orwell's predictions is beyond the range of possibility, and
> almost any of the social and political trends described could be brought
> to head by just a single triggered incident."

TODAY'S REALITY: This story was written in the Futurist magazine in December 1978. This was a providential 40 years ago. George Orwell would be shocked at how today's international society and every race and age is voluntarily fulfilling 1984s PROPHETIC VISION. The spying through algorithms by mega-tech companies has been abused and their CEO'S have had to testify before the United States Congress. It is no longer a dark secret how technology can be hacked, corrupted and profiled.

THE TRIGGERING INCIDENT

"ORWELL wrote 1984 partially to deprecate the excesses that the SOVIET and GERMAN states committed before and during World War II, but the novel is simply a polemic against collectivist societies or a diatribe against dictatorship. During most of his adult life, Orwell was disturbed by the wave of totalitarianism sweeping the world, and he often pointed out how the mentality leading to its spread was growing in England. In his 1939 novel COMING UP FOR AIR, Orwell's English protagonist muses about "all the things you've got in the back of your mind, the things you're terrified of, the things you tell yourself are just a nightmare or can only happen in foreign countries. The bombs, the food queues, the rubber truncheons, the barbed wire, the colored shirts, the machine guns squirting out of bedroom windows. It's all going to happen...it's just something that's going to happen."

"In the course of Orwell's novels, it finally did happen in 1984. Orwell did not believe that the state described in the novel would come from the West in just that form, but he did believe that something resembling it could arise. In 1949, right after the book was published, he said: "I believe...that totalitarian ideas have taken root in the minds of intellectuals everywhere, and I have tried to draw these ideas out to their logical consequences. The scene of the book is laid in Britain in order to emphasize that the English-speaking races are not innately better than anyone else and that totalitarianism, if not fought against, could triumph everywhere."

"Today, the fight against totalitarianism in America has been scaled down from the national obsession of the 1940s and 1950s to become a concern of a limited number of specialists. And yet many of the features of totalitarianism are still growing. If these trends continue, how many years will pass before the tyranny of totalitarianism overtakes the west?"

"Moreover, what if these trends suddenly quicken? The prospect is so distressing that most people would sooner not think about it. But the facts suggest that a number of different types of events could bring about the abrupt appearance of a 1984-type government. One such development is the sudden appearance of terrorist groups armed with atomic weapons."

"The terrorists would not even have to use atomic weapons to cause a massive reshuffling of social priorities. If they simply issued a clearly credible threat of nuclear attack, governments would have to take drastic steps to stop them or minimize possible damage. Such governmental action would almost inevitably result in some curtailment of individual rights. Furthermore, most people would willingly agree to give up those rights, as shown by airline passengers to waive some of their rights in the face of a real or imagined threat by terrorists." Ibid p 353

This article was written 23 years before September 11, 2001, and the infamous 9-11 terrorist attack. The United States Congress then unanimously passed the FREEDOM ACT to help protect American citizens from major terrorist attacks.

POLICE SCIENCE

"The technology of police surveillance and citizen control has kept abreast of progress in military science. Orwell accurately foresaw the development of large data banks—today's ELECTRONIC COMPUTERS—that would contain detailed information about all party members. Furthermore, the invention of FIBER OPTICS and MICROWAVE communications allows modern technologists to store and retrieve this information with the same speed as the inquisitors of Oceania." The Futurist p 348

"Orwell also predicted that television would help solve the police problems of 1984."

[Today, many criminal acts are captured on video cameras and viewed nationally. Video cameras were used intensively in the United Kingdom because of the Irish Republican Army (IRA) terrorist bombings during the 1980s. The popular music group THE POLICE and vocalist STING wrote the hit song SOMEONE IS WATCHING YOU and a popular MTV video showed cameras watching people on the streets of Britain. The TV surveillance helped stop the IRA's violence. Famous Irish pop singer BONO's SUNDAY BLOODY SUNDAY also helped end the bloody awful political/religious conflict. BLOODY IS A VERY BAD WORD IN BRITAIN.]

"Orwell also predicted that television would help solve the police problems of 1984. He writes of large public television screens in every meeting hall that continuously pour forth news, spurious statistics, and political propaganda. All home televisions are two-way flush mounted tele-screen, equipped with scanning lenses, powerful omnidirectional microphones, and remote sensors of heartbeat. With the tele-screen, the government keeps its citizens under almost constant surveillance. Externally and internally, big brother is watching you." The Futurist p 348

TECHNOLOGY UPDATE: Television was in its infancy in 1948. Today with micro-cameras they are literally invisible. In the movie SNOWDEN I was surprised by the scene where Snowden puts a piece of tape on his small TV screen camera. One of his high-tech friends had told him he could be monitored in his home. Ironic, that one of America's greatest techies didn't know this. He allegedly had just crashed an alleged 200 Communist Chinese hacking programs stealing America's technology and military secrets. He then is helped to illegally escape to sanctuary in Putin's Russian Federal State RFS, the Soviet Union minus its southern Islamic republics and the Ukraine.

"To improve the tele-screens, the scientists of Oceania are hard at work devising tone-of-voice analyzers and brain-wave sensors. Eventually, they hope to enable the secret police to reach their ultimate goal: "To discover, against his will, what another human being is thinking." The Futurist. p 348

PROPHETIC TECHNOLOGY: Orwell didn't perceive the SUB-DERMAL MICROCHIP implant first used to track animals. Today, Sweden allows citizens to voluntarily receive a microchip to clock into work and get paid their salary. Its so much easier than finding and punching your payroll TIME-CARD. Orwell doesn't make any reference to religion in 1984, because it apparently didn't exist in his dystopian world of hate and warfare. Orwell, as few people then, would have read the passage in Revelation that in the End-Time tribulation no one can buy or sell without having a number a sub-dermal implant?

AMERICA'S #1 FUTURIST GEORGE ISSUES SHOCKING PREDICTION

The GEORGE GILDER REPORT February 19, 2020

"This tiny piece of plastic will transform our world forever, Mr. President."
"The idea GEORGE GILDER proposed as he handed [President] RONALD REAGAN one of the world's first silicon MICROCHIPS was an impossible one."
At the time, most people said that he was crazy. Computers did not even exist.
But today we know that George's prediction came true—in explosive fashion."
"The microchip has gone on to generate trillions in profits and power the greatest economic explosion in the history of the human race."
"It was even voted by CNN to be the most important invention of all time, decades after his prediction!"
"But for George Gilder, the rise of the computing era was only one of many accurate predictions he made over his 53 year career."

"To the surprise of most, George has consistently seen the future."
'It's earned him nicknames like "The Technological Prophet", "King George" and "The Greatest Stock Picker in the World."
"During the 80s, Reagan quoted George more than any other person on the planet."
"During the tech boom of the 90s, Wall Street analysts lined up to get George's next stock market pick."
"And during the early 2000's, he was the first to predict companies like Youtube and Netflix would radically transform the media landscape."
"You see, George's looks at the world though a different lens than most—and his predictions are rarely   wrong."
"His ability to see 3 steps ahead of even the biggest thinkers has cemented his status as America's #1   futurist."
"It's also established him as the advisor Silicon Valley and Wall Street heavyweights consult when they're facing big problems."
"Eric Schmidt, former CEO of Google, said this about George's predictions.
                    "I listen very closely to what George has to say"
"And Ari Emmanuel, arguably the most powerful man in Hollywood, praised George's forward-thinking saying:
        "The internet, mobile and streaming revolutions happened just as George
        predicted. Watching George's predictions happen, living though them…I
        learned that the cycle of innovation doesn't stop after TV. Surviving the
        next revolution means connecting the dots early."

"But 17 years ago, after a 3-decade long run, George mysteriously decided to hang up his hat. And since then, he has remained largely out of the game."
"Happily resting at his New England estate on the millions in profits he made investing ahead of his predictions over the years. a few weeks ago, when George started to make some noise about a new prediction.
"A breakthrough that challenges everything we know about technology."
"It's been slowly building for 11 years, and now George believes the revolution has reached critical mass, it's here.
According to him this is "So big it will shake our economy to the core."
"So to share his prediction before it is too late. George has taken action.
"The goal—help Americans everywhere prepare for what's about to come.'
'To spread the word, he created a special breakdown of his shocking prediction."
"In this groundbreaking presentation, George explains the revolution he sees coming and shows Americans exactly how they can prepare."
"This information may sound shocking, confusing, or simply unbelievable. But it's not the first time George has predicted something like this."   5G?
PERSONAL STORY: George Gilder wrote the book WEALTH and POVERTY (1981) the Reaganomics textbook. ISRAEL TEST (2009) Israel's high tech. My friend Christopher Niebuhr went to church in the Berkshires in Massachusetts with George. His father was a B-17 bomber pilot killed in World War II. His father's Harvard classmate DAVID ROCKEFELLER "adopted" him. My grandmother passed in a nursing home near his dairy farm in Tyringham, MA. He graduated Phillips Exeter Academy and Harvard. A great-grandson of stained glass designer LOUIS TIFFANY. Kendra Stern O'Donnell, my 7th grade classmate, was the first woman dean of Phillips Exeter. There is a "Tiffany" window of her, she initiated the new computer science program at EXETER Academy.

Orwell Was a Disillusioned Communist

Orwell had been a human rights Communist who volunteered to fight in the deadly Spanish Revolution which Catholic Fascist FRANCO won. He saw Communist Russian Revolutionist advisors living an elitist life in battle scared Barcelona. Orwell was a brave anti-fascist against HITLER, MUSSOLINI and FRANCO'S SOCIALIST FASCISM. He wrote 1984, after World War II, as a warning of JOSEF STALIN'S COMMUNIST TOTALITARIAN brutality to his Russian and Ukrainian Christian and Jewish population in the hidden SIBERIAN GULAG.
AMAZING HIDDEN HISTORICAL STORY: At a MARY WASHINGTON University, Fredericksburg, Virginia, GREAT BOOKS LECTURE, an author of a biography about Orwell revealed that Orwell wanted to publish 1984 during World War II. The British government prevented its publication when they realized that his book THE LAST MAN IN EUROPE criticized Communist dictator JOSEF STALIN not FASCIST/SOCIALIST ADOLF HITLER. My daughter graduated Mary Washington College, a B.A. in German.
WHY??? Brutal Communist dictator STALIN and his huge army and air force were vital in defeating Hitler's powerful military forces controlling mainland Europe. The author revealed that Orwell's attempt to publish his book was prevented when the British government claimed there was a shortage of paper needed for the war effort.
The Futurist magazine reveals: "ALL OF THESE DEVICES ARE WITHIN THE STATE OF THE ART OF TODAY'S TECHNOLOGY."
"OURS COULD BE THE MOST SNOOPED-ON, COMPUTER-ANALYZED SOCIETY IN HISTORY. Television scanners equipped with electronic detectors of heartbeat, brainwaves, and

voice stress could collect physiological and behavioral date which could then be conveyed by microwaves or fiber optics to a central data bank for instantaneous cross matching with the ELECTRONIC PROFILES OF KNOWN SUBVERSIVES AND DISSIDENTS. SUSPECTED PERSONS COULD BE TRACED, ARRESTED, AND IMPRISONED—JUST AS IN 1984." The Futurist p 348

WHAT PRICE FREEDOM AND SAFETY?

"The possibility of Orwell's 1984 becoming reality—perhaps even before the date he specified—is clear."
"The vicarious pleasure taken in violence is one of the strongest parallels between modern society and the world of 1984."
"These triggering incidents might even make the world of 1984 a PREFERABLE FUTURE, because ETERNAL WARFARE and a LOSS OF LIBERTY would be VIEWED AS THE PRICE THAT MUST BE PAID TO AVOID CATASTROPHIC DESTRUCTION."

AS FICTION BECOMES FACT

"The 100-plus realized predictions that author DAVID GOODMAN and his colleagues found in 1984 show that GEORGE ORWELL'S FORESIGHT WAS ACCURATE in MANY SPHERES of LIFE. Among Orwell's specifications that have since come true are:

*Lotteries run by the state.
*Lack of heating fuels and electricity.
*Books written by computer.
*The construction of helicopter gunships.
*Forced metrification.
*Three-dimensional effects in art.
*Machines that translate voice into print.
*The merging of gender identities.

Goodman has found that all of Orwell's scientific and technological predictions have either come true or could come true. Today, governments command the technological ability to fashion a world like that of 1984. The need, Goodman says, is for some way to consciously shape the future so that Orwell's unfulfilled social and political predictions do not also come to fruition." The Futurist. p 351

HOLLYWOOD HAS DONE MANY EVEN MORE DYSTOPIAN FUTURISTIC FILMS.

DENIAL OF OBJECTIVE REALITY: "The Party in 1984 teaches its members that "Reality is not eternal. Reality exists in the human mind, and nowhere else. In this way, the good Party member learns how to sift his sense impressions through and ideological filter, acknowledging acceptable information and ignoring everything else." Ibid p 351
"Such solipsism [theory that the self is all that can be known to exist] is now widespread in our age of growing social confusion and ERODING TRADITIONAL VALUES. The increasing USE OF ALCOHOL and other DRUGS may be an attempt to AVOID A LOOK AT LIFE THAT WOULD BE

TOO PAINFUL TO BEAR. POLITICIANS ALSO DENY OBJECTIVE REALITY BY BACKING POLICIES THAT ARE UNRELATED TO THE ACTUAL NEEDS OF THEIR CONSTITUENCIES." Ibid p 351

In August 2019, former 8-year vice president JOSEPH BIDEN proclaimed: "I BELIEVE IN TRUTH NOT IN FACTS." Has Joe Biden read 1984 or is this a PARADOX of 1984 and HISTORY or just self-righteous elitist $$ prideful ignorance? "THOSE WHO FORGET HISTORY ARE CONDEMNED TO REPEAT IT." Novelist GEORGE SANTAYANA. I FORGOT 1984 IS A FICTIONAL BOOK NOT HISTORY.

SO WHAT IS TRUTH?

SO WHAT IS TRUTH? The BEST ANSWER TO THAT QUESTION IS JESUS.
PONTIUS PILATE asked JESUS:

"ARE YOU THE KING OF THE JEWS?" "Is that your own idea."
Jesus asked, "or did others talk to you about me?" "AM I A JEW?"
Pilate replied. "It was your people and your chief priests who
handed you over to me. What is it you have done?"
Jesus said, "My kingdom is not of THIS WORLD. But now my
kingdom is from another place."
"You are a king, then!" said Pilate. Jesus answered, "You are right
in saying I am a king. In fact, for this reason I was born, and for
this I came into the world, to testify to the TRUTH. EVERYONE
ON THE SIDE OF TRUTH LISTENS TO ME."
"WHAT IS TRUTH?" Pilate asked. With this he went out again to
the JEWS and said, "I find no basis for a charge against him. But
it is your custom for me to release to you one prisoner at the time
of the PASSOVER. Do you want me to release 'the king of the Jews.'?"
They shouted back, "No, not him! Give us Barabbas!" Now Barabbas
had taken part in a rebellion."   John 18:33-40 NIV

Tell me is there any BETTER DEFINITION OF TRUTH anywhere else in HIS-tory?
This truthful historical fact is not religion, it is God the Creator's providence. It is interesting that Pontius Pilate actually used a very sacred Jewish holiday PASSOVER custom to release a criminal sentenced to death. Did Pilate know the Biblical story of God's Passover blood covenant with the Hebrews of Egypt who were told to place lamb's blood on their door posts which spared their first born sons from God's angel of death? Pharaoh then freed the 400-year oppressed Hebrews allowing them to return to their homeland in Israel.

Ironically, Pilate, allowed a mob to free from death a Zealot murderer BARABBAS, who wanted to overthrow Rome's rule in Judah. So a rebellious "Jewish", maybe also some pagans, mob fulfilled Jesus predestined death for all of Humankind's salvation if they put their faith in Jesus' Grace through his shed blood on the the Jewish PASSOVER. A Passover lamb is sacrificed commemorating the Israelites release from bondage and their freedom to return to their Promised land, Israel.

Jesus Crucifixion released Humankind from their bondage to sin and their promise of Eternal life with Jesus and their loved ones and the saints.

I never heard a Sermon connecting these providential Passover connections. Of course, a rabbi couldn't preach that connection. YOUR FIRED or excommunicated!

THREE KINDS OF LIES, DAMNED LIES, AND STATISTICS

Samuel Clemens aka Mark Twain popularized in his Autobiography
"Lies, damned lies, and statistics" is a phrase describing the persuasive power of numbers, particularly the use of statistics to bolster weak arguments. It is sometimes colloquially used to doubt statistics used to prove an opponent's point."
PERSONAL CONNECTIONAL: My senior editor LUMAN LONG (1969-1974) at THE WORLD ALMANAC AND BOOK OF FACTS was from ROLLA, Missouri near Hannibal where SAMUEL CLEMENS aka MARK TWAIN lived. Mr. Long was an old school journalist and had worked for THE WORLD TELEGRAM AND SUN newspaper in New York City when it folded. The newspaper also published THE WORLD ALMANAC and BOOK OF FACTS which had been initiated by JOSEPH PULITZER in 1868, at the St. Louis POST DISPATCH. The Almanac editor was HARRY HANSEN who wrote historical books, I have his one volume CIVIL WAR book, one of the best. I meet him once when he visited our office at 230 Park Avenue in the unique GRAND GENERAL building. Shown in many New York City films it has the unique green triangular roof and straddles Park Avenue. We were on the fourth floor and could look down on Park Avenue. Mr. Hansen was in his 80s, I didn't know much about my grandfather in the Civil War then. He had just written a book on THE BOSTON MASSACRE.
The World Almanac was saved by chance from being discontinued by BOYD LEWIS, president of NEWSPAPER ENTERPRISE ASSN. of the SCRIPPS HOWARD 600-newspaper chain. EDWARD KENNEDY was a vice president who traveled throughout the United States and promoted the Almanac, getting the city newspapers to sell it on their newsstands with their newspaper's name imprint on the cover. When I left the Almanac in 1975, after 65 months as the History/Political editor etc. I believe sales had reached about 1,000,000 copies and almost 1,000 page computer printed book. The Reader's Digest. Information Please and The New York Times also had Almanacs.
LUMAN LONG took over as editor of the World Almanac and he hired me. I started work the Tuesday after Labor Day in 1969. I went through an employment agency who set up my appointment. Later, I learned that JACK ROSENTHAL, had left without notice, taking an English teacher job. His departing last words were that he was going to the WOODSTOCK ROCK CONCERT. My dad and I had a farm in Ghent, NY across from the Catskill Mountains from which we could see the whole range a breath-taking view. Bethel farm where Woodstock was held was at the south end of the Catskills almost within site from my house. I hadn't heard anything about the concert and was a Big Band fan. Some of America's best rock stars were there. I could see the town of WOODSTOCK in the Catskill Mountains, near Catskill.

YOU CAN'T COPY WRITE A FACT

JOURNALISTIC FACT: Mr Long told me that you CAN"T COPYRIGHT A FACT. A copyright is obtained to protect an original song, movie, poem, fictional work or a factual writing from another source which must be footnoted.
When LUMAN LONG passed we took a limo to the cemetery in SUMMIT, New Jersey, BLONDIE'S and MERYL STREEP'S hometown.

GREATEST NEWS SCOOP OF WORLD WAR II

GREATEST NEWS SCOOP IN HISTORY STORY: On the limo ride Ed Kennedy told a story how he had meet the reclusive HOWARD HUGHES. Years later, I was stunned to read in a book about famous World War II news stories that he without authorization reported the Victory in Europe peace meeting in Reims, France A DAY EARLY. THE MOST CONTROVERSIAL NEWSPAPER SCOOP IN HISTORY. General EISENHOWER, Pres. HARRY S TRUMAN and Prime Minister WINSTON CHURCHILL were outraged. YOUR FIRED! He was a civilian newsman and exempt from military or any punishment. I believe his newspaper editor-in-chief could have killed the story but didn't know about the European delay of announcing the most important story in History the defeat of HITLER and the end of the horrific war in Europe. His story went to Press and the world cheered. So it Goes. Kurt Vonnegut is freed as an American Army prisoner in DRESDEN, Germany. He then wrote his many exciting books including SLAUGHTER HOUSE FIVE where he survived the deadly RAF firebombing attack of Ash Wednesday 1945. So it Goes.   Rest in Peace Kurt.

MY DAD'S KURT VONNEGUT STORY: Dad was a fan of Vonnegut's books. One day he told me Vonnegut's daughter was one of GERALDO RIVERA'S wives. My dad was in the ABC TV Master Control room when Geraldo became famous with his shocking WILLOWBROOK MENTAL HOSPITAL video scandal. So it Goes or SMALL WORLD?

1984—THE SOCIAL AND POLITICAL PREDICTIONS

"Our studies indicate that all of Orwell's scientific and technological predictions have either already come true or could soon come true. But such judgment cannot be rendered easily on Orwell's social and political forecasts." Ibid p 350 Futurist magazine

"To some futurists, many of these social and political speculations still seem incredible. In Oceania, no part of a person's life is personal, not even his thoughts. The government, through the THOUGHT POLICE, works to convince everyone that EXTERNAL REALITY DOES NOT EXIST, that the only measure of the past is PEOPLE'S MEMORIES AND WRITTEN RECORDS, BOTH OF WHICH ARE ALTERED CONSTANTLY to SUIT the PARTY DOGMA. Oceania is a country of CONSTANT FEAR, where public executions, search without warrant, and imprisonment without cause are commonplace." Ibid p 350

"Some futurists, in fact, hardly acknowledge Orwell as a PROPHET at all. Both RICHARD FARMER in THE REAL WORLD OF 1984 (David McKay Company, NY, 1973) and JEROME TUCCILLE in WHO'S AFRAID OF 1984 (Arlington House, New Rochelle, NY, 1975) foresee a "satisfied plenty" and "exuberant democracy" ahead for the American people. Although they admit that technological change is altering people's lives, they believe that people will come to accept technological advancement as inevitable and learn to use technology to further, rather than destroy, human privacy."

UPDATE: They could not then perceive how massive data could be stored on the punch cards, magnetic tape, floppy discs and hard drives which processed slowly and stored limited amounts of data. Today, miniature SD and USB Flash drives can store vast amounts of written text data and photos and videos and can be sent to CLOUD servers as a backup for a small monthly fee. I have to take time to delete much unnecessary data. Everything connects to my iPads and MacBook and my written manuscript updates automatically. My newest iPad is helpful because its Pages program underlines all misspellings and typos with a red underline. This serves as a quick proofread for typos, two words together or a missing letter or a spelling error which can be checked by pressing the touch pad showing the correct spelling. I will not use SPELL CHECK IT IS STUPID. Recently my 15 year old granddaughter has sent me her vacation photos she has an iPhone 9S. She is now in 9th grade and has an iPad and a MacBook she is a left-handed techie really smart. I am worried about her surfing the Internet there is so much good but there is more and more dark side which pops up. Somebody is making money? This hasn't been brought to Congress attention? We know the Internet isn't FREE except the WIFI fee. Billions of dollars earned through profiling and pop up ads.

My new iPad began sending me photo selections based on locations I visited using its GPS locator. They are enjoyable and even seem professionally done, not random, except for a few superfluous photos. I think it is created by an algorithm program. It would cost money and there is nothing to buy. I have maybe a dozen of these photo montages which are enjoyable.

The 1978 Futurist article reflects: "But the trends of the last 30 years have brought the West closer to 1984 than ever before, and these trends could rapidly accelerate under certain circumstances. [read MOORE'S LAW on Wikipedia] Of course, the correspondence between Orwell's world and our own varies widely depending on the specific feature under consideration, but the overall drift is obvious."   Ibid p 350

DOUBLETHINK

"In 1984, DOUBLETHINK is a mental facility required of every good Party member. Orwell defines it as "THE POWER OF HOLDING TWO CONTRADICTORY BELIEFS IN ONE'S MIND SIMULTANEOUSLY, AND ACCEPTING BOTH OF THEM." Furthermore, "THE PROCESS HAS TO BE CONSCIOUS, OR IT WOULD NOT BE CARRIED OUT WITH SUFFICIENT PRECISION, BUT IT HAS TO BE UNCONSCIOUS, OR IT WOULD BRING WITH IT A FEELING OF FALSITY AND HENCE OF GUILT."

HITLER-STALIN PACT EXAMPLE OF DOUBLETHINK

"Essentially, DOUBLETHINK is Orwell's PROJECTION OF THE TENDENCY HE SAW IN PEOPLE TO SUBVERT REALITY TO IDEOLOGICAL ABSTRACTIONS. Orwell especially detested the trait in the LIBERAL SOVIET SYMPATHIZERS WHO BECAME APOLOGISTS FOR GERMANY AFTER THE HITLER-STALIN PACT, and this FORMED MUCH of the BASE FOR DOUBLETHINK in 1984. But doublethink MARKS ALL POLITICAL PROPAGANDA TO SOME EXTENT."   Ibid p 350

NEWSPEAK

"The linguists of Oceania are busy replacing traditional English with NEWSPEAK, a language so impoverished that "A HERETICAL THOUGHT...SHOULD BE LITERALLY UNTHINKABLE, AT LEAST SO FAR AS THOUGHT IS DEPENDENT ON WORDS."

"Today the STEADY DEGRADATION of the English language is a constantly lamented fact. Verbal test scores have fallen for a decade; bureaucratic gobbledygook grows more dense as problems of government grow more complex; and politicians continue to mangle the language with their neologisms (as when bombing raids become "protective reaction strikes"). Ibid p 351

WHO CONTROLS THE PAST CONTROLS THE FUTURE

"MUTABILITY OF THE PAST: In Oceania, HISTORY IS COMPLETELY REWRITTEN every day to suit the needs of the Party. Day-to-day FALSIFICATION OF PUBLISHED RECORDS HELPS ASSURE THE STABILITY OF REGIME IN POWER. One of the Party's slogan is "WHO CONTROLS THE PAST CONTROLS THE FUTURE; WHO CONTROLS THE PRESENT CONTROLS THE PAST."   Ibid p 351

MAXIM: HISTORY IS WRITTEN BY THE VICTORS.

The Futurist retorts: "REVISING THE RECORDS OF THE PAST TO FIT CURRENT POLICIES HAS LONG BEEN STANDARD PROCEDURES IN MANY COUNTRIES AND HAS BECOME INCREASINGLY COMMON IN THE WESTERN WORLD." HISTORIES are REWRITTEN, TAPE RECORDING ERASED, records deliberately "lost," and past statements dismissed as "inoperative."

BREAKUP OF THE FAMILY

"One of Oceania's greatest methods of personal disorientation is the DISSOLUTION OF THE FAMILY. BREAKING THE EMOTIONAL TIES BETWEEN MAN AND WOMAN, PARENTS AND CHILDREN, ELIMINATE BONDS that would detract from a PERSON'S ABSOLUTE DEVOTION TO THE STATE."

"In America, the divorce rate more than doubled between 1963 and 1973, with more than one out of every three marriages now ending up in divorce. The subsequent WITHDRAWAL INTO SELF has contributed to a growing to a growing aimlessness and a wide search for something to replace personal relationships."   Ibid p 352

UNWARRANTED SEARCH AND SURVEILLANCE

"In Oceania, as in most totalitarian states, DUE PROCESS OF LAW IS MERELY A TOOTHLESS LEGALISM. A man's home is the government's castle. Any citizen can have his dwelling ransacked and possessions seized as evidence to be used against him. Tele-screens provide almost complete physical surveillance, and even the mind is not exempt from probe. Personal privacy has steadily eroded in recent years. The surveillance of alleged subversives by U,S, government agencies has been documented by congressional testimony. Both government agencies and private companies employ investigators to make a personal credit check. Some journalists use hidden microphones to collect information for their articles. And satellites orbit the earth maintaining constant surveillance of areas as small as a square yard."   Today, Drones.
TODAY: Early morning FBI raids and arrests of President Donald Trump's friends. 1984

Some Scientific and Technological Predictions from 1984

PREDICTIONS IN MILITARY SCIENCE

1 Think tanks where experts plan future wars.
2 Improved missiles and bombs.
3 Planes independent of earth.
4 Lenses suspended in space.
5 Floating fortresses to guard important sea lanes.
6 Germs immunized against all antibodies.
7 Self-propelled bombs to take the place of bombing planes.   Drones
8 Earthquake and tidal wave control.
9 Efficient defoliants that could be spread over wide areas.
10 Soil submarines that could bore through the ground.

PREDICTIONS IN POLICE TECHNOLOGY

1 Data banks containing detailed personal information.
2 Rapid access to and retrieval of data.
3 Two-way, flush mounted televisions.
4 Remote sensor of heartbeat.
5 Tone-of-voice analyzer.
6 Sensitive omnidirectional microphone.
7 Police patrol helicopter.
8 Large tele-screens for public viewing.   Jumbotron at rock concerts
9 Memory holes for rapid destruction of information.   Shredder/burn bag
10 Scanner to detect and analyze human thought.

PREDICTIONS IN PSYCHOLOGY

1 Improved electrotherapy.
2 Better techniques for hypnosis.
3 Improved truth drugs.
4 Control of the sex drive, specifically by abolishing orgasm.
5 The ability to artificially inseminate.
6 Reconditioning by implosive therapy or flooding.
7 New forms of physical and psychological torture.
8 A science determining thoughts by facial expressions and gestures.
9 Televised group therapy.
10 Subcortical psychosurgery.

CONTINUOUS WAR

"The THREE SUPERPOWERS of 1984 have adopted CONTINUOUS WAR as an expedient to "use up the products of the machine without raising the standard of living," In this way, "the consequences of being at war, and therefore in danger, makes the handing-over of all power to a small caste the natural, unavoidable condition of survival." Today's ARMS RACE is the equivalent of Orwell's continuous war. In addition, the current struggles in Africa, the Middle East, and

Southeast Asia show many of the same qualities as the war in 1984. With regards to the Orwellian purpose of continuous war, the experiences of the 1960s are enough to remind us that some of the worst violations of personal liberties have occurred during time of war, usually in the time of national security."   Ibid p 353

MUST WE LIVE THIS FUTURE?

"The possibility of Orwell's 1984 becoming reality—perhaps even before the date he specified—is clear. Whether or not it really happens WILL DEPEND ON WHAT WE DO TODAY. We must prepare to act on two fronts—to prevent the triggering incidents from taking place, and to REVERSE THE SOCIAL TRENDS THAT ARE LEADING THE WESTERN DEMOCRACIES TOWARDS 1984." Ibid p 355

"In pondering these problems, we should not expect answers from government bureaucracies. As Willis W. Harman of SRI International has noted: "SOCIETY TENDS TO HIDE KNOWLEDGE FROM ITSELF that is superficially THREATENING to the STATUS QUO, even though this knowledge may b badly needed to resolve its most fundamental problem."   Ibid p 355

"NINETEEN EIGHTY-FOUR: A NOVEL—The story was mostly written at Barnhill, a farmhouse on the Scottish island of JURA, at times while Orwell suffered from sever tuberculosis. Thematically, Nineteen Eighty-Four centers on the risks of GOVERNMENT OVERREACH, TOTALITARIANISM, and REPRESSIVE REGIMENTATION of all persons and behaviors within society."

PERSONAL STORY: The island of Jura in the Scottish Outer Hebrides is the domain of the CAMPBELL clan which my father said the Louden clan is related. President DONALD J. TRUMP'S mother was born on a Scottish Outer Hebrides island.

"The story takes place in an imagined future, the year 1984, when much of the world has fallen victim to PERPETUAL WAR, OMNIPRESENT GOVERNMENT SURVEILLANCE, HISTORICAL NEGATIONISM, and PROPAGANDA."

HISTORICAL NEGATIONISM DEFINITION: Also called DENIALISM [deny scientific or historical reality as a way to avoid a psychologically uncomfortable truth, an essentially irrational action that withholds the validation of a historical experience or event, when a person refuses to accept an empirically verifiable reality.] and propaganda."   Wikipedia

"Great Britain, known as Airstrip One, has become a province of a superstate named ORANIA that is ruled by the Party who employ the THOUGHT POLICE to PERSECUTE INDIVIDUALITY and INDEPENDENT THINKING."

[HISTORY GREAT BRITAIN TODAY: Is the EUROPEAN UNION the SUPERSTATE OF 1984? The new PARLIAMENTARY GOVERNMENT of Great Britain formed in August 2019 under Prime Minister BORIS JOHNSON who wants to restore Britain's sovereignty through the BREXIT vote effective on October 31, HALLOWEEN, 95 THESES DAY, In September 2019, his conservative party is deserting him, including his brother and Winston Churchill's grandson. This has created a "CIVIL W. Great Britain has had a large number of immigrants who want to stay in the GLOBALIST EUROPEAN UNION. The conservative English people want to maintain their traditional democratic, religious and economic freedoms. In October a new "DEMOCRATIC" election could keep Great Britain in the GLOBALIST EUROPEAN UNION with its economic restrictions that it has created. Will Britain's expensive royalty be preserved? Queen ELIZABETH II, the longest serving monarch, has been a very popular beloved Queen. Though the royal family has had its controversies making international news, the present royal prince sons and their children are popular. Who will be Great Britain and the Commonwealth next King? A British friend of mine say the ROYAL LINE OF SUCCESSION calls for PRINCE CHARLES to be KING. Will he step down and allow his popular son WILLIAM to be the next King?]

"BIG BROTHER, the leader of the Party, enjoys an intense CULT OF PERSONALITY despite that he may not exist. The protagonist, WINSTON SMITH, is in the party and is a diligent skillful rank-and-file worker and Party member who secretly hates the Party and dreams of rebellion' He enters a forbidden relationship with a co-worker, Julia."

"Nineteen Eighty-Four has become a CLASSIC LITERARY example of political and DYSTOPIAN FICTION. Nineteen Eighty-Four also popularized the adjective "ORWELLIAN", connoting things such as OFFICIAL DECEPTION, SECRET SURVEILLANCE, BRAZENLY MISLEADING terminology, and MANIPULATION OF RECORDED HISTORY by a TOTALITARIAN or AUTHORITARIAN STATE." Wikipedia

HISTORY AND ORWELL'S TITLE

"Orwell "encapsulated the thesis at the heart of his unforgiving novel" in 1984. the implications of DIVIDING THE WORLD up into ZONES OF INFLUENCE. which had been conjured by the TEHERAN [Iran 1944] CONFERENCE. By 1989, it had been translated into 65 languages, more than any other novel in English until then." Wikipedia

"The title of the novel, its themes, the NEWSPEAK language and the author's surname are often INVOKED AGAINST CONTROL AND INTRUSION BY THE STATE, and the adjective ORWELLIAN describes a TOTALITARIAN DYSTOPIA that is characterized by GOVERNMENT CONTROL and SUBJUGATION OF THE PEOPLE." Wikipedia

"Orwell's inventive language, NEWSPEAK, SATIRIZES HYPOCRISY and EVASION BY THE STATE: the MINISTRY OF LOVE (MINILUV) oversees TORTURE and BRAINWASHING. the MINISTRY OF PLENTY (MINIPLENTY) oversees shortage and Rationing, the MINISTRY OF PEACE (MINIPAX) oversees WAR and ATROCITY and the MINISTRY OF TRUTH (MINITRUE) oversees PROPAGANDA and HISTORICAL REVISIONISM. [erasing History]" Wikipedia

"Throughout its publication history, 1984 has been either BANNED OR LEGALLY CHALLENGED, AS SUBVERSIVE OR IDEOLOGICALLY CORRUPTING, like the DYSTOPIAN novels WE (1924) by YEVGENY ZAMYATIN, [the first book banned by Soviets] BRAVE NEW WORLD (1932) by ALDOUS HUXLEY, DARKNESS AT NOON (1940) by ARTHUR KOESTLER, KALLOCAIN (1940) by KARIN BOYE, FAHRENHEIT 451 (1953) by RAY BRADBURY." Wikipedia

Some believe the Russian novel WE and the plot and characters of DARKNESS AT NOON by Koestler, a personal friend of Orwell, influenced the plot of 1984.

THE CLASS HIERARCHY OF OCEANIA HAS THREE LEVELS:

* The upper-class INNER PARTY, the elite ruling minority, who make up 2% of the population.
* The middle-class OUTER PARTY, who make up 13% of the population.
* The lower-class PROLETARIAT, who makes up 85% of the population and represent the uneducated working class.

As the GOVERNMENT, the PARTY CONTROLS the POPULATION with 4 MINISTRIES:

* The MINISTRY OF PEACE deals with war and defense.
* The MINISTER OF PLENTY deals with economic affairs (rationing and starvation).
* The MINISTRY OF LOVE deals with law and order (torture and brainwashing).

* The MINISTRY OF TRUTH deals with the news, entertainment, education and art (propaganda). Wikipedia

REWRITING HISTORY AND DESTROYING THE PAST

"The protagonist Winston Smith, a member of the Outer Party, works in the ReCords Department of the Ministry of Truth as an editor, REVISING HISTORICAL RECORDS, TO MAKE THE PAST CONFORM to the ever-changing PARTY LINE and DELETING REFERENCES TO UNPERSONS, people who have been "vaporized, i.e., not only killed by the state but DENIED EXISTENCE EVEN IN HISTORY OR MEMORY."

IN THE BEGINNING OF OCEANIA'S DYSTOPIA

"The story of Winston Smith begins on 4 April 1984: "It was a bright cold day in April, and the clocks were striking 13." Yet he is uncertain of the true date, given the regime's continual rewriting and manipulation of History."

DOUBLETHINK—"The keyword here is BLACKWHITE. Like so many NEWSPEAK words, his word has two mutually contradictory meanings. Applied to an opponent, it means the habit of impudently claiming that BLACK IS WHITE, in CONTRADICTION OF THE PLAIN FACTS. Applied to a Party member, it means a loyal willingness to say that black is white when Party discipline demands this. But it means also the ability to believe that black is white, and more, to know that black is white, and to forget that one has ever believed the contrary. This demands a continuous alteration of the past, made possible by the system of thought which really embraces all the rest, and which is known in Newspeak as doublethink. Doublethink is basically the power of holding two contradictory beliefs in one's mind simultaneously, and ACCEPTING BOTH of them."
—Part II, Chapter IX—The Theory and Practice of Oligarchical Collectivism   Wikipedia

Political Geography—3 perpetually warring totalitarian super-states control the world:

*OCEANIA (ideology: INGSOC, i.e. ENGLISH SOCIALISM), whose core territories are the Western Hemisphere, the BRITISH ISLES, AUSTRALASIA, POLYNESIA and Southern AFRICA.

* Eurasia (ideology: NEO-BOLSHEVISM), whose core territories are CONTINENTAL EUROPE and RUSSIA, including SIBERIA.
* EAST ASIA (ideological: Obliteration of the Self or Death Worship), whose core territories are CHINA, JAPAN, KOREA and INDOCHINA.

"The perpetual war is fought for control of the "disputed area" lying "between the frontiers of the super-states", which forms "a rough parallelogram with its corners at TANGIER, BRAZZAVILLE, DARWIN and HONG KONG", and Northern AFRICA, the MIDDLE EAST, INDIA and INDONESIA are where the superstates capture and use SLAVE LABOR. Fighting also takes place between EURASIA and EASTASIA in MANCHURIA, MONGOLIA and Central ASIA. and all three powers battle one another over various Atlantic and Pacific islands."   Wikipedia

THE DAY THE WORLD DIED Nov. 23, 1963

Pres. JOHN F. KENNEDY, CLIVE C.S. LEWIS and ALDOUS HUXLEY ALSO DIED.

SYMPHONIC HOLLYWOOD THEMES BY AIRMEN

HENRY MANCINI AND JOHN WILLIAMS

Yes, JOHN WILLIAMS and HENRY MANCINI who played piano in the post-war GLENN MILLER big band.

"It happened quite by accident, HENRY MANCINI, who had toiled in obscurity as a staff composer at UNIVERSAL PICTURES for the previous six years, had been let go by the studio. On one of his last days, he happened to stop in the studio's barbershop for a haircut. Sitting in the next chair over from Mancini was director BLAKE EDWARDS [JULIE ANDREWS husband]. The two had a lot in common —two years apart in age, both had learned their craft (Edwards also working as an actor and writer) in the final years of the old Hollywood studio system."

"Edwards only recently had been promoted to director. It was at the barbershop that Edwards asked Mancini a question that would not only change both of their lives, but PERMANENTLY WOULD ALTER THE HISTORY OF MOVIE MUSIC."

"Hey" said Edwards, "would you be interested in doing a TV show for me?" that show, needless to say, was PETER GUNN."   [Review from my Peter Gunn soundtrack CD]

"Mancini was 34 years old then, having been born Enrico Nicola Mancini in Cleveland, Ohio, in 1924. He grew up ENAMORED OF BOTH MOVIES AND MUSIC and at an early age, became determined to make both. He studied composition and arranging and had the opportunity, as a student, to conduct the PITTSBURGH SYMPHONY, and, while still a teenager, was encouraged by BENNY GOODMAN. He played piano in military bands during World War II and, immediately after the war, joined the refurbished GLENN MILLER ORCHESTRA under the leadership of singing saxist TEX BENEKE."

"Much as he LOVED THE BIG BANDS, however, MANCINI'S DREAM WAS TO WRITE MUSIC FOR THE MOVIES, and with the support of his wife, former Beneke vocalist GINNY O'CONNOR, he gradually made it in the back door of Hollywood, where he started with LOST IN ALASKA (1952), a grade-B ABBOTT & COSTELLO comedy. Mancini's big band background served him well when Universal asked him to work on the BENNY GOODMAN STORY (1955) and THE GLENN MILLER STORY (1954), the latter introducing one of Mancini's first and best themes, "SO LITTLE TIME." But it wasn't until Universal was closing down as a studio that Mancini, who earlier in 1958, had shown the world what he could do with a crime movie score in his brilliant writing for ORSON WELLES'S classic A TOUCH OF EVIL, bumped into Blake Edwards."

"When Mancini and Edwards began work on Peter Gunn, as the composer told biographer GENE LEES." The IDEA OF USING JAZZ IN THE GUNN SCORE WAS NEVER EVEN DISCUSSED, IT WAS IMPLICIT IN THE STORY. Peter Gunn [actor CRAIG STEVENS] hangs out in a jazz house called "Mothers," where there was a five piece jazz group. It was the time of so-called "'COOL" West coast jazz, and that was the sound that came to me, the walking bass and drums." Peter Gunn signified the most through use of jazz that had ever been pulled off in HOLLYWOOD up 'til that time. Before Mancini, as ANDRE PREVIN once noted, "the only time you hear jazz in a movie is when somebody steals a car." but Gunn, although it was a crime story, took a major step in the direction of making jazz socially acceptable in Tinseltown."

236

"Gunn almost instantly made Mancini a HOUSEHOLD NAME: Mancini also arranged the theme for band leader RAY ANTHONY (who earlier had scored a hit with a boogie version of the DRAGNET music), and soon RCA Victor had decided to do an album of the Gunn music." "GUNN MUSIC can not be described as anything other than orchestral jazz of the highest caliber."
[The album featured the finest West Coast studio solo jazz musicians] "featuring former GLENN MILLER band, bassist ROLLY BUNDOCK and trombonist JIMMY PRIDDY (also ON PIANO Mancini's SUCCESSOR as MOVIE LAND'S FUTURE MOST CELEBRATED THEME WRITER——JOHN WILLIAMS). Mancini, became RCA's grand guru of "easy listening" music, the rough equivalent of what PERCY FAITH was to Columbia."
"For Mancini, PETER GUNN was only the beginning. Within a year or so he followed it with his equally well-received theme to MR. LUCKY, and the OSCAR-WINNERS —MOON RIVER (from BREAKFAST AT TIFFANY'S) and DAYS OF WINE AND ROSES, and eventually THE PINK PANTHER, CHARADE and dozens of others. The Peter Gunn title theme actually derives more from Rock and Roll than jazz." Mancini once pointed out, and it wasn't long before rock and rollers took him at his word, starting with Duane Eddy in 1960. Sarah Vaughn recorded Bye, Bye, a lyricize version of the theme.
"The Peter Gunn theme has that kind of effect on people - once heard, it is not easily forgotten."
WILL FRIEDMAN, premier jazz reviewer/critic on my PETER GUNN CD

[I have many Mancini LP albums Sousa Marches and VISIONS OF EIGHT is unique. It is music from the original soundtrack for theme music for the 1972 Munich Olympics. This Olympic meet was held 36 years after the infamous 1936 Berlin Olympics which Hitler used as a showcase for his "ARYAN master race". THE ISRAELI OLYMPIC team was killed by Palestinian terrorists at the Furstenfeldbrueck German airbase where my Bitburg AB unit had been stationed until January 1953. The original Greek Olympics were made international in 1896 to create a world competitive brotherhood. The former Communist Russia, like Hitler also politicized the Olympics. The Palestinians through terrorism used the Olympics to bring "sympathy" for their cause. Violence does not bring sympathy for a cause. My son and daughter swam with three Olympic gold, silver, bronze medal recipients. In Germany I dated Sheri from Oregon who said she swam in Lake Oswego with DON SCHOLLANDER who won four gold medals swimming at the Mexico City Olympics in 1968.]
VISIONS OF EIGHT—"His vision of life is what sets the artist apart. Sunflowers are familiar to millions, yet no one ever saw them the way VINCENT VAN GOGH did. So it is hoped, with the Olympics: a recurring spectacle familiar to people around the world, yet now seen, as if for the first time, through the perceptions of eight directors."
"VISIONS OF EIGHT" is a film about the personal dreams which make the Olympic games transcend the physical into the spiritual. When granted the authority to record the 1972 official film of the games, the Wolper Organization elected to eschew the traditional documentary approach in favor of the human stories spelled out during the contests. Although the cameras recorded the TRAGIC EVENTS surrounded the DEATHS of the ISRAELI ATHLETES, the film remains a NON-POLITICAL TRIBUTE to all the contestants, and to the spirit of the Olympic games."
"This, then, is no chronological record of the 1972 Olympics, of the winners and losers."
"It is a film of the separate visions of eight of the world's foremost motion picture directors. Each director projects his contribution to the film against a separate segment of the game, hence the title."
"The production company numbered more than 100, with some 50 camera crews assigned to report the human stories projected against the background of the athletic pageant."
"To enhance the international spirit projected in the film, Wolper and Marguiles commissioned three-time ACADEMY AWARD WINNER, Henry Mancini, to create the musical score. Dedicating

himself to underscoring the events that are the theme of the picture. Mancini maintains the difficult balance between the artistic levels generated by the eight directors…different in tone and technique. His stunning score is the music you will hear within." [Visions of Eight record album cover notes.]

"Transcending the physical, Mancini has underscored the mood and thoughts of the athletes. What he has created could justifiably be called the ninth vision."

"That LOVE OF SPORTS and the challenge of scoring the supreme quadrennial event come through with the same vision that the eight international directors devoted to this Olympic-sized project." Harvey Siders West Coast editor DOWN BEAT MAGAZINE

JOHN WILLIAMS HOLLYWOOD BLOCKBUSTER COMPOSER

"JOHN T. WILLIAMS is an American composer, conductor, and pianist. Widely regarded as one of the GREATEST AMERICAN COMPOSERS of all time. He has composed some of the MOST POPULAR, RECOGNIZABLE, and critically acclaimed FILM SCORES IN CINEMATIC HISTORY in a career spanning over six decades. Williams has composed for many popular movies: the STAR WARS series, JAWS, CLOSE ENCOUNTERS of the THIRD KIND, SUPERMAN, E.T. the EXTRATERRESTRIAL, the INDIANA JONES series, HOOK, the first two JURASSIC PARK films, SCHINDLER'S LIST, and the first three HARRY POTTER films. He has been associated with director STEVEN SPIELBERG since 1974, composing music for all but five of his feature films. Other works by Williams include theme music for the 1984 SUMMER OLYMPIC games [Los Angeles], NBC SUNDAY NIGHT FOOTBALL, "THE MISSION" THEME used by NBC NEWS AND SEVEN NEWS in Australia, the TV series LOST IN SPACE and LAND of the GIANTS, and incidental music for the first season of Gilligan's Island."

"He served as the BOSTON POPS'S principal conductor from 1980 to 1993. [ARTHUR FIEDLER created the POPS orchestra from 1930-1979, 50 years, until his death.]"

Williams has won 24 GRAMMY awards, seven BRITISH ACADEMY FILM AWARDS, BAFTA, five ACADEMY AWARDS, and four GOLDEN GLOBE awards. With 51 Academy Award nominations, he is the second most-nominated person, after WALT DISNEY. The LIBRARY OF CONGRESS also entered the STAR WARS soundtrack into the National Recording Registry for being "culturally, historically, or aesthetically significant." Williams was inducted into the HOLLYWOOD BOWL'S HALL OF FAME in 2000, and received a KENNEDY CENTER HONOR in 2004 and the AFI LIFE ACHIEVEMENT award in 2016. He has composed the score for eight of the top 20 highest-grossing films at the U.S. box office (adjusted for inflation.)"

"In 1952, Williams was drafted into the U.S. Air Force, where he played the piano, and conducted an arranged music for the U.S. AIR FORCE BAND. He also attended music courses at the University of Arizona as part of his service. In 1955, following his Air Force service, Williams moved to New York City and entered the JUILLIARD SCHOOL, where he studied piano with ROSINA LHEVINNE. During this time Williams worked as a jazz pianist in the city's many jazz clubs." Wikipedia

MUSIC TRIVIA: Britain's conductor of symphonic pop music is JOHN WILSON. J WIL!

"Rosina was born in 1880 in Kiev, Ukraine, moving to Moscow in 1882, because of violent anti-Semitic riots. Her teacher and later husband Josef Lhevinne both studied at the MOSCOW IMPERIAL CONSERVATORY under pianist VASILY SAFONOV, whose father was a COSSACK general. After the RUSSIAN REVOLUTION they emigrated to New York City, where they joined the faculty of the Institute of Musical Art which later became the JULLIARD School. She trained dozens of famous pianists [read Wikipedia] including Williams, who because of his father's jazz heritage, first wrote jazz but then created America's cinemas FANFARE and BACKGROUND

MUSIC which billions around the world have heard. Rosina passed—-Nov. 9, 1976, age 96."
Wikipedia
My Orthodox Jewish wedding in Brooklyn was Nov. 9, 1974. — November 9-10, 1938, was CHRYSTAL NIGHT when the Nazis openly burned Jewish Synagogues and destroyed and robbed stores and appropriated Jewish homes.
I had nothing to do with wedding plans being on that day, Nov. 9, 1974. It was a Sabbath Saturday and had been planned about six months earlier. I later learned this was a wedding Temple and there are just so many Sabbaths for booking. I had heard about and seen videos of KRYSTALNACHT but didn't connect the date. Temple Beth Shalom's in Fredericksburg, Virginia, student rabbi just before my son's Bar Mitzvah asked my family if we knew the significance of November 10th in Jewish History? In my research I had just read that date. I said, "Chrystal Night." My son's BAR MITZVAH was on the Sabbath/Saturday Nov. 10, 1990. MARTIN LUTHER was born on Nov. 10, 1483, baptized on Nov. 11, named for birthday of St. Martin of Tours, who had a Jesus dream, and began the military chaplains. My son was born on Nov. 8, 1977, at the old MARY WASHINGTON hospital in Fredericksburg, Virginia. DONALD J. TRUMP was elected president of the United States of America on Nov. 8, 2018, my son's 39th birthday, one year short of the providential Biblical 40 years.

I was christened Lutheran at St. JOHN'S Lutheran—Missouri Synod Church in Lexington, KY, in May 1943. I was Confirmed Lutheran at 1800s EMMANUEL Lutheran Church in Hudson, NY, in May 1958, just after my 15th birthday. Everything I have just written was providential. At my Jewish wedding I had many Catholic family friends and an Episcopal couple. I didn't have any Lutheran friends. Reflecting back, I think some of my wife's Jewish friends must have know this was Chrystal Night. Conservative Rabbi PHILIP BOOK must have known that fact. Past HIS-tory.]

SEMANTICS TRIVIA: Rosina was considered a famous PEDAGOGUE. PEDAGOGY (most commonly understood as the approach to teaching) referred broadly to the theory and practice of learning, and how this process influences, and is influenced by, the psychological development of learners.

.

"Instructing strategies are governed by the pupil's background knowledge and experience, situation, and environment, as well as learning goals set by the student and teacher. One example would be the SOCRATIC METHOD."— "A form of cooperative argumentative dialogue between individuals, based on asking and answering questions to stimulate critical thinking and to draw out ideas and underlying presuppositions. It is a dialetic method, involving a discussion in which the defense of one point of view is questioned; one participant may lead another to contradict themselves in some way, thus weakening the defender's point. This method is named after the Classical Greek philosopher SOCRATES and is introduced by him in PLATO'S THEAETEUS. The Socratic method is a method of hypothesis elimination, in that better hypotheses are found by steadily identifying those that lead to contradictions. The Socratic method searches for general, commonly held truths that shape beliefs and scrutinizes them to determine their consistency with other beliefs. The basic form is a series of questions formulated as tests of logic and fact intended to help a person or group discover their beliefs about some topic, exploring definitions or LOGOI (singular LOGOS) and seeking to characterize general characteristics shared by various particular instances."   Wiki

JOHN WILLIAMS AND PETER GUNN ON TELEVISION

"After moving to Los Angeles, Williams began working as a session musician, most notably for composer HENRY MANCINI. He worked with Mancini on the PETER GUNN soundtrack and later MR. LUCKY television series." He actually played the piano on TV.

"While skilled in a variety of 20th-century compositional idioms, Williams's most familiar style may be described as a form of NEO-ROMANTICISM, inspired by the late 18th century's large-scale orchestral music—in the STYLE of TCHAIKOVSKY or RICHARD WAGNER and their concept of LEITMOTIF— that inspired his film music predecessors."

"Williams was a studio pianist, performing on film scores by composers such as JERRY GOLDSMITH, ELMER BERNSTEIN, and HENRY MANCINI. With Mancini he recorded the scores 1959's PETER GUNN, 1962's DAYS OF WINE AND ROSES, and 1963's CHARADE. (Williams played the popular opening riff of Mancini's Peter Gunn theme.)"

"In 2005, the AMERICAN FILM INSTITUTE (AFI) selected William's score to 1977's STAR WARS as the GREATEST AMERICAN FILM SCORE OF ALL TIME. His score of JAWS and E.T. also appeared on the list, at Number 6 and Number 14, respectively. He is the only composer to have three scores on the list. Williams received the AFI LIFE ACHIEVEMENT in June 2016, becoming the first composer to receive the award."

ACADEMY AWARDS
1971—FIDDLER ON THE ROOF, Best Scoring Adaptation and Best Song Score, WON
1975—JAWS, Best Original Dramatic Score, WON
1977—STAR WARS, Best Original Score, WON
1982—E.T. THE EXTRA-TERRESTRIAL, Best Original Score, WON
1993—SCHINDLER'S LIST, Best Original Score, WON
2000—THE PATRIOT, Best Original Score, nominated
Check internet for dozens of other nominated scores and theme songs.
BAFTA AWARDS—British Academy Film Awards
1975—JAWS, best Film Music, WON
1978— STAR WARS, best Film Music, WON
1978—CLOSE ENCOUNTERS OF THE THIRD KIND, best Film Music, nominated
1980—THE EMPIRE STRIKES BACK, best Film Music, WON
1981—RAIDERS OF THE LOST ARK, best Film Music, nominated
1982—E.T. THE EXTRA-TERRESTRIAL, best Film Music, WON
1988—EMPIRE OF THE SUN, best Film Music, WON
1993—SCHINDLER'S LIST, best Film Music, WON
1998—SAVING PRIVATE RYAN, best Film Music, nominated
2005—MEMOIRS OF A GEISHA, best Film Music, WON
2011—WAR HORSE, best Film Music, nominated
2012—LINCOLN. best Film Music, nominated
2013—THE BOOK THIEF, best Film Music, nominated
2015—STAR WARS: THE FORCE AWAKENS, best Film Music, nominated
Partial List
GOLDEN GLOBE AWARDS
1975—JAWS, best Original Score, WON
1977—STAR WARS, best Original Score, WON
1977—CLOSE ENCOUNTERS OF THE THIRD KIND, best Original Score, nominated

1978—SUPERMAN, best Original Score, nominated
1980—THE EMPIRE STRIKES BACK, best Original Score, nominated
1982—E.T. THE EXTRA-TERRESTRIAL, best Original Score, WON
1989—BORN ON THE FOURTH OF JULY, best Original Score, nominated
1993—SCHINDLER'S LIST, best Original Score, nominated
2005—MEMOIRS OF A GEISHA, best Original Score, WON
2011—WAR HOUSE, best Original Score, nominated
2012—LINCOLN, best Original Score, nominated
2013—THE BOOK THIEF, best Original Score, nominated
2017—THE POST, best Original Score, nominated
Partial list
EMMY AWARDS—TELEVISION   see Wikipedia
GRAMMY MUSIC AWARDS   see Wikipedia

Col. Gabriel Air Force Symphony Conductor—D DAY Survivor

"Colonel ARNALD D. GABRIEL (born May 31, 1925) in Cortland, New York was the Commander and Conductor of the United States AIR FORCE BAND, U.S. Air Force SYMPHONY ORCHESTRA, and SINGING SERGEANTS from 1964 to 1985. In 1990, he was named the FIRST CONDUCTOR EMERITUS of the United States AIR FORCE BAND and the 29th DIVISION BAND of the Virginia Army National Guard."

PERSONAL SMALL WORLD STORY: The 29th Division was the first unit to land on Omaha Beach taking the heaviest casualties. The unit's BEDFORD BOYS from the small town BEDFORD, VIRGINIA, had so many young men killed that the U.S. government placed the National D DAY MEMORIAL there. It is located in the beautiful rolling mountain farm countryside between Lynchburg and Roanoke, Virginia. Appomattox is nearby where Gen. ROBERT E. LEE and Gen. ULYSSES S. GRANT signed the peace terms which ended America's most deadly WAR OF SECESSION, CIVIL WAR. MEDAL OF HONOR recipient Pvt. DESMOND DOSS was born in Lynchburg. He was the first conscientious objector awarded America's highest combat award. ANDREW GARFIELD portrayed him in the Academy Award nominated movie HACKSAW RIDGE directed by American/Australian MEL GIBSON. A great film about the true horror of war. VINCE VAUGHN played a serious role as Doss' tough, frustrated drill sergeant, but interjects comedy. AUDIE MURPHY, America's most decorated soldier, airplane crashed in fog into Brush Mountain within "sight" of Roanoke airport. I visited Murphy's monument there after I saw the premier of Hacksaw Ridge in Lynchburg about 60 miles away. I stopped at D DAY memorial and had tour on the way there. In 1956, when I was 13, I shook Audie Murphy's hand after Hudson, New York movie premier of WALK THE PROUD LAND, he portrayed Christian Indian agent JOHN CLUM from Claverack, where I graduated High School, where I was on 6 boy track team with Larry North, later Lt. Col. OLIVER NORTH. Walk Proud Land is on U Tube, it was Audie Murphy's favorite film role, a great film. His film TO HELL AND BACK. was his life story, but was difficult because Murphy had PTSD, from horrific front line combat where his fellow soldiers were killed next to him. Audie Murphy heard about the bravery of Desmond Doss and visited him and wanted to portray him in a movie. Doss turned America's most decorated American soldier down. He probably told him it would be PRIDEFUL if he allowed Murphy to put his story on the big screen. Doss was a very devout SEVENTH DAY ADVENTIST. Gail in my small Bible study class said she knew the Doss family and was invited to two of his family weddings in Richmond, Virginia.

"During World War II, Gabriel served as an infantryman (as a machine gunner) with the US Army's 29th Infantry Division in Europe. For his service in Europe he received two Bronze Star medals, the Combat Infantry Badge, and the French Croix de Guerre.

"After leaving the Army, Gabriel worked at a canning factory due to not being able to go to college. Later on, his High School Band director decided that Gabriel was too talented to waste his days in a canning factory. Gabriel's old High School director paid for Gabriel to attend ITHACA COLLEGE in 1946. He earned both Bachelor and Master of Science degrees in Music Education there."

"Colonel Gabriel retired from the US. Air Force Band and the Air Force in February 1985. In 1990, he was named the FIRST CONDUCTOR EMERITUS of the United States Air Force Band at DAR CONSTITUTION HALL in Washington, D.C. Colonel Gabriel is also a Professor Emeritus of GEORGE MASON University."

HONORS—"Gabriel's honors include the FIRST CITATION OF EXCELLENCE awarded by the National Band Association."   Wikipedia

PERSONAL STORY: I videoed Colonel Gabriel at his Air Force Symphony concert under the Air Force Memorial in Washington, D.C., in May 2018. At age 93, he conducted the PRIVATE RYAN theme of the Omaha Beach landing where he was in 1944! As Colonel Gabriel conducted the Air Force Symphony with the PRIVATE RYAN Omaha Beach landing film music playing. Another former airman JOHN WILLIAMS wrote the RYAN soundtrack music. Read my list of Williams soundtracks, AWESOME.

There is a U Tube video of 94-year-old Colonel Gabriel conducting the Air Force Symphony Orchestra on the 70th D DAY anniversary on June 6, 2019.

There is also a great U Tube biographical tribute to Colonel Gabriel D DAY to Greatness. An amazing story of how he was the only survivor of his unit, machine gunners like him, were killed in three days. Maybe his name GABRIEL WAS HIS GUARDIAN ANGEL? God's providence?

Composer DAVID ROSE Connection to GLEN MILLER AAF Band

"During World War II, Rose entered the Army, in 1942, Rose wrote HOLIDAY FOR STRINGS still recognized as a classic American composition its pizzicato strings and soaring melodies give this composition its distinctive sound." The song was used by the GLENN MILLER Army Air Force Concert Orchestra which played on the radio in Great Britain. "Rose meet RED SKELTON in the Army and they became friends. Skelton used "Holiday for Strings" as the theme song for THE RED SKELTON SHOW for 21 years on his CBS and NBC TV shows with DAVID ROSE as his music conductor."   Wikipedia

"In 1942, Rose and his orchestra provided the music for TUNE UP, AMERICA! on MUTUAL radio. The program provided "RECOGNITION OF THE EFFORTS OF WOMEN ENGAGED IN WAR WORK."   Wikipedia

"In 1955, Rose was commissioned by MGM Studios to compose the score for their forthcoming science fiction project FORBIDDEN PLANET." He was discharged because his electronic music was replaced by others. I was 12, when I saw this film with ROBBIE THE ROBOT, very low tech, but a beginning. In 1977, 22 years later, I saw STAR WARS and LUCAS and his light technology opened a new UNIVERSE. My birthday is on May 4, MAY THE FOURTH FORCE BE WITH ME! I saw the film in Charlottesville, Virginia.

Rose composed 15 movie SOUNDTRACKS. The most popular ones: PLEASE DON'T EAT THE DAISIES (1960) DORIS DAY, DAVID NIVEN and JANIS PAGE; NEVER TOO LATE (1965) CONNIE STEVENS, JIM HUTTON, PAUL FORD, MAUREEN O'SULLIVAN. O'Sullivan was the first JANE in 1932, TARZAN THE APE MAN with Austro-Hungarian JOHNNY WEISSMULLER, who had won five Olympic swimming Gold medals. Jim Hutton has a sad dramatic death scene at the end of the film GREEN BERETS (1966). His son TIMOTHY HUTTON, two years after his father's death, won the 1981 ACADEMY AWARD for his Supporting Actor role in ORDINARY PEOPLE (1980). He dedicated his OSCAR to his father. Hutton's first uncredited movie role was as a 4-yr. old boy running to his daddy in Never Too Late, 1965. In "Ordinary People" his father was the enigmatic Canadian actor DONALD SUTHERLAND, action actor KIEFER'S father. MARY TYLER MOORE was Hutton's mother. Rose also wrote soundtrack with Henry Mancini, uncredited, for OPERATION PETTICOAT (1959) with CARY GRANT, TONY CURTIS and DINA MERILL." Wikipedia

"Rose also wrote music for many TV series, including IT'S A GREAT LIFE, THE TONY MARTIN SHOW, LITTLE HOUSE ON THE PRAIRIE, HIGHWAY TO HEAVEN, BONANZA, and HIGHWAY PATROL." He won four EMMY's. Wikipedia

"In 1962, he released THE STRIPPER instrumental song composed in 1958 for a TV Special saluting burlesque. The song featured especially prominent trombone lines, giving the tune its lascivious signature, and evokes the feel of music used to accompany burlesque strip tease artists." MGM Records needed a side B on a 45-rpm single for his string composition of the standard EBB TIDE. It is alleged in the Gettysburg Times that an office boy looked through Rose's old tapes and found the Stripper. It became a surprise hit, receiving much radio play." Wikipedia. I heard on radio and bought a;bum.

"David Rosenberg Rose was born in London, England on June 15, 1910. Rose first wife was the popular actress, radio and TV star MARTHA RAYE, October 1938-May 19, 1941. On July 28, 1941, Rose married actress and singer JUDY GARLAND. They had no children, though Garland, according to biographer Gerald Clarke, underwent at least one abortion during the marriage, at the insistence of her mother, her husband, and the studio that employed her, MGM. They divorced in 1944." Wikipedia Abortion was illegal at that time with jail time for the doctor and the woman. It was considered murder.

MARTHA RAYE—"Raye was honored in 1969 at the ACADEMY AWARDS as the JEAN HERSHOLT HUMANITARIAN AWARD recipient for her volunteer efforts and service to the troops." She joined the USO, United Service Organizations, in 1942, soon after the U.S. entered World War II." "On Nov. 2, 1993, she was awarded the PRESIDENTIAL MEDAL OF FREEDOM by President BILL CLINTON for her service to her country. The citation reads:

"A talented performer whose career spans the better part of a century,
Martha Raye has delighted audiences and uplifted spirits around the
globe. She brought her tremendous comedic and musical skills to her
work in film, stage, and television, helping to shape American entertainment.
The great courage, kindness, and patriotism showed in her many tours
during World War II, the Korean conflict, and the Vietnam conflict earned her
the nickname "COLONEL MAGGIE". The American people honor Martha
Raye, a woman who has tirelessly used her gifts to benefit the lives of
fellow Americans."

"From 1935-38, she was a featured cast member in 39 episodes of AL JOLSON'S weekly CBS radio show. Martha sang both solos and duets with Jolson. Over the next quarter century, she would appear with many of the leading comics of her day, including JOE E. BROWN, BOB HOPE, W.C. FIELDS, ABBOTT AND COSTELLO, CHARLIE CHAPLIN, and JIMMY DURANTE." Wikipedia

"Raye's personal life was complex and emotionally tumultuous. She was married seven times."
DId her many visits to the troops in three wars and film, radio and TV give her any time to be a wife and keep a conventional home?

"Raye was a devout Methodist who regularly attended church [7 church weddings], read the Bible daily, and even taught Sunday school classes." Wikipedia

"Politically, Raye was CONSERVATIVE, affirming her political views by informing an interviewer in 1984, "I am a Republican because I believe in the Constitution, strength in National Defense, limited government, individual freedom, and personal responsibility as the concrete foundation for American government." They reinforce the resolve that the United States is THE GREATEST COUNTRY IN THE WORLD AND WE CAN ALL BE ETERNALLY GRATEFUL TO OUR FOUNDING FATHERS FOR THE BEAUTIFUL LEGACY THEY LEFT US TODAY."   The HOLLYWOOD REPORTER,1984

"Martha Raye was the FIFTH PERSON to be awarded honorary GREEN BERET, When in Vietnam she would assist those in combat hospitals instead of performing because she was a LPN." She also brought the patients humor.

Raye starred in the film BILLY ROSES'S JUMBO with DORIS DAT, STEPHEN BOYD and JIMMY DURANTE in 1962. Raye has two stars on the HOLLYWOOD WALK OF FAME—one for motion pictures and one for television. She has one daughter.

THE AIRMEN OF NOTE GLENN MILLER TRIBUTE BAND

"The AIRMEN OF NOTE is the premier jazz ensemble of the United States Air Force and part of the United States Air Force Band. Created in 1950 to carry on the tradition of Major GLENN MILLER'S ARMY AIR CORPS dance band, the "NOTE" is a touring big band that has attracted 18 professional jazz musicians from across the United States."

"The band has presented jazz performances to audiences throughout the United States, Europe, and Asia and produces broadcasts and recordings, with one release reaching #2 on the JAZZ WEEK jazz album chart. [COOL YULE 2010]. In 1954 the Airmen of Note played Miller's band in the movie THE GLENN MILLER STORY." Wikipedia

"The GLENN MILLER SOUND has remained central, but the band adopted a more contemporary sound in the 1950s and 1960s largely due to staff arrangers such as SAMMY NESTICO. Over the past four decades, MIKE CROTTY and ALAN BAYLOCK have taken the role. To augment the writing staff, the Airmen of Note has commissioned works by BOB FLORENCE, BOB MINTZER, ROB MCCONNELL, and BILL HOLMAN. [Florence arrangement of HOAGY CARMICHAEL'S (Up A) LAZY RIVER was trombonist SI ZENTNER big band hit in 1962, he won a Grammy for Best Pop Instrumental. Wikipedia lists LAZY RIVER being recorded by 64 artists! This must be a record? Every band, vocalist and soloist played it, BOBBY DARIN in 1961 #14, may have been the most famous version because he sang it on DICK CLARK'S AMERICAN BANDSTAND.]

"Sammy Nestico and former band member TOMMY NEWSOM have composed works for the group." "Newsom was a tenor saxophone player in the NBC Orchestra on THE TONIGHT SHOW STARRING JOHNNY CARSON, for which he later became assistant director. Newsom was frequently the band's substitute director, whenever DOC SEVERINSEN was away from the show or filling in for announcer ED MCMAHON. Nicknamed "MR. EXCITEMENT" by JOHNNY CARSON as an ironic take on his low-keyed, reserved persona, he was often the FOIL FOR CARSON'S HUMOR. His conservative brown or blue suits were a marked contrast to SEVERINSEN'S FLASHY STAGE CLOTHING." "Newsom joined the TONIGHT SHOW BAND in 1962, and left it when Carson retired in 1992. Newsom then performed with the orchestra for the MERV GRIFFIN SHOW." Wikipedia

"Newsom was as well known within the music industry as much as he was as a performer. He arranged for groups as varied as the Tonight Show ensemble and the Cincinnati Pops Orchestra, and musicians SKITCH HENDERSON, WOODY HERMAN, KENNY RODGERS, CHARLIE BYRD, JOHN DENVER, opera star BEVERLY SILLS."

"Newsom won two EMMY AWARDS as a music director, in 1982 with NIGHT OF 100 STARS and in 1986 for the 40th Annual TONY AWARDS. He recorded six big band albums." NEWSOM JOHNNY CARSON QUIPS: "One night, Newsom wore a very bold (for him) yellow suit, CARSON commented, "Look at that big, dumb canary. "Newsom's response: "You'll know what kind of bird I am when I fly over you." "During one episode Newsom appeared in a sport coat similar to Carson's own. Noticing the similarity, Carson asked Newsom where he got his; he responded simply. "It was in my closet at home, John". "Another time, Carson, who just returned from vacation, said, "I really missed you guys." Newsom: "Why didn't you write?" "During a March 1991 episode, Johnny asked drummer ED SHAUGHNESSY, who was going to perform in Illinois, if he was going to a concert for a clinic; Shaughnessy replied he was doing just a concert. When Johnny asked Tommy Newsom if he ever did clinics, Tommy replied "I go to clinics" which yet again brought down the house. Johnny temporarily walked offstage in mock offense." Wikipedia

SMALL WORLD STORY: In March 1962, at a University of Maine, dance the first time I saw LES ELGART'S band, Les introduced drummer Ed Shaughnessy from Las Vegas, and we listened to his drum solo on the song MAR CHA CHA from Les greatest album DESIGNS FOR DANCING with many great standard songs. It was my first stereo Elgart record December 1960, the most swinging dance album I have. A couple of blocks from my college dormitory, my local record store manager DAVE BROWN used it as a demo record and wouldn't sell it to me until Christmas! Les Elgart said the University of Maine dance was the first time they played his new TWIST GOES TO COLLEGE album songs.

[The Tonight orchestra under Doc Severinsen and Newsom featured top instrumental soloists. In the 1960s The Airmen of Note were almost disbanded and Doc Severinsen gave his support saving the band. I first heard the Airmen of Note on the East Capitol side in the summer of 1993. I have heard the band in many locations and am like the band's "mascot". I have taken VHS videos of their concerts which I converted to DVD which I have given the band. Today, only a few remain because of their retirement. Band members are still active and alto saxophonist ANDY AXELRAD is today in BROADWAY SHOW orchestras. Andy told me he has an aunt who was related to Senator BARRY GOLDWATER. I was a friend of his for 20 years telling him I was virtuoso alto saxophonist LARRY ELGART band "photographer" to get into closed concerts. I asked Andy how did Larry Elgart play solos higher and smoother than any other musician. Andy said his range was "altisimo" which required tremendous breath control and practice. Larry did not smoke cigarettes, drink alcohol or take any drugs. Many great jazz musicians took heroin, cocaine and especially marijuana.]

PROVIDENTIAL MUSIC STORY: I told Larry Elgart that I thought his music recordings sounded "ethereal". Larry Elgart recalled, "We recorded in the COLUMBIA CHURCH STUDIO in downtown New York City." I had no idea what that meant. Wikipedia says that the COLUMBIA CHURCH STUDIO had been several different churches, it had a high ceiling and remarkable acoustics better than a recording studio. African American trumpeter MILES DAVIS and EUGENE ORMANDY and other classical orchestras also recorded there. ETHEREAL: dictionary definition heavenly, spiritual, other worldly seems too perfect for this world. LES AND LARRY ELGART were Jewish. SHALOM

Les was the band leader but Larry was the perfectionist. In 1953, even before stereophonic, two speaker separation, begun in 1958, their arrangements by tenor saxophonist CHARLIE ALBERTINE were dimensionally interplayed and they divided the five saxophones on the left and the three trombones, emphasizing the deep bass trombone, and four trumpets on the right. On tour they had a problem with out of tune pianos. They made an innovative decision to drop the piano and highlighted the guitar, bass and drums giving their band a more rhythmic swinging modern sound. Albertine and both Elgarts are credited with writing the 1954 song BANDSTAND BOOGIE which became DICK CLARK'S AMERICAN BANDSTAND theme song played across America at 4:00 PM. My dad was the senior engineer in the ABC TV Master Control room who often connected DICK CLARK'S Philadelphia dance studio to America's youth, addicted to America's new popular music artists who visited and they danced to. I asked my dad to get me that song. He gave me the Elgart's Columbia record album BAND OF THE YEAR (1954) with the BANDSTAND BOOGIE in March 1960, my first LP record album. I have all their some 55 record albums, many have been reissued on two-album CDs. Check U Tube most of the Elgart's music is played some just showing the record player but some have slide photo presentation of female models and montages shown along with the song. Larry's WILLOW WEEP FOR ME will mesmerize you. Type in any artist and I guarantee, you will go from one song to another and forget what is on TV. ENJOY.

Wikipedia CHARLES ALBERTINE SPACE AGE MUSIC and see the complete Elgart discography and his other later big band arrangements, Hollywood film soundtrack, and many TV music scores. He went to JULLIARD MUSIC for a year, but left to pursue his own ideas which were more innovative and modern.

LARRY ELGART'S BIG BAND BEGINNINGS

SMALL WORLD FACT: Albertine was playing tenor saxophone in the TOP BANANA BROADWAY show with PHIL SILVERS, TV's SERGEANT BILKO. Larry Elgart played alto sax in the "PIT" band and they discussed their musical ideas. Before LES and LARRY ELGART'S big band, Albertine wrote the unique BAREFOOT BALERINAS, 1953, used by dance classes, I saw it at University of Maine dance studio in 1963. In 1953, UFO extraterrestrial Hollywood films about aliens were shown after pilot KENNETH ARNOLD'S report of "saucer-shaped" craft flying very fast in the Rocky Mountains in Washington State, the ROSWELL crash incident and flying saucers UFOs photographed over the Washington, D.C. Capitol, when HARRY S TRUMAN was president. As a young child I remember the scary H.G. WELLES WAR OF THE WORLDS in color and black and white THE DAY THE EARTH STOOD STILL. The extraterrestrial British actor MICHAEL RENNIE warned the world about the hazard to the earth of nuclear warfare. A TRUE FACT OR WAS IT RUSSIAN PROPAGANDA? Albertine wrote a unique jazz space suite called IMPRESSIONS FROM OUTER SPACE featuring Larry Elgart's alto saxophone in 1953. In 1982, I visited my favorite record store DAYTON'S on 12th and Broadway. I bought this Decca 10 inch LP for $30, a lot of money then. I usually got FOR DEMONSTRATION USE ONLY radio copies for $2 in stereo. Recently, I found its songs on U Tube, way ahead of its time. ENJOY.

INA RAE HUTTON FIRST FEMALE SWING BAND

PERSONAL STORY: My dad attended Transylvania College 1939-42, and said he knew a girl who played trumpet in Ina Rae Hutton's MELODEARS all female Big Swing band. The school had been famous trumpeter BILLY BUTTERFIELD's alma mater. She was born in Chicago to an

African American piano player mother. Hutton had been a tap dancer from age 8 and at 15 she appeared in the ZIEGFELD FOLLIES. Her Wikipedia photo shows her as a white blonde. Her band began in 1934 and had talented female musicians. In the 1950s she had a TV show. She was married six times, her fourth husband was virtuoso trumpeter RANDY BROOKS who in 1946 had a #1 song Tenderly. Brooks at age 11 gave concerts with RUDI VALLE's orchestra in Maine where they lived. Valle was an alumnus of the University of Maine and played saxophone. .He also made Hollywood movies and sang using a megaphone. When married to Ina Rae Hutton he had a stroke and was incapacitated. He made a short comeback but the days of the Big Bands was over except the most famous ones. Brooks passed in Sanford/Springvale, Maine, in 1967, where I graduated college in 1964. Her half sister JUNE HUTTON became a popular singer in 1941 in CHARLIE SPIVAK's STARDUSTERS, then in 1944 she replaced JO STAFFORD IN TOMMY DORSEY'S PIED PIPERS and sang hit "Deam". In 1951, she sang on FRANK SINATRA'S TV show meeting AXEL STORDAHL and married, he led her TV band. U Tube has clips. In 1968, she married Hollywood actor KENNETH TOBY, TV's Whirlybirds, sci-fi films, see big list on Wikipedia. She passed May 2, 1973, I was born May 4, 1943. Toby never remarried he passed at 85. Charlie Spivak featured the young Elgart brothers and also a trombonist NELSON RIDDLE whose swing arrangements and Axel's made Sinatra great again.

HOLLYWOOD'S UNSEEN HERO OF 500 + FILMS

In 1976 and 1977, I worked as a licensed Metropolitan Life insurance sales representative in White Plains, New York. Another salesman Dennis Cerullo said his uncle AL CERULLO was a helicopter pilot who was helping film a new Pink Panther movie in nearby New York City. He piloted almost all famous movie stars in 500 plus Hollywood films but was not shown until the CAPTAIN AMERICA: CIVIL WAR movie. I had a chance to call him years ago and tell him that I worked with Dennis, his "distant cousin." Al Cerullo recalled working with dozens of Hollywood's most famous action actors whose lives and safety was literally in his hands. Many dangerous daring scenes were filmed using his "Space Camera" attached to the nose of his helicopter.
Al Cerullo literally was the UNSUNG HERO of Hollywood's BLOCKBUSTER ACTION films only excluding CGI space war films. There are several U TUBE video clips, one New York City TV station did a news story with him highlighting his heroism as a helicopter pilot in Vietnam, and then helicopter pilot for the Hollywood stars and dangerous film close-up scenes using his unprecedented 17,000 helicopter flight hours. Al Cerullo has a helicopter agency where he gives scenic tours of New York City and surrounding areas. He must be well known by air traffic controllers and may have clearances other pilots aren't given.

REPUBLIC BUILDER OF AMERICAN TACTICAL AIRCRAFT

His helicopter is at Republic Airport, near my hometown Amityville. Republic Aircraft factory built about 10,000 P-47 Thunderbolt fighter in World War II, about 7,000 F-84 Thunderjet, F-84F Thunderstreak jet fighters and RF-84 Thunderfash photo reconnaissance jets, 822 F-105 Thunderchief, internal bomb-bay supersonic low-level nuclear jet fighter bombers. It finally built the Republic-Fairchild A-10 Thunderbolt II, "Warthog" tank buster jet fighter bombers which won the First Gulf War destroying SADDAM HUSSEIN's thousands of tanks, Bull long range artillery and SCUD long range rockets, single handed using its 30mm Gatling gun and Hellfire missiles mostly at night using INFRARED sensors which detected the "hidden" Russian T-72 steel tanks and Canadian engineer Bull's superior long range artillery, gun barrels. The A-10's were shipped to the Fairchild factory in Hagerstown, Maryland for final assembly. I was with my family at Myrtle Beach in the summer of 1982. I looked up and saw the strangest looking jet I had ever seen the A-10, we drove by the nearby airbase but couldn't get a close view, it was one of the first airbases to fly this aircraft. Arizona Senator (R) MARTHA MCSALLY was one of several women A-10 Middle East combat pilot's, to fly the jet that our enemies fear the most. Some senior Air Force people want to retire this aircraft, but American and Allied ground forces known this aircraft has saved their unit's many deaths and casualties. Many A-10 aircraft have received new wings and modern glass computer cockpit instrumentation making it more effective.

AL CERULLO'S HOLLYWOOD LEGACY

MARVEL CINEMATIC UNIVERSE WIKI—FANDOM

"Al Cerullo, Jr., was the helicopter pilot in THE INCREDIBLE HULK; IRON MAN 2; THE AVENGERS: IRON MAN 3; CAPTAIN AMERICA: THE WINTER SOLDIER; DOCTOR STRANGE; SPIDER-MAN: HOMECOMING; AVENGERS: INFINITY WAR and THE PUNISHER episode TROUBLE THE WATER."
TRIVIA: Al Cerullo was the helicopter pilot in the SONY PICTURES studios productions SPIDER-MAN; SPIDER-MAN 2, SPIDER-MAN 3; THE AMAZING SPIDER-MAN and THE AMAZING SPIDER-MAN 2."
"Al Cerullo was a stunt performer in the 20TH CENTURY FOX productions X-MEN, DAREDEVIL and FANTASTIC FOUR."
"He was the helicopter pilot in the 20TH CENTURY FOX productions X-MEN, DAREDEVIL, FANTASTIC FOUR: RISE of THE SILVER SURFER and X-MEN: DAYS FUTURE PAST."
"He was a helicopter pilot in the DC EXTENDED UNIVERSE production BATMAN V SUPERMAN: DAWN OF JUSTICE."
"He was the helicopter pilot in the DC ENTERTAINMENT productions SUPERMAN; SUPERMAN RETURNS and GOTHAM."
CHECK IMDb for full movie credits which is incredible click actor and stunts fo access
A PARTIAL LIST BEGINS AT END some of biggest: ESCAPE FROM NEW YORK, 1981; NIGHTHAWKS, 81; THE SOLDIER, 82; THE WORLD ACCORDING TO GARP, 82; TEMPEST, 82; HEAVEN HELP US, 85; THE PROTECTOR, 85; THE MANHATTAN PROJECT, 86; BLACK WIDOW, 87; CROCODILE DUNDEE II, 88; BLUE STEEL, 90; BOOMERANG, 92; HOME ALONE 2: LOST IN NEW YORK, 92 [Donald Trump cameo in his hotel close-up on Empire State Bldg.]; GUARDING TESS, 94; MIGHTY APHRODITE, 95; BED OF ROSES, 96; THE JUROR, 96; ERASER, 96; CONSPIRACY THEORY, 97; THE DEVIL'S ADVOCATE, 97; BIG DADDY, 99; MICKEY BLUE EYES, 99; WEDDING CRASHERS, 2005; CAPTAIN AMERICA; CIVIL WAR, 2016."
HELICOPTER PILOT HIGHLIGHTS: THE IRISHMAN, 2019; JOHN WICK: CHAPTER 3 PARABELLUM, 2019; OCEANS EIGHT, 2018; AVENGERS INFINITY WAR, 2018; SPIDER-MAN: HOMECOMING, 2017; COLLATERAL BEAUTY, 2016; DOCTOR STRANGE, 2015; GHOSTBUSTERS, 2016; BATMAN Vs SUPERMAN: DAWN OF JUSTICE, 2016; TRAIN WRECK, 2015; TED 2, 2015; PIXELS, 2015; RUN ALL NIGHT, 2015; BEIJING, NEW YORK, 2016; ANNIE, 2014; DUMB AND DUMBER TO, 2014; JOHN WICK, 2014; THE EQUALIZER, 2015; TEENAGE MUTANT NINJA TURTLES, 2014; DELIVER US FROM EVIL, 2014; X-MEN: DAYS OF FUTURE PAST (DC), 2014; THE AMAZING SPIDER-MAN 2, 2014; CAPTAIN AMERICA; THE WINTER SOLDIER (DC), 2014; NOAH, 2014; NEED FOR SPEED, 2014; WINTER'S TALE, 2014; NON-STOP, 2014; JACK RYAN: SHADOW RECRUIT, 2014; THE

HUNGER GAMES: CATCHING FIRE, 2013; DELIVERY MAN, 2013; THE SECRET LIFE OF WALTER MITTY, 2013; THE HEAT, 2013; THE GREAT GATSBY, 2013; IRON MAN 3, 2013; BROKEN CITY, 2013; GUILT TRIP, 2012; DISCONNECT, 2012; GIRL MOST LIKELY, 2012; THE ICEMAN, 2012; MADEA'S WITNESS PROTECTION, 2012; THE AMAZING SPIDER-MAN, 2012; ARBITRAGE, 2012; NEW YEAR'S EVE, 2011; TOWER HEIST, 2011; ARTHUR, 2011; SKYLINE, 2010; SALT, 2010; SORCERER'S APPRENTICE, 2010; GROWN UPS, 2010; SEX AND THE CITY 2, 2010; IRON MAN 2, 2010; THE BACK-UP PLAN, 2010; COP OUT, 2010; SHUTTER ISLAND, 2010; G.I. JOE: THE RISE OF COBRA, 2009; THE TAKING OF THE PELHAM 123, 2009; ANGELS AND DEMONS, 2009; GHOSTS OF GIRL FRIENDS PAST, 2009; STATE OF PLAY, 2009; KNOWING, 2009; DUPLICITY, 2009; BROOKLYN'S FINEST, 2009; MARLEY AND ME, 2008; PRIDE AND GLORY, 2008; THE WOMEN, 2008; BURN AFTER READING, 2008; BABYLON A.D., 2008; HELLBOY II: THE GOLDEN ARMY, 2009; HANCOCK, 2008; THE INCREDIBLE HULK, 2008; YOU DON'T MESS WITH THE ZOHAN, 2008; STOP-LOSS, 2008; 21, 2008; JUMPER, 2008; I AM LEGEND, 2007; THE BRAVE ONE, 2007; THE BOURNE ULTIMATUM, 2007; HAIRSPRAY, 2007; FANTASTIC 4: RISE OF THE SIVER SURFER, 2007; PERFECT STRANGER, 2007; SPIDER-MAN 3, 2007; BREACH, 2007; MUSIC AND LYRICS, 2007; THE GOOD SHEPHERD, 2006; CHARLOTTE'S WEB, 2006; THE HOAX, 2006; WORLD TRADE CENTER, 2006; THE DEVIL WEARS PRADA, 2006; SUPERMAN RETURNS, 2006; CLICK, 2006; THE SENTINEL, 2006: FAILURE TO LAUNCH, 2006; 16 BLOCKS, 2006; FUN WITH DICK AND JANE, 2005; KING KONG, 2005; RENT, 2005; DARK WATER, 2005; WAR OF THE WORLDS, 2005; MISS CONGENIALITY 2: ARMED & FABULOUS, 2005; HITCH, 2005; HIDE AND SEEK, 2005; MEET THE FOCKERS, 2004: TAXI, 2004; THE FORGOTTEN, 2004; SPIDER-MAN 2, 2004; THE DAY AFTER TOMORROW, 2004; 13 GOING ON 30, 2004; LAWS OF ATTRACTION. 2004; MONA LISA SMILE, 2003; STUCK ON YOU, 2003; Dave Matthews Band Central Park concert, 2003: THE ITALIAN JOB, 2003; ANGER MANAGEMENT, 2003; DAREDEVIL, 2003; MAID IN MANHATTAN, 2002; GANGS OF NEW YORK, 2002; ANALYZE THAT, 2002; RED DRAGON, 2002; ASSASSINATION TANGO, 2002; THE EMPEROR'S CLUB, 2002: MEN IN BLACK 2, 2002; MR. DEEDS, 2002; SPIDER-MAN, 2002; CHANGING LANES, 2002; EMPIRE, 2002; VANILLA SKY, 2001; OCEANS 11, 2001; ZOOLANDER, 2001; THE ART OF WAR, 2000; AUTUMN IN NEW YORK, 2000; X-MEN, 2000; THE PERFECT STORM, 2000: SHAFT, 2000: FREQUENCY, 2000: KEEPING THE FAITH, 2000; END OF DAYS, 1999; AFTERSHOCK: EARTHQUAKE IN NEW YORK, TV, 1999; THE BONE COLLECTOR, 1999; MICKEY BLUE EYES, 1999; THE THOMAS CROWN AFFAIR, 1999; PUSHING TIN, 1999; ENTRAPMENT, 1999; ANALYZE THIS, 1999; IN DREAMS, 1999; YOU'VE GOT MAIL, 1998; THE SIEGE, 1998; MEET JOE BLACK, 1998; ARMAGEDDON, 1998; GODZILLA, 1996; DEEP IMPACT, 1998; U.S. MARSHALS, 1998; THE PEACEMAKER, 1997; CONSPIRACY THEORY, 1997; MEN IN BLACK, 1997; THE DEVIL'S OWN, 1997; THE PREACHER'S WIFE, 1996; JERRY MCGUIRE, 1996; RANSOM, 1996; CITY HALL, 1996; THE JUROR, 1996; BED OF ROSES, 1996; MONEY TRAIN, 1995; DIE HARD WITH A VENGEANCE, 1995; THE RIVER WILD, 1994; NORTH, 1994; WOLF, 1994; PHILADELPHIA, 1993; SIX DEGREES OF SEPARATION, 1993; SLEEPLESS IN SEATTLE, 1993; THE BABE, 1992; JFK, 1991; BUGSY, 1991; THE BUTCHER'S WIFE, 1991; Billy Joel Live at Yankee Stadium TV, 1990; THE GODFATHER III. 1990; GOODFELLAS, 1990; COMMUNION, 1989; WHEN HARRY MEET SALLY, 1989; TRUE BELIEVER, 1989; WORKING GIRL, 1988; WALL STREET, 1987; POPEYE DOYLE, 1986; A CHORUS LINE, 1985; DEATH WISH 3, 1985; COMMANDO, 1985; STAYING ALIVE, 1983; SOPHIE'S CHOICE, 1982; Q, 1982; WOLFEN, 1981; SUPERMAN, 1978; HEROES, 1977; THE GUMBALL RALLY, 1976"

[Many of Al Cerullo films say he is uncredited. He has flown helicopters for many TV film episodes for DESIGNATED SURVIVOR, SHOW ME A HERO, POWER, ALLEGIANCE, THE STRAIN, THE

BLACKLIST, COVERT AFFAIRS, SUITS, ZERO HOURS, BEAUTY AND THE BEAST, REVENGE, DOGS IN THE CITY, THE WHOLE TRUTH, LIVE TO DANCE, DELOCATED, TOP CHIEF, V, MERCY, UGLY BETTY, BRICK CITY, GOSSIP GIRL, DIRTY SEXY MONEY, WITHOUT A TRACE, HEROES, THE WIRE, THE MAN IN THE HIGH CASTLE and BILLIONS." HOORAY FOR HOLLYWOOD'S HERO.

MULTIPLEX THEATERS MAKE HOLLYWOOD BOOM

"A multiplex is a movie theater with multiple screens within a single complex. They are usually housed in a specifically designed building. The largest of these complexes can sit thousands of people and are referred to as a megaplex. Around 1915, two adjacent theaters in Moncton, New Brunswick, under the same ownership were converted to share a single entrance with separate ticket booths. The arrangement was so unusual that it was featured by ROBERT RIPLEY in his BELIEVE IT OR NOT comic strip. In 1937 James Edwards twinned his Alhambra Theater in the Los Angeles area by converting an adjacent storefront into a second "annex" screen."   Wikipedia PERSONAL STORY: My dad told me that his longtime ABC TV fellow worker JOE KELLY who was head of ABC's Kinescope film department since 1949, when my dad was hired to work at the new ABC TV. In 1953, Joe Kelly told a young evangelist to put his one-hour 16mm promotion film on 35mm and his voice and image would be better visually on the small home TV screens. Later, the evangelist BILLY GRAHAM returned with a half-hour 35 mm film. GRAHAM then began his National TV MINISTRY. In the late 1960s ABC discontinued using Kinescope recordings adopting the new Video tape technology. My dad said, "Joe Kelly later worked with SPYROS SKOURAS, who had been a senior executive at the 20TH CENTURY FOX film production company." Temporarily, Skouras worked with Joe Kelly on a mini-theater idea but then owned the Prudential Lines shipping oil tankers. I found Joe's son on the Internet and spoke with him at his theater lighting company in Northport, Long Island. His Website has a World War II photo of his father as a projectionist at the BROOKLYN NAVY YARD where he showed Hollywood films to Navy sailors and ship construction shipyard workers. His son Joe recalled, "My dad was in the Navy and received orders to ship out to active duty. The Brooklyn Shipyard personnel petitioned that he stay as their film projectionist. He stayed and his assigned ship, a destroyer was sunk by a submarine."
The battleship MISSOURI was built there. In October 1945, Navy Day, I was 30 months old, and my mother and father took me aboard the Missouri, a few weeks after the Japanese peace armistice was signed aboard the ship. The first event I can recall in my life, is being on a big gray ship with big gray sticks (16 inch guns)—THE MISSOURI. I just bought a sheet of Missouri postage stamps as a souvenir.
"SPYROS SKOURAS was a Greek-American motion picture pioneer and movie executive who was president of the 20TH CENTURY FOX from 1942 to 1962."
"In May 1935 Skouras took the initiative for the merger of FOX STUDIOS with TWENTIETH CENTURY PICTURES. He served as president of the merged company 20TH CENTURY FOX from 1942 to 1962. Skouras oversaw the production of such classics as THE SEVEN YEAR ITCH, THE HUSTLER, THE KING AND I, GENTLEMEN PREFER BLONDES and THE ROBE. He signed a young model named Norma Jean Baker, MARILYN MONROE, who rose to fame as the most famous Hollywood sex symbol of the 20th century. Monroe, who never knew her father, developed a special relationship with Skouras, and sometimes called him "Papa Skouras"." Wikipedia
"During Skouras' tenure, the longest in the company history, he worked to RESCUE THE FALTERING MOVIE INDUSTRY from the LURE OF TELEVISION. Movies are better than ever,

gained credibility in 1953 when Spyros introduced CINEMASCOPE in the studio's groundbreaking feature film THE ROBE. The wide screen CinemaScope increased the appeal of movies, helping them maintain audiences against television. This new technology soon became the standard of the industry." Wikipedia

"Cost overruns on such films as CLEOPATRA (1963) resulted in a shareholder revolt demanding a change in management DARRYL F. ZANUCK was elected president of the company while Skouras served as chairman of the company for several years."

"His son Plato produced five films, including FRANCIS OF ASSISI (1961)."

"HIGHEST GROSSING FILMS—The ACADEMY FILM ARCHIVES houses the 20TH CENTURY FEATURES COLLECTION which contains features, trailers, and production elements mostly from the FOX, TWENTIETH CENTURY, and TWENTIETH CENTURY-FOX studios, from the late 1920s-1950s." Box Office Mojo July 8, 2016   N. America NA

1 AVATAR —2009—$760,507,625 NA— $2,789,679,794 World Wide

2 TITANIC —1997—$659,363,944 NA— $2,187,463,944 World Wide

3 STAR WARS: EPISODE 1 — THE PHANTOM MENACE—1999—$474,544,677 NA
      $1,027,044,677 World Wide

22 BOHEMIAN RHAPSODY—2018— $216,428,042—NA #4 $903,655,259 World Wide

25 ICE AGE: DAWN OF THE DINOSAURS —2009—$196,573,705 NA
      #5 $886,686,817 World Wide

4 STAR WARS—1977—$460,998,007 NA— #11 $775,398,007 World Wide

5 STAR WARS: EPISODE III — REVENGE OF THE SITH—2005—$380,270,577— NA

6 DEADPOOL—2016— $363,070,709 NA —#10 $783,112,979 World Wide

7 DEADPOOL 2—2018—$324,535,803 NA—#9 $785,046,920 World Wide

8 STAR WARS: EPISODE II — ATTACK OF THE CLONES — 2002 $310,676,740 NA
      #15 $649, 398, 328 World Wide

9   RETURN OFTHE JEDI—1983—$309,306,177 North America

10 INDEPENDENCE DAY — 1996— $306,169,268 NA—#8 $817,400,891 World Wide

11 THE EMPIRE STRIKES BACK —1980— $290,475,067 NA—#22 $547,969,004 WW

12 HOME ALONE — 1990— $285,761,243 NA

13 NIGHT AT THE MUSEUM— 2006 $250,863,268 NA —#21 $574,480,841 Worldwide

15 X-MEN: DAYS OF FUTURE PAST —2014— $233,921,534 NA #12 $747,862,775 W

17 THE MARTIAN —2015— $228,433,663 NA —#16 $630,161,890 World Wide

18 LOGAN —2017— $226,277,068 NA #18 $616,225,934 World Wide

19 LIFE OF PIE — 2012 — $609,016,565 World Wide

24 DAWN OF THE PLANET OF THE APES—2014 $208,545,589 NA #13 $710,644,566

23 THE DAY AFTER TOMORROW —2004— $544,272,402 World Wide

These 20TH CENTURY FOX films have netted trillions of dollars especially worldwide equal to the American National Debt of $26,000,000,000 + trillion. In 1963, the Fox studios almost closed because of the over budgeted CLEOPATRA which was a box office failure. It was the last cast of thousands film not using computer CGI technology.

HOLLYwOOD TRIVIA: JOE MANUCHIN, Secretary of the Treasury is a mega producer.

WHERE ARE HOLLYWOOD'S FILMS?

The PACKARD CAMPUS storage facility located in Culpeper, Virginia has more than 90 miles [500,000 feet] of shelving beneath MOUNT PONY'S fields and woodland, the library's Packard Campus stores an preserves more than 6,000,000 of the nation's motion pictures, audio recordings, television programs, plus manuscripts, posters and screenplays. Its 124 vaults safely store highly combustible nitrate films [pre 1950] from HOLLYWOOD'S GOLDEN ERA.

Philanthropist David Woodley Packard, son of the co-founder of Hewlett-Packard, and his Packard Humanities Institute acquired the property and converted the FEDERAL RESERVE'S catastrophe bunker into temperature-controlled storage for many of the nation's movie and sound treasures. In 2007, after 10 years of intensive effort, the institute donated the complex to the LIBRARY OF CONGRESS. At $160,000,000, its project was the largest ever private gift to the country's legislative branch, and the second largest to the federal government after the SMITHSONIAN INSTITUTION.

CULPEPER'S PACKARD CAMPUS STARS IN 1992 FILM

Culpeper Star-Exponent Clint Schemmer Thursday March 5, 2020

I was surprised to find an almost full 215-seat Packard theater filled motivated by this newspaper article. The theater is free but has been "sold out" when a major film shows. I have seen about 20 films there: DR. ZHIVAGO, LOVE STORY, MEMPHIS BELLE, GOOD MORNING VIETNAM, BATTLEGROUND, THE BATTLE OF THE BULGE, THE BIG RED ONE, MRS. DOUBTFIRE, HACKERS, ALICE'S RESTAURANT, CHARADE silent films GREAT TRAIN ROBBERY, HULA, and SPARTACUS on March 7, 2020.

The headline film was the 1992 film SNEAKERS about hackers who steal an encryption device which can decipher the passwords of top secret computer systems allowing access to view or steal data. A spokes lady discussed the plot and how where the audience was seated was part of the plot. She said, "You are allowed to applaud during that scene." We did. The first hacking attempt is the Federal Reserve secure site which closed four months before the film premiered on September 11, 1992. The film was shown on Mar. 6, 2020, which was also "DISCONNECT ELECTRONIC DEVICE DAY".

The Culpeper newspaper reveals the background for the film. "Larry Smith, a nitrate film specialist at the center, was reviewing director Phil Robinson's "FIELD OF DREAMS" filmology and learned that his film "Sneakers" had woven into its plot the place he worked. "My jaws dropped when I heard the actors in 'Sneakers' mention not only Culpeper, but the Federal Reserve bank located inside Mount Pony," he recalled in an interview this week."

"That super-secure U.S. government facility a relic of the nation's COLD WAR with the Soviet Union, formed the nucleus of library's Packard Campus. Smith scarcely expected to hear it or Culpeper referenced in a mass-market movie."

"But the ROBERT REDFORD film not only notes Culpeper but the very building that the Packard Campus was built around." "For its time, "Sneakers" was an edgy film that foresaw some of privacy, data theft an online security issues that are so much a part of Americans' lives today."

He said, "It has something to do with computer security, politics, a team of former criminals [hackers] trying to do the right things, mistaken identity, the CIA, romance, and a blind sound expert."

"The all-star cast [later Academy Award winners and nominees] includes ROBERT REDFORD, SIDNEY POITIER, BEN KINGSLEY, DAVID STRATHAIRN, DAN AYKROYD, RIVER PHOENIX and MARY MCDONNELL (DANCES WITH WOLVES)."

"What for Smith is when a key scene shows the protagonists—maverick computer and espionage experts who become involved in a government scheme to steal code-breaking technology—

clustered around a computer monitor as they try to break in the Federal Reserve. They need to test the technology's ability to PENETRATE ENCRYPTED PASSWORDS."

"River Phoenix's character, Carl, is asked what is the hardest computer to hack into? Whistler, played by DAVID STRATHAIRN, says: "Give me something impossible to access." Carl answers, "What about this? FEDERAL RESERVE transfer node, Culpeper, Virginia.' Mother, DAN AYKROYD's character, replies, "Yeah, sure good luck." Carl adds, "900 billion a day go through there." They broke the password and access it.

FEDERAL RESERVE BANK REPOSITORY CULPEPER

"Between Dec. 10,1969, and July 1982, the Federal Reserve's radiation hardened, 145,000 square-foot building housed four computers through which it processed the majority of the 5,700 U.S. banks' transmissions. The steel-and-concrete structure, buried in the side of Mount Pony, held about $4,000,000,000 in cash and could serve as a self-contained bunker to shelter important federal officials in case of nuclear war."

"The Mount Pony site was part of an extensive network of facilities that Uncle Sam built during the Cold War to provide "continuity of government" in case an atomic strike decapitated the government in Washington, D.C. These cash reserves and computers could be used to keep business transactions going on throughout the eastern half of the United States in the event that Washington was bombed in a nuclear war, making cash there radioactive and unusable," Smith said." "The idea was that Culpeper's cash reserve would be used to restore banking after a nuclear calamity. The Federal Reserve's building was decommissioned in June 1992, just months before "Sneakers" opened in September 1992. In 1997, Congress transferred the former Federal Reserve property to the library."

SMALL WORLD STORY: Actor CHRISTOPHER REEVE had his tragic horse accident at the Commonwealth Equestrian Center steeplechase meet about two miles away.

MY DAD, KING KONG, HITLER and MERYL STREEP

How can there possibly be a connection between these four?

KING KONG has had four Hollywood films three ending with Kong's death falling off the EMPIRE STATE Building. In 1949, I was six years old and my father was hired by ABC TV, Channel 7 Seven in New York City. ABC was a new television station along with CBS, Channel 2; NBC, Channel 4; DUMONT, Channel 5. I remember watching my father on the very top of the Empire State building tower installing the new TV antenna to connect ABC to the public. The Internet tells about these TV connections.

He had told me as a child, 14, his mother took him to see the movie KING KONG (1933) at America's largest movie theater RADIO CITY MUSIC HALL. He said it was a scary film which it was at the time even though he knew it was fictional because he lived in Amityville, about 30 miles away and the theater was a few blocks away from the film location. He said he had a teenage crush on Canadian born actress FAY WRAY. She had previously done scary damsel-in-distress B films and became an early "scream queen". At the end of the film at Kong's deceased body the police officer says 'the airplanes, biplanes, got him." The promoter disagrees proclaiming:

"BEAUTY KILLED THE BEAST!"

HOLLYWOOD FACT: MARLENE DIETRICH entrained American troops on the frontline.

Adolf Hitler is known to have been an avid movie fan of German, blonde LENI REIFENSTAHL and MARLENE DIETRICH who were popular film heroines and singer, and American films especially WALT DISNEY, German American, cartoons. It is alleged King Kong was one of Hitler's favorite films. Why? Fay Wray was a beautiful blonde in a black and white film. She in 1933, was an example of Hitler's ARYAN (Nordic) blonde woman which he wanted propagated through his secret LEBENSBORN blonde parenthood and children program for his German Master Race. My 19 year old, waist length platinum blonde haired mother left Hitler's Germany in January 1935, 6 month tourist visa, and was illegal for five years until she married my father in his hometown Amityville, Long Island in August 1940. My mother's Frankfurt high school girl friend Gertie went to England in 1938. In June 1973, she told me my mother's boyfriend Guenther told my Lutheran mother Elisabeth Frank to leave Germany. Guenther warned: "Elisabeth for God's sake leave Germany before it is too late! The Nazis have a new secret program called Lebensborn to have blonde German girls have blond Aryan babies for the Third Reich."
She recalled, "Guenther was a wonderful young chap, I wonder what became of him. He was an SS lieutenant." Guenther is my godfather, he made me an American.
So what is MERYL STREEP's connection? Meryl Streep began her acting career in OFF BROADWAY plays.
According to Wikipedia; "Although Streep had not aspired to become a film actor. ROBERT DE NIRO'S performance in TAXI DRIVER (1976) had a profound impact on her; she said to herself, "That's the kind of actor I want to be when I grow up." Streep began auditioning for film roles, and underwent an unsuccessful audition for the lead role in DINO DE LAURENTIIS's KING KONG (1976). Laurentiis, referring to Streep as she stood before him said in Italian to his son:

"This is so ugly. Why did you bring me this?"

Unknown to Laurentiis, Streep understood Italian, and she remarked,
"I'm very sorry that I'm not as beautiful as I should be, but you know —
this is it. This is what you get."

Wikipedia continues: "ROBERT DE NIRO spotted Streep in her stage production of the CHERRY ORCHARD suggested that she play his girl friend in the [Vietnam] war film THE DEER HUNTER (1978). PAULINE KAEL, who would later become a strong critic of Streep, remarked that she was a "REAL BEAUTY" who brought much freshness to the film with her performance. The film's success exposed Streep to a wider audience and earned her a nomination for the Academy Award for Best Supporting actress. Was director De Laurentiis a mysoginist bully? Kael, a woman film critic. called Streep a real beauty. New actress JESSICA LANGE was selected making her film debut as the damsel-in-distress in KING KONG. Her husband was SAM SHEPHARD best known for his portrayal of CHUCK YAEGER in THE RIGHT STUFF (1983).They live in Charlottesville, Virginia. PATTY JENKINS, director of WONDER WOMAN (2017) wanted to produce a film on Yaeger. Her father was a jet fighter pilot awarded a Silver Star NAM
Pauline Kael in her film review wrote "She [Lange] has a facial structure that the camera yearns for, and she has talent, too." A director has to have an "eye" for the cast which will project to the public on the big screen."
MOTHER'S PERSONAL CONNECTION: Meryl Streep looks more like my mother than any Hollywood actress. My mother had the blonde hair and the long "Roman" nose like Meryl Streep. Streep's grandparents were from the northern Black Forest and central Switzerland, Germanic like my Frankfurt born mother. Mom passed in 1967, before any Meryl Streep films. My mother was a movie fan and would have loved Streep's films.

Wikipedia says, "In 1978 TV miniseries HOLOCAUST, Streep played a leading role of a German woman married to a Jewish artist in Nazi era Germany. An estimated audience of 109,000,000, Holocaust brought a wider degree of public recognition to Streep, who found herself "on the verge of national visibility". She won the Primetime Emmy Award for Outstanding Lead Actress in a Miniseries or Movie for her performance,

In 1982, Streep starred in SOPHIE"S CHOICE portraying a Polish survivor of Auschwitz. Wikipedia says, "WILLIAM STYRON wrote the novel with [Swiss actress] URSULA ANDRESS in mind for the role of Sophie, but Streep was determined to get the role of Sophie. Streep filmed the "choice" scene in one take and refused to do it again, finding it extremely painful and emotionally exhausting. That scene, in which Streep is ordered by an SS [officer] guard at Auschwitz [railcar] to choose which of her two children would be separated from her. She selects her daughter to be sent away not her son? Steep won the Academy Award for Best Actress for her performance.

PERSONAL HOLLYWOOD HISTORY FACT: Suzanne Dassel's father was a German/Russian artist who painted famous movie billboards for German artists including LENI REIFENSTAHL, who he meet. I meet him when he was in his 80s. During the war he was forced to paint propaganda posters. He made a famous GONE WITH THE WIND poster. He lived in the area where my grandfather was born near his hamlet named Dassel in northeast HESSE district near my grandfather's cemetery.

MY SIX DEGREES OF SEPARATION CONNECTION

The SIX DEGREES OF SEPARATION refers to the "game" of connecting Hollywood actors who were in the many KEVIN BACON films. I searched the Internet and learned that this began during a TV Kevin Bacon marathon of his films FOOTLOOSE, ABOVE THE TOP and many others. It was during a snowstorm at ALBRIGHT COLLEGE in Reading, Pennsylvania, when three college students decided to make it a game. It became popular and TV personality JOHN STEWART featured the students on his show with KEVIN BACON making it viral across the United States and worldwide.

My manager lady's grandfather taught at Albright College. Professor FELIX GINGRICH compiled the GREEK-ENGLISH dictionary. My Lutheran MO Synod pastor has a copy.

Dealing with Pride: In Life and in D.C.

Capitol Ministries founder-president Ralph Drollinger May 1, 2018
"Some view PRIDE as a VIRTUE, but SCRIPTURE IS CLEAR that the BELIEVER is to DETEST IT. Charles Bridges states in his excellent commentary on Proverbs, "On no point is the mind of God more fully declared than AGAINST PRIDE. Unfortunately, in our increasingly backward culture, pride is often valued as a prized commodity.

"The Apostle PAUL heralds in stark contrast to self-importance. "I HAVE BEEN CRUCIFIED WITH CHRIST, AND IT IS NO LONGER I WHO LIVE..." (Galatians 2:20). The biblical orientation of one's thought life more than suggests that we get our minds off of ourselves and focus instead on the One who saved us! Biblical thinking at this point — this mental exercise of exchange — is the only way to truly and completely mortify personal PRIDE."

"The acceptance of pride in our culture is so prevalent that some will argue with what I've said. Allow me to illustrate its prevalence."

FRANK SINATRA AND WHITNEY HOUSTON HIT SONGS

"Frank Sinatra sang, "I DID IT MY WAY" and Whitney Houston popularized "THE GREATEST LOVE OF ALL…is LEARNING to LOVE YOURSELF." Both made millions from the sale of such albums. "Taking pride in one's work" is a commonly held axiom."

IN ESSENCE, PRIDE IS THE REBEL THAT DOES BATTLE AGAINST
GOD'S DOMINION.

REALIZE WHAT IS GOOD IS FROM GOD

"Isaiah 64:6 is a sobering passage for anyone who thinks he is self made."
.   SUMMARY
"Similar to what Jesus said in the Gospel of Luke (18:14), James 4:10 exclaims a great takeaway promise worthy of memorization, HUMBLE YOURSELVES IN THE PRESENCE OF THE LORD, AND HE WILL EXALT YOU. Be careful to always deflect praise to HIS GLORY, and remember: GOD WILL NOT SHARE HIS GLORY WITH ANYONE, SO BE CAREFUL NOT TO COMPETE!"

MAN AS SINNER—THE SIN OF PRIDE—REINHOLD NIEBUHR

"THE NATURE AND DESTINY OF MAN —A CHRISTIAN INTERPRETATION" 1941

"The will-to-power is thus an expression of insecurity even when it has achieved ends which, from the perspective of an ordinary mortal, would seem to guarantee complete security. The fact that human ambitions know no limits must therefore be attributed to the infinite capacities of the human imagination but to an uneasy recognition of man's finiteness, weakness and dependence, which become the more apparent the more we seek to obscure them, and which generate ultimate perils, the more immediate insecurities are eliminated. Thus man seeks to MAKE HIMSELF GOD because he is betrayed by both his greatness and his weakness; and there is no level of greatness and power in which the lash of fear is not at least one strand in the whip of ambition."
"The intellectual pride of man is of course a more spiritual sublimation of his PRIDE OF POWER. Sometimes it is so deeply involved in the more brutal and obvious pride of power that the two cannot be distinguished. Every ruling oligarchy of history has found ideological pretensions as important a bulwark of authority as its police power. But intellectual pride is confined neither to the political oligarchs nor to the savants of society. All human knowledge is tainted with an "ideological" taint. It pretends to be more true than it is. It is finite knowledge, gained from a particular perspective; but it pretends to be final and ultimate knowledge. Exactly analogous to the cruder pride of power, the pride of intellect is derived on the one hand from ignorance of the finiteness of the human mind and on the other hand from an attempt to obscure the known conditioned character of human knowledge and the taint of self-interest in human truth."   p 194-5
"INTELLECTUAL PRIDE is thus the PRIDE OF REASON which forgets that it is involved in a temporal process and imagines itself in complete transcendence over history." It is this appearance of independent history of state constitutions, systems law, of ideologies in every special field which above all has blinded so many people," declares FRIEDERICH ENGELS. [Toward an Understanding of Karl Marx, Sidney Hook, p 341]   p 195

"Despite the tremendous contribution of MARXIST thought in the discovery of the ideological taint in all culture, it is precisely the element of pretense which it fails to understand. It is too simple a theory of human consciousness betrays it here. Thus ENGLES declares: "The real driving force which moves it [ideology] remains unconscious otherwise it would not be an ideological process," Ibid p 341 But the real fact is that all pretensions of final knowledge and ultimate truth are partly prompted by the uneasy feeling that the truth is not final and also by an uneasy conscience which realizes that the interests of the ego are confounded with this truth."   p 195-6

"A particular significant aspect of INTELLECTUAL PRIDE is the inability of the agent to recognize the same or similar limitations of perspective in himself which he has detected in others. The MARXIST detection of ideological taint in the thought of all bourgeois culture is significantly unembarrassed by any scruples about the conditioned character of its own viewpoints. "SOCIALIST THOUGHT," declares Karl Mannheim, "which hitherto has unmasked all its adversaries' utopias as ideologies, never raised the problem of determinateness about its own position. It never applied this method to itself and checked its own desire to be absolute." [IDEOLOGY AND UTOPIA, p 225] The fanaticism which springs from this blindness becomes particularly tragic and revealing when it is expressed in conflict between various schools of Marxist thought as for instance the STALINISTS and TROTSKYITES. Each is forced to prove and to believe that the opponent is really a covert capitalist or Fascist, since ideological taint in genuine proletarian thought is inconceivable." Ibid p 196-7

"The PROUD achievement of MARXISM in discovering the intellectual pride and pretension of previous cultures therefore ends in a pitiful display of the same sin. It is no inkling of the truth of the Pauline observation: "For wherein thou judgest another, then condemnest thyself; for thou that judgest doest the same things" (Romans 2:1)."   p 197

"The MARXIST PRIDE may, as in other instances of similar pride, be regarded as merely the fruit of the ignorance of ignorance. The Marxist has mistakenly confined ideological taint to economic life and therefore erroneously hopes for a universal rational perspective when economic privileges would be equalized. But one has the right to suspect that something more than ignorance is involved. The vehemence with which the foe is accused of errors of which the self regards itself free betrays the usual desperation with which the self seeks to hide the finiteness and determinateness of its own position from itself.There is in short no manifestation of intellectual pride in which the temptations of both human freedom and human insecurity are not apparent." p 197

"The explicit character of pride is fully revealed in all cases in which the universalistic note in human knowledge becomes the basis of an imperial desire for domination over life which does not conform to it. The modern religious nationalist thus declares in one moment that his culture is not an export article but is valid for his nation only. In the next moment he declares that he will SAVE the world by destroying inferior forms of culture."

"Moral pride is the pretense of finite man that his highly conditioned virtue is the final righteousness and that his very relative moral standards are absolute. Moral pride thus makes virtue the very vehicle of sin, a fact which explains why the New Testament is so critical of the righteous in comparison with "publicans and sinners." This note in the Bible distinguishes Biblical moral theory from all simple moralism, including Christian moralism. It is the meaning of Jesus' struggle with the pharisees, of ST. Paul's insistence that MAN IS SAVED "NOT BY WORKS LEST ANY MAN SHOULD BOAST," in fact of the whole Pauline polemic against the "righteousness of works"; and it is the primary issue in the PROTESTANT REFORMATION. Luther rightly insisted that the unwillingness of the sinner to be regarded as a sinner was the final form of sin." p 199

"The final proof that man no longer knows God is that he does not know his own sin. The sinner who justifies himself does not know God as judge and does not need God as Savior. One might add that the sin of self-righteousness is not only the final sin in the subjective sense but also in the objective sense. It involves us in the greatest guilt. It is responsible for our most serious cruelties, injustices and defamations against our fellowman. The whole history of RACIAL, NATIONAL, RELIGIOUS and other social struggles is a commentary on the objective wickedness and social miseries which result from SELF-RIGHTEOUSNESS." Ibid p 200

"Christianity rightly regards itself as a religion, not so much of man's search for God, in the process of which he may make himself God; but as a religion of REVELATION in which a Holy loving God is revealed to man as the source and end of all finite existence against whom the SELF-WILL of man is shattered and his pride is abased." Ibid p 201

"But as soon as the PROTESTANT ASSUMES that his more prophetic statement and interpretation of the Christian Gospel guarantees him a superior virtue, he is also lost in the sin of self-righteousness. The fact is that Protestant doctrine of the priesthood of all believers may result in an individual SELF-DEIFICATION against which Catholic doctrine has more adequate checks." Ibid p 202

"Religion, by whatever name, is the inevitable fruit of the spiritual stature of man; and R and RELIGIOUS INTOLERANCE and PRIDE is the final expression of sinfulness. A religion of revelation is grounded in the faith that God speaks to man from beyond the highest pinnacle of the human spirit; and that this voice of God will discover man's highest not only to be short of the highest but involved in the dishonesty of claiming that it is the highest." Ibid p 203

"Prophetic religion had its very inception in a conflict with NATIONAL SELF-DEIFICATION. Beginning with AMOS, all the great Hebrew prophets challenged the simple identification between God and the nation, or the naive confidence of the nation in its exclusive relation to God. The prophets prophesied in the name of a Holy GOD who spoke judgment upon the nation; and the basic sin against which this judgment was directed was the sin of claiming that Israel and God were one or that God was the exclusive possession of Israel." (Amos 7:16,17)

"Judgment would overtake not only Israel but every nation, including the great nations who were also equally guilty of exalting themselves beyond measure." (Is. 47; Jer, 25:15; Ez. 24-39). Ibid p 214

"This genius of prophetic faith enables AUGUSTINE in the Christian era to view the destruction of the Roman Empire without despair to answer the CHARGE THAT CHRISTIANITY WAS RESPONSIBLE FOR ITS DOWNFALL with the assertion that, on the contrary, destruction is the very law of the life of the "city of this world" and that PRIDE IS THE CAUSE OF ITS DESTRUCTION." Ibid p 215

"The prophetic insight of Augustine was partially obscured by his identification, however qualified, of the city of God with the historic church, an identification which was later to be stripped of all its Augustinian reservations to become the instrument of the spiritual pride of a universal church in its conflict with the political pride of an Empire."

"The fact that human pride insinuated itself into the struggle of the Christian religion.

"Against the pride of men can avail itself of the very instruments intended to mitigate it. The church, as well as the state, can become the vehicle of collective egotism."

"EVERY TRUTH CAN BE MADE THE SERVANT OF SINFUL ARROGANCE, including the PROPHETIC TRUTH THAT ALL MEN FALL SHORT of the TRUTH." Ibid p 217

GERMAN SOCIALISTS REGARDED CHRISTIAN FAITH INCOMPATIBLE

"The most demonic form of nationalism today is expressed rather than in a Christian culture. The GERMAN NAZIS were quite right in regarding the Christian faith as incompatible with their national egoism. While Christianity may itself be made the tool of Nationalism, the Christian faith, if it retains any vitality, is bound to mediate some word of divine judgment upon the nation, which the Nazis find intolerable. No nation is free of the sin of pride, just as no individual is free of it.

Nevertheless it is important to recognize that there are "Christian" nations, who prove to be Christian because they are still receptive to prophetic words of judgment spoken against the nation. It may be that only a prophetic minority feels this judgment keenly. But there is a genuine difference between nations which do not officially destroy the religious-prophetic judgment against the nation and those which do. Here, as in individual life, the final sin is the unwillingness to hear the word of judgment spoken against our sin."   Ibid p 219

"CAPITALISTS ARE NOT GREATER SINNERS than poor laborers by any natural depravity. But it is a fact those who HOLD GREAT ECONOMIC AND POLITICAL POWER ARE MORE GUILTY OF PRIDE AGAINST GOD AND OF INJUSTICE AGAINST THE WEAK THAN THOSE WHO LACK POWER AND PRESTIGE." p 225

THE NATURE AND DESTINY OF MAN—A CHRISTIAN INTERPRETATION, Vol. I. HUMAN NATURE — REINHOLD NIEBUHR— GIFFORD LECTURES, Edinburg University, Scotland; Charles Scribner's Sons, New York Copyright 1941

(To my wife Ursula who helped, and To my children Christopher and Elisabeth who frequently interrupted in the writing these pages) Christopher told me he wanted to play.

The Sermon You Will Not Hear?

PERTINENT LESSONS FROM THE BOOK OF JOB

Ralph Drollinger president founder Capitol Ministries Feb. 26, 2019
"There are certainly occasions while serving in public office that your world falls apart whether by the orchestration of Satan or not. When that happens, Job stands as an example to us of the way we should respond — with an inalterable and unshakable confidence in the God of the Bible who has revealed Himself to us and mankind. Like Job, will we stand on the promises of God during these times? Absent personnel abilities or resources of our own, will we hold steady as God leads us through insurmountable hurdles that only HE can provide the solutions to or deliver us from? On a much larger scale, can the truth of the book of Job — God's removal of HIS restraining GRACE — be possible on a national level as well? As evidenced by the almost daily tumultuous events in America. I think so."
Like Job, God calls us to FAITHFULNESS, both personally and professionally, no matter what crisis we may be encountering. May Job encourage you this week to stand firm and be rock-solid in your perseverance through the myriad of present national difficulties!"   Pastor Drollinger

YOUR NAME'S MEANING

"As with many OT books the title is derived from the chief character of its narrative. The Hebrew word JOB means "PERSECUTION". Most appropriate."
                    "(Be careful what you name your children!)"
"The book states that Job never knew of the drama unfolding in Heaven; it follows then, that he could not have been the author. The leading candidate for authoring is SOLOMON. Although Job lived at a different time. Solomon could have written about Job, just as MOSES wrote about ADAM

and EVE, with divine enablement. The style of writing is reminiscent of Solomon's book of Ecclesiastes.

BACKGROUND

"SATAN, an angel who, when tempted, had himself fallen not long before the account here to Job had tempted Adam and Eve, who as a result, feel as well. This is an important perspective. After the flood, God, in a sense, is starting over. Satan, perhaps feeling flush with victory, thought he could tempt and defeat one of God's most faithful individuals (1:1) in the beginning of the start over. Perhaps Satan thought the defeat of Job was as strategic a victory as the defeat of Adam and Eve, it makes parallel sense. Accordingly, the book of Job begins with the overall insight to the reader (1:6-2:10). Satan, ever the accuser, asserts to God that Job is only faithful because of God's blessings, and so God allows Satan to test Job. In the end, Job illustrates the power and perseverance of true saving faith.

"Why do you TRUST IN GOD? Why do you serve Him? Is it because of the benefits? Job's faith was tested and all such thinking was forever removed. His only reason for belief was pure: He believed because of the attribution of God — who He is. God is deserving of worship, adoration and respect, if for no other reason, because He is one's creator. If He is who is revealed in Scripture then ultimately it matters not what He may or may not do for those He created. That is a huge message of the book.

Another main theme relates to suffering. Even when one cannot figure our personal plight, one need never trust in the sovereign integrity of Holy God."

PRESENTED WITH THE MYSTERY OF SUFFERING, INTIMACY WITH GOD SOON BECOMES THE ONLY SALVE

"And in that light, suffering always makes perfect sense. Why? Because God declares communion, now and for eternity. As FRANCIS SCHAEFFER has insightfully noted, the very fact that God is Triune in His being serves to inform of His want for fellowship and close proximity, the suffering of the saint fulfills those objectives. If sometimes the reason for suffering is unknown, and accomplished by personal innocence, think of God's desire to commune throughout it.

THE CREATED ARE SOMETIMES IGNORANT PAWNS IN A HEAVENLY CHESS MATCH

"Scripture also teaches that there are other purposes for suffering and any study would be incomplete and imbalanced without mention of them. Suffering can also relate to humanly knowable reasons. A brief description of each of these follows:

SUFFERING FOR STRENGTHENING

"In 2 Corinthians 12:7-10 the Apostle Paul states why God allowed a "thorn in (his) flesh." Unlike Job, he knew exactly why he suffered per verse 10:

Therefore I am well content with weaknesses, with insults, with distresses, with persecutions with difficulties, for Christ's sake, for when I am weak, when I am strong.

God intended continual suffering in Paul's life for the purposes of keeping him dependent on Him in contrast to "exciting myself" (12:7), God's strength, states this message, is perfected in one's weakness (12:9).

TRUST BEFORE REASONING

"Job three friends tried their best to explain what was happening to Job, but in the end, their theology was rebuked by God (42:7). Perhaps this is why the book is so long the length serves to illustrate, express, and then dismiss the futility of their reasoning."

The greatest and most profound lesson of the book is that one need trust in God over and above one's limited, finite and fallen personal reasoning. Job hugely underscores the necessity of this kind of mindset in this life. Born from such is humility and subsequent God given strength: "God is opposed to the proud, but gives grace to the humble" (James 4:6)

HEAVENLY MATTERS AFFECT EARTHLY LIVES

"Satan sought from God the right to test Job (1:9-12) — just as he asked permission of God to "sift Peter like wheat" (Luke 22:31), Again, Job knew nothing about this heavenly matter. One's adversity in this world could relate to unknowable heavenly matters.

Even though Job was blessed in the end, God never informed him about the heavenly matters behind the scene. In a similar sense, the reasons why injustice and evil might befall a righteous governing authority may never be known in this life; Job says that's okay: Don't necessarily expect them to be.

THE RIGHTEOUS SUFFER

James 1:2-5 is a good principled NT distillation of the overall narrative of Job:

GOD MIGHT NOT UNVEIL THE REASONS FOR SUFFERING, BUT HE PROMISES
TO GIVE WISDOM IN SUFFERING

As a governing authority, view righteous suffering as a good thing. It is God's means of achieving a more intimate relationship with Jesus. What could be of greater value?

DON'T JUDGE SPIRITUALITY IN RELATION TO SUFFERING

"Since bad things happen to good people all the time, one need always refrain from judging another's spirituality based on their gainful circumstances (cf. Matthew 7:1-2). Don't be like Job's buddies. Job had neither material wealth nor physical health during his time of intense trial — yet the remained throughout a very godly man."

GOD IS FAITHFUL AND BLESSES THE RIGHTEOUS

"Suffering may be intense, but for those chosen of God (cf. John 15:15), it always ultimately ends in blessing, if not in this life, in the heaven lies. Stated in James 1:12 and echoed in the last chapter of Job (42:10) are these marvelous attentions in the faithfulness and blessings of God Almighty.

Blessed is a man who perseveres under trial for once he has been approved, he will receive the crown of life which the Lord has promised to those who love him.

The Lord restored the fortunes of Job when he prayed for his friends, and the Lord increased all that Job had two fold.

SUMMARY

"If one's suffering is not explainable via strengthening comforting, or sinning, the book of Job affords much insight into how the believer should deal with suffering when at a loss for explanations. Here is how he or she should think and react."

SUFFERING

"My spirit is broken; my days are extinct; the graveyard is ready for me." Job 17:1
Also read Job 17 + Psalm 25

"The name of JOB is synonymous with "suffering." God allows Satan to attack Job and take away everything important to him. Job has some friends who give him bad counsel. They try to find a reason behind Job's suffering. Surely, it is a result of this or that SIN of Job's PAST, for which God is now punishing him, they say.

Much of the Book of Job is God speaking with Job to humble him. In effect, God tells Job that He alone if and has the answers. Job shouldn't try to pry into God's hidden Will and find answers to questions that God hasn't answered. With Job, we learn to acknowledge that we can't always answer the why of our suffering—the reason for it often remains hidden with God.

But we do learn something positive from Job, In his suffering, Job takes comfort in his redeemer: "I know that my Redeemer lives, and at the last He will stand upon the Earth: (Job 19:25). While much of God's will for him is hidden, Job believes that God loves him. Job learned this from the sacrifices. Through the blood, God redeems him."

"The same is true for us. When you are suffering, run to the part of God's Will that has been revealed to you. You have a redeemer. He loves you and died for you. Though you lose all, you have everything in Him."

"God strengthen me in times of suffering." AMEN
Lutheran Missouri Synod PorTals Prayer Friday,February 22, 2019 Mom born 2-22-1915

Put Off the Evil Culture of Deception

Ralph Drollinger president-founder of Capitol Ministries March 26, 2019

"It is becoming more commonly accepted in our society to shade the truth, sidestep, use qualifying words, narrowly defined meanings, or other devious methods to mask the true meaning of what is being said. We have become a culture that is more and more accepting of, or at least more tolerant and perhaps desensitized to, deception than past generations. It's become part of our norm."

But the Bible takes a strong position against deception. Matthew 5:37 says, "But let your statement be, 'Yes, yes' or 'No, no'; anything beyond these is evil."

"In this week's study, Put Off the Evil Culture of Deception, I would like to investigate, build your awareness of, and stimulate the creation of convictions regarding the evil nature of the deception. Unfortunately, in our culture, deception has become an acceptable practice.

What exactly is DECEPTION? It is the act of causing someone to believe something that is not true, typically in order to gain some personal advantage. It is to intentionally give a mistaken impression. It is viewed, often, as a political necessity.

May I however, proffer an alternative? There is always a better way than lying and deceiving: Be Honest. Read on."

INTRODUCTION

"Lincoln's insistence on honesty and putting away deception is apparent throughout his life. One such illustration comes from Mark Steiner's book an honest calling: The law practice of ABRAHAM LINCOLN. He notes:

"A relative by marriage, Augustus Chapman, recalled: "In his law practice on the Wabash Circuit he was noted for unswerving honesty. People learned to love him ardently, devotedly, and juries listened intently, earnestly, receptively to the sad-faced, earnest man...I remember one case of his decided[ly] honest trait of character. It was a case in which he was for the defendant. [Previously] satisfied of his client's innocence, it depended mainly on one witness. [But] that witness told on the stand under oath what Abe knew to be a lie, and no one else knew. When he arose to plead the case, he said: "Gentlemen, I depended on this witness to clear my client. He has lied. I ask that no attention be paid to his testimony. Let his words be stricken out [even] if [it means] my case fails. I do not wish to win in this way."

"For clever, seasoned public servants the intentional use, omission, or manufacture of misleading impressions comes easily. In stark contrast to the TEMPTATION TO DECEIVE is Proverbs 19:22."

IT IS BETTER TO BE POOR THAN A LIAR.

"Abraham Lincoln modeled the essence of that principle many times in many ways. God's Word has much to say about this subject and the capital community has much to learn in response. Habitual truth-telling needs to be the goal even - and especially — when it costs you something.
"

HOW ARE YOU IN TERMS OF HABITUAL TRUTH-TELLING?

"Is this the habit of your heart and tongue? Are you a card-carrying member of the HONEST ABE society? Never jeopardize your integrity for short-term gain. Let's look to the book of Proverbs, which has much to say about telling the truth. One Proverb from this lesson that you should memorize is 12:19."

"Truthful lips will be established forever, but a lying tongue is only for a moment."

SUMMARY

"Deception is the act of causing someone to believe something that is not true, typically in order to gain some personal advantage. It is to intentionally give a mistaken impression. It is often viewed as a political necessity. But you can see from this study the tremendously deleterious effects deception has on lawmakers, governmental leaders, and the nation's justice system. Don't be a contributor to that cause, deception destroys both individuals and nations."

"It is critically important that public servants completely abandon the manufacturing of mistaken impressions and instead practice honest — the strictest honesty, as practiced by ABRAHAM LINCOLN. So be it."

DECLARATION OF CONSCIENCE

Maine U.S. Senator Margaret Chase Smith
U.S. Senate June 1, 1950

The Declaration of Conscience was a speech made by [Maine Republican] U.S. Senator MARGARET CHASE SMITH on June 1, 1950, less than four months after Senator JOE McCARTHY's "Wheeling Speech," on February 9, 1950. Her speech was endorsed by six other liberal-to-moderate Republicans. In it, she criticized national leadership and called for the country, the United States Senate, and the Republican Party to re-examine the tactics used by the HOUSE UN-AMERICAN ACTIVITIES COMMITTEE (HUAC) and (without naming him) Senator Joe McCarthy. She stated the basic principles of "AMERICANISM" were:

* The right to criticize;
* The right to hold unpopular beliefs;
* The right to protest;
* The right of independent thought.

Smith voiced concern that those who exercised those beliefs at that time risked unfairly being labeled COMMUNIST or FASCIST.
In the Declaration of Conscience, Smith said:

DEMOCRATS COMPLACENT T0 COMMUNIST THREAT

The Democratic administration has greatly lost the confidence of the American people by its complacency to the threat of communism and the leak of vital secrets to Russia through key officials of the Democratic administration. There are enough proved cases to make this point without diluting our criticism with unproved charges.
Surely these are sufficient reasons to make it clear to the American people that it is time for a change and that a Republican victory is necessary to the security of this country. Surely it is clear that this nation will continue to suffer as long as it is governed by the present ineffective Democratic Administration.

Four Horseman of Calumny—Fear, Ignorance, Bigotry and Smear

Yet to displace it with a Republican regime embracing a philosophy that lacks political integrity or intellectual honesty would prove equally disastrous to the nation. The nation sorely needs a Republican victory. But I don't want to see the Republican Party ride to a political victory on the FOUR HORSEMAN OF CALUMNY— FEAR, IGNORANCE, BIGOTRY and SMEAR.

Don't Place Political Party above National Interest

"I doubt if the Republican Party could —simply because I DON'T BELIEVE the American people will uphold any political party that puts POLITICAL EXPLOITATION ABOVE NATIONAL INTEREST."
The other Senators who signed onto the Declaration were WAYNE MORSE of Oregon, GEORGE AIKEN of Vermont, EDWARD THYE of Minnesota, IRVING IVES of New York, CHARLES TOBEY

of New Hampshire, and ROBERT HENDRICKON of New Jersey. While the initial reception was chilly, the full-fledged outbreak of the KOREAN WAR on June 25, 1950 had made it unlikely that Smith's views would prevail.

BERNARD BARUCH proclaimed, "IF A MAN HAD GIVEN THE DECLARATION SPEECH "HE WOULD BE THE NEXT PRESIDENT."

The speech was listed as #41 in American Rhetoric's Top 100 Speeches of the 20th Century (listed by rank).

Senator Joseph McCarthy Censured by U.S. Senate 1954

Although it would be another four years before McCarthy would be censured, THE FACT THAT A WOMAN WAS THE FIRST TO SPEAK OUT IN THE SENATE AGAINST SUCH TACTICS HOLDS SIGNIFICANCE FOR FEMINISTS, HISTORIANS." Wikipedia

A Declaration of Conscience Classic Senate Speech

U. S. Senator Margaret Chase Smith—Republican Maine
"One of the most early challenges to JOSEPH R. McCARTHY's charges of Communists in government was made by MARGARET CHASE SMITH of Maine in her "Declaration of Conscience" speech in June 1950.

In the controversial aftermath of [Wisconsin Senator] Joseph McCarthy's speech at Wheeling, West Virginia, Maine Senator Margaret Chase Smith was initially impressed with McCarthy's accusations about subversives in the State Department. "It looked as if Joe was on to something disturbing and frightening," she decided, refusing to join with those senators taking issue with McCarthy. But then she asked to see the documents he was citing as evidence. Reading through McCarthy's materials, she failed to see their relevance to his charges. The more she read, and the more she listened to McCarthy, the less comfortable she felt. Smith began to question the "validity, accuracy, credibility, and fairness" of his charges and came to believe that McCarthy was CREATING AN ATMOSPHERE OF POLITICAL FEAR IN WASHINGTON, PARTICULARLY AMONG FEDERAL EMPLOYEES.

Smith had succeeded her late husband, Clyde H. Smith, in the House of Representatives in June 1940 and was reelected four times. Then, in 1948, she won election to the Senate. As a freshman, a fellow Republican who considered herself a friend of McCarthy's, and the ONLY WOMAN MEMBER of the Senate at the time, Smith felt reluctant to speak out publicly. However, friends in the media, including the eminent newspaper columnist WALTER LIPPMAN, encouraged her to take a stand, and Senator Smith and her administrative assistant WILLIAM LEWIS began drafting her "Declaration of Conscience." She circulated the draft among a half dozen other liberal Republicans and collected their endorsements. As Smith headed to the Senate chamber on June 1, 1950, they encountered Senator McCarthy at the subway to the Capitol. "MARGARET, YOU LOOK VERY SERIOUS," McCarthy said, "ARE YOU GOING TO MAKE A SPEECH?" "YES, AND YOU WILL NOT LIKE IT!" Smith replied. "Remember Margaret, I control Wisconsin's 27 convention votes!" he rebutted. Smith took this as an unsubtle threat that HE WOULD BLOCK HER CHANCES OF RECEIVING THE REPUBLICAN VICE PRESIDENT NOMINATION IN 1952." [President Eisenhower chose California Senator RICHARD NIXON twice.]

When Smith rose to deliver her fifteen-minute speech in the Senate chamber, McCarthy sat two rows behind her. Smith began her brief remarks by denouncing the fact that some members were turning the Senate into "a FORUM of HATE and CHARACTER ASSASSINATION." She called for a renewal of "THE RIGHT TO INDEPENDENT THOUGHT" and a return to the principles of the Republican party as "the CHAMPION of UNITY and PRUDENCE." Her party should base its opposition to the Democrats on "PROVEN CAUSES" rather than "UNPROVED CHARGES" Smith concluded with a five-point "Declaration of Conscience," in which she was joined by 6 Republican colleagues.

After Smith finished, although she had not mentioned McCarthy by name, she fully expected him to respond. Instead, McCarthy quietly left the chamber. A few senators spoke in praise of her remarks, but for the most part the Senate remained silent, fearing to engage McCarthy in further recriminations. The MAIL, however, showed an 8 to 1 APPROVAL FOR SMITH'S STAND. Newspaper editorials endorsed her position, and numerous organizations awarded her recognition for her courageous stand in favor of civil liberties against the POLITICS OF FEAR."

PRESIDENT TRUMAN PRAISES SENATOR SMITH'S PATRIOTISM

"The next time that [Democrat] President HARRY S TRUMAN came to the Capitol for lunch, he invited [Republican] Margaret Chase Smith to join him. "Mrs. Smith," he told her, "Your DECLARATION OF CONSCIENCE was ONE OF THE FINEST THINGS that has happened here in Washington in ALL MY YEARS in the SENATE and the WHITE HOUSE." [Truman was the best Democrat president a Bible reader who created Israel.]

MCCARTHY saw things differently. He ridiculed Smith and her cosigners as "SNOW WHITE AND THE SEVEN DWARFS." MCCARTHY VIOLATED SENATE CUSTOM TO REMOVE HER AS A MEMBER OF THE PERMANENT SUBCOMMITTEE ON INVESTIGATIONS, and gave her place to the NEW SENATOR from California, RICHARD M. NIXON. McCarthy's allies took every occasion to smear Senator Smith. But in 1954 she had the satisfaction of casting a vote for McCarthy's CENSURE and effectively ENDING HIS CAMPAIGN OF FALSEHOOD AND INTIMIDATION—ending what she had so effectively denounced as a political attempt to ride "THE FOUR HORSEMEN OF CALUMNY—FEAR, IGNORANCE, BIGOTRY and SMEAR."

Reprinted from ROBERT C. BYRD, THE SENATE, 1789-1989: CLASSIC SPEECHES, 1830-1993. Washington, D. C. Government Printing Office, 1994

AFTERWORD: "Four months earlier, McCarthy had ROCKED TO NATIONAL ATTENTION. In a well-publicized speech in Wheeling, West Virginia, he claimed to possess the names of 205 card-carrying communists in the State Department. Smith, like many of her colleagues, shared McCarthy's concerns about communist subversion, but she grew skeptical when he repeatedly ignored her requests for evidence to back-up his accusations. "It was then," she recalled, "that I began to wonder about the validity and fairness of Joseph McCarthy's charges." Wikipedia

FRESHMAN SENATOR MARGARET SMITH NOT "SILENT"

"At first, Smith HESITATED TO SPEAK, "I WAS A FRESHMAN SENATOR," she explained, "AND IN THOSE DAYS, FRESHMAN SENATORS WERE SEEN AND NOT HEARD." She hoped a senior member would take the lead. "This great psychological fear...spread to the Senate." she noted. "where a considerable amount of mental paralysis and muteness set in for fear of offending McCarthy." As the weeks passed, Smith grew increasingly angry with McCarthy's attacks and his defamation of individuals she considered above suspicion. Bowing to Senate rules on comity, Smith chose not to attack McCarthy, but to denounce the tactics that were becoming known as "MCCARTHYISM." "Mr. President," she began, "I would like to speak briefly and simply about a serious national condition…The United States Senate has long enjoyed worldwide respect as the greatest deliberative body…But recently that deliberate character has…been debased to…a forum of hate and character assassination." In her 15-minute address, delivered as McCarthy looked on, Smith endorsed every American's right to criticize, to protest, and to hold unpopular beliefs. "Freedom of speech is not what it used to be in America," she complained. "It has been so abused by some that it is not exercised by others." She asked her fellow Republicans not to ride to political victory on the "Four Horseman of Calumny—Fear, Ignorance, Bigotry, and Smear." Her speech triggered a public explosion of support and criticism. "This cool breeze of honesty from Maine can blow the whole miasma out of the nation's soul," commented the Hartford Courant. "By one act of political courage, [Smith has] justified a lifetime in politics," commented another. Newsweek magazine ran a cover story entitled "Senator Smith: A Women Vice President?" Critics called her "Moscow-loving," and much worse, McCarthy dismissed her and her supporters as "Snow White and the Six Dwarfs."

Smith's Declaration of Conscience did not end McCarthy's reign of power, but she was one of the first senators to take such a stand. She continued to oppose him, at great personal cost, for the next four years. Finally, in December of 1954, the Senate belatedly concurred with the "lady from Maine" and censured McCarthy for conduct "contrary to senatorial traditions." McCarthy's career was over. Margaret Chase Smith's career was just beginning."   Senate Historical Office

PERSONAL NOTE: I thank Kentucky Sen. MITCH MCCONNELL for mentioning Sen. MARGARET SMITH's DECLARATION OF CONSCIENCE on FOX News. I thank Wikipedia and the Internet for this important American historical information. I attended Nasson college in Maine from 1960-1964. In 1960-61 I was a Maine Civil Air Patrol cadet, when Senator Smith was a Lt. Col. in the Maine Air National Guard. Go Air Force.

FAITH AND FREEDOM

Barbara Ward OBE

Circa 1983, while researching Hitler and his Socialist domination of the Church, I found this testimony in Barbara Ward's 1954 book FAITH AND FREEDOM. A "stimulating inquiry into the History and relationship of political freedom and religious faith." John Fischer, editor of "HARPER'S." once said, "Barbara Ward is probably the most brilliant writer on economics and political affairs in all of Europe. Her themes are that FAITH AND FREEDOM are the TWIN PILLARS OF THE WEST, that our free institutions depend on religious Faith, and that the West itself CANNOT SURVIVE unless both these great concepts flourish."

In her Chapter "ECONOMICS OF WELFARE" she makes the following prophetic statements regarding HITLER AND COMMUNISM: "Yet the aberrations of humanity need not, any more than the errors of individual lives, entail pure loss. The warnings are there to be heeded. The lessons can be learned, the challenge is to learn them in such a way that the typical swing of the pendulum of error—from one extreme to its opposite—is avoided; and this, as the whole post-Communist History of the West makes clear, is anything but an easy operation.

NAZISM A BLIND REACTION TO COMMUNISM

"The National Socialist counter-revolution in Germany is the extreme example of the false reaction to Communism. The root of the evil lay, in the first place, in the extent to which NAZISM WAS A BLIND REACTION TO FEAR. If Hitler had not been able to EXPLOIT COMMUNISM AS A THREAT TO EVERYTHING THE WEALTHY, THE PROFESSIONAL PEOPLE, or the SHAKEN MIDDLE CLASSES HOPED TO PRESERVE—their status, their respectability, their property—he could never have used the METHODS OF VIOLENCE, DECEIT, and TOTAL ILLEGALITY TO DEFEAT THE EQUALLY VIOLENT, DECEITFUL, AND UNCONSTITUTIONAL COMMUNIST PARTY organization. Nazi propaganda painted Communist aims and methods in a BESTIAL light to cover its own BESTIALITY. ONLY FEAR COULD HAVE BLINDED DECENT, CONSERVATIVE PEOPLE TO VIOLENCE that was being committed in the name of anti-Communism. And BLIND, IRRATIONAL FEAR APPEARS TO HAVE THE PSYCHOLOGICAL CONSEQUENCE: That it lays panic-stricken men and women open to precisely those terrors they fear the most. Thus Hitler was able to DESTROY LAW ON THE PRETEXT OF SAVING IT, UNDERMINE FREE GOVERNMENT ON THE GROUND THAT HE WAS ITS ONLY SAFEGUARD, BRING ALL PROPERTY UNDER STATE CONTROL with the explanation that he was the CHAMPION OF PRIVATE ENTERPRISE. And finally OPEN THE GATES OF EUROPE TO RUSSIAN COMMUNISM on the excuse that HE ALONE KNEW HOW TO FIGHT IT.

"HITLER'S ARROGANCE OF WESTERN NATIONALISM"

"Barbara Ward continues, "So much for the negative reaction, the positive basis of the Nazi counter-revolution was no less destructive. In order TO FIGHT COMMUNISM, HITLER DREW ON THE ARROGANCE, THE UNLIMITED PRETENSIONS, THE UNBRIDLED ASSERTIVENESS OF WESTERN NATIONALISM. The force, which had already unleashed one appalling war on the world, in Germany had the additional bitterness of remembered defeat. [World War One] In Hitler's hands, it became the instrument of paranoiac unreason. He attempted to base a world system on the alleged innate SUPERIORITY OF A SINGLE RACIAL GROUP. He carried the exclusiveness of nationalism to the pitch of scientifically murdering practically the entire community of European Jewry. He reduced the Slavs in his brief empire to the status of slaves and helots. He worked out in extreme institutional form and with total logic of the lunatic the unlimited pretensions of Western nationalism. In other nations, some modesty, some respect for Law, some lingering sense of a wider worldwide community had put a certain restraint on the arrogance of national sovereignty. In Nazism, each Western people had to see its own worst instincts with the mask down and all restraints thrown off. This is what revolutionary nationalism could look like 'in extremis'. This was the monster of pure violence and pure irrationality that had been growing up in Europe for the last 400 years and now stood revealed, a mystery of nihilism and pure destruction." [Luther 1517-39]

"MCCARTHYISM'S" FEAR AND INTOLERANCE

"Ms Ward asserts, "This frightful experience revealed once and for all the destructive forces concealed within the drives of national arrogance and irrational fear, as in the release of atomic power itself, their conjunction let loose more or less incalculable and unpredictable violence. Nor is there any reason to suppose that the experience, once made, could not be repeated. It is for this reason that many people in Europe, who have lived through the Nazi Revolution at close quarters, observe with what some Americans think is EXAGGERATED ALARM the phenomenon known as "MCCARTHYISM" in the United States. It is not that they deny the RISKS OF COMMUNISM or question for one moment the DANGERS OF THE SOVIET GOVERNMENT'S WORLDWIDE CONSPIRACY. It is not that they equate the deeply rooted American Democracy with the flimsy facade of the WEIMAR REPUBLIC. as they recoil from METHODS which recall ominously those of the NAZI DICTATOR. The exploitation of unreasoning fear and the creation of general distrust on the one hand, the emphasis on nationalist separation on the other, have in them the seeds at least of a type of anti-communism which, in Europe only two decades ago, destroyed law, destroyed government, destroyed all forms of freedom, destroyed enterprise and free trade unions, and opened the way to unlimited war. COMMUNISM MUST BE COUNTERED; but if it is to be countered by the wrong methods, the results are ultimately undistinguishable from Communism itself."

"ALL AMERICA HAS TO FEAR IS FEAR ITSELF"

"Barbara Ward faithfully concludes, "COMMUNISM, in short, WILL NOT BE DEFEATED IF THE WESTERN WORLD TRIES TO COUNTER IT BY FALLING BACK ON THE UNCONTROLLED VITALITIES OF OUR AGE. Unlimited defense of absolute property or unrestrained reliance upon nationalism offer no answer to the Communist challenge—for they are, in fact, the destructive forces which helped to bring Communism into being and would, even without Communism, tear the world apart with social strife and international conflict. Nor will Communist criticism, to reconsider its own basic institutions and, in the face of the false philosophy of Communism, to re-examine its own fundamental beliefs. Communism is at once the cumulative effect of Western errors and the inexorable criticism of them."   FAITH AND FREEDOM Barbara Ward OBE

MCCARTHYISM IN AMERICA TODAY

"Professor Agar recalls, " 'They were wild with passion and frenzy, doing they know not what.' ALEXANDER STEPHENS' words apply to Nazi Germany as well as to the southern mobs of his time and ours. We must force ourselves to understand that they could apply to each one of us tomorrow, the best defense against demagogues is to admit our vulnerability. Each crisis will bring its own demagogues. The press must be left free because it can help us keep an eye on the government, muzzled the press is a catastrophe and can undermine our hope of freedom, furthermore, McCarthyism is a disease from which we cannot wholly protect ourselves. The disease will recur whenever we become slack or frightened. The roots of McCarthyism were, first. the failure of American liberals during the 1930s to preserve the liberal faith."

U.S. REPRESENTATIVE JEANNETTE RANKIN REFUSES TO DECLARE WAR ON JAPAN

"On December 8, 1941, JEANNETTE RANKIN was the ONLY MEMBER of EITHER HOUSE OF CONGRESS to VOTE AGAINST the DECLARATION OF WAR ON JAPAN following the attack on Pearl Harbor. Hisses could be heard in the gallery as she cast her vote; several colleagues, including Rep. (later Senator) EVERETT DIRKSEN, asked her to change it to make the resolution unanimous—or at very least, to abstain—but she refused. "As a woman I can't go to war," she said, "and I refuse to send anyone else."

"After the vote, a crowd of reporters pursued Rankin into a cloak room. There, she was forced to take refuge in a phone booth until Capitol Police arrived to escort her to her office, where she was inundated with angry telegrams and phone calls. One cable from her brother, read, "Montana is 100 percent against you". Rankin remained unapologetic.

"Everyone knew that I was opposed to the war, and they elected me," she said. "I voted as the mothers would have had me vote." Wikipedia

"Two days later, a similar war declaration against Germany and Italy came to a vote; Rankin abstained. Her political career effectively over she did not run for election in 1942. Asked years later if she ever regretted her action, Rankin replied, "Never. If you're against war, you're against war regardless of what happens. It's a wrong method of trying to settle a dispute."

Later Rankin visited India, where she studied the pacifist views of MAHATMA GANDHI."

Jeannette Rankin was a women's rights advocate, and the FIRST WOMAN TO HOLD FEDERAL OFFICE in the United States. She was elected to the U.S. House of Representatives as a Republican from Montana in 1916, and again in 1940. Each of Rankin's Congressional terms coincided with initiation of U.S. military intervention in the two World Wars. A lifelong PACIFIST, she was one of 50 House members who opposed the declaration of war on Germany in 1917."

"Shortly after her term began, Congress was called into an extraordinary April session in response to Germany's declaration of UNRESTRICTED SUBMARINE WARFARE on all Atlantic shipping. On April 2, 1917, President WOODROW WILSON, addressing a joint session, asked Congress to "MAKE THE WORLD SAFE FOR DEMOCRACY" by declaring war on Germany. After intense debate, the war resolution came to a vote in the House at 3:00 am on April 5; Rankin cast one of the 50 votes in opposition. Although 49 male Representatives and 6 Senators also voted against the declaration, Rankin was singled out for criticism. "I wish to stand for my country," she said, "but cannot vote for war." "By 1937, Rankin believed that a SECOND WAR IN EUROPE was UNLIKELY, on the assumption that Germany and Italy would SEEK DIPLOMACY. She opposed Pres. Franklin Roosevelt's attempts to aid the British, and testified before multiple Congressional committees in opposition to a variety of preparedness measures.

"A SUFFRAGIST during the PROGRESSIVE ERA, Rankin while in Congress, introduced legislation that eventually became the 19th Amendment, granting unrestricted voting rights to women nationwide." Wikipedia

Rankin passed on May 18, 1973, in Carmel, California, age 92. My Jewish wife was born May 18, 1948, four days after Israel became a nation. My church Old Testament Bible teacher Phil's wife Betty's birthday is May 18. Judy, my realtor, who sold me my house in April 2005, had also been in Phil's Bible class, her birthday was May 18, two weeks after my May 4, 1943 birthday. Pope St. JOHN PAUL II was born on May 18.

Maine Sen. Susan Collins Clears the Way for
Brett Kavanaugh's Supreme Court Confirmation
October 5, 2018 6:23 PM ET

"I will vote to confirm Judge Kavanaugh," Collins said at the end of a 45-minute speech laying out her argument for supporting the judge. During the speech, she spoke in detail about Kavanaugh's record and explained that she believed he was a qualified justice.

When Collins got to the recent allegations against Kavanaugh, she said that she believed some more than others. While she did not believe allegations that Kavanaugh had been at parties where girls were gang raped, she said she took more seriously the testimony of Christine Blasey Ford, the California psychology professor who accused Kavanaugh of sexually assaulting her when the two were in high school, Collins said she believes that Ford is a survivor of assault, but that there was not enough evidence to convince the Senator that Kavanaugh was involved. A "presumption of innocence and fairness" had to prevail," she said.

MY GRANDFATHER VOTED FOR LINCOLN TWICE

PERSONAL MAINE STORY: My dad's father JOHN LOUDEN was born in Calais, Maine in 1839. He was one of the 50,000 first volunteers in the American Civil War of Secession to preserve the Union. He was a corporal in the 12th Maine Volunteer Regiment under General BENJAMIN BUTLER who occupied New Orleans and Louisiana in May 1862. My grandfather contracted typhoid and malaria from a mosquito. He should have died. He left Ship Island, Mississippi in April 1862, and sailed to Boston where in May he had a relapse and was taken to America's "best" hospital Massachusetts General. He had no pulse and had turned cold. The doctors told a nurse "Take this man to the morgue he is deceased!" On the way to the morgue the nurse saw his toe twitch. "Bells on your toe" and "dead ringer." His second wife from Eastport, Maine, was 38 when my father Alexander Bruce was born on Jan. 28, 1919, in his Louden-Knickerbocker Brunswick hospital in Amityville, New York. The same hospital where actor ALEC BALDWIN, from neighboring Massapequa was born. John Louden was 79 years old when my father was born. He voted for ABRAHAM LINCOLN TWICE! His grave stone says John Louden 1839-1933. Maine magazine article May 1985, headline says he voted Republican all his life. His last election in 1932, would have been for President HERBER HOOVER he was 94. Pres. FRANKLIN D. ROOSEVELT had a home CAMPOBELLO next to Eastport, but is actually in New Brunswick, Canada which is across the Passamaquoddy Bay. Roosevelt was afflicted with POLIO there. Eastport and Calais, Maine are the easternmost part of the United States "DOWN EAST" and gave President Donald Trump one of Maine's three electoral votes.

My grandfather had a 5th Grade "LITTLE RED SCHOOLHOUSE" education. My father's maybe 60 year older brother was a doctor who graduated from JOHNS HOPKINS UNIVERSITY medical college in Baltimore, Maryland. He ran the hospital in the late 1880s which was for alcohol and drug addicts. After the Civil War there was a major opiate laudanum morphine pain-relief addiction because thousands Civil War soldiers had arms and legs amputated to prevent gangrene and blood poisoning.

One TV episode of DR. QUINN MEDICINE WOMAN featured a young man who had an amputated arm and stole morphine from the doctor's medicine cabinet to relieve his excruciating pain. I have been told and seen on TV that Long Island, like all of America, has a drug addiction problem not because of pain but to get "high." It is not Oxycontin, for pain relief, which is more expensive than street heroin! Dr. Quinn was portrayed by British actress JANE SEYMOUR. Seymour was on the REGIS AND KATHIE LEE show. I was amazed when she said her mother was a Dutch citizen who was a Japanese prisoner in World War II in Java, Dutch East Indies, today's Indonesia. My Dutch aunt was also a Japanese prisoner in a work camp in Java. Jane Seymour also said her father was Jewish and Kathie Lee said her father was also Jewish. He was in the U.S. Navy and played saxophone in the Navy band. Kathie Lee Gifford was born in Paris.

My grandfather's hospital in 1880s also advertised it worked with nervous disorders. A NEW YORK TIMES newspaper has a front page article then about a lawsuit by people claiming they were practicing mental health not legal then!

Through GOOGLE I found an article about the hospital's alcohol history. It seems that the great character actor JOHN BARRYMORE received treatment there and passed away in my grandfather's Brunswick hospital. Alcoholism is one of America's major accepted illnesses. Hollywood actors are exposed to alcohol and much more dangerous drugs a hazard of the business.

DREW BARRYMORE when a child actress was exposed to alcohol through her acting environment and her family's alcoholism. She has done many lovely films I enjoyed and have VHS tapes and DVDs of. I pray her need for addictive substances has ended. I read on Internet that she has a film company making family orientated movies in partnership with JIMMY FALLON's wife. God bless them and their children.

PERSONAL NOTE: When I joined the Air Force on Apr. 3, 1965, my enlistment papers misspelled my first name Olive not Clive not a typo. DREW BARRYMORE's first daughter is named Olive and her movie production company is named OLIVE PRODUCTIONS. At LACKLAND AFB I got the clerical error corrected and was sent to the men's barracks which had rooms for four not an open bay. Our barracks was across from the women's barrack. Our TI technical instructor T/Sgt. KEYSER and S/Sgt. ADAMS warned us not to look across at the WAF barracks. We sneaked peeks but the hallway was about a football field distance away. So it Goes.

FBI Director Comey "Exonerates" Secy. of State Hillary Clinton

Statement by FBI Director James B. Comey on the Investigation of Secretary Hillary Clinton's Use of a Personal E-Mail System Washington, D.C. FBI National Press Office July 5, 2016   (Remarks prepared for delivery at press briefing. Patriotic Holiday?)

"Good morning. I'm here to give you an update on the FBI's investigation of Secretary Clinton's use of a personal e-mail system during her time as Secretary of State.

After a tremendous amount of work over the last year, the FBI is completing its investigation and referring the case to the Department of Justice for a prosecutive decision. What I would like to do today is tell you three things: what we did; what we found; and what we are recommending to the Department of Justice.

This will be an unusual statement in at least a couple of ways. First, I am going to include more detail about our process than I ordinarily would, because I think the American people deserve those details in a case of intense public interest. Second, I have not coordinated or reviewed this statement in any way with the Department of Justice or any other part of the government. They do not know what I am about to say.

I want to start thanking the FBI employees who did remarkable work in this case. Once you have a better sense of how we have done, you will understand why I am so grateful and proud of their efforts.

So, first, what we have done:

The investigation began as a referral from the Intelligence Community Inspector General in connection with Secretary Clinton's use of a personal e-mail server during her time as Secretary of State. The referral focused on whether classified information was transmitted on that personal system.

Our investigation looked at whether there is evidence classified information was improperly stored or transmitted on that personal system, in violation of a federal statue making it a felony to mishandle classified information either intentionally or in a grossly negligent way, or a second statute making it a misdemeanor to knowingly remove classified information from appropriate systems or storage facilities.

Consistent with our counterintelligence responsibilities, we have also investigated to determine whether there is evidence of computer intrusion in connection with the personal e-mail server by any foreign power, or other hostile actors.

I have so far used the singular term, "e-mail server," in describing the referral that began our investigation. It turns out to have been more complicated than that. Secretary Clinton used several different servers and administrators of those servers during her four years at the State Department, and used numerous mobile devices to view and send e-mail on that personal domain. As new servers and equipment were employed, older servers were taken out of service, stored, and decommissioned in various ways. Piecing all of that back together—to gain as full an understanding as possible of the ways in which personal e-mail was used for government work—has been a painstaking undertaking, requiring thousands of hours of effort.

For example, when one of Secretary Clinton's original personal servers was decommissioned in 2013, the e-mail software was removed. Doing that didn't remove the e-mail content, but it was like removing the frame from a huge finished jigsaw puzzle and dumping the pieces on the floor. The effect was that millions of e-mail fragments end up unsorted in the server's unused—or "slack"—space. We searched through all of it to see what was there, and what parts of the puzzle could be put back together.

FBI investigators have also read all of the approximately 30,000 e-mails provided by Secretary Clinton to the State Department in December 2014. Where an e-mail was assessed as possibly containing classified information, the FBI referred the e-mail to any U.S. government agency that was likely "owner" of information in the e-mail, so that agency could make a determination as to whether the e-mail contained classified information at the time it was sent or received, or whether there was a reason to classify the e-mail now, even if its content was not classified at the time it was sent (that is the process sometimes referred to as "up-classifying").

From the group of 30,000 e-mails returned to the State Department, 110 e-mails in 52 e-mail chains have been determined by the owning agency to contain classified information at the time they were sent or received. Eight of those chains contained information that was Top Secret at the time they were sent 36 chains contained Secret information at the time; and eight contained Confidential information, which is the lowest level of classification. Separate from those, about 2,000 additional e-mails were "up-classified" to make them Confidential; the information in those had not been classified at the time the e-mails were sent.

The FBI also discovered several thousand work-related e-mails that were not in the group of 30,000 that were returned to Secretary Clinton to State in 2014. We found those additional e-mails in a variety of ways. Some had been over the years and we found traces of them on devices that supported or were connected to the private e-mail domain. Others we found by retrieving the archived government e-mail accounts of people who had been government employees at the same time as Secretary Clinton, including high-ranking officials at other agencies, people with whom a Secretary of State mught naturally correspond.

This helped us recover work-related e-mails that were not among the 30,000 produced to State. Still others we recovered from the laborious review of the millions of e-mail fragments dumped into the slack space of the server decommissioned in 2013.

With respect to the thousands of e-mails we found that were not among those produced to State, agencies have concluded that three of those were classified at the time they were sent or received, one at the Secret level and two at the Confidential level. There were no additional Top Secret e-mails found. Finally, none of those we found have since been "up-classified."

I should add here that we found no evidence that any of the additional work-related e-mails were intentionally deleted in an effort to conceal them. Our assessment is that, like many e-mail users, Secretary Clinton periodically deleted e-mails or e-mails were purged from the system when devices were changed. Because she was not using a government account—or even a commercial account like Gmail—there was no archiving at all of her e-mails, so it is not surprising that we discovered e-mails that were not on Secretary Clinton's system in 2014, when she produced the 30,000 e-mails to the State Department.

It could also be that some of the additional work-related e-mails we received were among those deleted as "personal" by Secretary Clinton's lawyers when they reviewed and sorted her e-mails for production in 2014.

The lawyers doing the sorting for Secretary Clinton in 2014 did not individually read the content of all of her e-mails, as we did for those available to us, instead, they relied on header information and used search terms to try to find all work-related e-mails among the reportedly more than

60,000 total e-mails remaining on Secretary Clinton's personal system in 2014. It is highly likely their search terms missed some work-related e-mails, and that we later found them, for example, in the mail boxes of other officials or in the slack space of a server.

It is also likely that there are other work-related e-mails that they did not produce to State and that we did not find elsewhere, and that are now gone because they deleted all e-mails they did not return to State, and the lawyers cleaned their devices in such a way as to preclude complete forensic recovery.

We have conducted interviews and done technical examination to attempt to understand how that sorting was done by her attorneys. Although we do not have complete visibility because we are not able to fully reconstruct the electronic record of that sorting, we believe our investigation has been sufficient to give us reasonable confidence there was no international misconduct in connection with that soaring effort.

And, of course, in addition to our technical work, we interviewed many people, from those involved in setting up and maintaining the various iterations of Secretary Clinton's personal server, to staff members with whom she corresponded on e-mail, to those involved in the e-mail production to State, and finally, Secretary Clinton herself.

Last, we have done extensive work to understand what indications there might be of compromise by hostile actors in connection with the personal e-mail operation.

That's what we have done. Now let me tell you what we found.

Although we did not find clear evidence that Secretary Clinton or her colleagues intended to violate laws governing the handling of classified information, there is evidence that they were extremely careless in their handling of very sensitive, highly classified information,

For example, seven e-mail chains concern matters that were classified at the TOP Secret/Special Access Program level when they were sent and received. These chains involved Secretary Clinton both sending e-mails about those matters and receiving e-mails from others about the same matters. There is evidence to support a conclusion that any reasonable person in Secretary Clinton's position, or in the position of those government employees with whom she was corresponding about these matters, should have known that an unclassified system was no place for that conversation. In addition to this highly sensitive information, we also found information that was properly classified as Secret by the U.S. Intelligence Community at the time it was discussed on e-mail (that is, excluding the later "up-classified" e-mails).

None of these e-mails should have been on any kind of unclassified system, but their presence is especially concerning because all of these e-mails were housed on unclassified personal servers not even supported by full-time security staff, like those found at Departments and Agencies of the U.S. Government—or even with a commercial service like Gmail.

Separately, it is important to say something about the making of classified information. Only very small number of the e-mails containing classified information bore markings indicating the presence of classified information.But even if information is not marked "classified" in an e-mail, participants who know or should know that the subject matter is classified are still obligated to protect it.

While not the focus of our investigation, we also developed evidence that the security culture of the State Department in general, and with respect to use of unclassified e-mail systems in particular, was generally lacking in the kind of care for classified information found elsewhere in the government.

With respect to potential computer intrusion by hostile actors, we did not find evidence that Secretary Clinton's personal e-mail domain, in its various configurations since 2009, was successfully hacked. But, given the nature of the system and of the actors potentially involved, we assess that we would be unlikely to see such direct evidence. We do assess that hostile actors gained access to the private commercial e-mail accounts of people with whom Secretary Clinton was in regular contact from her personal account. We also assess that Secretary Clinton's use of a personal e-mail domain was both known by a large number of people and really apparent. She also used her personal e-mail extensively while outside the United States, including sending and receiving work-related e-mails in the territory of sophisticated adversaries. Given that combination of factors, we assess it is possible that hostile actors gained access to Secretary Clinton's personal e-mail account.

So that's what we found. Finally, with respect to our recommendation to the Department of Justice. In our system, the prosecutors make the decisions about whether charges are appropriate based on evidence the FBI has helped collect. Although we don't normally make public our recommendations to the prosecutors, we frequently make recommendations and engage in productive conversations with prosecutors about what resolution may be appropriate, given the evidence. in this case, given the importance of the matter, I think unusual transparency is in order. Although there is evidence of potential violations of the statues regarding the handling of classified information, our judgment is that no reasonable prosecutor would bring such a case."

Prosecutors necessarily weigh a number of factors before bringing charges, There are obvious considerations, like the strength of factors before bringing charges. There are obvious considerations, like the strength of the evidence, especially regarding intent. Responsible decisions also consider the context of a person's actions, and how similar situations have been handled in the past.

In looking back at our investigations into mishandling or removal of classical information, we cannot find a case that would support bringing criminal charges on these facts, All the cases prosecuted involved some combination of: clearly intentional and willful mishandling of classified information; or vast quantities of materials exposed in such a way as to support an inference of intentional misconduct; or indications of disloyalty to the United States; or efforts to obstruct justice. We do not see those things.

To be clear, this is not to suggest that in similar circumstances, a person who engaged in this activity would face no consequences. To the contrary, those individuals are often subject to security or administrative sanctions. But that is not what we are deciding now.As a result, although the Dept. of Justice makes final decisions on matters like this, we are expressing to Justice our view that no charges are appropriate in this case.

I know there will be intense public debate in the wake of this recommendation, as there was throughout this investigation, What I can assure the American people is that this investigation was done competently, honestly, and independently. No outside influence of any kind was brought to bear.

I know there were many opinions expressed by people who were not part of the investigation— including people in the government—but none of that mattered to us. Opinions are irrelevant, and they were all uninformed by insight into our investigation, because we did the investigation in the right way. I couldn't be prouder to be part of this organization."

This WHITEWASH was delivered on July 5th, a holiday week, when few people were interested in watching or listening to a legalistic dissertation like this. How much did this investigation cost? It has since been revealed that Comey decided Hillary's innocence before she was interviewed without even being put under oath. Democrats praised Comey for his decision, until just before

Election day Comey made a statement about finding a laptop of Abedin Weiner's which her perverted husband Anthony had access to with some of Hillary's e-mails. The Democrats then blamed Comey for Hillary Clinton losing the election. COMEY YOUR FIRED! Comey's former mentor Robert Mueller then spent 20 months and spent $30-35,000,000 on a "Russian collusion" special investigation finding that President Trump and his family and associates had no collusion with Russia. Are the taxpayers going to get a refund?

Is former FBI Director James Comey Self Righteous?

"A HIGHER LOYALTY —TRUTH, LIES, AND LEADERSHIP" JAMES COMEY

"WHO AM I TO TELL others what ethical leadership is? Anyone claiming to write a book about ethical leadership can come across as sanctimonious. All the more so if that author happens to be someone who was quite memorably and publicly been fired from his last job."   p ix

"I understand the impulse to think that any book written about one's life experience can be an exercise in vanity, which is why I long resisted the writing of a book of my own. But I changed my mind for an important reason. We are experiencing a dangerous time in our country, with a political environment where basic facts are disputed, fundamental truth is questioned, lying is normalized, and unethical behavior is ignored, excused, or rewarded. This is not just happening in our nation's capital, and not just in the United States. It is a troubling trend that has touched institutions across America and around the world—boardrooms of major companies, newsrooms, university campuses, the entertainment industry, and professional and Olympic sports. For some of the crooks, liars and abusers, there has been a reckoning. For others, there remain excuses, justifications, and a stubborn willingness by those around them to look the other way or even enable the bad behavior."   Ibid p ix

"So if there ever was a time when an examination of ethical leadership would be useful, it is now. Although I am no expert, I have studied, read, and thought about ethical leadership since I was a college student and struggled for decades with how to practice it. No perfect leader is available to offer those lessons, so it falls to the rest of us who care about things to drive the conversation and challenge ourselves and our leaders to do better."   Ibid   p x

"Ethical leaders do not run from critics, especially self-criticism, and they don't hide from uncomfortable questions. They welcome them. All people have flaws and I have many. Some of mine, as you'll discover in this book, are that I can be stubborn, prideful, overconfident, and driven by ego." Ibid p x

"I have learned that ETHICAL LEADERS lead by seeing beyond the short-term, beyond the urgent, and take every action with a view toward lasting values. They might find their values in a religious tradition or a moral worldwide view or even an appreciation of history. But those values—like truth, integrity, and respect for others, to name just a few—serve as external reference points for ethical leaders to make decisions, especially hard decisions in which there is no easy or good option. Those values are more important than what may pass for prevailing wisdom or the groupthink of a tribe. Those values are more important than the impulses of the bosses above them and the passions of the employees below them. They are more important than the organization's profitability and bottom line. Ethical leaders choose a higher loyalty to those core values over their own personal gain." Ibid   p x-xi

"ETHICAL LEADERSHIP is also about understanding the truth about humans and our need for meaning. It is about building workplaces where standards are high and fear is low. Those are the kinds of cultures where people will feel comfortable speaking the truth to others as they seek excellence in themselves and the people around them."

"Without a fundamental commitment to the truth—especially in our public institutions and those who lead them—we are lost. As a legal principle, if people don't tell the truth, our justice system cannot function and a society based on the rule of law begins to dissolve. As a leadership principle, if leaders don't tell the truth, or won't hear the truth from others, they cannot inspire trust among those who follow them."   Ibid   p xi

"The good news is that integrity and truth-telling can be modeled in powerful ways, shaping cultures of honesty, openness, and transparency. Ethical leaders can mold a culture by their words and, more important, by their actions, because they are always being watched. Unfortunately, the inverse is also true. Dishonest leaders have the same ability to shape a culture, by showing their people dishonesty, corruption, and deception. A commitment to integrity and a higher loyalty of truth are what separate the ethical leader from those who just happen to occupy leadership roles. We cannot ignore the difference. I spent a lot of time thinking about the title of this book. In one sense, it came out at a bizarre dinner meeting at the White House, when a new president of the United States demanded my loyalty—to him, personally—over my duties as FBI director to the American people. But in another, deeper sense, the title is the culmination of four decades in law, as a federal prosecutor, business lawyer, and working closely with three U.S. presidents…The higher loyalty is to lasting values, most important the truth. I hope this book is useful in simulating all of us to think about the values that sustain us, and to search for leadership that embodies those values."   Author's Note Ibid   p xi-xii

A HIGHER LOYALTY, James Comey Copyright 2018, Flatiron Books, 175 Fifth Avenue, New York, N.Y. 10010

PERSONAL OBSERVATION: Every American and freedom loving person in the world should agree with these words. This is not a legalistic lawyer's words. After a two year "RUSSIAN COLLUSION" FBI investigation of our freely elected President DONALD J. TRUMP they have found nothing incriminating and have revealed there was none! Why is the MUELLER investigation continuing? Hundreds of FBI agents and more than $32,000,000 American taxpayer dollars have been spent. It is ironic, or an oxymoron, because of these hearings we now know that many high level FBI agents and Obama administration top security officials colluded through leaks and prejudicial statements during candidate Trump's campaign after he was selected, from 17 Republican candidates, and even after his election have colluded to "impeach" President Donald Trump. That is TREASON. Their radical anti Trump comments on liberal cable TV aren't going to change the TRUTH. Their motive to not conclude this "Witch Hunt" appears to be to create anger and doubt before the mid-term election to regain Democrat party seats to obstruct conservative Republican laws and appointment of judges and presidential officials.The decision on Hillary Clinton's unauthorized personal computer server and her obliterating 33,000 e mails was not "intentional" and Bill Clinton's "coincidental" private 20 minute meeting on an FBI Gulfstream 5 jet with Attorney General LORETTA LYNCH calling Hillary's e mail not an investigation but a "matter" and not "gross negligence" helped Donald Trump become president. Their June 27, 2016 meeting at Phoenix airport tarmac FBI director Comey recalls, "When I first heard about this impromptu meeting, I didn't pay much attention to it.. I didn't have any idea what they talked about. But to my eye, the notion that this conversation would impact the investigation was ridiculous. If Bill Clinton was going to try to influence the attorney general, he wouldn't do it by walking across a busy tarmac, in broad daylight, and up a flight of stairs past a group of FBI special agents. Besides, Lynch wasn't running the investigation anyway. But none of these basic realities had any impact on the cable news punditry. As the firestorm grew in the media. I paid more attention, watching it become another corrosive talking point about how the Obama Justice Department couldn't be trusted to complete the Clinton email investigation."p178

MEDIA DOES ITS JOB: A local journalist actually "scooped" this "chance" meeting and reported it. The left wing pro Hillary media tried to coverup this controversial meeting before her presidential campaign. The conservative FOX NEWS questioned the motive of this meeting. Comey in his testimony explains how Lynch, his superior, told him to call his investigation a "matter" and not use the felony term "grossly negligent" in Hillary's use of her unauthorized unsecured private home server which Comey testified had secret messages compromised. On July 4th weekend Comey gives the FBI's conclusion on Hillary Clinton's email. Who saw that? U TUBE. After 12 minutes criticizing Clinton's inappropriate actions Comey concluded saying there was no indictable intent! If Hillary was indicted for security violations she would have been ineligible to run as the first woman president. That means it would have been Independent democrat/socialist BERNIE SANDERS against DONALD J. TRUMP. Who would have won that election?

You are JUDGED BY YOUR DEEDS. The leftist politicians and media have been able to not report or downplay many coverups and treasonous acts. Now these people are calling President Trump a traitor or Quisling? The truth is actually the opposite. The liberal media rarely give positive news about President Trump's many great accomplishments as if they never happened. I am stunned when I watch them and see only one-sided NEGATIVE attacks? American media should serve as a WATCHDOG not as ATTACK DOGS! There is a Latin word which explains this duplicitous thinking , NON SEQUITAR which the "tolerant" secular humanists have promoted for generations. They win the popular vote provide entitlements "free stuff democracy" not a Constitutional Republic.

[BENJAMIN FRANKLIN was asked by a lady, "What kind of government do we now have Sir?" Franklin retorted, "A Constitutional Republic If we can keep it!"]

"James Comey graduated from the college of WILLIAM & MARY, Williamsburg, Virginia in 1982, majoring in chemistry and religion. His senior thesis analyzed the theologian REINHOLD NIEBUHR and the televangelist JERRY FALWELL, emphasizing their common belief in public action." "Mr. Comey Goes To Washington", New York magazine, October 2003."   Wikipedia

PERSONAL NOTE: I have been a close friend of Reinhold Niebuhr's only son Christopher for 29 years until he passed on June 1, 2018, age 86. I have told my providential story how we meet at a Tanglewood, MA, symphony when we sat together.

> "Man's capacity for justice makes democracy possible, but man's
> inclination to injustice makes democracy a necessity."

REINHOLD NIEBUHR   INTRODUCTION   Ibid p 1

"I still thought that I wanted to be a doctor, and became a premed student with a chemistry major at the College of William & Mary. But one day I was headed to a chem lab and noticed the word DEATH on a bulletin board. I stopped. It was and advertisement for a class in the religion department…I took the course, and everything changed. The class allowed me to explore a subject of intense interest to me and see how religions of the world dealt with death. i added religion as a new second major."

"The religion department introduced me to the philosopher and theologian REINHOLD NIEBUHR, whose work resonated with me deeply. Niebuhr saw the evil in the world, understood that human limitations make it impossible for any of us to really love another as ourselves, but still painted a compelling picture of our obligation to try to seek justice in a flawed world…And justice, Niebuhr believed, could be best sought through the instruments of government power. Slowly it dawned on me that I wasn't going to be a doctor after all. Lawyers participate much more directly in the search for justice, That thought, I thought, might be the best way to make a difference."   Ibid p 13-14

James Comey talks about leaving his Yonkers, New York childhood neighborhood which he loved, probably fellow Irish heritage. Then his family moved to Allendale, New Jersey in the Palisades cliffs across the Hudson River from New York City. His accent and being short and chubby caused him to be bullied. After high school he grew tall to about 6 foot 8. In college he regrets being in a group that bullied a student and they damaged his property which he did because "I was one of the guys. Finally I belonged." "I was raised by parents who consistently emphasized the importance of resisting the group. A thousand times, in many contexts, my mother said, "If everyone is lined up to jump off the George Washington Bridge, are you going to go in line?" I gave a speech at my high school graduation about the evils of peer pressure. I carried in my wallet from the age of 16 a quotation by Ralph Waldo Emerson: "it is easy in the world to live after the world's opinion; it is in solitude to live after our own; but the great man is he who in the midst of the crowd keeps with perfect sweetness the independence of solitude."   Ibid p 38-39

"Despite all that training, all that reflection, and in the face of whatever guilt or hesitation I felt, I surrendered to the loud laughter and the camaraderie of the group and maybe to a feeling of relief that I wasn't the target. I harassed and bullied another boy, who wasn't very different from me. I was a timid hypocrite and a fool."

"I was a living example of something I knew then and have come to know even better decades later. We all have a tendency to surrender our moral authority to "the group," to still our own voices and assume that the group will handle whatever difficult issue we face. We imagine that the group is making, thoughtful decision, and if the crowd is moving in a certain direction, we follow, as if the group is some moral entity larger than ourselves. In the face of the herd, our tendency is to go quiet and let the group's brain and soul handle things. Of course the group has no brain or soul separate from each of ours. But by imagining that the group has these centers, we abdicate responsibility, which allows all groups to be hijacked by the loudest voice, the person who knows how brainless groups really are and uses that to his advantage."   Ibid   p 39

PERSONAL NOTE: CHARLOTTESVILLE, Virginia ended in tragedy with an innocent beautiful young girl who helped the needy being killed by an outsider from Ohio, not connected to the two violent groups. Black masked, stick wielding ANTIFA (anti-fascist) leftist MARXIST communists attacked the right-wing NEO-NAZI Brownshirts. Each side was allowed freely to assemble and speak though their First Amendment right of assembly but didn't because of violence. The police were ordered to "stand down" and not allowed to take away weapons and masks? What did they expect would happen? I watched it on cable TV and knew this was what my Lutheran refugee German mother Elisabeth Frank saw during 1927-1933 in her hometown Frankfurt, Germany before Adolf Hitler was elected chancellor on Jan. 30, 1933, to restore "LAW AND ORDER"! The Communist party was soon outlawed, then sent to camps, and Christian Germany saw no further rioting by unemployed "atheists". There was then peace and law and order in Germany. My waist length platinum blonde haired Lutheran mother received her 6 month tourist visa in January 1935, lived with her Brooklyn, NY, sponsors. She told the Ritter family she would jump off the ship before she would return to Hitler's Germany. She was illegal for 6 years until she married my father in his hometown Amityville, Long Island, NY, in August 1941. My mother would be very disturbed by what is happening to America today. In September 1982, when I learned that Hitler was trying to replace Christianity with Nazism I began my shocking research about Germany's Christian Apostasy. Then, I could not foresee that America would REPEAT HISTORY.

SNOWDEN, APPLE I PHONE SECURITY HACK ISSUE

"Before I became the FBI director EDWARD SNOWDEN, a contractor at the National Security Agency, stole a huge trove of classified data about the NSA's activities and then shared a very large amount of that data with the press. One obvious result of this theft was that it dealt a devastating blow to our country's ability to collect intelligence. Another result was that, in the year after his disclosures, bad actors across the world began moving their communications to devices and channels that were protected by strong encryption, thwarting government surveillance, including the kind of court-authorized electronic surveillance the FBI did. We watched as terrorist networks we long had been monitoring slowly went dark, which is a scary thing."   Ibid   p 131

"In September 2014, after a year of watching our legal capabilities diminish, I saw Apple and Google announce that they would be moving their mobile devices to default encryption. They announced it in such a way as to suggest—at least to my ears—that making devices immune to judicial orders was an important social value. This drove me crazy. I just couldn't understand how smart people could not see the social cost to stopping judges, in appropriate cases, from ordering access to electronic devices. The Apple and Google announcements came on the eve of one of my regular quarterly sessions with the press corps that covered the FBI and the Department of Justice. I hadn't planned to talk about encryption, but I couldn't help myself. I expressed my frustration with the move to default encryption.:   Ibid   p 151

> "I am a huge believer in the rule of law, but I also believe
> that no one in the country is beyond the law. What concerns
> me about this is companies marketing something expressly
> to allow people to place themselves beyond the law."

"With these comments, I joined an incredible complicated and emotional battle.

"The divide between the FBI and companies like APPLE can be explained, in large measure, by how each sees the world, and the limitations of each of these perspectives. And frankly, there is not a lot of true listening going on between the parties. The leaders of tech companies don't see the darkness the FBI sees. Our days are dominated by the hunt for people planning terrorist attacks, hurting children, and engaging in organized crime. We see humankind at its most depraved, day in and day out. Horrific, unthinkable acts are what the men and women of the FBI live, breathe, and try to stop. I found it appalling that the tech types couldn't see this. I would frequently joke with the FBI "Going Dark" team assigned to seek solutions. "Of course the Silicon Valley types don't see the darkness—they live where it's sunny all the time and everybody is rich and smart." Theirs was a world where technology made human connections and relationships stronger…I thought the tech community did not fully appreciate the costs when good people from law enforcement were unable to use judicial orders to get evidence."

"Because both sides are biased by our places in the world, I thought it critical that the resolution shouldn't be dictated by either Apple or the FBI, the American people should decide how they want to live and govern themselves. But what exactly that means as a practical matter is an incredibly hard question to answer. The collusion between privacy and public safety in the encryption context touches on not just privacy amid public safety but also issues of technology, law, economics, philosophy, innovation, and international relations, and probably other interests and values."   Ibid   p 152-153

"THE EASY LIE"

"He who permits himself to tell a lie once, finds it much easier
to do it a second time and third time, till at length it becomes
habitual; he tells lies without attending to it, and truths without
the world's believing him. This falsehood of the tongue leads
to that of the heart, and in time depraves all its good dispositions."
President Thomas Jefferson   (Comey chapter heading)

"When MARTHA STEWART was released from prison in March 2005, the press was making much of the fact that her net worth grew during her time in custody. As if the goal of prosecution had been to destroy her, rather than punish her for LYING during an investigation and send a message that people no matter who they are, CAN'T OBSTRUCT JUSTICE."

A reporter asked, "Mr. Comey, Martha Stewart is getting out of prison today worth two hundred million dollars more than when she went in. How does that make you feel?" "Well," I said slowly, "We at the Department of Justice are all about the successful reentry of our inmates into society. Mrs. Stewart may have done better than most of our convicts, but that's certainly no cause for concern."   Ibid p 50-51

[Martha Stewart's crime was determined to be insider Stock Market information and her selling around $100,000 worth of stock which lost great value the following day.]

"In 1995, I had worked briefly for the Senate committee investigating BILL and HILLARY CLINTON's investments in an Arkansas development called WHITEWATER and a variety of related issues. One of those issues involved the suicide of President Clinton's deputy White House counsel VINCE FOSTER and the subsequent handling of documents left in his office…One of the questions the committee had was whether First Lady HILLARY CLINTON or anyone acting on her behalf went to Foster's office after his death and removed documents. I left the investigation long before any conclusions were reached."   Ibid   p 63-64

"Keep your friends close, but your enemies closer."
AL PACINO (As Michael Corleone), THE GODFATHER, Part II

"THERE ARE NINETY-FOUR [94] Federal districts in the United States, each presided over by a United States Attorney nominated by the president and confirmed by the Senate. The offices vary greatly in size and reach. The office in Manhattan, known as the Southern District of New York, is both one of the largest and the most well regarded. It is famous for its energy and its expansive sense of its own ability to bring cases. The office has long been accused of considering only one question relevant to its claims of jurisdiction: "Did it happen on the earth?""

"I joined the Attorney's office in Manhattan in 1987. It was my dream job. I would work for a man who was becoming legendary: RUDY GIULIANI."   Ibid   p 15

[Giuliani ended the historic Italian mobs dynasties in the New York area with indictments of Mafia/La Cosa Nostra mob leaders overseen by Comey's justice department. A prosecuting attorney Italian-American Rudi Giuliani said he profiled Italian-Americans. In Boston the underworld was organized by Irish-Americans." [Read Wikipedia to learn about ROBERT MUELLER's FBI involvement with the Boston mob. Hollywood's DEPARTED and WHITEY BOLGER movies are about Boston's mob and FBI connection. FAKE NEWS? Comey graphically reveals how he interrogated a Mafia hit man who described how he strangled 21 opponents rather than shooting them as being more honorable. His incriminating testimony convicted a mob boss, he got new identity under FBI WITNESS PROTECTION program.The original GODFATHER movie graphically depicts a strangulation. Guns are also used and the GODFATHER, portrayed by MARLON BRANDO, son Sonny is machine gunned to death in a classic slow motion scene. Actor JAMES CAHN didn't know there would be sequels?]

[Mueller and Comey also were involved in a wrongful ARTHUR ANDERSON indictment sending four people to prison and hundreds lost their honest jobs through prosecutor ANDREW WEISSMAN, who heads Mueller's President Trump investigation all Democrat FBI lawyers team. Weissman's decision was later overturned 9-0 by US Supreme Court! Also read about Comey's JOHN ASHCROFT hospital incident. Today, I heard CNN make a comment that Comey wasn't close to Mueller maybe because of his anti-Trump investigation and Comey's connection through his leaked statement to the media. The Anderson auditors where also involved with Houston based ENRON CORP which had close ties with both Republican BUSH presidents. A biased motive?]

"Before I was sworn in as FBI director in 2013, I spent a week shadowing BOB MUELLER…Mueller was characteristically disciplined about preparing me to follow him as director. During the first week of shadowing, he explained that he had arranged for me to talk with leaders of the FBI's major divisions. I was to meet with them one-on-one, he said, and they would each brief me on their area's challenges and opportunities. Then, Mueller explained, without a hint of a smile, he would meet with me after each of these sessions, "to tell you what's really going on." That comment rocked me. The FBI is an institution devoted to finding the truth. Why would the director tell me "what's really going on" after each meeting? The assumption in Bob's comment was that senior officials either weren't aware of what was happening at the FBI or weren't going to be truthful to me, their new boss, about it. My guess was the later."   Ibid   p 121-122

"Let me not seek as much…to be understood as to understand."
Peace prayer of Saint Francis

"ERIC GARNER, TAMIR RICE, WALTER SCOTT, FREDDIE GRAY. Those are the names of some of the black men who died during encounters with the police in 2014 and 2015. Those encounters were captured on video, and those videos went viral, igniting communities that had been soaked in the flammable liquid of discrimination and mistreatment. And although it didn't include a video of the shooting, one death, in particular, rocked the country. On August 9, 2014, a young man named MICHAEL BROWN was shot and killed by a white police officer in Ferguson, Missouri, touching off weeks of unrest in that community and bringing attention in America to the use of deadly force by police against black people."   Ibid   p 139

[WHAT REALLY HAPPENED? If you watched the left and right cable channels you saw what happened? Personal videos and the media agitated these tragic events and profited. It was found that videos don't show everything and people gave false information and actually lied to the media and were not charged with inciting rioting. Innocent businesses were looted and burned by outside agitators not local residents.

The videos should have been taken by police and secured in a judicial office as evidence. The media should not be allowed to interview numerous people who will prejudice the case. These cases were proven to have been justified but ruined police officers lives and endangered their families. Local police could not control the civil disobedience and State Police and the state National Guard had to bring order.]

"In the months after the shooting, the federal investigation discovered some important truths. The Ferguson police had been engaged in a pattern of discriminatory behavior directed at African Americans, and the town government—from ticketing practices to the bail system—operated to oppress black people. As in so many American towns and cities, the police needed to change before African Americans would trust them. It was understandable that Michael Brown's death

was a tragic spark that ignited a powder keg built by oppressive policing in that community."
Ibid   p 139-140

"The Gentle Giant" whose Death Burned a Missouri Town

PERSONAL EVALUATION: One of my news emails about Michael Brown's death featured a story in the St, Louis Post Dispatch titled "The Death of a Gentle Giant" by Elissa Crouch. I spoke to her on the phone and asked her if Michael Brown had received any head injuries when he played football which could have caused his actions. She said she didn't believe he had football injuries and he was going to soon attend college. I told her I had been a researcher/editor for the World Almanac which was created by Joseph Pulitzer in 1868 when he was editor of her newspaper. She knew that. I asked her if she knew JOSEPH PULITZER's statement: "OUR REPUBLIC AND ITS PRESS WILL RISE AND FALL TOGETHER." She answered, "We have that quote in our press room." I thanked her for her time.
James Comey does reveal that there were false statements. Brown's friend said he had his hands up when he was shot, he LIED. HANDS UP DON'T SHOOT! He received no punishment? Comey said DNA tests shows he tried to grab the police officer's pistol.
I recall that the officer fired a few shots as Brown charged him hitting him in the arms. The fatal shot was in the top of his head. What Comey didn't see? was the video of Brown stealing a pack of Cigarello cigars and pushing BULLYING the store owner who was oriental or from India. The officer was on an emergency call but was confronted by Brown on the highway. These cigars are often stripped and repacked with marijuna. Brown's step-father, who had been in prison, told the crowd and TV cameras "Burn this bitch down" then the rioting and looting began. Great for media. Did he go back to jail? Brown's birth father seemed to be the only rational person I saw on TV. SO SAD.

I Never Heard this Before—A Lutheran since 1943

"YOU ARE NOT ONLY RESPONSIBLE FOR WHAT YOU SAY, BUT ALSO FOR WHAT YOU DO NOT SAY."   MARTIN LUTHER   Ibid   p 250

[Attorney General Comey is a Roman Catholic. His confessional priest knows his truth?]
FACEBOOK PROVIDENCE: In October 2019, I learned that fired-FBI director COMEY had a secret FACEBOOK account using the name REINHOLD NIEBUHR. I providentially met his son CHRISTOPHER NIEBUHR in August 1988, read my story, and have been one of his closest friends. He passed in June 2018. Rest in Peace Chris.

COMEY'S LAW

VANITY FAIR magazine March 2017 BETHANY MCLEAN

Photo: Comey with right hand raised at his U.S. Congressional hearing testimony.
Caption: I SOLEMNLY ERR—F.B.I. director James Comey at the JULY 7 House-oversight committee hearing on the FBI's probe into Hillary Clinton's use of a private e-mail service.
"When [President OBAMA chose him as FBI. director, in 2013, James Comey was widely admired for his principles and probity. But his investigation into Hillary Clinton's e-mails—culminating in the infamous "Comey letter," which may have cost her the presidency—enraged both parties and

led to serious questions about his motives. Bethany McLean explores why a law-enforcement hero ignored some of his agency's most fundamental roles in the early summer of 2013—what seems like a lifetime ago—James "Jim" Comey was nominated by President Barack Obama to serve a 10-year term as the director of the Federal Bureau of Investigation agency. Even in a time of fierce political divides, there was little divide about Comey, who at the time was a Republican. (He has since changed his party registration but not said to what) He was confirmed by a vote of 93-1. "Jim is a natural leader of unquestioned integrity," said Obama. And he was."

"…Comey made his name prosecuting terrorism cases in the Eastern District of Virginia, and then served in the powerful position of U.S. attorney for the Southern District of New York and as President George W. Bush's deputy attorney general (D.A.G.), in the aftermath of 9/11. Those who have worked with him describe him as intelligent and charismatic, processing both humor and humanity. "He knows the names of your family members, pops into your office to chat, and sends handwritten thank-you notes," says a prosecutor who worked under him. "He inspires incredible loyalty," says another. "People who worked for him feel like they would have marched up any hill for him.""

"A former Southern District attorney recounts how on every new prosecutor's first day in the office, Comey would tell the person that he loved his job as a prosecutor because it involved by definition, doing the right thing. He cites as a formative influence the 20th-century realist theologian REINHOLD NIEBUHR, who URGED CHRISTIANS TO BECOME ACTIVELY INVOLVED IN POLITICS TO ENSURE THE MORAL GOOD,"

[Read my story of my providential 29-year friendship with his son Christopher Niebuhr.]

"How the perception of Comey has changed."

"Today he stands at the center of the raging storm of rumors, reality, and rancor that was the FBI's investigation into Hillary Clinton's use of an unsecured server to send and receive e-mails during her tenure as secretary of state. In early July 2016, after a year-long investigation that reportedly cost more than $20,000,000, Comey pronounced that "no reasonable prosecutor would bring such a case" against her for mishandling classified information. This caused Republicans to erupt in rage."

"Four months later—11 days before the 2016 presidential presidential election—Comey sent a letter to Congress saying he was reopening the investigation in light of new information found, but not yet examined, by the FBI. It was now the Democrats' turn to erupt in rage—a rage that only grew when two days before the election Comey announced there was nothing new or incriminating about the new information."

[An FBI agent went public that a laptop computer of Secretary Clinton's assistant Abedin
Weiner allegedly accessed some of Clinton's Congressionally subpoenaed missing 30,000 e-mails of Chelsie's wedding "plans" and yoga e-mails which were destroyed beyond retrieval "wiped with a cloth?" through expensive radical "bleach bit" and destroyed electronic devices? CLINTON GUILT?]

"The "October surprise" dominated the news cycle in the crucial last days of the election, allowing DONALD TRUMP to claim on the campaign trail that Hillary would soon be indicted, and to lead the followers [rally crowds] in chanting, "Lock her up!""

"After Hillary lost, BILL CLINTON summed up what many Democrats and some Republicans still believe: "James Comey cost her the election.""

[Russian collusion on Internet, 3rd party JILL STEIN Green Party votes, 50 per cent "deplorable" Republicans, Bill Clinton's adultery and abused women at presidential debate, biased/prejudicial poll figures in favor of Hillary continuously broadcast by the liberal media, Hillary spending about $1,000,000,000 in her campaign on TV etc., about triple what Donald Trump spent aided by liberal media's continuous coverage of candidate Trump claiming he could never win the presidency, Hillary's failure as secretary of state the red button reset with Putin, Obama "off mike" telling

Medvedev to tell Putin he can talk with him when reelected, Bill Clinton's $$$ speech to Russian bank and millions of $$$ from Russia to Clinton Foundation, Benghazi cover-up, Hillary claims MARGARET SANGER, Planned Parenthood birth control/abortion racist eugenist as her "hero". America's Constitutional Republic state ELECTORAL COLLEGE votes rule 270 votes decides presidency. President DONALD J. TRUMP received 322-263 vote landslide. President Trump didn't receive the popular vote majority about 63,000,000 to Hillary Clinton's about 65,000,000 votes. Her votes were from America's liberal Northeast, Illinois and the radical West Coast. DEMOCRACY came from Greece and demos means destruction, demolition. The majority of people can be deceived by "free stuff" even when their "wealthy" states and cities are bankrupt. The Golden Goose has died, America's NATIONAL DEBT is more than $25,000,000,000,000 trillion.]

"Just days before her defeat, an open letter circulated among former federal prosecutors and Justice Department officials accusing Comey of unprecedented actions that had left them "astonished and perplexed"—as well as angry. In our network, we are sad," says the former Southern District attorney. 'He was an American hero. Now who knows how he will go down in history?' "

"He left himself exposed to charges that he acted in a way that affected the outcome of a political election," says someone who was close to the e-mail investigation. "It has affected the reputation of the Justice Department and the FBI in ways that are profound and will take years to comprehend."

"It was a mistake of world historic proportions," argues another person, who was close to events."

"In mid-January, the inspector general for the Department of Justice announced that he was opening an investigation into Comey's conduct. In other words, it is far from over."

"Was Comey's October announcement a naked political gambit, planned in collusion with the Trump campaign and Republican operatives? None of the people I spoke with who had worked for Comey or knew him well believe this, not even those who are infuriated with his actions."

"The more complicated and interesting question, then, is why someone who prides himself on being apolitical became embroiled in a great political scandal. On top of that, why, long before October, did he set himself on a course where he began violating strongly publicly about investigations, particularly of people you don't charge and particularly when doing so might interfere with the election?"

"For original sin, you have to start with Hillary Clinton, who began using a private e-mail account tied to a server in the basement of her and Bill's Chappaqua house in 2009, when she was Obama's secretary of state."   [Hillary was 4th in the line of succession.]

"In early July 2015, after reporters and congressional investigators looking into the 2012 attacks in Benghazi filed Freedom of Information Act (FOIA) requests but came up empty on Clinton's e-mails, the inspector general of the intelligence community notified the potential compromise of classified information. This sort of security review isn't uncommon—one source says that hundreds of such cases are referred every year—and the very option of what's classified is contentious in and of itself, with many arguing that the U.S. government has a huge over-classification problem. A former U.S. attorney observes, "[The classification system] is a huge cloud. Who classifies what? Who has the right to classify? Everyone is sloppy."

"But the probe into Clinton's server quickly escalated, as reports appeared that she had deleted 30,000 e-mails that she considered personal. After an original review of the matter, the FBI opened a criminal investigation."

FIDELITY, BRAVERY AND INTEGRITY

"There is a mystique about the FBI, but the organization is still made up of human beings…"It is supposed to be apolitical, but in a world where criminal investigations have an impact on politics it is going to be complicated."

"FBI agents still tend to be white males. In a way, this situation is systemic: to be promoted, you have to be willing to relocate, which can be difficult for women and children. A current agent also says that there is a strong conservative bent: if a TV is on in an FBI building, it is likely to be Fox News."   [A good influence?]

"But even in the FBI, there are tensions. "There are three FBI's," this agent tells me. "There are the [56] field offices, there's [headquarters in] Washington, and then there's [the field office in] New York."

"Often, a retired agent says, those in the field are suspicious of Washington. "Dreamland," they called it in his day, because they believed those who weren't on the ground investigating cases were clueless. "[Agents] out in the field never want to give a case to D.C. because they believe headquarters is a hindrance to their investigations," says the agent, who also notes there is a paranoia that politics might interfere at headquarters. New York has an especially dim view of Washington and a reputation for fierce independence. "There is a renegade quality to the New York F.B.I.," says a former prosecutor, which, he claims, can take the form of agents leaking to the press to advance their own interests or to influence an investigation. "New York looks like a sieve," concurs another former prosecutor."

"There is a tension with the prosecutors in the Justice Department. The FBI's job is to investigate potential crimes, but they need one of the 93 U.S. Attorney's Offices, or an attorney at so-called Main Justice, in Washington, to open a case. Agents often feel that prosecutors aren't told enough to bring the cases the FBI has investigated.

"When RUDY GIULIANI was the U.S. attorney for the Southern District of New York, he brought the young Comey into the highly prestigious office, where from 1987 to 1993 he was in charge of the case against the financier MARC RICH, who had fled the U.S. after being indicted for tax evasion and illegal dealings with Iran. In 1996, Comey served as deputy special counsel for the Senate Whitewater Committee and later that year became and assistant U.S. attorney for the Eastern District of Virginia. In 2002, he was named the U.S. attorney for the Southern District of New York, where his most widely know case resulted in putting life style guru MARTHA STEWART behind bars for obstruction of justice and making false statements. As the U.S. attorney for the Southern District, he also lead a criminal investigation into BILL CLINTON'S highly controversial pardon of Rich, which resulted in no prosecution. President GEORGE W. BUSH then appointed him deputy attorney general, in 2003."

[I believe Rich is living in Switzerland and his wife has contributed large amounts of presidential campaign funds to both the Clinton's. Democrats have denounced the U.S. Supreme Court allowing large donations to political campaigns under the CITIZEN'S UNITED bill. Democrat candidates have received millions of dollars from Weinstein, Epstein and Soros who they have protected knowing of their perversions and anti democratic motives.]

[Comey invokes REINHOLD NIEBUHR'S Christian beliefs which were Neo-Orthodox which were Biblical which were secularized or mocked during the mid 1800s by DARWIN, MARX, NIETZSCHE, SCHOPENHAUER Their beliefs have killed hundreds of millions of innocent men, women, children and fetuses. A rejection of Almighty God caused these deaths. I will not blame Satan because humankind was given FREE-WILL to choose right from wrong. Our Creator did not create robots? We are in HIS IMAGE.]

"But two cases established his reputation in legal and political oracles. The first involved obtaining indictments for the 1996 KHOBAR TOWERS incident, when 19 American military personnel were killed in a terrorist attack in Saudi Arabia. The career prosecutors at Main Justice had been working on the case for nearly five years, so long that the statute of limitations was about to expire on some of the possible charges. Comey and another prosecutor named John Davis worked on it for about three months, and then, over a weekend, Comey holed up in his office and wrote a detailed indictment of one Lebanese and 13 Saudi suspects."

"Even more famous is Comey's dramatic hospital-room confrontation with the Bush administration, in early March of 2004, over the secret warrantless domestic-eavesdropping program, which caused a national furor when the press revealed its existence in late 2005. In what The Washington Post later called "the most riveting 20 minutes of Congressional testimony. Maybe ever," Comey told the story of how he, as acting attorney general, filled in for his boss, JOHN ASHCROFT, who was hospitalized. After refusing to re-authorize the program, which he believed was illegal, Comey discovered that other members of the administration were planning an end run to get an incapacitated Ashcroft to sign off on it in his hospital bed. Comey "ran, literally ran," up the stairs to prevent that, he testified. The next day he considered resigning."

"Well, yes. But did Comey really believe that the program was "fundamentally wrong"?

"President BUSH quickly gave his support to making changes to the program—changes that have never been disclosed publicly—and Comey stayed on at D.A.G. until August 2005, as the wire-tapping program continued."

"Many would argue that legal technicalities are critically important, but some of Comey"s former D.O.J. colleagues carped to The New York Times that his actions had not been as heroic as they were portrayed. One observer cites Comey's willingness to say. "I know what is right," even when doing so causes potentially avoidable drama. Another person who knows Comey well says, "There is stubbornness, ego. and some self-righteousness at work."

LAW AND DISORDER

"In 2014, [President] Obama chose LORETTA LYNCH to be his attorney general after ERIC HOLDER resigned…Technically, the FBI falls under the jurisdiction of the Justice Department, and technically Comey reported to Lynch. But it was always apparent that, as a former agent puts it, he was not going to say to an attorney general, "Mother, may I?" Although views differ on both Lynch and Comey's relationship with her, several people saw the seeds of problems to come. While she has inspired deep loyalty among some who worked for her in the Eastern District, one source close to the Justice Department says that as attorney general she was aloof internally and didn't cultivate relationships."

"On January 14, 2016, the inspector general notified the Senate that [Hillary] Clinton's private server had been flagged for classified information. Comey made the decision to run the investigation out of D.C., not New York, despite the fact that Clinton and her server were in [Chappaqua] New York. A core group of investigators and analysts were vetted and given security clearance, meaning that only those who were working on the case knew what they were doing."

"Comey chose Washington because he wanted to to be close enough to get daily updates, according to CNN, but he may have been worried about leaks from New York. A former D.O.J. official says that, as early as 2015, a rumor was floating around that FBI agents in New York were cracking jokes about HILLARY CLINTON in handcuffs. "it was widely understood that there was a faction in that office that couldn't stand her and was out to get her," this person says."

"In the fall of 2015, President OBAMA told 60 MINUTES that the Clinton e-mail issue was "not a situation in which America's national security was endangered." A former prosecutor who is close to the case says that the remarks sparked outrage in the FBI. "Disparaging the seriousness of something his A.G. is supposed to take responsibility for is not cool," he says."

"On February 24, Lynch told Congress that she had assigned career prosecutors—that is, non-political appointees—to work on the case and that it would be conducted as "every other case." But efforts to stay outside of politics created its own politics, particularly between the FBI, and the DOJ. One person who was close to events says, "The DOJ was afraid of the FBI, afraid if it did anything that the FBI perceived as impeding the investigation they could be criticized and there would be a political fallout. So the DOJ at every level abdicated the assertiveness we expect of prosecutors. It came from the very top.""

"To make matters worse, on June 27, 2016, BILL CLINTON went aboard Loretta Lynch's plane on the tarmac in Phoenix for a chat, an event that is epic in the annuals of bad decisions because it gave the appearance he was pleading his wife's case. Lynch was in Phoenix for a routine meeting with local police officers, while Clinton was finishing a fund-raiser for his wife. Lynch's staff had no chance to intervene: they had already gotten off the plane. He told Lynch, who has a reputation for being polite, that he just wanted to say hello. "It would have been very awkward for her to say no," says a source close to events. But Clinton then proceeded to talk for nearly half an hour about his grandchildren, about golf, and about travel, according to Lynch."

[This chance meeting was reported by a local reporter or it would have been unknown.]

"The furor among Republican conservatives over the tarmac visit was immediate, with Trump citing it as a perfect example of how "special interests are controlling your government." The right-wing JUDICIAL WATCH sued the FBI for records of the plane meeting. After the outcry, Lynch told the press that not only would she "fully expect to accept" the recommendations of the FBI and the career prosecutors on the case but she'd been planning to do so all along."

"But neither did she rescue herself and turn the case over to D.A.G. SALLY YATES. A source says there was an internal debate over what to do and the decision was made that it would be bad for the Justice Department "if the A.G. relinquished her decision-making power," as this person puts it, because then, "with every political case going forward, there would be an expectation that the A.G. would recuse." Instead they went with a middle ground."

"Under no circumstances should something like this be left to career lawyers without supervision...All of the people with the authority to make decisions are political appointees. The statutes do not give career lawyers the authority to make decisions. That is for a good reason: the political appointees are accountable via the electoral process. That is how it works. It was an unfathomable decision to make." This person adds, "Lynch created the situation where the FBI director could freelance.""

"One source, who is willing to excuse Lynch's poor judgment, nevertheless says, "What she did and what the DOJ did [after the tarmac incident] is inexcusable. To say that a political appointee can't sit in judgment is insane. It's saying the Justice Department cannot do its job. The director of the FBI is a political appointee!" This person adds, "Lynch was more than happy to have Comey take responsibility. It was complete and total abdication.""

CASE NOT CLOSED

"Into the vacuum created by Lynch's refusal to either dismiss the tarmac incident or move out of the way stepped JIM COMEY. That he would do so is not a surprise to anyone who knew him. On July 5, 2016, Comey held the press conference in which he announced that agents had found thousands of e-mails that contained government secrets, all of which had traveled insecure, unclassified channels on Clinton's private e-mail network. Nonetheless, he said, "WE CANNOT FIND A CASE that would SUPPORT BRINGING CRIMINAL CHARGES," in large part because they DID NOT FIND INTENT, which is a critical element of most criminal cases."

"Comey certainly knew that the career prosectors, who had been working hand-in-glove with the FBI agents, would agree with the decision. But he made it clear he hadn't even informed the DOJ, whose responsibility it is to decide whether to authorize an indictment, that he was holding a press conference. Lynch corroborated this, admitting that the DOJ had learned of the press conference only "right before." Indeed, some at the DOJ turned to CNN to find out what Comey was saying."

"Plenty of Comey's longtime admirers were appalled that he had spoken at all, because by doing so he blew through several of the Justice Department's long-standing policies. "It was an unprecedented public announcement by a non-prosecutor that there would be no prosecution," says someone who once worked for Comey. The FBI does not talk publicly about investigations, and it does not make prosecutorial decisions full stop."

"Comey has said he did not consult with anyone at the DOJ beforehand so he could say it as the FBI's recommendation," observes another former prosecutor. "But right there that is a massive act of insubordination."

"Comey then, according to his critics, compounding his mistake by declaring Clinton's conduct and that of her aides "EXTREMELY CARELESS." This was another breach of protocol. Neither prosecutors nor agent criticize people they don't change. "We don't dirty you up," says Richard Frankel, who retired from the FBI in early 2016 and now consults ABC News. And Comey's choice of language opened another can of worms. Unlike other criminal statutes, which as a rule, require intent, the ESPIONAGE ACT does allow for prosecutions of those who display "gross negligence.""

"Those close to the case were also shocked by what Comey didn't say. For instance, he didn't point out that the "CLASSIFIED" e-mails had been marked that way when they were sent or received, and didn't point out that all the e-mails were to people who work in government—not to outsiders who aren't supposed to receive such information. "He gave a very skewed picture," says one person involved in the case. "The goal has to be that people understand the decision, and it came out exactly the opposite.""

"Those who know Comey say that, while the decision for him not to recommend prosecution was an easy one, his unprecedented decision to speak about it publicly wasn't…There's also speculation that Comey's decision to criticize Clinton was influenced by his prior experience, from WHITEWATER to MARC RICH with her and her husband. But sources close to Comey insist that isn't true, and that his decision to go into more detail was influenced by his desire to make people believe the process had been fair despite the appearance of impropriety. An FBI source says that since the details of the investigation were going to come out, framed in hyper partisan ways via congressional hearings and FOIA [Freedom of Information Act] requests. Comey wanted to offer an apolitical framing of the facts first."   [Clinton Justice?]

"Some factions within the FBI were not in Comey's corner—particularly New York. One agent even heard about a petition to have Comey removed. "All of a sudden people who thought he was the best guy ever were saying he should resign," says this person. Hosko adds, "There was tremendous frustration about the notion that someone [like Clinton] could carelessly traffic in very sensitive material and walk away unscathed, arrogantly walk away and wait for her coronation."

"The disquiet within the FBI was made public, largely by James Kallstrom, head of the FBI's New York office from 1995 to 1997. He is close to former U.S. attorney (and former New York mayor) RUDY GIULIANI, about whom he says, "When I was a young agent, he was a young prosecutor. We've known each other for 40 years." During the campaign Giuliani was one of Trump's most prominent supporters. In the weeks following COMEY'S July announcement, both Kallstrom and Giuliani were all over conservative news outlets, talking about the "revolution" as Giuliani called it, among the FBI rank and file, who viewed the failure to indict as "almost a slap in the face of the FBI's INTEGRITY." By late September, Kallstrom was telling the DAILY BEAST that he had been talking to hundreds of people, "including a lot of retired agents and a few on the job" who were "basically disgusted" and felt they had been "stabbed in the back."

"There is another piece to the internal issues at the FBI. Agents, primarily in New York, had been trying over the last few years to put together a case involving financial crimes or influence peddling against the CLINTON FOUNDATION. One knowledgeable source says that agents went to several U.S. Attorney's offices, trying to get prosecutors to open the case, before finally going to the Justice Department's public-integrity office. This person says that the agents did not have any facts that would support prosecutors taking further steps. But angry agents leaked to THE WALL STREET JOURNAL."

MUCH ADO ABOUT NOTHING

"On October 26, 2016, Rudolph Giuliani appeared on FOX NEWS and said, "We got a couple things up our sleeve that should turn this around. Even the liberal pollsters will get to see." When pressed about what these surprises would be, Giuliani broke into a smile and said, 'You'll see, Ha, ha, ha."

"Two days later, on October 29, just 11 days before the election, Comey sent his letter to Congress saying that "in connection with an unrelated case, the FBI has learned of the existence of e-mails that appear to be pertinent to the investigation" of Clinton."

"Fox News obtained the internal memo Comey had sent to the FBI staff, in which he wrote he felt "an obligation" to update Congress. Although he noted that we "don't know the significance of this newly discovered collection of e-mails." He thought it would be "misleading to the American people were we not to supplement the record.""

"The e-mails, between Clinton and her aide HUMA ABEDIN, were discovered during the FBI's investigation into unrelated allegations that Abedin's husband, ANTHONY WEINER, had been sending illicit text messages to a 15-year-old girl in North Carolina from the silver Inspiron laptop he shared with his wife."

"The story broke in the [British] DAILY MAIL on September 21, and the FBI seized the laptop on October 3. Within a couple of days, the New York FBI agents, who had a warrant to look only at Weiner-related information, knew there were Clinton e-mails on the laptop, and the prosecutors in D.C. were informed. But investigating electronic information can be a lengthy process, and it wasn't until the middle of the month that the agents said there were a lot of Clinton e-mails and that they appeared to cover a three-month period at the start of Clinton's tenure at State that had previously been missing, says an official familiar with the investigation. This was a big deal, because her e-mails from that period had not been recovered. On the 27th, Comey was briefed, and agents argued that they needed to get a warrant to go through the new e-mails."

"Comey agreed with his agents, and that afternoon the FBI alerted the Department of Justice that he planned to write the letter updating Congress..."If we had known we would have been able to reach a conclusion quickly, that might have colored the decision-making," says an official familiar with events. But most of all, the FBI was worried that if it came out that they had kept silent, and the existence of the e-mails was revealed after the election, it would give credence to claims, which were already being circulated by Trump, that the election results were illegitimate."

"Officials at the DOJ tried to convince the FBI that all Comey had promised Congress was that he would take a look at new information, that he risked creating another misinterpretation by sending a letter, that doing this so close to an election was insanity, and that "the overwhelming odds are that this will amount to nothing," as one former official puts it."

"One argument that the FBI gave in response was that now that the circle had become much bigger, including agents in New York, the probably of a leak was high and would only increase once the request for the warrant was filed. "Yes, it was absolutely explicit that one reason for the letter was that the agents in New York would leak it," says a Justice Department source."

"Multiple sources say, the Justice Department never ordered Comey not to send the letter, and neither Lynch nor Yates personally called Comey. Instead, staff called over to the FBI. A source says, "I do know that [Lynch] never spoke directly to Comey, and she didn't allow the DAG [Yates] to speak to him…In his position, I would have understood this as permission to do what I wanted." He adds. "Before something this consequential would occur, you would at least want the A.G. to look Jim Comey in the eye and say. 'DO NOT DO IT!' ""

"On November 6, two days before the election, Comey informed Congress that the FBI had seen the e-mails and that the bureau had not changed its conclusion that Clinton should face charges over her handling of classified information."

"The result was predictable: Republicans again insisted the game must be RIGGED, and the Democrats couldn't believe Comey had re-ignited the issue on the eve of the election. Even the Justice Department joined the blame game, leaking a story to The New York Times in which officials claimed they had done practically everything possible to dissuade Comey from sending the   letter.""

"One source disagrees, saying: "As immense as my criticism for Comey, it is greater for the AG and DAG. If they had said, 'You can't send that letter,' he wouldn't have done it."

"They claim that couldn't have stopped it, but that is bullshit," says a former prosecutor, who says that, even today, "They don't get it, don't admit responsibility. They say, "We couldn't do anything—you know what he's like."

"Another observer, who is deeply familiar with the Justice Department, adds, "I know exactly why they didn't call themselves! THEY WERE ALL THINKING, HILLARY IS GOING TO WIN. If you could look back and say that would swing DONALD TRUMP, you would do anything to stop it, but they were worried that, if they told Comey not to do it, that would LEAK [from the FBI], and they would be ACCUSED OF INTERFERING."   (Lynch, Comey, and Yates declined to comment for this article.)

"People say that [Lynch] should have ordered him not to do it. I get with 20/20 hindsight why people feel that way," a Justice Department source responds. "But it was not a situation where [Comey] said, 'We need to talk.' It was presented as 'The director intends to do this. He has an obligation to correct a misimpression that Congress will be misled,' all of the A.G.'s options are bad. Either he obeys, and she is accused of obstructing justice. Or he disobeys and does it anyway. Or he resigns. All of these are terrible. He put her in an impossible situation."

"Lynch and Jim Comey were engaged in the same dance," says another source. "He wasn't going to have history judge him negatively as having covered things up, and she wasn't going to have history judge her negatively with political interference. Both were protecting their own reputations and legacies at a great cost to the country."

"There is certainly some TRUTH THAT THE FBI MIGHT HAVE LEAKED. but few who knew Comey think that was the reason he wrote the letter. Friends say it was not even a hard decision for him, because he'd already set himself on this course of total transparency. "If he had given no indication that the FBI had potentially had e-mails and those came out in January, that would be a bet-your-agency decision," says Richman."

"But to critics the dilemma was still of Comey's own making, because if he hadn't said anything in July, and compounded that by testifying before Congress, he wouldn't have found himself in a situation where there was no easy right answer. "He is a man of integrity, and he holds himself to high standards," says a person who knew him well. "But he didn't see the bigger issue. All he could see was "Will they question my integrity?" I think it was his integrity he was worried about,

291

not the bureau's, and the bureau's integrity suffered a devastating blow as a result of his decision making. He would have protected the agency by playing by the book."

"Even Comey's close friends acknowledge that his great strength is also his great weakness: a belief in his own integrity. "He believes this in a way that creates big blind spots, because he substitutes his judgment for the rules,' says Matt Miller, a former director of public affairs for the DOJ."

"Neither publicly nor privately has Comey shown any doubt about how he handled things. "I would be lying if I said the external criticism doesn't bother me at all," he wrote in a New Year's memo to employees, "but the truth is, it doesn't bother me much because of the way we? [I] made the decision." At a holiday lunch for former agents, Comey even called his July decision the best one he had made."

"On January 24, The New York Times reported that President TRUMP had asked Comey to remain as FBI director. One close observer speculates that Trump likes the fact that Comey has been weakened, although the politics of removing him would have been terrible, given that Comey's fiercest critics [Hillary and Republicans] say they are glad. As one of them puts it, "If Trump says, 'Let's shut down AMAZON' because he doesn't like something The Washington Post wrote, Comey won't do it, and in this environment, the country need someone like that."   [Pres. DONALD TRUMP hasn't]

[Bethany McLeans's article is an epic investigative report using FBI comments on America's most controversial historical-political election which Comey unleashed and continued to unleash against a Constitutionally elected President. The liberal media, Democrat politicians and RINO Republicans mocked DONALD TRUMP right up to his electoral upset which shocked their elitist, self-righteous pride and arrogance. I watched PRESIDENT DONALD J.TRUMP'S victory at about 2:20 AM on Nov. 9, 2016, when the state of Pennsylvania gave him the electoral votes needed to succeed Pres. BARACK OBAMA and VP JOE BIDEN'S 8-year economically failed Democrat administration.]

COMEY'S REAL MOTIVE? I have read and listened and have a theory which no one will dare say. On the day after President Trump was elected hundreds of thousands of American women marched in protest against President Trump. JAMES COMEY'S wife and daughters were there. MADONNA said. "I would like to burn down the WHITE HOUSE!" Feminists spoke and despicable signs against America's new president were displayed. I had never seen anything so hateful in my 77 years. The liberal media promoted it because it was news Fox had to also show this freedom of speech and assembly. Why do they hate the president? President Trump and VP MICHAEL PENCE are PRO LIFE and only for a woman's right to kill their baby in extreme cases. They are calling President Trump like HITLER. Ironically, they may unwillingly be telling a HISTORICAL TRUTH. In Nazi Germany it was a capital crime for a German woman to have an ABORTION punishable by guillotine! Hitler was not against racial and ethnic abortions, which America has done millions of legally since 1973. My Lutheran German mother Elisabeth Frank had waist length platinum blonde hair and came to America in January 1935, age 19, on a 6-month tourist visa. She was illegal until August 1940, when she married my father in his hometown Amityville, Long Island. In June 1973, I visited her high school girl friend Gertie at her home in Golder's Green, NW London. In her garden having 4 o'clock tea I asked her an important question. I asked Gertie, "Mom told me once when I was young someone told her: "Elisabeth for God's sake leave Germany before it is too late." "Do you know who told her that?" Gertie recalled, "That was Guenther your mother's boy friend, a wonderful chap, I wonder what became of him? He was an SS lieutenant and told her about the new Lebensborn program to have "aryan" blonde babies out of wedlock." My mother wasn't persecuted like so many innocent people were. She would have

been prostituted. I can thank Guenther for my being an American. He is my godfather and I know I will meet him in Jesus Eternity with my mother, father and my German grandparents.]
PERSONAL PROVIDENCE: This election was held on my son's 39th birthday November 8, 1977. My Jewish inter-faith wedding was on Nov. 9, 1974, in Brooklyn, NY, I learned in October 1990, that Nov. 9-10, 1938, was CHRYSTAL NIGHT, the beginning of Hitler's persecution of the German Jewish population. The wedding was planned six months earlier and I had heard about KRISTAL NACHT but was unaware of it when I broke the wedding glass symbolizing the fragility of marriage and the destruction of the two Jerusalem Temples. My Christian friends Lutheran, Catholic and Episcopal would not have known this. I am sure their were Jewish family members and friends who knew this providential fact. My mother-in-law Helen Denker, got the earliest date, probably knew this fact. I once heard that some of her distant Polish relatives were killed in the Holocaust. My son's BAR MITZVAH was on the Sabbath Nov. 10, 1990. MARTIN LUTHER was born on November 10, and the US Marine Corps was founded on Nov. 10, 1775, in Philadelphia. My wife was a non observant Jewess and I began attending Missouri Synod Lutheran services. I was confirmed Lutheran May 1958, age 15, at Emanuel Lutheran church in Hudson, NY, and also had services in historic small chapel in Harlemville. Pastor Grisliss had been a prisoner in a Communist Lithuanian jail before coming to America.]
[This article was written before FBI director James Comey leaked a memo to a friend which was published in the New York Times.]
Mueller investigated for 20-months and $35,000,000 hateful "RUSSIAN/TRUMP COLLUSION" which destroyed many people's lives some guilty of personal felonies and received long jail sentences. Lt. Gen. MICHAEL FLYNN, who headed America's intelligence during the Afghanistan/Iraq conflict was treated worse than any convicted enemy combatant or terrorist. FBI agent [s] lied to him that he didn't need a lawyer {MIRANDA RIGHTS VIOLATION] and was indicted on "LYING TO FBI agents" because of a "legal" FISA wiretap at the Trump Tower in New York. Once I heard on FOX NEWS a report that General Flynn was treated so badly because he was an early supporter of candidate Donald Trump and along with the cheering Trump audience shouted "LOCK HILLARY UP, LOCK HER UP". The liberal news network supporters of HILLARY CLINTON showed no compassion for what the FBI did illegally to General Flynn a combat decorated American hero. Today, December 2019, I hear the liberal, hateful media calling President Trump's rally followers a "CULT". In May 2020, FBI memos reveal that General Flynn was treated illegally, going to court.]

FIDELITY, BRAVERY, INTEGRITY

The Villages "Daily Sun" Florida   Katie Tammen 2008

Retired agents remember why they wanted to serve with the 100-year-old Bureau.
"THE VILLAGES—They helped put jewel thieves, mobsters, spies, terrorists, and even federal judges, behind bars. In a century of work, the men and women of the FBI protected, fought country and taught evolving in an ever-changing world to best serve the country and the people in it.

As the bureau celebrates its centennial retired special agents living in and around The Villages recalled their years with the FBI. Their love and loyalty for the bureau is something they all shared."

PERSONAL FRIEND FRANK DUNPHY'S PROVIDENTIAL STORY

"Frank Dunphy never thought that he could be an FBI agent. At age 12, his family moved to the United States from Nova Scotia, Canada, so he wasn't a born-and-bred American. By age 18, he had received his American citizenship and joined the U.S. Military Police Corps."

"It was my intention to go to work for the Los Angeles County sheriff. I never really thought about the FBI," he said. "I figured No. 1, they wouldn't hire any immigrant; and No. 2, you had to be a lawyer (to become an agent)."

"Then after returning home from a tour of duty in Vietnam, Dunphy RECEIVED A MESSAGE FROM GOD."

"Actually, the messenger came in the form of a Catholic priest who had been a counselor at Dunphy's high school."

"He said, I want you to think about the FBI," Dunphy recalled.Then Father Jorge DaSilva handed him a contact name and the rest is history."

"If someone were to walk up to me with a plate full of gold and say, "We'll trade you this for your career in the FBI. Dunphy said with a smile, shaking his head, "THERE COULD NEVER BE ENOUGH GOLD TO MAKE ME DO THAT."

The Villages Daily Sun article features two photographs of Frank Dunphy. One shows him, a former Supervisory Special Agent, on the front page smiling holding a collection of four special agent badges from the agency's 100-year History. The other photo is a plaque showing his FBI PHOTO ID CARD, his FBI BADGE encompassed with a wreath with three medallion pendants, and his retirement certificate FRANCIS DUNPHY.

Frank's wife Kim was my son and daughter's 3rd grade teacher in Stafford, and was from Long Island like me. On a visit to the Villages in July 2006, my wife, daughter and granddaughter stayed overnight at their home. I have a beautiful photo of Frank smiling holding my 10 month old granddaughter with his wife Kim also smiling.

One night Frank and I had a providential discussion, after his wife and my family went to sleep. Frank suggested I apply for Veterans medical insurance to supplement my Medicare insurance. Since then I have had some very expensive surgeries which VA insurance completely paid a great financial relief. Thank you Frank for your advise.

SMALL WORLD STORY: Frank told me his father was in the Canadian Army fighting in Europe in World War II. I told Frank my dad was in the 8th Air Force in Britain and didn't want to fly home on his unit's B-24 bomber to Iceland, Greenland and Hartford, CT. Instead, he took the Queen Mary with 15,000 Canadian soldiers in June 1945. Frank said his father was on that ship returning home after three years of brutal combat.

I told Frank that my father said a Canadian soldier told him that the Canadian soldiers were told that some of the Canadians would be required to stay in devastated Germany as occupation soldiers. The Canadian soldiers, were part of the British Commonwealth, became angered when the war ended wanting to go home to their families. Some of the soldiers got drunk and disorderly and damaged a small English town. My father may have told the soldiers his grandfather was born in St. Stephens, New Brunswick, and his father was born in Calais, Maine, on the Canadian border.

To appease the soldiers they were told they would be sent home on a long overdue leave if they "volunteered" to fight the Japanese. These soldiers must have seen newsreels of the fanatic fighting and the brutal massacres committed by Japanese soldiers against civilians and beheading of soldiers taken as prisoner. These soldiers must have known about the Japanese Bushido Code where a Japanese soldier fought to his death, surrender was dishonorable. Even the SS units which the Canadians fought in Normandy, France were not as fanatic, except the HITLER JUGEND SS PANZER tank Division of HITLER YOUTH which executed Canadian prisoners. They were tried for war crimes under Geneva Convention terms. The Japanese did not sign the Geneva Convention. Japan was allied to England and America during World War I.

The atomic bomb was unknown until it was dropped on two Japanese cities prompting the Japanese emperor HIROHITO to order his fanatic generals to surrender. The Canadians soldiers must have been very thankful.

Frank told me he was an MP at Army MACV HQ at DANANG, Vietnam in 1964. He escorted NY Cardinal SPELLMAN when he visited. Later, when Frank was in the FBI he arranged to be on Pope John Paul II guard detail in Texas. He and Kim took a tour to Vietnam and visited DANANG and Frank said he meet a nun he had meet about 43 years earlier. Dale, an FBI forensic agent, I have known in my Missouri Synod Lutheran church since 1968, said he knew Frank. Frank had a glass case with a dozen Bobbie police hats he received when he did training liaison visits to Canada and Great Britain. His Canadian heritage qualified him for this special duty.

Frank proudly showed me his FBI citation signed by FBI director J. EDGAR HOOVER. My wife gave me this beautiful forgotten article which I just found, Sept. 16, 2019, in one of my file boxes. I have added this after JAMES COMEY's HIGHER LOYALTY book excerpts. Frank passed from a heart attack before the FBI corruption and seditious/treasonous spying on a candidate and then an elected president DONALD J. TRUMP.

100 YEARS OF THE FBI 1908-2008

VILLAGES DAILY SUN Katie Tammen June 2008

"June 26, 1908—Attorney General Charles Bonaparte and President TEDDY ROOSEVELT create Bureau of Investigation, the forerunner of the FBI. BOI agents primarily investigated national banking, naturalization, antitrust and land fraud. 1917—World War I causes an expansion of the BOI's responsibilities to include ESPIONAGE. May 10, 1924—J. EDGAR HOOVER selected as Acting Director of the BOI. July 1924—National Identification division set up. January 1928—BOI establishes first course to train agents. June 1930—BOI begins handling Uniform Crime Statistic reports. July 1932—Name changed to the United States Bureau of Investigation. Summer 1934—Role of BOI in criminal investigation expands and agents are permitted by Congress to carry guns and make arrests. January 1936—U.S. BOI becomes the Federal Bureau of Investigation. 1940s—World War II changes the face of the FBI again and agents are assigned to posts worldwide to gain information on espionage. March 14, 1950–First "TEN MOST WANTED FUGITIVES" list released. 1960s—Congress passes law expanding FBI jurisdiction to investigate certain murders after the assassination of President JOHN F. KENNEDY. September 1975—J. Edgar Hoover building dedicated. January 1982—Drug Enforcement Administration begins reporting to the FBI. August 1983—Hostage Rescue Team fully operational. July 1984—National Center for the Analysis of Violent Crime established at Quantico. March 1992—Consolidated services—NOC—AFIS and Uniform Crime Reports—into the Criminal Justice Information Service. December 1997—National DNA Index System introduced allowing agencies to link serial violent offenders through DNA—also began using mitochondria DNA like a strand of human hair. October 2001—Joint terrorism task forces establishment through out all offices following September 11, [terrorist attacks on New York City, Pentagon, Pennsylvania jet airliner] President GEORGE W. BUSH signs the PATRIOT ACT."

FBI agent MARK FELT was the DEEP THROAT informant to Washington Post reporters WOODWARD and BERNSTEIN. This was kept secret until his death. In 1972, President RICHARD NIXON was elected with 62% of the vote, 49 States, except Massachusetts, because South Dakota Senator GEORGE MCGOVERN was too Socialist!

IRONIC HISTORICAL FORGOTTEN FACT: How could media hated NIXON get such an unprecedented vote? In July 1971, the U. S. Congress passed an Amendment lowering the voting age to 18. The young voters who had been in the streets protesting the Vietnam War saw that Nixon was withdrawing American troops and ended the unfair military draft. President Nixon began Vietnamizing the war. President LYNDON JOHNSON was elected with 62% of the vote when he told the American public, "American boys shouldn't fight an Asian boys war." HE LIED. My first election the year I graduated from college was in 1964. I had heard this lie and voted for Johnson. I really liked Conservative Senator BARRY GOLDWATER, an Air Force general. The press slandered him saying he would start World War Three in Vietnam. We dropped 6 times more tonnage of bombs on Vietnam than we dropped to win World War II. Johnson actually said, "Our aircraft can't bomb an outhouse without my permission."

As a child I had wanted to be a jet pilot because I lived 3 miles from Republic aircraft where they built 4,400 F-84 Thunderjet fighter bombers. In April 1965, I enlisted in the U.S. Air Force and was assigned to the Army Information Journalism school with 21 other airmen, all were college graduates. In October 1966, I was assigned to Bitburg AB, Germany, which had several 5 minute nuclear ready F-4D Phantom jets during the Cold War. I had previously spent a year at Andrews AFB, Washington, DC. The day I was doing my transfer paperwork an airmen said President Johnson is boarding Air Force One. I have a color photo of him walking to Air Force One 26000.

My church FBI friend Dale did forensics in New York on the PAN AM 747 which exploded over Long Island and then he had to go to the Atlanta bombing case. He left the FBI because he was away from his family wife and two sons too long.

I had a neighbor who was in the FBI who gave me wood for my stove. He was fired from the FBI for having an adulterous affair. This is a standard policy because adultery can compromise an agent through blackmail. I was a TRAK AUTO store manager in Fairfax, Virginia in 1987. One day an Armored truck guard came to pick up my store's deposit. It was my former FBI agent neighbor. FBI agent STROZK had a well publicized adulterous affair. YOUR FIRED? Apparently high ranking agents cover for each other, "band of brothers" Is this in the regulations book? Director Mueller was Comey's mentor.

What was the motivation for so many top FBI agents to attempt to remove an elected president? The liberal, socialist media also supported their corrupt deeds covering up true facts. FOX NEWS has revealed the truth the facts many of their lawyer commentators have written books which will not be read by highly paid liberal pundits.

WHY MEN COMMIT SEDITION/TREASON?

THE MOTIVE EVEN FOX NEWS WON'T TELL: All of these treasonous Trump haters have one thing in common. THEIR WIVES AND MISTRESS! These women hate and despise TRUMP and PENCE and their Christian values. There is a video of Comey's wife and daughters at the disgraceful women's march the day after President Trump's inauguration. They fear the Roe-Wade 7-2 Supreme Court abortion tolerance law will be repealed by Trump/Pence and their Supreme Court originalist appointments. Director McCabe's wife ran as a Democrat U.S. Senate candidate in Virginia with Clinton money. The OHR husband and wife collusion. FBI agent Peter

Strozk and his FBI lawyer girl friend Lisa Page's emails against DONALD TRUMP being elected president. FBI director Rob Rosenstein's wife was a Clinton lawyer. "Politics makes strange bedfellows." It is all on Wikipedia, it's no secret. John Durham knows the FBI truths, Attorney Gen. Bill Barr and Inspector General Horowitz? will restore justice in America.

Media Silence to America's Genocide of Minority Babies

These people invoke Hitler, Nazi and Holocaust against President Trump. Trump had nothing to do with 55,000,000 babies aborted/killed since 1973. The majority of these abortions are of minority children. Is this not genocide?   MEDIA SILENCE
Conservative African American Candace Owens reports 19,000,000 black abortions.
I am on a long email list 60+ which has several writers who make insane hateful self-righteous President Trump comments. I have tried to get off this chain which I will not respond to and don't see any familiar name connection? One "liberal" justified abortion of "unwanted, unloved" babies and said "Who would care from them?" This is MARGARET SANGER's racist Planned Parenthood agenda. Hillary Clinton called her her heroine. When Sanger visited Europe Hitler would not allow her to visit Germany and promote her birth control. She visited Communist dictator Stalin's Soviet Union and her program was rejected. Sanger was not allowed to visit Europe's devout Roman Catholic countries who forbade abortion.

VILLAGES ARTICLE CONCLUSION—retired and still working—The fraternal atmosphere of the Bureau doesn't dissipate with retirement and today all these men gather once a month and remember living and working during some of the FBI'S most influential decades."
"They recall the impact of a national finger printing data base and expansion of jurisdiction not just within the nation, but in the world."

Former Reagan Attorney General Ed Meese:
   Bill Barr is Restoring Faith in the DOJ
THE DAILY CALLER Amber Athey, White House correspondent Nov. 18, 2019

"Former Attorney General ED MEESE, who served under President RONALD REAGAN, told the Daily Caller in an exclusive interview that he believes Attorney General BILL BARR is working to restore trust in the Department of Justice."
"I think that Bill Barr has done an outstanding job as attorney general, having to take over and look at situations that go all the way back to the Obama administration," Meese said when asked to evaluate Barr's performance in the role thus far. "I think Bill is continuing to do what JEFF [SESSIONS] did, and that is to restore the dignity and integrity to the Department of Justice."
"Meese weighed in on Barr's handling of the release of the MUELLER REPORT, which contained Special Counsel ROBERT MUELLER'S FINDINGS on whether the Trump campaign COLLUDED with Russia during the 2016 election and whether President DONALD TRUMP obstructed justice during the investigation. Meese praised Barr's decision to release his own summary of the report and to reach a conclusion on the obstruction of justice charge against President Trump."
"I think what Barr did was an accurate summary…there's no question if you compare what Bill Barr said in the report, when it was ultimately released in its entirety, that what he said was an accurate summary," Meese asserted."
"He continued, "Bill Barr had no choice but to make a choice on the obstruction of justice charge because it was standing out there before the public, and the Mueller commission did not carry out their responsibility to make a determination if there was adequate evidence to charge a person

with a crime, and in the absence of that, you couldn't just leave that out there for the public to speculate."

"Meese also challenged the notion that the report did not "exonerate" the president, explaining that the purview of an investigation is not to exonerate anyone, but to determine if there is enough evidence to charge someone with a crime."

[Attorney General EDMUND MEESE is a Missouri Synod Lutheran like I am. He had spoken at a luncheon to my community's Women's Republican Club about conservative Constitutional Republican values which for 6 years of President BARACK OBAMA's progressive-liberal Democrat party implemented Obama's publicly stated plan to "fundamentally change" "modernize" the U.S. Constitution. Obama graduated from HARVARD University with a "constitutional law" degree. Meese autographed my copy of his Encyclopedia of Constitutional laws. President Obama with a Democrat majority in the House of Representatives passed laws America's FOUNDING FATHER's would find existentially completely opposite what was written in their Judeo-Christian original U.S. Constitution. Our Founding father JAMES MADISON attended the College of NEW JERSEY, today's PRINCETON University. James Madison's home MONTPELIER is located 25 miles south of my home. MICHELLE OBAMA graduated from Princeton University and publicly stated. "I felt out of place there." It was an IVY LEAGUE white college. Madison studied Hebrew a difficult language my son and daughter learned.

PERSONAL STORY: Attorney General Ed Meese is a resident of my community. I have a photo with him at our community clubhouse in front of pictures of Virginia's 8 American Presidents— GEORGE WASHINGTON, THOMAS JEFFERSON, JAMES MADISON, JAMES MONROE, WILLIAM HENRY HARRISON, JOHN TYLER, JAMES POLK, and WOODROW WILSON. I also have an autographed photo of Attorney General Ed Meese siting with President RONALD REAGAN. President DONALD J. TRUMP presented Attorney General ED MEESE the PRESIDENTIAL MEDAL OF HONOR at his STATE OF THE UNION address on Jan. 28, 2020. Dad's birthday Jan. 28,1919.]

VOTER GUIDE 2016 US President FAITH & FREEDOM COALITION

First Amendment Defense Act—Trump NO—Clinton—YES
Defund Planned Parenthood—Trump—YES—Clinton—NO
Iran Nuclear Deal—Trump—NO—Clinton—YES
Amnesty for Illegal Aliens—Trump—NO—Clinton—YES
School vouchers—Trump—YES—Clinton—NO
Common Core—Trump—NO—Clinton—YES
Same Sex Marriage—Trump—NO—Clinton—YES
Federal Tax Increase—Trump—NO—Clinton—YES
Repeal Obamacare—Trump—YES—Clinton—NO
Abortion on Demand—Trump—NO—Clinton—YES

THE CASE FOR GEORGE MCGOVERN ADVERTISEMENT

The New York Times Sunday October 15, 1972 Full Page 5 AD
We are attorneys in New York City. We have studied the critical problems facing
our nation and have compared the records and proposals of the candidates.
On the basis of our evaluation we wholeheartedly support Senator George
McGovern and urge his election as President of the United States. We present
for your consideration some of the reasons for our endorsement of Senator McGovern.

We are deeply distressed by the failures of the Nixon Administration to deal effectively with the pressing problems facing our nation.

We are persuaded by Senator McGovern's character and record that he will succeed where Richard Nixon has failed.

1. Richard Nixon has failed to fulfill his pledge to make our lives free from violent crimes, as evidenced by
   * A 32% increase in serious crimes over the last three years.
   * His refusal to support effective gun control legislation.
   * An increase of over 100% in the number of heroin-addicted men and women.

   * Inadequate funding of job training and drug education programs to combat the causes of crime.
   * Inept and wasteful handling of Law Enforcement Assistance Administration funds appropriated by Congress to fight crime.

1. Senator McGovern has developed a sound program to deal with the rising crime rate. It includes
   * A tougher crackdown on heroin trafficking and more effective treatment for heroin addicts.
   * Stricter control on the sale and possession of handguns and more stringent penalties for their use in violent crimes.
   * A Policeman's Bill of Rights to make police work an even more professional career.
   * A detailed legislative program for court reform.
   * Improvement of corrective facilities to provide genuine rehabilitation.

2. Richard Nixon has run a scandal-ridden administration with special favors for the rich, as evidenced by
   * A $10,000,000 secret campaign fund in defiance of the Federal Election Campaign Act which President Nixon praised and signed.
   * The advance tip-offs to grain exporters who made millions of dollars on the SOVIET wheat deal at the expense of American farmers and consumers.
   * The controversial settlement of the I.T.T. anti-trust suit following the promise of a substantial contribution to the benefit of the Republican Party by an ITT subsidiary.
   * The BUGGING and burglarizing of the Democratic headquarters at the WATERGATE.

2. Senator McGovern is committed to public interest of the American People rather than the special interests of the favored few, as evidenced by his
   * Voluntary disclosure of all his campaign financing.
   * Advocacy of a Consumer Protection Agency and sponsorship of a Truth in Advertising Bill.
   * Call for reordering of national priorities including emphasis upon environmental protection and public transportation.

3. The Nixon administration has exhibited incompetent management of the economy, as evidenced by
   * A four year budgetary deficit ($90.1 billion) exceeding the combined deficits of the Eisenhower, Kennedy and Johnson

3. Senator McGovern, working with leading economists, has a sound plan for full employment and economic justice. He urges reforming our tax system and eliminating unnecessary military

administrations.

*An 85% increase in the number of unemployed, from 2.6 million to 4.8 million people.

* A 66% increase in the welfare roles, from 6.2 million people to 10.3 million people.

* An inflationary increase of 17.6% in the consumer price index.

4. The Nixon administration has continued the unconscionable and inhumane war in Southeast Asia which has resulted in

* Another 20,000 American servicemen dead (40% of all American combat deaths).

* Another 110,000 wounded American servicemen.

* Another 500 prisoners of war and missing in action.

* Another 3.7 million tons of bombs dropped on Indochina

* An enormous increase of the flow of HEROIN from Southeast Asia.

* A daily war cost to the American public of $425 million.

5. Richard Nixon has shown disrespect and contempt for the law and contempt for the law and our civil liberties as evidenced by his

* Attempts to undermine the Voting Rights Act.

* Failure of the Justice Department to enforce the 14th Amendment and the civil rights laws enacted under it.

* Demeaning of our Federal Courts by the consistent selection of mediocre nominees, such as Carswell and Haynsworth for the Supreme Court.

* Attempts to suppress publication of the PENTAGON PAPERS in newspapers throughout the country.

* Persistent intimidation of the press and other news media.

* Encouragement and defense of the illegal arrest of 13,000 citizens during the May Day demonstrations in Washington.

* Introduction of no-knock entry and preventive detention legislation and the widespread use of wiretapping, eavesdropping, and other forms of surveillance.

* Encouragement of defiance and disobedience of Federal Court desegregation orders.

* Use of criminal prosecutions and federal

expenditures to make $52 billion in revenue available in order to

* Build schools and hospitals.

* Clean up our environment.

* Create millions of new jobs in private industry.

* Pay 1/3 of the cost of elementary and secondary schooling.

* Provide decent minimum care for dependent mothers and children, the aged, the blind, the handicapped and the sick.

4. Senator McGovern has long articulated a constructive approach to foreign policy, including

* A complete halt to American intervention in Indochina.

* An immediate return of our Prisoners of War and accounting of our missing in action.

* A long-standing call for re-examination of America's China policy.

* Consistent support for the State of ISRAEL and vigorous condemnation of the Soviet Union's restrictive policy on emigration to Israel.

* Genuine international cooperation and consultation rather than the Nixon policy of militarism, unilateralism and power politics.

* Cooperation with Congress in the formulation of foreign policy

5. Senator McGovern has shown his devotion to the Constitution, as evidenced by his

* Co-sponsorship of all major civil rights legislation enacted during the last decade.

* Support of the Equal Rights For Women Amendment.

* Dedication to First Amendment freedoms by actions such as support for disclosure of the

grand juries to stifle dissent.

————

Nixon elected 62%-38% 49-1 States

PENTAGON PAPERS.
* Opposition to nominations of Haynsworth, Carswell and Rehnquist.
*Opposition to the District Columbia Crime Bill (with provisions for no-knock entry and preventive detention) and to electronic eavesdropping and government use of computerized dossiers.

THE DANGER of the ATTACKS on the ELECTORAL COLLEGE

Trent England, director, SAVE OUR STATES Hillsdale College April 30, 2019

"Once upon a time, the ELECTORAL COLLEGE was not controversial. During the debates over ratifying the CONSTITUTION, Anti-Federalist opponents of ratification barely mentioned it. But by the mid-twentieth century, opponents of the Electoral College nearly convinced Congress to propose an amendment to scrap it. And today, more than a dozen states have joined in an attempt to hijack the Electoral College as a way to force a national popular vote for president.

What changed along the way? And does it matter? After all, the critics of the Electoral College simply want to elect the president the way we elect most other officials. Every state governor is chosen by a statewide popular vote. Why not the popular vote for the President of the United States?

Delegates to the Constitutional Convention in 1787 asked themselves the same question, but then rejected a national popular vote along with several other possible modes of presidential election. The Virginia Plan—the first draft of what would become the new Constitution—called for "a National Executive…to be chosen by National Legislature." When the Constitutional Convention took up the issue for the first time, near the end of the first week of debate, Roger Sherman from Connecticut supported this parliamentary system of election, arguing that the national executive should be "absolutely dependent" on the legislature. Pennsylvania's James Wilson, on the other hand, called for a popular election. Virginia's GEORGE MASON thought a popular election "impracticable," but hoped Wilson would "have time to digest it into his own form," Another delegate suggested election by the Senate alone, and then the Convention adjourned for the day.

When they reconvened the next morning, Wilson had taken Mason's advice. He presented a plan to create districts and hold popular elections to chose electors. Those electors would then vote for the executive—in other words, an ELECTORAL COLLEGE. But with many details left out, and uncertainty remaining about the nature of the executive office, Wilson's proposal was voted down.

A week later,   ELBRIDGE GERRY
of Massachusetts proposed elections by state governors. [Gerry created voting districts Gerrymandering, which Obama and Soros are now trying to redistrict as Democrat.]

This too was voted down, and a consensus began to build. Delegates did not support the Virginia Plan's parliamentary model because they understood that an executive selected by Congress would become subservient to Congress. A similar result, they came to see could be expected from reassigning the selection to any body of politicians.

There were other oddball proposals that sought to salvage congressional selection—for instance, to have congressmen DRAW LOTS to form a group that would then choose the executive in secret. But by July 25, it as clear to JAMES MADISON that the choice was down to two forms of popular election: "The option before us,'" he said, "[is] between an appointment by Electors chosen by the people—and an immediate appointment by the people." Madison said he preferred popular election, but he recognized two legitimate concerns. First, people would tend toward supporting candidates from their own states. Second, a few areas with HIGHER concentrations of VOTERS MIGHT COME TO DOMINATE. MADISON SPOKE POSITIVELY of the idea of ELECTORAL COLLEGE, finding that "there would be very little opportunity for cabal or corruption" in such a system.

By August 31, the Constitution was nearly finished—except for the process of electing the president. The question was put to a committee comprised of one delegate from each of the 11 states present at the Convention. The committee, which included Madison, created the Electoral College as we know it today. They presented the plan on September 4, and it was adopted with minor changes. It is found in Article II, Section I"

> Each State shall appoint, in such Manner as the Legislature thereof may
> direct, a Number of Electors, equal to the whole Number of Electors, equal
> to the whole Number of Senators and Representatives to which the State
> may be entitled in the Congress.

Federal officials were prohibited from being electors. Electors were required to cast two ballots, and were prohibited from casting both ballots for candidate from their own state. A deadlock for president would be decided by the House of Representatives, with one vote per state. Following that, in case of a deadlock for vice president, the Senate would decide. Also under the original system, the runner up became vice president.

This last provision caused misery for President JOHN ADAMS in 1796, when his nemesis, THOMAS JEFFERSON became his vice president. Four years later it nearly robbed Jefferson of the presidency when his unscrupulous running mate, AARON BURR, tried to parlay an accidental deadlock into his own election by the House. The Twelfth Amendment, ratified in 1804, fixed all this by requiring electors to cast separate votes for president and vice president.

It is easy for Americans to forget that when we vote for president, we are really voting for electors who have pledged to support the candidate we favor. Also, perhaps, the Electoral College is a victim of its own success. Civics education is not what it used to be. Most of the time, it shapes American politics in ways that are beneficial but hard to see. Its effects become news only when a candidate and his or her political party lose a hard fought and narrowly decided election.

So what are the beneficial effects of choosing our presidents through the Electoral College? Under the ELECTORAL COLLEGE SYSTEM, presidential elections are decentralized, taking place in the states. Although some see this as a flaw—U.S. Senator ELIZABETH WARREN opposes the Electoral College expressly because she wants to increase federal power over elections—this decentralization has proven to be of great value.

Disputes over mistakes of fraud are contained within individual states. Illinois can recount its vote, for instance, without triggering a nation-wide recount. This was an important factor in America's messiest presidential election—which was not in 2000, but in 1876. That year marked the first time a presidential candidate won the electoral vote while losing the popular vote. It was a time of organized suppression of black voters in the South, and there were fierce disputes over vote totals in Florida, Louisiana, and South Carolina. Each of those states sent Congress two sets of electoral vote totals, one favoring Republican RUTHERFORD HAYES and the other Democrat SAMUEL TILDEN. Just two days before Inauguration Day, Congress finished counting the votes—which included determining which votes to count—and declared Hayes the winner. Democrats declared this "THE FRAUD OF THE CENTURY," and there was no way to be certain today—nor was there probably a way to be certain at that time—which candidate actually won. At the very least, the

Electoral College contained these disputes within individual states so that Congress could endeavor to sort it out. And it is arguable that the Electoral College prevented a fraudulent result. PERSONAL CONNECTION: Samuel Tilden was born in Columbia County, New Lebanon, New York, about 20 miles from my boyhood home. President MARTIN VAN BUREN was also born in Columbia County, Old Kinderhook, OK, 8 miles from my farm. Van Buren's presidential campaign coined OK as his slogan. Tilden became nationally popular because he legally ended the corrupt New York City TAMMANY HALL Democrat political ring which stole millions of dollars from taxpayers. Tilden ran as a Democrat anti-corruption candidate. Ironically, Tilden received the popular vote but lost the election because of corrupt electoral votes in three Southern Democrat states. Tilden should have become President of the United States. So it Goes.]

"Four years later, the 1880 presidential election-demonstrated another benefit of the Electoral College system: it can act to amplify the results of a presidential election. The popular vote margin that year was less than 10,000 votes—about one-tenth of one per-cent—yet Republican JAMES GARFIELD won a resounding, with 214 electoral votes to Democrat WINFIELD HANCOCK's 155. There was no question who won, let alone any need for a recount. More recently, in 1992, the Electoral College boosted the legitimacy of Democrat BILL CLINTON, who won with only 43 percent of the popular vote but received over 68 percent of the electoral vote." [Hancock was a great Civil War general.]

[ROSS PEROT's Third Party gained millions of popular votes but no electoral votes.]

"But there is no doubt that the greatest benefit of the Electoral College is the powerful incentive it creates against regionalism. Here, the presidential elections of 1888 and 1892 are most instructive. In 1888, the incumbent Democratic President GROVER CLEVELAND lost reelection despite receiving a popular vote plurality. He won this plurality because he won by very large margins in the overwhelmingly Democrat South. Altogether he won in six southern states with margins greater than 30 percent, while only tiny Vermont delivered a victory percentage of that size for Republican BENJAMIN HARRISON. In other words, the Electoral College ensures that winning supermajorities in one region of the country is not sufficient to win the White House. After the Civil War, and especially after the end of Reconstruction, that meant that the Democratic had to appeal to interests outside the South to earn a majority in the Electoral College. And indeed, when Grover Cleveland ran again for president four years later in 1892, although he won by a smaller percentage of the popular vote, he won a resounding Electoral College majority by picking up New York, Illinois, Indiana, Wisconsin, and California in addition to winning the South.

Whether we see it or not today, the Electoral College continues to push parties and presidential candidates to build broad coalitions. Critics say that swing states get too much attention, leaving voters in so-called safe states feeling left out. But the legitimacy of a political party rests on all of those safe states—on places that the party has already won over, allowing it to reach farther out. In 2000, for instance, GEORGE W. BUSH needed every state that he won—not just Florida—to become president. Of course, the Electoral College does put a premium on the states in which the parties are most evenly divided. But would it really be better if the path to the presidency primarily meant driving up the vote total in the deepest red or deepest blue states?

Also, swing states are the states most likely to have divided government. And if divided government is good for anything, it is accountability. So with the Electoral College system, when we do wind up with a razor-thin margin in an election, it is likely to happen in a state where both parties hold some power, rather than the state controlled by party.

HOROWITZ PROPOSES CHANGES FOR THE FBI

"FBI officials could have avoided many of their troubling mistakes and omissions, Mr. Horowitz concluded in his report, offering nine 9 recommendations for changes in the bureau to prevent similar failures."

"The FBI opened the Russia investigation without the approval of the Justice Department and didn't notify national security lawyers at the department after the investigation was opened. Though that is allowed under existing policies, the inspector general said officials should require informing the deputy attorney general."

"The inspector general also said that top officials at the FBI needed to do a better job running investigations from headquarters."

[Adam Goldman reports on the FBI from Washington and is a two-time PULITZER PRIZE winner. Charlie Savage is a Washington-based national security and legal policy correspondent and is a PULITZER PRIZE recipient.

"OUR REPUBLIC AND ITS PRESS WILL RISE AND FALL TOGETHER." JOSEPH PULITZER who created THE WORLD ALMANAC AND BOOK OF FACTS in 1868. I worked for the almanac from 1969–1975 as one of four editors. I edited History/Government, Religion, Associations/Societies, World Almanac Fact to 600 newspapers.

President ABRAHAM LINCOLN proclaimed: "It is true that you may FOOL ALL THE PEOPLE SOME OF THE TIME; you can even FOOL SOME OF THE PEOPLE ALL THE TIME; but you CAN'T FOOL ALL OF THE PEOPLE ALL THE TIME." This well known maxim was recorded in "Lincoln's Yarns and Stories" by Alexander McClure who said that Lincoln added: "IF YOU ONCE FORFEIT THE CONFIDENCE OF YOUR FELLOW CITIZENS, YOU CAN NEVER REGAIN THEIR RESPECT AND ESTEEM."]

[After being renominated for president Abraham Lincoln quipped: "I do not allow myself to suppose that either the convention of the League have concluded to decide that I am either the greatest or the best man in America, but rather that it is not best to swap horses while crossing the river, and have further concluded that I am not so poor a horse that they might not make a botch of it trying to swap."

Abraham Lincoln speaking at a Republican State Convention in 1858 proclaimed: "A HOUSE DIVIDED AGAINST ITSELF CANNOT STAND." Lincoln concluded foretelling: "I believe this government cannot endure permanently half slave and half free, I do not expect the Union to be dissolved—I do not expect the house to fall—but I do expect it will cease to be divided."

"A PUBLIC OFFICE IS A PUBLIC TRUST"

"A public office is a public trust." is attributed to Pres. GROVER CLEVELAND. The phrase was originated by Sen. CHARLES SUMNER in a speech on May 31, 1872, and was later adopted as Cleveland's presidential slogan. In his inaugural address March 4, 1885, Cleveland retorted: "Your every voter, as surely as your chief magistrate exercises a public trust!"

"In 1835, South Carolina Sen. JOHN CALHOUN remarked: "The very essence of a free government consists in considering offices as public trusts, bestowed for the good of the country, and not for the benefit of an individual or a party."

NEW YORK TIMES ADMITS IT SPIED ON PRESIDENT TRUMP

TTN Trump Train News Email Dec. 20, 2019

"In a new report about how easy it is to track people from cell phone data the NEW YORK TIMES admitted that they spied on Trump and tracked his movements."

"According to THE DAILY WIRE:

In an extensive report that was part of its "PRIVACY PROJECT," The New York Times revealed Thursday that it has gained access to cell phone tracking data for millions of Americans and was able to rather easily track the movements of regular Americans as well as high-profile and powerful figures, including President TRUMP HIMSELF—details of whose actions THE TIMES published in a follow-up report.

"In its initial report, titled "TWELVE MILLION PHONES, ONE DATASET, ZERO PRIVACY," THE TIMES warns that if you are able to see the data which they obtained from a single private cell phone APP company, "you might never use your phone again."

"In a follow-up report titled "HOW TO TRACK PRESIDENT TRUMP," THE TIMES reveals that it easily followed the movements of Trump — by simply identifying a cell phone owned by a person in his entourage:

"The device's owner was easy to trace, revealing the outline of the person's work and life. The same phone pinged a dozen times at the nearby Secret Service field office and events with elected officials. From computer screens more than 1,000 miles away, [GPS] we could watch the person travel from exclusive areas at Palm Beach International Airport to Mar-a-Largo."

"It seems disconcerting that President Trump is so easily tracked. Do you think THE TIMES should have given this information to the secret service or transmitted it to OUR ENEMIES as they did here?"

[This is stealth spying not intentional. It would be easy for an agent to voluntarily be tracked which would be seditious/treasonous.]

The Culpeper Minutemen Flag: The History

of the Banner Flown by a Militia of Patriots

Culpeper news Kelly Dec. 9, 2019 e-mail

THE CULPEPER MINUTEMEN
LIBERTY   coiled   OR DEATH
                rattlesnake
DON'T   TREAD   ON   ME

"The CULPEPER FLAG is often mistaken as a modern variation of the iconic "DON'T TREAD ON ME" GADSDEN FLAG —and rightly so. What many don't know is that the Culpeper Flag was inspired by its Gadsden counterpart, and both have become touchstones of the SECOND AMENDMENT MOVEMENT."

"While remarkably similar to its Gadsden relative, the flag of the Culpeper MINUTEMAN is arguably cooler—and significantly more obscure. While it has the same coiled rattlesnake and

"Don't Tread on Me" legend, the Culpeper Flag is white, it carries the additional motto "LIBERTY OR DEATH," and when historically correct, a banner bearing the name of the Culpeper Minutemen."

"The rattlesnake had been a symbol of American patriotism since the time of the FRENCH AND INDIAN WARS. In 1751, BENJAMIN FRANKLIN wrote an editorial satirically proposing that, in return for boatloads of convicts being shipped to the American colonies, that the Colonies should return the favor by shipping back a boat filled with rattlesnakes to be dispersed. Three years later in 1754, Franklin published his famous "JOIN OR DIE" comic. [photo showed a snake cut into parts with states names] This early symbol of American unity urged colonists in ALBANY to join the collective defense of the American Colonies during the French and Indian wars. The rattlesnake symbol once again became a popular mascot of American unity after the STAMP ACT."

THE ORIGINS OF THE CULPEPER MILITIA

"The Culpeper Minutemen were formed on July 17, 1775, in a district created by the THIRD VIRGINIA CONVENTION. This district consisted of the ORANGE, FAUQUIER and titular CULPEPER counties. In September of that year, 200 men were recruited for four companies of 50 men from Culpeper and Fauquier, with an additional 100 men for two companies from ORANGE. By order of the District Committee of Safety, the Culpeper Minutemen met under a large oak tree in a large field currently part of YOWELL MEADOW PARK in Culpeper, Virginia."

[In 2008, my wife and three year old granddaughter went to this park 24 miles from my home. I was surprised to see the park sign with the rattlesnake, I recalled from a history book, and story of how the Culpeper Minutemen were sent to protect Virginia's capital in WILLIAMSBURG. There was also a sign about how Culpeper was a major encampment for Union soldiers in the WAR OF SECESSION, a staging area before the major battles of CHANCELLORSVILLE and THE WILDERNESS where my house is located.]

"When the Revolutionary War came, the Culpeper Minutemen chose the Patriot side. It was at this time that they also adopted their standard bearer that can be seen adorning pickup trucks of modern-day patriots from sea to shining sea. Their first action during the AMERICAN REVOLUTION was to defend Virginia's capital Williamsburg after the Royal Governor, JOHN MURRAY, Lord Dunmore, confiscated the gunpowder."

THE CULPEPER BOYS ARRIVE IN WILLIAMSBURG

"'They cut quite a sight arriving in the aristocratic capital, wearing heavy linen shirts dyed the color of the local foliage and carrying tomahawks and knives for scalping. Philip Slaughter, who served with the Culpeper boys as a 16 year old, said that the colonists looked at them much as they might the Indians themselves. The Culpeper Minutemen, however, were no roughnecks, but a disciplined and orderly squad who quickly earned the respect of their new charges."

"During the Revolutionary War, the area where the Culpeper boys were organized was still the frontier. So they were often called to more populated and settled areas. For example, the Culpeper Minutemen fought in HAMPTON when the British tried to land troops there, at the request of the local authorities, The Culpeper Militia successfully mounted an attack on the arriving ships, shooting the men who were manning the cannons and guns on the ship, preventing the British from landing."

THE BATTLE OF GREAT BRIDGE

"The Culpeper Minutemen were also involved in the December 1775 Battle of Great Bridge, which is one of the places where historians agree that their flag [Don't Tread on Me] was carried in battle. Here they met the troops of their old enemy Dunmore. This was an American rout. It marked the final gasp of colonial power in Virginia."

[Dec. 11, 2019, on FOX NEWS TUCKER CARLSON interviewed a Virginia sheriff who said he will deputize all the citizens in his county for their protection. This is an unprecedented state's rights constitutional act. His motivation reason is because the Virginia state legislature will vote in January 2020 on banning and confiscating the AR-15 "assault" rifles the most popular hunting and protective rifle weapon used in Virginia and 49 other states. The sheriff revealed that presently 68 counties in Virginia will refuse any law passed by the newly elected Democrat government majority. Carlson asked what their motivation is? The sheriff retorted, "I believe they are trying to initiate a national precedent." I first heard this at the Richmond, Virginia Veterans Hospital on December 10, from a man and his wife who live in the Shenandoah Valley and own guns. His wife said that America is becoming a Communist country. In the few minutes I talked to them I quickly told them my mother's story about leaving Hitler's Germany in January 1935, when 19, and was illegal for 5 years. I was impressed with their knowledge of history, the wife says she reads a lot. They live in what was the breadbasket of the South the fertile farmland of the beautiful Shenandoah Valley. They must know how General Jackson famously routed Union advances there. During the WAR OF NORTHERN AGGRESSION more Confederate and Union soldiers die and were wounded in Virginia than any other state. My wife and daughter moved to Garrisonville, Stafford County, Virginia on July 4, 1977. My son was born on November 8, 1977, at the old Mary Washington Hospital in Fredericksburg, VA. My daughter graduated from MARY WASHINGTON College, now university, in 1997. My son graduated from VIRGINIA TECH in 2000. I continue to learn historical stories about the CIVIL WAR, I and my daughter live in two of the battlefields and two others are with 12-17 miles away. I have visited most of the president's and general's homes. On April   15, 2005, I moved into The Lake of the Woods community and the WILDERNESS 2nd day General SEDGWICK trench is 22 paces into the woods behind my house within sight from my living room. I was surprised to learn that in 1724, this neighborhood FORT GERMANNA was the western frontier. There is a map/sign at the local WalMart which shows that in 1724, Orange County included 4 western states Kentucky, Ohio, Indiana, Illinois, and southern part of 2 states, Michigan, Wisconsin and western Pennsylvania. I was born in Lexington, Kentucky on May 4, 1943, 220 years earlier had been part of my county. Ft. Germanna is where the first Germans in Virginia came to mine iron. They cut down about 1,000 acres of trees to smelt the pig iron shipped to Britain. This created the "Wilderness" undergrowth an ecological anomaly which was a disaster in the battle where wounded soldiers were burned alive. The miners came from SIEGEN, Germany. in August 1958, when 15, I visited German cousins Anneliese and Werner in Siegen which was 22 miles west of where my grandfather Karl Frank was born. Small World.]

"While it doesn't get as much attention in history books, the situation in Revolutionary Virginia was arguably as tense as it was in Revolutionary Massachusetts. Dunmore had dismissed the colonial assembly, the House of Burgesses, as well as the aforementioned confiscation of gunpowder. The gunpowder was confiscated without incident, but Dunmore feared for his life and fled the colonial capital."

"In October, Dunmore had finally gained enough military support among Loyalists in the colony to begin military operations. This included attacks on the local civilian populations in an attempt to confiscate military materials that might be used by the rebels. On November 7, Dunmore declared martial law and even went so far as to offer emancipation to all the slaves willing to fight in the British Army. Indeed, he was able to raise an entire regiment to that effect."

"The local forces numbered a scant 400. However, reinforcements from neighboring areas, including the Culpeper boys, helped to ballon this number. Dunmore, however, had old intelligence that left the numbers at the original 400. The battle ended with the British forces spiking their guns to avoid capture by the Revolutionary forces."

"When all was said and done, there were 62 British casualties by British count and 103 by the count of the rebels. The rebels had only a single 1 casualty—A slight thumb wound. The Virginians considered this to be their BUNKER HILL. The Patriots refused to allow the overcrowded ships (where the Tories sought refuge) to be resupplied, which resulted in the bombardment of Norfolk and its looting and destruction by rebels, Dunmore, considered the greatest threat to the Revolution by many senior rebel officers, was eventually forced out of Virginia entirely in August 1776."

"Reports indicated that the British were highly intimidated by the reputation of the frontiersmen who would be arriving at the battle. This undoubtedly provided them with a psychological advantage in what was an important battle."

THE DEATH AND RESURRECTION OF THE CULPEPER MINUTEMEN

'The Committee of Safety ordered the group to disband in January 1776, however, almost all of the Culpeper boys kept on fighting—either as continental militiamen or underneath officers such as DANIEL MORGAN."

"The fourth Chief Justice of the United States, JOHN MARSHALL, was one of the first Culpeper boys."

"When the War Between the States came, the Culpeper Minutemen were reconstituted under the old oak tree where they first organized generations prior. This was in 1860, and they once again carried the same flag as their forefathers. They were eventually integrated into the regular army of the Confederate States of America, as part of Company B of the 13th Virginia Infantry, where they served to the end of the Civil War."

"The Minutemen came together again during the Spanish-American War, but were never activated. During World War I, the Culpeper boys organized once again, this time under the auspices of the 116th Infantry. The modern-day Alpha Company Detachment, 2nd Regiment of the Virginia Defense Force, considers themselves to be a descendent of the Culpeper Minutemen, probably with their roots in the First World War."

"While many of the Revolutionary War flags flown by the Patriots today have dubious origins, the Culpeper Flag is one of the few banners that we know for certain was flown by Patriots during the Revolutionary period. It also offers a succinct statement of the values of the American nation: LIBERTY OR DEATH—and a stern warning to those who would threaten our liberty."

"We are committed to preserving liberties like the Second Amendment. This article is licensed under a Creative Commons Attribution 4.0 International License."

[At my local Veterans group Christmas party in 2017 I talked with the DJ about music. I told him about my special Fight Terrorism Virginia license plate, with Pentagon, I bought in January 2002. He showed me on his cell phone a photo of him with the Virginia license he designed. It was the yellow Virginia license with the rattlesnake Don't Tread on Me flag with number 00 rattlesnake 00. Providence. He lives in Culpeper but was born in Portland, Maine. I told him my grandfather enlisted at Cape Elizabeth near Portland. He walked from Calais on the New Brunswick, Canadian border about 200 miles, as one of Lincoln's first 50,000 volunteers to preserve the Union. He voted for Abraham Lincoln twice. He was 79, when my father was born in 1919, and his wife from Eastport, Maine was 38. His Amityville, Long Island tombstone is on FIND A GRAVE JOHN LOUDEN 1839-1933, He voted Republican until Hoover. I told him I graduated from Nasson College in 1964, about 35 miles from Portland. I had my graduation dinner in KENNEBUNKPORT, Maine at the Shawmut Inn. The inn was on the Atlantic Ocean the inlet past the BUSH'S presidential house. This was 1964, my French teacher 3 1/2 years in high school was Miss Bush, no relation. Really SMALL WORLD.

The Personal and Cultural Benefits of Truthfulness

Ralph Drollinger founder-president Capitol Ministries October 22, 2018

"I'm sure you have lived long enough, as have I, to experience the fact that time and truth run hand in hand. TRUTH WINS OUT IN THE END."
"Accordingly, the importance of truth in the capitol community cannot be understated. Notice in this week's Bible study the following Proverbs that depict the various benefits of being a man or woman of truth. When you understand the benefits of being truthful, versus the detriments of lying or bearing false witness, it proves motivational to say the least." [Read the 9TH COMMANDMENT about bearing FALSE WITNESS]

TRUTHFULNESS: WHAT WILL IT DEMAND OF YOU?

"Having established the foundational need for both kindness and truth coexisting in the soul of man, notice in addition the further proverbial admonition: Proverbs 4:24 Put away from you a deceitful mouth and put devious speech from you."
It follows that deceit and deviousness, in that they are far from God's nature, must be far from ours as well! The idea of devious speech — speech opposite of kind and truthful speech — includes speaking GOSSIP, SLANDER, or harm toward others, which encompasses the idea of the 9th Commandment stated in Exodus 20:16:

"YOU SHALL NOT BEAR FALSE WITNESS."

Solomon further impresses this idea on his son, Rehoboam, the future Public Servant of Israel who will one day be tasked with the leadership of a nation, stating: Proverbs 23:23 buy truth, and do not sell it, get wisdom and instruction and understanding.
"All too often people do not buy into truth, but instead sell it out in the capital for reasons of POLITICAL EXPEDIENCY. How sad it is to see the oft selling out of truth in the extremely COMPETITIVE atmosphere of ELECTIONS. The following Proverb helps us to not succumb to such pressures:

"Proverbs 28:6 Better is the poor who walks in his integrity than he who is crooked though he be rich."
"The desire to be rich relates to more than monetary wealth; often in our culture it relates to power and upward mobility in one's career, like getting elected to office. Do NOT SACRIFICE TRUTH and PERSONAL INTEGRITY on the ALTAR OF POLITICAL EXPEDIENCE, my beloved friend.

Such haste in the moment of battle is not beneficial in the long run because time and truth do run hand in hand."

DEEM TRUTH TO BE MORE VALUABLE THAN YOURSELF OR YOUR CAREER

"I am afraid this idea is largely lost in America today. Is your highest good in your career, winning the next election? Is truth subservient to that? May it not be so; God will honor your being principled versus expedient. Commit yourself to being a man or women of truth today. Think of it this way in the specific terms of an election; being TRUTHFUL today may cost me an election, but in so doing it may set me up for what God has next in store for me. This is what truth demands of me."

PEOPLE IN THE CAPITAL COMMUNITY SHOULD BE ARDENT
SEARCHERS FOR TRUTH, STRONGLY CONDEMNING ANY AND ALL
FORMS OF DEVIATION IF FOR NO OTHER REASON THAN THEIR
SENSE OF CLOSENESS TO GOD

DO YOU TAKE THE CARE OFTEN NECESSARY TO MENTALLY ARREST
YOUR SINFUL NATURE AND ITS PROPENSITY FOR EVIL THINKING?

IF YOU ARE LOOKING FOR LONGEVITY AND PERSEVERANCE IN
OFFICE, THEN BECOME A HABITUAL TRUTH TELLER

THE STABILITY OF THE GOVERNMENT RESTS PRIMARILY UPON THE
LOYALTY AND VERACITY OF THE ONES WHO GOVERN
Pastor Ralph Drollinger Capitol Ministries Washington, DC

The Longest Day PorTals Prayer June 21, 2018
"Today in the northern hemisphere, it is the summer solstice, the longest day of the year. Solstice comes from the Latin sol (sun) and sistere (to stand still): on the solstice, the sun seems to stand still before beginning its long descent into sunset.
The science of the solstice is fascinating, an amazing tribute to our infinitely wise, powerful, and creative God. His first words to us were, "Let there be light," and there was light…And God made the two great lights—the greater light to rule the day and the lesser light to rule the night—and the stars. And God set them in the expanse of the heavens to give light on earth. And God saw that it was good" (Genesis 1:3, 16-17,

SING OF GOD'S POWER AND LOVE

"I will sing of the steadfast love of the Lord, forever; with my mouth I will make known Your faithfulness to all generations." PSALM 89:1-18 Also read Ephesians 5:17-21

"Perhaps you've experienced the power that music has to stick with us (for good or evil). Memorizing words set to music has consistently been shown to be easier than memorizing words not attached to music.

In Psalm 89, the author [David] writes of singing of the love of the Lord so that all generations will know the faithfulness of the Lord. Singing is important enough that Ephesians 5 calls us to sing in place of evil thoughts and debauchery and to sing as a way of giving thanks to God from the heart.

Music is a gift from God. It helps us learn His Word and recall His promises. It helps us give witness to our family and friends about what God has done. "Psalms and hymns and spiritual songs" (Ephesians 5:19) help keep our minds focused on Christ and give thanks for all He has done for us."

Dear Lord, help me to sing a new song to you always. Thank You for the gift of music. Help me to use it for good.   Amen   PorTals Prayer May 23, 2018

CHRISTIAN HYMNS AND CREEDS AMAZING GRACE

Amazing grace! How sweet the sound
That saved a wretch like me!
I once was lost but now am found;
Was blind, but now I see.
'Twas grace that taught my heart to fear,
And grace my fears relieved.
How precious did that grace appear
The hour I first believed.
The Lord has promised good to me;
His Word my hope secures.
He will my shield and portion be
As long as life endures.
Thro' many dangers, toils and snares
I have already come.
'Tis grace hath brought me safe thus far,
And grace will lead me home.
When we've been there ten thousand years,
Bright shining as the Sun,
We've no less days to sing God's praise
Than when we'd first begun

JOHN NEWTON [1725-1807] stanza 5, JOHN P. REES [1828-1903]

GLORIOUS THINGS OF THEE ARE SPOKEN

JOHN NEWTON

Glorious things of thee are spoken, Zion, city of our God; He whose
Word cannot be broken formed thee for His own abode: on the
Rock of Ages founded, what can shake thy sure repose?
With salvation's walls surrounded, thou mayst smile at all thy foes.

See the streams of living waters, springing from Eternal Love,
Well supply thy sons and daughters and all fear of want remove:
Who can faint while such a river ever flows their thirst to assuage?
Grace which, like the Lord, the Giver, never fails from age to age.
Round each habitation hovering, see the cloud and fire appear
For a glory and a covering, showing that the Lord is near!
Glorious things of Thee are spoken, Zion, city of our God;
He whose Word cannot be broken formed thee for His own abode.

I Heard the Bells on Christmas Day

"I heard the bells on Christmas day Their old familiar carols play, and wild and sweet the the words repeat Of peace on earth, good will to men.
I thought how, as the day had come, The belfries of all Christendom Had rolled along th'un unbroken song Of peace on earth, good will to men.
And in despair I bowed my head: "There is no peace on earth," I said, "For hate is strong, and mocks the song Of peace on earth, good will to men.
Yet peeled the bells more loud and deep: "God is not dead, nor doth He sleep; The wrong shall fail, the right prevail, With peace on earth, good will to men.
Then ringing, singing on its way, The world revolved from night to day—A voice, a chime, a chant sublime Of peace on earth, good will to men!"
Text: Henry W. Longfellow

This song is an ode to his wounded son at a nearby Civil War battle MINE RUN in December 1863. It is about two miles south of where the WILDERNESS battle was fought in May 5-6, 1864. My home, community and church are built in this battlefield.

Google I heard the bells on Christmas Day there is an amazing U TUBE VIDEO about the tragic personal history which motivated Longfellow to write this poem put to music.

It is narrated by actor EDWARD HERMANN with the MORMON TABERNACLE CHOIR.

It is one of the greatest non-biblical Christmas hymns. In October 2014, I visited a former neighbor who was sent to a nursing home in Amesbury, Massachusetts. After I left him at 9 PM, I drove passed a nearby historic house Longfellow's.

HOW GREAT THOU ART

O Lord my God, when I in awesome wonder Consider all the worlds thy hands have made, I see the stars, I hear the rolling thunder, Thy pow'r thro'out the universe displayed. Then sings my soul, my Savior God, to Thee; How great Thou art! Then sings my soul, my Savior God, to Thee: How great Thou art, how great Thou art!

When thro' the woods and forest glades I wander And hear the birds sing sweetly in the trees, When I look down from lofty mountain grandeur, And near the brook and feel the gentle breeze. Then sings my soul, my Savior God, to Thee; How great Thou art, how great Thou art! Then sings my soul, my Savior God, to Thee: How great Thou art, how great Thou art!

And when I think that God, His Son not sparing, Sent Him to die, I scarce can take it in, That on the cross, my burden gladly bearing, He bled and died to take away my sin, Then sings my soul, my Savior God, to Thee: How great Thou art, how great Thou art! Then sings my soul, my Savior God, to Thee: How great Thou art, how great Thou art!

When Christ shall come with shout of acclamation And take me home, what joy shall fill my heart! Then I shall bow in humble adoration, And there proclaim, my God, how great Thou art, Then sings my soul, my Savior God, to Thee; How great Thou art! Then sings my soul, my Savior God, to Thee: How great Thou art, how great Thou art!

When Christ shall come with shout of acclamation And take me home, what joy shall fill my heart! Then I shall bow in humble adoration, And there proclaim, my God, how great Thou art! Then sings my soul, my Savior God, to Thee; How great Thou art, how great Thou art! Then sings my soul, my Savior God, to Thee: How great Thou art! How great Thou art, how great Thou art, how great Thou art!

TEXT and MUSIC Stuart K. Hine; Last stanza setting by Eugene Thomas

BLESSED ASSURANCE

"IS ANYONE HAPPY? LET HIM SING SONGS OF PRAISE."   James 5:13

Blessed assurance, JESUS IS MINE! O what a foretaste of GLORY DIVINE! Heir of SALVATION, purchase of God, Born of HIS SPIRIT, washed in HIS BLOOD. THIS IS MY STORY, THIS IS MY SONG, Praising my Savior all the day long; This is my song, Praising my Savior all the day long; This is my story, this is my song, Praising my Savior all the day long.

PERFECT SUBMISSION, perfect delight! Visions of Rapture now burst on my sight; Angels descending bring from above Echoes of mercy, whispers of love. This is my story, this is my song. Praising my Savior all the day long; This is my story, this is my song, Praising my Savior all the day long. This is my story, this is my song.

Perfect submission—all is at rest, I IN MY SAVIOR AM HAPPY AND BLEST; Watching and waiting, looking above, Filled with His GOODNESS, lost in HIS LOVE. This is my story, this is my song. Praising my Savior all day long.

TEXT: FANNY CROSBY   MUSIC: Phoebe P. Knapp; Descant by James C. Gibson

HISTORICAL FACT: Fanny Crosby wrote some 8,000 hymns and Gospel songs from 1864-1915 under nearly 200 pseudonyms, other names, because hymn music publishers were hesitant, couldn't cope? with so many hymns written by one person in their hymnals— a woman. Fanny Crosby, a Methodist, became know as the "Queen of Gospel song writers" and as the "Mother of modern congregational singing in America."

IRA DAVID SANKEY, known as "THE SWEET SINGER OF METHODISM", was an American Gospel singer and composer who accompanied evangelist preacher DWIGHT L. MOODY during the late 1880s REPENTANCE AND REVIVAL tour of America. Sankey attributed the success of the MOODY AND SANKEY evangelical campaigns largely to FANNY CROSBY'S HYMNS whose hymns were "paradigmatic of all revival music'" Crosby's best known hymns were BLESSED ASSURANCE, PASS ME NOT, O GENTLE SAVIOR, JESUS IS TENDERLY CALLING YOU HOME, PRAISE HIM, PRAISE HIM, RESCUE THE PERISHING, and TO GOD BE THE GLORY. Fanny may have been inspired by the spirit of Englishman JOHN WESLEY, father of Methodism Anglican church evangelist reformism, and his brother CHARLES WESLEY who composed some 6,500 hymns and by OUR LORD AND SAVIOR JESUS CHRIST.

FANNY CROSBY WAS BLIND

NICENE CREED

325 A.D.Turkey
I believe in one God,
the Father Almighty,
maker of heaven and earth
and of all things visible and invisible.
And in one Lord Jesus Christ,
the only-begotten Son of God,
begotten, not made,
being of one substance with the Father,
by whom all things were made;
who for us men and for our salvation came
down from heaven
and was incarnate by the Holy Spirit of
the virgin Mary
and was made man;
and was crucified also for us under
Pontius Pilate.
He suffered and was buried.
And the third day He rose again according
to the Scriptures
and ascending into Heaven
and sits at the right hand of the Father.
And He will come again with Glory to judge
both the living and the dead,
whose kingdom will have no end.
And I believe in the Holy Spirit,
the Lord and giver of life,
who proceeds from the Father and the Son,
who with the Father and the Son together
is worshipped and glorified,
who spoke by the prophets.
And I believe in one holy Christian and
Apostolic Church,
I acknowledge one Baptism for the remission of sins,
and I look for the resurrection of the dead
and the life + of the world to come. Ame

APOSTLES' CREED

325 A.D. Asia Minor
I believe in God, the Father Almighty,
maker of Heaven and earth.
And in Jesus Christ, His only son, our Lord,
who was conceived by the Holy Spirit,
born of the virgin Mary,
suffered under Pontius Pilate,

was crucified, died and was buried.
He descended into hell.   [Hades underworld]
The third day He rose again from the dead
I believe in the Holy Spirit,
the holy Christian Church,
the communion of saints,
the forgiveness of sins,
the Resurrection of the body,
and the life + everlasting. Amen.

A MIGHTY FORTRESS IS OUR GOD "Ein feste Burg ist unser Gott"

Martin Luther 1529 A.D.

A mighty fortress is our God, A sword and shield victorious;
He breaks the cruel oppressors rod. And wins salvation glorious.
The old satanic foe Has sworn to work us woe.
With craft and dreadful might He arms himself to fight.
On earth he has no equal.

No strength of ours can match his might. We would be lost rejected.
But now a champion comes to fight, Whom God Himself elected.
You ask who this may be? The Lord of hosts is He, Christ Jesus,
mighty Lord, God's only Son, adored. He holds the field victorious.
Though hordes of devils fill the land All threat'ning to devour us,
We tremble not, unmoved we stand; They cannot overpow'r us.
Let this world's tyrant rage; In battle we'll engage.
His might is doomed to fail; God's judgment must prevail!
One little word subdues him.
God's Word forever shall abide. No thanks to foes, who fear it;
For God Himself fights by our side With weapons of the Spirit.
Were they to take our house, Goods, honor, child or spouse,
Though life be wrenched away, They cannot win the day.
The Kingdom's ours forever!

MARTIN LUTHER's inspiration for writing A MIGHTY FORTRESS is found in the words of the Old Testament's PSALM 46:

"God is our refuge and strength, a very present help in trouble.
Therefore we will not fear though the earth gives way, though
the mountains be moved into the heart of the sea, though its
waters roar and foam, though the mountains tremble at its
swelling. There is a river whose streams make glad the city
of God, the holy habitation of the Most High. God is in the
midst of her; she shall not be moved; God will help her when
morning dawns. The nations rage, the kingdoms totter; he

utters his voice, the earth melts. The Lord of host is with us;
the GOD of JACOB is our fortress. Come, behold the works
of the Lord, how he has brought desolations on the earth. He
makes wars cease to the end of the earth; he breaks the bow
and shatters the spear; he burns the chariots with fire. Be still,
and know that I am God. I will be exalted among the nations.
I will be exalted among the nations, I will be exalted in the earth!
The Lord of hosts is with us, the God of all.   Psalm 46:1-11

Lift High The Cross

Lift high the Cross, the love of Christ proclaim, Till all the world adore His sacred name.
Come, Christians, follow where our Savior trod, Our King victorious, Christ, the   Son of God.

Led on their way by this triumphant sign, The hosts of God in conqu'ring ranks combine.
O Lord, once lifted on this glorious Tree, As Thou hast promised, draw men unto Thee.
Set up Thy throne, that earth's despair may cease Beneath the shadow of its   healing peace.

For Thy blest Cross which doth for all atone, Creation's praises rise before Thy throne.
Text: George W. Kitchin and Micheal Newbolt Music: Sydney H. Nicholson copy write Hymns
Ancient and Modern LTD

Onward Christian Soldier

Onward Christian soldiers, Marching us to war, With the cross of Jesus Going on before! Christ
the royal Master, Leads against the foe; Forward into battle See His banners go!
Onward ye soldiers, marching as to war With the Onward, Christian soldiers, marching as to war,
With the cross of Jesus going on before. Amen
At the sign of triumph Satan's host doth flee; On then, Christian soldiers, On to victory! Hell's
foundations quiver At the shout of praise; Brothers lift your voices, Loud your anthems raise!
Like a mighty army Moves the Church of God; Brothers, we are treading Where the saints have
trod. We are not divided, All one body we— One in hope and doctrine, One in charity.
Onward, then, ye people, Join our happy throng; Blend with ours your voices In the triumph song.
Glory, laud and honor Unto Christ the King — This thru countless ages Men and angels sing
Onward, ye soldiers, marching as to war. With the Onward, Christian soldiers marching as to war
With the cross of Jesus going on before. Amen
Text: Sabine Baring-Gould Music: Arthur S. Sullivan; Descant by David Allen copyright 1986 Word
Music

The Battle Hymn of the Republic

Mine eyes have seen the glory of the coming of the Lord, He is trampling out the vintage where
the grapes of wrath are stored; He hath loosed the fateful lightning of His terrible swift sword—
His truth is marching on. Glory! glory, hallelujah! Glory! glory, hallelujah! His truth is marching on.

I have seen Him in the watchfires of a hundred circling camps, They have builded Him an altar in the evening dews and damps; I can read His righteous sentence by the dim and flaring lamps— His day is marching on, Glory! glory hallelujah!

He has sounded forth the trumpet that shall never sound retreat, He is sifting out the hearts of men before His judgment seat; O be swift, my soul, to answer Him! be jubilant, my feet! Our God is marching on. Glory! glory, hallelujah! His truth is marching on.

In the beauty of the lilies Christ was born across the sea, With a glory in His bosom that transfigures you and me; As He died to make men holy, let us live to make men free, While God is marching on. Glory! glory, hallelujah! Glory, glory, hallelujah! His truth is marching on. Glory, glory hallelujah!

Text: Julia Ward Howe Music: traditional American melody copywrite 1986 Word Music

Land of Hope and Glory

Solo
Dear Land of Hope and Glory, thy hope is crowned,
God make thee mightier yet!
On Sov'ran brows, beloved, renowned,
Once more thy crown is set.
Thine equal laws, by Freedom gained,
Have ruled thee well and long;
By Freedom gained, by Truth maintained,
Thine Empire shall be strong.
Chorus
Land of Hope and Glory, Mother of the Free,
How shall we extol thee, who are born of thee?
Wider still and wider shall thy bounds be set;
God, who made thee mighty, make thee mightier yet,
God, who made thee mighty, make thee mightier yet.
Solo
Thy fame is ancient as the days,
    As Ocean large and wide,
A pride that dares, and heeds not praise,
    A stern and silent pride;
Not that false joy that dreams content
    With what our sires have won;
The blood a hero sire hath spent
    Still nerves a hero son.

Watch this rousing song sung by Dame VERA LYNN, Britain's World War II nightingale. She passed in June 2020, age 103. Watch her many U Tube music videos. Also watch on U Tube the large British audiences singing this song at the BBC PROMS music festivals. Only "God Save the Queen or King" and "Rule Britannia" are more patriotic. Its lyrics by A.C. Benson, written in 1902, are based on the original music theme taken from Sir EDWARD ELGAR's famous "Pomp and Circumstance March No. 1," used as the school processional music played at high schools, colleges and universities in Anglo-American nations. England currently has no agreed national anthem with "God Save the Queen" the anthem of the United Kingdom. A 2006 survey conducted by the BBC suggested that 55% of the English public would rather have "Land of Hope and Glory" than 'God Save the Queen" as their national anthem. Wikipedia [Queen Elizabeth II, 93, has been the longest reigning monarch, 70 years, in British History surpassing Queen Victoria and Queen Elizabeth I. I think King Charles or William would have to make a decision. "God Save the King" would still be the royal ceremonial song.] 'Audience participation in the second half of the program had become a ritual, and from 1947 a boisterous "tradition" was created by the conductor Malcolm Sargent, making "Land of Hope and Glory" part of a standard program for the event. The "Last Night of the proms" was broadcast annually on television from 1953 onwards, and Promenaders began dressing up outrageously and waving flags and banners during the climax of the evening." Interestingly, "Land of Hope and Glory" was the England team's victory anthem at the Commonwealth Games until 2010, when the public rejected it in a poll in favor of "JERUSALEM". Wikipedia [I heard a 10 year old boy play Jerusalem solo on his violin at a Seventh Day Adventist SDA Saturday sabbath. The 16 years I attended Beth Shalom "House of Peace" Reformed Temple in Fredericksburg, Virginia, I had never heard Jerusalem played. This young boy's solo was one of the most inspirational songs I have ever heard. The Seventh Day Adventists are more "Jewish" than most modern Jews.]

Ironically, "The writing of the song is contemporaneous with the publication of CECIL RHODES' will—in which he bequeathed his considerable wealth for the specific purpose of promoting "the extension of British rule throughout the world," and added a detailed list of territories which Rhodes wanted brought under British rule and colonized by British people." Wikipedia   [This song therefore glorifies Great Britain's continued 18th Century colonization "imperialism" to bring English civil law to the "Third World". The Rhodes scholarship has been given to some intellectual Americans of merit? Bill Clinton was a Rhodes scholar at Oxford University, not a graduate, which kept him out of service during the Vietnam War. His daughter Chelsea was selected as a Rhodes scholar and actually graduated. Wikipedia says MSNBC TV newswoman RACHEL MADDOW was the "first" Rhodes scholar to be openly gay. Does she know that she has an "imperialistic" degree? I don't have MSNBC but have seen some of her anti President Trump's Make America Great Again, nationalist Founding Father's beliefs. The Rhodes scholars are taught to promote global peace. Only Jesus Christ can do that! I once heard her supporting our troops. Her father was a Captain in the Air Force.]

SMALL WORLD FACT: Today, November 19, 2017, 40-year president Robert Mugabe, 93, of Zimbabwe, Northern Rhodesia, government resigned and the country is now under military control. The country was originally part of British Rhodesia, named after Cecil Rhodes! It was rich in mineral resources. It is also in the news now for having a large endangered elephant population which President Donald Trump has become involved with because his son-in-law is a big game hunter. Ironically, a couple of years ago Zimbabwe made international news and outrage when an American doctor, with a local guide, killed a legendary old bull elephant. What was the elephant's name? CECIL! The news media did not realize the elephant's name was connected with Cecil Rhodes buried there. As Kurt Vonnegut would retort: "So it Goes!" RIP Kurt.

JERUSALEM

And did those feet in ancient time
Walk upon England's mountains green?
And was the holy Lamb of God
On England's pleasant pastures seen?
And did the Countenance Divine
Shine forth upon our clouded hills?
And was Jerusalem builded here

Among these dark Satanic Mills?
Bring me my bow of burning gold!
Bring me my arrows of desire!
Bring me my spear! O clouds, unfold!
Bring me my chariot of fire!
I will not cease from mental fight,
Nor shall my sword sleep in my hand,
Til we have built Jerusalem
In England's green and pleasant land.

The words of Jerusalem, are from "Milton" by William Blake (1757-1827) OXYMORON: This is a British song not Jewish Israeli song! Why? The English royalty reigns over the British Commonwealth and Jerusalem! Britain from 1918-1948 had control over Palestine and its Balfour Declaration allowed a limited number of Jewish people to live in Palestine. On May 14, 1948, a close UNITED NATIONS vote allowed the restored Nation of Israel to be opened to Holocaust survivors. The Arab-Islamic nations and Communist nations opposed creating the nation of Israeli after 2,520 years! The Old Testament actually reveals this exact date through prophecies! Providential Prophecy!
"Cathedral bans popular hymn Jerusalem. Have your say: Is Jerusalem too nationalistic?" London Telegram April 10, 2008

SONG OF JOY

Ludwig von Beethoven
O friends, no more of these sounds!
Let us sing more cheerful songs,
More songs full of joy!
Joy!
Joy!
Joy, bright spark of divinity,
Daughter of Elysium,
Fire-inspired we tread
Within thy sanctuary.
Thy magic power re-unites
All that custom has divided,
All men become brothers,
Under the sway of thy gentle wings.
Whoever has created
An abiding friendship,
Or has won
A true and loving wife,
All who can call at least one soul theirs,
Join our song of praise;
But those who cannot must creep tearfully
Away from our circle.
All creatures drink of joy
At natures breast.
Just and unjust

Alike taste of her gift;
She gave us kisses and the fruit of the vine,
A tried friend to the end.
Even the worm can feel contentment,
And the cherub stands before God!
Gladly, like the heavenly bodies
Which He sent on their courses
Through the splendor of the firmament;
Thus, brothers, you should run your race,
Like a hero going to victory!
You millions, I embrace you.
This kiss is for all the world!
Brothers, above the starry canopy
There must dwell a loving father.
Do you fall in worship, you millions?
World, do you know your creator?
Seek Him in the heavens;
Above the stars must be dwell.

LUDWIG von BEETHOVEN, composed this in 1824, in the final movement of his last, and arguably his most famous symphony, Symphony No. 9. The premiere took place in Vienna on May 7, 1824, and despite its unpracticed and underrehearsed presentation, the audience was ecstatic. It was the first time Beethoven had appeared on stage in 12 years. At the end of the performance (though some sources say it could have been after the 2nd movement), it was said that Beethoven continued conducting even though the music had ended. One of the soloists stopped him and turned him around to accept his applause. The audience was well aware of Beethoven's health and hearing loss, so in addition to clapping, they threw their hats and scarves in the air so that he could see their overwhelming approval. This symphony is considered by many leading musicologists to be one of the greatest works in western music. What makes it so special is Beethoven's use of the human voice; he was the first major composer to include it within a symphony. This is why you'll often see Symphony No. 9 referred to as the Choral symphony. Beethoven's 9th symphony, with an orchestra bigger than any other at the time and a play time of well over an hour (longer than any other symphony), was a major turning point for classical music; it was a catapult into the Romantic Period, where composers began breaking rules of classical period composition, and exploring the use of large ensembles, extreme emotion, and unconventional orchestration."

The "Ode to Joy" text employed, and slightly modified, by Beethoven was written by the German poet, JOHANN von SCHILLER, in the summer of 1785. It was a celebratory poem addressing the unity of all mankind."   Wikipedia

[I have a large LP, CD and tapes collection of Swing bands and large pop symphonic orchestras. In grade school I couldn't learn notes and we all played the "Tonette" sweet potato, ocarina, not a melodic instrument. I had listened to my dad's first expensive London LP circa 1950 of Mantovani playing Charmaine. Dad had a large Latin American bands and marimba LP collection. Dad taught me to learn what instrument was playing. I learned arrangement styles and could name soloists in big bands. I never played a note. My dad learned one song "I Saw Stars" rote and could play a little by ear and read sheet music. He bought an old baby grand 4 foot 8 inch Kimball player roll piano. I would play it in our apartment across MaComb park by Yankee stadium, 1001 Jerome Avenue. I loved playing the American standard songs from the 1930s and 1940s. I opened the windows and never had a complaint even though the piano was louder than my big stereo. Most of the tenants were senior citizens. My granddaughter is 12 and in 7th grade and has just been selected as a First Chair Cellist in her school string orchestra. She is left handed not a problem? The cello is a soulful instrument which is becoming very popular, YO YO MA and FOUR CELLOS. Actor JAIME FOX was a gifted bipolar cellist in 2009 film THE SOLOIST with ROBERT DOWNEY, JR.

I have heard great recorded instrumental music and seen some great Big Bands and Symphonic orchestras. I have seen the sheet music arrangements. Beethoven had to be the world's greatest composer to be able to arrange such an amazing symphony when completely deaf. In the 1995 movie IMMORTAL BELOVED English actor GARY OLDMAN portrays Beethoven and reveals his deafness was caused by Napoleon's cannon fire on Dresden, Germany. Beethoven was divinely inspired and allegedly he wrote this symphony to redeem and repent his troubled sibling rivalry over a girl friend.

GOD BLESS AMERICA

God bless America Land that I love Stand beside her And guide her Through the night with the light from above From the mountains To the prairie To the oceans White with foam God bless America My home sweet home
From the mountains To the prairies To the oceans White with foam God bless America
My home sweet home

The song was originally written for a Ziegfield-style army revue,"Yip, Yip Yaphank", at Camp Upton near Yaphank, Long Island, New York, in the summer of 1918 during the Great War, World War I, but ironically wasn't released until World War II. Berlin then added a World War II introduction:

> "While the storm clouds gather far across the Sea, let us swear
> allegiance to a land so fair, as we Raise our voices in a solemn prayer."

Songwriter" Irving Berlin copy write Imaem Music Inc
Berlin was a Jewish Russian immigrant from Tashkent in Siberia, Russia.

ATHANASIAN CREED

The TRINITY explained
Whoever desires to be saved must, above all, hold the catholic faith.
Whoever does not keep it whole and undefiled will without doubt perish.
And the catholic faith is this, that we worship one God in Trinity
and Trinity in Unity, neither confusing the persons nor dividing the substance.
For the Father is one person, the Son is another, and the Holy Spirit is another.
But the Godhead of the Father and of the Son and of the Holy Spirit is one:
the glory equal, the majesty coeternal.
Such as the Father is, such is the Son, and such is he Holy Spirit:
the Father uncreated, the Son uncreated, the Holy Spirit uncreated;
the Father infinite, the Son infinite, the Holy Spirit infinite;
the Father eternal, the Son eternal, the Holy Spirit eternal.

And yet there are not three Eternals, but one Eternal.
Just as there are not three Uncreated or three Infinites,
but one Uncreated and one Infinite.
In the same way, the Father is almighty, the Son almighty, the
Holy Spirit almighty; and yet there are not three Almighty's, but one Almighty.
So the Father is God, the Son is God, the Holy Spirit is God;
and yet there are not three Gods, but one God.
So the Father is Lord, the Son is Lord, the Holy Spirit is Lord;
and yet there are not three Lords, but one Lord.
Just as we are compelled by the Christian truth to acknowledge each distinct
person as God and Lord, so also we are prohibited by the catholic religion
to say that there are three Gods or Lords.
The Father is not made nor created nor begotten by anyone.
The son is neither made nor created, but begotten of the Father alone.
The Holy Spirit is of the Father and of the Son, neither made nor created
nor begotten, but proceeding.
Thus, there is one Father, not three Father's; one Son, not three Sons;
one Holy Spirit, not three Holy Spirits.
And in this Trinity none is before or after another; none is greater or
less than another; but the whole three persons are coeternal with each
other and coequal, so that in all things, as has been stated above,
the Trinity in Unity and Unity in Trinity is to be worshipped.
Therefore, whoever desires to be saved must think thus about the Trinity.
But it is also necessary for everlasting salvation that one faithfully believe
the incarnation of our Lord Jesus Christ.
Therefore, it is the right faith that we believe and confess that our Lord
Jesus Christ, the Son of God, is at the same time both God and man.
He is God, begotten from the substance of the Father before all ages;
and He is man, born from the substance of His mother in this age:
perfect God and perfect man, composed of a rational soul and human flesh;
equal to the Father with respect to His divinity, less than the Father with
respect to His humanity. Although He is God and man, He is not two,
but one Christ: one, however, not by the conversion of the divinity into
flesh, but by the assumption of the humanity into God;
one altogether, not by confusion of substance, but by unity of person.
For as the rational soul an flesh is one man, so God and man is one Christ.
who suffered for our salvation, descended into hell, rose again the third day
from the dead, ascended into Heaven, and is seated at the right hand
of the Father, God Almighty, from whence He will come to judge
the living and the dead.
At His coming all people will rise again with their bodies and give an account
concerning their own deeds.
And those who have done good will enter into eternal life, and those who
have done evil into eternal fire.
This is the catholic faith; whoever does not believe it faithfully and firmly
cannot be saved.

The Lord's Prayer

Our Father who art in Heaven, hallowed be Thy name, Thy kingdom come, Thy will be done on earth as it is in heaven; give us this day our daily bread; and forgive us our trespasses as we forgive those who trespass against us; and lead us not in temptation,
but deliver us from evil.
For Thine is the kingdom and the power and the glory forever and ever. Amen

The Lord's Prayer Original Old Tradition

Our Father in heaven, hallowed be Your name, Your kingdom come. Your will be done on earth as it is in heaven. Give us this day our daily bread. Forgive us our SINS as we forgive those who SIN against us. Lead us not into temptation, but deliver us from evil.
For the kingdom, the power, and the glory are Yours now and forever. Amen   Matt 6:9

ONE FAITH

"Now there are varieties of gifts, but the same Spirit; and there are varieties of service, but the same Lord; and there are varieties of activities, but it is the same God who empowers them all in everyone." 1 Corinthians 12; 4-6   Also 1 Cor.12, Psalm 115
"Each of us has a different personality, and every person, with his or her uniqueness, also has a special God-ordained purpose.
I believe God has given each of us a different personality type for reaching out to others with the news of the Gospel. In ways and circumstances unique to each person, we are called to be disciples of Christ and tell others of Jesus and His love.
God has built our personalities, given us spiritual gifts, and placed us in our communities for a divine purpose—to share the one message of Jesus and the life and salvation that is found only in Him."
O Lord, help me to trust that You have made me and placed me exactly where you want me. Empower me to share the one true faith, using my unique gifts in the specific community in which You have placed me. AMEN
PorTals Prayer Tuesday April 17, 2018 Concordia Publishing House 3558 S. Jefferson Ave. St. Louis, MO 63118
This prayer was on the day BARBARA PIERCE BUSH passed at age 92.

FAITH PRODUCTION

"Not only that, but we rejoice in our sufferings, knowing that suffering produces endurance." Romans 5:3 Also Romans 5:2-5, Psalm 8
"Faith also produces. By faith, we have forgiveness and salvation, which gives us comfort, peace, strength, and joy. But as we live by faith, we will at times face difficulties. When we wear our faith on our sleeves for the world to see how we believe in Jesus, we will face persecution. Many people do not want to hear about Jesus because it offends what they believe.
"We will get weary and grow tired as others who don't want to hear the Gospel may cause us emotional and physical hurt. We are never to shy away from sharing our faith because of the hurt

323

that it may bring. But we can stand in times of persecution, knowing faith is producing awesome qualities in us so we can continue spreading the Gospel."

Dear Jesus, we will at times suffer because of our faith, but we know that faith produces all that we need to continue in our mission of bringing Your love to the world. AMEN

PorTals Prayer Thursday April 19, 2018   The anniversary of Oklahoma City bombing.

Also, the birthday of my Air Force friend Johne Westfall who lives in Tulsa, OK. We both graduated from the last Defense Information School of Information journalism class at Ft. Slocum, NY in September 1965. He was editor of the 17th AF Command "Ramjet" newspaper at Ramstein AB, Germany 1968, I was editor of the Bitburg AB "Skyblazer".

DECLARE GOD'S GLORY

"Declare His Glory among the nations, His marvelous works among all the peoples!"
Psalm 96:3 Also 1 Peter 2:9-12

"God has called us though the Gospel to be His people. He therefore gives each of us the task of proclaiming "The excellencies of Him who called you out of darkness into His marvelous light." (1 Peter 2:9) and living lives that glorify Him makes it clear throughout the Scriptures that the Good News is ——————FOR ALL PEOPLE IN ALL NATIONS.

"Our vocation of proclaiming God's Glory begins in our own home as we teach and encourage our family. We may have the opportunity to share our faith in Jesus with our neighbors through our work, in our neighborhoods, or through congregational ministries of outreach. Many times, God brings "all nations" to our doorstep and gives us the opportunity to declare His Glory through our daily lives."

"Be encouraged that this is God's work and promise, not another law to fulfill. We know that God uses us to speak the Good News about all that He has done to those who are around us.As we see what God is doing in and through our lives, we can give to God.

Dear Jesus, thank You for redeeming us from sin, death, and the devil. Help us to see how You work through Your people for Your Glory. AMEN
PorTals Prayer Friday May 4, 2018   My 75th birthday

God's Light Shines Through Us

"The Lord is my light and my salvation whom shall I fear?" Psalm 27:1 Also Philippians 2:12-18
"In Philippians 2, Paul reminds us that we "shine as lights in the world" (v 15). Psalm 27 reminds us where the light comes from: "The Lord is my light." God's light shines through us."

Dear Jesus, YOU are the light of the world. Be a light to our path. Help us to shine like stars with the light that You give us. Amen. PorTals May 14, 2018, Israel's 70th birthday.

BENJAMIN BRITTEN BRITAIN'S BEETHOVEN/HANDEL

My German mother ELISABETH FRANK lived with BENJAMIN BRITTEN at the TITLEY HOUSE on 123 LOUDEN AVENUE in AMITYVILLE, Long Island circa 1938-40. My mother's 6-month tourist visa expired in July 1935. I found 23 post cards to my mother from her German parents Karl and Susanna, and high school girl friend Gertie. I was able to learn her six addresses where she lived. I have 1939 post cards and an envelope addressed to my dad in 1939 with he World Fair postage stamp. The 1940 U.S. Census lists my mother as born in Frankfurt, Germany and was a waitress. The Titley's were psychiatrists and had housed expatriates from Europe. Providential LOUDEN AVENUE is named for my father's father whose large LOUDEN HALL/KNICKERBOCKER/BRUNSWICK hospital was also on that street. It was founded in 1888, specializing in ALCOHOL, DRUG and NERVOUS "Mental" DISORDERS. America had a serious drug problem with laudanum morphine addiction for pain. There were many Union Civil War soldiers who had amputations and war wounds and needed OPIATES to relieve their serious pain. Today, America has an opiate problem which has become a serious addiction. Some may be for pain but it has also become addictive for its "high". Britten has a book "LETTERS TO MY MOTHER" in England, I have found it on the Internet. He drew a map with a sketch of the Titley House and told his mother how he liked their friendship. The 1940 Census said they had a daughter Rachel, 5. My dad said when he meet my mother she was their nanny. He said the doctors had a private practice and weren't connected to his father's hospital down the street.

The Internet has a lot about SIR BENJAMIN BRITTEN. There are also U Tube Videos of him playing piano accompanied by his Suffolk County, England, childhood friend and partner PETER PEARS, who was a brilliant tenor soloist singer in his operas. When I was a child we played his THE YOUNG PERSONS GUIDE TO THE ORCHESTRA, so I was familiar with his name. Mom said he was GAY, I was 8-9, and thought that meant HAPPY. I believe he may have been, though Britain jailed homosexuals and legally medicated them. He wrote his mother that Amityville was in Suffolk County and on the ocean like their home in Suffolk, England. My mother may have learned some English from him because she had been America for only four years, and Germany didn't teach English, she graduated in 1934. Hitler was elected Chancellor on Jan. 30, 1933.
SIR BENJAMIN BRITTEN'S story is remarkable as I will reveal from the following book. THE GIFT OF MUSIC—GREAT COMPOSERS AND THEIR INFLUENCE by JANE STUART SMITH, an Opera singer, and BETTY CARLSON, who also both co-authored FAVORITE MEN HYMN WRITERS and FAVORITE WOMEN HYMN WRITERS. They both live and work in Lausanne, Switzerland at the L'ABRI FELLOWSHIP founded by the great evangelist FRANCIS SCHAEFFER. Therefore, this information is a Christian and un-prejudicial tribute to Britain's greatest composer of symphonies and operas.

It doesn't matter what style a composer chooses to write in,
as long as he has something definite to say and says it clearly.
Benjamin Britten

"Another of England's prolific composers [preceded by RALPH VAUGHAN WILLIAMS] in the mid-twentieth century was BENJAMIN BRITTEN. He was born in 1913, on the FEAST DAY OF ST. CECILIA, the PATRON SAINT OF ALL MUSICIANS. His parents' home faced the North Sea, and one could hear in his music his love for the sound of the sea. After his parents died, he moved to a converted windmill in a little fishing village. He spent long hours walking the windswept coast sorting out his musical ideas."

"As a child the first music he heard was his mother singing to him selections from SCHUBERT, SCHUMANN, BACH, HANDEL, and MOZART. At 2 he began to play the piano, and at 5 he started composing. When he was 7, he read himself to sleep with musical scores of operas and symphonies. When he was 16, he received a scholarship to the ROYAL COLLEGE OF MUSIC. The only thing he wanted to do was to compose, and at 19 he was determined to earn his living through composition. It was not easy, but he accomplished what he set out to do."

"From these early beginnings flowed a distinguished career in both secular and sacred music. He rejected the tendencies of many composers to ignore the church as a vehicle for great music and Christianity as a subject for it. Some of his best-known sacred compositions are A BOY WAS BORN, A WAR REQUIEM, the delightful CEREMONY OF CAROLS, REJOICE IN THE LAMB, and THE HOLY SONNETS OF JOHN DONNE."

"He is best remembered for his operas PETER GRIMES, THE TURN OF THE SCREW, and BILLY BUDD. His opera THE RAPE OF LUCRETIA includes two narrators who make Christian comments on the PAGAN TRAGEDY. Many in the audience when this opera was performed were troubled and demanded, "WHY DRAG IN CHRISTIANITY?" But in the mind of Britten there was no question of "dragging in Christianity." It had been there all the time. He felt it was morally wrong to set a cruel subject to music without linking the cruelty to the hope of redemption."

"After the performance Britten said, "I used to think that the day when one could shock people was over—but now I've discovered that being simple and considering things spiritual of importance produces violent reactions!""

"It was to the tune of one of HENRY PURCELL'S hornpipes that Britten wrote one of the his most popular works, THE YOUNG PERSONS GUIDE TO THE ORCHESTRA—a lively and most exhilarating introduction to instrumentation. Purcell greatly influenced Britten's creativity."

BRITTEN'S GREATEST SYMPHONY — THE WAR REQUIEM

"The WAR REQUIEM, OP. 66, is a large-scale setting of the REQUIEM composed by BENJAMIN BRITTEN mostly in 19611 and completed in January 1962. The War Requiem was composed for the consecration of the new COVENTRY CATHEDRAL, which was built after the original 14th Century structure was destroyed in a World War II bombing raid. The traditional Latin texts are interspersed, in telling juxtaposition, with extra-liturgical poems by WILFRED OWEN, written during World War I."   Wikipedia

THE GREATEST SYMPHONIC PRESENTATION IN HISTORY

"The work is scored for soprano, tenor and baritone soloists, boys' choir, organ, and two orchestras (a full orchestra and a chamber orchestra). The chamber orchestra accompanies the intimate settings of the English poetry, while soprano, choirs and orchestra are used for the Latin sections; all forces are combined in the conclusion. The Requiem has a duration of approximately 80-85 minutes. In 2019, War Requiem was selected by the LIBRARY OF CONGRESS for preservation in the National Recording Registry for being "culturally historically, or aesthetically significant."   Wikipedia

COMPOSITION

"The War Requiem was first performed on 30 May 1962. Britten a pacifist and conscientious objector, was inspired by the commission, which gave him complete freedom in deciding what to compose. He chose to set the traditional LATIN MASS FOR THE DEAD interwoven with nine 9 poems about war by the English poet Wilfred Owen. Owen, who was born in 1893, was serving as the commander of a rifle company when he was killed in action on 4 November 1918 during the crossing of the Sambre-Oise Canal in France, just one week before the Armistice [November 11] Although he was virtually unknown at the time of his death, he has subsequently come to be revered as one of the great war poets."   Wikipedia

"Britten himself acknowledged the stylistic influence of Requiems by other composers, such as GIUSEPPE VERDI'S, on his own composition. Britten dedicated the work to Roger Burney, Piers

Dunkerley, David Gill, and Michael Halliday, who died in the war, were friends of PETER PEARS [his childhood friend and partner] and BRITTEN. According to the Britten-Pears Foundation's War Requiem website, Dunkerley, one of Bitten's closest friends, took part in the 1944 NORMANDY landings. Unlike the other dedicatees, he survived the war and committed suicide in June 1959, two months before his wedding. None of the other dedicatees have known graves, but are commemorated on memorials to the missing." Wikipedia

ORCHESTRATION

"The musical forces are divided into three groups that alternate and interact with each other throughout the piece, finally fully combining at the end or the last movement. The soprano soloist and choir are accomplished by the full orchestra, the baritone and tenor soloists are accomplished by the chamber orchestra, and the boys' choir is accompanied by a small positive organ (this last group being situated at some distance from the full orchestra). This group produces a very strange, distant sound. The soprano the choir and boys' choir sing the traditional Latin Requiem text, while the tenor and baritone sing poems by Wilfred Owen, interspersed throughout." Wikipedia

PREMIERE AND PERFORMANCES

"For the opening performances, it was intended that the soloists should be [soprano] Galina Vishnevskaya (a Russian), PETER PEARS [tenor] (an Englishman) and Dietrich Fischer-Dieskau (a German), to demonstrate a spirit of unity. Close to the premiere, the Soviet authorities did not permit Vishnevskaya to travel to Coventry for the event, although she was permitted to leave to make the recording in London. With only ten days notice, HEATHER HARPER stepped in to perform the soprano role." Wikipedia

"Although the Coventry Cathedral Festival Committee had hoped Britten would be the sole conductor for the work's premiere, shoulder pain forced his withdrawal from the main conducting role. He did, however, conduct the chamber orchestra, and this spawned a tradition of separate conductors that the work does not require and Britten never envisaged. The premiere took place on May 30, 1962, in the rebuilt cathedral with the City of Birmingham Symphony Orchestra, conducted by Meredith Davies." Wiki

Wikipedia recalls, "At Britten's request, there would be ———————————————
NO APPLAUSE FOLLOWING THE PRGRAM."

"It was a triumph, and critics and audiences at this and subsequent performances in London and abroad hailed it as a contemporary masterpiece." Writing to his sister after the premiere, Britten said of his music, "I hope it'll make people think a bit." On the title page of the score score he quoted Wilfred Owen:

> My subject is War, and the pity of War.
> The Poetry is in the pity.
> All a poet can do today is warn.

Watch the symphony on U TUBE it is a great Tribute to the departed of the World Wars.
HISTORICAL FACTS: A new cathedral was built and one wall is glass to view the old cathedral.
LADY GODIVA rode naked on a horse in Coventry as a protest against taxes.

[Britten's Children's Guide to the Orchestra was my first exposure to music. My dad bought the great Italian-English symphonic popular music conductor MANTOVANI first London LP album circa 1949, and my dad would tell me what instrument was playing. My Father and I attended a Mantovani concert in White Plains, NY, circa 1971. When in college I had heard Mantovani at the Portland, Maine auditorium and was able to get his autograph across the New York City skyline on his songs of Manhattan LP album cover in 1963. I had previously heard RAY CHARLES there.

My dad had an extensive collection of Latin-American records in the early 1950s. In 1940, he had taken my mother to see the great XAVIER CUGAT orchestra at the Waldorf Astoria with his vocalist wife ABBY LANE. Later, he married CHARO, who also sang with his orchestra. I saw her on TV, I think the ABC REGIS AND KATHIE LEE show, play classical Spanish guitar. I bought her CD she is a serious virtuoso. My dad in 1937-39 studied Spanish at AMITYVILLE High school. He listened to Guatemalan marimba bands on his short wave Hallicrafter radio the size of a refrigerator. In the 1950s Latin-American/Puerto Rican dances and music were popular. When the family drove in our black 1949 "woody" sides FORD station wagon dad would play the PEANUT VENDORS Latin-American music. New York symphony conductor LEONARD BERNSTEIN choreographed Latin American dance into his American "Romeo and Juliet" THE WEST SIDE STORY.

PERSONAL PROVIDENTIAL CONNECTION: ERNESTO LECUONA CUBA'S "GERSHWIN" wrote MALAGUENA, SIBONEY and ANDALUSIA "THE BREEZE AND I and dozens of Cuban folk songs. My dad was a big Latin American music fan. And listened to Guatemalan marimba bands on his radio. He had a large collection of Latin American records CUGAT, PEREZ PRADO, RAFAEL HERNANDEZ and PANCHITO 78 rpm and 33 rpm LP records. The mambo, Merengue, Cha Cha, Samba and Rumba were popular dance melodies. ROSEMARY CLOONEY, George's aunt, even had a hit song PAPA LOVES MAMBO. My father's favorite was Lecuona for his beautiful songs. In 1968, he was driving home to our farm in upstate New York when he saw a large funeral procession pass by near the Hawthorne Circle. My dad recalled, "I had a premonition that a friend was passing by." He learned this was Ernesto Lecouna's funeral at GATE OF HEAVEN Cemetery in Hawthorne, New York. FIND A GRAVE shows his purple granite grave stone. ANOTHER PROVIDENTIAL CONNECTION? When my dad was stationed at DREW FIELD, today Tampa International airport, he walked through the Cuban neighborhood to take a bus into Tampa. Dad heard someone playing the song MALAGUENA probably on a grand piano. My dad may have actually heard Lecuona himself on the piano? My dad didn't smoke and Tampa had a large Cuban community making cigars. If my father had knocked on the door he may have meet Ernesto Lecuona himself? This would have been in 1944. Small World?

"Britten-the-pianist closely resembles Britten-the-composer," said ROSTROPOVICH. Britten had the ability to play songs by SCHUBERT or SCHUMMAN or HAYDN with such concern that he made the music sound like it was his own."

"In our Chesalet record collection there is a recording of the WAR REQUIEM conducted by Britten with the great Russian soprano GALINA VISHVEVSKAYA, the wife of ROSTROPOVITCH, singing. She and her husband were good friends of Benjamin Britten and his collaborator, PETER PEARS. Her autobiography GALINA (1984), is immensely readable and exposes the cruelty of the Soviet Union to their great artists. Galina and her husband befriended SOLZHENITSYN AND LITERALLY SAVED HIS LIFE before he was expelled from Russia."

"BOTH BRITTEN and PEARS WERE PACIFISTS, but they were granted military exemptions from going to war because they toured England giving recitals in small towns and villages, cheering the people who had never been to a concert before."

"Benjamin Britten was undoubtedly one of the century's most gifted and disciplined composers. As in the parable of the talents, he multiplied his and proved a good steward of what God had given him. He was a metropolitan composer with a longing for a "micropolitan" existence. Whenever he could, he returned to the little fishing village. Being an intensely private person, there was a "Beware of the dog" sign on his gate in 7 languages. His pet was a tiny dachshund as gentle as his master.

"In 1973 he became partially paralyzed after heart surgery. He died in 1976, and a friend said his end was "peaceful."

GIFT OF MUSIC—Great Composers & Their Influence reviews

"There will be no one who will not find stimulating insights [in The Gift of Music]…I look for this book to open the doors to a new affirmation of life in the area of music."—FRANCIS A. SCHAEFFER, Founder, L'ABRI FELLOWSHIP.

"[The authors'] joyous enthusiasm …should serve to ignite the curiosity of many readers and lure them on to sample more liberally the magnificent sound structures of BACH and HANDEL, HAYDN and MOZART—not to mention both their forerunners and their heirs."—"CHRISTIANITY TODAY"

"The most valuable contribution of THE GIFT OF MUSIC is the way the authors integrate the lives, philosophies, and music of these great composers. It is their discussion of the cross-pollination of thought and the interaction of one composer and artist with another. This approach makes the men come alive and places the reader in the 18th and 19th centuries as observers, not historians…Whether readers are new to classical music or graduates of a classical music program, they will find the book a good resource and an excellent overview of the development of musical thought."—"CONTEMPORARY CHRISTIAN"

""Reading about these great composers has been most inspiring to me. This is a book to read and enjoy."—George Beverly Shea, renowned Opera soloist

"I found THE GIFT OF MUSIC hard to lay down until I had read it from cover to cover. I feel this book is a must."—Jerome Hines, Metropolitan Opera Company

[I have more than 4,000 books I have read, researched and mostly only used the index looking for WHATEVER. I found this book for its TRUTH, very spiritually inspiring and most composers were of Germanic heritage, Britain is ANGLO-SAXON. After reading Benjamin Britten's only two pages which were concise on his Christian musical beliefs. I had to read the other Germanic composers and was amazed how they highlighted their music to Christianity and the historical events and their providential locations to Reformation leader MARTIN LUTHER. On the DARK SIDE they reveal the powerful philosophical-ideologies of other Germanic legends like SCHOPENHAUER and NIETZSCHE who inspired RICHARD WAGNER. Wagner's powerful visual music inspired the false heroes and utter Nordic pagan nihilistic death and glory of VALHALLA which inspired ADOLF HITLER and his false ARYAN RELIGION of NATIONAL SOCIALISM which was anti-Biblical and ANTICHRIST. They reveal that Wagner's last Opera, PARSIFAL about the CRUCIFIXION OF JESUS is considered his most spiritual music, it is pseudo-Christian based on secular Holy Grail legends from WOLFRAM VON ESCHENBACH book PARSIFAL about the innocent Grail Knight and the Holy Lance that pierced Jesus side.

In 1998, my daughter and I visited his small museum in Eschenbach near Nuremberg. It was not listed in three tour books? They don't mention that Parsifal's music was so profound "THE GOOD FRIDAY BELLS theme" that its Jewish conductor was baptized Roman Catholic. Wagner became very anti Semitic and therefore had no use for the Old Testament and to Wagner Jesus was not heroic in His death on the Cross. I have a Wagner CD which tells his biography saying that his father dies shortly after his birth and that he soon had a step father, born in Eisleben Martin Luther's birthplace. a theatrical producer who inspired him, who also died in Wagner's childhood. The authors allege Ludwig Geyer may have been his real father and may have been of Jewish heritage not investigated in the early 1800s.]

THE TWO-FACED SENATOR—KIRSTEN GILLIBRAND

America's 1st Freedom magazine August 2019 Frank Miniter, editor in chief

"Those who don't know New York state, as opposed to "the city that never sleeps." might be surprised to learn the U.S. Senator KIRSTEN GILLIBRAND'S [D.N.Y.] old House district [NY 20] is mostly a bucolic mix of rolling hardwood hills and small towns separated by apple orchards, cornfields and horse farms. There are urban areas, too. To win in such an upstate New York district, it helps if a politician goes to the county fair and is seen eating apple pie as they embrace the rest of what is traditionally American, especially our right to bear arms."

[I lived in her Columbia County earlier in 1954-1974, and from my hilltop farm in Ghent/Harlemville could "see" Gillibrand's house in Hudson, the county seat, in the valley across from the 30 mile long Catskill Mountain range. One of the best views in Eastern America. When I visited my dad in 1993, my dad warned me, "Don't drive in Hudson because I had a Virginia license plate and the police would probably pull me over to check for drugs or maybe cheap cigarettes. Gillibrand running on a "Blue Dog" Democrat ticket had said she slept with two "guns" under her bed. Her British husband probably never fired a gun unless he was of the upper class country gentry.]

"Gillibrand did just that when she ran for a seat in Congress in 2006. She was a then-unknown politician. What was known in the 1990s was she had been a defense attorney for the tobacco company PHILLIP MORRIS [ALTRIA CORP.]. Gillibrand even defended Phillip Morris' executives in a criminal investigation probing whether they'd committed perjury when they testified to Congress THEY HAD NO KNOWLEDGE OF A CONNECTION BETWEEN SMOKING AND CANCER."

[This law firm also represented the NFL in its case against football head injury suicides. Watch the movie CONCUSSION where WILL SMITH plays the Ibo Christian medical examiner who proves the NFL's negligence. I knew he would not get an Academy Award nomination for Best Actor. The National Football League is bigger than Hollywood.]

Senator Gillibrand proclaims: "The NRA is Worst Organization in America."

"Gillibrand's adamant beliefs were only opportunistic. She now says, though in 2008 she was an experienced congresswoman and previously had been an attorney representing Phillip Morris, that she doesn't understand American FREEDOM. Now she thinks you and your rights are to blame for the actions of murderers. Now she adamantly thinks your civil-liberties organization, the NRA, is "worst organization in the country."

"As anyone can plainly see it is hard to judge what Gillibrand really thinks now and what she might have thought in 2008. The 2020 election is sure shaping up to be a referendum on OUR FREEDOM." page 17

"Senator Kirsten Gillibrand withdrew from the presidential race August 28, 2019, after failing to qualify for the third debate." Wikipedia

20 HISTORICAL QUOTES ABOUT GUN OWNERSHIP

American Action News Match 22, 2018

1 THOMAS JEFFERSON: "What country can preserve its liberties if their rulers are not warned from time to time that their people preserve the spirit of resistance. Let them take arms." "Thomas Jefferson was a leading Founding Father and the principal author of the Declaration of Independence. After the Revolutionary War, he served as the third President of the United States and is universally regarded as one of the nation's best chief executives."

2 ALAN DERSHOWITZ: "Foolish liberals who are trying to read the Second Amendment out of the Constitution by claiming it's not an individual right or that it's too much of a public safety hazard, don't see the danger in the big picture. They are courting disaster by encouraging others to use the same means to eliminate portions of the Constitution they don't like."

Alan Dershowitz is an American lawyer, constitutional and criminal law scholar, and best selling author. He spent most of his career at Harvard University, where at age 27 he became the youngest professor in the prestigious institution's 381 year history.

3 ADOLF HITLER: "The most foolish mistake we could possibly make would be to allow the subjugated races to possess arms. History shows that all conquerors who have allowed their subjugated races to carry arms have prepared their own downfall by doing so. Indeed, I would go so far as to say that the supply of arms to the underdogs is a sine qua non for the overthrow of any sovereignty."

"Adolf Hitler rose from obscurity to become the infamous leader of the Nazi Party and eventually Fuehrer of Germany. He led the German people to catastrophe in the Second World War, which claimed the lives of between 60 to 80 million people — including six million Jews and five million other "undesirables" in Europe. Almost all of whom were unarmed and helpless to slow the Nazi war machine."

4 GEORGE MASON: "To disarm the people...[is] the most effectual way to enslave them."

"George Mason was a Virginian farmer, politician, and delegate to the constitutional convention of 1787."

5 JAMES MADISON: "The right of people to keep and bear arms shall not be infringed. A well-regulated militia, composed of the body of the people, trained to arms, is the best and most natural defense of a free country." Another Founding Father, James Madison served as the fourth President of the United States."

6 MAO ZEDONG: "All political power comes from the barrel of a gun. The communist party must command all the guns, that way, no guns can ever be used to command the party." "Mao Zedong was a communist revolutionary, founder of the People's Republic of China, and has the dishonorable distinction of being one of the worst human beings in history. The estimated number of Chinese who died during his 27-year-reign range from 40 to 70 million."

7 FREDERICK DOUGLASS: "A man's rights rest in three boxes: the ballot box, the jury box, and the cartridge box." "Douglass was a famous abolitionist, orator, and writer."

8 BENITO MUSSOLINI: "The measures adopted to restore public order are: First of all, the elimination of the so-called subversive elements.They were elements of disorder and subversion. On the morrow of each conflict I gave the the categorical order to confiscate, which continues with the utmost energy, has given satisfactory results."

"Mussolini was an Italian politician who rose to become the leader of his country's National Fascist Party. He was elected Prime Minister, but shortly after that dropped any pretense of democracy and established a dictatorship. In World War II, he threw his support behind the Axis Powers, thereby sealing his fate."

9 NICCOLO MACHIAVELLI: "When you disarm the people, you commence to offend them and show that you distrust them either through cowardice or lack of confidence, and both of these opinions generate hatred." "Machiavelli was an Italian diplomat and philosopher during the Renaissance period. He is regarded by many as the father of modern political science."

10 DIANE FEINSTEIN: "If I could have banned them all—'Mr. and Mrs. America turn in your guns' — I would have!" "Feinstein is the senior U.S. Senator from California. She's a member of the Democratic Party. Her first high-profile office held was as Mayor of San Francisco from 1978 to 1988."

11 SAINT AUGUSTINE: "Though defensive violence will always be 'a sad necessity' in the eyes of men of principle, it would be still more unfortunate if wrongdoers should dominate just men."

"Augustine was a 3rd century Christian theologian and philosopher whose teachings were instrumental in shaping the core tenets of the early church."

12 VLADIMIR LENIN: "One man with a gun can control 100 without one." "Lenin was a communist revolutionary who brought about the end of the 300-year Romanov Dynasty in Russia. After defeating anti-Communist forces in a bloody civil war, he established the Soviet Union, which he ruled from 1917 to 1924. Although his reputation is relatively intact, both inside Russia and among leftists worldwide, the body count for seven year's in power exceeds GENGHIS KHAN'S."

13 JOE WURZELBACHER: "In 1911, Turkey established gun control. From 1915 to 1917, 1.5 million Armenians, unable to defend themselves, were exterminated."

"Wurzelbacher, also known as Joe the Plumber, is an entrepreneur, conservative activist, and political commentator."

14 ROSIE O'DONNELL: I don't care if you want to hunt, I don't care if you think it is your right. I say 'Sorry.' it's 1999. We have had enough as a nation. You are not allowed to own a gun, and if you own a gun, I think you should go to prison." "She is a comedian, actress, and longtime TV personality. She's known for her far-left views."

15 THOMAS SOWELL: "As for gun control advocates, I have no hope whatever that any facts whatever will make the slightest dent in their thinking — or lack of thinking."

"At the age of 87. Sowell remains a Senior Fellow at the conservative Hoover Institution. He is one of America's preeminent economics and prolific authors."   [African American]

16 GEORGE ORWELL: "That rifle on the wall of the laborer's cottage or working class flat is the symbol of democracy. It is our job to see that it stays there."

"Orwell was one of the 20th century's most famous novelists. Although an outspoken liberal on most issues he had a healthy distaste for totalitarianism." [1984, Animal Farm]

17 JOSEF STALIN: "We don't let them have ideas. Why would we let them have guns?"

"Hitler, Mao, and Stalin are all finalist for the most brutal dictators in history. Millions of Stalin's citizen's went to Siberian gulags for trivial offenses. Meanwhile, his political enemies —both real and imagined—were executed en masse over perceived threats. His iron-fist rule led to the deaths of some 20 million Soviets and initial shortsightedness contributed to the massive loss of life in the war with Hitler's Germany."   [25,000,000]

18 CLINT EASTWOOD: "I have a very strict gun control policy. If there's a gun around, I want to be in control of it." "Eastwood is an iconic actor, Academy Award-winning director, and leading conservative."

19 BARACK OBAMA: "I don't believe people should be able to own guns." — Obama (during a conversation with economist and author John Lott, Jr. at Univ. of Chicago Law School in the 1990s.) Obama is a Democrat Party leader who served as the 44th President of the United States."

20 "RONALD REAGAN" "Freedom is never more than one generation away from extinction. We didn't pass it to our children in the bloodstream. It must be fought for, protected, and passed on or we will spend our sunset years telling our children's children what it was like in the United States when men were free."

"Reagan was an actor-turned-conservative politician who became the 40th president of the United States, and whose policies hastened the demise of the Soviet Union."

What Secular Media Doesn't Get

"I'm thankful I could speak up for the Lord on CNN and MSNBC."
"The media doesn't seem to understand that conservative Christians
want a spiritually great nation."

"During Easter week, the Lord allowed me to speak up for HIM during two interviews on CNN and one on MSNBC. The interviewers asked me about Stormy Daniels who alleged she had a one-night stand 11 years ago with DONALD TRUMP.

As soon as the news about Daniels broke, the media had a storyline: "How could a president this immoral deserve to serve as president? Surely any Christians supporting him are hypocrites." They only needed some evangelical leader to give them their soundbites.

Our public relations company had been pitching me to be on some talk shows to discuss GOD AND DONALD TRUMP, to little avail. Suddenly, I received three invitations to talk about Daniels. I prayed about what to say.

My first interview was with ALISYN CAMEROTA on CNN. She began by saying "Explain to us again how it is that evangelicals are willing to overlook these reports of infidelity, and other things, to support President Trump."

That was easy to answer, I told her, because Trump has had a reputation as a playboy going back to the 80's, yet evangelicals still voted for him. "I didn't support Donald Trump for a long time because I didn't approve of his lifestyle," I said.

"Then what changed?" Camerota asked, "which gave me the opening I wanted."

I replied: "I think he changed. I really do, I talk about this in my book, GOD AND DONALD TRUMP.

But Camerota didn't seem satisfied with my answer. "But in order to receive forgiveness, don't you have to confess your sins?" she said. "Isn't that a tenet in the Bible? You know, Donald Trump has famously said he has never asked God for forgiveness."

I said, I was glad she was quoting the Bible and then shifted the discussion to policy matters. Each time an interviewer asked me why evangelicals could vote for a man so flawed?, I replied that millions of Christians had prayed that somehow God would shift the direction of this nation. I said, "God answered in a way we didn't expect with a person we didn't necessarily like."

TRUMP'S CONNECTION TO PERSIAN KING CYRUS?

Before the election, I was aware of the comparisons between TRUMP and the pagan KING CYRUS, whom God used to let the Israelites return to Jerusalem from Persia [Iran]. The Scriptures in ISAIAH 45 says: "Thus says the Lord to CYRUS, His anointed…I have called you by name; I have named you, though you have not known Me." [Isaiah prophesied this some 500 years earlier. Trump is the 45th president providence?] If God could use Cyrus, he could use Trump. Later, I understood his policies and strong support for Christian and Israel Jewish issues.

I was surprised to get an invitation to be on a CNN show hosted by RYAN NOBLE on Easter. Noble asked about Trump's behavior and quoted FRANKLIN GRAHAM, who said Trump has changed since the time of these alleged affairs. This gave me the best opening of any of the interviews.

"You know, the whole essence of Christianity is that God is able to CHANGE PEOPLE through the power of the GOSPEL," I told him.

I began to see they wouldn't contradict me when I spoke up for the Gospel, probably because it was HOLY WEEK. In my interview GOOD FRIDAY with CRAIG MELTON on MSNBC, I turned a question on policy to say: "Millions of evangelical Christians believed the country was going in the wrong way, and we prayed. We prayed that God would somehow do something to shift the direction of our country, and here He raised up a man who we didn't necessarily like, in the form of DONALD TRUMP. He has done more for religious liberty and helping persecuted Christians—

and the kinds of causes that Christians feel are important—than any president, I think in my lifetime."

The media doesn't seem to understand that conservative Christians want a spiritually great nation. Although we are interested in tax cuts and foreign policy, the real issue is how policies help or hurt the Christian community and move our nation in the right or wrong direction.

Melton cited a poll that seemed to prove his point that Trump was losing evangelical support. I cited my own "poll"—all the people I've talked to, none of whom are changing their minds about Trump.

"There have been many, many opportunities to change our minds about Trump." I told Melton, "But he has come through again and again. He's standing strong, he's trying to make AMERICA GREAT AGAIN, and most evangelical Christians, like me, are praying that somehow America will become morally and spiritually great again."

STEPHEN STRANG is the founder of CHARISMA and CEO of CHARISMA MEDIA. He is author of the best selling book GOD AND DONALD TRUMP.

THE "CYRUS LEGEND" AND BABYLON

"CYRUS II-called "the GREAT"—was King of PERSIA [IRAN in 1935] form c. 558 to 528 B.C. He brought the whole of the NEAR EAST—including MIGHTY BABYLON—under his rule, from the Aegean Sea to the Indus River [India]. Significant among his deeds was his granting permission to the Jewish captives of Babylonia to retun to their homeland."   p 13

"That much is History. But what is not widely realized is that almost two centuries before CYRUS, the prophet ISAIAH recorded (Isaiah 44:28) that a man named CYRUS would permit the exiled Jews to rebuild JERUSALEM and the TEMPLE—which, in ISAIAH'S DAY, had not yet been destroyed! Isaiah also prophesied CYRUS' overthrow of Babylon." (Isaiah 45:1-3)."   p13

"Not only did GOD call Cyrus by name long before he was born, he saw to it that SATAN the devil was prevented from putting the infant CYRUS to death and thwarting his plan. Greek sources—HERODOTUS, XENOPHON and CTESIAS—provide considerable information about Cyrus' early life. Notice the remarkable story surrounding Cyrus' birth and childhood, according to a version related by Herodotus in hIs HISTORY (1.107-130): Astyagus, king of the MEDES, was overlord of the Persians. Astyages gave his daughter Mandane in marriage to his vassal Cambyses, king of the Persians."

"From the marriage of Mandane and Cambyses, CYRUS was born. Astyages, however, had a dream that the baby would grow up to overthrow him. So he ordered his adviser, Harpagus, to personally kill the infant (Cyrus}. Harpagus, however, entrusted the execution to a herdsman named Mitradates. On finding that his wife had just given birth to a stillborn child, the herdsman substituted CYRUS, and reared him as his own son. When Cyrus was 10 years old, Astyages discovered the deception. In spite of the dream, the king was persuaded to let the boy live."   p 13

"When he reached manhood, Cyrus ascended the Persian throne (c. 558 B.C.). In 553 he led a rebellion against his maternal grandfather. In 550 Astyages marched against Cyrus, but his army deserted him and surrendered to the Persians. Astyages—the last ruler of MEDIA—was captured and dethroned, though he was permitted to live out his life in peace. Thus CYRUS became king of the MEDES and PERSIANS, firmly established on his throne and poised to fulfill his amazing PROPHETIC DESTINY." p 13

BABYLON-PAST, PRESENT AND FUTURE—Worldwide Church of God 1992

"IS NOT THIS GREAT BABYLON?"

"Under NEBUCHADNEZZAR'S leadership, Babylon became the greatest and most impressive city in the world,"

"Warfare often rocked the cradle of civilization. Mesopotamia was the scene of many battles in the centuries that followed the attempt to build the Tower of Babel. The city of BABEL—or BABYLON as we know it in later history—waxed and waned. Built on the banks of the EUPHRATES RIVER. Babylon was attacked and destroyed several times, but rose from its ruins even more magnificent than before." p 7

"Under HAMMURABI the Babylonians controlled an empire that stretched from the Persian Gulf to the upper reaches of the TIGRIS RIVER. In the mid-second millennium B.C., this dynasty fell into the hands of enemies and Babylon's power declined." p 7

"Others now had control over Mesopotamia. For several centuries, Babylon's influence would only play a secondary role. But in 612 B.C. the Assyrian capital, NINEVEH, fell to a combined force of Babylonians and Medes. Seven years later, the Babylonians (also known by this as the Chaldeans) defeated the Egyptian forces of Pharaoh NECHO at Carchemish, and Babylon once again became the dominant power in the region under the leadership of the brilliant Nebuchadnezzar." p 7

"What Nebuchadnezzar did not realize was that his rise to power was part of a divine plan. The proud king saw himself as undisputed master of the world. God chose this moment to teach him, and all who followed him, who really controlled the destiny of nations. His empire would now confront a nation that was not like the others he had subdued." p 11

"BELSHAZZAR was as proud and arrogant as Nebuchadnezzar once had been. Although Babylon was besieged by enemies, Belshazzar remained unconcerned, trusting that the city's formidable defenses would keep him safe. In Daniel, chapter 5, we read that he planned a great feast. In a great show of conceit, he ordered the drinks and the meal be served in golden goblets and plates plundered from the TEMPLE in Jerusalem." p 12

"Even as he sat feasting, the party was stunned into silence as a mysterious hand appeared and began writing on the wall of the throne room. None of the king's magicians could understand. Once again Daniel was summoned. He explained that the writing was a message from God. God was bringing the proud rule of Belshazzar to an end. Babylon was finished. The kingdom would be divided between the Medes and the Persians, who were even as they spoke entering the city." p 12

"On that night, in October 539 B.C., God intervened in the affairs of Babylon again. What happened was a dramatic confirmation of God's earlier hand in History. God had prophesied the end of Babylon, in a detailed prophecy delivered through Isaiah, nearly 200 years before!" p 12 [Isaiah 45 about Persian/Mede King Cyrus].

"THE FALL OF BABYLON—ISAIAH prophesied that God would make it possible for a king, Cyrus by name, to conquer the many kingdoms that ultimately would make up his empire." p 12

"Thus says the Lord to His anointed, to Cyrus, whose right hand I have held—to subdue nations before him and loose the armor of kings, to open before him the double doors [or, two levered gates], so that the gates will not be shut" (Isaiah 45:1)." p 12

"The "double doors" that would not be shut or locked is a reference in the remarkable way in which Cyrus was able to capture Babylon. With its massive high walls, Babylon appeared impregnable from the outside. When Cyrus' main army encamped around the city, the Babylonians laughed. Aware of his advance, they stored up provisions for many years, and could survive a siege indefinitely." p 12

"Unknown to the Babylonians, however, Cyrus was implementing an ingenious plan. Some of his men were busy upstream diverting the EUPHRATES RIVER, which normally flowed through massive river gates into the city. They dug a channel to redirect the river into an old lake. The river level soon sank, permitting the Persians to wade under the gates and into Babylon under cover of darkness."   p 13

"CYRUS apparently had also gotten a spy into the city, who on the appropriate night had unlocked a set of gates—the prophesied "double door"—in the wall that stretched along the bank of the river. Through those gates, Cyrus' army swarmed into the metropolis. The Babylonians were surprised and offered no effective resistance."   p 13

"So large was the city that when the outer parts were already taken, those living in the center of Babylon remained unaware of the city's demise. Celebrating what may have been the New Year Festival, they continued their merriment until the truth became all too apparent."   p 13

"The greatest city of the ancient world had fallen! (Over the next few centuries, it slowly declined and finally crumbled into ruins.)" [The Bible prophesied this and its existence was actually questioned.]   p 13

"EXCAVATING BABYLON—It was the German architect and archeologist ROBERT KOLDEWEY (1855-1925) who revealed the Babylon of the Bible as an historical reality."

"In 1897, Dr, Koldewey announced his intention to uncover Nebuchadnezzar's Babylon. He mounted a major excavation under the auspices of the Deutsche Orient-Gesellschraft (German Orient Society). Digging began on March 1899 among desolate mounds of crumbled mud bricks near the village of HILLA, south of BAGHDAD. It would continue for the next 18 years."   p 10

"Slowly and painstakingly, Koldewey began uncovering the metropolis of Nebuchadnezzar. Among Koldewey's first discoveries were the remains of the cities massive walls."   p 10

"Koldewey's workmen—some 200 strong—next cleared the PROCESSIONAL WAY, the main north-south avenue bisecting the city. The way led to the magnificent ISHTAR GATE. [In June 1998, my Jewish daughter, after her first year teaching high school German, and I walked through the ISHTAR GATE in the PERGAMON museum located in Berlin, Germany. The Pergamon museum has the PERGAMON ALTAR to goddess DIANA which was removed from near today's BERGAMA, Turkey. The Pergamon altar looks similar to the LINCOLN MEMORIAL with Greek Doric columns and steps.

"An assistant wrote that Koldewey "lived for Babylon and thought of Babylon…day and night" The approach of the British Expeditionary Force in March 1917 forced him to close down the excavations with much of his work was unfinished."   p 10

BABYLON—Past, Present…and Future—Worldwide Church of God

"The little, baked brick tower, protruding impudently out of the plain posed no threat to God, but it was a symbol defiance and expression of the self-confident, independent attitude. The Lord came down to see the city and the tower that had gotten Adam and Eve and their descendants in trouble. God could not let it to continue unchecked."   p 5

"So as God reviewed the progress at Babel, he knew what had to be done. He would not prevent humans from following their chosen course, but he would slow them down."

"Genesis tells us what happened. "And the Lord said, 'Indeed the people are one and they ALL HAVE ONE LANGUAGE, and this is what they begin to do, now nothing that they propose to do will be withheld from them. Come, let Us go down and there CONFUSE THEIR LANGUAGE, THAT THEY MAY NOT UNDERSTAND ONE ANOTHER'S SPEECH' " (Genesis 11:6-7). p 5

"The builders were UNABLE TO COMMUNICATE clearly with each other, and so the building of the Tower of Babel came to a halt. Families went their separate ways, TO BE SCATTERED over the face of the EARTH and eventually to become tribes and nations."

"It was the first time that God intervened in the development of a "Babylon," but it would not be the last."   p 5   Worldwide Church of God 1991

[Hungarian Jewish-"Catholic-convert" hedge-fund billionaire GEORGE SOROS' father before World War II, wanted a new universal world language called ESPERANTO. Today, this can be done through computer technology translators. I have seen Wikipedia listings which can be translated into many languages. As the Tower of Babel story reveals God doesn't want the world speaking a common language, Why? In the later days END-TIME the WORLD DICTATOR THE ANTICHRIST wants all the world to be deceived by his lies. Jesus is the Word. Bibles have been translated into hundreds of languages. There are still hundreds of dialects which haven't had Bible translations yet.

REBUILDING BABYLON

"Today, certain of Babylon's major buildings are being restored by the Iraqi government as an archeological park.

Bible prophecies, however, say Babylon will never again become a thriving inhabited city, Isaiah 13:19-20 tells us: "And Babylon, the glory of kingdoms, the beauty of the Chaldeans' pride, will be as when God overthrew SODOM AND GOMORRAH. It will never be inhabited, nor will it be settled from generation to generation; nor will the Arabian pitch tents there, nor will the shepherds make their sheepfolds there."   p 17

The book of JEREMIAH says "Babylon shall become a heap, a dwelling place for jackals, an astonishment and a hissing, without an inhabitant" (Jeremiah 51:37).

THE GOD OF THIS WORLD

"It is impossible to really appreciate the significance of Babylon in History and prophecy without also understanding the role of Satan the devil.

The concept of a malevolent spirit that is the embodiment of all evil sounds far fetched and superstitious today. But the Bible shows that there is a devil who has played an invisible, but significant role in the HISTORY OF MANKIND. It tells us that he was once a powerful angel, LUCIFER, the "light bringer" holding a high position at first at God's throne and later on earth. He became warped through jealousy and pride and ultimately led one-third of the angels in a rebellion against God. Thus Lucifer the angel of light became Satan the adversary and the leader of the powers of darkness.   p 4

Satan works behind the scenes, quietly and insidiously. He often appears as a benefactor, a friend and servant of mankind. The apostle PAUL warns that Satan "transforms himself into an angel of light. Therefore it is no great thing if his ministers also transform themselves into ministers of righteousness" (II Corinthians 11:14-15). Much of what is done through his influence may appear to be good at first. Its true intent is not exposed until it is too late, It is important to understand this if we are to fully understand the lesson of Babylon.   p 4

DIREST PREDICTIONS FOR WAR IN IRAQ—"BABYLON"

End-Time Interpreters See Biblical Prophecies Being Fulfilled
Bill Broadway The Washington Post Staff Writer 1991

"Ever since Jesus said that ONLY GOD [THE FATHER] KNOWS THE HOUR OR DAY OF THE SECOND COMING, preachers and self-appointed doomsayers have been trying to predict when it will happen — and watching the sun rise on another generation. Even those who despise date-setters nearly always say, God's final judgment is coming soon, probably in our lifetime, so get ready."

"In recent weeks, the prophetic interpreters have been citing a new reason to believe the end is coming: the IMPENDING WAR WITH IRAQ. Anxious decisions have arisen on prophecy Web sites, in Bible study groups and churches and at such gatherings as last night's 20th International Prophecy Conference in Tampa, its title: "Shaking Nations Living in Perilous Times.""

"Many see evidence evidence of Iraq's significance in End-Time scenarios in key passages of the apocalyptic book of Revelation, Chapter 16, which includes the mention of ARMAGEDDON in the Bible carries a direct reference through modern-day Iraq,"

"The sixth angel poured out his bowl upon the great river EUPHRATES, and its water was dried up to prepare the way for the kings of the East, writes JOHN, possibly the apostle, of a container of angel's anger emptied on the ancient land BABYLON, now IRAQ. The kings will drive their armies through the Euphrates Valley en route to Har Megiddo (Armageddon) in northern ISRAEL."

"The Euphrates appears a second time being one of seven [7] angels whose blaring trumpets warn that the FINAL JUDGMENT is near. "Release the four angels who are found at the great river Euphrates," an angel commands the sixth angel of God, whose compliance unleashes agents of death who "had been kept ready for this future hour and day and month and year were released to kill a third of mankind.""

"Then comes the clincher. In Chapter 9, Verse 11—John says the leader of an army of locusts released to fight humankind is named ABADDON in Hebrew, APOLLYON in Greek. Both words mean Destroyer," one of several meanings for the name "SADDAM.""

"Iraq fits like hand in glove, Irvin Baxter Jr., founder of END-TIME magazine and pastor of Oak Park Church in Richmond, Indiana, said of the role he believes the country will play in world-ending   events   if   U.S.-led   forces   invade   Iraq."

"Baxter, a lifelong student of OLD and NEW TESTAMENT prophecies, said casualties will be tremendous, not only of combatants in Iraq but of people in neighboring countries hit by retaliatory missiles of mass destruction and Americans who fall victim to terrorists armed with portable nuclear weapons."

"And other countries will take the opportunity to pursue their own interests—China trying to retake Taiwan, or India making and all-out assault on KASHMIR—leading to WORLD WAR III, he said. The result, Baxter concludes, could be a nuclear holocaust that takes the lives of 2,000,000,000 people, the "one third of mankind" stated in Revelation." [World population estimates in 1 A. D.— 188,000,000; A.D. 100—195,000,000; 1900—1,654,000,000; 1940—2,307,000,000; 1970— 3,691,172,616 UN; 2000—6,127,700,428 UN; 2015—7,349,472,000—today 2,500,000,000 people die?]

"Such talk bothers Craig C. Hill, professor of new Testament at Wesley Theological seminary in northwest Washington and one of many biblical scholars who say end-time interpreters distort Scripture to fit their own point of view. Most claim to read the Bible "literally" yet take bits and pieces from both written centuries apart under different circumstances, he said."

"EZEKIEL, one of the most popular End-Time texts, was written in the 6th century B.C. by a Judaean priest exiled in BABYLON who dreamed of the Jews returning to Israel and the RESTORATION OF THE TEMPLE. Revelation was written 600 years later about A.D. 95, by an exiled Christian leader encouraging churches in Asia Minor or to preserve under the hardship of Roman control."

"Yet prophetic interpreters will take verses from each and combine them and create a reading that justifies their point of view, said Hill, author of "In God's Time: The Bible and The Future.""

"In trying to create one overarching interpretation, they are not allowing for the complexity of the Biblical witnesses to come through," he said. "The irony is, in their quest for accuracy, biblical literalists are forced to misread the Bible."

IS AMERICA MENTIONED IN BIBLE PROPHECY?

Christ's Gospel Fellowship Church—Spokane, Washington magazine advertisement

"Is it possible that, re-gathered here in the United States of America, we have a representative number of all of the 12 Tribes of Israel? And if this is so, could it be possible that these 12 Tribes of Israel are the peoples which comprise the Anglo-Saxon, Celtic, Germanic, Irish, Scottish, French, Dutch, Scandinavian and kindred peoples?"

"Have you ever wondered why the peoples which comprise Anglo-Saxondom are called "CAUCASIANS"? Is there some special historical significance to the name Caucasian?"

"Is there a reason why America has become the greatest, most powerful and prosperous nation ever known? The prophets ISAIAH and MICAH both prophecy that, in the last days, the mountain(i.e. kingdom) of the Lord would become the greatest most blessed Christian nation upon the Earth. Is is possible the United States is that nation?"

"Why has it been the peoples of Anglo-Saxondom who have taken the Gospel of the Lord Jesus Christ to all nations of the world? Could it be that the Israelites were never "lost", but were simply blinded to their National identity until these latter times, and God has been using them all along to teach and preach those things concerning the Lord Jesus Christ and his COMING KINGDOM?"

"America today is experiencing tremendous problems nationally, just as did Israel of old. And it is for the same reason. There is sin in the land! Immorality abounds, and our courts seem to be powerless to slow this process, much less to stop it. Politically we are in confusion, (see Daniel 9:7-11 for the reason only), and things are getting worse. Our economy is in decline, putting millions out of work, while taxes, inflation, and business failures are increasing. Spiritual values are lowered on every hand. We are living in the time that the Prophet JEREMIAH referred to as "THE TIME OF JACOB'S TROUBLE." (Jeremiah 30:7)

"Are there any answers to these problems which now plague America? Yes, there are! Since approximately 70% of the Holy Bible deals with Government and National issues we find in it the solution to every problem which now troubles America!"

"Therefore we encourage you write and ask for the following articles:

#1 "AMERICA'S DIVINE DESTINY"
#2 "WHO HAS GIVEN AMERICA TO THE ROBBERS AND SPOILERS"
#3 "SUPPOSE WE ARE ISRAEL, DOES IT MAKE A DIFFERENCE?"

#4 "Our colorful 11x17 Migration Map which is entitled "THE REFORMATION OF ISRAEL IN THE WEST". This map shows the routes taken by the 12 Tribes of Israel as they migrated from the land of Assyria into Asia Minor, Europe, the British Isles, the Scandinavian countries, and then in God's time, to America."

"Some 3,000 years ago, Solomon, the wisest King to ever rule over a Kingdom, was informed by God: "If my people, which are called by my name, shall humble themselves, and pray, and shall seek my face. and turn from their wicked (sinful) ways; then will I hear from HEAVEN and will forgive their sin, and will heal their land."(II Chronicles 7:14)

SOCIALISM MUST BE REJECTED

Dan Weber president-founder Association of Mature American Citizens JAN/FEB 2019

"America's excellence can largely be credited to the great engine of prosperity known as enterprise. Yet 2018 showed an alarming trend towards socialism. among the Democrats. Socialism is currently ravaging once prosperous Venezuela, and in Paris the civilians have been rioting in the streets to protest increased taxes to pay for their socialist programs. In the United States, Marxist professors teach students that CAPITALISM IS EVIL, while progressive socialists in Congress push for more government control and the higher taxes that come with it.

This edition of AMAC Magazine is a rebuttal to the socialist movement seeking to fundamentally alter our country and way of life, point blank, socialism is a dead end. Human nature drives us to compete for success, while socialism encourages laziness and apathy. In the end, freedom outperforms socialism every time. We urge parents and grandparents to pass this lesson down to the younger generation.

For a prime example of Americans working to preserve our values, look no further than this edition's report on the "red wave" that swept into the Capitol in December: AMAC had its first legislative fly-in as Delegates and Chapter Presidents met with over 80 Congressman, Senators, and their staffers. We received support from numerous elected representatives for our proposals to cut the cost of health care, guarantee Social Security, and address the growing National Debt. With the 116th Congress in session, we face new challenges ahead. The Democrats have taken the House and brought back Nancy Pelosi as Speaker, while the Republicans have retained control of the Senate. Despite the divided Congress, AMAC is determined to work with both sides of the aisle as we pursue solutions to the issues faced by American seniors.

MARGARET THATCHER ON SOCIALISM: 20 BEST QUOTES

Eddie Johnson Self Reliance Central Feb. 17, 2020

"This autumn will mark 30 years since MARGARET THATCHER departed 10 Downing Street as the first woman and longest-serving British Prime Minister of the 20th Century. What an amazing tenure it was!"

A "DO-IT-YOURSELF" VISION—In 1979, the IRON LADY assumed the premiership of a country divided with labor strife, racked by stagflation and run down by decades of nanny government. Britain struggled on all fronts as the sick man of Europe. For the most part, Thatcher didn't propose to fix big problems through small tweaks as other cowardly or unprincipled politicians were suggesting. She set about, in her words, to "roll back the frontiers of the state." She wanted to reinvigorate the country restoring a culture of entrepreneurship and respect for private property. [Her father ran a grocery.]

She reminded the nation of these objectives during her second of three terms when she declared: "I came to office with one deliberate intent: to change Britain from a dependent to a self-reliant society—from a give-it-to-me. To a do-it-yourself nation. A get-up-and-go, instead of a sit-back-and-wait-for-it Britain."

"A woman of convictions, she thought the unprincipled in government deserved to take the fall because they were too afraid to take a stand. She was more interested in doing what was right than what was politically palatable [correct], as evidenced in this well known remark: "To me, consensus seems to be the process of abandoning all beliefs, principles, value and policies in search of something in which no-one believes, but to which no-one objects.""

"At a policy meeting once, she famously pulled out a copy of F. A. HAYEK's "The Constitution of Liberty" from her handbag, slammed it down on the table and declared, "This is what we believe! On another occasion, she observed that Marxists get up early in the morning to further their causes. We must get up earlier to defend our freedom.""

"She defied conventional wisdom about the "glass ceiling" women in British politics faced. She understood the issues that ordinary people faced, noting in a 1971 interview that "I started life with two great advantages: no money, and good parents.""

DEREGULATION AND PROGRESS—"Painfully at first, her policies wrenched the country from its doldrums to a new era of progress and confidence. Her 11 years in Britain's top job proved that a vigorous program of privatization, deregulation, and tax reduction is an effective antidote for disastrous collectivism. She was increasingly skeptical of the EUROPEAN UNION, partly because of its enchantment for bureaucracy and regulation and partly because of its effort to homogenize the features that made each country special."

"Thatcher died in 2013 but had she lived another seven years, she would likely be cheering BREXIT, which finally happened last month. She told the HOUSE OF COMMONS in 1991, "Our sovereignty does not come from Brussels—it is ours by right and by heritage." In her 2002 book, STATECRAFT: STRATEGIES FOR A CHANGING WORLD she states: "Europe" in anything other than the geographical sense is a wholly artificial construct…If Europe charms us, as it has so often charmed me, it is precisely because of its contrasts and contradictions, not its coherence and continuity."

"As I wrote in this 2013 tribute at the time of her passing, titled "UGLINESS FROM UGLY IDEAS.""

"Socialists despised her because she stood up to them, questioned their false compassion, and dared to expose STATISM as the senseless, dehumanizing cult that it is. She rhetorically ripped the velvet glove from he iron fist and spoke of welfare-state socialism as a wolf in sheep's clothes. Those are things state worshipers cannot abide."

PRIME MINISTER THATCHER'S THOUGHTS ON SOCIALISM

1 "It is good to recall how our freedom has been gained in this country—not by great abstract campaigns but through the objections of ordinary men and women to having their money taken from them by the State. In the early days, people banded together and said to the then Government. 'You shall not take our money before you have redressed our grievances.' It was their money, their wealth, which was the source of their independence against the Government."

2 "The philosophical reason for which we are against nationalization and for private enterprise is because we believe that economic progress comes from the inventiveness, ability, determination and the pioneering spirit of extraordinary men and women. If they cannot exercise that spirit here, they will go away to another free enterprise country which will then make more economic progress than we do. We ought, in fact, to be encouraging small firms and small companies, because the extent to which innovation comes through these companies is tremendous,"

3 "I was attacked for fighting a rearguard action in defense of 'middle-class interests.'…Well, if 'middle class values' include the encouragement of variety and individual choice, the provision of

fair incentives and rewards for skill and hard work, the maintenance of effective barriers against the excessive power of the State and a belief in the wide distribution of individual private property, then they are certainly what I am trying to defend.This is not a fight for 'privilege'; it is a fight for freedom for every citizen."

4 "Our challenge is to create the kind of economic background which enables private initiative and private enterprise to flourish for the benefit of the consumer, employee, the pensioner, and society as a whole. I believe we should judge people on merit and not on background. I believe the person who I prepared to work the hardest should get the greatest reward and keep them after tax. That we should back the workers and not the shirkers: that it is not only permissible but praiseworthy to want to benefit your own family by your own efforts."

5 "I place a profound belief—indeed a fervent faith—in the virtues of self-reliance and personal independence. On these is founded the whole case for the free society, for the assertion that human progress is best achieved by offering the freest possible scope for the development of individual talents, qualified only by a respect for the qualities and the freedom of others. For many years there has been a subtle erosion of the essential virtues of the free society. Self-reliance has been sneered at as if it were an absurd suburban pretension. Thrift has been denigrated as if it were greed. The desire of parents to choose and to struggle for what they themselves regarded as the best possible education for their children has been scorned."

6 "I do not believe, in spite of all this, that the people of this country have abandoned their faith in the qualities and characteristics which made them a great people. Not a bit of it. We are still the same people. All that has happened is that we have temporarily lost confidence in our own strength. We have lost sight of the banner. The trumpets have given an uncertain sound. It is our duty, our purpose, to raise those banners high, so that all can see them, to sound the trumpets clearly and boldly so that all can hear them. Then we shall not have to convert people to our principles. They will simply rally to those which truly are their own."

7 "I shall never stop fighting. I mean this country to survive, to prosper and to be free. I haven't fought the destructive forces of socialism for more than twenty years to stop now, when the critical phase of the struggle is upon us."

8 "What are the lessons then that we've learned from the last thirty years? First, that the pursuit of equality itself is a mirage. What's more desirable and more practicable than the pursuit of equality of opportunity. And opportunity means nothing unless it includes the right to be unequal and the freedom to be different. One of the reasons that we value individuals is not because they're all the same, but because they're all different…Because we must build a society in which each citizen can develop his full potential, both for his own benefit and for the community as a whole, a society in which originally, skill, energy and thrift are rewarded, in which we encourage rather than restrict the variety and richness of human nature."

9 "Let me give you my vision. A man's right to work as he will to spend what he earns, to own property, to have the State as servant and not as master; these are the British inheritance. They are the essence of a free economy. Freedom all our others depend."

10 "Some socialists seem to believe that people should be numbers in a State computer. We believe they should be individuals. We are all unequal. No one, thank heavens, is like anyone else, however much the socialists may pretend otherwise. We believe that everyone has the right to be unequal but thus every human being is equally important."

11 "The socialists tell us that there are massive profits in particular industry and they should not go to the shareholders—but that the public should map the benefits. Benefits? What benefits? When you take into public ownership a profitable industry, the profits soon disappear. The goose that laid the golden eggs get broody. State geese are not great layers. The steel industry was nationalized some years ago in the public interest—yet the only interest now left for the public is

in witnessing the depressing spectacle of their money going down the drain at a rate of a million pounds a day."

12 "There are others who warn not only of the threat from without, but of something more insidious, not readily perceived, not always deliberate, something that is happening here at home. What are they pointing to? They are pointing to the steady and remorseless expansion of the socialist State. Now none of us would claim that the majority of socialists are inspired by other than humanitarian and well-meaning ideals. At the same time few would, I think, deny today that they have made a monster that they can't control. Increasingly, inexorably, the State the socialists have created is becoming more random in the economic and social justice it seeks to dispense, more suffocating in its effect on human aspirations and initiative, more politically selective in its defense of the rights of its citizens, more gargantuan in its appetite—and more disastrously incompetent in its performance. Above all, it poses a growing threat, however unintentional, to the freedom of this country, for there is no freedom where State totally controls the economy. Personal freedom and economic freedom are indivisible.You can't have one without the other, you can't lose one without losing other."

13 "One of our principal and continuing priorities when we are returned to office will be to restore the freedoms which the Socialists have usurped. Let them learn that it is not a function of the State to possess as much as possible. It is not a function of the State to grab as much as it can get away with. It is not a function of the State to act as ring-master, to crack the whip, dictate the load which all of us must carry or say how high we may climb. It is not a function of the State to insure that no-one climbs higher than anyone else. All that is the philosophy of socialism. We reject it utterly for, however well-intended, it leads in one direction only: to the erosion and finally the DESTRUCTION OF THE DEMOCRATIC WAY OF LIFE."

14 "There is no such thing as 'SAFE SOCIALISM" If it's safe, it's not socialism. It's not safe. The signposts of socialism point downhill to less freedom, less prosperity, downhill to more muddle, more failure. If we follow them to their destruction they will lead this nation into bankruptcy."

15 "The economic success of the Western world is a product of its moral philosophy and practice, The economic results are better because the moral philosophy and practice. The economic results are better because the moral philosophy is superior. It is superior because it starts with the individual, with his uniqueness, his responsibility, and his capacity to choose. Surely this is infinitely preferable to the socialist-statist philosophy which sets up a centralized economic system to which the individual must conform, which subjugates him, directs him and denies him the right to free choice. Choice is the essence of ethics: if there were no choice, there would be no ethics, no good, no evil; good and evil have meaning only insofar as man is free to choose."

16 "In our philosophy the purpose of the life of the individual is not to be servant of the State and its objectives, but to make the best of his talents and qualities. The sense of being self-reliant, of playing a role in the family, of owning one's own property, of paying one's way, are all part of the spiritual ballast which maintains responsible citizenship, and provides the solid foundation from which people look around to see what more they might do, for others and for themselves. That is what we mean by a moral society; not a society where the State is responsible for everything,no-one is responsible to the State."

17 "Once you give people the idea that all this can be done by the State, and that it is somehow second-best or even degrading to leave it to private people, then you will begin to deprive human beings of one of the the essential ingredients of humanity—personal moral responsibility. You will in effect dry up in them the milk of human kindness. If you allow people to hand over to the State all their personal responsibility, the time will come — indeed it is lose at hand — when what the taxpayer is willing to pride for the good of humanity will be seen to be far less than what the individual used to be willing to give from love of his neighbor. So do not be tempted to identify

virtue with collectivism. I wonder whether the State services would have done as much for the man who fell among thieves as the Good Samaritan did for him?"

18 "Popular capitalism, which is the economic expression of liberty, is proving a much more attractive means of diffusing power in our society. Socialists cry "Power to the people," and raise the clenched fist as they say it. We all know what they really mean—power over people, power to the State. To us Conservatives, popular capitalism means why it says: power through ownership to the man and woman jn the street, given confidently with an open hand."

19 "I think we have gone through a period when too many children and people have been given to understand 'I have a problem, it is the Government's job to cope with it' or 'I have a problem, I will go and get a grant to cope with it!' 'I am homeless, the Government must house me!' And so they are casting their problems on society and who is society? There is no such thing! There are individual men and women and there are families and no government can do anything except through people and people took on themselves first. It is our duty to look after ourselves and then also to help look after our neighbor and life is reciprocal business and people have got the entitlements too much in mind without the obligations. There is no such thing as society."

20 "I set out to destroy socialism because I felt it was at odds with the character of the people. We were the FIRST COUNTRY IN THE WORLD to roll back the frontiers of socialism, then roll forward the FRONTIERS OF FREEDOM. We reclaimed our heritage; we are renewing it and carrying it forward."

This is a guest post by Lawrence W. Reed President Emeritus, Humphreys Family Senior Fellow, and Ron Manners Ambassador for Global Liberty at the Foundation for Economic Education. He is author of EXCUSE ME, PROFESSOR: is author of CHALLENGING THE MYTHS OF PROGRESSIVISM and REAL HEROES: INCREDIBLE TRUE STORIES OF COURAGE, CHARACTER, AND CONVICTION.

Prime Minister Margaret Thatcher's analysis on Socialism leaves no doubt to it being the opiate of the people not religion as KARL MARX professed as he and VLADIMIR LENIN told workers to unite. This is important to Americans because it sounds very similar to the tyranny and taxation forced on the British colonies in America to pay for the debts incurred during the French and Indian 7 Years War which extended to India which became a British colony under General ROBERT CLIVE.

The Collapse of Communism and End of the Cold War

August 1991 (unofficial view of Lincoln Landis, USMLM, 1961-63)

1. "Political stability in central Europe was sustained by the continuing presence of USMLM, BRIXMIS and FMLM tours throughout East Germany.
2. Communism collapsed and the Cold War ended when, in response to the sudden disintegration of Party authority in August 1991 — long suffering, yet "detente-minded," ordinary Russians delivered a revolution in Moscow's streets.

This brief essay reflects ideas gained during a succession of government assignments that "opened the door" to attitudes of Russians at all levels discounting communism as a way of life.
- 2nd lieutenant, 7th US Army guard-posts, Russian zonal border, Germany, 1945-46;
- 1st lieutenant, US Constabulary Liaison to Soviet Eighth Guards Army, East Germany, 1947-48;

- Captain, Ground Liaison Officer to 86th Fighter-Bomber Wing, W. Germany, 51-54
- Major/Lieutenant colonel, USMLM to Group, Soviet Forces, Germany, 1961-63;
- White House advisor, US-USSR cooperative exchanges under detente, 1976-77;
- Senior analyst, Defense intelligence Agency. 1979-91.

The three Allied Military Liaison Missions, I suggest, served, as a persisting brake upon possible, radical consequences regarding both the internal and external reach of Communist Party rule. Meanwhile, Kremlin-watchers remained solely focused upon Russian economic advisers and entertained little thought about the possible strategic result of popular unrest. Consequential, when radical change in the political climate surfaced in August 1991, their fateful error occurred, as noted by D. James H. Billington,
Library of Congress:

"We are living in the midst of a great historical drama that we did not expect, do not
understand, and cannot even name." (Remarks to the American Academy of Arts
and Sciences, 1992) and restated last year as "implosion of the Soviet system...totally
unanticipated...we still don't understand it." (Russia House website, August 26, 2011)."

Lost on Kremlin-watchers was the possibilities that, with Party authority under attack by "Party regulars," citizen unrest would crystalize and persuade President BORIS YELTSIN to abolish Communism. (Sovietologists could not imagine that crucial insights, routinely available to the Allied Missions, might lurk behind their isolated scrutiny of "geopolitical" factors.)

Consider, for example, casual actions of one Soviet sentinel who, apparently unimpressed by tensions unfolding during the Berlin Wall crisis, chose to interrupt his detention of a USMLM tour:

"After properly admonishing the Americans about impending Soviet troop
maneuvers (thus conveying useful intelligence information), he allowed
personal preference to overtake his sworn duty as a security guard.
While expecting a lieutenant to arrive shortly, he hastily shouldered his
machine gun (to the delight of fellow soldiers in a nearby ditch) and grasped
the tour officer's battery-razor "to give it a try." With word of his lieutenant's
approach, he again returned to "on-guard.""

(Lecture to the Lake of the Woods Veteran's Group about his first assignment to the East German forest border occupied by the Russian army in 1945) February 2019

KARL MARX RICH MAN — CHOOSES TO BE POOR MAN

"A famous lecturer said, "The credence given to Marx's economic interpretation of history is extraordinary. Why, Marx's own life denies his theory. Born the son of a lawyer with a comfortable place assured to him for the asking, still he chose the hard and penniless life of a political exile. If economic motivation had so little appeal for Marx himself, how could he believe all History to be determined by the economic motivations of mankind?"

"The lecturer's observation is thought provoking. Marx's own life does indeed provide a striking instance of a man whose primary motivations were non-economic. Even if Marx's point is right that society organizes itself along the class lines of economic interest, it would be an instance of fallacy of division to suppose that what is true of all taken together, need to be true of each individual. Economic motivations might be a least common denominator sufficient to determine class interests even though no one person was primarily motivated by them." p. 29-30

The Berlin Wall: 30 Years on, What has Changed?

THE WEEK November 22, 2019

"The real elephant in the room is SOCIALISM, said Helen Raleigh in   TheFederalistcom
The centrally planned, Communist economy of East Germany failed miserably, leaving those living under Soviet control in drab near-poverty, while capitalist West Germany boomed. Yet, "like a zombie, socialism refuses to die" and has even taken root here in the U.S. Far-left candidates like Bernie Sanders and Elizabeth Warren are riding high in the polls, buoyed by young, self-styled, "Democratic Socialists" who never knew the horrors of the Soviet Union. Nearly half of Millennials describe themselves as "SOCIALIST." said John Harley in USATodaycom the plans they support—most notably, Alexandria Ocasio-Cortez's "Green New Deal"— would bring much of the economy under government control and drag the U.S. toward the collectivist oppression that was so dramatically proved a failure in 1989."

"It isn't just the left that's sliding backward, said Brian Klass in the Washington Post. Behind the "would-be strongman" DONALD TRUMP, the Republican Party has shown some troubling, anti-majoritarian tendencies. In 2014, fully 1 in 6 Americans said that military rule would be "good" or "very good," whereas back in 1995 that figure was only 1 in 16. Let's face it, said Fred Kaplan in Slatecom The lesson of 1989 is that history isn't a simple, linear narrative with a happy ending. "History is an unending whirlwind, and we're caught in it."

"So much for "the END OF HISTORY," said Ishaan Tharoot in The Washington Post. When the BERLIN WALL came down 30 years ago this past weekend, the free world reacted with giddy euphoria. That revolutionary moment didn't just mean the reunification of Germany, we were told, or even the defeat of communism and the end of the Cold War. The peaceful fall of the wall was hailed as history's joyous finish line, after which the global triumph of liberal democracy and capitalism was no longer in serious question. But History, it turns out, "never ended"

Thirty years later, Communist China is the world's "looming hegemony"; Hungary and Poland are embracing authoritarian, one-party rule; forces of tribalism and "demagogic population" are ripping Europe apart; after a fleeting "ARAB SPRING," the Middle East has backslid into sectarian bloodshed and tyranny; and in Russia, de facto one-party rule has been re-established by a former KGB officer [Vladimir Putin] with all-too-familiar territorial ambitions."

"I was there when the Wall came down, Serge Schmemann in the New York Times, and while the hope we all felt seems "quaintly utopian" with the benefit of hindsight, "I refuse to accept that nothing changed." That exhilarating moment proved that peaceful protest can bring down an empire—and it is still inspiring people from Hong Kong to Chile to rise up and demand their freedom."   [What about Venezuela Iran and Hong Kong?]

[The Defense Department, DIA, CIA and FBI spent trillions of taxpayer dollars and didn't see that the Soviet Union was collapsing.Wall street must have known that   Russia's economy was bankrupt with virtually no exports. The one fact I remember from my college Economics course was the GUNS AND BUTTER RULE. A nation has to have a strong economy to build today's expensive high tech weapons. When President RONALD REAGAN said the United States would build a STAR WARS anti-ballistic missile system. The Communist Russian government took Reagan seriously and began spending excessive rubles to respond to his challenge. The Russian government controlled economy then couldn't provide basic needs to the general Russian population unless you were a Communist party member. I think any tourist to Russia could have seen the Russian people weren't happy. President REAGAN, Prime Minister MARGRET THATCHER, the Russians called the "IRON LADY" and the Polish POPE JOHN PAUL II and GORBACHEV's reform policies allowed the Union of Soviet Socialist Republics USSR to vote for separation and the UKRAINE, the BALTIC STATES and the southern Muslim republics voted for freedom. Democracy?]

[The American media "remarkably" didn't report excessively the MOST EPIC EVENT IN WORLD HISTORY? It was a REPUBLICAN President REAGAN and President GEORGE H. W. BUSH victory not a Democrat president victory—Presidents JOHN F. KENNEDY, LYNDON B. JOHNSON, JIMMIE CARTER. After 70 years of MARXIST-LENINIST-STALINIST repression of the Russian Orthodox Christians, non Communist millions of people died in the GULAG Siberian work camps and Ukrainian starvation.

I also give credit to Western pop culture. I recently listened to BILLY JOEL'S CD Leningrad concert which I have seen on TV, was Billy Joel the first singer to be flung into the arms of his fans "MOSH PIT"? STING sang his song to Mr. GORBACHEV DO THE RUSSIANS LOVE THEIR CHILDREN TOO? Of course, they do! And still do. Even the Beatles songs of love and brotherhood included BACK IN THE USSR.]

[Lincoln Landis graduated from WEST POINT in the three-year "short class" of 1945. He learned basic Russian language at West Point which "guaranteed" a long tour in Germany maybe a record? 1945-1963 is almost 18 years. I previously told Linc Landis connection to my commander Col. CHARLES PATTILLO at Bitburg AB, Germany. Colonel Patillo's twin brother's daughter is married to one of his son's. They were World War II North American P-51 Mustang fighter pilots over Germany. After the war they were stationed at Fuerstenfeldbruck AB near Munich with the 36th Tactical Fighter Group. There the Patillo, twin brothers, flew as right and left wingmen in the first Air Force jet team the SKYBLAZERS. In 1953, they flew in the first THUNDERBIRDS jet exhibition team in Republic F-84 Thunderjets, built three miles from my home Amityville.

The 36th was deployed to the new Bitburg AB, December 1952, 10 miles from Luxembourg. His former commander Col. ROBERT SCOTT flew to Bitburg in his Republic F-84 Thunderjet which had a Tiger insignia on its nose. Scott was the leader of the famous FLYING TIGER volunteer American pilots who defended China from Japanese bombers in 1939 until World War II, then they became part of the USAAF.

My college roommate for two years enlisted in the US Army stationed at FORT, DIX, New Jersey, and then two years at the HEIDELBERG, Germany U.S. Army Europe (USEUR) headquarters Patton Barracks. He was a SPEC 4 specialist in the HQ top secret message center from 1967-69. Ed's landlord in Neckargemund, east of Heidelberg, was PAUL SKODA who was General ERWIN ROMMEL's chef in the AFRICA KORPS. An Army Times article said he cooked ADOLF HITLER a vegetarian meal in a Berlin restaurant before World War II, and apples from his father's apple orchard in Remagen. I was at BITBURG AIR BASE from 1966-1969, a longer tour. I was editor of the SKYBLAZER newspaper in 1968, when Colonel Patillo was my wing commander.]

Eight year old Linc sat with his uncle KENNESAW MOUNTAIN LANDIS, the baseball commissioner, at the 1932 World Series game in Chicago where BABE RUTH was heckled after two strikes and in response pointed his bat where he would HIT HIS HOME RUN. This home run became legendary. Linc gave me a copy of Kennesaw Landis GREEN LIGHT letter to Pres. FRANKLIN ROOSEVELT about ending baseball during World War II. At the COOPERSTOWN BASEBALL MUSEUM in New York a guide took my photo by the 10 foot poster of the GREEN LIGHT letter. President Roosevelt told Landis to keep America's only big league sport open for the American public to attend games or listen to on national and local radio.

Legendary BOSTON RED SOX player TED WILLIAMS was drafted and was a US Marine aerial gunnery officer trainer at Pensacola. His 20-10 vision made him one of the most accurate gunners. Recalled during the Korean War he was a Marine Grumman F-8F Panther jet bomber pilot flying very dangerous missions on the frontline. PAUL JANNSEN, a member of my Missouri Synod Lutheran church told me he was Ted Williams tent mate in Korea for four months. Williams wingman was JOHN GLENN.

I asked him if he was related to actor RICHARD JANNSEN? He said,"A distant relative."

Communism and its Relation to the First Amendment:
    Freedom of Speech, Freedom of Assembly,
        and Freedom of the Press
Nasson College Springvale, Maine term paper Political Science course, submitted 1962
by Clive D. Louden

"The first Amendment of the BILL OF RIGHTS states the following:
    "Congress shall make no law respecting an establishment of religion,
    or prohibiting the free exercise thereof; or abridging the freedom of
    speech, or of the press; or the right of the people PEACEABLY to
    assemble, and to petition the Government for a redress of grievances." 1

Communism is today the greatest threat faced by our democracy. Communism is not a large organization in the United States but is powerful. "The average number of members in the Communist party in the United States for the last twenty three years was 40,000 or about two-hundredths of one-per-cent of the population." 2

On the other hand about 700,000 men and women have left the Communist Party. This shows Americans are not accepting Communism in our country.

Though the Communist Party is weak in numbers its strength is far more significant. The Communist Party operates a press in English and foreign languages. They dominate seven unions with a total membership of between 300,000 and 400,000. 2

1 Norman Thomas, "The Test of Freedom", New York, 1954, p. 198
2 A. Powell Davis, "The Urge to Persecute," Boston, 1954, p. 76

"There were numerous pro-communists in the State Department." 3

There have been many laws that deal with treason, espionage, sedition and sabotage. No issues of civil liberty have been involved by these laws, however. The important issue is that of the changing of the government by illegal means using the freedom of speech and the press. This crime may be punished as sedition under the First Amendment." 4

The most important federal law dealing with this issue is the Smith Act of 1940, "This law makes it unlawful to conspire to advocate bringing about the forceful overthrow of the government." 5

During the end of 1940, the Supreme Court made a decision which was published by the American Civil Liberties Union and deserves mention. The Smith Act was interpreted by the majority of the court as follows:

"1. To prohibit a number of persons (but not an individual), 2, from advocating
(but not discussing), 3. under certain circumstances (but not under all
circumstances), 4. violent overthrow of the government but not necessarily any
other end." 6

348

"This court decision convicted William Z Foster and 11 other Communist leaders during the late forties. This decision of the court can be best summed up by a statement of Justice Black. "To assemble and to talk and publish certain ideas at a future date: the indictment is that they conspired to organize the Communist Party and to use newspaper or other publications in the future to teach and advocate forcible overthrow of the government." 7

"We cannot defend liberty by denying the danger of the organized Communist conspiracy even if at the moment it is weak within the United States." 8

3 Ibid p 66-67 4 Thomas op. cit. p 103 5 Ibid p104 6 Ibid p 108 7 Ibid p108 8 Ibid p78

"Communism is a monstrous threat to our practice of freedom within our country. Under a false allegiance they are conspiring against our democracy with the ultimate goal of revolution." 9

"Thomas Jefferson himself would be among the first to admit that laws against subversive acts, including espionage and sabotage, and their rigorous enforcement violate no principle or precept of the Bill of Rights." 10 He would also admit "that special provisions must be made to ascertain the loyalty and reliability of persons in positions to injure a country through espionage, sabotage, or plain carelessness." 11

What rights should Communists still loyal to the Party possess under our theory of freedom? The Communist Party should be entitled to the same protection of freedom of speech and of the press as all other American citizens. Speech within a conspiratorial organization should not, however, fall under the full protection which the First Amendment gives to public speech.

Morris Ernest's Constitutional argument on the freedom of speech follows this proposal in the Columbia Law Review of May 1953.

(1) "Protect all private and secret speech regarding the advisability of changes in government…so long as such discussion does not involve the "overt act" necessary to establish any criminal conspiracy, (2) In the event that, as a result of private and secret speech, any one or more persons were to undertake any activity toward an unlawful end, the speech could not be protected any more than would a bank robber's conference." 12

9 Ibid p 80 10 Ibid p 81-82 11 Ibid p 82 12 op. cit. p 84

"The overt act in furtherance of such a criminal conspiracy need not, of course, criminal itself. 13

"Mr. Ernest believes there is a three-fold advantage to this legal distinction between secret and public speech:

1. Distinguish between a secret speech and a public speech which the First Amendment was designed to protect.
2. Determine if a secret speech is an "overt act". If a secret speech contains no "overt act" it will not be restricted.
3. Give protection to public speech and not to secret speech, which will cause more ideas to be formed by the general public. These ideas can then be subjected to public ridicule and debate and can then be accepted or rejected without resort to violence. 14

"Despite the conspiratorial nature of the Communist movement, the Communist party should not be outlawed." 15

"This idea is not only according to the principles of the Bill of Rights, but is a sound public policy. We must protect the rights of men to form radical parties, Outlawing such a party, even with a majority objection is denying a basic democratic principle. This condition may lead to subversive and ultimately violent action in place of political action." 16

"If the Communist Party was outlawed, an appeal would be created of both mystery and martyrdom especially in the youth of our country. It would be a very sad affair to create a greater threat from Communism by outlawing it. This would be an ironic injustice if such an event would occur due to our democracy making foolish decisions. These steps are, in effect, undemocratic even if they are thought justified by the majority." 17

"The Communists have the right to stay out of jail, to speak openly for their cause, to organize their own open party, and participate in elections. This does not, however, imply an equivalent right to seek and hold every sort of office in a democratic state. If Communists are to exist as members of the normal community, they must have a right to work. "But not at tasks or in public positions where they may, under orders, practice a type of espionage, sabotage, or subversion, which might jeopardize the republic." 18
No such right exists in the common sense in the Bill of Rights. [CIA Brennan vote 1976]

13 Norman Thomas, "The Test of Freedom" p 85 14 Ibid p 85 15 Ibid p 86 16 Ibid p 87
17 Ibid p 88 18 Ibid p 88

"Some people have protested that the Communists are not entitled the protection which is given to other Americans. They are not considered to be Americans because of their conspiring to overthrow our system of government. Should we give the Communists freedom? This is not an easily answered question.
"It is true that the Communists are trying to use our freedoms with the intention of destroying them." 19
"One example of a radical move to outlaw was Senator McCarthy's Senate investigations. He attacked the Communists ruthlessly. On one occasion he made a very unjust attack. The following story will show why we must be gradual about reforming the Communist Party.
"Senator McCarthy implied that the "CAPITOL TIMES" of Madison, Wisconsin was a pro-communist newspaper. He urged the advertisers not to contribute, "to bringing the Communist Party line into the homes of Wisconsin." 20 However, this newspaper was not pro-communist as [Wisconsin Senator] McCarthy had wrongly accused it. It was in reality strongly anti-communist."
"This is a case in which there was an uncalled for slander of an innocent newspaper due to prejudice. This is why it is important to be careful on any action which is to be taken to limit any subversive organization. There is only one sure method of reforming a subversive group such as the Communists. That is by slow, methodical, democratic legislation."
19 Davis op. cit. p 183 20 Ibid p 133

Russia Became A Communist Hellhole Because of This Man

Richard Lim The DAILY SIGNAL November 6, 2019
"In Vladimir Lenin's eyes, human lives were expendable
in the pursuit of the worker's paradise."

"To understand Communism, it's important to look at the man who was the first to institute a government dedicated to Karl Marx's ideals: VLADIMIR LENIN."
"When I was in college, I recall the conversation with several classmates who joked about throwing a get together and naming it "The Communist Party." They mocked the idea that anyone would fear this supposedly well-meaning ideology."

"I wonder if they would have been laughing if they were in the presence of gulag survivors."

"This November 7 marks the 102nd anniversary of the Lenin's rise to power in Russia, and November 9 will mark the 30th anniversary of the fall of the BERLIN WALL, the symbol of tyranny built by the regime it forged."

"Victor Sebestyen's 2017 biography on Lenin—the first major biography of the Soviet leader to hit Western bookshelves in two decades—documents his many crimes against humanity."

"Lenin's streak of cruelty began long before he came to power. By his early 20s, his zealous dedication to MARXISM led him to believe that anything justified revolution."

CRUELTY WITHOUT A CONSCIENCE

"When a famine broke out in the Volga region in 1891—one that would kill 400,000 people—Lenin welcomed the event, hoping that it would topple the CZARIST REGIME. His sister, dedicated revolutionaries themselves, assisted with relief efforts for the starving and were shocked by his callous refusal to help."

DOES HISTORY REPEAT ITSELF? AntI-PRESIDENT TRUMP media and politicians have called for Trump's, best American economy and highest employment in 50-years, to collapse. This would force millions of American men, women and children to return to government taxpayer food stamps EDT. Many families could loose their expensive, homes, vehicles and electronic devices with no government aid except limited Unemployment benefits. They would loose their Health insurance requiring Medicade aid. Families would have difficulty paying their monthly bills: Electricity fo heat and AC, water, phone and Internet. Unemployed people also don't pay Federal and State taxes, County school and vehicle Personal Property taxes or pay into the almost bankrupt SOCIAL SECURITY and MEDICARE Socialist government plans from 1935, FDR, 1965, LBJ. The unfunded future liabilities for retiring people's federal benefits and a $23.000,000,000,000 trillion NATIONAL DEBT will in my granddaughter's lifetime, make America a 1984 COMMUNIST/SOCIALIST/FASCIST government which will destroy our REPUBLIC and "democracy". BENJAMIN FRANKLIN after signing the U.S. CONSTITUTION was asked by a lady Sir. "What kind of government do we now have?"

Franklin retorted: "A REPUBLIC IF WE CAN KEEP IT."

"Later, in 1905, when Czarist forces killed hundreds of striking workers and 86 children in Moscow, Lenin refused to mourn for the dead and, instead, hoped the event would further enflame class antagonisms. In his eyes, human lives were expendable in the pursuit of the workers' paradise."

"Lenin would spend a career castigating and eliminating competitor's who he believed had deviated from what he considered: TRUE MARXISM. As Sebestyen notes, though, "The first major 'deviationist' was Lenin, who frequently turned Marxism on its head when it didn't suit his tactical purposes."

"In other words, Lenin was a hypocrite who would purge others for revisioning Marx, but reserved that right for himself."

"Marx had asserted that broad, impersonal (not individual), and material forces controlled the course of History. He also didn't envision the revolution of urban proletariat happening in the largely agrarian Russian Empire."

"No matter—it could happen in Russia, because Lenin said so and would make it happen (which he did). So much for broad, impersonal forces."

"Thus Lenin ushered in the longtime communist practice of manipulating ideology to obtain whatever was desired."

STOKING THE FLAMES OF REVOLUTION

""Before taking power, Lenin spent much of his life under house arrest in Siberia or in exile abroad, living in the United Kingdom, France, and Switzerland—countries that one day would face an existential threat from the regime he would create."

"He established himself as a major leader in the underground communist movement. Reading Sebestyen's account makes it seem that Lenin was the head of some sort of secretive startup enterprise."

"Lenin was constantly raising funds and generating support. He wrote and printed subversive literature, distributing it through underground networks."

"At times, it looks as though Lenin's venture was on the brink of collapse and no one else seemed to believe he would amount to anything-except, it seemed, Lenin himself."

  [ADOLF HITLER had a parallel beginning from obscurity. TRIUMPH OF THE WILL.]

"He survived, in part, by living off his mother's funds. History seems to indicate that dependency combined with radicalism is rarely a going thing. OSAMA BIN LADEN, too, was an extremist who lived off his family's wealth while financing his Islamist activities."

  [ADOLF HITLER received a stipend from an aunt when he lived in Vienna, Austria.]

"A series of tragic incidents led this foundering communist to eventually take control over the world's largest country by land mass. Germany invaded Russia, the Czar showed disastrous leadership, and Berlin ultimately sent the exiled Lenin back to Russia to destabilize it and remove it from the war."

[General ERICH LUDENDORFF gave an unwilling   LENIN gold to go back to Russia to initiate a MARXIST revolution and overthrow Czar NICHOLAS II, which he did, to take Russia out of THE GREAT WAR, World War I. Ludendorff transported Lenin from neutral Switzerland in an armored military train to Russia. In the WONDER WOMAN movie Wonder woman kills General Ludendorff with her sword thinking he is the Greek god of war. To Wonder Woman's dismay the Great War didn't end. Hollywood ending probably not well received in Great Britain, but showed how Humankind has been deceived and that evil is on both sides. The Old Testament has many examples of this. Jesus New Testament is the truth and the answer.]

PERSONAL STORY: My German mother's father KARL FRANK fought on the Russian Front for three years not on the Western Front. He was there at the beginning when the Czarist Russian armies were in EAST PRUSSIA and almost to Germany's capital BERLIN. Artillery General FRANCOIS decimated the Russian armies in September 1914, at TANNENBERG and also at MAUSARIAN LAKES ending a victory which would have ended the "WAR TO END ALL WARS" The Great War. My grandfather's commander in chief was General LUDENDORFF. My mother was born on Feb. 22, 1915, Washington's birthday. She was three when he came home to Frankfurt am Main. My mother's middle name is Francois, in honor of the only "hero" of the GREAT WAR.]

"It also helped Lenin's cause that he had the perfect slogan for a suffering populace: "PEACE, LAND, and BREAD." [Hitler proclaimed the same Socialist utopia to Germany.]

"While in exile, Lenin railed against the Imperial government for its oppressive ways—for instance, its censorship of the opposition and dismissal of parliament. Of course, once in power, Lenin repeated these policies and usually exceeded their cruelty, prisoning and confiscating the property of his opponents."

  [Hitler did this after REICHSTAG FIRE a month after his election on Jan. 30, 1933]

A REGIME OF TORTURE AND MURDER

"Lenin appointed the homicidal Felix Dzerzhinsky to head up the CHECKA (the secret police) with orders "to fight a merciless war against all enemies of the revolution. We are not in need of justice, it is war now."   [Hitler created the GESTAPO and SS.]

"In less than a year, hundreds, if not thousands, were executed—including Nicholas II and his family. He would be the last Emperor of Russia."

"In a move that prefigured MAO ZEDONG'S later CULTURAL REVOLUTION in China. Lenin incited class warfare across the Soviet Union." [40,000,000 died in China/Russia.]

"He marked wealthy peasants, or kulaks, as enemies of the revolution and encouraged violence against them. He imposed fixed grain prices at low rates, straining peasants who where already living on the margins, seized their grain, and left them to starve."

"When the peasants began resisting, Lenin ordered government officials to torture them or apply poison gas. He specifically ordered his henchman, JOSEF STALIN, to be ruthless in taking grain from Tsaritsyn."

[5-6,000,000 Ukrainians died on collectivized communist farms. They were Russian Orthodox Christian and Jew who were God-fearing capitalists not atheist Communists.]

"When those tactics contributed to yet another famine in the Volga area, he refused to provide relief and did so only after being forced by his advisers. American official HERBERT HOOVER, who was running humanitarian efforts in Europe during World War I, offered his services to the Soviet   government,"

"For those who scoff at the idea that communism was an inherently expansionist regime, Lenin created the Communist International, or "Comintern," to spread the revolution around the world. At times, more funds were spent to spread propaganda abroad (including in the United States) than on famine relief."

THE END OF ONE MAN, THE BEGINNING OF A DISASTER

"An assassination attempt and a series of strokes weakened Lenin and, by 1923, he was dying. By then, he came to believe Stalin was too heavy-handed to be his successor (he would know), even saying as much in his famed Last Testament (which was later suppressed)."

"Lenin died in January 1924, having failed to dislodge Stalin from power. As bad as Lenin was, somehow,   even   greater   suffering   awaiting   the   Russian   people."

"After a lifetime of serving the Soviet government at the highest levels, MOLOTOV reflected on the two men, saying that both were "hard men…harsh and stern." He added, "Without a doubt, Lenin was harsher.""

"The regime that Lenin founded would eventually impose totalitarian dictatorships over its Eastern European neighbors and threaten the existence of the West, but ultimately would collapse in 1991 under   the   weight   of   its   own   contradictions.""

"The Soviet Union may no longer exist today, but the Communist Party in China remains firmly entrenched. Few regimes can match the levels of totalitarianism practiced under LENIN, STALIN and MAO, yet Beijing continues to disregard human life in its pursuit of the promised MARXIST UTOPIA."

"The United States has never been a perfect country, but we can be thankful that it avoided the autocratic   and   ideological   extreme   of   the   20th   Century."

"The far left is always looking to publicize injustices here at home. By that standard, the story of Lenin   ought   to   receive   more   attention   than   any   other."

CHURCHILL'S ANALYSIS OF SOCIALISTS BECOMING CONSERVATIVE

WINSTON CHURCHILL—"Socialism is a philosophy of failure, the creed of ignorance, and the gospel of envy. its inherent virtue is the equal sharing of misery."
"When you are a youth you are for socialism or you have no heart. When you are 40 you become conservative if you have a brain."

HILLARY CLINTON CAMPAIGNED FOR ULTRA-CONSERVATIVE GOLDWATER

Socialism Promises Utopia, but Delivers Suffering

Walter E. Williams, African-American economics professor George Mason University columnist for The Daily Signal

"Presidential contenders are in a battle to out give one another."

Sen. Elizabeth Warren, D-Mass., proposes a whopping $50,000 per student college loan forgiveness. Sen. Bernie Sanders, I-VT., proposes free health care for all Americans plus illegal aliens. Most Democratic presidential candidates PROMISE FREE STUFF that includes college, universal income. "Medicare for All," and debt forgiveness.

Their socialist predecessors made promises, too.

"Freedom and Bread" was the slogan used by ADOLF HITLER during the National Socialist German Workers' Party (NAZI) campaign against President PAUL von HINDENBURG. Hitler even promised, "In the THIRD REICH every German girl will find a husband." [A lie because millions of men were killed or prisoners in World War II.]

Stalin promised a great socialist-Marxist society that included better food and better worker conditions.

China's Mao Zedong promised democratic constitutionalism and the dream that "farmers have land to till." These, and other promises, gave Mao the broad political support he needed to win leadership of the entire country in 1949.

Socialism promises a utopia that sounds good, but those promises are never realized. It most often results in massive human suffering.

Capitalism fails miserably when compared with a heaven or utopia promised by socialism. But any earthly system is going to come up short in such a comparison. Mankind must make choices among alternative economic systems that actually exist.

It turns out that for the common man capitalism, with all of its alleged shortcomings, is superior to any system yet devised to deal with his everyday needs and desires. By most any measure of human well-being, people who live in countries toward the capitalistic end of the economic spectrum are far better off than their fellow men who live in countries toward the socialist end. Why?

Capitalism, or what some call free markets, is relatively new in human history. Prior to capitalism, the way individuals amassed great wealth was by looting, plundering, and enslaving their fellow man. With the rise of capitalism, It became possible to amass great wealth by serving and pleasing your fellow man.

Capitalists seek to discover what people want and produce and market it as efficiently as possible as a means to profit. A historical example of this process would be John D, Rockefeller, whose successful marketing drove kerosene prices down from 58 cents a gallon in 1865 to 7 cents in 1900. Henry Ford became rich by producing cars for the common man.

Both Ford's and Rockefeller's personal benefits pale in comparison to the benefits received by the common man who had cheaper kerosene and cheaper and more convenient transportation.

There are literally thousands of examples of how mankind's life has been made better by those in the pursuit of profits.

Here is my question to you: Are the people who, by their actions, created unprecedented convenience, longer life expectancy, and a more pleasant life for the ordinary person—and became wealthy in the process—deserving of all the scorn and ridicule heaped upon them by intellectuals and political hustlers today?

In many intellectual and political circles, the pursuit of profits is seen as evil. However, this pursuit forces entrepreneurs to find ways to either please people efficiently or go bankrupt. Of course, they could mess up and avoid bankruptcy if they can get the government to bail them out or give them protection against competition.

Nonprofit organizations have an easier time of it. As a matter of fact, people tend to be the most displeased with services received from public schools, motor vehicle departments, and other government agencies. Nonprofits can operate whether they please people or not. That's because they derive their compensation through taxes I'm sure that we'd be less satisfied with supermarkets if they had the power to take our money through taxes, as opposed to being forced to find ways to get us to voluntarily give them our money."

By the way, I'm not making an outright condemnation of socialism. I run my household on the Marxist principle, "From each according to his ability, to each according to his needs."

That system works when you can remember the names of all involved." Copywrite 2018

SOCIALISM A FALSE FAUSTIAN DYSTOPIA—SPENGLER

German historian OSWALD SPENGLER wrote THE DECLINE OF THE WEST Vol. 1 published in Germany in 1918, and Volume 2 was published in 1922. It was translated and published in the United States in 1926 (Vol.1) and 1928 (Vol. 2). The books are Spengler's exhaustive investigations of the background and origins of our [Western] civilization. He passed of a heart attack in 1936, age 56, in Munich. He loved the Harz mountains. Spengler's following critique of Socialism would have gotten his book banned or this passage deleted by the Nazis and Communists.

"Let us, once more, review Socialism (independently of the economic movement of the same name) as the FAUSTIAN EXAMPLE of Civilization-ethics. Its friends regard it as the FORM OF THE FUTURE, its enemies as a sign of ITS DOWNFALL, and both are equally right. WE ARE ALL SOCIALISTS, wittingly or unwittingly, willingly or unwillingly. Even resistance to it wears its form."

"SOCIALISM—in its highest and not its street-corner sense is, like every other FAUSTIAN IDEAL, exclusive. It owes its popularity only in the fact that it is completely misunderstood even by its exponents, who present it as a sum of rights instead of as one of duties, an abolition instead of an intensification of the KANTIAN imperative, a slackening instead of a tautening of directional energy. The trivial and superficial tendency towards ideals of "WELFARE," "FREEDOM," "HUMANITY," the doctrine of the "greater happiness of the greatest number," are negations of the FAUSTIAN ETHIC —a very different matter from the tendency of EPICUREANISM towards the ideal of "happiness," for the condition of happiness was the actual sum and substance of the classical ethic. Here precisely is an instance of sentiments to all outward appearance much the same, but meaning in the one case everything and in the other nothing." THE DECLINE OF THE WEST Oswald Spengler Vintage Books NY April 2006   p 185-186

"The Socialist feels the FUTURE as his task and aim, and accounts the happiness of the moment as worthless in comparison….And here Socialism becomes tragic. It is of the deepest significance that NIETZCHE, so completely clear and sure in dealing with what should be destroyed, what transvalued, loses himself in nebulous generalities soon as he comes to discuss the Whither, the Aim. His criticism of decadence is unanswerable, but his theory of the SUPERMAN is a castle in the air." Ibid p 187

FLOGGING A DEAD HORSE—THE DEMOCRAT PARTY

"FLOGGING A DEAD HORSE—BEATING A DEAD HORSE is an idiom that means a particular EFFORT IS A WASTE OF TIME AS THERE WILL BE NO OUTCOME."

"EARLIEST USE—According to the Oxford English Dictionary, the first recorded use of the expression in its modern sense was by an English politician and orator JOHN BRIGHT in reference to the REFORM ACT of 1867, which called for more democratic representation in Parliament. Trying to rouse Parliament from its apathy on the issue, he said in a speech, would be like trying to "flog a dead horse to make it pull a load."   Wiki

"However, an earlier insistence is attributed to that same John Bright 13 years prior: speaking in [House of] COMMONS on SUFFRAGETTE [woman's vote] protests, March 28, 1859. LORD ECHO remarked that Bright had not been "satisfied with the results of his winter campaign" and that "a saying was attributed to him [Bright] that he [had] found he was 'flogging a dead horse.' " Wikipedia

BRITAIN'S "SOAK THE RICH" 1909 TAX NOT PASSED BY HOUSE OF LORDS

"The HOUSE OF LORDS was reformed in 1911 due to controversy over the previous BUDGET of 1909. In 1909 the Lords had to pass a bill to make it law, and as the "SOAK THE RICH" Budget would have affected them, they refused to pass it, so it could not become law."   Wikipedia

"A reference could be made to previous conflicts. 1909 was not the first time the CONSERVATIVE LORDS had gone against the LIBERAL COMMONS."

"The conflict within the [House of] LORDS is an excellent topic for exam questions since it is complicated yet only lasted a short time. It is easy to get mixed up over the details."

"The KING [Edward II] threatened to knight liberal Lords so that the budget would be passed. The previous Conservative majority would have been a minority, and would be frightened into passing the Budget. This gave rise to the reform which stated that if a bill was passed three times it would have become law no matter what the Lords said, passed abolishing their "veto" and stopping them forbidding an Act…This meant that Acts could be passed in the interest of the people without the Lords preventing them, so making the whole system more democratic." Wikipedia

"PICTURE SOURCE: Shows democracy as a "Government of the People", symbolizing the liberal government of the time, winning over the huge monster of the Lords with its veto lain down beside it. The sheer size of the symbolic Lord and the phrase 'The Monster Slain' shows the Act as a massive achievement in democracy." Wikipedia

(AOA/NEAB Modern World Revision copy write Stanley Thomes 2000)

MAKING A MOUNTAIN OUT OF A MOLEHILL

"MAKING A MOUNTAIN OUT OF A MOLEHILL is an idiom referring to over-reactive, histrionic behavior where a person makes too much of a minor issue. It seems to have come in existence in the 16th century."

METAPHOR—"The idiom is a metaphor for the common behavior of responding disproportionately to something — usually an adverse circumstance. One who makes a mountain out of a molehill is said to be greatly exaggerating the severity of the situation. In cognitive psychology, this form of distortion is called magnification or overreacting. The phrase is so common that a study by psychologists found that with respect to familiarity and image value, it ranks high among the 203 common sayings they tested."

"The earliest recorded use of the alliterative phrase making a mountain out of a molehill dates from 1548. The idiom is founded by play write and cleric Nicholas Udall, a student of Thomas Cromwell, English statesman who was beheaded by King Henry VIII."

DEFINITION COGNITIVE PSYCHOLOGY: "Is the scientific study of mental processes such as "attention," language use, memory, perception problem solving, creativity, and thinking." Wikipedia

DEFINITION OF MAGNIFICATION: "Exaggeration is a representation of something in an exclusive manner. MUNCHAUSEN SYNDROME by proxy is a controversial term for a behavior pattern in which a caregiver deliberately exaggerates, fabricates, or induces physical, psychological, behavioral, or mental health problems in those who are in their care." [Adam Shiff's false story of President Trump telling the newly elected (72% vote) Ukrainian president Zelensky that "I tell you 7 times, I said 7 times to investigate Joe Biden and I won't tell you again." The transcript of the call was immediately made public and revealed this was a LIE. Presidential conversations with world leaders are normally kept confidential. A member of Congress can't be prosecuted or censured for telling a falsehood? Shiff is a caregiver to the American people as an elected representative. "A PUBLIC OFFICE IS A PUBLIC TRUST." TERM LIMITS. Actor ROBIN WILLIAMS portrayed BARON VON MUNCHAUSEN who was a habitual false boaster telling tall tales. The German people love fairy tales. Americans love fairy tales also. German American WALT DISNEY and his ABC DISNEY films all have happy endings.This has generated billions of dollars and created thousands of jobs.]

SHOCK JOCK: "A shock jock, a type of radio broadcaster, entertains or attracts attention using humor and/or melodramatic exaggeration that some portion of the listening audience may find offensive." Wikipedia   [Shiff, Nadler, Shumer are lawyers.]

PATHOLOGY: "Psychoanalysis considered that neurotic exaggerations were the products of displacement — overvaluations for example being used to maintain a repression elsewhere. The grandiose sense of self-importance observed in NARCISSISTS also USES EXAGGERATION to thwart any recognition of moderate fallibility, seeing any departure from complete success as total and hopeless failure."

"Self-dramatization, theatrically, and exaggerated expression of emotion" can be observed in those with histrionic personality disorder, while "catastrophizing" is associated with depressive, neurotic or paranoid behavior."

MEDIA: "German philosopher SCHOPENHAUER SAW EXAGGERATION as ESSENTIAL to journalism. He may have exaggerated the case slightly, but YELLOW JOURNALISM [later] thrived on exaggeration, not FACT-CHECKING and independent verification." Wikipedia [Hitler read Schopenhauer as Leni Reifenstahl learned when she visited his apartment when he was running for political office. Hitler retorted, "My beliefs are based on Schopenhauer's "WILL TO POWER" not NIETZSCHE's Superman.]

POLITICS: "Politicians can EXAGGERATE. In the electoral process one may EXPECT EXAGGERATION. Outside the electoral process the exaggerations of propaganda can bolster the position of incumbents." Wikipedia   [TERM LIMITS]

CHARACTER ASSASSINATION: "Is a deliberate and sustained effort to damage the reputation or credibility of an individual. The term could also be selectively applied to social groups and institutions. Agents of character assassinations employ a mix of open and convert methods to achieve their goals, such as raising FALSE ACCUSATIONS, planting and fostering rumors, and MANIPULATING INFORMATION."   Wikipedia

"Character assassination (CA) happens through character attacks. These can take many forms, such as spoken insults, speeches, pamphlets, campaign ads, cartoons, and internet memes. As a result of character attacks, individuals may be rejected by their professional community or members of their social or cultural environment. The process of CA may resemble an annihilation of human life as the damage sustained can last a lifetime. For some historical figures, that damage endures for centuries."Wikipedia

"CA may involve exaggeration, misleading HALF-TRUTHS, or MANIPULATION OF FACTS to present an UNTRUE picture of the targeted person. It is a form of defamation.

"The phrase "character assassination" became popular from around 1930." Wikipedia

"Similar idioms include MUCH ADO ABOUT NOTHING and MAKING A SONG AND DANCE ABOUT NOTHING." Wikipedia

THE PARADOX: "By means of "noting" (which in Shakespeare's day, sounded similar to "nothing" as in Shakespeare's MUCH ADO ABOUT NOTHING play's title, which means GOSSIP, RUMOR, and OVERHEARING).   Wikipedia

BLOW OUT OF PROPORTION: "TO OVERREACT or to OVERSTATE; to treat too seriously or be overly concerned with." Wikipedia

QUISLING the NAME for a TRAITOR

I once met a man after a church service with my father in Bethany, Connecticut, third oldest Episcopal church. He saw my Swedish 1969 SAAB 99. I told him I had been to Sweden and bought it in Kaiserslautern, Germany. The man then proudly told me and my father, "My Norwegian father was in VIDKUN QUISLING's firing squad!" QUISLING's name has become an English synonym for TRAITOR. Not ARNOLD?

PROVIDENTIAL FACT: The week that FOX TV news commentator BILL O'REILLY was dismissed at the end of one show posted his word of the day QUISLING. He said that is an interesting word? Few Americans know this word. I have several Norwegian friends who know this infamous man's name. Wikipedia has a remarkable story about Quisling. He actually believed that his Norwegian countrymen where a NORDIC MASTER RACE blondes not ARYAN like Hitler and the Nazis propaganda. In the Winter Olympics Norwegians are dominating especially considering Norway's small population. Many American Winter Olympic Gold medalists are of Norwegian or of Scandinavian heritage. My Scottish heritage, my father once told me, has "Viking" genes his auburn brown and my red hair. My German mother had platinum blonde hair also Nordic, not Aryan, a term derived from Afghanistan and Persia which became Iran, Aryan, in 1935. This pigmentation is unique to a north temperate climate. In September 1968, I was on an Air

Force exchange to Norway at Bodo Air Base, 50 miles north of the Arctic Circle. I have a photo on a mountain top of grade school children all with platinum blond hair, their teacher had red hair.

ARNOLD HERO OF STRATEGIC SARATOGA BATTLE The Treasonous Name of BENEDICT ARNOLD Still Rings Out

by Charles Jameson CULPEPER TIMES Aug.15-21, 2019

"The name BENEDICT ARNOLD has been synonymous throughout American History with the WORD TRAITOR. You might be surprised to know that Arnold built a very impressive military career, and his generalship during the [American] Revolution probably saved America through the year 1776. That's what made his defection to the British army such a shock, and one that we still talk about over two centuries later."

"Born in the British colony of Connecticut in 1741, he was the only child out of 11 to survive to adulthood. He spent his young adulthood as an apothecary and merchant, but served in the militia as well,"

"Arnold quickly established himself as one of George Washington's BEST GENERALS. In 1775 ARNOLD, along with ETHAN ALLEN and his GREEN MOUNTAIN BOYS, planned and executed an attack on the British at FORT TICONDEROGA. The Fort was secured by the patriots, but most importantly, so were the 100 ARTILLERY PIECES [cannons] which were quickly transported to the American positions supporting the SIEGE OF BOSTON." [My father circa 1988, told me to see the Taconic State parkway marker 1/2 mile down our dirt road, near Harlemville, NY. The granite marker shows an engraving of General Knox wagons towing cannons toward Hillsdale then to Great Barrington, Massachusetts over the rugged Berkshire Mountains to Boston.]

"The overall British strategic plan to end the war was to ISOLATE New England by SECURING THE HUDSON RIVER VALLEY up through LAKE CHAMPLAIN. During 1776, GENERAL ARNOLD engineered a brilliant defense of the lake, frustrating BRITISH EFFORTS to take both the lake and upper Hudson. He would again show his bravery and dedication to the American cause during the battles of Saratoga in 1777."

"Arnold believed the Continental Congress insufficiently rewarded his efforts. But Arnold isn't the only leader on the American side that had been slighted by Congress. In order to ensure the fledgling union would stay together, Congress tended to make sure each state held an equal number of generalships. So it was obvious that promotion to General or Major General was a political process rather than a meritorious one. This chaffed a number of America's early military leaders including DANIEL MORGAN and NATHANIEL GREENE, both of whom had to be coaxed back into service after being snubbed by Congress."

"After being appointed Brigadier General, Arnold watched as Congress passed him over for promotion to the post of Major General five times in favor of subordinates. Arnold had every intention of resigning from military services following these outrages, but stayed on after Washington's insistence. He was rewarded in 1777 with a promotion to Major General and a post as military commander of Philadelphia."

"During his career, Arnold had difficulty getting along with other continental officers and officials, having open feuds with several officers in the continental army. In Philadelphia, Arnold began to associate with British loyalists and became smitten with 18 year old PEGGY SHIPPEN. Peggy was the daughter of wealthy Philadelphia loyalist Edward Shippen. [founder of Shippensburg, PA] Arnold began to live extravagantly and many began to question if his wealth came from covert dealings with the British. Although he successfully secured Peggy's hand, his extravagance and imprudence ultimately drove him into debt."

"Continental officials could not confirm Arnold's suspected betrayal until 1780, when hard evidence of his treason was uncovered. After receiving command of West Point in 1779, Arnold willingly provided the British with vital information for taking control of it. West Point was the most important defensive site along the Hudson River. Although by this time the British had turned their attention to the southern colonies, West Point was still a critical point along the communications and transportation routes for the Patriots. On September 23, 1780, after meeting with Arnold and receiving documents on West Point's defenses, British spy, Major JOHN ANDRE was captured trying to make his way back to the British ship, Vulture. The three unsuspecting New York militiamen John Spaulding, David Williams and Eric Van Wert stepped out of the woods, stopped Andre, questioned, undressed him and found the hidden documents in Andre's stockings beneath his feet. Andre tried to bribe the three to release him, but instead they turned him over to Col. JOHN JAMESON — one of original CULPEPER [Virginia] MINUTEMEN— who was commander of the TARRYTOWN area of New York. Unfortunately, his commanding officer was General Benedict Arnold."

"Col. Jameson received and questioned Andre, but Andre convinced Col, Jameson that he should be sent to General Arnold for questioning. Col. Jameson agreed, but soon countermanded the order after discussions with BENJAMIN TALMADGE, George Washington's SPYMASTER. Col. Jameson instead sent a note to Arnold, unknowingly tipping Arnold off that he was about to be unmasked, and had the papers sent to General Washington. When Arnold realized what had been uncovered, he made haste to the Vulture. Arnold successfully escaped. Andre was not as he was not so lucky. He was hanged a couple of weeks later. [He was a British spy.]

"Arnold would go on to lead a British invasion of the Virginia Tidewater area in 1781. [Arnold also burned New London, CT]. While his military maneuvers were successful, lack of support from the British loyalists and the zeal of British loyalists and the zeal of the American Patriots would end the war at YORKTOWN later that year. After that, the British didn't have much use for Arnold, and sidelined him from military service. He and his family lived alternately between London and New Brunswick. He struggled with poor business decisions, debt and his reputation and ultimately died in London in 1801."

"For his part, Col. Jameson was chastised by General Washington for allowing Arnold to get away. It was later said that Col. Jameson only did what was correct as an officer following the chain of command, so no lasting punishment came from the incident. The important part was that WEST POINT remained safely in American hands thus preventing a disastrous end of the Revolutionary War. This allowed the United States of America to become the country it is today. ALEXANDER HAMILTON stated that "the conduct of Andre to that of his captors formed a striking contrast. He tempted them with the offer of his watch, his horse and any sum of money they should name. They rejected his offers with indignation and the gold that could seduce a man high in esteem and confidence of his country who had memories of past exploits the motives of present reputation and future glory to prop his integrity, had no charms on three simple peasants leaning only on their virtue and an honest sense of their duty. While Andre is handed with execration to future times posterity will repeat the names VAN WERT, SPAULDING and WILLIAMS."

(Charles C. Jameson is a member and past president of the George Washington Carver Regional High School Alumni Association, vice president of the Culpeper Minute Men Chapter of the Sons of the American Revolution, member of the Board of Trustees for Museum of Culpeper History, member of the Culpeper Branch #7058 of the NAACP.)

[Mr. Jameson is an African American, his family may have an historical connection to Col. Jameson who was an original Culpeper Minuteman. The Minuteman were from my Orange County, Culpeper County, and Madison County and defended Virginia's capital then located at

Williamsburg not Richmond, Virginia. They designed the "DON'T TREAD ON ME" Revolutionary war flag which shows a coiled, striking rattlesnake. Virginia sells a personalized yellow license plate with this rattlesnake. I met the man who designed this license plate who showed it to me on his cell phone 00 rattlesnake 00. He was the DJ at my Lake of the Woods veterans group 2017 Christmas party. I talked to him and mentioned I had the Virginia FIGHT TERRORISM Pentagon license plate, and in Florida had met the daughter whose Texas father designed the license plate. He lives in Culpeper, but was from Portland, Maine. I told him I graduated from a college in Maine about 35 miles from Portland. SMALL WORLD.]

FORGETTING THE HOLOCAUST

Breakpoint Daily May 18, 2018
Eric Mataxas with Roberto Rivera

INEXCUSABLE IGNORANCE OF THE PAST

"In the 1930s and 40s, six million Jews perished at the hands of the Nazis, But amazingly, this would be news to many among us."

"Just about the only unequivocal example of evil most Americans can agree on are the Nazis. It's why what's known as "GODWIN'S LAW" holds that the longer an online argument about some issue goes on, the more likely it is that someone is going to invoke Adolf Hitler: We all agree that being like Hitler is bad."

"But a disturbing new report suggests, an increasing percentage of Americans don't really know why Hitler and his henchmen are considered to be evil incarnate."

"A study conducted by the Conference on Jewish Material Claims Against Germany, or "Claims Conference" for short, found that forty-one percent of all respondents, and two-thirds of millennials, could not correctly identify Auschwitz. Not surprisingly, 45 percent couldn't name a single concentration camp."

"Only half knew that 6,000,000 Jews perished in the Holocaust. One-third out the number of murdered at 2,000,000 or less. Even worse, "Twenty-two percent of millennials in the poll said they haven't heard of the Holocaust or are not sure whether they've heard of it." Paradoxically, nearly three-in-five of those interviewed "believe the Holocaust could happen in the United States." Given the overall level of ignorance about the Holocaust itself, it's not clear what they've basing their opinions on."

"The head of the Claims Conference, Julius Berman, told the Times of Israel that, "We are alarmed that today's generation lacks some of the basic knowledge about these atrocities." The Conference's vice-president added that "there remain troubling gaps in Holocaust awareness while survivors are still with us; imagine when there are no longer survivors here to tell their stories."

"What makes this report especially troubling is that there has been a rise in anti-Semitism both in the United States and, especially, abroad. While anti-Semitism is, in the words of historian Daniel Jonah Goldhagen, "The Devil That Never Dies," it was, for a while at least, driven mostly underground by the Third Reich's crimes against the Jews of Europe."

"Now, to paraphrase the book of Exodus, a generation has arisen that knows not Auschwitz. On the left, criticism of Israeli policy, some of which is arguably warranted, has fostered alliances with

loathsome anti-Semites, Hamas, and Holocaust deniers. One prominent left-wing British politician even called Hitler a "ZIONIST."
"I wish I were making that up."

"On the right, ask any prominent Jewish commentator about how quickly his or her comment boxes fill up with anti-Semitic bile. Sometimes, you don't even have to be Jewish: David French of the National Review, who is an Evangelical Christian, was subjected to pictures of his seven-year-old daughter in a gas chamber."
"On a personal note, when my father was a teenager, German troops massacred thousands of their former Italian allies on his home island of Cephalonia in Greece."
HOLLYWOOD STORY: The film CAPTAIN CORLEON'S MADOLIN with Italian-American actor NICHOLAS COPPOLA CAGE vividly shows this massacre after Italy left the AXIS and joined the ALLIES.

"The Spanish philosopher GEORGE SANTAYANA famously wrote that "Those who cannot remember the past are condemned to repeat it." Growing up, especially in the New York area, I can't imagine that people could ever forget the lessons of World War II and the Holocaust, much less not know what Auschwitz is."
"Well, it appears that people not only have forgotten the past, they never bothered to learn about it in the first place."
"It's and ignorance that leaves us, effectively, without a Devil, which is as dangerous as it is inexcusable."

[Eric Metaxas has written books on Pastor Martin Luther, Pastor Dietrich Bonhoeffer, Wilberforce who ended the slave trade to Great Britain, 4 days before his passing, Seven Men and Seven Women. I have all these epic historical Christian books.]

SMALL WORLD FACT: This FORGETTING THE HOLOCAUST date MAY 18 is providential. My Jewish wife was born May 18, 1948, 4 days after Israel became a nation. Phil my Baptist Bible OLD TESTAMENT prophetic Bible study teacher's wife Betty was born on May 18. My realtor lady Judy's birthday was May 18, 1943, my birthday May 4, 1943. She had been in Phil's Bible study until she moved South before I joined his class. I joined after I meet Phil at local resident EDWIN MEESE's presentation to the Susan Allen Republican women's luncheon. I spoke with Phil who led the six-man LAKERS a cappella GOSPEL singing group. He invited me to his LOW church Bible study group. I am more Jewish now than in the 13 years I attended Reform Temple. Finally, Pope ST. JOHN PAUL II, born May 18, friend Andre his second cousin.

THE CHUCK COLSON CENTER FOR CHRISTIAN WORLDVIEW
PERSONAL STORY: This Holocaust story was written on my Jewish wife's 70th birthday. She was born four day's after Israel was restored as a nation by a close United Nations vote. She was born in MAIMONIDES hospital in Brooklyn. After giving birth her mother Helen Denker heard some nurses talking about the beautiful red haired baby girl. She then was shown her daughter.

The HOLOCAUST and Dutch CHRISTIAN CORRIE TEN BOOM

PLAIN THRUTH magazine March 1995 Paul Kroll
"Through this time of trial, the living words of Jesus Christ sustained her spirit."

"The TEN BOOM family was from the small city of HAARLEM, Holland. The center of their work was a small watch repair shop, run out of their home by the elderly ten Boom father and two of his daughters, Betsie and Corrie.

Their triumphant story was documented a quarter of a century ago in the book THE HIDING PLACE. This ever popular story of the ten Boom family's accomplishments has been reprinted many times.

The ten Booms were the unlikeliest heroes. At the time, Corrie was 50, her sister was 7 years older, and father ten Boom was 80.

Yet heroes they were. The ten Booms lodged numerous Jews on a temporary basis. They then spirited them out to safe houses throughout the Dutch countryside. A brother Willem, and another sister Nollie, also participated in helping Jews.

Ultimately, some 80 Dutch citizens—from elderly women to teenage boys—participated in the ten Boom "cell." It was called, affectionately. "God's underground."

Beginning in May 1942—-and for more than a year and a half—they led, as Corrie put it, "double lives." On the surface, the ten Booms ran a struggling repair shop. But the shop was the hub of an underground organization with spokes throughout Holland.

The ten Booms knew it would be only a matter of time before the Nazis would discover them. On Feb. 28, 1944, their worst fears came true.

The Gestapo raided the watch shop. Willem, Corrie, Betsie, Nollie, their elderly father and others were arrested and taken to the police station.

The ten Booms were then transported to a federal penitentiary at Scheveningen,Holland

PERSONAL CONNECTION: In July 1967, when stationed at Bitburg AB, Germany, I went to the popular beach at Scheveningen with another airman a Mexican-American from California. We drove there from "MOM'S" B&B in the Square in EINDHOVEN, where Bitburg airmen, American army and even some Canadian army soldiers stationed in Germany would stay there. A great large breakfast. I met one American soldier born the same day as me May 4, 1943, in Detroit. We didn't have a beer together? Is that an astrology "same karma" thing? Detroit is due north of my birthplace Lexington, Kentucky, also a geographic astral connection?

I am not a beach person my red hair and "lily" white skin are very sunburn prone. I did not know about skin cancer until age 75, in 2019, when my VA Vietnamese lady surgeon Dr. Phan removed two melanoma cysts on my left chin at the HUNTER HOLMES MCGUIRE VA hospital, named after Dr. MCGUIRE who amputated Gen.THOMAS "Stonewall" JACKSON's left arm after being shot by friendly fire. Later I fell and made a "one point" landing disconnecting my left elbow. I have a plate reconnect done by VA Dr. JEB STAURT. I commented, "Dr. Stuart you know this VA hospital is named after Dr. MCGUIRE who amputated Gen. Stonewall JACKSON's left arm." Dr. JEB STUART retorted. "Don't worry." Then, I was given anesthesia. Then I went to LA LA LAND.

HISTORY PROVIDENCE: During the battle of CHANCELLORSVILLE, Virginia, May 5, 1862, General JACKSON was shot in the arm, two balls, by friendly fire, during his overly zealous recon in the dark woods of the Wilderness, where I have lived since April 15, 2005. I have passed his site's memorial monument hundreds of times.This was after Jackson's famous 12-mile bold FLANK MARCH, which Quantico Marines today reenact, which completely surprised and routed Gen.THOMAS HOOKER's, twice as large, Union Army's western Flank. Gen. ROBERT E. LEE's greatest victory. Gen. AMBROSE BURNSIDE's (burnsides) disastrous battle at Fredericksburg in December 1962, was more disastrous and a shock to the incredibly brave Union soldiers moral. At GETTYSBURG on July 2, 1863, General LEE would order his Virginian's to cross the one mile open field in General GEORGE PICKETT's immortal famous "charge" into carnage. One of Gen. GEORGE PATTON's relatives died there. The film GETTYSBURG (1992) shows Gen. WINIFRED HANCOCK's soldiers barely hold back Pickett's charge at MISSIONARY RIDGE central target of the attack. His troops victoriously cheer shouting FREDERICKSBURG!

FREDERICKSBURG! They had suffered many casualties there during one of the 7 suicidal charges against MARYE'S HEIGHTS sunken road "trench". Calvary Gen. J.E.B. STUART, next highest in rank officer, becomes the Confederate army's commander. General "FIGHTING" JOE HOOKER retreated North still suffering for shell shock. Hooker, at the start of the battle, was sitting on the porch of the Chancellor family's roadhouse when a cannonball landed close to him almost killing him. The term "HOOKER" was coined in his dishonor for allowing women camp followers to visit his soldiers for illicit relationships.

The Veterans hospital is in south Richmond behind the huge ALTRIA Philip Morris/Marlboro cigarette factory. Dr. SCHUTZER was my VA hospital chief of radiology for my 20 lower right chin 30 minute, 10 minute intermittent radiation scans. I asked Dr, Schutzer if he had German relatives. He said his German grandfather's family left Germany when he was a child in 1933. ADOLF HITLER, 44, was elected as Germany's Chancellor on Jan. 30, 1933, 40% of vote. Gen. PAUL VON HINDENBURG, 88, World War I, German Army commander-in-chief, was elected President HEAD OF STATE of Germany. I gave Dr. Schutzer a copy of what I wrote about my dad's 8th AAF B-24 unit's best bombing record, including my refugee mother's story about why she left Hitler's Germany, January 1935. My mother was a 19 yr. old platinum blonde Lutheran, who had a 6-month tourist visa. She was an illegal alien for five years until August 1940, when she married my father in his hometown Amityville, Long Island. My mother Elisabeth Frank was born on February 22, 1915, George Washington's birthday.]

"Happily, Willem and Nollie were released within a few weeks. But father ten Boom—"Opa" as the 80-year-old gentleman was affectionately known—died in prison 10 days after the arrest. When Corrie got the news, she scratched the following on the prison wall behind her cot: "March 9, 1944. Father. Released."

CONCENTRATION CAMP

"In September of 1944, Betsie and Corrie were transported to the German concentration camp for women at RAVENSBRUECK, Germany.

Here they suffered the same terrible privations and fears so well portrayed in the film SCHINDLER'S LIST. Betsie and Corrie were DEHUMANIZED INTO MERE NUMBERS, Prisoner 66729 and prisoner 66730.

"Betsie died in the camp at Ravensbreuck in late December 1944, an eerie shell of skin and bone. Corrie described her sister as she lay on a cot:

"It was a carving in old yellow ivory. There was no clothing on the figure: I could see each rib, and the outline of the teeth through the parchment cheeks. It took me a moment to realize it was Betsie." (THE HIDING PLACE, page 218}

"Corrie's life was saved when she was released on New Year's Day in 1945, because of a clerical error. [PROVIDENCE.] One week after her release, all women her age were sent to the gas chambers."

"Few times have been darker than the holocaust of World War II. It threatened to extinguish spiritual light and to destroy all that is good—truth, mercy, justice, life, truth."

"NOBEL PEACE PRIZE winner ELIE WIESEL, who survived AUSCHWITZ and then BUCHENWALD, wrote of what the holocaust could do to a human being."

He said in his book NIGHT: "Never shall I forget the little faces of the children, whose bodies I saw turned into wreaths of smoke beneath a silent blue sky."

"Never ever shall I forget those flames which consumed my faith forever."

"Never shall I forget that nocturnal silence which deprived me, for all eternity, of the desire to live."

"Never shall I forget those moments which MURDERED MY GOD and MY SOUL and turned my dreams to dust."   (page 32)

PERSONAL HISTORY STORY: These words are engraved on the wall at the exit of the HOLOCAUST MEMORIAL museum in Washington, DC, across from the WASHINGTON MONUMENT obelisk. At the beginning of my testimony/witness I reveal in my opinion that these words by ELIE WIESEL's are sad because he has lost his faith in his God JEHOVAH for not intervening to save the Jewish people from the holocaust. JEHOVAH/JESUS/YESHUA was there and the Christian Allies defeated Hitler's Nazi socialist anti-Christian regime and Israel became European Jewish survivors homeland again, as the Old Testament prophecies predestined in the year 1948! Jesus predestined countdown to the End-Times. HIS-tory.

LIGHT OF GOD'S WORD

"Yet Corrie ten Boom and her sister found a light in that blackest concentration camp nights that saved their faith in God, even as Betsie wasted away and died."
"While Corrie was still in her native Holland, she became ill and was taken to a hospital. A sympathetic nurse asked her if she could help.

"Corrie asked for several items, including a bible, not really expecting to receive anything. But the nurse slipped a small package to her."
"Corrie described in her book what she found when she unwrapped it. There it was—"Not indeed a whole Bible, but in four small booklets, the four Gospels." (THE HIDING PLACE, page 146).

"Corrie called these "the precious books I clutched between my hands." Here, then, was the God-given gift that would sustain her and Betsie through the worst of times in the prison camp."
"In those Gospels, we find a profound statement by Jesus: "The words I have spoken to you are spirit and they are life" (John 6:63). Those were the very words that spoke to Corrie, Betsie and others at the concentration camp."
"'Like waifs clustered around a blazing fire," she wrote in THE HIDING PLACE, we gathered about it, holding our hearts to its warmth and light. The blacker the night around us grew, the brighter and truer and more beautiful burned the word of God." (page 194).

GOD IN HIS WORD

"Corrie described life at Ravensbrueck as living on two different planes. The black world of the camp was horrific, capable of destroying mind and body."
"But the words of scripture portrayed a different world to them—a world of spirit, of light, of life and truth."
"The bible was like a newly written book to Corrie. The scriptures described and spoke to the life-and-death world she lived in."
"She wrote: "It was simply a description of the way things were—of hell and heaven, of how men act and how God acts. I had read a thousand times the story of Jesus arrest—how soldiers had slapped him, laughed at him, flogged him. Now such happenings had faces and voices." (page 195)

A LIVING BOOK

"The Bible became a living book to Corrie.There in its pages, Jesus spoke to Corrie's pain, suffering, fear—and hope."

"Christ's words brought wholeness to Corrie's and Betsie's brokenness, blazing like a blinding spiritual light in rank darkness."

"To us as well, the words of Jesus can bring healing and hope, light and — truth—even to the blackest darkness of our lives."

"Our part is simply to respond in faith to these words of life."

"THE HIDING PLACE, a movie produced in 1975, is based on the best-selling book by the same name. It is a gripping look at the story of the ten Boon family. Refusing to deny their faith in Christ, the ten Boons opened their doors to Jews and others in Holland seeking refuge from the Nazis oppression."

"The ten Booms ran "GOD'S UNDERGROUND," helping people escape from the Nazis for a year and a half before the Gestapo raided there home. After the dramatic scene in which the family is arrested by the Gestapo, the movie focuses almost exclusively on two of the sisters, Betsie and Corrie."

"Taken to the Ravensbrueck concentration camp, the women become an inspiration to their fellow prisoners, teaching them that "no pit is so deep that He is not deeper still."

"At the end of the film, the 80-year-old Corrie ten Boom reflects on her life and the strength she gained from her relationship with Jesus."

"The Hiding Place was filmed at authentic sites in Holland and other European countries." —Bill Palmer   PLAIN TRUTH magazine March 1995

PERSONAL PROVIDENTIAL CONNECTION: Read my story about my Dutch aunt who lived in Java and was a Japanese work camp prisoner for 3 1/2 years. I had a customer who had an accent similar to my aunt, whose father was my mother's German father's brother. He went to neutral Holland circa beginning of the Great War. He became a Dutch soldier and was sent to the Dutch East Indies, today Indonesia. She learned English from Australian prisoners in the Java work camp.

I asked the man are you Dutch? He said, "Yes." I told him I have a Dutch aunt who lives in NIJKIRK, Holland, but had lived in Java. He responded, "I lived in Java." I was surprised and asked him. "What is your name?" Thinking he could be related to me. He replied, "PETER TEN BOOM." I was stunned and asked, "Like Corrie ten Boom?" He replied. "Corrie was my aunt, but I only met her once because of her worldwide mission." I told him I was writing a book about my German blonde Lutheran mother leaving Hitler's Germany in 1935, and not returning being illegal for six years. I told him my book is about Hitler trying to replace Christianity with Nazi socialism. I told him I married a red haired Jewish girl and "converted" to Judaism to have a Jewish Temple wedding. He said his wife was Jewish and is a member of his Baptist church in Dale City/Woodbridge. He later brought his wife with him to my job so I could meet her for only a few minutes. I had just begun attending my Lutheran Missouri Synod church services. This was one of my many very SMALL WORLD providential experiences. The big wide world gate leading me to Jesus narrow gate Kingdom."

The BIG LIE—Hitler and The Holocaust Never Happened

"No retreat, no surrender; One American's fight is a 2007 book by TOM DELAY, elected House Majority Whip in 1995, and Republican House Majority Leader in 2002. Quote from the book— "On charges that Delay violated campaign finance laws "I believe it was Adolf Hitler who first acknowledged that the big lie is more effective than the little lie, because the big lie is so audacious, such an astonishing immorality, that people have a hard time believing anyone would say if it wasn't true. You know, the big lie — like the holocaust never happened or dark-skinned people are less intelligent than light-skinned people. Well, by charging this big lie liberals have finally joined the ranks of scoundrels like Hitler."   Wikipedia

17 REASONS WHY DEMOCRATS NAZI ANALOGIES INSANE

AMERICAN ACTION NEWS July 7, 2018 received Oct. 4, 2019

"We all know that historical literacy isn't what it used to be. Unfortunately. the radical left takes that to new heights when they flippantly compare their political opponents to Adolf Hitler. We know that you're savvier than that. However, liberals might need a refresher on that subject; given the frequency with which they play the Nazi card and how abhorrent the Nazis were. To that end, we have provided a small glimpse into the horrors of the Third Reich to emphasize that Nazis comparisons are more than merely tawdry and dumb—they're incredible offensive."

1 MASS MURDER OF POLISH CIVILIANS
"The German Army invaded Poland on September 1, 1939, justifying the slaughter with a false flag operation against a German radio station at the Polish border by Wehrmacht commandos in Polish uniforms. Behind the advancing panzers [tanks], SS death squads operated with impunity. Around 6,000,000 Polish civilians—one out of fiveONE —perished under Nazis occupation."

2 MASS KILLING OF SOVIET POWS

"Nearly 6,000,000 Red Army soldiers— including one of Stalin's sons—were taken prisoner by the Wehrmacht, mostly in the opening stages of the invasion of the Soviet Union [June 22, 1941]. At least 3,300,000 died in German custody; with the vast majority perishing in the second half of 1941." [These were mostly Ukrainian and Russian Orthodox Christians not Communist leaders.]

3 NIGHT AND FOG DECREE
"The Gestapo seized untold numbers of French, Dutch, and Belgian citizens in the middle of the night under Hitler's NIGHT AND FOG DECREE. The Fuerhrer wanted to squash the fledgling resistance movement in Western Europe by any means. Patriots took for questioning, usually died from prolonged torture, execution, or starvation/exposure in the concentration camps."
4 LIDICE MASSACRE

"After Czech partisans assassinated REINHARD HEYDRICH, second-in-command of the vaunted SS, the German units raised the village of LIDICE to the ground and systematically executed its 5,000 inhabitants." [American poet EDNA ST. VINCENT MILLAY, born in Rockland, Maine, wrote a poem honoring Lidice. She lived on Rt. 22 in New York, overlooking the Massachusetts border, about 8 miles from my home in Ghent/Harlemville. The film REDS, director/actor WARREN BEATTY'S all star cast film about the Russian Revolution in World War I, portrays MILLAY and EMMA GOLDMAN as American Communist supporters of the new Soviet nation during its Civil War with the ALEXANDER KERENSKY's Christian WHITE PARTY. The film DOCTOR ZHIVAGO also portrays this Civil War. A friend told me in 1950s he delivered ice to Millay's home which today has an art studio museum. My German mother drove me on the dirt road where she lived because it was near her lady friend NAOMI FOSTER'S house on Rt. 22. I remember Naomi telling my mother that her daughter was FRED FRIENDLY's secretary at CBS TV in New York City. Friendly produced TV reporter EDWARD R. MURROW's show PERSON TO PERSON where Murrow interviewed famous people. Friendly was the CBS TV producer of Murrow's TV shows which were critical of Wisconsin Republican Senator JOSEPH MCCARTHY'S "Witch Hunt" for Communists. In the black and white film GOOD NIGHT, GOOD LUCK, about McCarthy's harassment of an American airman was produced by GEORGE CLOONEY, who portrayed not Murrow, but Fred Friendly the producer, a minor role. GEORGE CLOONEY was born in St. JOSEPH'S HOSPITAL in Lexington, Kentucky on May 6, 1961. I was born in St. JOSEPH HOSPITAL on May 4, 1943. My dad received his B.A. degree from Transylvania College in Lexington on June 1942. My original birth certificate says father's occupation "Avon depot Canadian radio" which was radar. It was a new 1940 high tech school located near Lexington. My mother lived in a house on Fontaine Road in Lexington, a block from HENRY CLAY'S home ASHLAND. We moved to my dad's hometown Amityville in October 1945, after my brother was born in Lexington, KY, on September 30, 1945. Saint JOSEPH was Jesus foster-father with his wife MARY who was JESUS earthly Jewish mother prophesied in the Old Testament. In the New Testament ANGEL GABRIEL revealed to MARY her son's immaculate virgin birth.

My German family connection to GEORGE CLOONEY in his film MONUMENTS MEN. The mine in Siegen, Germany is where the Nazis hid the stolen Dutch paintings. In 1715, indentured German miners from Siegen were brought to my Wilderness community. In 1958, when 15, I visited cousins Anneliese and Werner in Siegen. It was near where my grandfather was born.

There were socialist/Communist ideology citizens in our federal government, schools, and actors and screen writers in Hollywood. During the 1930s GREAT DEPRESSION the Socialist SOCIAL SECURITY law was passed in 1935. Millions of Americans were unemployed and needed federal, state and local government assistance because the 1929 Wall Street economy failed because of easy limits on investments. Hollywood actors and thousands of its film making personnel were underpaid or unemployed. Some of them were enticed by socialist and Communist groups, capitalism seemed to have failed. Ironically, during the GREAT DEPRESSION Hollywood served as an escape for the unemployed in the large big screen theater "palaces" if only for a couple of hours. Movie tickets were reasonably priced. The theaters had been built during the ROARING TWENTIES many for silent films which required a large theater pipe organ for the sound track with screen captions. In the early 1970s, my dad and I were in the Connecticut Valley and New York theater organ societies and heard many concerts given on restored theater pipe organs by veteran organists who were virtuosos.

During the 1930's there were some great classic movies, cowboy and Indian, gangsters and comedies. Then in 1939 technicolor came to Hollywood and GONE WITH THE WIND and THE WIZARD OF OZ captured the eyes, hearts and minds "psyches" of Americans and the world. Director FRANK CAPRA's films captured the hearts and souls through "Christian" scripts of the good guy overcoming the bad guy. JIMMY STEWART'S MR. SMITH GOES TO WASHINGTON just before America entered World War II disturbed many in the CONGRESS of the United States showing there could be corruption in the hallowed halls of Washington, D.C. Senator JEFFERSON SMITH, the appointed "safe" hayseed Boy Scout leader from Montana is up against a political juggernaut machine. When Smith is being censured with lies he is about to concede defeat. Then his female assistant tells Senator Smith how he can use the Senate filibuster rule to fight for his case. The local kids and friends help rescue him.

HISTORICAL FACT: After the Nazis defeated France they allowed the French people to play one last Western film. They chose MR. SMITH GOES TO WASHINGTON. American patriot and brave bomber pilot JAMES STEWART must have learned that France had honored him by showing his democratic film against tyranny in America's great Republic. Stewart was decorated with two Distinguished Flying Crosses and the CROIX DE GUERRE, France's highest award.

Today, President DONALD J. TRUMP is undergoing a similar hypocrisy from the left wing/socialist progressive government of the U.S. House of Representatives which moderate Democrats regained from Trump blue districts because they convinced their voters they were for middle class health care, law and order, better gun control, and more educational funding. This happened in my Virginia 7th JAMES MADISON district to my friend U.S. Representative DAVE BRAT. The 50 year conservative 7th District had been redistricted. Representative Brat won 8 counties but lost the two large districts HENRICO and CHESTERFIELD around Richmond which gave his opponent ABIGAIL SPANBERGER their votes 6,600 more than he received. I meet Spanberger at a local Germanna College Q & A meeting. She is much more articulate and focused than the overly publicized Cortez "gang of four" rookies who were placed on committees they have no qualifications for? They have destroyed the Democrat party and Speaker PELOSI'S authority. Pelosi won't admit it but Cortez defeated by a few votes the 25 year Bronx/Queens incumbent FOLEY, who had been named as a possible replacement as Speaker of the House replacing NANCY PELOSI. Pelosi must have been happy about Cortez victory but probably doesn't sleep so well lately. Today, the TRUMPED UP Ukrainian phone call leading to impeachment inquiry of President Trump has made my Representative Spanberger side with the impeachment Democrats.

I agreed with her platform of necessary legitimate needs people are concerned about. She is using her background with the CIA connected to mail fraud as grounds for her concern for constitutional "crimes and misdemeanors" concerning JOE BIDEN and asking Ukrainian president Zelensky to check his son's connection to the billion dollar American grant to their gas company, TAX PAYERS MONEY? Fox News has showed Biden joke about how he got the Ukrainian fired who was obstructing his son's position on a video which I have seen on Fox for two years. All America knows about this now.

What even FOX news hasn't commented on is that Vice President Biden was speaking at the COUNCIL OF FOREIGN RELATIONS, its logo was behind him. This is what should scare everyone. This is the organization which is GLOBALIST and its members of many American and International companies, bankers, and top American and world political leaders. This is in open sight OPEN YOUR EYES. Read Wikipedia this is DEEP STATE and the global ILLUMINATI who intend to control everyone's lives except most of the elitist wealthy that the socialist Democrats claim they will tax and control. You wonder why Populist Trump is hated by the globalist media and socialist Democrats? He is the antithesis to this as an AMERICAN NATIONALIST.

Now, it is revealed that the "Whistleblower" only heard about the call from others who were there. The whistleblower law required that the "facts" had to be first-hand but that rule law had just been changed? BY WHO? Representative ADAM SHIFF was asked if he had met or talked to the whistleblower. He said NO. Now, it appears he not only talked to the whistleblower, but his staff prepared what is a lawyer's legal statement. The person is reportedly a CIA analyst. This again sounds like the "DEEP STATE." It is reported that the person is a registered Democrat 52-54% of the population. When this "LEAK" whistleblower report first was released to the media, someone on FOX news? thought the person did it to hurt Joe Biden who was the Democrat's front runner in the polls, even with some serious memory "gaffes". Bernie the Communist isn't a contender though young people like him, FREE STUFF. Elderly people like me know better not to let the government get bigger. Who would benefit? The Republican Senate will never impeach President Trump and let America become a Socialist country.

PERSONAL STORY: I was the first person to speak directly to Representative Spanberger. I showed her my xeroxed black and white copy of my mother's 1935 modeling photo with her waist length platinum blonde hair. I told her my mother a Lutheran left Hitler's Germany in January 1935, and was an illegal alien for 5 years until she married my father in August 1940. Then I noticed her security guard edging close to me through the crowd. I ended my comments telling her my mother would not like what is happening in America today. I finished telling her America cannot become a Socialist country. She said it won't. She is only one of 435 representatives and her party is unanimously heading to the leftist socialist path to "buy votes" which is hard to do when we have the best peacetime economy in History. Impeachment is their only hope.

5 ORADOUR-sur-GLANE MASSACRE
'The French village of Oradour-sur-Glane stood for over 600 years, until June 10, 1944. On that fateful day, a Waffen SS battalion on its way to stop the Allied advance in Normandy encountered resistance fighters who had kidnapped a local SS commander. Several hundred fanatical Nazis proceeded to seal off the village and murdered all but 20 of its 662 inhabitants — who fled as soon as they saw the approaching column. Hundreds of men, women, and children were burned alive."
My college girlfriend Joanne said she lived near there for awhile.

6 MALMEDY MASSACRE
"During the confusion surrounding the initial stages of the Battle of the Bulge, the Wehrmacht captured several thousand American soldiers. On December 17, 1944, a column of German tanks routed an American convoy two miles south-east of the Belgium hamlet of Malmedy.

Approximately 120 American troops surrendered and were marched by German infantry to an adjacent field when, for unknown reasons, SS troops opened up with machine gun fire, They killed 84 American prisoners of war in cold blood."

7 GARDELEGEN MASSACRE
"With liberation at the hands of the rapidly approaching U.S. Army only hours away, local firefighters, Volkssturm, and Hitler Youth forced over 1,000 slave laborers into a large barn near the town of Gardelegen. The Germans then set the structure ablaze. There were no survivors."
8 THE INTENTIONAL DESTRUCTION OF CULTURALLY SIGNIFICANT SITES
"The German Army, particularly when in retreat, did not want to leave anything of value behind. Prominent examples include the intentional destruction of priceless medieval Russian cathedrals, like the one at Novgorod or historic monasteries near Moscow and the grand palaces of the Czars in Saint Petersburg [Leningrad]. Although recognized as a UNESCO World Heritage Site today, retreating German troops in 1944 left it in ruins."
9 THE COMMANDO ORDER
"In October 1942, the Nazis decreed that any Allied Commandos would be summarily executed upon discovery, regardless if they were in uniform or not. At the Nuremberg Trials after the war, the Commando Order was found to be a direct breach of the laws of war, German officers who carried out the illegal executions were guilty of war crimes."
10 BABI YAR
"Numerous massacres occurred at this ravine in Kiev. Most abhorrent, the retaliatory killing of 33,771 Jews between September 29-30, 1941. German forces and Ukrainian collaborators killed as many as 150,000 people here during the two years the region was under Nazi control."

11 ODESSA MASSACRE
"Refers to the mass murder of Odessa's Jewish population during the winter of 1941-42 by Romanian and German forces. Depending on the scope and time frame, upwards of 100,000 Jews were executed."
12 RUMBULA MASSACRE

"A Nazi Einsatzgruppen death squad with the help of local collaborators exterminated over 25,000 Jews in a two-day period near Riga, Latvia in the fall of 1941."

13 WOLA MASSACRE

"After being taken by surprise in the early days of the WARSAW UPRISING, a ruthless SS General took command of all German forces in the city. In 7 days, the Nazis brutally and systematically murdered resistance fighters and civilians in mass executions. Between 40,000 and 50,000 Jewish people died.

14 THE PLANNED DESTRUCTION OF WARSAW

After the failed uprising by Polish patriots, who expected help that never came from nearby Russians [massive Army], the German Army put unprecedented effort to systematically destroy anything that remained standing in Warsaw and exterminating its inhabitants. By the time Red Army tanks rolled past the smoldering ruins months later, the city's cultural heritage had ceased to exist, and barely 100,000 residents (out of a prewar population of 1,200,000) were still breathing.

[In September 1939, the Nazi Blizkrieg began, a week later the Russian army invaded Poland from the East. Stalin and Hitler had signed a non-aggression pact in August 1939, the week before Poland was invaded. which agreed to let Russia occupy Poland to the Vistula River dividing Poland. The Versailles Treaty after the GREAT WAR, World War I, had taken this land from the defeated German/Austro-Hungarian Empires and the former Czarist Russia which became the atheist Marxist/Leninist Communist Soviet Union which was anathema to Christian Europe. This land was returned to the Polish people restoring the historic nation of Poland for 20 years.]

15 THE HOLOCAUST

"In total, the monstrous crimes of the Third Reich against the Jews, invalids. Roma [gypsies], Slavs, Soviet POWs, and other "UNDESIRABLES" claimed the lives of 6,000,000 Jews and 17,000,000 victims in total."

16 TOTAL WAR AGAINST THE SLAVIC POPULATION ON THE EASTERN FRONT

"Roughly 70,000 towns and villages burned to the ground at the hands of the Germans in the Soviet Union. By the war's end, approximately 25,000,000 Soviets had died. In Belarus alone, 25 percent of the population succumbed during the three-year German occupation."

[The slavic population of Yugoslavia lost a higher proportion of its population than Poland. There were Royalists under Mikalovic, Communists under TITO, and pro Nazi sympathizers creating a civil war killing 50 percent of its population. There was even a Muslim SS mountain unit which was the only dark skinned SS unit. Serbian people helped thousands of American bomber crewmen who had parachuted over Serbia from damaged aircraft. Many Serbian civilians were killed for aiding enemy airmen who they hide and helped escape capture. These airmen from the 15th Air Force stationed at airbases in Italy were captured by Allied forces in brutal fighting. These airmen flew missions beyond the range of the 8TH Air Force in Great Britain. They bombed the Nazi key oil field and refinery at Ploesti, Romania about 28 times devastating it. The Nazis had to then use synthetic oil made from coal. The 15th AAF bombed German factories in Italy, Austria, Czechoslovakia, Yugoslavia, Greece, Albania and Poland, including one raid on AUSCHWITZ, the BUNA synthetic rubber factory on Christmas Eve 1944. The bombers also targeted Hungary, Bulgaria and Romania who were allied to Hitler.]

Who Needs God When You've Got Government

Breakpoint Daily May 22, 2018
Eric Metaxas with Stan Guthrie

"We need a surgeon general's warning: "This government program may be hazardous to your spiritual health."

"Jesus said we're to render unto Caesar what is Caesar's, and unto God what is God's, so it's clear we have responsibilities both to God and to government. You could fill whole libraries with the volumes that have been written on this rich and vital topic. But what do we do when Caesar attempts to usurp the place of Christ in our hearts?"

"Sometimes, as when Nebuchadnezzar commanded the people of God [Jews] to bow down to his golden image, the answer is simple—you obey the Lord and leave the consequences to Him. But sometimes the challenge from those who rule over us is far more subtle. Instead of facing a fiery furnace, [or hungry lion] we may encounter a temptation that, at its heart, says. "In government we trust."

"That seems to be the conclusion of two psychology researchers who say that better government services are correlated with lower levels of strong religious belief, both in the U.S. and internationally. Their study's title says it all: "Religion as an Exchange System: The Interchangeability of God and Government in a Provider."

"If a secular entity provides what people need, they will be less likely to seek help from God or other super natural entities," the researchers say. "If the benefits acquired in the religious exchange can be acquired elsewhere, religion becomes less useful." They add that, when it comes to social stability, "the power and order emanating from God can be outsourced to the government."

"Now to my mind that's a fairly cynical take, as if the only reason people turn to God is for what they can get out of Him. But I know it has an element of truth. God in His sovereign mercy sometimes uses our physical and emotional needs to awaken in us our desperate spiritual need for Him."

"But if all our felt needs are meet by government, what room will God find in our hearts for Him? I'm not here to argue against effective and targeted government programs, which are good things, and I'm certainly not saying the church ought to keep the poor in misery. But what I am saying is that the church needs to continue to be the church. God has designed the world so that people are best served, and He is most glorified, when government keeps its place and His people do His work in His way."

"My colleague John Stonestreet reminds us of the Catholic social teaching of subsidiarity, which holds that "functions of government, business, and other secular activities should be as local as possible." The more local we can be, the more loving and effective we can be. The government can start a program, but it cannot love."

"Then there is the Reformational concept of "sphere sovereignty," which Chuck Colson summarized as "society giving equal respect to all the social structures ordained by God. Family, church, school, business—each has its own distinctive task that no other group can do. The role of the state is to protect these little platoons so they can carry out their God-given tasks."

"That's often not what happens, as government takes more and more areas that belong to others—including God. As John says, "In the absence of rivals or challenges to its authority, the reach of the modern state will not and cannot be checked. It will expand to fill the void left by the absence of intermediate institutions like the family, local communities, and the Church."

"So the challenge to God's people to this encroachment by Caesar couldn't be clearer. We must strengthen our families, the churches, and our communities. We must stop sitting around waiting for "the government" to "do something." We need to do something—support a pregnancy care center, feed the hungry, visit the sick, teach the ignorant, befriend the lonely— proclaim the Good News of Jesus with our lips and in our lives."

THE CHUCK COLSON CENTER FOR CHRISTIAN WORLDVIEW

[The European nations have for many years had socialist governments with "CRADLE TO GRAVE" entitlements paid for by taxes around 50 per cent of their income. One tax Europeans pay is a church tax. Church attendance at Europe's great cathedrals is mostly tourists, "I gave at the office." I have visited many of these great, ancient cathedrals. I have been told the Norwegian State Lutheran church has stopped taking state-taxes and is now taking free-will tithe donations like the Bible requests. Norwegians are returning to churches. After Martin Luther's Reformation's 500th anniversary in 2017, I think many Lutherans are returning to their churches?]

PERSONAL STORY: I once saw a bumper sticker WASHINGTON IS NOT MY GOD.

PROVIDENTIAL STORY: In 1982, I was driving to work on I-95 to Fredericksburg, Va, home of religious freedom statute law January 1777, when an old Cadillac de Ville sped past me with an elderly white bearded man driving, he wasn't Santa Claus. He had a personalized Virginia license plate which read ATHEST. Right behind him a large Dodge Marauder car sped past me with a personalized Virginia license plate which read BAPTST! At work I told my WOOLCO automotive manager, a lay Baptist minister, what I had seen. Bill Logan retorted, "Us BAPTISTS are always chasing those ATHEISTS!" Later, I read in the Washington Post the driver lived in Augusta County near Staunton, VA, and that a Christian women tried to have this license plate revoked. It wasn't. I have seen many biblical inspirational personalized license plates in Virginia.

ONE NATION, UNDER GOD

Dr. John W. Howe, Senior Pastor Lake of the Woods Church
Cross Currents bulletin July 2019

"The Lord your God is bringing you into a good land…where you will lack nothing. Take care that you do not forget the Lord your God…and say to yourself, "My power and the night of my own hand have gotten me this wealth."   Deuteronomy 8:7ff

"First of all, then, I urge that supplications, prayers, intercessions, and thanksgivings be made for everyone, for kings and all who are in high places, so that we may lead a quiet and peaceable life in all godliness and dignity." 1 Timothy 2:1,2

"Tom Phillips, who was then Chairman of the Raytheon Corporation, speaking at a Mayor's Prayer Breakfast in Dayton some years ago, suggested there is a historical cycle in the rise and fall of nations. He said: bondage leads to faith, and faith leads to courage. Courage leads to freedom, and freedom produces abundance. Abundance leads to selfishness, which produces complacency. Complacency leads to apathy, which produces fear. Fear leads to dependency, and dependency ends in bondage.

And he added: "Where in the cycle are we?"

As we pause to celebrate America's Birthday once again, it may be good to ponder that question. On the one hand, there is so much to be thankful for. It is beyond any argument that the average American today lives more comfortably than most royalty ever did down through the ages. Materially, physically, economically, socially, culturally—we are the richest people in human history.

It is equally beyond dispute that the role America has played in the community is unparalleled. It has been said that the United States of America has sent out more missionaries, more doctors and nurses, more teachers and educators, more agricultural specialists and industrial consultants…we have built more schools, hospitals and churches…and we have given away more billions of dollars than all the other nations in the world in all of history put together!

On the other hand, we live in a moment of deeper political division than we have known since the Civil War. The animosity in Washington and throughout the country is so toxic it seems we can do nothing but fight with each other.

Just a generation ago, John F. Kennedy began his presidency with the promise: "Let every nation know, whether it wishes us well or ill, that we shall pay any price, bear any burden, meet any hardship, support any friend, oppose any foe, in order to assure the survival and the success of liberty."

We can hardly imagine anyone running for office today saying anything even vaguely similar. And if they said it, how would they even begin to accomplish it?

So, how shall we think about these things? How shall we pray for our country and its leaders?

First, let us remember that our true homeland is in Heaven (cf. Hebrews 11, especially verses 14-16). But that must not mean we see our earthly citizenship as irrelevant. God told the people of Jeremiah's day to "seek the welfare" of the city of BABYLON —where they were being held captive! —and to "pray to the Lord on its behalf, for in its welfare you will find your welfare." Jeremiah 29:7

To pray for our leaders in government is not to "take sides" with them. We may agree with some of their decisions, and deeply disagree with others. We may greatly support-or greatly oppose - an individual or a party. Still we are to pray for them."

St. PAUL said it was a matter "of first important" that we pray for all those on high positions, "so that we may lead a quiet and peaceable life in all godliness and dignity." 1 Timothy 2:1,2

And PETER said, "honor the emperor" (1 Peter 2:17) even though the emperor at the time was NERO — who was happily torturing and executing Christians for their faith!

Most of the men who have lived in the White House have been driven to their knees by the responsibilities of office. Equally, many members of Congress and the judiciary call out to God for wisdom and guidance. Even — and especially — when we find we are in such disagreement with some of them that we consider them our enemies Jesus specifically commanded us to pray for them. Matthew 5:43

Ask God to let our leaders feel the weight of their responsibilities: let it drive them to their knees. Ask him to give them wisdom and his guidance in the difficult decisions they must make. Ask him to show them where they are wrong, especially in their moral choices. Ask him to help them repent and seek his forgiveness. Ask him to give them the courage to acknowledge publicly their dependence on Him. Ask Him to help them seek out the strength that comes from fellowship with other believers.

And for the nation as a whole, pray that we will heed the warning of Deuteronomy: "Take care that you do not forget the Lord your God, by failing to keep his commandments, His ordinances, and His statutes, which I am commanding you today. When you have eaten your fill and have built fine houses and live in them, and when your herds and flocks have multiplied, and all that you have is multiplied, then do not exalt yourself, forgetting the Lord your God…Do not say to yourself, 'My power and the might of my own hand have gotten me this wealth.' But remember the Lord your God, for it is He who gives you the power to get wealth, so that He my confirm his covenant…If you forget the Lord your God and follow other gods to serve and worship them, I solemnly warn you today that you shall surely perish." Deuteronomy 8:11-20   Pastor John Howe

A PRAYER TO CONSIDER

Rev. Joe Wright May 21,1996 8:50 AM

"This is a prayer that was offered by Reverend Joseph Wright as the Kansas House of Representatives began their daily business."

Heavenly Father:

"We come before you today to ask your forgiveness and seek your direction and guidance. We know your word says, "Woe to those who call evil good," but that's exactly what we've done. We have lost our spiritual equilibrium and inverted our values."

"We confess that we have ridiculed the absolute truth of your Word and called it moral pluralism.

"We have worshiped other gods and called it multiculturalism.

"We have endorsed perversion and called it an alternative lifestyles.

"We have exploited the poor and called it the lottery.

"We have neglected the needy and called it self-preservation.

"We have rewarded laziness and called it welfare.

"We have killed our unborn and called it choice.

"We have shot abortionists and called it justifiable.

"We have neglected to discipline our children and called it building self-esteem.

"We have abused power and called it political savvy.

"We have coveted our neighbors' possessions and called it ambition.

"We have polluted the air with profanity and pornography and called it freedom of expression.

"We have ridiculed the time-honored values of our forefathers and called it enlightenment."

"Search us, O God, and know our hearts today, try us and see if there be some wicked way in us, cleanse us from every sin and set us free."

"Guide and bless these men and women who have been sent here by the people of Kansas, and who have been ordained by you, to govern this great state. Grant them your wisdom to rule, and may their decisions direct us to the center of your will. I ask it in the name of your Son, the Living Savior, Jesus Christ."   Amen

"As you can imagine, Rev. Wright's prayer elicited a wide variety of responses that reflect the hearts of believers and unbelievers alike. It is a bold prayer. You may like it or you may not. It reminds me of the kind of bold prayers one finds in Psalms. For me personally, it is a prayer that needs to be prayed. It is a prayer of "national" confession. More than a prayer that cites many of the moral failures now institutionalized in our culture, it acknowledges the grave influence sin has on us all."

"This is a time to look closely at who we really are, poor sinful beings. It is a time to look with greater intensity at the cross of Christ that we might reflect upon the tremendous price paid by Him on account of our sin."

"This is also a time of hope as we reflect upon the eternal hope we receive by faith in Christ Jesus. With repentant hearts we receive, by God's grace, forgiveness of our sins, and, with that welcome relief, the promise of life eternal in heaven with God. Father Son and Holy Spirit."

"TRUE NORTH" OUTLINES 14 CONSERVATIVE PRINCIPLES

THE DAILY SIGNAL Rachel del Guidice October 21, 2019

"The Heritage Foundation will introduce a set of 14 conservative principles Monday at the outset of the influential think tank's annual President's Club meeting in Washington."

'Heritage Foundation President KAY COLES JAMES said the laser-focused definition of conservatism in the document, called "True North: The Principles of Conservatism," is destined to unite the movement."

"While good conservatives may have differing viewpoints about some aspects of conservatism, there are certain fundamental principles where we must remain resolute. These are our True North principles," James said in an email to Heritage staff announcing the set of conservative principles."

"They're called True North because they represent a fixed direction on which to stay focused, regardless of which way forces may be pressuring us," she said."

"James who became Heritage president in January 2018, is a former director of the U.S. Office of Personnel Management and former secretary of health and human resources for Virginia as a trustee at the THINK TANK since 2005."

"The President's Club meeting, held each Fall, brings together the leading think tank's supporters to network with and hear from leaders in the Conservative movement, including lawmakers, policy experts, and commentators."

"Vice President MIKE PENCE is scheduled to deliver the KEYNOTE ADDRESS Tuesday evening at the inaugural Heritage Honors gala."

"The 14 principles laid out in "True North" cover much ground, beginning with the importance of the federal government's role in society, namely that it "EXISTS TO PRESERVE LIFE, LIBERTY, AND PROPERTY, and it is instituted to PROTECT THE RIGHTS OF INDIVIDUALS according to natural law."

"These rights, some laid out in the DECLARATION OF INDEPENDENCE and others specified in AMENDMENTS to the CONSTITUTION, include LIFE, LIBERTY, and the PURSUIT OF HAPPINESS, the FREEDOM OF SPEECH, RELIGION, PEACEFUL ASSEMBLY, and the PRESS: and the RIGHTS TO BEAR ARMS, to be treated equally and justly under the law, and to enjoy the fruits of one's labor."

"The second point of "True North" establishes that government only has the power given to it within the confines of the Constitution, quoting THOMAS JEFFERSON as saying:

"THE GOVERNMENT CLOSEST to the PEOPLE SERVES THE PEOPLE THE BEST."

"The document recognizes that individuals and families as the primary and most important decision-makers when it comes to their lives and those of their children, including employment, education, and health care."

"It defines the FAMILY as the "ESSENTIAL FOUNDATION OF CIVIL SOCIETY" and calls marriage between one man and one women the "cornerstone of the family."

"The Daily Signal is the multimedia news organization of the Heritage Foundation."

"Here is the full list of "True North" principles for CONSERVATISM:

1 The federal government exists to preserve life, liberty, and property, and it is instituted to protect the rights of individuals according to natural law. Among these rights are the SANCTITY OF LIFE; the freedom of speech, religion, the press, and peaceful assembly; the right to bear arms, the right to be treated equally and justly under the law; and the right to enjoy the fruits of one's labor.

2 The federal government's powers are limited to those named in the Constitution and should be exercised solely to protect the rights of the citizens. As THOMAS JEFFERSON said, "The government closest to the people serves the people best." Powers not delegated to the federal government, not prohibited by the Constitution, are reserved to the states or to the people."

3 Judges should interpret and apply our laws and the Constitution based on their original meaning, not upon judges' personal and political predispositions."

4 Individuals and families—not government—make the best decisions regarding their and their children's health, education, jobs, and welfare.

5 The family is the essential foundation of civil society, and traditional marriage serves   as the cornerstone of the family.

6   The federal deficit and debt must not place unreasonable financial burdens on future generations.

7 Tax policies should raise only the minimum revenue necessary to fund constitutionally appropriate functions of government.

8 America's economy and the prosperity of individual citizens are best served by a system of free enterprise, with special emphasis on economic freedom, private property rights, and the rule of law. This system is best sustained by policies promoting free trade and deregulation, and opposing government interventions in the economy that distort markets and impair innovation."

9 Regulations must not breach Constitutional principles of limited government and the separation of powers.

10   America must be a welcoming nation—one that promotes patriotic assimilation and is governed by laws that are fair, humane, and enforced to protect its citizens.

11 Justice requires an effective criminal justice system—one that gives defendants adequate due process and requires an appropriate degree of criminal intent to merit punishment.

12 International agreements and international organizations should not infringe on Americans' Constitutional rights, nor should they diminish American sovereignty.

13 America is strongest when our policies protect our national interests, preserve our alliances of free peoples, vigorously counter threats to our security, and advance prosperity through economic freedom at home and abroad.

14 The best way to ensure peace is through a strong national defense.

"With the DEMAND FOR SOCIALISM at an all-time high among our young people—our future leaders and decision makers—the experts at Heritage stopped and asked a question that not many have asked: IS SOCIALISM REALLY MORALLY SOUND?

"The researchers at The Heritage Foundation have put together a guide to help you and our fellow Americans better understand the 9 WAYS THAT SOCIALISM WILL MORALLY BANKRUPT AMERICA

9 WAYS SOCIALISM WILL MORALLY BANKRUPT AMERICA

Free Online eBook available

1 Socialism directly OPPOSES the AMERICAN DREAM.

2 POLITICIANS IN POWER make your most important decisions for you.

3 FREEDOM OF CHOICE is severely limited or eliminated.

4 All under Socialism WILL SUFFER EQUALLY.
5 If EVERYONE OWNS the resources, NOBODY TRULY OWNS THEM.
6 "Robbing Peter to pay Paul" is MORALLY WRONG.
7 POWER IS CONSOLIDATED within the Government.
8 SOCIALISM CREATES DISSENT and stifles FREEDOM OF SPEECH.
9 SOCIALISM CREATES DEPENDENCE instead of FREEDO

REPUBLICAN LINCOLN'S GETTYSBURG ADDRESS

"Four score and seven years ago our fathers brought forth on this continent, a NEW NATION, conceived in LIBERTY, and dedicated to the proposition that ALL MEN ARE CREATED EQUAL.

"Now we are engaged in a GREAT CIVIL WAR, testing whether that nation, or any nation so conceived and so dedicated, CAN LONG ENDURE. We are met on a great battlefield of that war. We have come to dedicate a portion of that field, as a final resting place for those who HERE GAVE THEIR LIVES that that NATION MIGHT LIVE. IT IS ALTOGETHER FITING AND PROPER THAT WE SHOULD DO THIS.

But, in a larger sense, we can not dedicate—we can not consecrate—we can not hallow—this ground. The brave men, living and dead, who struggled here, have struggled here, have consecrated it, far above our poor power to add or detract. The WORLD WILL LITTLE NOTE, NOR LONG REMEMBER WHAT WE SAY HERE, but IT CAN NEVER FORGET WHAT THEY DID HERE. It is FOR US THE LIVING, rather to be dedicated here to the unfinished work which they who fought here have thus far so nobly advanced. It is rather for us to be here dedicated to the great task remaining before us—that from these honored dead we take increased devotion to that cause for which they GAVE THE LAST FULL MEASURE OF DEVOTION—that we here highly resolve that THESE DEAD SHALL NOT HAVE DIED IN VAIN—that THIS NATION, UNDER GOD, shall have a NEW BIRTH OF FREEDOM—and that GOVERNMENT OF THE PEOPLE, BY THE PEOPLE, SHALL NOT PERISH FROM THE EARTH."   President ABRAHAM LINCOLN November 19, 1863

WHAT EVERYONE SHOULD KNOW ABOUT IMPEACHMENT

The "Impeachment" of President DONALD J. TRUMP THE HERITAGE FOUNDATION
Hans von Spakovsky, Senior Legal Fellow at the Heritage Foundation

"The CONSTITUTION gives the "SOLE POWER OF IMPEACHMENT" to the House [of Representatives], which can approve articles of impeachment by a simple majority. As a practical matter, therefore, it might be said that the category of "High Crimes and Misdemeanors" includes whatever the House says it does. But America's founders took this phrase from English common law, where it had developed a definition. It is a narrow category of serious misconduct that requires removing the president now, rather than waiting for the next election."

"Articles of impeachment approved by the House are similar to a criminal indictment by a grand jury: they are a list of unproven accusations. The House has adopted 19 of the more than 60 resolutions of impeachment introduced since our Founding. Fifteen of those have been for federal judges, including Supreme Court Associate Justice Samuel Chase in 1804. The last resolution of impeachment approved by the House concerned former U.S. District Judge Thomas Porteous, Jr. in 2009. He was accused of receiving gifts, cash payments and other valuable items from lawyers practicing before him."

"The Senate has the "Sole Power to try all Impeachments," although the Constitution does not explicitly require the Senate to act on the articles of impeachment or to hold a trial. Under congressional rules, members of the House who are designated as impeachment "managers" have the role as prosecutors. The impeachment trial of a president is presided over by the Chief Justice of the Supreme Court and held before the entire Senate. Impeachment trials of other officials (under rules established by the Senate) take place before an impeachment trial committee of Senators. In these trials, Senators have a role that combines features of both judge and jury, with the authority to govern the conduct of the trial and decide any evidentiary issues that may arise."

"If the House votes to impeach, then the Senate will ultimately try the case against President Trump, and determine if he should be removed from office."

"Two presidents have been impeached, ANDREW JOHNSON in 1868 and BILL CLINTON in 1998, neither was convicted by the Senate. There were efforts to impeach presidents JOHN TYLER and RICHARD NIXON (Nixon resigned before proceedings began)." [President Nixon had received 62%, including the youths, of the popular vote winning 49 states, except Massachusetts, because his opponent Sen. GEORGE MCGOVERN ran on a "socialist" big government platform.]

PRESIDENT JOHNSON LIED ABOUT VIETNAM WAR

[Providentially, in 1971, the U.S. Congress passed a Constitutional amendment lowering the voting age from 21 to 18. Ironically, Nixon ended the draft and "Vietnamized" the war rapidly withdrawing American troops. The Vietnam War and its unfair draft had mobilized young Americans against the Democrat government under President JOHNSON who got elected proclaiming, "American boys shouldn't fight an Asian boys war." HE LIED. President Nixon didn't perceive this because the American press was supporting the anti-war protests because they felt betrayed by President Johnson and his false MCNAMARA war deceptions. This was illegally reported. "FREEDOM OF THE PRESS" by the Nixon-hating WASHINGTON POST. Richard Nixon had been a New York lawyer and had no involvement with the Vietnam conflict. The POST released the PENTAGON PAPERS in June 1971. This event caused President Nixon to finally go rogue and allow the intentionally "bungled" WATERGATE burglary. The Cubans put tape on the door to be found by the security guard, Wikipedia, because they had felt betrayed by Nixon who went to China and meet with Communist dictator MAO and KISSINGER meet with the Communist Russians in Moscow. The Cubans had escaped CASTRO's brutal Communist Cuba. Nixon resigned and the weak Vietnamese democracy was subdued by Communism. Many Vietnamese people died. I know three who are today patriotic American citizens.]

ACTOR VOGT LEAVES DEMOCRATS FOR REPUBLICANS

HOLLYWOOD FACT: Actor JON VOGT said he left the Democrat party after it ended any further aid to the Vietnamese people. Vogt had won the Best Actor OSCAR for COING HOME (1978) where he portrayed a disabled Vietnam veteran. Ironically, JANE FONDA was his adulterous companion won the Best actress Oscar. During World War II we had a Japanese/American "TOKYO ROSE" who broadcast anti-American messages to American soldiers fighting bravely in the Pacific Theater. She went to prison. Fonda's photo helmeted on a Vietnamese anti-aircraft gun was accepted by Hollywood? I know GREEN BERETS JOHN WAYNE, CLINT EASTWOOD and World War II B-24 bomber pilot JIMMIE STEWART didn't accept it. Stewart flew on a B-52 mission in Vietnam as an Air Force brigadier general. Stewart"s wife's son was killed in Vietnam. There were many other American actors and servicemen upset by this anti-American act.
PERSONAL FACT: JON VOGT's birthday in Yonkers, NY was on December 29, 1938. My Jewish mother-in-law Helen was born in Brooklyn, NY on December 29.

GEORGE WASHINGTON'S FAREWELL ADDRESS

September 19, 1796 newspaper article
"GEORGE WASHINGTON'S FAREWELL ADDRESS is a letter written by President George Washington as a valedictory to "friends and fellow-citizens" after 20 years of public service to the United States. He wrote it near the end of his second term of his presidency before retiring to his home at Mount Vernon in Virginia."
"The letter was first published on The Address of General Washington to the People of America on His Declining the Presidency of the United States in the AMERICAN DAILY ADVERTISER on Sept. 19, 1796, about 10 weeks before the presidential electors cast their votes in the 1796 election. It is a classic statement of REPUBLICANISM, warning Americans of the political dangers which they must avoid if they are are to remain true to their values. If was almost immediately reprinted in newspapers throughout the country, and later in pamphlet form."

"The first draft was originally prepared by JAMES MADISON in June 1792, as Washington contemplated retiring at the end of his first term in office. However, he set it aside and ran for a second term because of heated disputes between Secretary of the
Treasury ALEXANDER HAMILTON and Secretary of State THOMAS JEFFERSON which convinced Washington that the growing tensions would rip apart the country without his leadership. This included the state of foreign affairs, and divisions between the newly formed FEDERALIST and Democratic-Republican parties."
"As his second term came to a close four years later, Washington prepared a revision of the original letter with the help of Hamilton to announce his intention to decline a third term in office. He reflects on the emerging issues of the American political landscape in 1796, he expresses his support for the government eight years after the adoption of the Constitution, defends his administration's record, and gives valedictory advise to the American people."   Wikipedia

FAREWELL ADDRESS HIGHLIGHTS: ALLIANCES WITH FOREIGN NATIONS

"Washington's hope that the United States would END PERMANENT ALLIANCES with FOREIGN NATIONS was realized in 1800 with the CONVENTION of 1800, the Treaty of Mortefontaine which officially ended in 1778 Treaty of Alliance, in exchange for ending the ending of the Quasi-War and establishing most favored nation trade relations with Napoleonic France. In 1823, Washington's foreign policy goals were further realized in the MONROE DOCTRINE, which promised non-interference in European affairs so long as the nations of Europe did not colonize or interfere with the newly independent Latin American nations of Central and South America. The United States did not enter into any permanent military alliances with foreign nations until the 1949 NORTH ATLANTIC TREATY which formed NATO.

DEFENSE OF THE PROCLAMATION OF NEUTRALITY

"Washington then explains his reasoning behind the Proclamation of Neutrality which he made during the FRENCH REVOLUTIONARY WAR, despite the standing TREATY OF ALLIANCE with France. He explains that the United States had a right to remain neutral in the conflict and that the correctness of that decision "has been virtually admitted by all" nations since. Justice and humanity required him to remain neutral during the conflict, he argues, and the neutrality was also necessary to allow the new government a chance to mature and gain enough strength to control its own affairs."

CHECKS AND BALANCES AND SEPARATION OF POWERS

"Washington continues his defense of the Constitution by stating that the system of CHECK AND BALANCES and SEPARATION OF POWERS within it are important means of preventing a single person or group from seizing control of the country. He advises the American people that, if they believe that it is necessary to modify the powers granted to the government through the Constitution, it should be done through constitutional amendments instead of through force."

RELIGION, MORALITY AND EDUCATION

"One of the most referenced parts of Washington's letter is his strong support of the importance of religion and morality in promoting private and public happiness and in promoting the political prosperity of the nation. He argues that the religious principles promote the protection of property, reputation, and the life that are the foundations of justice. HE CAUTIONS AGAINST THE BELIEF THAT THE NATION'S MORALITY CAN BE MAINTAINED WITHOUT RELIGION."

CONSTITUTION AND POLITICAL FACTIONS

"Washington goes on to state his support for the new constitutional government, calling it an improvement upon the nation's original attempt in the ARTICLES OF CONFEDERATION. He reminds the people that it is the right of the people to alter the government to meet their needs, but it should only be done through constitutional amendments. He reinforces this belief by arguing that violent takeovers of the government should be avoided at all costs and that it is the duty of every member of the
republic to follow the Constitution and to submit to the laws of the government until it is constitutionally amended by the majority of the American people."

"Washington warns the people that political factions may seek to obstruct the execution of the laws created by the government, or to prevent the branches of government from enacting the powers provided them by the Constitution, Such factions may claim to be trying to answer popular demands or solve pressing problems, but their true intentions are to take the power from the people and place it in the hands of unjust men."

"Washington calls the American people to only change the Constitution through amendments, but he then warns them that GROUPS SEEKING to OVERTHROW the GOVERNMENT may strive to pass constitutional amendments to WEAKEN THE GOVERNMENT to a point where it is unable to defend itself from political factions, enforce its laws, and protect the people's rights and property. As a result, he urges them to give the government time to realize its full potential, and only amend the Constitution after thorough time and thought have proven that it is truly necessary instead of simply making changes based upon opinions and hypotheses of the moment."

POLITICAL PARTIES DANGER

""Washington continues to advance his idea of the dangers of sectionalism and expands his warning to include the dangers of political parties to the country as a whole. These warnings are given in the context of the recent rise of two opposing parties within the government—the DEMOCRAT-REPUBLICAN Party led by JEFFERSON, and HAMILTON'S FEDERALIST Party. Washington had striven to remain neutral during the conflict between Britain and France brought about by the FRENCH REVOLUTION, while the Democratic-Republicans had made efforts to align with France and the Federalists had made efforts to ally with Great Britain."

"Washington recognizes that it is natural for people to organize and operate within groups such as political parties, but he also argues that every government has recognized political parties as an enemy and has sought to repress them because of their tendency to seek more power than other groups and to take revenge on political opponents, he feels that disagreements between political parties weakened government and "provide foreign nations access so they can impose their will on us."

"Moreover he makes the case that "the alternate domination" of one party over another and coinciding efforts to exact revenge on political opponents have led to horrible atrocities, and "is itself a frightful despotism. But this leads at length to a more formal and permanent despotism." From Washington's perspective and judgment, political parties eventually and "gradually incline the minds of men to seek security in the absolute power of the individual", leading to despotism. He acknowledges the fact that parties are sometimes beneficial in promoting liberty in monarchies, but argues that political parties must be restrained in a popularly elected government because of their tendency to distract the government from their duties, create unfounded jealousies among groups and regions, raise false alarms among the people, promote riots and insurrection, and provide foreign nations and interests access to the government where they can impose their will upon the country."   [CHINA]

UNITY AND SECTIONALISM

BEWARE OF SECESSION IDENTIFY AS AMERICAN, NOT BY STATE OR REGION
"Washington warns the American people to be suspicious of anyone who seeks to ABANDON THE UNION, to SECEDE a portion of the country from the rest, or to weaken the bonds that hold together the Constitutional Union. To promote the strength of the Union, he urges the people to

place their identity as Americans above identities as members of a city, or region, and focus their efforts and affection on the country above all other local interests. He reminds the people that they do not have more than slight differences in religion, manners, habits, and political principles, and that their triumph and possession of independence and liberty is a result of working together."
"Washington goes on to warn the American people to question the ulterior motives of any person or group who argues that the land within the borders of the United States is TOO LARGE TO BE RULED as a REPUBLIC, an argument made by many during the debate on the proposed purchase of the LOUISIANA TERRITORY, calling on the people to give the EXPERIMENT of a large republic a chance to work before deciding that it cannot be done. He then offers strong warnings on the dangers of SECTIONALISM, arguing that the true motives of a sectionalist are to create distrust or rivalries between regions and people to gain power and take control of the government."   Wikipedia

BEST PARTS OF TRUMP'S LETTER TO SPEAKER PELOSI
American Action News Staff 12/18/2019 12:00 AM

"Impeachment is the topic of the day and debate is rampant over whether or not the impeachment of President is just. The Democrats are looking to put Trump's head on a platter and the Republicans are defending him on all angles."
"Recently Pelosi announced that the vote was going to be held and Trump wrote a scathing letter in return. Here are the best parts of Trump's scathing letter to Pelosi:

1.) YOU HAVE CHEAPENED THE IMPORTANCE OF THE VERY UGLY WORD, IMPEACHMENT.

"Trump put this line in the letter and it speaks to Pelosi and her gang of partisan hacks looking to overturn the results of the 2016 election. What the Democrats are doing is little more than a political impeachment, there is no evidence that suggests Trump has done anything wrong."

2.) YOU DARE TO INVOKE THE FOUNDING FATHERS.

"You dare to invoke the Founding Fathers in pursuit of this election-nullification scheme?
"This line takes apart Pelosi and companies move with elegance. It shows the hypocrisy of their move to overturn the results of the 2016 election. This is the last thing the Founders would have wanted!"

3.) IT IS A TERRIBLE THING YOU ARE DOING, BUT YOU WILL HAVE TO LIVE WITH IT, NOT I.

"This quote from Trump is in reference to the precedent the Democrats are setting by going with a political impeachment. Democrats may end up seeing a Democrat President impeached by a Republican President in the future."

4.) YOU VIEW DEMOCRACY AS YOUR ENEMY.

"This captivates the state of the Democrat party, they are brooding over the fact that their awful policies are rejected by Americans!"

383

5.) MORE DUE PROCESS WAS AFFORDED TO THOSE ACCUSED IN THE SALEM WITCH TRIALS

"This line from the letter is no more than a quip but the mainstream media commentators are reading into it way too much. The media is using this as the focus of the letter and raving over all kinds of conspiracy theories about it, it's as much of a conspiracy as the Russian Collusion story!"

WHY SOME REVOLUTIONS FAIL

Joseph Laconte THE DAILY SIGNAL July 14, 2020

"Soon after the start of the French Revolution on July 14, 1789, the English statesman EDMUND BURKE saw storm clouds on the horizon. Under the banner of "LIBERTY, EQUALITY, and FRATERNITY," the French revolutionaries not only attacked the dreaded BASTILLE PRISON in Paris. They assaulted the most important historic institutions in France: the monarchy, the aristocracy, and the Christian religion."

"In his "REFLECTIONS ON THE REVOLUTION IN FRANCE," Burke warned of political revolutions that despise everything that came before them: "People will not look forward to posterity, who never look backward to their ancestors.""

"We know the rest of the story. Barely a decade after executing their hated monarch—and after years of political instability, social chaos, and the remorseless violence of the guillotine—the freedom loving revolutionaries installed an emperor to replace him. NAPOLEON, dictator for life, would plunge continental Europe into war."

"Near the heart of America's cultural crisis today is a failure to grasp the profound differences between the two great revolutions for freedom in the 18th century—between the events of 1776 and those of 1789."

"Intoxicated by lofty visions of an egalitarian society, the revolutionaries in Paris took a wrecking ball to the institutions and traditions that shaped France for centuries. Virtually nothing, including the religion that guided the lives of most of their fellow citizens, was sacrosanct. We must smother the internal and external enemies of the Republic." warned Maximilien ROBESPIERRE, "or perish with them." Their list of enemies—past and present—was endless."

"The men who signed the Declaration of Independence in Philadelphia, by contrast, did not share this rage against inherited authorities."

"Although the Americans, in the words of JAMES MADISON, did not suffer from a "blind veneration for antiquity," neither did they reject the political and cultural inheritance of Great Britain and the Western tradition. They did not seek to invent rights, but rather to reclaim their "chartered rights" as Englishmen."

"From both classical and religious sources, the American Founders understood that human passions made freedom a vulnerable state of affairs: Political liberty demanded the restraints of civic virtue and Biblical religion."

"The French revolutionaries took a different view, Paul-Henri Thiry, one of the most influential philosophers of his days, spoke for many: "To learn the true principles of morality, men have no need of theology, of revelation, or gods: They have need only by reason. This sanguine—and thoroughly secular—view of human nature underwrote the French political project. In their democratic society, all of the base and cruel passions would be unchained, while the sentiments of generosity and brotherhood would be awakened by the laws. The revolutionaries sang an anthem in political utopianism the likes of which had never been heard before in Europe."

"The Americans rejected it as dangerous nonsense. Instead, the Founders—living in a. Society animated by Protestant Christianity—held a hopeful but deeply sober view about the prospects for republican self government."

"Benjamin Franklin captured the essence of it when, emerging from the Constitutional Convention, he was asked what kind of government the Framers were delivering to the American people. "A republic," he said, "If you can keep it!"

"A major concern of the "Federalist Papers," perhaps the most significant reflection on the nature of political societies ever written, is the problem of human self-interest. The threat of factions—what would be called tribalism—weighed heavily on their minds."

"Though defending, along with JOHN JAY and ALEXANDER HAMILTON, the American Constitution, MADISON identified factions as the "mortal disease" of popular govt."

"Here is the most challenging aspect of any democratic revolution preserving freedom over the long haul. A sound constitution—embodying concepts such as limited government, the separation of powers, and equal justice under the law—is essential."

"Good political leadership is also important. But so is civic virtue: the capacity to govern oneself and to work for the common goal. And for that, the Founders believed, democracies needed the moral ballast of religious belief."

"In his farewell address as president GEORGE WASHINGTON took a swipe at the French "philosophies": 'Whatever may be conceded to the influence of refined education…reason and experience both forbid us to expect that national morality can prevail in exclusion of religious principle."

"Reverend JOHN WITHERSPOON—the only minister to sign the Declaration of Independence—reinforced the prevailing view: "that he is the best friend to American liberty who is most sincere and active in promoting true and undefiled religion."

"Ironically, it was a Frenchman, ALEXIS de TOCQUEVILLE, who confirmed BURKE's worst fears about the events in France. "Because the Revolution seemed to be striving for the regeneration of the human race even more than the reform of France." De Tocqueville wrote, "it lit a passion which the most violent political revolutions had never before been able to produce. This zeal, he added, took on the appearance of "a new kind of religion…WITHOUT GOD, without ritual, and without life after death."

"Thus in the American and French revolutions, we encounter starkly different journeys toward freedom: two conflicting visions of human nature and the nature of political societies. A republic—if you can keep it—or the dawn of universal bliss."

"Herein lies the source of our current crisis: the willingness to trade the legacy of the American Revolution for that of the French Revolution.What path will we take? Perhaps the welfare of the City of Man really does depend, after all, on our belief in the City of God.   Joe Laconte, dir. Kenneth Simon Center for Amer. Studies Heritage Foundation

THE MONROE DOCTRINE— NO EUROPEAN COLONIZATION

December 2, 1823—Washington, District of Columbia
"The MONROE DOCTRINE was a United States policy of opposing European colonialism in the Americas beginning in 1823. It stated that further efforts by European nations to take control of any independent state in North and South America would be viewed as "The manifestation of an unfriendly disposition toward the United States. At the same time, the doctrine noted that the U.S.

would recognize and not interfere with existing European countries. The Doctrine was issued on Dec. 2, 1823 at a time when nearly all Latin American colonies of Spain and Portugal had achieved, or were at the point of gaining, independence from the Portuguese and Spanish Empires."

"The U.S. government feared the victorious European powers that emerged from the CONGRESS OF VIENNA (1814-1815) would revive monarchial government. France had already agreed to restore the Spanish monarchy in exchange for CUBA. As the revolutionary NAPOLEONIC WARS (1803-1815) ended, PRUSSIA, AUSTRIA, and RUSSIA formed the HOLY ALLIANCE to defend monarchism. In particular, the Holy Alliance authorized military incursions to reestablish BOURBON rule over Spain and its colonies, which were establishing their independence." Read LOUISIANA PURCHASE.

SEEDS OF THE MONROE DOCTRINE—ISOLATIONIST COUNTRY

"Despite America's beginnings as an ISOLATIONIST COUNTRY, the seeds for the Monroe Doctrine were already being laid even during George Washington's presidency."

"ALEXANDER HAMILTON desired to control the sphere of influence in the western hemisphere, particularly in North America but was extended to the Latin American colonies by the Monroe Doctrine.   Hamilton, writing in the FEDERALIST PAPERS, was already wanting to establish AMERICA AS A WORLD POWER would suddenly become strong enough to keep the European powers outside of the Americas, despite the fact that European countries controlled much more of the Americas than the U.S. itself. Hamilton expected that the United States would BECOME THE DOMINANT POWER IN THE NEW WORLD and would, in the future, act as an intermediary between, the European powers and any new countries blossoming near the U.S."   Wikipedia

THE DOCTRINE

"The full document of the MONROE DOCTRINE, written chiefly by future—President and then Secretary of State JOHN QUINCY ADAMS asserts that the NEW WORLD is no longer subject to colonization by the European countries."

> The occasion has been judged proper for asserting, as a principle in which
> the rights and interests of the United States are involved, that the American
> continents, by the free and independent condition which they have assumed
> and maintain, are henceforth not to be considered as subjects for future
> colonization by any European powers.

"The second key passage, which contains a fuller statement of the Doctrine, is addressed to the "ALLIED POWERS" of Europe (that is, the HOLY ALLIANCE); it clarifies that the U.S. remains neutral on existing European colonies in the Americas but is opposed to "interpositions" that would create new colonies among the newly independent Spanish American republics."

> We owe it, therefore, to candor and to the amicable relations existing
> between the United States and those powers to declare that we should
> consider any attempt on their part to extend their system to any portion
> of this hemisphere as dangerous to our peace and safety. With the
> existing colonies or dependencies of any European power, we have not
> interfered and shall not interfere. But with the governments who have
> declared their independence and maintained it, and whose independence
> we have, on great consideration and on just principles, acknowledged,

we could not view any interposition for the purpose of oppressing them, or controlling in any other manner their destiny, by any European power in any other light than as the manifestation of an unfriendly disposition toward the United States.   Wikipedia

INTERNATIONAL RESPONSE

"Because the U.S. lacked both a credible navy and army at the time, the doctrine was largely disregarded internationally. PRINCE METTERNICH of Austria was angered by the statement, and wrote privately that the doctrine was a "NEW ACT OF REVOLT" by the U.S. that would grant "New strength to the apostles of sedition and reanimate the courage of every conspirator." Wikipedia

"The doctrine, however, met with tacit British approval. They enforced it tactically as part of the wider PAX BRITANNIA, which included enforcement of the NEUTRALITY OF THE SEAS. This was in line with developing British policy of LAISSEZ-FAIRE FREE TRADE against MERCANTILISM. Fast-growing British industry sought markets for its manufactured goods, and, if the newly independent Latin American states became Spanish colonies again, British access to these markets would be cut off by Spanish mercantilist policy."   Wikipedia

LATIN AMERICAN REACTION

"The reaction in Latin America to the Monroe Doctrine was generally favorable but on some occasions suspicious. John Crow, author of THE EPIC OF LATIN AMERICA, states, "SIMON BOLIVAR, Venezuela, himself, still in the midst of his last campaign against the Spaniards, Santander in Colombia, Rivadavia in Argentina, VICTORIA in Mexico—leaders of the emancipation movement everywhere—received Monroe's words with sincerest gratitude." Crow argues that the leaders of Latin America were realists. They knew that the President of the United States wielded very little power at the time, particularly without the backing of the British forces, and figured that the Monroe Doctrine was unenforced if the United States stood alone against the Holy Alliance."

MEXICO AND NAPOLEON III

"In 1862, French forces under NAPOLEON III invaded and conquered MEXICO, giving control to the puppet monarch EMPEROR MAXIMILIAN. Washington denounced this as a violation of the [Monroe] doctrine but was unable to intervene because of the American CIVIL WAR. In 1865 the U.S. stationed a large combat army on the border to emphasize its demand that France leave. France did pull out, and Mexican nationalists executed MAXIMILIAN."

"in 1842, U.S. President JOHN TYLER applied the MONROE DOCTRINE to HAWAII and warned Britain not to interfere there. This began the process of annexing Hawaii."
"On December 2, 1845, U.S. President JAMES POLK announced that the principle of the MONROE DOCTRINE should be strictly enforced, reinterpreting it to argue that no European nation should INTERFERE with the AMERICAN WESTERN EXPANSION ("MANIFEST DESTINY")."   Wikipedia   [Read LOUISIANA PURCHASE 1803]

ZIMMERMANN TELEGRAM—AMERICA'S MOTIVE FOR ENTERING WORLD WAR ONE

"The ZIMMERMANN TELEGRAM was a secret diplomatic communication issued from the German foreign office in January 1917 that proposed a MILITARY ALLIANCE BETWEEN GERMANY AND MEXICO. In the event that the United States entered WORLD WAR I, The Great War, against Germany. Mexico would recover TEXAS, ARIZONA and NEW MEXICO, The telegram was intercepted and DECODED BY BRITISH INTELLIGENCE. Revelation of the contents enraged Americans, especially after German Foreign Secretary ARTHUR ZIMMERMANN publicly admitted on March 3 that the telegram was genuine, helping to generate support for the United States declaration of war on Germany in April."   Wikipedia

THE SECRET—SECRET THAT BROUGHT NEUTRAL AMERICA TO WAR

"The decryption was described as the most significant intelligence triumph for Britain during World War I, and one of the earliest occasions on which a piece of signal intelligence influenced world events."

TELEGRAM CONTENT—"The message came in the form of a CODED TELEGRAM dispatched by Arthur Zimmermann, a Staatssekretar (a top-level civil servant) in the Foreign Office of the German Empire on 19 January 1917, The message was sent by the German ambassador to Mexico, HEINRICH VON ECKARDT. Zimmermann sent the telegram in anticipation of UNRESTRICTED SUBMARINE WARFARE by Germany on 1 February, an act the German government presumed would almost certainly lead to war with the United States. The telegram instructed Ambassador Eckardt that if the United States appeared certainty to enter the war, he was to approach the Mexican Government with a proposal for military alliance with funding from Germany."

THE DECODED TELEGRAM IS AS FOLLOWS:

We intend to begin on the first of February UNRESTRICTED SUBMARINE WARFARE. We shall endeavor in spite of this to keep the United States of America neutral. In the event of this not succeeding, we make war with Mexico a proposal of alliance on the following basis: Together, make peace together generous financial support and an understanding that Mexico is to reconquer the lost territory in Texas, New Mexico, and Arizona. The settlement in detail is left to you. You will inform the President of the above most secretly as soon as the most secretly as soon as the outbreak of the war with the United States of America is certain, and add the suggestion that he should, on his own initiative, invite Japan to immediate adherence and at the same time mediate between Japan and ourselves. Please call the President's attention to the fact that the ruthless employment of our submarines now offers the prospect of compelling England in a few months to make peace.
Signed, ZIMMERMANN"   Wikipedia

PREVIOUS GERMAN EFFORTS TO PROMOTE WAR

"Germany had long sought to incite a war between Mexico and the United States, which would have tied down American forces and slowed the export of American arms to the ALLIED POWERS. The Germans had engaged in a pattern of actually arming, funding and advising the Mexicans, as shown by the 1914 YPIRANGA INCIDENT and the presence of German advisors during the 1918 Battle of AMBOS NOGALES. German Naval Intelligence officer Franz von Rintelen had attempted to incite a war between Mexico and the United States in 1915, giving VICTOIANO HUERTA $12 million for that purpose. The German saboteur Lothar Witzke—responsible for the March 1917 munitions explosion at the MARE ISLAND NAVAL SHIPYARD in the San Francisco Bay Area, and possibly responsible for the July 1916 BLACK TOM EXPLOSION in New Jersey—was based in Mexico City. The failure of United States troops to capture PANCHO VILLA in 1916 [General Pershing and Patton] and the movement of President CARRANZA in favor of Germany emboldened the Germans to send the ZIMMERMANN note-telegram."   Wikipedia

"The German provocations were partially successful. WOODROW WILSON, president at the time, ordered the military invasion of VERACRUZ in 1914 in the context of the Ypiranga Incident against the advice of the British government. War was prevented thanks to the NIAGARA FALLS PEACE conference organized by the ABC NATIONS, Argentina, Brazil, Chile, but the occupation was a decisive factor in MEXICAN NEUTRALITY IN WORLD WAR I. Mexico refused to participate in the embargo against Germany and granted full guarantees to the German companies for keeping their operations open, specifically in Mexico City. These guarantees lasted for 25-years—coincidentally, it was on 22 May 1942 that Mexico declared war on the AXIS POWERS following the loss of two Mexican-flagged tankers that month to Kriegsmarine U-boats."

GERMAN MOTIVATION FOR THE TELEGRAM

"The Zimmermann Telegram was a part of an effort carried out by the Germans to postpone the transportation of supplies and other war materials from the United States to the ALLIED POWERS that were at war with Germany. The main purpose of the telegram was to make the Mexican government declare war on the United States in hopes of tying down American forces and slowing the export of American arms. The GERMAN HIGH COMMAND believed they would be able to defeat the British and French on the Western Front and strangle Britain with unrestricted submarine warfare before American forces could be trained and shipped to Europe in sufficient numbers to aid the Allied Powers, The Germans were encouraged by their successes on the Eastern Front into believing that they would be able to divert large numbers of troops to the Western Front in support of their goals, The Mexicans were willing to consider the alliance but declined the deal after the Americans were informed of the Telegram."

MEXICAN RESPONSE—"Mexican PRESIDENT CARRANZA assigned a military commission to assess the feasibility of the Mexican takeover of their former territories contemplated by Germany. The [Mexican] generals concluded that it would be neither possible not even desirable to attempt an enterprise for the following reasons:

*Mexico was in the midst of a civil war and Carranza's position was far from secure. A declaration of war by his regime would have provided an opportunity for opposing factions to align with the U.S. and Allied Powers in exchange for diplomatic recognition."

*The United States was far stronger militarily than Mexico was. Even if Mexico's military forces were completely united and loyal to a single regime, no serious scenario existed under which they could invade and win a war against the United States."

*Germany's promises of "generous financial support" were very unreliable. The German government had already informed Carranza in June 1916 that they were unable to provide the necessary gold needed to stock a completely independent Mexican national bank. Even if Mexico received financial support, the arms, ammunition, and other needed war supplies would presumably have to be purchased from the ABC nations (Argentina, Brazil, and Chile), which would strain relations with them."

*Even if by some chance Mexico had the military means to win a conflict against the United States and reclaim the territories in question, Mexico would have severe difficulty accommodating and pacifying a large English-speaking population that was better supplied with arms than most civilian populations."

BUILD THE WALL

[BUILD THE WALL is being called racist. Latinos are CAUCASIAN which is of the white racial classification. In July and August 2019, in the lot next to my house, I saw a 7-man Latino work crew build a large two-story house with basement in 5 weeks! I watched and photographed the foundation, the frame, siding and roof, windows and roof shingles. I spoke with them and complimented them. I am sure they all were vetted and had green cards and may have been naturalized citizens. I am sure every one of them would be upset if a skilled illegal immigrant entered the United States and took their job working for a lower wage. The media doesn't tell you that.]

ATLANTIC CHARTER FUTURE FREEDOMS

"The ATLANTIC CHARTER was a statement on 14 August 1941 that set out American and British goals for the world after the end of World War II. The joint statement stated: no territorial aggrandizement, no territorial changes made against the wishes of the people (self-determination), restoration of self-government, global cooperation, FREEDOM FROM FEAR AND WANT, FREEDOM OF THE SEAS, and abandonment of the use of force, and disarmament of aggressor nations. The adherents to the Atlantic Charter signed the DECLARATION OF THE UNITED NATIONS on 1 January 1942, which was the basis for the modern UNITED NATIONS.

ALDOUS HUXLEY THE SURVIVAL OF DEMOCRACY

"The survival of democracy depends on the ability of large numbers of people to make realistic choices, in the light of adequate information. A dictatorship, on the other hand, maintains itself by CENSORING or DISTORTING THE FACTS, and by appealing, NOT TO REASON, not to enlightened self-interest, but to PASSION and PREJUDICE, to the powerful "HIDDEN FORCES" as HITLER called them, PRESENT IN THE. UNCONSCIOUS DEPTHS OF EVERY HUMAN MIND." Brave New World Revisited   47

What A Terrifying Government Database Knows About You

TRUE DAILY Website June 4, 2019

"An FBI photo database has been exposed for using facial recognition technology, essentially allowing for a police state, WTOP [DC] reports:
"A government watchdog says the FBI has access to about 640,000,000 photographs—including from driver's licenses, passports and mugshots—that can be searched using facial recognition technology.

The figure reflects how the technology is becoming an increasingly powerful law enforcement tool, but is also stirring fears about the potential for authorities to intrude on the lives of Americans. It was reported by the Government Accountability Office (GAO) at a congressional hearing in which both Democrats and Republicans raised questions about the use of the technology.

The FBI maintains a database known as the Interstate Photo System of mugshots that can help federal state and local law enforcement officials. It contains about 36,000,000 photographs, according to Gretta Goodwin of the GAO.

But taking into account the bureau contracts providing access to driver's licenses in 21 states, and its use of photos and other databases, the FBI has access to about 640,000,000 photographs, Goodwin told lawmakers at the House oversight committee.

Could this database be politicized and used to oppress conservatives? We've seen how the government turned on Pres. Trump, does that make any American safe from this?"

[In June 2019, a million protestors in HONG KONG protested sending its citizens to mainland Communist China for political trials. Chinese technology has developed a vast camera and photo recognition network.]

HISTORICAL FACT: A major use of surveillance cameras began in London in the early 1980s in response to Irish Republican Army IRA terrorist bomb attacks. The British pop singing group THE POLICE, later STING, had a song SOMEONE IS WATCHING YOU music video showing people in London's streets recorded on police video cameras.]

Traffic cameras have sent millions of driver's tickets for "running" red lights a dangerous act to other drivers. Millions of dollars have been collected and in some locations there have been protests that it has been used excessively for profit?

The state of Virginia has several State Police cars equipped with license plate recognition cameras which can be relayed to a data base computer probably in Richmond. Several years ago a female Virginia state trooper's license plate camera detected a license connected to a double homicide. She followed the vehicle at a distance and called for backup. The vehicle was blocked on I-66 and pulled over. The driver shot himself, a suicide. The man had worked for the Roanoke, VA newspaper and was fired. He had stalked a woman reporter who was doing an early morning news report at Smith Lake. Her TV cameraman was shot, as he fell to his death, he videoed the shooter. His fiancé was a TV producer on duty and tragically witnessed her future husband's death. They were able to identify the assailant. The cameraman was a recent graduate of VIRGINIA TECH from nearby Salem. I met a man wearing a Salem T shirt, they were on football team together. My son graduated VA TECH in 2001. Small World?

The Unchanging Principles of Conservatism Defined

by Kay Coles James The Daily Signal August 22, 2019
"As the left continues to push policies like "Medicare for All," free
college tuition, open borders, and depleting the strength of the military,
conservatives must counter these policies with a strong voice."

"At The Heritage Foundation, we're always about ways to talk to new and nontraditional audiences about how conservative principles can create the greatest freedom, opportunity, prosperity, and civil society for the American people.

We realize that these ideas to take hold, we have to counter the false narratives of left-leaning media outlets, educational institutions, and politicians.

We also see how messaging to new audiences can be diluted when some institutions and politicians who bear the "conservative" label drift far from fundamental conservative principles.

This not only hurts the conservative brand, but it also leaves these audiences thinking we're not authentic about our views and that we change them based on convenience. It harms our credibility and leaves them thinking what we told them was right and true really wasn't.

Many institutions and politicians start out as conservative, but if they're not firmly rooted in principles, they can deviate from the path.

In politics and policy, the forces that create a curved trajectory—deviating from principles—include pressure from the media or political opponents, pressure from those you normally agree with deviating from principles, or not wanting to be seen as the only one advocating for a position that's right but not popular.

Since principles are meant to represent our highest ideals and should be based on fundamental truths, they should mostly be unchanging.

While most conservatives may have differing viewpoints about some aspects of conservatism, there are certain fundamental principles where we must remain resolute. In fact, at The Heritage Foundation, we call them the True North principles because they represent a fixed direction on which to stay focused, regardless of which ways the forces may be pressuring us.

Some of these major principles include:

* The federal government is instituted to protect the rights bestowed on individuals under natural law. It exists to preserve life, liberty, and property—a mission that includes not only protecting the sanctity of life, but DEFENDING FREEDOM OF SPEECH, RELIGION, THE PRESS, and ASSEMBLY, and the right of the individuals to be TREATED EQUALLY and justly under the law and to enjoy the fruits of their labor.
* The federal government's powers should be limited to only those named in the U.S. Constitution and exercised solely to protect the rights of its citizens.
* Government functions best when it is closest and most accountable to the people and where power is shared between the federal government and the states.
* Individuals and families make the best decisions for themselves and their children about health, education, jobs, and welfare.
* America's economy and the prosperity of individual citizens are best served by a system built on free enterprise, economic freedom, private property rights, and the rule of law. This system is best sustained by policies that promote general economic freedom and eliminate governmental preferences for special interests, including free trade, deregulation, and opposing government interventions in the economy that distort free markets and impair innovation.
* Tax policies should raise the minimum revenue necessary to fund only constitutionally appropriate functions of government.
* Regulations should be limited to those that produce a net benefit to the American people as a whole, weighing both financial and liberty costs.
* Judges should interpret and apply our laws and the Constitution based on their original meaning, not upon judges' own personal and political predispositions.
* America must be a welcoming nation—one that promoted patriotic assimilation and is governed by laws that are fair, humane, and enforced to protect its citizens.
* America is strongest when our policies protect our national interests, preserve our alliances of free people, vigorously counter threats to our security and interests, and advance prosperity through economic freedom at home and abroad.

These are just some of the unchanging principles of conservatism.

As the left continues to push policies like "Medicare for All," free college tuition, open borders, and depleting the strength of the military, conservatives must counter these policies with a strong voice.

We must convince more and more people that our ideas work better and can assure a more free and prosperous future for all Americans. If we don't do that, and more Americans succumb to the false promises of the STATISTS, we soon won't recognize America. If ever there was a time we needed to be clear about our principals, it is now.

Originally published in THE WASHINGTON TIMES.

Kay James is president of the HERITAGE FOUNDATION. She formerly served as director of the U.S. OFFICE OF PERSONNEL MANAGEMENT and as Virginia's secretary of health and human resources. James is African American.

GOD WAS AT THE CHARLOTTESVILLE TRAGEDY

I watched CNN'S ANDERSON COOPER'S interview with the two African American ladies whose white car was rear ended by a car. They told Anderson the police directed them to that scene. One woman recalled, "I think God brought us there or more people would have died." What the media didn't know is that she was telling God's truth. I saw the incident replayed on my iPad and was able to enlarge their license plate which said GODKPME! GOD did they were uninjured. I have their interview on my iPhone.

A man in my church, who sings in the choir, said his sister lives in Charlottesville. She said the liberal mayor allowed the ANTI-FA and NEO-NAZIS confrontation with no police control. It was a liberal set-up to begin racist tensions in America over historical statues. Today, all historical statues even Jesus are being destroyed by angry cheering mobs.

I give CNN credit for showing the neo-Nazis nighttime torchlight parade. Millions of Southern heritage Americans like General PATTON bravely destroyed the THIRD REICH and Imperial Japan. Read my Virginian Desmond Doss Medal of Honor story.

"How Many Success Stories Do You Need Before WRITING YOUR OWN?" RYAN SEACREST

"THE UPSIDE" GUIDEPOSTS March 2018
Quotes from today's "POSITIVE THINKERS"

Retrieved at Hunter Holmes McGuire Veterans's Hospital Chapel Richmond, Virginia.
Named after Gen. Thomas "Stonewall" Jackson's doctor who amputated his left arm.

MY "TEN DEGREES" OF SEPARATION

FIRST DEGREE: My personal connection to a subject.
SECOND DEGREE: My family connection to a subject.
THIRD DEGREE: My friend's connection to a subject.
FOURTH DEGREE: My friend's friend's connection to a subject.
FIFTH DEGREE: My church and fellow workers connection to a subject.
SIXTH DEGREE;   My customers through name, area phone #, hat, shirt connection.
SEVENTH DEGREE: Hollywood actors my personal and film connection to a subject.
EIGHTH DEGREE: Facebook groups connection to a subject.

NINTH DEGREE: Wikipedia, Google and Internet connection to a subject.
TENTH DEGREE: Casual friends met at movie theaters, book author lectures/signings, veterans, AARP, Civil War Group, Veteran's Club, air shows, air, army, navy ships historical museums and historical sites signs connections.

GODDESS IDOLS IN AMERICA COLUMBIA Goddess of America

I lived in beautiful Columbia County, New York from September 1954-October 1974, with a panoramic, breath-taking view of the 35 mile long Catskill Mountains across the Hudson River Valley about 20 miles to the West. I enjoyed watching the sunset behind the 3,000 foot Catskill mountain range, much different than my Amityville, Long Island home 1945-1954. I didn't know the great American historical significance of the name Columbia though its name is very prominent throughout the United States.
I have seen dozens of Columbia motion picture films which begin with the beautiful radiant sunlit red haired lady in a full length white gown standing mightily holding a bright torch in her right hand with billowing white thunder clouds behind her. Billions of people in America and throughout the world have seen her image and enjoyed some of America's greatest films.

Through the Internet I have found how amazingly historic this "goddess" LADY COLUMBIA is actually a feminized version of CHRISTOPHER COLUMBUS "discover" of America. Columbus never set foot on mainlined America only the Bahama islands and Santo Domingo, Dominican Republic/Haiti. Columbus sailors almost threw Captain Columbus overboard when he headed West which some of the crew thought they would fall of the Flat Earth. Columbus learned the Earth was a sphere through ancient Egyptian/Greek documents that he could reach the East Indies Spice Islands, today's Indonesia, by sailing West. He discovered the West Indies. Spanish Queen Isabella gave Columbus money for his expedition because the eastern trade route was unsafe or was taxed by the Middle East Islamic muslims.
OXYMORON FACT: Americans can thank Mohammad and his Islamic muslim religion conquering the Christian Middle East for the discovery of America. I was an A student in History and don't remember reading that major historical fact. I doubt today's History textbooks tell this fact either. If they tell this story the textbook's today would probably praise the Middle East muslims for "creating" America. In the 1950s and 1960s the Islamic muslim nations and the Muslim religion were never mentioned. Only when the Arab nations unsuccessfully tried to destroy the new nation of Israel did the Middle East make the news.The atheist Communist Soviet Union supplied the Arab nations Egypt, Syria and Iraq with massive supplies of jet fighters, tanks, missiles and guns.
A PARADOX: Islam claims to be an ultra-orthodox religion praying 5 times a day, believing in only one god ALLAH, monotheism. The only more horrific historical parallel I
have mentioned earlier is the non-aggression pact that HITLER AND STALIN signed in August 1939, the week before they both invaded the peaceful nation of Poland. This started World War II, causing 55,000,000 mostly civilian deaths.
AMERICA FACT: America is named after another Italian explorer AMERICO VESPUCCI. Norseman LIEF ERICKSON sailed to Greenland and Labrador part of North America circa 1,000 A.D. HISTORY.
GODDESS—A female DIETY: A temple to ATHENA NIKE, GODDESS OF VICTORY

Goddess Columbia and General Washington

How did this "woman" Columbia become a symbol of America? Until being replaced by another goddess a gift commemorating our Revolutionary War friendship from France the STATUE OF LIBERTY "LIBERTY ENLIGHTENING THE WORLD" in New York city harbor. She is also holding "a torch of freedom" high in her right hand.   The reason:

"During the dark hours of the American Revolutionary War General GEORGE WASHINGTON received a letter from PHILLIS WHEATLEY.

A slave women's poetry:

To His Excellency, General Washington.

"Celestial choir! enthron'd in realms of light, Columbia's scenes of glorious foils I write. While freedom's cause her anxious breast alarms. She flashes dreadful in refulgent arms. See mother earth her offspring's fate bemoan, And nations daze at scenes before unknown! See the bright beams of heaven's revolving light. Involved in sorrows and veil of night!"

"The goddess comes, she moves divinely fair. Olive and laurel bind her golden hair; Wherever shines this native of the skies, Unnumber'd charms and recent graces rise.

Muse! bow propitious while my pen relates How pour her armies through a thousand gates, As when Eolus heaven's fair face deforms, Enwrapp'd in tempest and a night of storms; Astonish'd ocean feels the wild uproar, The refluent surges beat the sounding shore. Or thick as leaves in Autumn's golden reign, Such, and so many, moves the warrior's train. In bright array they seek the work of war. Where high unfurl'd the ensign waves in the air. Shall I to Washington their praise recite? Enough thou know'st them in the fields of fight. Thee, first in peace and honours,—we demand the grace and glory of thy martial ban. Fam'd for thy valour for thy virtues more, Hear every tongue thy guardian aid implore!

One century scarce perform'd its destined round.

When Gallic powers Columbia's fury found; And so may you, whoever dares disgrace The land of freedom's heaven-defended race Fix'd are the eyes of nations on the scales, For in their hopes Columbia prevails. Anon Britannia droops the pensive head, While round increase the rising hills of dead. Ah! cruel blindness to Columbia's state!

Lament thy thirst of boundless power too late.

Proceed, great chief, with virtue on thy side, Thy ev'ry action let the goddess guide, A crown, a mansion, and a throne that shine, With gold unfading, Washington! be thine."

Washington became America's first president. The Capitol is in the District of Columbia.

"HAIL COLUMBIA!"

"Hail Columbia" was he unofficial national anthem until in 1931, "THE STAR BANGLED BANNER " was selected.

"Hail Columbia, happy land! Hail ye heroes, heav'n-born band, Who fought and bled in freedom's cause, And when the storm of war was gone. Enjoy'd the peace of your valor won. Let independence be our boast, Ever mindful what it cost; Ever grateful for the prize, Let its altar reach the skies.   Chorus

Firm, united let us be, Rallying round our liberty, As a band of brothers joined, Peace and safety we shall find.

Immortal patriots, rise once more, Defend your rights, defend your shore! Let no rude foe, with impious hand, Let no rude foe with impious hand, Invade the shrine where sacred lies of toil and blood, the well-earned prize, While off'ring peace, sincere and just, in Heaven's we place a manly trust, That truth and justice prevail, And every scheme of bondage fail.   Chorus

Firm, united, and true, united let us be, Rallying round our liberty, As a band of brothers joined, Peace and safety we shall find.

Behold the chief who now commands, Once more to serve his country stands. The rock on which the storm will break, But armed in virtue, firm, and true, His hopes are fixed on Heav'n and you. When hope was sinking in dismay, When glooms obscured Columbia's day, His steady mind, from changes free, Resolved on death or liberty.   Chorus

Firm, united let us be, Rallying round our liberty, As a band of brothers joined, Peace and safety we shall find.

Sound, sound the trump of fame, Let Washington's great fame Ring through the world with loud applause, Ring through the world with loud applause, Let ev'ry clime to freedom dear, With equal skill, with God-like power He governs in the fearful hour of horrid war, or guides with ease The happier time of honest peace.   Chorus

Firm, unified let us be, Rallying round our liberty, As a band of brothers joined, Peace and safety we shall find."

WASHINGTON'S VISION AND PROPHECY FOR AMERICA

Dr. JOHN GRADY, M.D. American Freedom Crusade Benton, TN 37307

"Various accounts of GEORGE WASHINGTON'S vision and prophecy all agree in content. There have been only minor variations in some details as the story was repeated over the years by those whom it was related by George Washington."

"The place was VALLEY FORGE, in the cold and bitter of 1777. Washington's army suffered several reverses and the situation was desperate. Food was scarce. The CONTINENTAL CONGRESS was not sending supplies of money. Some of the troops did not even have shoes to wear in the snow. Many soldiers were sick and dying from disease and exposure. Morale was at an all-time low and there was great agitation in the Colonies against continued effort to secure our freedom from England, Nevertheless, General Washington was determined to see the struggle through."

"These are the words of a first-hand observer, ANTHONY SHERMAN, who was there and describes the situation. "You doubtless heard the story of Washington's going into the thicket to pray in secret for aid and comfort from God, the interposition of whose DIVINE PROVIDENCE brought us safely through the darkest days of tribulation."

"One day, I remember it well, when the chilly winds whistled through the leafless trees, though the sky was cloudless and the sun shown brightly, he remained in his quarters nearly all the afternoon alone. When he came out, I noticed that his face was a shade paler than usual. There seemed to be something on his mind of more than ordinary importance...Washington related the event that occurred that day."

WASHINGTON'S OWN WORDS

"This afternoon, something seemed to disturb me. Looking up, I beheld standing opposite me a singularly beautiful female. So astonished was I, for I had given strict orders not to be disturbed, that I was for some moments before I found language to inquire the cause of her presence. A second, a third and even a fourth time did I repeat my question, but received no answer from my mysterious visitor except a slight raising of her eyes."

"By this time I felt a strange sensation spreading through me. I would have risen but the riveted gaze of the being before me rendered volition impossible. I assayed once more to address her, but my tongue had become useless, as though it had become paralyzed

"A new influence, mysterious, potent, irresistible, took possession of me. All I could do was to gaze steadily, vacantly at my unknown visitor. Gradually the surrounding atmosphere seemed as if it had become filled with sensations, and luminous. Everything about me seemed to rarefy, the mysterious visitor herself becoming more airy and yet more distinct to my sight than before. I now begin to feel as one dying, or rather to experience the sensations which I have sometimes imagined accompany dissolution. I did not think, I did not reason, I did not move, all were alike impossible. I was only conscious of gazing fixedly, vacantly at my companion."

"Presently I heard a voice saying:

"Son of the Republic, look and learn," while at the same time
my visitor extended his arm eastwardly. I now beheld a heavy
white vapor at some distance rising fold upon fold. This
gradually dissipated, and I looked upon a stranger scene.
before me lay spread out in one vast plain all the countries
of the world — EUROPE, ASIA, AFRICA and AMERICA. I saw
rolling and tossing between EUROPE and AMERICA the billows
of the Atlantic, and between ASIA and AMERICA lay the Pacific.

""Son of the Republic,' said the same mysterious voice as before, 'look and learn,'
At that moment I beheld a dark shadowy being, like an angel, standing or rather floating in mid-air, between EUROPE and AMERICA. Dipping water out of the ocean in the hollow of each hand, he sprinkled some upon America with his right hand, while with his left hand he cast some on Europe. Immediately a cloud raised from these countries, and joined in mid-ocean. For a while it remained stationary and then moved slowly westward, until it enveloped America in its murky folds. Sharp flashes of lightning gleamed through it at intervals, and I heard the smothered groans and cries of the American people."

COMMENT: This part of the vision is probably the war of independence

"A second time the angel dipped water from the ocean, and sprinkled it out as before. The dark cloud was then drawn back to the ocean, in whose heaving billows it sank from view. A third time I heard the mysterious voice saying, 'Son of the Republic, look and learn,' 'I cast my eyes upon America and beheld villages and towns and cities springing up one after another until the whole land from the Atlantic to the Pacific was dotted with them."

"Again, I heard the mysterious voice say, 'Son of the Republic,
the end of the century cometh, look and learn." At this the dark
and shadowy angel turned his face southward, and from Africa
I saw and ill omened specter approach our land. It filled slowly
over every town and city of the latter. The inhabitants presently
set themselves in battle array against each other. As I continued

looking I saw a bright angel, on whose brow rested a crown of
light, on which was traced the word 'UNION,' bearing the
American flag which he placed between the divided nation, and
said. 'Remember ye are brethren.' Instantly, the inhabitants,
casting from them their weapons became friends once more,
and united around the NATIONAL STANDARD."

COMMENT: This part of the vision is most likely describing the Civil War
over which involved the slave trade that was brought to America from Africa.

"And again I heard the mysterious voice saying, 'Son of the
Republic, look and learn." At this the dark, shadowy angel
placed a trumpet to his mouth, and blew three distinct blasts:
and taking water from the ocean, he sprinkled it upon Europe,
Asia and Africa. Then my eyes beheld a fearful scene: From
each of these countries arose thick, black clouds that were
soon joined into one. Throughout this mass there gleamed a
dark red light by which I saw hordes of armed men, who,
moving with the cloud, marched by land and sailed to America.
Our country was enveloped in this volume of cloud, and I saw
these vast armies devastate the whole country and burn the
villages, towns and cities that I beheld springing up. As my ears
listened to the thundering of the cannon, clashing of the sword,
and the shouts and cries of millions in mortal combat, I heard
again the mysterious voice saying. 'Son of the Republic, look
and learn.' When the voice ceased, the dark shadowy angel
placed his trumpet once more to his mouth, and blew a long
and fearful blast."   [The World Wars?]
"Instantly a light as of a thousand suns [atomic bombs] shone
down from above me, and pierced and broke into fragments the
dark clouds which enveloped America. At the same moment the
Angel upon whose head still shone the word UNION, and who
bore our National flag in one hand and a sword in the other,
descended from the heavens attended by legions of white
Spirits. These immediately joined the inhabitants of America.
Instantly the dark cloud rolled back, together with the armies
it had brought, leaving the inhabitants of the land victorious!"
"Then once more I beheld the villages, towns and cities springing
up where I had seen them before, while the bright angel,
planting the azure standard he had brought in the midst of them,
cried with a loud voice. 'While the stars remain, and the heavens
send down dew upon the earth, so long shall the Union last.'
And taking from his brow and crown on which was blazoned
the word 'UNION,' he placed it upon the Standard while the
people, kneeling down, said. 'AMEN.' "
"The scene instantly began to fade and dissolve, and I at last
saw nothing but the rising, curling vapor I at first beheld. This
also disappearing, I found myself once more gazing upon the
mysterious visitor, who, in the same voice I had heard before,

said, 'Son of the Republic, what you have seen is thus interrupted: Three great perils will come upon the Republic. The most fearful is the third, but in this greatest conflict the WHOLE WORLD UNITED shall not prevail against her. Let every child of the Republic learn to LIVE FOR HIS GOD, his land and the Union. With these words the vision vanished, started from my seat and felt that I had seen a vision wherein had been shown to me the birth, progress, and destiny of the United States."

WAS GENERAL WASHINGTON'S SPIRIT AT GETTYSBURG? GEORGE WASHINGTON'S GHOST SAVED THE UNION.

GHOSTS OF NEW YORK

"During the desperate days of early July 1863 during the Civil War GEORGE WASHINGTON'S ghost came to the rescue of the union."
"The ghost of American president and FOUNDING FATHER George Washington came to the rescue of a group of Union soldiers waging a battle against draft rioters during the Civil War on Broadway and Duane Street. Dressed in the uniform of the American Revolution, the man was Washington, who then issued the command, "Fix bayonets! Charge!" The Union soldiers charged down the hill, forced the rioters into a full retreat."

REMEMBRANCE

"When an officer was interviewed years later about the ghost of George Washington, the old soldier replied cautiously: "Yes, that report circulated through our lines, and I have no doubt that it inspired the men doubtless it was a superstition." Then he paused and added, "Who among us can say that such a thing was impossible? We have not yet sounded or explained the immortal life that lies out beyond our earthly plane. We do not know what mystic powers may be possessed by those who are now bivouacking with the dead. I only know the effect, but I dare not explain or deny the cause.I do believe that we were enveloped by the powers of the other world that day and who shall say Washington was not among the number of those who aided the country he founded?"

WASHINGTON'S SPIRIT AT LITTLE ROUND TOP

"Perhaps a day apart, George Washington appeared before the 20th Maine Division [volunteer Regiment] as they approach Gettysburg. As they approached a fork in the road, they were unsure which direction to take? Suddenly a very tall, imposing figure wearing a tri-cornered hat on horseback then waved them in the right direction and commanded them to follow him."
"Did you know that George Washington is credited by some as helping the Union Army in one of the most decisive engagements at Gettysburg? Wait a minute...GEORGE WASHINGTON? He was a general during the Revolutionary War and died in 1799, well before the Civil War. Yet Washington — or rather his ghost — is said to have appeared to the 20th Maine Division as they approached Gettysburg. At first they thought he was a Union general but they began to scratch their heads that he looked remarkably like George Washington. The horseman led the Union soldiers to LITTLE ROUND TOP where they were able to repel the Confederates."

"As rumors of a ghostly presence of the Founding Father of the country, Lincoln's Secretary of War EDWIN STANTON investigated. Colonel JOSHUA CHAMBERLAIN, the regiment commander, testified, "We know not what mystic power may be possessed by those who are now bivouacking [residing] with the dead. I only know the effect, but I dare not explain or deny the cause. Who shall say that Washington was not among the number of those who aided the country that he founded."

"Although Washington died in 1799, his spirit continued to serve his country during one of its darkest moments when it was at war with itself.

GETTYSBURG GHOSTS—There are many ghost stories killed civilian JENNY WADE has a statue and ghost tour. Park rangers at all Civil War parks are forbidden to discuss apparition stories. I have heard one from my next door neighbor, a retired Air Force colonel. I live on Wilderness battlefield land with a General Sedgwick's Corps trench within sight from my living room. At Colonel Patton's Winchester cemetery two lady's gave me his ghost pamphlet story killed in action near there. Valley Forge park rangers had told the story of the angel and Washington. My local friend Doctor Andre, a 2nd cousin to Pope Saint John Paul II, told me the park rangers no longer tell the angel story at Valley Forge. He had lived in nearby Princeton, New Jersey. I have been told that MARTIN LUTHER tours at the Wartburg Castle, where Luther was hiding from the Pope as a "heretic", don't tell how Luther threw his inkwell at the devil. During his 10 month stay there, Luther translated the New Testament from Greek into German. Gutenberg printing presses allowed the German people to read Jesus Gospel for the first time. Only the religious clergy had access to the few handwritten Latin Vulgate Bibles.

Did Martin Luther throw his ink well at the devil? I believe it is a true story.

A Ghost at Gettysburg: The 20th Maine's Mysterious Encounter

Posted by MBHENRY July 11, 2018
Following the Path to the Past

"It was a difficult march to say the least. The road was clouded with dust, and they had to move fast in the oppressive July heat. In the dead of night, just as they approached the guns of Gettysburg, the regiment came upon a fork in the road. One path would lead them to the assistance of their countrymen, and the other would lead them on a wild goose chase. The maps were out of date and they had no idea which one to take. Suddenly, in the bright moon light, there appeared a mysterious rider on a magnificent pale horse. He was adorned with a brightly colored tricorn hat. He urged the horse down one of the paths, and then he waved for Colonel Chamberlain's confounded troops to follow him. The strange man led them to the Union battle lines, and soon the 20th Maine was rushed to the aid of their Union brothers."

"But who was the rider?"

"Until the critical moment of the fighting on LITTLE ROUND TOP. As the frightened soldiers prepared to charge the rebel line with nothing but bayonets [they had no bullets], the mysterious man reappeared. This time he was at the front of the Union line and bared a sword that glowed with fire. His identity was unmistakeable. It was George Washington. Now under the supernatural command of the general that helped give birth to their nation, the Union boys blasted down the hill and into the pages of Gettysburg history."

"It is one of the most fantastical accounts from the battle of Gettysburg and it circulated in Civil War circles for decades. On our own ghost tour, our guide saved this incredible tale for last and it sure made a fitting finale, as would any story that involves George Washington with a flaming sword."

"But is it true? Most historians and academics will give you a quick answer —hell no. There is no way that George Washington came back from the dead to lead Union troops to a spectacular victory. However, that might not convince some of the fighters from the 20th Maine. Even Chamberlain himself later noted that his troops were inspired by some curious vision that day."

"When questioned on the subject after the battle, he had this to say — "Now from a dark angle of the roadside came a whisper, whether from earthly or unearthly voice one cannot feel quite sure, that the august form of George Washington had been seen that afternoon at sunset riding over the Gettysburg hills. Let no one smile at me! I half believed it myself."

"In another interview on the matter much later in life, he also said —"I have no doubt that it [the Washington tale] had a tremendous psychological effect in inspiring the men. Doubtless it was a superstition, but who among us can say that such a thing was impossible? We have not yet sounded or explored the immortal life out beyond the Bar…I only know the effect, but I dare not explain or deny the cause."

PERSONAL STORY: My 9 yr. old granddaughter took the Gettysburg bus tour on Little Round top a one-star General Porter picked her, the only child, to tell her a story. He showed her a rare little grey graphite pencil which he told her was given by General Robert E. Lee to General Ulysses S. Grant at Appomattox, Virginia, to add a change to the Peace agreement to end the American Civil War.Two weeks later my granddaughter completed the quiz at Appomattox and raised her hand to take an honorary oath. We saw the original pencil on display. I took an iPhone photo and noticed in the background a sign saying "With malice to none." Lincoln's Biblical quotation in 2nd Inauguration.

This was at the time the distressed South Carolina boy killed pastors, elders and other members of the African American Baptist church in Charleston, South Carolina. He was upset by all the media reports and violence on the TV media especially cable networks about the BLACK LIVES MATTER and anti police murders and obscene protests. He was shown with a Confederate flag which caused South Carolina and other states to remove Confederate flags. This led to the defiling and destruction of Civil War memorial statues and culminated in the Charlottesville, Virginia confrontation over General Lee's and General Jackson's statues ending in the death of an innocent young girl. The conflict between antifa "anti-fascist' and neo-Nazi groups. The police were ordered to stand down because of the right of freedom of speech. A riot broke out and no-one got to speak. The whole nation and the whole world thanks to CNN saw "Americans" at their worst. The boy was from a suburb of the capital of South Carolina, Eastover. My street in Virginia is Eastover Parkway. Small World?

My 9 year old granddaughter also toured Harper's Ferry and John Brown's courthouse and the spot where he was hanged for treason. Major Thomas Jackson and cadets from the Virginia Military Institute VMI attended the hanging of the notorious abolitionist who wanted all slaves freed in 1859. John Wilkes Booth attended in a stolen VMI uniform. We then walked around the ANTIETAM battlefield, America's bloodied day, and walked across the BURNSIDE bridge. We also took the First Manassas battlefield tour and walked the Second Manassas battlefield. I spoke to the Manassas Park Ranger England and learned his father was a mechanic on the Enola Gay, which dropped the first atomic bomb. Small World. My granddaughter lives on the eastern end of the Chancellorsville battlefield and I drive through it past where General Jackson was seriously wounded driving from my home in the Wilderness battlefield. My granddaughter has visited Marye's wall which held back 7 Union attacks at Fredericksburg, General "sideburns" Burnside great defeat. She has also driven around the large Spostsylvania battlefield, where General SEDGWICK, was killed by a long-range sniper, 2,000 ft.?, the highest ranking Union soldier killed in the War of Secession.

Statue of Freedom

"The STATUE OF FREEDOM, also known as Armed Freedom, is a bronze statue which has crowned the U. S. Capitol building in Washington, District of Columbia since 1863, originally named Freedom Triumphant in War and Peace. The Statue of Freedom is a colossal bronze standing figure 9 1/2 feet (5.9m) tall, weighing approximately 15,000 pounds (6,800 kg). Her crest peaks at 288 feet (88m) above the east front plaza of the U. S. Capitol. The Statue of Freedom is a female, allegorical figure whose right hand holds the hilt of a sheathed sword, while a laurel wreath of victory and the Shield of the United States are clasped in her left hand. Her chilton, an ancient Greek unisex draped shoulder garment, is secured by a brooch inscribed "U.S." and is partially covered by a heavy, Native American-style fringed blanket thrown over her left shoulder. She faces east towards the main entrance of the building and the rising Sun. She wears a military helmet adorned with stars and an eagle's head which is itself crowned by an umbrella-like crest of feathers. Although not called "Columbia", she shares many of her iconic characteristics. Freedom stands atop a cast-iron globe encircled with one of the national mottoes, E PLURIBUS UNUM, OUT OF MANY ONE The lower part of the base is decorated with fasces and wreaths. The fasces were a symbol of ancient Rome which symbolized a magistrate's power and jurisdiction. The U.S. Capitol is America's national center for its 435 House of Representatives and the 100 Senators who represent our 50 states. The Roman fasces was a prehistoric symbol identified with female divinities. Wiki

HOLLYWOOD CONNECTION: In the film GODS AND GENERALS (2001) Virginia Militia Colonel ROBERT E. LEE (ROBERT DUVALL) rides in a horse carriage and behind him the Capitol building is shown without its dome and the Freedom statue in May 1861. The Secretary of War Gen. WINFIELD SCOTT offers Colonel Lee the command of the Union Army. Lee declines his offer claiming his allegiance to his home state of Virginia which was seceding from the Union.
HISTORY FACT: The building of the U.S. Capitol was initiated by Mississippian JEFFERSON DAVIS, a former Secretary of War. He was elected as the president of the 11 secessionist Confederate states. A West Point graduate, Davis modernized the American Army replacing muzzle loading rifles, increased military pay and enlarged the Navy. When 14, Davis attended Transylvania College in Lexington, Kentucky, the oldest college west of the Appalachian Mountains (1790). My dad graduated from Transylvania College in June 1942. I was born in Lexington in May 1943, when my dad was learning "Canadian" radio actually secret radar at the nearby Avon "Bluegrass" Army depot. This is on my original birth certificate as my father's occupation.
"The U.S. Mercury dime (1916-1945) depicts a fasces, symbolizing unity and strength, and an olive branch, signifying peace. The coin also depicted a young Lady Liberty wearing a Phyrgian cap which in early modern Europe became a symbol for freedom and the pursuit of liberty. It became known as the liberty cap because it was worn by emancipated slaves in ancient Rome.
"The coin was replaced after the death of President Franklin D. Roosevelt in April 1945. President Roosevelt, was stricken with polio and needed a wheel chair and braces, had greatly promoted the March of Dimes program to find a cure for polio. There was no need for congressional action and the Treasury chose that denomination to honor the nation's beloved four-time elected president. He had led Americans through the Great Depression and the brutality of World War II. In 1946, after 25 years, Mint Director NELLIE TAYLOE ROSS, said a total of 2,877,232,488 dimes were struck. Polio was eradicated by Dr. JONAS SALK in the 1950s to the relief of everyone [including myself.]" Wikipedia   Watch the movie BREATHE another brave ANDREW GARFIELD role. He and his wife fought his hospital polio confinement in an "iron lung" going home and then a friend devises a mobile system. A very inspirational film.

OXYMORON FACT: The fasces Roman symbol was revived by Italian dictator BENITO MUSSOLINI. The word Fascist which the Nazis also became was derived from this word. Today, the media has coined the word ANTIFA to describe left wing violent protestors of the "right-wing" neo-Nazis, Brownshirts and Klu Klux Klan—KKK. ANTIFA radicals are Marxist-Leninist Communists American media. My 5'9" waist length platinum blonde haired Lutheran mother Elisabeth Frank left Hitler's Germany in January 1935, on a 6 month tourist visa. She was an illegal alien for 5 years until she married my father in August 1940, in his hometown Amityville, Long Island. As a child my mother told me about the Nazis and Communists rioting during the Depression over a lack of jobs in her beautiful hometown Frankfurt am Main. Later, I will write what I saw at Charlottesville, Virginia which ALL THE MEDIA didn't understand. It was all captured on the media. I will explain it through what I saw and heard as a biblical providential parable. HIStory.

Washington's Tallest Buildings

The Height of Buildings Act in Washington was passed by Congress in 1899. The highest object in Washington, everyone is familiar with, the Washington Monument obelisk is 555 ft. (169m), a Masonic symbolic number? The tallest building is the Catholic Basilica of the National Shrine of the Immaculate Conception, 325 ft. (100m). The second tallest building is the Old Post Office Pavilion, now the Trump International hotel, 315 ft. (96m). The third tallest is the Washington National Cathedral, 301 ft. (92m). The fourth highest is the U.S. Capitol, 289 ft. (88m). The sixth tallest is Georgetown University's Healy Hall, 200 ft. (61m). The 27th tallest is the Watergate Hotel and Office building, 157 ft. (48m). This building became infamous because of the "bungled" burglary of the Democratic Party Committee safe.

THE REAL COVERUP: Later, I will tell the untold story of why there was tape on the DNC door shown at the end of THE POST (2017) movie with MERYL STREEP and TOM HANKS. The African-American guard removes the tape which he later finds again on door and calls the DC police. It wasn't FORREST GUMP portrayed by TOM HANKS who in THE POST portrays, the anti President RICHARD NIXON, zealous editor of the WASINGTON POST, BEN BRADLEE. An ironic oxymoron? Actor Tom Hanks received the Best Actor Oscar for Forrest Gump; Best actor nomination for his role in THE Post.

SMALL WORLD STORY: Watergate was where MONICA LEWINSKY lived with her mother within walking distance of the WHITE HOUSE where as a 22 yr. old unpaid intern who worked for President WILLIAM JEFFERSON "Bill" CLINTON. Monica Lewinsky was a close friend of LINDA TRIPP who taped her conversations about her affair with President Clinton which she gave to JONAH GOLDBERG's mother who broadcast it on her radio show. Jonah Goldberg's book LIBERAL FASCISM - The SECRET HISTORY of the AMERICAN LEFT from Mussolini to the POLITICS OF MEANING (2007) is the best book of my 4,000 plus book library, about Fascism/Communism and its influences on America and the world today. An epic History book.

AMERICA'S MORALITY DESTROYED: President Clinton's Oval Office adulterous affair and his other very abusive non consensual affairs became international stories. Today, in June 2018, President Clinton is defending his adultery in interviews saying it cost him $16,000,000. Today, he and Hillary are worth more than $100,000,000. The ME TOO abused women are now not happy with the hypocrite Clinton's who were very close friends with big political donor HARVEY WEINSTEIN, as were many of their liberal Democrat Hollywood friends. Hillary's closest aide HUMA ABEDIN WEINER's husband ANTHONY WEINER is now serving a prison sentence for his online perversion with an underage girl. I was shocked when I heard a FOX news commentator say that President Clinton received support from the most famous "feminists", many of whom were lesbians, who supported the Clinton's because they were PRO-CHOICE "HEALTH CARE" allowing women to terminate their baby's lives of their own "free" will. Abortion was "legalized" by the 1973 ROE VS WADE Supreme Court decision by 7 of 9 elderly male justices. FREEDOM to break three of GOD JEHOVAH/JESUS COMMANDMENTS. YOU SHALL NOT MURDER THE INNOCENT, HONOR YOUR FATHER AND MOTHER. How many innocent babies lives have been terminated because of breaking GOD'S YOU SHALL NOT COMMIT ADULTERY COMMANDMENT? I am not the judge.

Read the Old Testament story of King AHAB and Queen JEZEBEL and Prophet ELIJAH'S destruction of their BAAL idols and priests and the destruction of their evil idolatrous regime. Elijah was taken to Heaven and gave his ministry to ELISHA to restore Israel. I have never heard a sermon about Elisha, the 14 years I attended my Reform Jewish Temple, or the many different denominational sermons? I believe America and Germany and Apostate Europe need to hear a sermon about Elisha restoring Israel through REPENTANCE and REVIVAL.

Who is the judge? All of the Old Testament is the HIS-tory of God's judgment of his chosen people the Jews when they disobeyed His laws given to His prophets. The New Testament is Jesus/Yeshua's fulfillment of the prophecies "

REPAIRING THE REAL BREACH

SHOULD THE PRESIDENT [CLINTON] REPENT?
BREAKPOINT with CHUCK COLSON March 5, 1997

"What is the president up to now? That's the question in Washington media hounds have been asking for the last two weeks, as both President BILL CLINTON and Mrs. Clinton have reached out to America's religious leaders. Even NIGHT-LINE devoted a program to it, during which I was interviewed."

"What the president is up to began when Rev. ROBERT SCHULLER [CHRYSTAL CATHEDRAL church] sent the president a CONGRATULATORY NOTE after the election. Schuller quoted ISAIAH 58:12 — a verse that says, in part "THOU SHALT BE CALLED, THE REPAIRER OF THE BREACH, THE RESTORER OF PATHS TO DWELL IN." [Isaiah preached the supremacy of the God YAHWEY of Israel, Isaiah 52 proclaimed the suffering Messiah, he promoted God's moral demands on worshippers.]

[The scandalous Clinton impeachment destroyed America's morality and the Democrat party. I blame Hillary Clinton and her attacks on her misoginist husband's truthful accusers "standing by her man" but actually was for her later presidential aspirations.]

"Apparently Clinton liked this verse, because he used it in his INAUGURAL ADDRESS. He said that Americans "call on...us...to be repairers of the breach." In the next few weeks, the president made several more references to the need to heal the breach. The Clintons also meet with various religious leaders."

"WHAT'S GOING ON?" the press asked, "The president quoting SCRIPTURE, reaching out to religious leaders. Is this some kind of political ploy?"

[They were shown leaving the FOUNDARY METHODIST church in Washington, D.C. holding hands. I have read during this time this liberal, tolerant church also hosted gay rights services. Two of my closest college friends, I learned years later are gay. I truly believe the good Lord Jesus loves them. One was a pastor for 30 years, the other I met at a 50th college reunion and learned a providential personal story which connects his partner as a classmate to my brother at Husson Business college in Bangor, Maine. They had attended Albany Business college. He was from Saranac Lake, NY. I met him once at their beautiful oceanside home in Bar Harbor. Another Small

World providential story the good Lord has given me. Jesus knows what is in everyone's heart and why.]

"No I don't believe it was a ploy. After all, a president quoting SCRIPTURE is nothing new Presidents BUSH, REAGAN, CARTER — and even NIXON — did it."

"And the president is right to reach out and try to heal America's racial and religious divisions and, particularly as a Christian, to heal the ranks of his own church. But by quoting Isaiah 58, or just saying we want to heal things, the president is missing and essential ingredient. The most famous rebuilder of walls is Nehemiah. But before Nehemiah undertook this task, he prayed that God would forgive him. He repented of his own sins and asked forgiveness for the sins of his fathers."

"President LINCOLN once did exactly the same thing. During the CIVIL WAR, a time when both America and the church were bitterly divided. President Lincoln didn't talk about healing breaches. Instead, he called the nation to repentance. "It behooves us," Lincoln said, "to humble ourselves before [God], to confess our national sins and pray for forgiveness.""

"This is the lesson for President Clinton — that healing America's breaches won't take place unless we repent first. Otherwise, it's cheap grace. And it has to begin on both sides. If the president were to say to the country — and especially to his own Baptist church — that he was wrong to defend partial-birth abortion, and wrong to ignore persecuted Christians in China and Sudan, the reaction in this country would be electric. I personally would rush to him as a Christian brother and offer him love. I suspect that many of us would ask to be forgiven ourselves."

"In fact, wouldn't it be wonderful if all of us set aside some time to repent of our own sins. We evangelicals could repent of our arrogance and triumphalism." Political leaders might repent of condoning practices contrary to God's will."

"If this happened, I suspect that there would be a healing like this country has not seen in this century. Had President Nixon done it, WATERGATE might have been a footnote in history. Presidents, however, don't do these things easily."

"As I told Night Line, yes, President Clinton is right to try to repair the breach. But the answer is not in rhetoric or quoting Bible verses."

"The answer is for each of us to seek forgiveness first from God, then from one another."

Sexual Sin and the Aphrodisiac of Power

Ralph Drollinger founder-president Capitol Ministries May 30, 2019

"Given the nature of the capital community, many people live away from their home environments for extended periods of time. The temptation for sexual sin is ever present—and I have seen too many legislators, staff and lobbyists fall prey to it. Accordingly, here are some key biblical insights related to staying sexually pure in a surreal environment like the U.S. capitol.

INTRODUCTION

"Power is an aphrodisiac that makes those elected to high office much more susceptible to sexual sin than someone who is not in power This is an important Bible study, therefore, for someone in the public eye. The following are some biblical insights that relate to avoiding sexual temptation and sin in this area.

OBEY GOD REGARDING SEXUAL PURITY

"No pragmatic means of avoiding sexual sin will ever supplant this first and primary necessity. One must first come to Faith in Christ and experience the power of the indwelling Holy Spirit to bring their sexual passions under control. Even then it is difficult in a sex-laden culture like

America. Galatians 5:16, however, does provide a promise that the believer can have a victory and control over sinful sexual desire."

"…walk by the Spirit, and you will not carry out the desire of the flesh."…

PROTECT AND NURTURE THE SEXUAL ASPECT OF MARRIAGE

"Since most everyone possesses sexual desire, get married. Marriage is God's intended means to satisfy and fulfill the God-given desire for sexual relations. If one does not have the gift of celibacy (and very few do.) then he should be seeking to get married. That is God's delightful design for most people. Genesis 2:24 states in this regard:

"For this reason a man shall leave his father and his mother, and be joined to his wife, and they shall become one flesh."…

BE SEXUALLY UNSELFISH WITH YOUR SPOUSE

"Once married. one's body becomes the property of his or her spouse. 1 Cor 7:1-5 says:

"Now concerning the things about which you wrote, it is good for a man to touch a woman. But because of immoralities, each man is to have his own wife, and each woman is to have her own husband. The husband must fulfill his duty to his wife, and likewise also the wife to her husband. The wife does not have authority over her own body, but the husband does; and likewise also the husband does not have authority over his own body, but the wife does." …

"Beloved in the capital [D.C.] community, sexual sin can destroy your life, and it will destroy your life if you let it get hold of you."

"You have to discipline yourself to achieve a sexually fulfilling life. As in all things, you have to discipline yourself to do it God's way. My prayer for you."   Ralph Drollinger

GOD Chose the Prophet Jeremiah in the Womb

[How many babies were aborted because of breaking God's Commandment "You shall not commit adultery Women or Men? Every life human and animal begins at conception when the male sperm fertilizes the female egg. Biology 101]

THE CALL OF JEREMIAH Jeremiah 4-5 NIV
"Then the word of the Lord came into me saying,
"Before I formed You in the womb I knew [chose] You, before you
were born. I set you apart; I appointed you as a prophet to the nations."
Jesus has a mission for every believer in him. Have you found yours?

You shall have no other gods before [besides] me 'You shall not make for yourself an idol in the form of anything in Heaven or on the Earth beneath or in the waters below. You shall not bow down to them or worship them for I, the Lord your God, am a jealous God, Punishing the children for the sin of the fathers to the third and fourth generation of those who hate me, but showing love to a thousand generations, of those who love me and keep my commandments."   Exodus 20-3-6 NIV

The ancient CANAANITE/AMMONITE fertility (IDOL) god MOLOCK is found five times in Leviticus 18:21, 20:2, 20:3, 20:4, 20:5. "And he (King of Judah) defiled Topheth/Moloch, which is in the valley of the children of Hinnom, that no man might make his son or daughter the fire to Moloch. 2 Kings 23:10 "And they built the high places of BAAL, which are in the valley of the son of Hinnom, who cause their sons and their daughters to pass through the fire unto Moloch which I commanded them not, neither came it into mind, that they should do this abomination, to cause JUDAH TO SIN" Jeremiah 32:35 "The practice of "passing through the fire" associated with the name Moloch in the citations above also occurs without reference to Moloch in Deuteronomy 18:10-13, 2 Kings 16:3 and 21:6 and Ezekiel 20:26,31 and 23:37."

There is no IDOL of Moloch in existence today but there are depictions either a bull with horns with hands raised high and a "bear faced" creature with hands outstretched to receive the child or baby sacrifice.

A 12th Century French Rabbi SHLOMO YITZCHAKI, commenting on the BOOK OF JEREMIAH Jeremiah 7:31 stated:

Tophet is Moloch, which was made of brass; and they heated him from his
lower parts; and his hands being stretched out, and made hot, they
put the child between his hands, and it was burnt; when it vehemently cried out;
but the priests beat a drum, that the father might not hear the voice of his son,
and the Heart might not be moved."

NOTE: The term "DIED LAUGHING" allegedly originated from this horrendous sacrifice which was also practiced by other ancient pagan civilizations around the world.

The child was not "laughing" but crying in excruciating pain being burned alive.

ABRAHAM took his "first" born fruit of GOD son ISSAC as an offering to YAHWEH on MT. MORIAH in Jerusalem not far from where 1,000 years later Jesus Christ would be crucified on CALVARY another mountain top in Jerusalem, a sacrifice for the sins of all humankind for all who are faithful believers in Jesus Christ. It was God's "test" of elderly Abraham's faith in his GOD YAHWEH. Abraham passed the test and God provided a lamb as his offering. A happy ending for the boy Issac.

Later, the story of ELIJAH and the idol BAAL and its priests. Also, the story of "wise king SOLOMON" and his multitude of wives and concubines and how he and his priests brought his wive's PAGAN IDOLS into the JERUSALEM TEMPLE he built to GOD YWHW/JEHOVAH Creator of the Universe, Man and Jesus. Why? the priests and rabbis didn't want to possibly "offend" the pagan idols and incur their wrath?

The GOLDEN CALF "fertility" idol was forged when MOSES was gone for 40 DAYS on MT. SINAI receiving God's 10 Commandments. The Hebrews who had been protected from Pharaoh and were directly aided by GOD during the 10 plagues in Egypt, PASSOVER protection with the blood of the lamb on door posts, and the crossing of the RED SEA broke God's first commandment. God commanded the Hebrews to stay in the Wilderness desert of northern Arabia for 40 years, the span of a generation, before being allowed to reenter their promised Holy Land Canaan.

"The sacrifices were held in the Valley of the children of HINNOM surrounding Jerusalem's Old City, including MOUNT ZION, from the West and South, it meets and merges with the KIDRON VALLEY, the other principal valley around the Old City, near the southeastern corner of the city. In the New Testament it is called GEHENNA, in rabbinic literature it is a destination for the wicked. The biblical names SHOEL/HADES is called the abode of the dead, which the King James Version of the Bible translated into the Anglo-Saxon word HELL. This one FOUR LETTER WORD has become ANATHEMA in the English language and has caused many "good" people not to read the multitude of biblical truths of the Old and New Testaments. It is HIStory.

THE KORAN refers to HELL FIRE'S for evildoers hundreds of times. All major religions especially MONOTHEISTIC believe in a god who determines a final judgment for HUMANKIND who are all created in his image.

How the March for Life Highlights the Value of Women's Voices

THE DAILY SIGNAL Abigail Mereno-Riano January 23, 2020

"Actress Michelle Williams' Golden Globe Awards was something that confirmed my desire to have an abortion was the reason for her success both saddened and shocked me into thinking of my own dreams and designs for the future."

"I'm very passionate about the dignity of women, and for that reason, all forms of sexual exploitation—whether it be pornography, prostitution, or sex trafficking—anger me, because they shatter a woman's perception of herself."

"My desire to see all woman treated with respect and dignity is what has caused me to want to dedicate my life to freeing women from exploitive situations. But as a young person, I recognize that I can never expect to see the end of sexual exploitation in my lifetime until the idea of aborting a living, vulnerable human being is not first made inconceivable."

"For that reason, I couldn't agree more with the theme of this year's March for Life: "LIFE EMPOWERS: PRO-LIFE IS PRO-WOMAN.""

"The pro-life movement is pro-women. It rightly advocates for a woman's personal dignity by fighting for her unborn child to be seen as a person, not as an object. When women are encouraged to see their own sense of worth and dignity—one that extends past the usefulness of their bodies—they are empowered to see their unborn children in the same way."

"Though I have been passionate about the dignity of women and children for a while, this is the first year I will attend the March for Life. In understanding the gravity of this fight for the unborn and women alike, I have never seen it as more crucial for young women and future leaders to attend."

"Ironically, actress Michelle Williams' Golden Globe Award speech was something that confirmed my desire to attend this year. Her statement that the freedom to have an abortion was the reason for her success both saddened and shocked me into thinking of my own dreams and desires for the future."

"As a young woman, I recognize there are many challenges to having children and a career. To say women do not have to sacrifice anything to be mothers is false."

"But as former model Leah Darrow encouraged women everywhere: "Babies don't keep us from dreams." She reminded women, me included, that babies won't keep us from professional growth, but will "make [us] better because of it.""

"The speakers for the March for Life this year include Louisiana state Sen. Katrina Jackson; abortion survivors Claire Culwell and Melissa Ohden; Elisa Martinez, executive director of the New Mexico ALLIANCE FOR LIFE; and Marjorie Dannenfelser, president of the SUSAN B. ANTHONY LIST. All are women who have used their diverse platforms to represent the voiceless."

"As a young woman, I look up to these leaders who have ignored party lines for the worthy cause of life."

"This year, I'm compelled to go to the March of Life because it is also the CENTENNIAL [100th] anniversary of the 19th Amendment, granting women the right to Vote."

"It's a monumental year to remember that we are not marching without influence, not without the ability to truly change the culture. Those who fought for a woman's right to vote, fought for women to use voices not to shout-but to speak for those without a voice.

"The industries of sexual exploitation survive by camouflaging exploitation as "FREEDOM," indoctrinating women to believe that their body makes them valuable, and therefore, that it is "empowering" to have an abortion."

"Through these industries, women are deprived of their sense of hope, worth, and identity—aspects that make us human—and see themselves as objects instead.

"The cycle of degrading womanhood through sexual exploitation does not end at the woman's body. It continues to the living child within her. And I realize that the fight for the honor and worth of women starts at the womb."

"It starts with our privilege, strength, and ability to bring life into the world. It starts with fighting for the respect and consideration of unborn children, not because of their ability to be useful but because they are human beings, already filled with the ability to dream and hope for the future." Abigail is a student at REGENT University

PERSONAL STORY: Michelle Williams has two daughters and is pregnant with a baby. Her partner Australian actor HEATH LEDGER passed from medication for jet lag.

Trump Becomes the First President To Attend March For Life: "EVERY PERSON IS WORTH PROTECTING"

THE DAILY CALLER Amber Athey—White House Correspondent Jan. 24, 2020

"President DONALD TRUMP became the first U.S. President to attend the annual March For Life, telling the crowd that he believes "Every person is worth protecting."

"Hundreds of thousands of people gather every year in Washington, D.C. for the march in opposition to abortion. Vice President MIKE PENCE has attended the march in the past and Trump has addressed the rally goers in video messages, but this is the first year that the President attended in person."

"It is my profound honor to be the first president to attend the March for Life!" Trump told the crowd. "We're here for a very simple reason — to defend the right of every chid, born and unborn. "Every. Life brings love into the world," Trump said. "every person is worth protecting."

"Trump knocked several Democrats during his speech for their pro-abortion comments, particularly Virginia Governor RALPH NORTHAM, who suggested that mothers and doctors should be allowed to kill children after they are born!"

FORGOTTEN HISTORICAL FACT: Northam is a licensed doctor. Coincidentally, the next day a photo from Northam's college year book was televised showing him in black-face and another student wearing a racist KKK Klansman's white hood. Northam confessed in a TV report he was in the photo. However, the next day he recanted being in the photo because you couldn't identify him. His nickname was "COON MAN" which is an anti-Negro racist slur and would have been in black-face. Immediately, a women alleged that Virginia's part-time Lt. Governor FAIRFAX had raped her at a previous President OBAMA Convention in Boston. Another women then made a rape complaint against Fairfax. Complete silence on these cases even in the ME TOO era where women are revealing abuse by powerful political and Hollywood personalities. Some have been fired and some have female lawyers. Furthermore, then Virginia's Attorney General MARK HERRING "admitted" having a black-face incident? These are all elected Democrat representatives in the great Constitutional Commonwealth of Virginia. The Founding Father's would be appalled as Republicans, Independents, and some Democrats justly are appalled. Nothing has been done There is a maxim: "Politics makes strange bedfellows." Republicans resign when they commit transgressions like this because "A public office is a public trust." Providential justice? These three men should have resigned and then the Republican leader of the Virginia House of Representatives ALEX COX would have been sworn in as temporary governor. Remarkably his election was so close Governor Northam had to toss a coin to decide the winner, 50—50 a providential act.

SMALL WORLD PERSONAL STORY: A lady friend in my church told me her son lives and works in Barcelona Spain for 12 years. Mrs. NORTHAM said she was waiting for her airliner flight and had her name on her baggage. She said several women approached her and asked: "Are you related to the "baby killing governor of Virginia?" She retorted, "I am not related to him." The Spanish people are Catholic and are devoutly against abortion and taking a baby's life after birth is INFANTICIDE—MOLOCH idol in Old Testament. The killing of an innocent newborn baby was completely forgotten trumped by racism and rape. All religions believe in an almighty's judgment for unethical acts. Apparently, self righteous elected elitists think they can rape and murder in this lifetime? KURT VONNEGUT would write: "SO IT GOES."

"If a mother is in labor, I can tell you exactly what would happen. The infant would be delivered The infant would be kept comfortable. The infant would be resuscitated if that's what the mother and the family desired, and then a discussion would ensue between the physicians and the mother," Northam said during an interview last year."

"Trump has implemented several pro-life policies since taking office, including declaring that taxpayer funds can no longer be used for abortion referrals under Title X. Planned Parenthood opted out of Title X program funding rather than stop referring women for abortions. "We will not be bullied into withholding abortion information from our patients," acting Planned Parenthood President Alexis McGill Johnson said at the time."

"The president also noted during his speech that he nominated two conservative justices in the Supreme Court: NEIL GORSUCH and BRETT KAVANAUGH."

"Trump received cheers and applause after he completed his speech."

ALLAH'S CREATION OF ADAM REVEALED IN THE KORAN

THE HEIGHTS—"IN THE NAME OF ALLAH, THE COMPASSIONATE, THE MERCIFUL
          WE CREATED YOU and gave you form. Then WE said to the angels:
          "prostrate yourselves before ADAM, " They all prostrated themselves
          except SATAN [LUCIFER], who refused.
          "Why did you not prostrate yourself?" ALLAH asked.
          "I am nobler than ADAM," he [LUCIFER] replied. "You CREATED ME
          of FIRE and HIM OF CLAY,"
          He [ALLAH] said: "Begone from PARADISE! This is NO PLACE
          FOR YOUR CONTEMPTUOUS PRIDE Away with you! Henceforth
          you shall be HUMBLE."
          Satan replied: "REPRIEVE me till the DAY OF RESURRECTION."
          "You are REPRIEVED," said HE [ALLAH].
          "Because You have led me into SIN," Satan said, "I will waylay [deceive]
          your servants as they walk on Your straight path, and spring upon them
          from the front and from the rear, from their right and from their left.
          Then you [ALLAH] shall find the greater part of them ungrateful."
          [APOSTATE—leaving the faith written in the KORAN]
          "Be gone!" said ALLAH, "A despicable outcast you shall henceforth be.
          With those who follow you I fill the pit of Hell."
          "To Adam He [ALLAH] said: "Dwell with your wife in Paradise, eat of
          any fruit you please; but never approach this tree or you both
          will become transgressors." [beyond the moral principals of the KORAN.]
          "But SATAN TEMPTED THEM, so that he might reveal to them their
          nakedness, which they had never seen before. He [Satan] said:

"Your Lord [ALLAH] has forbidden you to approach this tree
only to prevent you [Adam and wife] from becoming angels or immortals."
[A New Age heresy] Then he Satan/Iblis swore to them that he would
give them friendly counsel."
"Thus he [Satan] cunningly seduced them. And when they had eaten of
the tree, their shame became visible to them, and they both covered
themselves with the leaves of the garden."
"Their Lord {ALLAH] called out to them, saying: "Did I [ALLAH] not
Forbid you to approach that tree, and did I [ALLAH] not
warn you that Satan [Lucifer] was your sworn enemy?"
"They [Adam and wife] replied: "Lord, [ALLAH] we have wronged our
souls. Pardon us and have mercy on us, or we shall surely be
Among the lost."
"He [ALLAH} said: "Go hence, and may your descendants be enemies
to each other. The earth will for a while provide your sustenance
and dwelling place. There you shall live and there you
shall die, and thence you shall be raised to life."
"Children of Adam! Let Satan not deceive you, as he deceived your
parents out of Paradise."
"We have made the devils guardians over unbelievers."

HISTORICAL NOTE: This story of Humankind's creation is similar to GENESIS.
However, I find this revelation of Satan disobeying GOD YAHWEH "ALLAH" explaining the
premise of my Testimony/Witness I have written.

This creation of Adam accounts begins with the word WE. The Islamic faith proclaimed in the
QU'RAN/KORAN is monotheistic like JUDAISM and only revers a single GOD [ALLAH].
CHRISTIANITY IS TRIUNE/TRINITARIAN—GOD THE FATHER—GOD THE SON—GOD THE
HOLY SPIRIT revealed in the ATHANASIAN CREED.
The use of the plural WE is called the ROYAL MAJESTY WE not the TRINITY.

Biblically GOD personally judged in the Old Testament. The FLOOD and Noah's Ark. The TOWER
OF BABEL in UR today's IRAQ when GOD stopped the prideful construction of the Babel tower
by creating many languages "babble" and dispersed the population throughout the world. The
destruction of SODOM AND GOMORRAH for their great sins which LOT pleaded for God's mercy.
Lot even amazingly offered his virgin daughter's to the debauched SODOMITES. They rejected
Lot's offer and demanded he give them the guest he housed. God's angel told Lot to leave with
his family the only righteous people. Lot was told to tell his family not to look back on their former
home or they would die. Why did Lot's wife disobey and look back? and turn into a pillar of "salt"
and die. Her stone image is still visible. Lot's wife didn't want to leave her treasurers. Jesus said
in the Last Days all Christians should be ready to be with Him and your loved ones quickly without
any warning.

Then the last major intervention by GOD was when Moses was on Mt. SINAI receiving the TEN
COMMANDMENTS. The HEBREWS who GOD had just freed from 400 years of slavery in Egypt
had made a GOLDEN CALF idol breaking HIS FIRST COMMANDMENT worship no other gods
and HIS SECOND COMMANDMENT not to make a GRAVEN IMAGE. The Hebrews are ordered

411

to stay in the Wilderness desert of Arabia for 40 years until the unfaithful generation died. Why a bull idol? It was the Egyptian god of fertility. This was a worldwide pagan belief. In Canaan the Canaanites actually sacrificed baby's to the deity MOLOCH. Since 1973, American women have "legally" sacrificed 62,000,000 babies—calling it health care. God doesn't divinely intervene any longer? "Life begins at conception!" JOHN MCCAIN in OBAMA DEBATE.

African American Candace Owens says 19,000,000 abortions were black babies.

NAZIS GERMANY FORBIDS ARYAN ABORTIONS

"Nazi Germany's eugenics laws severely restricted abortion for ARYAN women. Abortion was only permitted if the fetus was deformed or disabled. During World War II, anti-abortion laws were increased again, and it became a capital offense. [I have read beheading by guillotine.] Non-Aryan women meanwhile were often "encouraged" to utilize contraception and abortion in order to reduce their populations." Wikipedia

"When Germany became a country in 1871, section 218 of the Constitution OUTLAWED ABORTION, required a penal term for both the woman and doctor involved. During the WEIMAR REPUBLIC , such discussion led to a discussion led to a reduction in the maximum penalty for abortion, and in 1926 a court's decision legalized abortion in cases of grave danger to the life of the mother."

[During Adolf Hitler's THIRD REICH —January 1933-May 1945—"Aryan" blond and other German women were rewarded with being mothers and having as many children as possible. They received government aid to care for their children. In America we have through government "poverty" welfare programs which help children and support birth control and abortion. It is well know that government programs have allowed families to break up in minority communities. KANYE WEST has just been outspoken about this in October 2019, greatly angering liberal white and African-American politicians who have spent trillions of taxpayer dollars and gained political reelection. TERM LIMITS. Kanye West, a billionaire black rapper, calls for people of his race to think for themselves and help themselves in today's historic booming economy. President Trump has helped by removing restrictive government regulations and lowering Capital Gains taxation stimulating business and cutting individual taxes giving Americans more money. Vice President JOE BIDEN helped reelect himself and Pres. BARACK OBAMA by repeating "We killed OSAMA BIN LADEN and SAVED GENERAL MOTORS." The American government gave GM taxpayer money paid back? I have owned GM cars Oldsmobile, Pontiac, Saturn now gone. Not everyone owns a General Motors car. VP BIDEN also gave a campaign speech to African-Americans falsely telling them "They [Republicans] want to PUT YOU BACK IN CHAINS!" Isn't that RACIST?

Ironically or providentially he spoke these racist words in DANVILLE, Virginia. In April 1865, the capital of the CONFEDERACY was moved there from Richmond, Virginia, for a week. HISTORY: Republican ABRAHAM LINCOLN FREED THE SLAVES. I have lived in Virginia with my family since July 4, 1977, in Garrisonville, Stafford County, 40 miles south of Washington, DC. I have lived in the WILDERNESS battlefield since April 2005, and am still learning about America's worst

CIVIL WAR, WAR OF SECESSION, WAR OF NORTHERN AGGRESSION. South Carolina started it at Fort SUMTER.

"VIRGINIA GOVERNOR NORTON ALLOWS ABORTION AFTER BIRTH"

HIPPOCRATIC OATH

"The HIPPOCRATIC OATH is an oath of ethics historically taken by physicians. It is one of the most widely known of Greek medical texts. In its original form, it requires a new physician to swear, by a number of HEALING GODS, to UPHOLD SPECIFIC ETHICAL STANDARDS. The oath is the earliest expression of medical ethics in the Western world, establishing several principles of medical ethics which remain of paramount significance today.These include the principles of medical confidentiality and non-maleficence. As the seminal articulation of certain principals that continue to guide and inform medical practice, the ancient text is of more than historic and symbolic value. Swearing a modified form of the oath remains a rite of passage for medical graduates in many countries"   Wikipedia

"The original oath was written in Ionic Greek, between the 5th and 3rd centuries BC. The Greek doctor HIPPOCRATES name is connected to the medical oath though scholars allege he didn't write the oath."

THE HIPPOCRATIC OATH:

> I swear by Apollo Physician, by Asclepius, by Hygieia, by Panacea,
> and by all the gods and goddesses, making them my witnesses,
> that I will carry out, according to my ability and judgment, this oath
> and this indenture,
> To hold my teacher in the art equal to my own parents; to make him
> partner in my livelihood; when he is in need of money to share mine
> with him; to consider his family as my own brothers, and to teach
> them this art, if they want to learn it, without fee or indenture; to
> impart precept, oral instruction, and all other instruction to my own
> sons, the sons of my teacher, and to indentured pupils who have
> taken the physicians oath, but to nobody else.
> I will use treatment to help the sick according to my ability and
> judgment, but never with a view to injury and wrong-doing. Neither
> will I administer a poison to anybody when asked to do so, nor
> will I suggest such a course. Similarly I will not give to a woman
> a pessary TO CAUSE ABORTION. But I will keep pure and holy
> both my life and my art. I will not use the knife not even, verily,
> on suffers from stone, but I will give place to such as are
> craftsmen therein.
> Into whatsoever houses I enter, I will help the sick, and I will
> abstain from all intentional wrong-doing and harm, especially
> from abusing the bodies of man or women, bond or free. And
> whatsoever I shall see or hear in the course of my profession,
> as well as outside my profession in my intercourse with men,
> if it be what should not be published abroad. I will never divulge,
> holding such things to be holy secrets.
> Now if I carryout his oath, and break it not, may I gain for ever

413

reputation among all men for my life and for my art; but if I break
it and forswear myself, may the opposite befall me. Translation WHS Jones

TERRI SCHIAVO LIFE SUPPORT CASE IN CONGRESS

"THERESA SCHINDLER SCHIAVO was a woman in an irreversible vegetative state. Terri apparently had a heart attack and fell. "On March 20, 2005, the U.S. Senate, by unanimous consent, passed their version of a relief bill; since the vote was taken by voice vote, there was no official tally of those voting in favor and those opposed. Soon after Senate approval the House of Representatives passed and identical version of the bill S.686, which came to be called the "Palm Sunday Compromise" and transferred jurisdiction of the Schiavo case to federal courts. President George W. Bush flew from Texas to sign the bill at 1:15 a.m." Terri's life support was removed Mar. 21, 2005."
PERSONAL CONNECTION: An employee in my company HQ dated her husband.

PERSONAL STORY: I attended a Wednesday night Bible study in Richmond at the African-American MT. OLIVE BAPTIST church. That evening in the parking lot I asked female Deacon Meadows a question. Why did Lot's wife, against God's orders, look back? Without hesitating she retorted, "She didn't want to LEAVE HER STUFF!" I never heard that preached when I was Jewish or Christian. I told this story to my Baptist Bible study teacher. He said, "The Bible says Lot had many worldly goods." Jesus said, "Keep your oil ready and have your wicks trimmed because you won't know the hour of MY return be ready." Every human on Earth can AGREE to ONE THING. YOU CAN'T TAKE YOUR STUFF WITH YOU when you pass from your earthly life. "Your heart is where your treasures are."
HISTORICAL NOTE: The Egyptian Pharaohs who thought they were gods did have a lot of stuff in the Pyramids for their afterlife. Mummies are dead Hollywood? Like films.
GOD'S NEW JUDGES: When the Israelites always didn't listen to HIS prophets Jehovah allowed their evil enemies to judge them. The evil Assyrians, the Greek Antiochus who defiled the Temple with unclean pig blood, then the even more evil Babylonian King Nebuchadnezzar whose army destroyed the Jerusalem Temple and the Romans who destroyed the second Jerusalem Temple on the same Jewish lunar calendar day the 9th of AV! This was a HIStory day of Providence not a coincidence.
SEPTEMBER 11, 2001 AMERICA'S DAY OF JUDGMENT? The almost 3,000 people who died that day were innocent victims of 29 fanatic jihadist muslims who martyred themselves. Rev. JERRY FALWELL called this most evil day in America's history as GOD'S JUDGMENT. He was actually referring to the Biblical HIStory I have just cited. Off course, his Biblical connection drew huge criticism from the liberal secular humanist media and Hollywood couldn't understand that our JUDEO-CHRISTIAN GOD JESUS OF LOVE could let something so evil happen to America. It was immediately known that the evil was perpetrated by one "evil" Muslim OSAMA BIN LADEN whose agents had just bombed two American embassies in Africa and the destroyer USS COLE damaged by a suicide boat bomb in Yemen. This happened during President GEORGE W. BUSH's term which started slowly because of the long Florida election recount with ALBERT GORE which was decided by one Supreme Court vote. The closest election America will ever have. President Bush led the fight to defeat this known enemy. Our intelligence agencies knew all this information but because it didn't connect some basic information partially because the CIA and the Federal Bureau of Investigation FBI weren't "legally" allowed to coordinate their secret data. The BOLAND AMENDMENT.

WHO WAS REALLY THE BLAME? VANITY FAIR magazine wrote an article alleging that HILLARY CLINTON, "co-president", was told by her husband President BILL CLINTON that Sudan, with no American embassy, wanted to give us the known terrorist OSAMA BIN LADEN who was living in the Sudan. HILLARY CLINTON allegedly retorted, "Bill we can't deal with the Sudanese government because of their harsh women's rights laws." Was that true? The Sudanese government uses strict Sharia Islamic law and has persecuted killing thousands of non Muslims for years. Bin Laden then was given sanctuary in Afghanistan under strict Sharia TALIBAN LAW. It was found that he had terrorist training camps there. President Clinton then had the U.S. Navy fire cruise missiles at the training camps in Afghanistan which had been abandoned. The Arab media had headlines MONICA'S MISSILES. A "chemical weapons" factory in Khartoum, Sudan was also hit with cruise missiles. It was a pharmaceutical pill factory?

IRONICALLY or PROPHETICALLY Israeli newspapers at the same time were headlining Monica Lewinsky as being like a modern-day QUEEN ESTHER to the Jewish people and nation of Israel. An OXYMORON? President CLINTON even during the long impeachment investigation was trying to do what President JIMMY CARTER did unsuccessfully, bring "peace" to Israel "two states" Palestine. He didn't.

Queen Esther's story in the Bible is one of the Old Testament's most providential stories. Esther even though made queen she had to discreetly through her faith in Jehovah save her Jewish people from annihilation from the hateful HAMAN, the Persian king's adviser, a former Canaanite, who convinced the king to kill the Jews living in PERSIA (IRAN in 1935) as traitors. Queen Esther prevents this and the feast of Purim celebrates this HIStoric salvation of the Persian Jewish people. Read my ESTHER story celebration of PURIM beginning on the day Reverend BILLY GRAHAM passed on February 21, 2018. Providence.

HISTORICAL FACT: Some Jewish people on Purim eat a cake called a HAMAN TASCHEN, which is literally eating the Biblical Jewish persecutor Haman who the Persian king hanged instead of MORDECAI. Do you think this is EVIL? Have you eaten a French croissant? It is crescent shaped, baked to commemorate the defeat of the Muslim army, after its defeat at the BATTLE OF TOURS in 732 AD in France. The symbol of Islam is the CRESCENT MOON. Charles MARTEL, a FRANK defeated Islam.

I believe this was submitted to the American public for the first time after DONALD J. TRUMP requested it as proof President OBAMA was born in America and was an American citizen. Barack Obama was elected president in November 2008, 30 months earlier. I would like to see the birth certificates before and after Obama's. A tabloid had a story that the registrar lady who submitted President Obama's "original" Hawaiian birth certificate died in a small aircraft accident soon after submitting the birth certificate. At the first Washington, DC TEA PARTY a TV reporter cameraman was interviewing a person about the controversy about President Obama's birth certificate. I then told the man how I received a copy, not original, of my Kentucky certificate of LIVE BIRTH. It is a clerical copy retrieved from the Frankfort state capital archives in August 2005. Everything looked correct except the clerk typed my first name as CLINE not CLIVE. Not a typo? I needed my birth certificate to apply for my Social Security retirement benefit monthly payment. I showed the Social Security lady my photo driver's license, IRS 1040 copy and a payroll check stub. I later found my original birth certificate and learned some very interesting personal information.

A birth certificate can be obtained quickly and is needed to obtain a PASSPORT. When "Barry" Obama was a student at Columbia University I "heard" he claimed to be a Kenyan "fraud"? Barry had a Pakistani friend he allegedly took a trip to Pakistan with him. I wonder what happened to his Passport? I still have my Passport I had issued at the Luxembourg Embassy when stationed at Bitburg AB, Germany in 1967. I didn't have my birth certificate but was an American airmen and had a military ID card. I have a 1973 Passport used to go to Europe for a month, and Passport to go with my daughter to Germany, Luxembourg, Holland, Switzerland and France for two weeks in June 1998. I also have an ID card Passport to go to Quebec, Canada with my family in July 2016.

I am a biblical HIStorical journalist who believes the TRINITARIAN GOD THE CREATOR OF THE UNIVERSE as MARTIN LUTHER wrote ERASMUS in 1525 that JESUS is in complete control of HIStory. Read my amazing Luther account of this. Luther revealed that HIStory is truly PREDESTINED by GOD JESUS. We all have FREE WILL but SATAN through many self righteous, prideful people of power in politics, media, Hollywood, business and religion and the church are being mislead by liberal secular humanist, progressive ideas which are promoted as being tolerant and inclusive of everyone. Everyone does not include the Judeo-Christian morality which is considered INTOLERANT of today's modern man's lifestyle new mores immorality.

HISTORICALLY ISRAEL'S JUDGE has been its Middle Eastern enemies. Today, America is being judged by these same countries who are today Islamic muslims. America and Israel are closer than any two nations in HIStory because of America's Judeo-Christian biblical beliefs. President Trump has finally put the American embassy in JERUSALEM which only Guatemala and Paraguay agree with? AMERICA AND ISRAEL are the only nations in the world which have populations with the some 160 nations of the United Nations within their borders. Israel's Jewish population was through the DIASPORA sent in slavery throughout the Roman Empire and further through pogroms persecution. America was created with refugees from the whole world seeking religious freedom or seeking economic or political freedom. Prophet Jeremiah spoke of the people of Israel becoming a worldwide people. Christianity which actually is Judeo-Christian has brought the Old Testament and New Testament Good News GOSPEL not only to America but through GREAT COMMISSION ministries to all the world even to persecuted underground churches.

IS ISLAM AND THE KORAN TODAY AMERICA'S JUDGE? Mohammad's third monotheistic religion is based on some of the Old Testament prophets and even accepts JESUS as a prophet born to an actual virgin mother. The Koran's Sharia laws require stoning an adulteress what about a male adulterer? Homosexual males are also stoned but pedophilia sodomy rape is accepted as an act of dominance bullying. This was revealed in the films LAWRENCE OF ARABIA, he was gay, MIDNIGHT EXPRESS and THE KITE FLYER. Women are completely subservient to their husband. A thief's hand can be cut off. These extreme acts are actually practiced by the Iranian theocracy and Taliban controlled areas of Afghanistan. In the film 12 STRONG, about the brave GREEN BERET horse soldiers in Afghanistan, there is a scene where a Taliban man asks pre teen girls to do math and recite from a secular book which they do well. He then says this is against Mohammad's teachings in the Koran and shoots their mother in the head. When I worked at the Pep Boys parts counter I had a bearded customer Alex who owned a high quality used car lot nearby. After 9-11, I asked Alex where he was from. He said Afghanistan. When I visited his car lot he told me how after his father passed in Afghanistan he as a teenage child managed his father's printing business. The Taliban appropriated his business and he said he was actually tortured by them. He showed me cigarette burn scars on his arm. I was stunned. Alex plays an ancient 12 string guitar like Buback giving extended hour long recitals at homes for the aged. It is like therapy. Alex is a holy Muslim.

Muslims think the TRINITY is heretical because they cannot conceive of God allowing HIMSELF TO DIE, to die for humanities sins. They believe Muslims can only enter PARADISE by following Mohammad's SIX PILLARS of faith. The ATHANASIAN CREED was written to explain the Trinity Godhead of Jesus Christ. It was written during the Nicean Council in Turkey in 325 A.D. to explain how Jesus wasn't just a human prophet.

The Statue of Liberty (Liberty Enlightening the World)

"The Statue of Liberty, La Liberte eclairant le monde, is a colossal neoclassical sculpture on Liberty Island in New York Harbor in New York City. The copper statue, a gift from the people of France to the people of the United States, was designed by French sculptor FREDERIC AUGUSTE BARTHOLDI and built by GUSTAVE EIFEL, who designed and built the 999 ft (333m) Eiffel Tower in Paris. The statue was dedicated on October 28, 1886. The Statue of Liberty is a figure of a robed woman representing Libertas, a Roman liberty goddess - also incorporating some elements of another roman deity, SOL INVICTUS. She holds a torch above her head with her right hand, and in her left hand carries a tabula ansata inscribed in Roman numerals with "July IV MDCCLXXVI" (July 4, 1776), the date of the DECLARATION OF INDEPENDENCE. A broken chain lies at her feet. The statue became an icon of freedom and the United States, was a welcoming sight to immigrants arriving from abroad."   Wikipedia

My mother sailed into New York harbor in January 1935, on a 6 month tourist visa. My 19 year old 5'9" waist length platinum blonde haired, blue eyed Lutheran mother Elisabeth Francois Frank was an illegal alien for 5 years until she married my father in his hometown Amityville, Long Island in August 1940. When I was a child my mother told me she cried when she entered New York harbor and saw the Statue of Liberty. She must have known she was not going back to her beloved fatherland Germany whose culture she loved. It was more than 10 years before her devastated homeland was free from Hitler and his Nazis evil.

"According to the National Park Service, the idea for the Statue of Liberty was first proposed by EDOUARD RENE de LABOULAYE the president of the French Anti-Slavery Society and a prominent and important political thinker of this time. The project is traced to a mid-1865 conversation between de Laboulaye, a staunch abolitionist and FREDERIC BARTHOLDI, a sculptor. In after-dinner conversation at his home near Versailles, Laboulaye, an ardent supporter of the Union in the American Civil War, is supposed to have said: "If a monument should rise in the United States, as a memorial to their independence. I should think it only natural if it were built by united effort—a common work of both our nations." The national Park Service suggested that abolition of slavery and the Union's victory in the Civil War in 1865. Laboulaye's wishes of freedom and democracy were turning into a reality in the United States. In order to honor these achievement of the United States, the French people would be inspired to call for their own democracy in the face of a repressive monarchy."

"According to sculptor Frederic Bartholdi, who later recounted the story, Laboulaye's comment was not intended as a proposal, but it inspired Bartholdi. Given the repressive nature of NAPOLEON III."

"Any large project was further delayed by the FRANCO-PRUSSIAN WAR, in which Bartholdi served as a major of militia. In the war Napoleon III was captured and deposed. Bartholdi's home province of ALSACE was lost to the Prussians, and a more liberal Republic was installed in France."

"In June 1871, Bartholdi crossed the Atlantic, with letters of introduction signed by Laboulaye. Arriving at New York Harbor, Bartholdi focused on Bedloe's Island (now named Liberty Island) as a site for the statue, struck by the fact that vessels arriving in New York had to sail past it. He was delighted to learn that the island was owned by the U. S. government."   Wikipedia

THE NEW COLOSSUS SONNET BY EMMA LAZARUS

"THE NEW COLOSSUS" is a sonnet by American poet EMMA LAZARUS (1849-1887) She wrote the poem in 1883 to raise money for the construction of a pedestal for the STATUE OF LIBERTY

(Liberty Enlightening the World). In 1903, the poem was cast onto a bronze plaque and mounted inside the pedestal's lower level."

"This poem was written as a donation to an auction of art and literary works conducted by the "Art Loan Fund Exhibition in Aid of the BARTHOLDI Pedestal Fund for the STATUE OF LIBERTY" to raise money for the pedestal's construction. Lazarus's contribution was solicited by fundraiser William Evarts. Initially she refused but writer Constance Harrison convinced her that the statue would be of great significance to immigrants sailing into the harbor.

"The New Colossus" was the first entry read at the exhibit's opening on Nov. 2,1883. It remained associated with the exhibit through a published catalog until the exhibit closed after the pedestal was fully funded in August 1885, but was forgotten and played no role at the opening of the statue in 1886. It was, however, published in JOSEPH PULITZER'S NEW YORK WORLD as well as THE NEW YORK TIMES during this time period. In 1901, Lazarus's friend Georgina Schuyler began an effort to memorialize Lazarus and her poem, which succeeded in 1903 when a plaque bearing the text of the poem was put on the inner wall of the pedestal of the Statue of Liberty."

"The original manuscript is held by the American Jewish Historical Society."

TEXT OF THE POEM:

"Not like the brazen giant of Greek fame,
With conquering limbs astride from land to land;
Here at our sea-washed, sunset gates shall stand
A mighty woman with a torch, whose flame
Is the imprisoned lightening, and her name
Mother of Exiles, From her beacon-hand
Glows world-wide welcome; her mild eyes command
The air-bridged harbor that twin cities frame.
"Keep, ancient lands, your storied pomp!" Cries she
With silent lips, "Give me your tired, your poor, your huddled
Masses yearning to breathe free, the wretched refuse of your
Teeming shore. Send these, the homeless, tempest tost to me,
I lift my lamp beside the golden door!"

INTERPRETATION

"The title of the poem and the first two lines reference the Greek COLOSSUS OF RHODES, one of the SEVEN WONDERS OF THE ANCIENT WORLD, a famously gigantic sculpture that stood beside or stranded across the entrance to the harbor of the island of RHODES in the 3rd century BC. In the poem, Lazarus contrasts that ancient symbol of grandeur and empire ("the brazen giant of Greek fame") with a "NEW" COLOSSUS—THE STATUE OF LIBERTY, a female embodiment of commanding "MATERNAL STRENGTH" ("MOTHER OF EXILES").

"The "sea-washed, sunset gates" are the mouths of the HUDSON and EAST RIVERS, to the west of Brooklyn. The "imprisoned lightning" refers to the electric light in the torch, then a novelty."

"The "air-bridged harbor that twin cities frame" refers to NEW YORK HARBOR between New York City and Brooklyn, which were separate cities at the time the poem was written, before being consolidated as boroughs of the City of Greater New York in 1898."

"The "huddled masses" refers to the large numbers of immigrants arriving in the United States in the 1880s. Lazarus was an activist and advocate for Jewish refugees fleeing persecution in Czarist Russia." [These were Russian Jews during the Czar's pogrom.]

INFLUENCE—IMMIGRATION TO THE UNITED STATES

"Paul Auster wrote that "BARTHOLDI'S gigantic was originally intended as a monument to the principles of international REPUBLICANISM, but 'The New Colossus' reinvented the statue's purpose, TURNING LIBERTY into a WELCOMING MOTHER, A SYMBOL OF HOPE to the outcasts and downtrodden of the world." [This is the theme of FIDDLER ON THE ROOF, Broadway and film, I had seen both before I became Jewish. This is the theme of the movie YENTL, a favorite BARBRA STREISAND film.]

"John T. Cunningham wrote that "The Statue of Liberty was not conceived and sculpted as a symbol of immigration, but it quickly became so as immigrant ships passed under the torch and the shining face, heading toward ELLIS ISLAND. However, it was [Lazarus's poem] that permanently stamped on Miss Liberty the role of unofficial greeter of incoming immigrants."

"The poem has entered the political realm. It was quoted in JOHN F. KENNEDY'S book A NATION OF IMMIGRANTS (1958) as well as a 2010 political speech by PRESIDENT OBAMA advocating immigration policy reform." Wikipedia

"On August 12, 2019, KEN CUCCINELLI, acting director of US Citizenship and Immigration Services, revised a line from the poem to defend an immigration policy that penalizes immigrants who apply for public assistance, stating: "Give me your tired, your poor who can stand on their own two feet and who will not become a public charge."

IN CULTURE

"Classical composer David Ludwig set the poem to music, which was performed at the worship service of President Obama's 2013 inauguration ceremony."

"Parts of the poem also appear in popular culture. The Broadway musical MISS LIBERTY, with music and lyrics by IRVING BERLIN, an immigrant himself, used the final stanza beginning "Give me your tired, your poor" as the basis for the song. [Israel Isadore Beilin was born in Tolochin, today Belarus, Russia on May 11, 1888, passed in Manhattan Sept. 22, 1989, age 101, the Nazis killed more than 2,000 Jews there. Berlin, a Jewish American wrote the lyrics and music to the beloved songs WHITE CHRISTMAS, EASTER PARADE, GOD BLESS AMERICA and BLUE SKIES.]

"It was also read in the 1941 film HOLD BACK THE DAWN as well as being recited by the heroine in ALFRED HITCHCOCK'S wartime film SABOTEUR."   Wikipedia

PERSONAL STORY: I visited Dr. ALBERT SCHWEITZER'S home in little Gunsbach, Alsace, France. I was told at his home to visit the nearby park Champs de Mars (March) in Colmar. There is a statue of a reclining Black man, a slave, which was sculpted by Bartholdi. This statue of the oppressed black man motivated Dr. Schweitzer to go to French Equatorial Africa, the nation of Gabon, where he opened a free hospital for the native population. Schweitzer going to Africa stunned Europe's elitist intellectuals.

NAZI STORY: During World War II, German soldiers in Colmar beheaded Bartholdi's statue of a pensive reclining black slave. I took a photo of the statue which was restored after the Americans occupied Colmar in World War II.

HISTORY FACT: At the time of the Battle of the Bulge in December 1945, Lt. AUDIE MURPHY received his Presidential Medal of Honor award for his bravery near Colmar. The town is in Alsace which was annexed to Germany in 1871-1919. In 1968, I visited its church where the famous EISENHEIMER ALTAR, the three-part panels, by the German artist "GRUENWALD" depicts —————— JESUS AND THE TWO THIEVES.

German shepherd dogs were originally called ALSATIANS.

AMERICA WHY I LOVE HER

written by John Mitchum [Robert's brother]
"My hope and prayer is that everyone know and love our country for
what she really is and what she stands for."   JOHN WAYNE
You ask me why I love her? Well, give me time, and I'll explain…
Have you seen a Kansas sunset or an Arizona rain?
Have you ever drifted on a bayou down Louisiana way?
Have you watched the cold fog drifting over San Francisco Bay?
Have you heard a Bobwhite calling in the Carolina pines?
Or hear the bellow of a diesel in the Appalachia mines?
Does the call of Niagara thrill you when you hear her waters roar?
Do you look with awe and wonder at a Massachusetts shore…
Where men who braved a hard New World, first stepped on Plymouth Rock?
And do you think of them when you stroll along a New York City dock?
Have you seen a snowflake drifting in the Rockies…way up high?
Have you seen the sun come blazing down from a bright Nevada sky?
Do you hail to the Columbia as she rushes to the sea…
Or bow your head at Gettysburg…in our struggle to be free?
Have you seen the mighty Tetons?…Have you watched an eagle soar?
Have you seen the Mississippi roll along Missouri's shore?
Have you felt the chill at Michigan, when on a winters day.
Her water's rage along the shore in a thunderous display?
Does the word "Aloha"…make you warm?
Do you stare in disbelief When you see the surf
come roaring in at a Waimea reef?
From Alaska's gold to the Everglades…from the Rio Grande to Maine…
My heart cries out…my pulse runs fast at the might of her domain.
You ask me why I love her?…I've a million reasons why.
My beautiful America…beneath God's wide, wide sky

THE HOUSE I LIVE IN—THAT'S AMERICA TO ME

FRANK SINATRA
WHAT IS AMERICA TO ME?
A NAME, A MAP, OR A FLAG I SEE
A CERTAIN WORD, "DEMOCRACY"
WHAT IS AMERICA TO ME
THE HOUSE I LIVE IN
A PLOT OF EARTH, A STREET
THE GROCER AND THE BUTCHER
AND THE PEOPLE THAT I MEET
THE CHILDREN IN THE PLAYGROUND
THE FACES THAT I SEE
ALL RACES AND RELIGIONS
THAT'S AMERICA TO ME
THE PLACE I WORK IN
THE WORKER BY MY SIDE

420

THE LITTLE TOWN THE CITY
WHERE MY PEOPLE LIVED AND DIED
THE HOWDY AND THE HANDSHAKE
THE AIR A FEELING FREE
AND THE RIGHT TO SPEAK YOUR MIND OUT
THAT'S AMERICA TO ME
THE THINGS I SEE ABOUT ME
THE BIG THINGS AND THE SMALL
THE LITTLE CORNER NEWSSTAND
OR THE HOUSE A MILE TALL
THE WEDDING AND THE CHURCHYARD
THE LAUGHTER AND THE TEARS
THE DREAM THAT'S BEEN GROWING
FOR A HUNDRED AND FIFTY YEARS
THE TOWN I LIVE IN
THE STREET, THE HOUSE, THE ROOM
THE PAVEMENT OF THE CITY
OR THE GARDEN ALL IN BLOOM
THE CHURCH THE SCHOOL THE CLUBHOUSE
THE MILLION LIGHTS I SEE
BUT ESPECIALLY THE PEOPLE
THAT'S AMERICA TO ME

[These words are the 2nd Stanza which were not sung because of controversy?]
View African-American Paul Robeson's U Tube soulful rendition]

THE HOUSE I LIVE IN, MY NEIGHBORS
WHITE AND BLACK, THE PEOPLE
WHO JUST CAME HERE,
OR FROM GENERATIONS.
THE TOWN HALL AND THE SOAP BOX,
THE TORCH OF LIBERTY.
A PLACE TO SPEAK MY MIND OUT,
THAT'S AMERICA TO ME.
THE WORDS OF OLD ABE LINCOLN,
OF JEFFERSON AND PAINE.
OF WASHINGTON AND DOUGLAS,
AND THE TASK THAT STILL REMAINS
THE LITTLE BRIDGE AT CONCORD,
WHERE FREEDOM'S FIGHT BEGAN.
OR GETTYSBURG AND MIDWAY
AND THE STORY OF BATAAN.
THE HOUSE I LIVE IN.
THE GOODNESS EVERYWHERE,
A LAND OF WEALTH AND BEAUTY
WITH ENOUGH FOR ALL TO SEE.
A HOUSE THAT WE CALL FREEDOM,
THE HOME OF LIBERTY,
AND THE PROMISE FOR TOMORROW,
THAT'S AMERICA TO ME.
THE TOWN I LIVE IN, THE STREET,

421

THE HOUSE, THE ROOM,
THE PAVEMENT OF THE CITY,
OR A GARDEN ALL IN BLOOM,
THE CHURCH, THE SCHOOL,
THE CLUBHOUSE, A MILLION LIGHTS.
BUT ESPECIALLY THE PEOPLE,
THAT'S AMERICA TO ME .
BUT ESPECIALLY THE PEOPLE,
THAT'S THE TRUE AMERICA.

(2,320,000 views; watch the U Tube RKO with preteen bullies 37,706 views 6-21-2011)
Lyrics Abel Meeropol—music Earl Robinson

SONG FACTS: "This became a patriotic anthem in America during World War II. The lyrics describe the wonderful things about the country…the "house" is a metaphor for the country. Meeropol used pen name Lewis Allen, had very liberal views and mixed feelings about America. He loved the constitutional rights and freedoms that America was based on, but he hated the way people of other races, religious, and political views were often treated. His lyrics do not reflect the way he thought America was but what it had the potential to be. With the country under attack, he wanted to express why it was worth fighting for."
"Meeropol was dogged by the government for his liberal (some would say Communist) views." [Meeropol and his wife adopted the two sons of JULIUS and ETHEL ROSENBERG convicted for passing nuclear secrets to STALIN'S Communist Russia, and both were executed in 1953. He felt they were wrongly accused.]   Wikipedia

"Meeropol wrote a lot of songs, including "STRANGE FRUIT," which was about the horrors of lynchings and became BILLIE HOLLIDAYS's signature song. Many songs he wrote were parodies of America, with commentary on racism and politics oppression. EARL ROBINSON, who wrote the music, also had very liberal views. During the MCCARTHY ERA, he was hounded for being a Communist and BLACKLISTED from HOLLYWOOD, making it hard for him to find work. Before his death in 1981, he wrote presidential campaign songs for FDR (1944), HENRY WALLACE (1948), and JESSE JACKSON (1984)."   Wikipedia
THE HOUSE I LIVE IN has also been recorded by MAHALIA JACKSON, PAUL ROBESON, SONNY ROLLINS, and JOSH WHITE. "SINATRA'S version is the most famous, as it was used in a short film he starred in with the same name in 1945. When Meeropol saw the film, he became enraged when he learned they deleted the second stanza of his song, which he felt was crucial to the meaning. He had to be removed from the theater. Its message of racial harmony, the second stanza, deemed too controversial for the film."   Wikipedia
"Sinatra loved this song and performed it many times, even as his political views moved from left to right as he got older. As an Italian-American, Sinatra experienced bigotry growing up, but he also loved the United States. He sang this at inaugural he produced for JOHN F. KENNEDY, and again in the NIXON WHITE HOUSE, and performed it for RONALD REAGAN at the re-dedication of the STATUE OF LIBERTY in 1986."   Wiki
"Charles Pignone, Vice President of Frank Sinatra Enterprises, also remembers watching him perform this in the '90s during the First Gulf War. "He would sing that every decade of his career," Pignone said in a Songfacts interview. "And that was another song that just stayed with him throughout his life." He added: "I remember sometimes HE WOULD TEAR UP after singing "The House I Live In."   Wikipedia
"Sinatra appeared in a 10-minute short for RKO, also titled THE HOUSE I LIVE IN, where he lectured a group of boys on racial and religious tolerance. Written by Albert Maltz, produced by

Frank Ross and directed by Mervyn LeRoy, the film won a special Academy Award in 1946."
Wikipedia   [It showed an orthodox Jewish boy being bullied.]
"THE HOUSE I LIVE IN regained popularity among Americans in the aftermath of the SEPTEMBER 11, 2001 attacks. A lot of people found it comforting at a difficult time."
[FRANK SINATRA passed on May 14, 1998, Israel's 50th anniversary. He could see Manhattan from his home in Hoboken, New Jersey and drove the girls "Bobbie Socksers" wild at the PARAMOUNT THEATER in Manhattan, long before ELVIS. He passed three years before 9-11 sparing him a deep sorrow worse than PEARL HARBOR. THE HOUSE I LIVE IN was his most personal song of many, many songs, Second, would have been one he wrote NANCY WITH THE LAUGHING FACE for his beloved baby daughter NANCY. Third, would be NEW YORK, NEW YORK. Fourth, I did it MY WAY. May 14, 1998, was also the 50th anniversary of the restoration of the Nation of Israel. Sinatra played a "rogue" American cargo pilot bringing supplies to the 1948 Israeli freedom fighters in CAST A GIANT SHADOW. He had many Jewish friends DON RICKELS loved to agitate him and everyone else even REGIS PHILBIN, great friends, that was his STIK. He loved talented SAMMY DAVIS and also with DEAN MARTIN would appear together in VEGAS shows and Hollywood movies.
AMAZING HOLLYWOOD STORY: Sinatra was married to AVA GARDNER who was co-starring with A-list actors while he was singing trite novelty songs at Columbia records under MITCH MILLER's direction because they were popular. Sinatra had acted with famous actors during World War II, and saw a role he could identify with in FROM HERE TO ETERNITY (1953). He didn't want the lead role BURT LANCASTER took. Sinatra was "OLD BLUE EYES" but wasn't the hunk Lancaster portrayed. He took the small role of MAGGIO, the Italian-American soldier which ERNEST BORGNINE portraying a sadistic, bigoted MP kills. Allegedly, Sinatra tells Borgnine to really beat him which he did. I don't believe the director realized what was going on, and it would have been difficult to find a double. I think Sinatra told Borgnine that he wanted it realistic because he hoped to get an Academy Award nomination. He did and received Best Supporting Actor in 1954, which launched his career which made him legendary. Borgnine won Best Actor as a like able bachelor in MARTY (1957).
HOLLYWOOD FUN TRIVIA: Watch Borgnine's U Tube tribute which plays DICK CLARK'S AMERICAN BANDSTAND theme song THE BANDSTAND BOOGIE. In the futuristic noire film ESCAPE FROM NEW YORK. Borgnine is a taxi driver who plays the song in his cab. In the climax scene the President actor DONALD PLEASANCE plays the cassette for the media and is stunned to hear THE AMERICAN BANDSTAND theme song rather than his audio tape. I wonder what DICK CLARK thought about that. I never had a chance to ask my friends LES AND LARRY ELGART what they thought about how their song was used. KURT RUSSELL was the star SNAKE. His first movie role as a pre-teenager was to kick ELVIS PRESLEY in the shin so he could get a date with a nurse in IT HAPPENED AT THE WORLD'S FAIR (Seattle). Elvis could date almost any girl he wanted as his films showed. Later, the amazing story of Elvis first screen kiss with a young actress DOLORES HART who made a few other films and then became a NUN. I read her inspirational autobiography HOLLYWOOD'S most providential story. I have visited her cloister in Bethlehem, Connecticut, where she is the mother superior. She had just left to Catholic University in Washington, D.C. beginning her book tour.]
PAUL HARVEY STORY: I heard Borgnine tell the story of how after the movie showed a group of Italian men surrounded him and said we are going to beat the Hell out of you for what you did to our brother Frank in the movie. He starts speaking Italian and says my name is BORGNINO, and tells them Sinatra told me to fight him rough to try to get an Academy Award nomination which he won. In the film the OSCAR (1968) great character actor STEPHEN BOYD is a street tough guy FRANKI FAIN who is nominated for the OSCAR and stands up when he hears name Frank called but it is Sinatra. He was mean to his friend TONY BENNETT (BENADETTO) and wife German

actress ELKE SOMMER. BOYD played many leading historical hunk roles with starlets except in BEN HUR where he is killed in the epic chariot race against CHARLTON HESTON. My favorite Boyd was DUMBO with DORIS DAY, a bad/good guy in a circus movie.

On Saturday Oct. 20, 1974, three weeks before our wedding in Brooklyn, my fiancé and mother-in-law attended Frank Sinatra's MAIN EVENT concert at MADISON SQUARE GARDEN in New York City, Sunday Oct. 21st. The concert was on TV we watched as HOWARD COSELL gave the MAIN EVENT'S SINATRA concert dramatic introduction. My father was the senior ABC Master Control room engineer that night. A really BIG SHOW as ED SULLIVAN so often gave. I have a photo with Ed Sullivan at the Waldorf Hotel BEST TIME OF THE YEAR awards ceremony in October 1969. I was a researcher/writer at THE WORLD ALMANAC AND BOOK OF FACTS who researched the celebrities who had record time in Hollywood and television: ED SULLIVAN. JOAN CRAWFORD, GINGER RODGERS, LASSIE, YVETTE MIMIEUX, GEORGE PLIMPTON. My friend ALEXANDER 'Alex' JOSEPH SALUSTRI craved the gravestones of ED SULLIVAN, JOAN CRAWFORD, JUDY GARLAND and JOHN GARFIELD at GATE OF HEAVEN cemetery in HAWTHORNE, New York. On Jan. 18, 2020 this fact was revealed at his memorial service sermon by Pastor MICHAEL LEMAY, Air Force Gen. CURTIS LEMAY's was his grandfather's brother's son, at the Lake of the Woods Church. He revealed his many artistic and mechanical talents but also emphasized his long voluntary service with our large LIONS group, Boy Scouts of America, our community AARP chapter, rated Virginia's best 2017, 2018, Knghts of Columbus and our large community Veterans group. Ten veterans gave an honorary FINAL SALUTE with a bugler playing TAPS. Pastor Lemay recalled Alex had been in the American 15th Divislon during World War II. Ales told me this was AUDIE MURHY'S unit, America's most decorated soldier. I had told Alex I had met Audie Murphy in 1956, when I was 13, at a local movie premier of WALK THE PROUD LAND. Murphy portrayed the Christian Indian agent JOHN CLUM. Clum was born in Claverack where my Regional School was located. Alex was 93, born January 23, 1926-December 25, 2019. He had been in hospital with pneumonia. He told his wife Madeline "I want to go home." He passed at home with his family on Christmas Day.

PERSONAL FAMILY STORY: My dad ALEXANDER BRUCE LOUDEN was born on January 28, 1919, 5 days later than Alex. My daughter was born on December 24, 1975, in Mt. Kisco, New York Northern Westchester hospital where CHRISTOPHER REEVES passed. He lived in nearby Bedford Village and had his horse accident in Culpeper, Virginia, about 22 miles from my home here in Lake of the Woods. The last time I saw Alex after the church service I believe I told him, "Alex my dad's name was Alexander but he wanted to be called Bruce because he didn't want to be called Alex."

My father was born in Amityville, Long Island in his father's Louden Knickerbocker Brunswick hospital. ALEC BALDWIN, Alexander Baldwin was born in the same hospital which is adjacent to his hometown Massapequa. Alec Baldwin please chill. My father's father built the LOUDEN HOME/KNICKERBOCKER hospital in 1880s for drug, alcohol and nervous disorders. "AMERICAN YANKEE INGENUITY" Mental health was not an accepted practice then. A New York Times front page article circa 1888, reported a family suing my grandfather for illegally practicing MENTAL HEALTH. I couldn't access inside page, but know he was exonerated an early precedent. He had a Calais, Maine LITTLE RED SCHOOLHOUSE 5th grade "3 Rs READING. RITHING, RITHMETIC and BIBLE" education. His mother was a relative of the famous frontiersman KIT CARSON who aided General Fremont and General KEARNEYin making California a state. His eldest son graduated JOHNS HOPKINS University, Baltimore medical school and was head physician running the hospital. In 1880s alcohol was a serious addiction as it is today in America. Ironically or providentially/prophetically there was a serious drug addiction problem. What drug? OPIATES, a major problem in America today killing thousands. Laudanum MORPHINE was legally used to alleviate the excruciating pain of thousands of CIVIL WAR amputees and wounded Union soldiers. I first saw this on a DR. QUINN MEDICINE WOMAN actress JANE SEYMOUR, TV show where a young Union soldier, whose arm was amputated, stole her Morphine to relieve his pain. Today, legal OXYCONTIN has been declared illegal and banned years after doctors knew that it was highly addictive. Billions of dollars the most horrendous BIG PHARMA SCANDAL. A 100 billion illegal pills a year smuggled into America. A national disgrace.

Frank Sinatra's THE HOUSE I LIVE IN nostalgic commentary:
SINATRA'S MAIN EVENT AT MADISON SQUARE GARDEN OCTOBER 1974
Sinatra's introduction to THE HOUSE I LIVE IN on Nationwide television

IT'S A SONG ABOUT THIS GREAT, BIG, WONDERFUL,
IMPERFECT COUNTRY. I SAY IMPERFECT BECAUSE
IF IT WERE PERFECT IT WOULDN'T BE ANY FUN TRYING
TO FIX IT, TRYING TO MAKE IT WORK BETTER, TRYING TO
MAKE SURE THAT EVERYBODY GETS A FAIR SHAKE AND
THEN SOME. MY COUNTRY IS PERSONAL TO ME BECAUSE
MY FATHER, WHO WASN'T BORN HERE, REST HIS SOUL, HE
MADE SURE THAT I WAS BORN HERE, AND HE USED TO
TELL ME WHEN I WAS A KID THAT AMERICA WAS A LAND
OF DREAMS AND A DREAMLAND. WELL I DON'T KNOW IF
MY COUNTRY FULFILLED ALL OF HIS DREAMS WHILE HE
WAS ALIVE, BUT TONIGHT WITH ALL OF US TOGETHER FOR
THIS HOUR, IT SURE FULFILLS MY DREAMS. AND TO ALL
OF YOU IN THE COUNTRY AND ALL OF YOU WATCHING
TONIGHT, HERE'S A SONG ABOUT A PLACE WE CALL HOME,
PROBABLY THE GREATEST NATION EVER PUT ON THIS EARTH.

A WORD ON BEHALF OF OUR COUNTRY

Gordon Sinclair Canadian Radio/TV commentator
Scripps-Howard News February 1974
The following is an excerpt from an editorial broadcast by Gordon Sinclair,
a Canadian radio and television commentator. It was headlined
"LET'S HEAR IT!"

"This Canadian thinks it is time to speak up for the Americans as the most generous and possibly the least appreciated people on all the earth.

"Germany, Japan, and, to a lesser extent, Britain and Italy are lifted out of the debris of war by the Americans who poured billions of dollars and forgave other billions of debts. None of these countries is today paying even the interest on its remaining debts to the United States.

"When the franc was in danger of collapsing in 1956, it was the Americans who propped it up, and their reward was to be insulted and swindled on the streets of Paris.

"I was there. I saw it."

"When distant cities are hit by earthquakes, it is the United States that hurries in to help...This Spring, 59 American town were flattened by tornadoes, Nobody helped."

"The MARSHALL PLAN and the TRUMAN POLICY pumped billions upon billions of dollars into discouraged countries. Now newspapers in those countries are writing about the decadent, warmongering Americans.

"I'd like to see just one of those countries that is gloating over the erosion of the United States dollar."
"Come on, let's hear it!"
"Why does no other land on earth even consider putting a man or woman on the moon?
"You talk about Japanese technocracy, and you get radios. You talk about Germany you get automobiles.
"You talk about American technocracy, and you find men on the moon—not once but several times—safely home again.
"You talk about scandals, and the Americans put theirs right in the store window for everybody to look at.
"Even their draft-dodgers are not pursued and hounded. They are here on our streets, and most of them—unless they are breaking Canadian laws—are getting American dollars from Ma and Pa at home to spend here.
"When the railroads of France, Germany and India were breaking down through age, it was the Americans who rebuilt them, When the Pennsylvania Railroad and the New York Central went broke, nobody loaned them an old caboose. Both are broke.
"I can name you 5,000 times when the Americans raced to the help of other people in trouble.Can you name even one time when someone else helped Americans in trouble?
"I don't think there was outside help even during the San Francisco earthquake?
"Our neighbors have faced it alone, and I'm one Canadian who is damned tired of hearing them kicked around.

"They will come out of this thing with their flag high. And when they do, they are entitled to thumb their noses at the lands that are gloating over their present troubles.
"I hope Canada is not one of these."
	[A truthful tribute of America's Judeo-Christian charity to our needy neighbors.]

Will There Be Animals or Pets in Heaven?

Seth Clemmer The Lutheran Witness-Missouri Synod August 2017
"Heaven is often imagined as a place where disembodied spirits float in the clouds. There's no earthly material and certainly no annoying pet hair sticking to our pants. Or perhaps its a place where we will more fully experience all the things we enjoyed on earth—better golf, tastier meals and perfectly behaved pets. But for an even clearer description of heaven, we look to the Scriptures to draw better conclusions about Fluffy's eternal faith."
"God created animals for man as a gift (Gen. 1:24-28). Before the fall, joy and peace existed between man and animals—no bug bits or cat scratches. But animals experienced death even before man (God killed an animal to clothe Adam and Eve), and animals have been dying ever since.
"It can be sad when our pets die. When our loved ones die in the faith. We find comfort in the bodily resurrection won for us by Jesus, but that promise of resurrection has not been made regarding animals. Jesus died and rose for mankind, but we cannot speak with certainty regarding animals; the Bible is silent on rhat topic."
Bringing joy.

"Paul explains the the fallen creation—including animals—longs to be set free from its bondage to corruption and obtain the freedom of the glory of the children of God (Rom. 8:21). What that looks like, though, has not been revealed."

Luther Says Animals Will be in the New Heaven

"Will there be any animals in heaven? Luther thought so. In response to that question, he wrote, "Certainly there will be, for Peter calls that day the time of restitution of all things." "All things" includes animals! John describes the "new heaven and new earth" and the "New Jerusalem" descending from heaven—that is, heaven comes down to the new earth (Rev. 21:1-2). Heaven will be a new earth, not necessarily different than the earth we enjoy now but certainly new and sinless."

"God created animals and called them good, and He made special provision to bring them through the flood. The new earth will likely contain new animals. But we'll enjoy those animals far more than we can enjoy Fluffy today—perhaps just as they enjoyed in the Garden of Eden."

St. Francis Confronts Tames the Ravaging Wolf

The Italian countryside sheepherders were being ravaged by a wolf. There was great fear and then Jesuit priest Francis went to comfort the scared farmers. When he confronted the wolf he raised his cross up and spoke Jesus name, allegedly the wolf prostrated itself. Francis then saw that the wolf was injured. This was a lone wolf. Wolves travel in packs and are very dangerous. He led the wolf into the Italian village where at first the residents were fearful. They cared for and fed the wolf which was an outcaste from its pack. I have a St. Francis with a deer birdbath statue in front of my house. My Bible church has a small statue of St. Francis.

St. Colomba Rebukes Attacking Loch Ness Monster

"The Vita Columae about St. Columba contains a story that has been interpreted as the first reference to the LOCH NESS MONSTER. According to Adomnan. Colmcille [Columba] came across a group of PICTS burying a man who had been killed by a monster. Colmcille saves a swimmer from the monster with the SIGN OF THE CROSS and the imprecation, "Thou shalt go no further, nor touch the man; go back with all speed." The beast flees, terrified, to the amazement of the assembled Picts who GLORIFIED Colmcille's GOD. Whether or not this incident is true, Adomnan's text specifically states that the monster was swimming in the RIVER NESS—the river flowing from the Loch—rather than in LOCH NESS [lake] itself."   Wikipedia

"SAINT COLUMBA born Dec. 7, 521, was an Irish abbot and missionary Evangelist credited with spreading Christianity in SCOTLAND at the start of the Hiberno-Scottish mission. He founded the important abby at IONA, which became a dominant religious and political institution in the region for centuries. He is the Patron Saint of DERRY [Londonderry]. He was highly regarded by both GAELS of Dal Riata [northeast Ireland, western Scotland] and is remembered today as a Catholic saint and one of the Twelve Apostles of Ireland."   Wikipedia

"In early Christian Ireland the DRUIDIC TRADITION collapsed due to the spread of the new Christian faith. In 563, he travelled to SCOTLAND with 12 companions. The ISLAND OF IONA was made over to him…He founded several churches in the HEBRIDES [islands], he worked to turn his monastery at Iona into a school for missionaries."   Wikipedia

"Through the reputation of its venerable founder and its position as a major European center of learning, Colomba's IONA became a place of pilgrimage. Colomba is historically revered as a warrior saint, and was often invoked for victory in battle. Colomba's relics were carried before SCOTTISH ARMIES in a reliquary made at Iona in the mid-8th century, called the BRECBENNOCH. Legend has it that the Brecbennoch was carried at the BATTLE OF BANNOCKBURN (24 June 1314) by the vastly outnumbered Scots army and the intercession of COLUMBA helped them to victory. The Inchcom Abby, the "Iona of the East" (situated on an island in the Firth of Fourth), a 14th century prayer begins "O Colomba, hope of the Scots".   Wikipedia [This battle is recreated in MEL GIBSON'S film BRAVEHEART about WILLIAM WALLACE who fought the English for Scotland's FREEDOM!]   "Wallace's last word."

ST. BONIFACE TAKES CHRIST TO GERMAN PAGAN FRANKS

"SAINT BONIFACE was a leading figure in the Anglo-Saxon mission to the Germanic parts of the FRANKISH EMPIRE during the 8th Century. He organized significant foundations of the Catholic Church in Germany and was made archbishop of Mainz by POPE GREGORY III. He was martyred in FRISIA [northeast Holland], along with 52 others, and his remains were returned to FULDA, Germany cathedral. He became the patron saint of Germania, known as the "apostle of the Germans."   Wikipedia

"Norman Cantor notes that the three roles Boniface played that made him "One of the truly outstanding creators of the first Europe, as the apostles of the Germans."As the apostle of Germania, the reformer of the Frankish church, and the chief fomenter of the alliance between the papacy and the CAROLINGIAN family." Through his efforts to reorganize and regulate the church of the FRANKS, he helped shape the Latin Church in Europe, and many of the diocese he proposed remain today. Boniface is celebrated (and criticized) as a missionary; he is regarded as a UNIFIER OF EUROPE, and he is seen (mainly by Catholics) as a GERMAN NATIONAL FIGURE. In 2019 Devon County Council with the support of the Anglican and Catholic churches in EXETER and PLYMOUTH, officially recognized BONIFACE as the Patron Saint of Devon where he was born."   Wikipedia

EARLY MISSIONARY WORK IN FRISIA AND GERMANIA—Boniface first left for the continent in 716. He traveled to UTRECHT, Holland, and met WILLIBRORD, THE "APOSTLE TO THE FRISIANS," had been working since the 690s. Willibrord returned to the abbey he had founded in ECHTERNACH (in modern-day LUXEMBOURG). He is the patron saint of Luxembourg." Wikipedia

PERSONAL CONNECTION: ECHTERNACH is 10 miles from Bitburg AB, where I was stationed from October 1966-March 1969. In April 1967, I picked up my 1967 SAAB 96, driven from the dealership in Luxembourg, 25 miles away. The salesman let me practice using the 4 speed column stick shift and learn how to use its free-wheeling shift without clutch except 1st gear. We did this in the large Willibrord Abby parking lot. It wasn't until June 1973, I learned some of its History. I met WILLA AMIDON in a hotel in Goteborg, Sweden, when I shipped my 1973 SAAB EMS to America. Mrs. Amidon was from Auburndale, Massachusetts. I told her I worked for the World Almanac as an historical editor. She sent me her manuscript about living in Echternach during World War II. She married a Luxembourg doctor before the war. She helped American soldiers with General Patton during the Battle of the Bulge find a route around Echternach to the SAUER RIVER on the German border. She said she was awarded the U.S. Bronze Star medal given for meritorious service. This award is usually given only to American servicemen not to a civilian. She was American but also a Luxembourg citizen. This award may have also been given Foreign Resistance fighters? She wrote she was in the little town of SPEICER near Bitburg. She said the town was bombed by American bombers and her infant daughter was killed. Later, a man in my Lutheran Church in Triangle, VA, told me he was stationed at nearby Spangdahlem AB, when I was stationed at Bitburg AB. He said his son was born in the Bitburg AB hospital in 1968. Chuck Bennetts told me a story about Speicer. The little hamlet dated back to Roman times and had an ancient pottery factory which was building V-1 rockets. The town was bombed a strategic target. Chuck said a bomber's crew had to bail out and crewmen were killed by angry town's people. Chuck said that this was seen by a bomber crew and later bomber crews said save "a bomb for Speicer!" I had never heard this story which was probably the reason Willa's daughter died? I wish I could have copied her manuscript or gotten it published. She wrote me that it was published in Luxembourg in the Luxembourgish native language.

SMALL WORLD PROVIDENTIAL STORY: I spent Christmas Day 1967, in Speicer. My assistant Information Officer Lt. RATLEY, had been invited by a German family and he asked me if I would go in his place. I had just arrived the end of October, but he may have known I spoke some German. I stayed over night Christmas Eve. I vaguely remember it but I know we didn't talk about the war. It was Christmas.

BONIFACE MEETS THE POPE

"BONIFACE went straight to ROME, where POPE GREGORY II renamed him "Boniface", after the (legendary) 4th Century martyr BONIFACE OF TARSUS, and appointed him missionary bishop for GERMANIA—he became a bishop without diocese for an area that lacked any church organization."

"According to the vitae Boniface felled the DONAR OAK, Latinized by Willibald as "JUPITER'S OAK," near todays town of FRITZLAR in northern HESSE. According to his early biographer Willibald, Boniface started to chop the oak down, when suddenly a GREAT WIND, AS IF BY MIRACLE, BLEW THE ANCIENT OAK OVER. When the god did not strike him down, the people were amazed and converted to Christianity." He built a chapel dedicated to SAINT PETER from its wood at the site. He is portrayed as a singular character who alone acts to root out paganism."

PROVIDENTIAL IRONIC FACT: The oak is a massive powerful tree, I have many surrounding my house and numerous squirrels. The Druidic-Celtic pagans of Germania would hang their enemies from oak trees as part of their Teutonic spiritual beliefs. Oak trees have a semi-parasitic plant, which extract water and nutrients, grow on it called MISTLETOE. Pre-Christian culture regarded the white berries as symbols of male fertility, with the seeds resembling semen. The CELTS, particularly, saw mistletoe as the semen of TARANIS, while the ancient Greeks referred to mistletoe as "oak sperm." Also in ancient Greek mythology, mistletoe was used by the hero AENEAS to reach the UNDERWORLD. Mistletoe played an important role in DRUID MYTHOLOGY in the ritual of oak and mistletoe. In NORSE MYTHOLOGY, LOKI tricked the blind god HODUR into murdering his own twin brother BALDER with an arrow made of mistletoe wood, being the only plant to which Balder was vulnerable."

"The ROMANS associated mistletoe with PEACE, LOVE and understanding, and hung it over doorways to protect the household. Hanging mistletoe was part of the SATURNALIA FESTIVAL."

"In the Christian era, mistletoe in the Western world became associated with CHRISTMAS as a decoration under which lovers are expected to kiss, as well as protection from witches and demons.The custom of kissing under the mistletoe is referred to as popular among servants in late 18th Century England: the serving class of Victorian England is credited with perpetuating the tradition. The tradition dictated that a man was allowed to kiss any woman standing underneath mistletoe, and that bad luck would befall any woman who refused the kiss."

VICTORIAN PURITANICAL STANDARD?

"In Germany, the Christmas tradition is that people who kiss under mistletoe will have an enduring love or are bound to marry one another."

"In the popular roleplaying game DUNGEONS AND DRAGONS, DRUIDS USE mistletoe as the default focus item for casting spells."   Wikipedia

"People have reportedly been poisoned and died from consuming mistletoe berries."

SAINT ODILE WHO PROPHESIED ALEMANIA'S DESTRUCTION BY ANGELS

"SAINT ODILE OF ALSACE born circa 662 at Mont Sainte Odile is a saint venerated in the Roman Catholic Church and the Orthodox Church. She is the patroness saint of good eyesight, and of ALSACE, France."

"ODILE was the daughter of ETICHON, Duke of Alsace and founder of the Etichon noble family. By tradition she was BORN BLIND. Her father did not want her because she was a girl and handicapped, so her mother Bethswinda had her brought to Palma (perhaps present day Baume-les-Dames in Burgundy), where she was raised by peasants. A 10th Century legend relates that when she was 12, Odile was taken to a nearby monastery. Whilst there, the itinerant BISHOP SAINT ERHARD of REGENSBURG WAS LED, BY AN ANGEL it was said, to Palma where HE BAPTIZED HER ODILE (SOL DEI), whereupon SHE MIRACULOUSLY RECOVERED HER SIGHT. Her younger brother Hughes had her brought home again, which enraged [her father] Etichon so much that he accidentally killed his son. Odile MIRACULOUSLY REVIVED HIM, and left home again."   Wikipedia

"She fled across the [nearby] RHINE RIVER to a cave or cavern in one of two places (depending on the source: the Musbach valley near FREIBURG im Breisgau, Germany [the entrance to the Black Forest I have driven through twice] or ARLESHEIM near Basel, Switzerland.) [This is near RUDOLF STEINER'S DORNACH spiritual center] Supposedly, the cliff face OPENED UP in order to rescue her from plight. In the cave, she hid from her father. When he tried to follow her, he was injured by falling rocks and gave up."   Hollywood story or God's providence?

"When Etichon fell ill, Odile returned to nurse him. He finally gave up resisting his headstrong [saintly loving] daughter and founded the AUGUSTINE monastic community of Mont Ste. Odile (also known as HOHENBURG ABBEY) in the Hochwald, Bas-Rhin, where Odile became abbess and where Eitchon was later buried. Some years later Odile was shown the site of NIEDERMUENSTER at the foot of the mountain by St. JOHN THE BAPTIST in a vision. There she founded a second monastery, including a hospital. Here, the head and an arm of St. LAZARUS of Marseilles were displayed but later sent to ANDLAU. [Lazarus was raised from the dead in Bethany near Jerusalem by Jesus Christ on the 4th day, the week before His Crucifixion.] Niedermuenster's buildings were destroyed by fire in 1542, but the local well is said to still cure eye diseases. [contains radon]"   Wikipedia

She died about 720 at the convent of Niedermuenster. At the insistent prayers of her sisters she was retuned to life, but after describing the BEAUTIES OF THE AFTERLIFE to them, SHE TOOK COMMUNION by herself and died again." Wikipedia

SAINT ODILE PROPHECY of DESTRUCTION OF GERMANY

"ALL NATIONS OF THE EARTH WILL FIGHT EACH OTHER
IN THIS WAR.THE FIGHTERS WILL RISE UP TO THE
HEAVENS TO TAKE THE STARS AND THROW THEM ON
THE CITIES, TO SET ABLAZE THE BUILDINGS,"

"This French saint was blind at her birth in the 7th century but while a young woman was miraculously healed by St. ERHARD, Bishop of Ratisbon.""Odile Daughter of Light"
"There will come a time when war will break out, MORE TERRIBLE THAN ALL OTHER WARS COMBINED, WHICH HAVE EVER VISITED MANKIND. A HORRIBLE WARRIOR [Hitler] will unleash it, and his adversaries will CALL HIM ANTICHRIST. All NATIONS OF THE EARTH WILL FIGHT each other in this war. The FIGHTERS WILL RISE UP TO THE HEAVENS to take the stars and throw them on the cities, to set ablaze the buildings and to cause immense devastations. OCEANS WILL BE BETWEEN THE GREAT WARRIORS, and the monsters of the sea, terrified by everything that happens on or under the sea, will flee to the deep."
CATHOLIC PROPHECY ORG ST. ODILE

[This prophecy was in the 7th Century this is before Columbus "discovered" America and the New World across the vast Atlantic Ocean and before the Norseman LIEF ERICKSON crossed to ICELAND, GREENLAND and the Canadian mainland circa 1000 A.D. There were great navies but not monsters under the sea predicting the horrific unrestricted submarine warfare of the GREAT WAR, World War I, 1914-1918, and WORLD WAR II, 1939-1945. There were some who considered Hitler an Antichrist, one was Pastor Bonhoeffer. German cities were fire bombed as were Japanese cities ending with two atomic bombs. Another prophetic voice from France NOSTRADAMUS predicted three antichrists NAPOLEON, HITLER [Hister] and ? in his 1555 visions written in his book CENTURIES. It is believed his predictions were perceived through occultism and drugs but some seem to have occurred later in History. PREDESTINED?]

"A person from the 7th century seeing high altitude bombers "angels" destroying cities might refer to them as "fighters" that will "rise up to the heavens to take the stars and throw them on the cities" causing them to burn and be demolished. Likewise, a vision of submarines might look like "monsters of the sea" that will "flee to the deep."
[In World War I and World War II we used piston propellor driven aircraft until July 1944, when Messerschmidt ME-262 twin engined jets went into combat. The Wright Brother's first heavier than air powered airplane made a very short flight at Kill Devil Hill, Nags Head, Cape Hatteras with the aid of ocean breezes in December 1904, on its second attempt. I was there on the 100 anniversary in December 2004, the replica failed to become airborne! Not enough wind. As KURT VONNEGUT would say "SO IT GOES".]
"Battles of the past will only be skirmishes compared to the battles that will take place, since blood will flow in all directions. The earth will shake from the violent fighting. Famine and pestilence will join the war. The nations will then cry "Peace, peace", but there will be no peace. Thrice will the sun rise over the heads of the combatants, without having been seen by them. But afterwards there will be peace, and all who have broken peace will have lost their lives."
NOTE: "The phrase "thrice will the sun rise" without ever being seen definitely sounds like a prediction of the three days of darkness, which other saints have warned about and which will bring about a lasting peace."
"On a single day more men will have been killed than the catacombs of Rome have ever held. Pyres will be erected greater than the greatest city, and people will ascend the highest mountains to praise God, and nobody will want to make anymore. Strange signs will appear in the skies: both horns of the moon will join the cross. Happy will be those who will have survived the war, since the pleasures of life will begin again, and the sun will have a new brilliance."
"Woe to those who, in those days, do not fear the ANTICHRIST, for he is the father of those who are propelled by crime. He will arouse more homicides and many people will shed tears over his evil customs. Men will set themselves one against the other and at the end will want to re-establish

order. Some will try to do so, but this will not succeed and thus will end up even worse off than before! But if things will have reached the summit and if the hand of man can no longer do anything, it will be put in the hands of Him, who can send down a punishment so terrible that it will not have been seen before. God has already sent the Flood, but he has sworn never to send one again. What he will do will be something unexpected and terrible." [The Jewish atomic bomb.]

THE DOOM OF GERMANY UNDER HITLER

(The 7th century Prophecy of St. Odile)
"STRANGE PROPHECIES THAT CAME TRUE" Stewart Robb 1967

"In the latter years of the 7th Century a little girl was born blind in the palace of great Lord Adalric of Alsace. He was a hard man and refused to have anything to do with his daughter, so she was turned over to the nuns. As years passed, the child "throve under the heavens" and grew into a beautiful character. The story goes that a miracle was performed on her. A visiting Bishop of Ratisbon healed her of her blindness. The holy man bestowed on her the name "Odile," which means "DAUGHTER OF LIGHT." He named her well, as she was no longer in darkness or of the night. And now her relenting father, abashed yet proud, invited her back to the ancestral castle into a nunnery. And henceforth, here on the heights of Hohenburg she lived out her days in piety and good works, ever to be known as the patron saint of Alsace." [A church lady lived near there.]
"To this holy maid a wondrous prophecy has been attributed, a Latin prose-poem on the recent Hitler war. Some critics have questioned her authorship of the work, saying that perhaps it was written by a modest monk, who not wishing to sign his name to it, dedicated it instead to "the Daughter of Light" who is the patroness of prophesy. But that is conjecture. The wonderful work is probably her own. And what matters most about it is that it was certainly written centuries before DER FUEHRER began to cast his ugly shadow over Earth. That is, this masterpiece of prophecy is unquestionably an authentic vision, so amazing, so perfect and circumstantial in its details— imperfect only in time-intervals (which are always hardest for the prophet to get)—that some who read it may think it is a gigantic hoax perpetrated after the event."   p 158
"At any rate, here it is in its entirety in a literal translation and with a running commentary where necessary:

> Listen, listen, O my brother, for I have seen the trembling of the forests
> and the mountains. The nations are in a stupor, for never in any place
> in the universe has like perturbation been witnessed. p. 159

"(The nations are in a stupor. This was truer of World War II than any previous wars. Hitler conquered the little nations one by one, hypnotizing them as a snake does a bird, petrifying them with a fear which prevented their acting until it was too late. And fifth columnists helped the stupor of the nations.)" Pres. Franklin D. Roosevelt addressed Americans proclaiming: "All we have to fear is fear itself." There were a few German-Americans "5th Column" who joined the American Bund and America First non-intervention isolationists.

> "The time has arrived when Germany will be called the
> most war-loving nation on Earth." p 159

"(As far back as the time of Caesar and Tacitus Germany was notorious for her cruelty and war likeness. Her literature expresses through countless writers the idea of world domination.

NIETZSCHE, perhaps Germany's greatest writer, wrote to his people, "Ye shall love peace—as a means to new wars, and a short peace better than a long one." BERHARDI proclaimed with pride, "We Germans are the most warlike nation in the world." A hundred years ago the German-Jewish poet HEINRICH HEINE prophesied, "In the past Christianity has to a certain extent, moderated the German delight in war. But once the charm that tames it, the cross is broken, [Twisted Cross-SWASTIKA] the savagery of those old warriors will burst forth anew…and when you hear a crash [Chrystalnight Nov. 9-10, 1938; then Blitzkrieg Sept. 3, 1939; Great War, World War I ended Nov. 11, 1918] such as the world has never heard before, you will know "The German thunder has found its mark.").   p 159-160

[Heine also prophesied: "Where books burn people will follow." My father said my German mother Elisabeth Francois Frank saw both books and people burned in her hometown Frankfurt am Main in 1934, my father told me when I asked him why she left her beloved homeland Germany. Frankfurt now holds BOOK FAIR. In August 1958, age 15, we visited the bombed rubble Frankfurt home of Goethe with a temporary memorial. In June 1998, my daughter and I visited Goethe's 3 story house/museum right after landing from Washington, DC. My Jewish daughter had just finished her first year teaching German at Stafford High School. In my daughter's senior year at Mary Washington college 1997, now university, she was assigned to translate GOETHE'S epic large prophetic novel FAUST. Dr. Faustus, makes a bargain with the devil, and SELLS HIS SOUL for fame and fortune for a period of 23 years. This is like translating JOHN BUNYAN'S PILGRIM'S PROGRESS or DANTE'S PARADISE LOST. A real metaphysical challenge or as the left wing media so often proclaims—EXISTENTIAL.

Media and socialist politicians and media here is an EXISTENTIAL FACT—Adolf Hitler was in power from 1922-1945—23 YEARS LIKE FAUST HAD. God's providence? How did that end? In 1521, Dr. MARTIN LUTHER wrote ERASMUS that HIS-tory is in GOD, JESUS' TRIUNE control. When Israel didn't follow JEHOVAH/YAHWEY, YWHW, YESHUA'S WORD-COMMANDMENTS God's prophets warn of judgment through their enemies. This is a truth every nation should fear, follow, and believe.]

Heinrich Heine may have influenced "fiction" novelist RAY BRADBURY to write FAHRENHEIT 451, the temperature books burn, when all books were burned because they all upset some group. I have more than 4,000 non fiction historical, theological books. My mother read hundreds of BOOK OF THE MONTH club books and dad read many World War II Ballantine books memoirs and a few new astronomy books, I also read. My only fiction books are the dystopian 451, 1984, ANIMAL FARM, BRAVE NEW WORLD, BRAVE NEW WORLD REVISITED, THE IRON HEEL and IT CAN'T HAPPEN HERE. The first three have been made into big screen films 1984, twice. All these books are prophetic warnings about totalitarian states which completely control their populations lives. None of these societies had guns just like Hitler's Germany, Mussolini's Italy, and all Communist governments. There was also a TV series V which featured "human-looking" extraterrestrials, actually REPTILIAN, which gave us medical technology which saved lives, can't be bad? Scarier than STEPHEN KING who is a "Mainiac" who lives in Maine. My father's father was from Calais, Maine and his mother was from Eastport, Maine. I graduated from Nasson College, Springvale, Maine 1960-1964. My class graduation dinner was at the SHAWMUT INN. It was on the Atlantic coast inlet past the BUSH family ocean side mansion. It was 1964, who were the Bush's? My high school French teacher 3 !/2 yrs. was Miss Bush. King's Jumanji was filmed in nearby Berwick, Maine featuring ROBIN WILLIAMS, KIRSTIN DUNST. The ROCK, KEVIN HART, JACK BLACK, KAREN GILLIAM, have done JUMANJI 2 & 3.

HEINE PARADOX? Heine proclaimed "Where books burn people will burn!" Heine cited a specific book THE KORAN! PARADOX or OXYMORON? Heine was Jewish and knew that Mohammedans, "not favored" by Muslims in Islam have persecuted their Jewish neighbors which is written in the KORAN/QURAN. Islam occupied the HOLY LAND ISRAEL where Jesus and Old

Testament prophets lived which caused the Roman Catholic church to initiate several 7 CRUSADES where thousands of Christians and Muslims died in "holy" warfare. Later, Europe was invaded by Muslims. Spain, Portugal and southern France were occupied for centuries by Saracen/Moor muslims. The Balkans were occupied by muslims for centuries. VLAD, "Dracula" soldiers killed many Ottoman Turkish muslims invading his Transylvania. Twice Vienna, Austria was under siege and almost captured. LUTHER wrote, his great hymn "A MIGHTY FORTRESS IS OUR GOD" which German Protestant soldiers sang marching to Roman Catholic Vienna. Burning or banning a Bible, Old and New Testament, Torah or the Koran is sacrilegious. However, the words of a divine power which promotes the morality of Humankind of all races and ethic backgrounds cannot be banned of burned.

"Stanley High, in an article entitled "Hitler's Ersatz Religion," reprinted in the Reader's Digest, wrote: "The whole power of the (Nazi) party is behind the effort to uproot Christianity and substitute for it a heathen tribalism. Instruction in the new faith is part of all teachers' training courses, its literature is required reading in the schools. The daily press and the movies are required to propagate the faith, its hymn book [MEIN KAEMPF, MY STRUGGLE] has been bought by more than a million German families...Frequently, Hitler is spoken of as "OUR REDEEMER." The famous Christian hymn, CHRIST, THOU LORD OF THE NEW AGE, has been changed for party gatherings to HITLER, THOU LORD OF THE NEW AGE." p 161

"In many government orphanages a prayer to Hitler is required of the children before every meal: "To Thee I owe, alone, my daily bread; abandon thou me never, with me fore'er abide, Fuehrer, my Fuehrer, my Faith and my Light..." p 161

"The Minister of the Interior warns German parents that names taken from the Bible or names of the saints or Christian martyrs will no longer be accepted by the state...Christians, solemnly affirm the Nazi researchers, did not originate with Christ at all. It originated with WOTAN—a 100 per cent German god and one of the first great Nazis ...GOOD FRIDAY is dedicated to BALDUR—another one of Nazism's mythological forebears. "The soldier," says a Nazi educator, 'who throws his last hand grenade, the dying seaman who pronounces the Fuehrer's name as his last word, these are, for us, divine figures much more than the crucified Jew.' "

"The National song of Nazi Germany was the HORST WESSEL LIED. Wessel was a young National Socialist who made his living by renting out whores [pimp], and was finally killed in a brawl over one of them. Yet he is the hero of the young Nazis and of the whole German nation. Their songs contained such lines as: "We follow not Christ but Horst Wessel. I am no Christian and no Catholic. Church can take a running jump!"

"Saint Odile was right. Hitler was an antichrist from every facet looked at, from every pore of his being." p 162

Observe how the saint predicts that the German tyrant will make Rachel weep. Rachel is a Jewish name, and the greatest sufferers of all under the antichrist were Jews). p162

SON OF THE RIGHT HAND—RACHEL'S HARD LABOR BIRTH OF BENJAMIN

"As her soul was departing...she called his name Ben-oni, but his father
called him Benjamin. So Rachel died, and she was buried on the way to
Ephrath (that is, Bethlehem). Genesis 35:18-19

"As Jacob's household travels to Bethlehem. RACHEL experiences very hard labor. Though she is dying, her midwife consoles her with news that she is having a son. This foreshadows the birth of a Son of God Himself in Bethlehem. For he is born to overcome the curse of death and bring consolation to all people."

"Rachel calls her son Ben-oni, meaning "son of my affliction." But JACOB gives him his lasting name, "Benjamin," which means "son of my right hand." In these names, we see the two parts of Jesus' saving ministry. He is born as the son of affliction, who suffers for the sins of mankind in

His state of humiliation. But in his state of exaltation, Jesus rises and ascends to the right hand of the Father as Lord of all."

"This is also how it is for us who believe in Jesus. Though we are now afflicted under the curse of death, we are given everlasting life and a new name through our Baptism in Christ. We are the blessed of the Father who will be gathered at Jesus' right hand on the Last Day." PorTals of Prayer Dec. 11, 2019 read Genesis 35:16-20 + Psalm 16

"The conqueror will come from the banks of the Danube."

[Hitler was born in Austria on the Inn River, a Danube tributary, across from Bavaria, Germany. His father was a border customs official. NOSTRADAMUS prophesied "HISTER" Hitler from Danube-Isr and would be the Second antichrist after NAPOLEON. He would begin a terrible war, he and his mistress would die in a cave "bunker".]

"He will be a remarkable leader among men. The war he has undertaken
is the most terrifying humans have ever undergone—in the height of the
mountains. [Berctesgarten mountain retreat] His arms will be flaming."
(Flame throwing tanks and other fiery horrors were used by the Germans
in the Battle of France.)
…And the helmets of soldiers are in the midst of bristling, shining
weapons, while their hands brandish flaming torches. How many of
the dead lie here!
"He will win victories on land and sea, and even in the air, and I see his war-skilled winded warriors, riding up with a clattering noise in the clouds, [bombers] there seizing stars [fire bombs] to throw down on the cities of the world, lighting gigantic fires." p 162
(This remarkable prediction of air warfare is perhaps even more surprising in the original Latin. A 100 years ago these lines would not have made sense.Today they do perfectly.)
"At that there is consternation among the nations, who exclaim:
"Whence comes his strength! How he has been able to
undertake such a war!"
(Exactly what all the world said while watching the course of Hitler's conquests.)
"The Earth will seem overturned by the collision of armies. Rivers of
blood will seem to flow. In the depths of the sea the monsters will be
stunned by the conflagration."
(Depth-bombs have done this.).   [submarines]
"While black tempests will lay all waste. Future generations will be
astonished that his enemies were not able to hold back the march of
his mighty victories."
And the war will be long, and the victory will have attained the height
of his triumphs about the middle of the sixth month of the second
year of the war."

(This specific statement terminates the "terrible mans" triumphs in March-April, 1941. In March, 1941, America passed the Lend-Lease Bill, at which isolationists held up their hands in horror, exclaiming, "Now we are committed to the defeat of Hitler!" But even more important Schickelgruber's [Hitler's original name] conquests ended in the period prophesied."). Ibid p 163

THE HUNCHBACK WHO "PLANNED" WORLD WAR II

"HOMER LEA was an American author and geopolitical strategist. He is best known for his involvement with Chinese reform and revolutionary movements in the early 20th Century and as a close advisor to Dr. SUN YAT-SEN during the 1911 Chinese Republican revolution that overthrew the QING DYNASTY, and for his writings about China." He became a Chinese lieutenant general and is buried in Taiwan."   Wikipedia

"Lea's book THE VALOR OF IGNORANCE, (1909) examined American defense and in part prophesied a war between America and Japan. The book contained maps of the hypothetical invasion of California and the Philippines. Gen. DOUGLAS MACARTHUR [read the book] and paid close attention in planning his defense of the Philippines. The Japanese military also read the [translated] book".   Wikipedia

"Lea in his book THE DAY OF THE SAXON, repeated the prophecy of war between America and Japan. In the "Day of the Saxon" Lea believed the entire Anglo-Saxon race faced a threat from the German (Teuton), Russian (Slav), and Japanese expansionism: "The fatal relationship of Russia, Japan, and Germany "has now assumed through the urgency of natural forces a coalition directed against the survival of Saxon supremacy." Lea believed that while Japan moved against the Far East and Russia against India, the Germans would strike at England the center of the British Empire. Two Pacts—Non-Aggression between Germany and Russia in 1939 and Neutrality between Russia and Japan in April 1941 prevented the prophecy from coming true. Lea considered the possibility of war between Germany and Russia but did not believe that this war will take place before the defeat of the British Empire because the German-Russian war would be mutual disastrous for both." Written (1912 p 124-125)   WW I began Sept. 1, 1914.

"In these books Lea viewed American and British struggles for political competition and survival as part of a larger Anglo-Saxon SOCIAL DARWINIST contest between the "survival of the fittest" races. He sought to make all English-speaking peoples see that they were in a global competition for supremacy against the Teutonic, Slavic, and Asian races. China figured prominently in his world-view as a key ally with the Anglo-Saxons in counterbalancing other regional and global competitors. Lea's THE SWARMING OF THE SLAVS, predicting that should Britain and America emerge victorious over Germany and Japan, they would then be forced to confront Russia was not completed because of his death in California on November 1, 1912, age 35."   Wikipedia

Vonnegut's "Slaughter House 5" Alien's Viewpoint of Christ

"She [Valencia] asked him if there was anything she could bring him from the outside, and he said, "No, I have just about everything I want."

"What about books?" said Valencia."

"I'm right next to one of the biggest private libraries in the world," said Billy, meaning Eliot Rosewater's collection of science fiction."

"Rosewater was on the next bed, reading, and Billy drew him into the conversation, asked him what he was reading at this time?"

"So Rosewater told him. It was THE GOSPEL FROM OUTER SPACE, by Kilgore Trout. It was about a visitor from outer space, shaped very much like a Tralfamadorian, by the way. The visitor from outer space made a serious study of Christianity, to learn, if he could, why Christians found it so easy to be cruel. He concluded that at least part of the trouble was slipshod storytelling in the New Testament. He supposed that the Intent of the Gospels was to teach people, among other things, to be merciful, even to the lowest of the low.—But the Gospels actually taught that."

"Before you kill somebody, make absolutely sure he isn't well connected. So it goes."

"The flaw in Christian stories, said the visitor from OUTER SPACE, was that Christ , who didn't look like much, was actually the Son of the mot powerful being in the Universe. Readers understood that, so, when they came to the Crucifixion they naturally thought, and Rosewater read out loud again:

"Oh, boy—they sure picked the wrong guy to Lynch that time!"

"And that thought had a brother: "There are right people to lynch?" Who? People not well connected. So it goes."

"The visitor from Outer Space made a gift to earth of a new Gospel. In it, Jesus was really a nobody [no Pride or beauty ISAIAH 52], and a pain in the neck to a lot of people with better connections than he had. [The Earthly powers—King Herod, the Pharisees and the Roman Empire's governor Pontius Pilate's dilemma, who found no guilt for Jesus' Crucifixion.]

He [Jesus] still got to say all the lovely and puzzling things he said in the other Gospels.

"So the people amused themselves one day by nailing him to a cross and planting the cross in the ground. There couldn't possibly be any repercussions, the lynchers thought. The reader would have to think that, too, since the new Gospel hammered home again and again what a nobody Jesus was."

"And then, just before the nobody died, the heavens opened up, and there was thunder and lightening. [Actually three hours of darkness and an earthquake which opened graves and "tore" the Holy Temple curtain.] The voice of God came crashing down. He told the people he was adopting the bum as his son. [Biblically this occurred at John the Baptist's baptism of Jesus in the Jordan River, Angel Gabriel told the virgin Mary she was going to have a boy child she should name YESHUA Immanuel, Jesus was born in David's Bethlehem as prophet Micah's prophesied fulfilled by Caesar's tax decree, Jesus' prayer in the Garden of Gethsemane, Isaiah 52 prophesied the suffering Messiah for the sins of Humankind who believe in HIS WORD like the penitent criminal on the Cross who Christ forgave.]

[Don't take only the word of the extraterrestrial or my brief synopsis. My testimony and witness has many biblical highlights. The Bible is the best historical thriller book ever written. Read the Bible yourself just open it anywhere. The first time I ever read the Bible at length was in the Virginia Unemployment office in January 1983 with 12% unemployment, a record high here. I opened my new gift red-letter King James Bible and read doctor Luke's story about Jesus birth and how Mary visited her cousin ELISABETH whose 6 month fetus John the Baptist leap [kicked] with JOY at the presence of Mary who arrived with her 3 month fetus baby Jesus. That was the first time I learned that my mother's name Elisabeth was also John the Baptist's mother's name.]

SMALL WORLD VONNEGUT FACT: His Army unit was captured in the snowy Ardennes Mountains during the brutal German army surprise attack the first day of the Battle of the Bulge. He was sent to Dresden and was there, sheltered in a meat slaughter house, during the horrendous fire storm bombing of Dresden providentially on ASH WEDNESDAY February1945. Vonnegut attended an Indianapolis high school. My Air Force friend Chuck Byler wrote a biography of Air Force Lt. Col. JAMES KASLER, who was the most decorated American airmen, a B-29 tail gunner Japan World War II, Korea, 6 MiG ace in F-86 and 92 missions in Republic F-105 Thunderchief, shot down, a tortured prisoner 6 years in Hanoi. Chuck said he attended the same high school at the same time as Kurt Vonnegut. So it goes. In Indiana, Pennsylvania, in June 2016, I meet two Indiana University students in James Stewart's hometown. I told them I was going to Stewart's museum and was writing a book about my dad and him both being in 8th Air Force units with B-24 bombers. I said something about Kurt Vonnegut and one of the students asked, "Are you going to have anything about extraterrestrials in your book like Vonnegut." I said yes, and told him about this biblical alien story. I told him I was Lutheran and his friend named KRUG said his mother was related to the man who designed the LUTHER ROSE [Lazarus] emblem. He said he was persecuted.

HOLLYWOOD CONNECTION: In the first FOOTLOOSE movie they are shown banning Vonnegut's SLAUGHTERHOUSE FIVE in the library. Actor KEVIN BACON retorts, "The book is a classic." After I saw the film, I searched the book and have the VHS video and couldn't find anything to ban not even four letter words but GOES. It must be the alien's interpretation of the JESUS STORY? OK it isn't KOSHER. The plot is about young people wanting to dance which had been banned, because of a tragic accident, by the town preacher actor JOHN LITHGOW, a great character actor. He is going to play ROGER AILES, the fired head of FOX NEWS in the movie BOMBSHELL. Footloose was a great beginning for Kevin Bacon "Six Degrees" movie career. SO IT GOES.

Microsoft and the Bavarian illuminati

Apple Sherlock Internet Web browser circa 1996

"These days most people have heard of Microsoft Corporation, and its founder BILL GATES. The majority of computers are today Microsoft system software, and those that do not often run applications from Microsoft. However, few people know the true story behind the rise of Microsoft and even fewer suspect the terrible cosmic secrets that are concealed beneath the facade of successful software company."

"In the Object Linking and Embedding 2.0 Programmer's Reference there is a very curious term. On page 78, the second paragraph starts with the sentence. "In the aggregate model, this internal communication is achieved through coordination with a special instance of IUNKNOWN interface known as the CONTROLLING UNKNOWN of the AGGREGATE." The term "CONTROLLING UNKNOWN" is a very interesting choice of words. It is not the most intuitively obvious term for what it is describing (a base class used for implementing an object-orientated data exchange/embedding system)."

"A term strikingly similar to "controlling unknown" was the term "UNKNOWN SUPERIORS", used by many OCCULT SECRET SOCIETIES. These included the Strict Observance Masonic lodge, whose members were sometimes referred to as "ILLUMINATI", and which had some connection with Adam Weishaupt's order "Unknown Superiors" is a term that refers to non-corporeal or superhuman agencies in command of secret societies or mystery cults. Such an agency is frequently known as the "inner head" of an order of organization, as opposed to the outer head, who is HUMAN."

"Organizations that claimed or were claimed to be commanded by such "unknown superiors" include the Ordo Templi Orientis of ALEISTER CROWLEY and the KNIGHTS TEMPLAR, whose INNER HEAD was apparently a being named BAPHOMET."

"Apart from the term "controlling unknown", another hint at the secrets behind Microsoft is the fact that MICROSOFT WINDOWS has a limit of FIVE window device contexts. FIVE is a decidedly ODD NUMBER for such an application, being neither a power of two nor one less than a POWER OF TWO, but let us not forget Adam Weishaupt's discovery of the LAW OF FIVES in the NECRONOMICON."

"Few people for sure know how many buildings there are in the Microsoft campus in Redmond, WA. No maps of the entire facility are known to exist. Some Microsoft employees put the estimate at six or three. An article in an Australian newspaper has claimed, "That there are 22 buildings. That is partly true; however, there is a building, hidden from the public and even from most Microsoft employees. The twenty-third building, or Building 7, is pentagonal in shape; is exact location known only to five people (of whom Bill Gates may be one), however it is believed that the building is accessible from elsewhere in the Microsoft campus by a secret passage."

438

"What is in the five sided building is not known. However, it is believed that the contents of Building 7 are of a supernatural nature. Apart from the Pentagon, there was a similar five-sided building in Nazi Germany. This has been carefully kept hidden from the public. One hypothesis is that Building 7 is inhabited, or used to communicate with, the Inner Head, or "controlling unknown". The identity of the Outer Head is unknown. Bill Gates may be the Outer Head, a high initiate of the conspiracy or just a figurehead whose purpose it is to divert attention."

I downloaded this from the Internet circa 1996 through the new Apple Sherlock Web browser possibly Altavista search engine server using a slow 18.8 kilobyte modem. This was long before GOOGLE connects everything. I have many "conspiracy" books some self published which give the history of the ILLUMINATI, KNIGHTS TEMPLAR,, FREEMASONS, NEW WORLD ORDER, TRILATERAL COMMISSION, COUNCIL OF FOREIGN RELATIONS. BILDERBERGS. BOHEMIAN GROVE and NEW AGE RELIGION which makes this Microsoft theory an interesting intrigue story. These organizations all exist today with members of immense wealth and political power. Twenty years later we can add the mega Internet intrigue which recently has been reported that FACEBOOK, U TUBE and GOOGLE through algorithms have profiled its billions of users. Their CEO's have been brought before the United States Congress and gave embarrassing testimonies. It showed that their sites weren't free. Users were indirectly sold through connected links generating billions of dollars. That was a "secret" business in capitalism. What wasn't alright was that through targeted algorithms conservative FACEBOOK and GOOGLE sites were targeted and unfairly deleted even when outspokenly patriotic but were judged "politically incorrect." U TUBE African-Americans DIAMOND AND SILK video in Congress about their critical comic anti-liberal FACEBOOK video being deleted. Liberal "politically correct" messages were promoted.

Here is What You Need to Know About Bill Gates' "ID2020" PROJECT

TRUMP TRAIN NEWS April 21, 2020

"A lot of online conspiracy theories have been raised around BILL GATES" involvement in a project called ID2020. Many of these conspiracies are while some are more on the tame side of things, the media has already stepped in to debunk many of these online rumors but someone needs to fact check the media as their credibility has been non-existent for years now."

1 WHAT IS ID2020?—"ID2020 is a program looking to give every human on earth a DIGITAL ID that can be verified and used by governments around the world the same way a passport or driver's license would be used. All in all the group is not really that strange and their motives are straight forward."

2 WHO IS INVOLVED?—"ID2020 was founded by the following organizations:

The Rockefeller Foundation—Accenture (a consulting firm)—Gavi, The Vaccine Alliance—Microsoft—IDEO (a consulting firm)

These organizations have board members who operate ID2020.

3 What were some of the Conspiracy Theories?—"Several conspiracy theories came to life over the organization that involved the topic of implanting microchips in individuals, mandatory vaccines, and 5G internet service. None of these things have been proven true nor is there any solid evidence to suggest any of them are remotely possible."

"The idea that this organization would provide individuals with microchips implanted in them as a digital ID is not their current goal, but the technology to do so is real. One company has offered microchips to individuals as a way to skip the ticket booth when getting on trains, although many ethical and security questions have been raised on this effort and will continue to be raised as the technology is explored further."

"While the idea of making vaccines mandatory for all has been popular among some circles of political thought for a long time it has been rejected time and time again. ID2020 has announced no plan to make a legislative effort that would mandate vaccines. 5G is a controversial subject on its own and has nothing to do with ID2020 despite what some are claiming online. 5G is an upgrade to the current telecommunications infrastructure that has been met with pushback from many in the scientific community and communities across the nation due to fears it does more harm than good."

4 Was the Media Honest in Covering ID2020?—"Has the media been honest in their coverage of ID2020? To put it simply, no. The media has a standard tactic where they cherry-pick a few tweets, Facebook posts, or comments and highlight them as if there are millions like them. What they are doing is poisoning the well, they intend to take the most fringe position and pretend that is what anyone who opposes ID2020 thinks. This is an extremely dishonest tactic and one the media uses often."

5 Issues With ID2020—"There are a lot of concerns with the objectives of ID2020, issues of security and abuse mainly. On the security front, many are concerned that these IDs may be stolen and abused in the same manner as social security numbers are stolen and abused every day around the world. Many are also expressing concern over governments abusing these IDs by tracking a user's digital footprint the same way communist China tracks the online presence of its citizens."

THE MICROCHIP AND THE MARK OF THE BEAST

"Dr. Carl W. Sanders is an electronic engineer, inventor, author and consultant for various government organizations as well as IBM, GENERAL ELECTRIC, HONEYWELL and TELEDYNE. He is also a winner of the Presidents and Governors Award for Design Excellence."

"Thirty two years of my life was spent in design engineering and electronic designing micro chips in the Bio Med field. In 1968, I became involved almost by accident in a research and development project in regard for a spinal by-pass for a young lady who had severed her spine. They were looking at possibly being able to connect motor nerves. It was a project we were all excited about. There were 100 people involved and I was senior engineer in charge of the project. This project culminated in the microchip that we talk about now a microchip that I believe is going to be the positive identification and MARK OF THE BEAST."

"Working on the microchip we had no idea about it ever being an identification chip. We looked at it as being a very humanitarian thing to do. We were all excited about what we were doing. We were doing high level integration for the very first time. This team was made up of people out of San Jose, people from Motorola, General Electric and Boston Medical Center it was quite a group of people."

"Over one and a half million dollars was spent finding out that the two places in the body that the temperature changes the most rapidly are the forehead (primary position) right below the hairline and the back of the hand (alternate position)"

"I was in one meeting where it was discussed: "How can you control a people if you can't identify them?"

Retrieved on Internet through Apple Sherlock App Dec. 5, 1998

[It was decided to end the program as a tracking chip was more lucrative.]

PERSONAL STORY: My grandfather was pronounced dead in the Massachusetts General hospital in Boston in May 1862. He passed age 94, in 1933, in Amityville, New York. The medical microchip project was discontinued for economic reasons when it was decided the chip technology was more profitable used as a location device used to track wild animals used for many years. Today Sweden has used personal microchips as IDs for entering work zones and even for financial transactions. Read the Mark of the Beast in Revelation passage which predestines that in the End Time all humanity will have to take a mark [chip] to buy or sell. This technology can fulfill a 2,000 year old prophecy. I may live to see this in my lifetime.

Will You GRIN for the MARK OF THE BEAST?

"Can a microscopic tag be implanted in a person's body to track his every movement? There's actual discussion about that. You will rule on that—mark my words—before your tenure is over."

U.S. Senator JOSEPH BIDEN, asked during. Senate Judiciary Committee hearings on the nomination of JOHN ROBERTS to be Chief Justice of the Supreme Court. Roberts was confirmed on September 29, 2005 as the 17th chief justice by a 78-22 vote.

"Author Nita Horn asked if the biblical mark of the Beast might be a conspiracy employing specific implantable technology only now available. Her theory was gripping. An occult elite operating behind the U.S. Government devises a virus that is a crossover between human and animal disease—let's say, an entirely new and highly contagious influenza mutation—and intentionally releases it into the public. A PANDEMIC ensues, and the period when a person contracts the virus and death is something like 10 days. A universal cry for a cure goes out. Seemingly miraculously, the government then steps forward with a vaccine. The government explains that given the nature of the animal-human flue, the "cure" uses animal DNA and nanobots to rewrite one's genetics so that the person is no longer entirely human. The point made was that those who receive this antidote would become part "beast," and perhaps thus the "mark of the Beast." No longer "entirely human" would also mean—according to this outline —that the individual could no longer be "SAVED" or go to Heaven, explaining why the book of Revelation says "whoever receives the mark" is damned forever. If one imagines the global chaos of such a pandemic, the concept of how the Antichrist "causes all," both small and great, to receive this mark becomes clearer. This scenario would mean that nobody would be allowed to "buy or sell" in the marketplace without the mark-cure due to the need to quarantine all but the inoculated, fulfilling all aspects of the mark of the Beast prophecy."
FORBIDDEN GATES THE DAWN OF TECHNO-DIMENSIONAL SPIRITUAL WARFARE
Tom and Nita Horn DEFENDER publishing Crane, Missouri 65633; 2010

Massive New Government Surveillance Program has Eerie Resemblance to "Mark of the Beast"

THE WESTERN JOURNAL Christine Fauvocci May 12, 2020

"PROPOSED DEMOCRAT 'TRACE' ACT IS LABELED WITH THE MOST HORRIFYING NUMBER POSSIBLE. If the possibility of granting massive surveillance powers to the government isn't frightening enough, the proposed COVID-19 Testing, Reaching, and Contacting Everyone Act also comes with an equally as ominous number: H.R. 6666."
"The number is eerily similar to one from biblical prophecy. "This calls for wisdom: let the one who has understanding calculate the number of the beast, for it is the number of a man and his number is 666," the Bible says in Revelation 13:18."

"Christians interpret the number from the apocalyptic Scripture as a symbol for the devil or the Antichrist, who will usher in the end times. With the world facing a global pandemic, giant Asian murder hornets, plagues of locusts, massive fires in Australia and California and so on, the faithful are   understandably   already   vigilant."

"If it were just the bill's number, however, it would be easy to overlook, but the U.S. House of Representatives proposed TRACE ACT would allot $100,000,000,000 billion to "conduct diagnostic testing for COVID-19, to trace and monitor the contacts of infected individuals, and to support the quarantine of such.""

"There aren't many specifics as to how the government would accurately "trace and monitor" American citizens but, as the saying goes, "the devil is in the details," which are notably absent. Considering that Rep. BOBBY RUSH's bill would provide funds to "hire, train, compensate, and pay the expenses" of entities charged with the aforementioned activities, the pieces come together into a "1984" existence where government representatives monitor private citizens' every move."

"In fact, the Illinois Democrat said in a statement on his own website that TRACE ACT includes for "door-to-door outreach.""

"There is also provision which states that individuals conducting testing should be hired from the community, meaning neighbors potentially would MONITOR NEIGHBORS, particularly in "hot spots" and "medically underserved communities.""

"Furthermore, for anyone who tests positive, the newly minted government employees would have the power to trace anyone who came in contact with the individual, exponentially expanding the number of people under surveillance at any given time."

"Those who test positive would also be confined to their homes or treated in one of the "mobile units" the bill would fund. The facts amount to widespread government surveillance. It's not a wild conspiracy theory, just a simple description of what the TRACE ACT seems to implement."

"This is problematic for many, as providing out of control governments with the excuse and the means to trace private citizens makes folks rightfully wary. Three weeks ago, I told you the virus pandemic would be used to track people in America,: Emerald Robinson at NEWSMAX tweeted. "And here we are: H.R. 6666 COVID-19 Testing, Reaching, And Contacting Everyone (TRACE) Act."

1% of Counties Home to Half of COVID-19 Cases, Over Half of Deaths

THE DAILY SIGNAL Norbert Michel May 13, 2020

30 Counties with most deaths.
Share of all counties .95%.

1,996 counties with 1 or fewer deaths
Share of all counties 63.5%

"As Heritage Foundation researchers have demonstrated throughout the pandemic, the spread of COVID-19 in the United States has been extremely concentrated in a small number of states— and among a small number of counties within all states."

"As of May 11, for example, 10 states accounted for almost 70% of all U.S. cases and nearly 75% of all deaths (but only 52% of the population). Together, New York and New Jersey alone account for 35% of all cases and 44% of total COVID-10 deaths, though only 9% of the U.S. population."

"The 30 counties with the most COVID-19 cases, for example, account for 48% of all the cases in the U.S. and 55% of all deaths, three or four times greater than their 15% share of the U.S. population."

"Of those 30 counties, 24 are in the Northeast corridor between Philadelphia and Boston, the passageway served by a commuter railway system that runs through Manhattan. Overall, only 10% of all counties contain 95% of all the COVID-19 deaths, even though they account for 64% of the population."

"Just as important, 50% of all counties (with 10% of the U.S. population) have ZERO COVID-19 deaths as of May 11. In fact, 63% of all counties (with 15% of the population) have no more than ONE COVID-19 death each."

"So, while 1% of counties (mostly in the Northeast) have more than half of all COVID-19 deaths in the U.S., 63% of counties have no more than ONE COVID-19 death each—and both groups represent the same share of the U.S. population."

WHAT IS THE ILLUMINATI?

"The nature of the universe is such that ends can never justify the means.
On the contrary, the means always determine the end." ALDOUS HUXLEY

"In 1785, a bolt of lightning struck a courier en route to Paris from Frankfort-am-Main. "Original Shift in Days of Illuminations," a tract written by ADAM "SPARTACUS" WEISHAUPT. founder of the ILLUMINATI, was recovered from the dead messenger. It contained the secret society's long-range plan for "The NEW WORLD ORDER through WORLD REVOLUTION.""

"The Bavarian Government promptly outlawed the society and in 1787 published the details of The Illuminati conspiracy in "The Original Writings of the Order and Sect of the Illuminati.""

"The illuminati was publicly founded May 1, 1776, at the University of Ingolstadt [Germany] by Weishaupt, a Professor of Cannon Law. It was a very "learned" society Weishaupt drew the earliest members of his new order from among his students."

"In Adam Weishaupt's own words:

"By this plan, we shall direct all mankind in this manner. And, by the simplest means, we shall start all in motion and in flames. The occupations must be so allotted and contrived that we may, in secret, influence all political transactions."

"There is disagreement among scholars as to whether or not the Illuminati survived its banishment. Nevertheless, under Weishaupt's guidance, the group had been quite successful in attracting members and through various manipulations had allied itself with the extensive MASONIC NETWORKS in Europe and the United States."

"On December 5, 1776, students at WILLIAM and MARY COLLEGE founded a secret society, PHI BETA KAPPA." A second chapter was formed at YALE, in 1780. The anti-Masonic movement which erupted in the United States during the 1820s denounced the secrecy of groups such as Phi Beta Kappa. The society responded to this pressure by going public. Some researchers note this as the direct cause of the appearance of YALE'S ORDER OF THE SKULL AND BONES."

"The alumni of Skull and Bones provide a direct link between the secret societies and the state department/national security apparatus."

"From "GEORGE BUSH: THE UNAUTHORIZED BIOGRAPHY":

"...Prescott Bush {Skull and Bones] was a U.S, senator from Connecticut, a confidential friend and golf partner with National Security Director GORDON GRAY, and an important golf partner with DWIGHT EISENHOWER as well. Prescott's old lawyer from the Nazi days, JOHN FOSTER DULLES, was Secretary of State, and his brother ALLEN DULLES, formerly of the Schroder bank, was head of the CIA."

"In the latter years of the Eisenhower presidency, Gordon Gray rejoined the government. As an intimate friend and golfing partner of Prescott Bush, Gray complemented the Bush influence on

Eisenhower The BUSH-GRAY family partnership in the 'secret government' continues up through the George Bush presidency

"Gordon Gray had been appointed head of the new Psychological Strategy Board in 1951 under AVERILL HARRIMAN's rule as assistant to President Truman for national security affairs. From 1958 to 1961 Gordon Gray held the identical post under President Eisenhower. Gray acted as IKE's intermediary, strategist and hand-holder, in the President's relations with the CIA and the U.S. and allied military forces."

"Eisenhower did not oppose the CIA's covert action projects; he only wanted to be protected from the consequences of their failure or exposure. Gray's primary task, in the guise of 'over-site' on all U.S. covert action, was to protect and hide the growing mass of CIA and related secret government activities."

"It was not only covert "projects" which were developed by the Gray-Bush-Dulles combination; it was also new, hidden "structures" of the United States government."

"From "THE IMMACULATE DECEPTION" by RUSSELL BOWEN:

"According to NIXON'S biography, his personal and political ties with the BUSH FAMILY go back to 1946, when Nixon claims he read an AD placed in an L.A. newspaper by the ORANGE COUNTY REPUBLICAN PARTY and wealthy group of businessmen led by Prescott Bush, the father of GEORGE H.W. BUSH."

"They wanted a young candidate to run for Congress. NIXON applied and won the job, becoming a MOUTHPIECE FOR THE BUSH GROUP, progressing to the U.S. SENATE and in 1952 the VICE PRESIDENCY."

"In 1960, Vice President Nixon was scouring the world seeking the presidency. At his side was PRESCOTT BUSH. Congressman GERALD FORD was helping raise funds, as was GEORGE H.W. BUSH."

"It took Nixon eight 8 more years to reach his goal. And the canny politician always remembered who helped get him there. So again it was payback time for George H.W. Bush. Nixon appointed him Chairman of the REPUBLICAN NATIONAL COMMITTEE, and later AMBASSADOR TO CHINA. "

"By 1976, Ford who succeeded Nixon after WATERGATE, paid his due bill. He picked out a big job for his old crony, GEORGE H.W. BUSH, the CIA.. But this time Bush would not be an underling. Now he would be head man."

[Vladimir Putin's 12 Russian hackers in the secret GRU, formerly KGB, were named the day before President DONALD TRUMP meet face to face with the Russian Federal States elected leader VLADIMIR PUTIN. A tremendous media storm followed when President Trump didn't tell Putin to his face to stop interfering in America's presidential elections. There was a media news frenzy and attacks, of course, by left socialist Democrats and even Conservative RHINO Republicans how this was a great diplomatic failure. President Trump the next day said he misspoke saying wouldn't instead of would? Semantics or just another brilliant President Trump plan to expose the far left wing progressive, socialist/communist hatred or love? All Americans should be shocked by these false "patriotic" attacks against President Trump being a traitor a pawn of Putin. Putin knows that President Trump has done more than draw a "Red Line" with no action. We have bombed Putin's mercenaries, not soldiers, in Syria killing 300?

The left wing media allowed TV "pundits" and former very high level American Bush/Obama administration "defenders" of America from Putin's "Communist" threat call President Trump a traitor and say he should be impeached. I heard unknowns and former Obama high ranking military and security officials refer to President Trump's failure to tell Putin to stop his spying as being like Pearl Harbor, 9-11, Chrystal Night, the Holocaust, Hitler, a Nazi. I don't know what History books these people have been reading? FAKE HISTORY. I have written my personal stories about my personal family connections to all these horrific HIStorical events. Ironically these irate media people don't call President Trump JOSEPH STALIN, the Communist dictator of Russia, a mass murder of some 8,000,000? Russian Christian and Jewish people about half were Ukrainians whose farms were collectivized and the farmers were starved. They didn't call Trump KARL MARX, VLADIMIR LENIN, MAO, POL POT, HO CHI MINH, MADURO, CASTRO, CHE GUEVERA, SADDAM HUSSEIN, GHADHAFFI, ASSAD, KHAMENI, MUSSOLINI, TOJO or Emperor HIROHITO who were responsible directly or indirectly for more than 100,000,000 innocent deaths. These men were/are unelected dictators. President Trump hasn't KILLED ONE AMERICAN or we would hear about it 24/7.

President Trump was freely elected wit 322 electoral votes, 270 were required. Trump won the states of Wisconsin, Michigan and Ohio which Hillary thought were Democrat. It has been revealed the Socialist JILL STEIN won a few thousand votes in these states which give these states to Trump. Ironically, EVERY VOTE DOES COUNT! Thus also happened to AL GORE in Florida in 2002, when a few thousand votes went to Independent RALPH NADER. This led to the infamous FLORIDA RECOUNT which went to the U.S. SUPREME COURT which elected GEORGE W. BUSH. The 5-4 vote was actually decided by African-American Justice CLARENCE THOMAS' vote. Was this KARMA or PROVIDENCE after his sexual/racist mistreatment before the U.S. Congress when he was nominated as a Conservative Supreme Court justice. His attractive red haired CAUCASIAN wife sat by his side quietly.]   Watch it on U TUBE.

Literally, EVERY POLL and media pundit, except some FOX news commentators believed Hillary would be the first woman president. When 16 Republicans were campaigning for President, ANNE COULTER was the first to say Trump would be elected president and she was laughed at by CNN pundits! Everyone said it was impossible for candidate Trump to reach the 270 Electoral votes! FAKE POLLS AND FAKE NEWS? Assistant FBI director ROSENSTEIN after announcing the names of 12 Russian spy hackers who meddled in the Clinton/Trump election, then revealed. "There is no evidence that this effected the American electoral vote." Is anyone listening? The Constitutional Republic ELECTORAL COLLEGE works. A DEMOCRACY popular vote would have made HILLARY CLINTON president. Liberal California, New England and Illinois are not America. I graduated from a college in Maine in 1964 and received a "Liberal Arts" History degree. My grandparents were born in Calais and Eastport, Maine. I have been everywhere in scenic New England. President JOHN TRUMP received one electoral vote from my grandparent's most easterly part of the United States next to Pres. Franklin Roosevelt's home CAMPOBELLO where he was afflicted with POLIO.

Seriously, voters were for Trump and his populist MAKE AMERICA GREAT AGAIN!

Putin wanted Hillary not Trump and soon it will be revealed Trump had NO COLLUSION with Putin and that Hillary, the Obama's top Justice department and top officials in the FBI were actually committing TREASON in trying to not get Trump elected and then when elected tried to un-elect him a CABAL or JUNTA! The "respected" MUELLER Russia "collusion" commission with 14 Democrats has spent $35,000,000? of taxpayers money in two years and has only sent Trump associates to jail for tax evasion and has bankrupted their families. FBI swat teams came to their homes in the dark. the CNN was invited to take a video shown on CNN and Trump haters loved it. The Gestapo came in the night in Germany for many Germans who disliked HITLER'S SOCIALIST unChristian deeds—HISTORY. It has been testified by many witnesses that no collusion has been found with Russia. I watch the far left wing media MSNBC and CNN and there nothing but HATE NEWS about Trump not FAKE NEWS. Many people on FOX NEWS lawyers have written books factually revealing the TRUTH about what fired FBI agents have done which is concealed from their viewers. They are very highly paid fo LIE. Do these self-righteous "journalists" really want the government and SOCIALISM to control America? Maybe they have colluded on a deal to keep their high salaries? Providentially, these pundits won't be needed anymore when America is SOCIALIST?

SCOTTISH STONE OF SCONE "STONE OF DESTINY"

"The STONE OF SCONE also known as the STONE OF DESTINY, and often referred to in England as THE CORONATION STONE—is an oblong block of red sandstone that has been used for centuries in the coronation of the monarchs of Scotland, and later the monarchs of Great Britain and latterly of the United Kingdom following the acts of union. Historically, the artifact was kept in the now-ruined Scone Abbey in Scone, near Perth, Scotland. It is also known as JACOB'S PILLOW STONE and the TANIST STONE. It weighs about 335 lb. (152 kg). The Stone of Scone was last used in 1953 for the coronation of QUEEN ELIZABETH II of the United Kingdom of Great Britain and Northern Ireland."   Wikipedia

ORIGIN AND LEGENDS—"Various theories and legends exist about the stone's history prior to its placement at Scone."

*One story concerns Fergus, son of Eric, the first king of the Scots in Scotland, whose transport of the stone from Ireland to Argyll, where he was crowned on it."

*Some versions identify the stone brought by Fergus with the LIA FAIL used at TARA for the High King of Ireland, Other traditions contend that the Lia Fail remains at Tara. (Inis Fail, The Island of Destiny, is one of the traditional names of Ireland.) Wikipedia

*Legends place the origins of the Stone in Biblical times and consider the STONE TO BE THE STONE OF JACOB, taken by Jacob while in Haran. (Genesis 28:10-22)

[Jacob slept on it "pillow" and had a dream of climbing to Heaven. He wrestled at night with an Angel of the Lord a reincarnation of Jesus. He asked to be blessed by the Lord and after his leg/hip is disjointed and the Lord name him Israel.]

"Geologists proved that the stone taken by EDWARD I of England (portrayed in movie Braveheart) to WESTMINSTER is a "lower Old Red Sandstone", which was quarried in the vicinity of Scone. In 1296, the stone was taken by Edward I as spoils of war and removed to Westminster Abbey, where it was fitted into a wooden chair—known as King Edward's Chair—on which most subsequent English and then British sovereigns have been crowned. Edward I sought to claim his status as the "Lord Paramount" of Scotland, with the right to oversee its King."   Wikipedia

There is a theory that monks may have switched the stone and hidden the real one. In 1950 some Scottish students stole the stone and hid it for awhile.

In 1996, in a symbolic response to growing dissatisfaction among Scots at the prevailing constitutional settlement, the British Government decided the stone should be kept in Scotland when not in use at coronations. On JULY 3 1996, Prime Minister JOHN MAJOR announced to the House of Commons that the stone would be returned to Scotland. On 15 November 1996, the stone was transported to Edinburgh Castle arriving on 30 November, St. ANDREWS DAY, where the official handover ceremony occurred. Prince ANDREW, Duke of York, representing Queen Elizabeth II, formally handed over the royal Warrant transferring the stone into the safekeeping of the Commissioner for the Regalia."   Wikipedia

PERSONAL STORY: I visited Scone Palace in Scotland in June 1973. Driving from the palace I saw a strange four horn sheep, when a child we had four sheep, and stopped to ask the caretaker what kind of sheep it was. He retorted, "They are Jacob's sheep from the Bible." They graze in the many "strays" parks throughout Britain he told me.

RELIGION, THE FOUNDERS, THE 2016 PRESIDENTIAL RACE

By Stephen Mansfield Liberty magazine September/October 2016

"Few observers of the American political scene could have predicted the prominent role religion is playing in the current 2016 presidential election."

"Indeed, this election might still become one of the most religiously contentious in our History. There were hints of this from the beginning. A Republican candidate launched his campaign from a leading Christian university [Liberty] and pledged repeatedly during the GOP debates to do the will of God in office. Another candidate accused his party's front-runner of being "unsaved," of being a religious fake, and of being so ignorant of the Christian faith that it "boggles the mind." The Democratic Party standard-bearer spoke boldly of her faith, while the leader of the Republican field even displayed a family Bible before cameras prior to the Iowa primary."

"Evangelicals have continued to be a potent force in U.S. politics, though in this election they have proven increasingly fragmented. Their leaders have splintered, variously endorsing every candidate running for office. Even the Pope [Francis] entered the fray, welcoming the most left leaning of all candidates, BERNIE SANDERS, [Jewish], to the VATICAN just prior to the decisive New York primary."

"Now that the race has narrowed to a Clinton-Trump contest, we are sure to see even more fiery faith-based battles. Part of the reason for this religiously infused politics of HILLARY CLINTON, the presumptive Democratic nominee. She is a lifetime social gospel Methodist who thought nothing of taking her Senate opponents to task for violating the ethics of Jesus on such issues as immigration and who has claimed that her religion is the basis of her positions on same-sex marriage and abortion. Donald Trump, for whom religion is clearly not a familiar language, will have his hands full."

"Yet this is what Americans seem to prefer. A recent Pew Forum survey revealed that more than half of all Americans would like to see wider discussion of religion in this year's presidential race. All indications are that they are likely to get it."

"None of this is new, of course, Americans have known religious bickering in their presidential politics since at least the moment THOMAS JEFFERSON announced his intentions to run for the office. What is new, however, is the current reticence among U.S. voters to press presidential candidates for specifics about their religious views. It is a reticence that does not serve our country well. Certainly we should hope for a change before the 2016 election ends."

"We live in a religiously contentious age. We live at a time when what a president believes religiously and what he or she knows about the world's religions is critically important. Yet we are used to pious mush and airy phrases when it comes to religion in presidential campaigns. We are used to "God bless America" at the end of a speech, and photos of a candidate attending church, Bible in hand."

"We have begun to settle for such symbols over the far more important religious content of what candidates believe. As a nation we are hesitant to press for specifics. Much of this stems from a false sense that our Founders did not want personal faith explored in elections and so forbade religious tests for public office. What we seem to have forgotten is that while our Founders prohibited government-mandated religious tests for public office, thy did expect and even hoped that the American people would always regard the religions of presidential candidates as important. This comes as a surprise to most Americans today, and so we should revisit the intentions of our Founders in this all-important matter of religion."

"The framers of our Constitution considered a ban on religious tests a natural extension of the First Amendment. If Congress should "make no law respecting an establishment of religion, or prohibiting the free exercise thereof," then no single religion should dominate the federal government. Banning religious tests for federal office would serve this cause. Thus the language of Article VI, clause 3, of the Constitution: ..."no religious test shall ever be required as a qualification to any office or public trust in United States.

"Obviously there were those who feared this provision. When the U.S. Constitution was being debated in state legislatures, there were loud protests over the exclusion of religious tests. More than a few were afraid that without such tests, non-Christians might ascend to public office. David

447

Caldwell, a Presbyterian minister in North Carolina, was in favor of a religious test that would eliminate "Jews and pagans of every kind." A Baptist minister named Henry Abbott complained, "As there are no religious tests, pagans, deists and Mahometans might obtain office."

"These were common fears of the time: If we don't have religious tests, then people of any faith can hold federal office. The answer of our Founders was clear and consistent: We want the people, not a simplistic religious test, to decide who is qualified for public office and who is not. The decision rests with the people."

"This confidence in the people's ability to examine the religion of candidates rings out from the writings of nearly every Founder. Consider, for example, the words of Richard Spaight, one of the signers of the Constitution."

"As to the subject of religion" "no power is given to the general [federal] government to interfere with it at all…No sect is preferred to another. Every man has a right to worship the Supreme Being in the manner he thinks proper. No test is required. All men of equal capacity and integrity are ever be chosen for any office, unless the people themselves be of the equally eligible to offices…I do not suppose an INFIDEL, or any such person, will ever be chosen to any office, unless the people themselves be of the same opinion."

"Clearly Spaight believed that while Congress may not establish a STATE Church or restrict individual liberties, and while no religious test for Federal office may exist, the people had the power to make religion a factor in their choices about political candidates. Consider also the words of Supreme Court Justice James Iredell, who was appointed to the bench by George Washington and who served from 1790 to 1799."

"But it is objected that the people of America may, perhaps, choose representatives who have no religion at all, and that pagans and Mahometans may be admitted into offices…But it is never to be supposed that the people of America will trust their dearest rights to persons who have no religion at all, or a religion materially different from their own."

"As with others in the founding generation, Iredell's confidence was in the scrutiny of the people. Finally, consider the words of Samuel Johnston, a member of the Continental Congress, a member of the United States Senate, and a governor of North Carolina."

"It is apprehended that Jews, Mahometans, pagans, etc., may be elected to high offices under the government of the United States. Those who are Mahometans, or any others who are not professors of the Christian religion, can never be elected to the office of President or other high office, but in one or two cases. First, if the people of America lay aside the Christian religion altogether, it may happen. Should this unfortunately take place, the people will chose such men as think as they do themselves. Another case is, if any persons of such descriptions should, notwithstanding their religion, acquire the confidence and esteem of the people of America by their good conduct and practice of virtue, they may be chosen."

"Clearly this eminent Founder took his case even further than the others whose words we've considered. He argued that while it would, in his opinion, be unfortunate should the American people elect a non-Christian to public office, they might do it if they ceased to be Christians themselves or if they found a member of a non-Christian to public office, they might do it if they ceased to be Christians themselves or if they found a member of a non-Christian faith to have good character and be of virtue. Clearly Samuel Johnson placed his entire faith about such matters in the decisions of the American people. They would pay attention. They would evaluate. They would make the best choice at the time."

"This was the counsel of the Founders regarding religion in the new American nation. Let the people be whatever religion they might choose. Let the states also be as religious as they wish. As important, be careful to deny the federal or general government any role in religion. Let it not establish a religion or prohibit the free exercise of religion—as the First Amendment would eventually say—not let the federal government require religious tests. Instead, the people will choose—as an expression of culture, of heart, and meaningful connection with God."

"The Founders trusted that the people would be vigilant. They trusted that Americans in every generation would recognize the power of religion to shape politics and choose their candidates with this power in mind, not as bigots. Not as those conspiring to cause their religion to prevail. Instead, the people would be vigilant because they would know the importance of religion in human affairs, and they consider what is best for the republic."

"The distinction our Founders made between federal and state governments has been removed through the years. The courts have read the 14th Amendment as requiring that the restrictions on the national government should also apply to the states. Now the states may no longer require religious tests either."

"What has not changed is the Founders' expectation that the people should be the ultimate decision-makers about faith in public office. There never has been a more important moment for a reclaiming of this responsibility. Faith is as much a factor in the challenges of our time as ever. There are also more varieties of faith than ever. Our elected leaders must understand these faiths, just as the people must understand what these leaders believe religiously. This is what the founding generations expected of us. It is vital today that we live out the hopes of the Founders."

"The conclusion is that asking the important religious questions of our candidates is not un-American. It is not contrary to the thinking of the Founders, nor is it something done only by the bigoted or the conspiring. It is what our Founders expected and our times demand. It is also in the best interest of the nation. There should be religious tests—the tests of the people, not tests imposed by the government."

"As we enter the general election of the 2016 presidential race, religion will move front and center. According to the Pew Forum, this is as a majority of the American people wish it to be. In light of the lifetime commitments of Hillary Clinton, it is an emphasis she will likely encourage, though some opponents on the right might disagree with her conclusions. Perhaps this emphasis will be welcomed by Donald Trump. Time will tell."

"What is certain that given the candidates involved in this all-important presidential race and given the religious underpinnings of our global challenges, there has rarely been a more important time for the American people to do the job entrusted to them by the Founders." Ask the questions of faith that must be asked. Make religion a part of their political decisions while always safeguarding religion from the intrusions of the state."

"It is time, then, to live out that time-honored Celtic maxim:

"That which thy fathers bequeathed thee—Earn it anew if thou would'st posses it."

AN OXYMORON: Providentially, there was a much closer election. In the 2000 presidential election the most infamous American election which the Democrat party has never gotten over elected President GEORGE W. BUSH by one Supreme Court justice vote in a 5-4 decision. One Supreme Court justice vote had to have been cast by the one African-American justice on the court CLARENCE THOMAS. Thomas' Congressional hearing was probably the most despicable event to ever be held in our Congress. The Democrats brought an African-American woman who had worked in Thomas' law office and claimed he spoke sexually unacceptable language to her but no physical acts. Thomas attractive red haired white wife sat nearby during this despicable hearing, trying not to be emotional, knowing it was directed at her because she was very outspokenly conservative. Today, with a new justice beginning a Congressional hearing soon for the Supreme Court the video of Thomas was shown on FOX news. Thomas forcibly exclaims, "This hearing has turned into a Hi Tech lynching!" Thomas lived in a suburb of Savannah, Georgia in a segregated black section which had little Civil Rights. He had lived with more discrimination than any Supreme Court justice. Congress voted to select him for the court. Thomas has been a strong Conservative Constitutional vote on the Supreme Court. There is justice in America.

449

It shouldn't be so biased or prejudicial. The election gave GEORGE W. BUSH the presidency over Senator ALBERT GORE because of poor paper ballots which were hard to read, I have heard that the votes for third party candidate RALPH NADER took the votes Gore needed to win. I meet Ralph Nader after the ABC intellectual DICK CAVETT show circa 1970, and gave him a copy of The World Almanac, I was an editor on, when he got in his taxi. He was a great lawyer for protecting American consumers from dangerous and fraudulent business practices. Muckrakers can't become presidents. Later, circa 1987, I meet Ralph Nader at a lecture at Mary Washington college in Fredericksburg, Virginia.

President BARACK OBAMA, three weeks before ELECTION DAY, after Russian meddling had been revealed jested, "There is no way for the Russians to "rig the election." Obama then retorted, "Mr. Trump should not worry about rigging and should keep campaigning." Donald Trump kept giving multi rallies flying there on his personal jetliner. He went to Wisconsin and Michigan, democrat blue states. He won them in very close count votes. I heard on FOX news a commentator say that HILLARY CLINTON lost those states because left wing progressive candidate GAIL STEIN received the votes Hillary needed to win the 2016 election. Is anyone listening? History does repeat.

There were dozens of reasons Hillary Clinton lost which were impossible to access until 2:22 A.M. Nov. 9, 2016. She didn't go to those states. I heard Bill Clinton told her to go there she didn't listen.

PERSONAL NOTE: I knew that Donald Trump had to be elected to cancel some of his unconstitutional executive orders and stop "leading from behind" 8 years under President Obama, Secretary of State Hillary Clinton and Secretary of State John Kerry..

Election Day was on Nov. 8, 2016, my son's 39th birthday. Trump became president after winning enough electoral votes on Nov. 9, 2016, my 42nd wedding anniversary Nov. 9, 1974, in an orthodox Jewish Temple in Brooklyn on CHRYSTAL NIGHT! I had seen a newsreel showing the burning of synagogues and theft of Jewish businesses on Chrystal Night, but didn't recall the date. I am sure most Jewish guests at my wedding would have known this. My son had his Bar Mitzvah on the Sabbath, Saturday Nov. 10, 1990, age 13, the second day of Chrystal Night. MARTIN LUTHER was born on November 10. Then my family left the Reform Jewish Temple Beth Shalom, House of Peace, in Fredericksburg, VA. I began regular services at Concordia Lutheran church Missouri Synod in Triangle, VA, which I first attended on Pentecost Sunday May 1989.

Hillary Clinton was in such shock that she wouldn't give a concession speech. The liberal media also literally went into shock no "thrill up their legs." Little did they know they colluded to destroy what was left of the benevolent, caring Democratic Party. She actually sent JOHN PODESTA out to concede the election to President-elect DONALD J. TRUMP. Ironically, Podesta's hacked password PASSWORD, gave access to Hillary's unauthorized private home computer server to be hacked by "Gucifer 2.0" believed to be a Romanian. He released information to Internet hacker ASSANGE, who leaked it to the public showing how the Democrat National Convention colluded against Independent Communist candidate BERNIE SANDERS and his electoral votes. DEBBIE WASSERMAN SCHULTZ, actually had to step down as the chairman at the Democrat National Party Convention. Is anyone listening? How could TRUMP LOSE? The liberal media reported as little as possible about this. FOX news covered it well. Hillary wrote another book "explaining" her loss even calling women voters "traitors."

President Trump is accused of ordering ICE to separate "tear children from their parents arms." ICE agents were doing their assigned duty which were actually initiated by President George Bush and President Barack Obama. Some of the children weren't brought by their parents but by criminal "coyotes" paid proxies. There was a time limit of 20 days separation of children impossible to complete with ICE's limited personnel and the illegal deluge. Now July 23, 2018, almost all the children have been vetted pending a decision on their future status. The photos of children behind anchor fences and caged like dogs were from 2014 under President Obama not today under President Trump. On FOX news an ICE agent said the anchor fences holding areas are actually for the children's safety. Walled rooms cannot be kept under watch for safety for large groups of children. The media is all guilty of showing crying children "separated" from their parents. This helped elevate the media attacks for our government to be more "compassionate". This has only radicalized the Democrat Party and its liberal left-wing media which has politicized these children making them "PAWNS NOT PEOPLE."

Representative of Bronx/Queens district defeated long time incumbent Crowley in a "big" upset 26,000 votes? The media won't say Crowley's Irish district has now become Latino demographically. TERM LIMITS? Cortez is now with Bernie Sanders in Iowa and Kansas selling their "HUEY LONG" free benefits populist, socialism with cheering crowds. President TRUMP has huge cheering crowds because he is creating jobs, making America energy independent now the top oil/gas producing nation, making NATO allies pay their minimum dues, rebuilt our defunded outdated military weapons, increased military pay delayed for many years, reject America being taxed by foreign Clean Air foreigners, end leading from behind with North Korea, restoring sanctions on Iran who used Obama's billions of dollars for terrorism, reforming hospital health costs, pharmacy medication prices, promoting community colleges and trade/tech schools, Ivanka's child care programs, lower Capital Gains tax to encourage small business entrepreneurship, all single and married 1040 taxpayer's get a 10 per cent immediate tax cut Pelosi calls "crumbs," She is a liberal millionaire. Is anybody listening? Russia and China are still to be resolved. The Quisling media dividing our country are traitors.

The 28 year old smiling Cortez is a sincere person but is actually hurting the Democrat party and has been called out for her extreme comments "eliminate ICE" and free education and free health care, by senior Democrats. She couldn't explain what socialism is? She said, "Capitalism will soon end because of its greed." Who is going to pay for her FREE STUFF?

PERSONAL STORY: As a child Alexandra Ocasio-Cotez moved from the Bronx to upper middle class Yorktown Heights in Westchester County. In August 1974 my fiancé and I looked at a house in Yorktown. I asked the realtor why the taxes were so high. She retorted: "We have the best schools in New York because the IBM Research Center is located here."

Democratic socialist countries have great benefits if you live to get them after paying up to 50 per cent taxes all your life. California and New York City when federal, state and local taxes are added together pay about that much and have Real Estate taxes that only the rich can afford. The middle income families are leaving. These are the economic centers of America on the verge of bankruptcy. President Trump will not "bail them out." He is a businessman not a politician. The unemployment rate for everyone are the lowest ever and Wall Street shows it because of his executive order taking away many "red tape" Obama administration unnecessary regulations.

HISTORY FACT: Does Cortez have a connection to the Spanish conquistador HERNANDO CORTEZ? She may want to keep that secret. His soldiers destroyed the AZTEC Indian civilization in his conquest of Mexico in the mid 1500s. He stole the Aztec's vast gold supply and took it to Spain making it the world's richest country. The liberals mistakenly call Mexican people and other Latinos a race. I haven't heard the Spanish, Italians, Greeks, Israeli, Turks and North African countries and Middle Eastern Muslim and Arabs calling themselves another race? They are all Caucasian which is white but with a browner skin which these Mediterranean and Middle Eastern people also have. This is an environmental determined pigmentation. Only Mestizo Mexicans are a different race through Spanish colonists intermarrying Native American Indians. I know several people who are intermarried with Cherokee and Sioux heritage. They are tan white and mulatto in skin color.

Then Spanish explorer FRANCISCO PIZZARO conquered and destroyed the wealthy INCAN civilization in Peru and also took their gold to Spain. Later, Spain with its great wealth built a great fleet the SPANISH ARMADA and tried to invade Great Britain. The Spanish fleet was annihilated in the English Channel. There was no gold in Great Britain but the British Empire controlled India, parts of Africa and most importantly the New World eastern coast of what became the United States. However, gold wasn't found in great quantity in the United States until 1849 in California, previously part of Mexico an independent republic, ceded to the United States in 1847.

MID APRIL TERRORISM AND DISASTERS

April 15, 2013 Boston Marathon terrorist bombing, 3 killed, 264 injured
April 16, 2002 Virginia Tech shooting, 32 killed, 17 injured
April 17, 1970 Apollo 13 returns safely through ingenuity
April 18, 1942 Lt. Col. Doolittle led 17 B-25 bomber raid on Tokyo
April 19, 1993 Waco ATF, FBI raid kils 76, 4 ATF agents
April 19, 1995 Oklahoma City bombing kills 168, 19 were children
April 19, 1989 Battleship Iowa 16 in. gun turret explosion kills 47 sailors

Saved By Grace, or Cake?

God shows His love for us in that while we were still sinners, Christ died for us. Rom 5:8
PorTals of Prayer November 2, 2019

"On this day, some Christians celebrate ALL SOULS' DAY. This day differs from yesterday's commemoration of All Soul's Day in that "saints" refers to Christians in Heaven, while "souls" refers to the penitent dead in Purgatory. Bells are rung to comfort the dead; soul cakes are shared with the poor as good works to reduce the suffering of those in Purgatory. Of course, other faith traditions reject the doctrine of purgatory, heeding the absence of its mention in the Bible. In one of his lectures on Genesis, MARTIN LUTHER stated, "PURGATORY is the GREATEST FALSEHOOD, because it is based on UNGODLINESS AND UNBELIEF; for they DENY THAT FAITH SAVES.""

"We are not called to have faith in our works to save us, nor does any good works of our departed loved ones merit God's good grace. Only in Christ's atoning sacrifice are we saved. As Christians, we live out our good works on Earth not to save those who have already passed from this life but to serve those around us who Christ calls our neighbors. In so doing, we share the love of Christ with a world so desperately in need of Jesus truth." Read Romans 5:1-11 & Psalm 29

Christ our Redeemer, thank You for giving Yourself as an atoning sacrifice for our sin, that we may give Glory to Your name for Eternity. Amen

Comforted By the Company of Saints

ALL SAINTS' DAY November 1, 2019   PorTals of Prayer
Therefore, since we are surrounded by so great a cloud of witnesses, let us also lay aside every weight, and sin which clings so closely, and let us run with endurance the race that is set before us. Hebrews 12:1 & Psalm 103

"The weight of the 21st Century world is heavy. Our personal burdens, combined with collective troubles of humanity that are shouted nonstop from news outlets and social media, tempt us to despair. But this temptation is not unique to this century. The saints who went before us may not have navigated land mines like social media, but they endured weighty troubles of their own times.

God encourages us through the stories of these men and women of faith, which are recorded throughout the Bible and in historical writings. We are inspired by their faith and comforted by their humanity. In our own lives, we can identify those who likewise shine a light for us by their endurance through tribulation and by their faithful confession of Jesus as Lord. We remember and give thanks for these examples of faith today—St. Peter, Martin Luther, flawed but faithful followers of Jesus, who finished their races but continue to guide us in our own."

> Father, thank You for the witness of the saints through the ages, who
> testify with their lives to one God—Father, Son, and Holy Spirit. Amen

Hammers and Nails

REFORMATION DAY October 31, 2019 PorTals of Prayer

For by Grace you have been saved through faith. And this is not your own doing it is the gift of God, not a result of works, so that no one may boast. Eph. 2:8-9,2:1-10; Psalm 46

"Whack! The sound of the hammer reverberated as MARTIN LUTHER nailed his 95 THESES to a church door 502 years ago; 95 propositions that started a REFORMATION.

A reformation is an improvement resulting in a condition superior to an earlier one. The church at that time taught that one could work or buy one's way into Heaven. After studying Scripture, Luther believed forgiveness and salvation are by GRACE ALONE THROUGH FAITH ALONE.

"Our condition is sinful. A just God requires sin to be punished. Divine punishment is eternal separation from God; that is hell."

"Whack! The sound of the hammer reverberated as Jesus was nailed to the cross—and another reformation was started. The sinless Son took God's righteous judgment upon Himself, completely paying the price for our sin. Baptism connects us to Christ's perfection—a condition far superior to our earlier one."

> Jesus—thank You for dying on the Cross, for paying the price for my sin,
> for Grace and mercy, and for Faith to believe.   Amen

NEW POLL SUGGESTS WHY CHRISTIANITY IS DECLINING

CNSnews The right news, right now Bill Donohue March 16, 2020

"The Pew Research Center survey on white evangelicals, President Trump, and Christianity's public role was released Thursday March 12. The data on Christianity's influence in American society is particularly interesting.

Over half of all Americans say Christianity's influence is declining (53 percent). A majority or plurality of respondents in all religious groups indicated that Christianity's influence is declining; those who were the least likely to ascribe to this point of view were Jews, the unaffiliated and non-believers.

The reasons posited for why this is happening vary. The number one reason given was the "growth in the number of people in the U.S. who are not religious" (60 percent). This was followed by "misconduct by Christian leaders" (58 percent) and "more permissive attitudes about sexual behavior and sexuality in popular culture" (53 percent). "Negative portrayals of Christianity in pop culture" was next (41 percent)."

White evangelicals and Catholics have much in common: the majority cited all four of the above reasons for the decline of Christianity's influence, the lone exception being white evangelicals who cited "misconduct by Christian leaders" (48 percent).

Not surprisingly, Catholics, having been burnt by the clergy sexual abuse scandal, were the most like (66 percent) to say "misconduct by Christian leaders" was a major cause of Christianity's decline. The other three most cited reasons are the most illuminating.

What does the growth of people who are not religious have in common with permissive attitudes about sexuality and negative portrayals of Christianity in pop culture? Answer: the sense that a more Christian nation would be a moral one.

This sentiment is not without reason. The rejection of Christian sexual ethics, with the emphasis on sexual reticence, is made manifest in sexual promiscuity and attacks on Christianity. This suggests that secular elites in the media, the entertainment industry, and education have crafted a culture that works to the detriment of most Americans. Yet they continue to see themselves as the enlightened ones. Most Americans know better. The country is split on whether Christianity's decline is permanent (27 percent) or temporary (24 percent). Comparing the faithful to those who are not religious, the former are more optimistic than the latter about this being a temporary condition. It would be interesting to know how many of the latter hope the condition is not temporary. Regrettably, there are lots of reasons to believe that today's atheists and agnostics are more intolerant of religion, especially Christianity, than in previous generations.

The decline of Christianity and the rise of secularism does not bode well for the future of American society. Self-giving and selflessness, which are hallmarks of Christianity, stand in stark contrast to the self-indulgence selfishness that mark the culture of secularism." (Bill Donohue is President and CEO of the Catholic League for Religious and Civil Rights, the nation's largest Catholic civil rights organization.)

TELL EVERYONE [The Great Commission] And Jesus charged them to tell no one. Mark 7:36—Mark 7:14-37 & Psalm 30

"Jesus' command in today's Gospel doesn't make sense. Sometimes a friend will talk to you in private and tell something bad he or she did or that has happened. The friend makes you promise to keep silent so "the whole world" doesn't know the bad news.

"Jesus had just healed a man who was deaf and had a speech impediment. Jesus' request for silence seems strange because what He had just done was not bad—it was miraculous!"

"This is not an isolated incident. Dead were raised Lazarus, blind were given sight, and 10 lepers were cleansed, Mary Magdalen had 7 demons cast out, and Legion had a multitude of demons cast into pigs. MOSES AND ELIJAH even came to visit JESUS on the MOUNT OF TRANSFIGURATION. All were incredible miracles, and yet Jesus often charged the people to tell no one else."

"What is our reaction to the GOOD NEWS of Jesus Christ? DO WE TELL NO ONE? Or are we so filled with joy and thankfulness that WE TELL EVERYONE? Looking at the last part of Mark 7:36, we see that "the more He charged them, the more zealously they proclaimed it." We know the best thing in the world: Jesus died and rose again to save us from our death. Salvation is by

Grace alone, through faith alone. We need to tell a lost and dying world the good news about the savior." PorTals of Prayer Oct. 16, 2019

Lord, please help me to zealously proclaim Your Good News of salvation
to everyone I meet.   Amen

New Virginia License Plate Exhorts Citizens to Fight Terrorism
By Gerry J. Gilmore American Forces Press Service July 2, 2002

"WASHINGTON, July 2, 2002 — Virginians soon will be able to sport vehicle license plates bearing a Pentagon-shaped logo and the words "FIGHT TERRORISM" emblazoned in REMEMBRANCE of the September 11 terrorism attacks on America,"
"The first plates are slated for delivery by the one-year anniversary of the attacks in New York, Virginia, and Pennsylvania, said Virginia House of Delegates representative Bob Hull today at an outdoor unveiling ceremony near the Pentagon."
"Hull sponsored the state legislature creating the license plates. He noted Virginians could obtain the new plates as a way to show solidarity for the first responders who came to help in the wake of the attacks, to remember victims and to demonstrate
"A NATIONAL EFFORT to RESIST THIS TYPE OF THING EVER HAPPENING AGAIN."
"The PENTAGON LOGO on the plates features an American flag and employs a silhouette of the New York WORLD TRADE CENTER'S TWIN TOWERS to form the "11" of the date of the attacks. The plates also commemorate the terrorist assault aboard the hijacked airliner that crashed into a Pennsylvania field."
"Arlington County Chief of Police Edward A. Flynn said the logo was discovered among items the public left as part of an informal memorial erected near the damaged Pentagon as police processed in the days just after the attack."
"The Arlington police were impressed with the logo's "simplicity and power to evoke those terrible days." Flynn said."the police wanted to adopt the logo. After much searching they discovered the logo's designer, a Texan named DAVID PARANTEAU, who gave them permission to use it for charitable fund raising, Flynn said."
"So the policemen decided to produce lapel pins, T shirts and decals featuring the design for sale, he said, with proceeds earmarked for September 11-related charities."
A "vanity-plate" costs $20, $10 more than the standard license plate."
PERSONAL STORY: I providentially meet David Paranteau's daughter in a Florida Turnpike rest stop at Kissimmee in July 2006. She thanked me for buying her father's license plate. She lives in Gainesville,Florida and has father's front Virginia plate on car.

Standing on the Nuernburg Gallows

"Nurnberg Trials, Germany: 1946—As the chaplain for the
Protestant Nazi criminals at Nurnberg, Chaplain
HENRY F. GERECKE provided spiritual comfort and
strength until their executions."

["They Shall not March Alone" Lutheran-MS Chaplain Ernstmeyer Concordia Pub. 1990]
"I stood next to them on the gallows as they were hanged—von RIBBENTROP, KEITEL, SAUKEL, FRICK, and ROSENBERG."

"I held a private devotion with each condemned Protestant criminal in his cell and then proceeded him down the long hallway to the place of execution. At the foot of the gallows, the prisoner climbed 13 steps to the top, and I followed. I accompanied the five Protestant prisoners: Chaplain O'CONNOR accompanied the five Catholic prisoners. Before the noose was adjusted, I stood next to the condemned and spoke a brief prayer. The trap was sprung. I remained there as the prisoner went down."

"They all took it as soldiers. Not one flinched. KEITEL, former chief of staff of the German army and devout Bible student, said to me just before the trap was sprung: "I want to thank you and the people who sent you for what you have done.""

"At SAUKEL'S turn, I almost passed out. I'd done considerable work in making future arrangements for his family of 11 children."

"The only man who refused prayer on the gallows was ROSENBERG. In my visits to Rosenberg's cell, I found him a gracious and polite man; but he always refused to read the Bible, to say a prayer, or even accept my saying the benediction for him. In the last hours of his life, I offered to read a psalm and a portion of the Gospel, but he refused. While he stood on the trap door, I again asked him if I might pray."

"He smiled and said 'No, thank you' at the moment of death."

"I ministered to Nazi war criminals' spiritual needs from November 1945 until Oct. 16, 1946. For almost a year, I called daily on the Protestant prisoners in their cells. I sat on their beds and spoke of things close to their hearts. Never did they criticize my country, flag, or uniform; never did they fail to say thanks for my calls. They asked me to return."

"During the Protestant services I conducted that year, 13 prisoners attended—ERICH RAEDER, ALBERT SPEER, HANS FRITZCHE, JOACHIM von RIBBENTROP, WILHELM KEITEL, FRITZ SAUKEL, BALDUR von SHIRACH, KARL DOENITZ, von NEURATH, FRICK, WALTER FUND, and HERMAN GOERING."

"I offered Holy Communion to HJALMAR SCHACHT, a former head of the REICHS BANK before the verdicts were in. He replied, "I thank you for the invitation, but I'm confident that I shall be a free man after the trials, and I intend to celebrate the Lord's supper with my wife by my side.""

"He was acquitted."

"After their sentence was passed, several prisoners became ardent Bible students. Von Ribbentrop reviewed the catechism and studied portions of the gospels and Paul's letter to the Romans. He asked, "CAN GOD LOVE ME, AS I AM, WITH ALL MY SINS?" I assured him he could and did.

"He also asked, "HOW CAN THE LEADER OF THE STATE BE A CHRISTIAN AND PATRIOTIC AT THE SAME TIME?" I told him that one must serve the state according to Romans 13 ("Let every soul be subject unto the higher powers," etc.) until it becomes a violation of Acts 5:29 ("We ought to obey God rather than men.")

"I was the last man to speak to HERMAN GOERING, the former Reichs marshal, at about 8:30 the night he died. When the guard told me he was having fits, I ran to his cell and spoke to him as he writhed. I don't believe he heard me. I also removed the letters, containing his last message, from his hand and gave them to the guard. They've never been made public."

"I had visited Goering, but it was difficult to conduct a devotion, because the former Reichs marshal questioned practically all fundamental doctrines of Christianity. Goering felt the church had remained too primitive, hadn't kept up — with the times, and had therefore lost much of its usefulness to society" [The apostasy in American and European liberal, tolerant churches.]

"I was with Mrs. Goering when she last visited her husband, At the hour's close, Goering asked his wife what their little daughter, Edda, had said about his impending death."
"Edda said, SHE WILL MEET YOU IN HEAVEN," Mrs. Goering answered."

PROVIDENTIAL PROPHETIC FACT: TRINITARIAN GOD ALMIGHTY AND CREATOR OF ALL has used many EVIL LEADERS to fulfill his predestined HIS-TORY of His Jewish chosen people and His Great Commission gentile Christians.

Will Edda meet her father in Heaven? Only Jesus can judge him. This story reveals Goering rejected the Bible and Jesus which should Eternally condemn him. it is know that Goering initiated the Gestapo's terror, ordered terror bombings of Warsaw, Rotterdam and London, and began Nazi persecution of the Jewish people and confiscated their property and then supported the Holocaust. Any Jew, or evangelical Bible Christian, would say that should surely condemn Goering to eternal punishment.

However, the Holocaust fulfilled the Old Testament prophecies that the Jewish people would return to their homeland Israel. Adolf Hitler and Herman Goering had no intentions for Israel becoming a nation in 1948. Today, in America the secular humanist socialist politicians and leftist hate media are showing a hatred for Israel. America and Israel have never been closer. President Trump's support for Israel has caused them to falsely call President Trump a racist.These people are personally biased and prejudicial because of their own racial or religious heritages. This only agitates false hatred in America agitating hate in people and groups. Satan, the devil is their deceiver.

CHI Receives Letter Signed by 21 Nazi War Defendants

The Lutheran Witness National News March 1999

"Concordia Historical Institute (CHI) is the recipient of a 1946 letter to the wife of a Lutheran Church—Missouri Synod Army Chaplain from 21 high-level Nazi officials on trial at Nuremberg for atrocities during World War II."
"Her husband was U.S. Army Chaplain HENRY F. GERECKE, who died in 1961.
"On March 16, their son, Henry H. Gerecke of Cape Girardeau, Mo., a retired U.S. Army colonel, presented a letter to the St. Louis-based institute, which houses the Synod's archives. Chaplain Henry F. Gerecke was chosen to minister to Nazi prisoners who identified themselves as "Protestant," because he spoke German, was Lutheran, and had been a prison chaplain."
"The handwritten letter to Alma Gerecke, who lived in St. Louis at the time, pleaded with her to "put off [her] wish" for her husband to return home. Alma Gerecke died in 1992."
"We simply have come to love him," the letter states. "In this state of the trial, it is impossible for any other man than him to break through the walls that have been built up around us, in a spiritual sense."
"Henry H. Gerecke remained in Germany through the NUREMBERG TRIAL and the Oct. 15, 1946, execution of Nazi war criminals."
"Among the signers of the 1946 letter were HERMANN GOERING, RUDOLF HESS, ERNST KALTENBRUNNER, HANS FRANK and ALBERT SPEER."

"This letter should dispel forever the commonly held MYTH THAT HISTORY IS BORING," said Rev. Daniel Preuss, director of CHI, in accepting the letter. "It shows God working through human instruments, in this case through an army chaplain and a member of our Synod. He reaches down even to the most contemptible of human beings and offers them Him."

PETER MARSHALL NEW U.S. SENATE CHAPLAIN 1947

"Our Father in Heaven we pray for the members of this body in their several responsibilities make them see dear Lord that you are not the God of any one party of any one nation or of any one race. Teach us that freedom may be seen not as right to do as we please but as the opportunity to do what is right. Give us the courage to stand for something lest we fall for anything save us from hotheads that would lead us to act foolishly and from cold feet that would keep us from acting at all. Create new warmth and love between the members of the Senate so that they may go at their work not head first but heart first. Help us Our Father to show other nations an America to imitate, an America that loves fair play, honest dealing, straight talk real freedom and faith in God help us make this God's own country by living like God's own people. AMEN"
A church friend told me he was related to Peter Marshall. He told me that President Eisenhower and other government personnel would hear him preach at the New York Avenue Presbyterian church and were inspired by his sermons. President Eisenhower was motivated to then propose that ONE NATION UNDER GOD be added to our NATIONAL ANTHEM in 1954. The movie A MAN CALLED PETER was based on his life. Irish actor RICHARD TODD portrayed Peter Marshall who was born in Scotland. He died Jan, 26, 1949. My dad was born Jan. 28, 1919, was of Scottish heritage.

LITANY FOR DICTATORSHIPS (1935)

Stephen Vincent Benet
"For all those beaten, for the broken heads, The simple the oppressed.
The ghosts in the burning city of our time. For those who still said
"God save the Crown!" And for those who were not courageous
But were beaten nevertheless. And kill the guard before they die,
For those slain at once. For those living through the months and years.
For those who planned and were leaders and were beaten and for those
Humble and stupid, who had no plan. The Jew with his chest crushed in
And his eyes dying. The revolutionist lynched by the private guards to make
Perfect states, in the name of perfect states. We heard the shots in the night
But nobody knew next day what the trouble was and a man must go to work.
For the women who mourn their dead in the secret night, For the children
Taught to keep quiet. We thought we were done with these things but we were
Wrong. We thought because we had power, we had wisdom. Our children know
And suffer the armed men."   [Excerpts not full text.]

SAINT EXUPERY WRITER AVIATOR HERO

French writer, poet, aristocrat, journalist and pioneering aviator Antoine de Saint Exupery's P-38 Lockheed Lightening aircraft crashed on a reconnaissance mission from the island of Corsica,

France on July 31, 1944. Word of his disappearance spread across the literary world. An unidentifiable French officers body was found south of Marseille in the Mediterranean Sea and was buried. "He was best remembered for his novand for his lyrical aviation writings WIND, SAND and STARS and NIGHT FLIGHT." The Little Prince was translated into 300 languages. His 1939 philosophical memoir became the name of an international humanitarian group; it was used as the central theme of EXPO 67 in Montreal, Quebec. He was an airline pilot and though elderly, 43, joined the Free French Air Force in North Africa. Swiss actor BRUNO GANZ portrayed Exupery in a 1997 biopic SAINT-EX, a British film biography of the French author-pilot. Google celebrated Saint-Exupery's 110th birthday with a special logotype depicting the little prince being hoisted through the heavens by a flock of birds. FLYING magazine ranked Saint-Exupery #41 on their list of the "51 Heroes of Aviation". A French fighter squadron has the Little Prince image on its jets tails. WING OF COURAGE, a 1995 docudrama was the world's first dramatic picture shot in the IMAX-format, and is a story of early airmail pilot Exupery portrayed by TOM HULCE. In the book THE RIGHT STUFF TOM WOLFE eulogizes Saint Exupery: "A saint in short, true to his name, flying up here at the right hand of God. The good Saint Ex! And he was not the only one. He was merely the one who put it into words most beautifully and anointed himself before the ALTAR of the RIGHT STUFF."   Wikipedia

ROD MCKUEN FILM THE LITTLE PRINCE: "Author Antoine de Saint-Exupery, belongs in the same category as KAHILL GIBRAN, ROD MCKUEN, and other gooey sentimentalists who coated their prose with a glaze of sincerity." In 1974, I saw this film song with theme sung by America's best selling poet ROD MCKUEN. Actor RICHARD KILEY, Man of La Mancha, is the voice of the aviator Saint Exupery downed with his aircraft in the Sahara desert. McKuen has collaborated with French composers and singers JACQUES BREL and CHARLES AZNAVOUR. U Tube has his Carnegie. I saw him three times on his birthday concert April 29, at CARNEGIE HALL and LINCOLN CENTER. My wife and I went to the stage where young girls gave him flowers. He bent down and kissed my red haired wife on the forehead. Rod never married and was gay. I met him after a previous concert and gave him a copy of the WORLD ALMANAC and told him I added his poetry to the Best selling books list which were excluded from Fiction listing. Rod passed on Jan. 29, 2015, age 81. My dad's birthday Jan. 28, 1919.
FUN FACT: The Little Prince is from Asteroid B-612. Influence to Kurt Vonnegut?

CHAUVINISM BLIND PATRIOTISM OF NAPOLEON

"NICOLAS CHAUVIN is a legendary possibly apocryphal French soldier and patriot who is supposed to have served in the First Army of the Republic and then in La Grande Armee of Napoleon. His name is eponym of chauvinism, originally a term for EXCESSIVE NATIONALISTIC FERVOR, but later used to refer to any form of bigotry or bias such as male chauvinism." Wikipedia

"He is said to have been wounded 17 times in his nation's service, resulting in his severe disfigurement and maiming. For his loyalty and dedication, Napoleon himself presented the soldier Nicolas Chauvin with a SABRE OF HONOR and a pension of 200 francs. Chauvin's distinguished record of service and his love and devotion for Napoleon, which endured despite the price he was willing to pay for them, is said to have earned him only ridicule and derision in RESTORATION FRANCE, when BONAPARTISM became increasing unpopular."   Wikipedia

"Historical research has not identified any biographical details of a real Nicolas Chauvin, leading to the claim that he may have been a wholly fictional figure."   Wikipedia

VICHY FRANCE'S NAZI COLLABORATION

"VICHY FRANCE is the common name of the French State headed by Marshal PHILIPPE PETAIN during World War II. Evacuated from Paris to VICHY in the unoccupied "Free Zone" in the southern part of France and French Africa and French colonial empire. From 1940 to 1942, while the Vichy regime was the nominal government of all of France except Alsace-Lorraine, the Germans and Italians militarily occupied northern and south-east France. Paris remained the de jure capital of France.
"Following the Allied landings in French North Africa in November 1942, southern France was also militarily occupied by Germany and Italy to protect the Mediterranean coastline."   Wikipedia
FACT: In July 1940, French forces left INDO-CHINA then U.S. embargoed oil to Japan.

DE TOCQUEVILLE AMERICA DEMOCRATIC QUOTATIONS

ALEXIS DE TOCQUEVILLE wrote DEMOCRACY IN AMERICA 2 Volumes 1835, 1840.
"Democratic nations care but little for what has been, but what will be; in this direction their unbounded imagination grows and dilates beyond measure…Democracy opens the future before him."   DEMOCRACY IN AMERICA 1840
"Thus not only does democracy make every man forget his ancestors, but it hides his descendants and separates his contemporaries from him." Ibid
"They [the Americans] have all the lively faith in the perfectibility of man." Ibid
"In order to enjoy the inestimable benefits that the LIBERTY OF THE PRESS ensures. It is necessary to submit to the inevitable EVILS THAT IT CREATES."   Ibid
"An American cannot converse, but he can discuss, and his talks falls into a dissertation. He speaks to you as if he was addressing a meeting."   Ibid
"Within these limits the power vested in the American courts of justice of pronouncing a statue to be UNCONSTITUTIONAL forms on one of the most powerful barriers that have been devised AGAINST TYRANNY of POLITICAL ASSEMBLY."   Ibid
"In a state where the citizens are all practically equal, it becomes difficult for them to preserve their independence against aggressions of power." Ibid
"I know of no country, indeed, where the love of money has taken stronger hold on the affections of men and where a profounder CONTEMPT is expressed for the theory of the PERMANENT EQUALITY OF PROPERTY." Ibid
"The LOVE OF WEALTH is therefore to be traced, as either a principal or accessory motive, at the bottom of all that the Americans do; this gives to all there passions a sort of family likeness…it is their desires that makes the Americans so methodical; it perturbs their minds, but it DISCIPLINES THEIR LIVES."   Ibid
"JUSTICE is the end of government, it is the END OF CIVIL SOCIETY. It has ever been and ever will be pursued, until it either will be obtained or until LIBERTY WILL BE LOST IN THE PURSUIT." Ibid
"The health of a democratic society may be measured by the equality of functions performed by private citizens." Ibid
"Americans are so enamored of EQUALITY that they would rather be EQUAL IN SLAVERY THAN UNEQUAL IN FREEDOM."   AMERICA IN DEMOCRACY

460

Henry Gerecke, Minister To Nazis During Nuremberg Trials

Examined by Tim Townsend in New Book Religion News Service 8-24-2014/12-6-2017

(RNS) HE WAS A MINISTER TO MONSTERS

"That's what Tim Townsend writes of HENRY GERECKE, the unassuming Lutheran pastor from Missouri who shepherded six of the most notorious Nazis to the gallows in "MISSION AT NUREMBERG: AN AMERICAN ARMY CHAPLAIN AND THE TRIAL OF THE NAZIS."

The book is one of a string of new titles that dust off a remote corner of World War II history — the role religion played both in and beyond the conflict.

"That's why I wanted to write this book," Townsend said from Washington, D.C. where he is a senior writer and editor for The PEW RESEARCH CENTER.

"A large part was trying to figure out why did the Allies provide spiritual comfort for men who were on trial for what was ultimately called the HOLOCAUST." He said. "They clearly did not have anyone's spiritual welfare in mind when they were murdering Jews, so why did we feel it was necessary and humane to provide them with chaplains to see to their spiritual comfort?"

Townsend combed the National Archives for some piece of paper, some order that explained why the Allies felt those charged with the most horrendous crimes of the century needed — even deserved — a chaplain of their own, beyond the fact that the GENEVA CONVENTION required it.

American culture has long accepted the idea of chaplains ministering to criminals from the common thief to the death row murderer. But what about genocidal killers overseas?

Townsend finds his answer in Gerecke, a Lutheran Church Missouri Synod pastor charged with caring for men such as HERMANN GOERING, ALBERT SPEER and WILHELM KEITEL— men responsible for the mass extermination of six million European Jews. How, he asks, did he understand his role in leading the condemned Nazis to their deaths?

Gerecke volunteered in 1943, when the Army was desperate for chaplains. His unit was sent from England to Germany after the Germans surrendered in 1945.

There, he visited DACHAU, where hundreds of thousands of Jews were gassed and cremated in ovens.

As the NUREMBERG TRIALS began, higher-ups heard there was a German-speaking Army chaplain and asked Gerecke to take on the role of ministering to 21 high-ranking Nazis on trial for their lives.

In saying yes, Gerecke played one of the most puzzling and under-examined roles in what Townsend calls "the judicial improvisation we now call the Nuremberg trials."

"Gerecke was the perfect choice," Townsend said. "He was able to go in with his mind and eyes wide open. He had seen DACHAU, he knew what these people were responsible for but he was able to move past that in terms of his ability to relate to them.

Townsend thinks Gerecke looked beyond the terrible men imprisoned in front of him to the children they had once been. One of the most lovely — and chilling — pieces in the book comes when Gerecke accompanies [General] Keitel up the 13 steps of the gallows and prays aloud with him a German prayer both were taught by their mothers."

"He knew that he NEEDED TO SAVE THE SOULS of as many of these men as he could before they were executed." Townsend said. "I think for him he thought it was a great gift he had been given."

And not one he took lightly. Gerecke did not give COMMUNION to any of the Nazis unless he believed they were truly penitent and made a profession of truth in Jesus. Only four of the 11 sentenced to hang meet Gerecke's standard.

One who did not was Goering, who many historians credit with helping to create "the FINAL SOLUTION." the genocide of the Jews. When he and Gerecke discussed the DIVINITY OF JESUS, Goering disparaged the idea.

"This Jesus you always speak of," he said to Gerecke, "TO ME HE IS JUST ANOTHER SMART JEW!"

Gerecke held that unless he ACCEPTED JESUS AS HIS SAVIOR, Goering could not receive communion.

"You are not a Christian," Gerecke told Goering, "and as a Christian pastor I cannot commune you."

Within hours, Goering was dead, robbing the hangman by swallowing cyanide he had secreted in his cell.

In the end, Gerecke walked five men to the gallows. After the war, he was criticized by some of his fellow pastors for not giving Goering communion. And he was criticized for ministering to such monsters in the first place.

During the trials, a rumor spread among the Nazis that Gerecke would go home before the end. They wrote a letter to his wife, ALMA, asking her to please let him stay. That letter which Townsend first saw in a St. Louis exhibit, led him to the story.

"Our dear Chaplain Gerecke is necessary not only for us as a minister but also as the thoroughly good man that he is," the letter reads above the signature of Goering, Keitel, Speer and others. Then it includes a word Townsend writes is not often associated with Nazis. "WE SIMPLY HAVE COME TO LOVE HIM."

[Pastor Gerecke or JESUS CHRIST? I believe it was both.]

#40

NOTE: In 1968, I was editor of the Bitburg Air Base, Germany "Skyblazer" newspaper , then The World Almanac and Book of Facts editor/researcher/writer of World Almanac Facts sent to about 1,200 Scripps Howard newspapers I ended World Almanac Facts with the #30 which is used in journalist news style to denote the end of the news article.

I used the #40 to conclude my TESTIMONY/WITNESS because it is the Biblical number of OUR LORD JESUS CHRIST USED IN 40 DAYS AND 40 YEARS in the NT/OT Bible.

GOERING'S DAUGHTER'S PRAYER FOR HER FATHER

"Chaplain GERECKE often recalled, in off-duty chats, his MOST TOUCHING MOMENT. When the prisoner's wives arrived to see their husbands, their children were left in the chaplains' offices. One day little EDDA GOERING,10, was left with Gerecke.

"Do you ever say your prayers?" he asked.

"I pray every night," the girl replied.

"And how do you pray?"

"I kneel down by my bed and look up to Heaven and ask God to open my daddy's heart and let Jesus in."   p xx "I Was a Nuremburg Jailer" Col. Burton C. Andrus 1969

#30

TAURUS

YOU ARE ABOUT TO ENTER A VERY EXCITING period in your life. Uranus, the planet of innovation, disruption, creativity, rebellion, independence and sudden change, will enter your sign of Taurus on March 6, 2020 and will remain there for seven 7 years, until April 2026. This is likely the first time in your life that you will experience Uranus in Taurus. Uranus takes 84 years to circle the SUN, spending seven years in each sign it visits, so it's not been since 1934 to 1942 that this planet has toured your sign.

During this span, YOU WILL ENTER INTO A HIGHLY CREATIVE PERIOD where ideas will initially spark your imagination at times, you may not know how you came up with such brilliant solutions to creative and practical matters, because they will stem from deep within you.

You will be on the cutting edge of all that is innovative and fresh, and others will be drawn to you to hear your perspective on a whole spectrum of current topics.
The creative influence of Uranus and its ability to fire up your imagination cannot be overstated and bears repeating, so it is important to voice your idea, some may be ahead of the curve, so give VIPs around you a chance to catch up, from now on your mind will be lit with 100,000 points of light.

You will feel a powerful need to be independent and make an important contribution to the world. Uranus rules humanitarian causes, charities and help for segments of society that have been overlooked or marginalized or are suffering and need attention. You may be moved to protect the environment, start a group to help battered women or start a licensed pre-K group for underprivileged children in poor neighborhoods. Now in the coming seven 7 years, you will be more determined than ever to make your time on earth count for something aligned with your beliefs.

If anyone close tries to heem you in or dominate you in the future, whether at work or in a close romantic relationship, you will bolt, for you will not be contained by anyone anymore. Uranus in Taurus will GIVE YOU STRENGTH OF YOUR CONVICTION, and no one will be able to "TALK YOU OUT" of YOUR MISSION you'll be your own person.
Uranus takes the gifts of Mercury and synthesizes these qualities into an even higher level, into the realm of genius.
Uranus is very different from other planets in the way he delivers his messages. Uranus strikes like lightening, rapidly and without warning. and instantly sweeps away anything he deems outworn and of no future value. Uranus will help you rebuild what was taken away, giving you ideas to replace what was "lost" to create new. Under Uranus's influence in 2019, you may find that you are feeling impulsive, anxious to move forward.

You will be confident and determined, and it will likely represent an exciting change in your lifestyle, a relationship or your career. YOU WILL FEEL A POWERFUL NEED TO BE INDEPENDENT AND TO MAKE AN IMPORTANT CONTRIBUTION TO THE WORLD. My birthday is May 4, 1943 born in the constellation of TAURUS. MAY THE FOURTH BE WITH ME.

CPSIA information can be obtained
at www.ICGtesting.com
Printed in the USA
LVHW061127260522
719454LV00010B/72